EDUCATIONAL PSYCHOLOGY:
A CENTURY OF CONTRIBUTIONS

EDUCATIONAL PSYCHOLOGY: A CENTURY OF CONTRIBUTIONS

Edited by

Barry J. Zimmerman
City University of New York Graduate Center

Dale H. Schunk
University of North Carolina at Greensboro

A project of Division 15 (Educational Psychology) of the
American Psychological Association

 LAWRENCE ERLBAUM ASSOCIATES, PUBLISHERS
2003 Mahwah, New Jersey   London

Senior Acquisitions Editor:	Naomi Silverman
Assistant Editor:	Lori Hawver
Cover Design:	Kathryn Houghtaling Lacey
Textbook Production Manager:	Paul Smolenski
Full-Service Compositor:	TechBooks
Text and Cover Printer:	Sheridan Books, Inc.

This book was typeset in 10/12 pt. Times, Italic, Bold, Bold Italic.
The heads were typeset in Americana, Italic and Bold.

Lawrence Erlbaum Associates, Inc., Publishers
10 Industrial Avenue
Mahwah, New Jersey 07430

Library of Congress Cataloging-in-Publication Data

Educational psychology : a century of contributions / edited by Barry J. Zimmerman,
    Dale H. Schunk.
      p. cm.
    Includes bibliographical references and index.
    ISBN 0-8058-3681-0 (case : alk. paper)—ISBN 0-8058-3682-9 (pbk. : alk. paper)
    1. Educational psychology—History.   2. Educators—Biography.
  3. Psychologists—Biography.   I. Zimmerman, Barry J.   II. Schunk, Dale H.

  LB1051 .E36214   2003
  370.15—dc21   2002010674

Table of Contents

Preface

This edited book examines the emergence of the field of educational psychology from its philosophical moorings in the late 19th century to its current scientific status at the dawn of the 21st century. The history of the discipline will be discussed in terms of three eras: a founding period (1890 to 1920), a rise to prominence period (1920–1960), and a modern period (1960 to the present). Each period commences with an overview chapter describing it in terms of key social, political, and historical events affecting educational theory, research, and practice. In addition, the authors of overview chapters describe major theoretical, methodological, and instructional contributions of the period and how they changed the course of educational psychology.

To understand this history in more personal terms, we included biographical chapters of individuals who made seminal contributions to the discipline during each period. We want readers to know these pioneering scholars as real humans who responded to the challenges of their time in personal and collective ways that changed the course of educational psychology. These biographical chapters include a description of the scholar's life—including historical events, social influences, and his or her personal reactions. The authors also describe major psychological contributions of the scholar to the field of education in terms of theory, research, and practice. Finally, the authors provide a description of the scholar's impact and legacy. This biographical approach was designed to extend beyond traditional descriptions of a scholar's theory and research to include insights regarding contributing events in his or her personal life. A special effort was made to describe intellectual events leading to a scholar's most prominent ideas and scientific discoveries when possible. In making these discoveries, many scholars had to struggle to overcome significant barriers of race, gender, religion, geographic region, or social status. Understanding the history of the discipline in human as well as scientific terms is especially important for young scholars who aspire to contribute to the discipline during the 21st century.

Although this book is, to our knowledge, the most comprehensive effort to capture this history to date, it is not the first effort to render a historical accounting for the field of educational psychology. There are several influential prior chapter-length articles (e.g., Hilgard, 1996; O'Donnell & Levin, 2001; Walberg & Haertel, 1992), which focused on chronological changes in research topics, theories, methodologies, and findings.

An advisory committee of the Educational Psychology Division of the American Psychological Association (Division 15) identified 16 scholars for inclusion in this book whose ideas and discoveries were judged to have greatly shaped the nature and direction of the discipline. These scholars were winnowed by the committee from a list of more than 60 nominees who made important contributions to the field. Because the historical impact of a scholar is often difficult to judge during his or her lifetime, the contributions of other scholars living near the end of the 20th century were undoubtedly underestimated and will be recognized more widely after the passage of time. The overview chapters were designed to complement the biographical chapters by describing the contributions of a broad range of scholars during each of the three major periods. The members of the advisory committee were: David Berliner, Anita Wolfolk Hoy, Richard Mayer, Wilbert McKeachie, Michael Pressley, the late Richard Snow, Claire Ellen Weinstein, and Joanna Williams. We would like to thank these committee members for their participation in the selection process and their helpful suggestions regarding authors for the various chapters. We are especially grateful to committee members who agreed to write chapters in this volume themselves.

Authors were chosen for each chapter who had particular expertise regarding the scholar or general period in question. Many of the authors of biographical chapters knew and worked personally with scholars who lived in the last half of the twentieth century. It was a special pleasure for us, as editors, to read these informative chapters, and we would like to thank the authors for their dedication and skill in capturing and explaining the contributions of these exemplary scholars. Finally, we would like to thank the Executive Committee of Division 15 (Educational Psychology) of the American Psychological Association for their generous support for this historic book.

REFERENCES

Hilgard, E. R. (1996). History of educational psychology. In D. Berliner & R. Calfee (Eds.), *Handbook of educational psychology* (pp. 990–1004). New York: Macmillan.

O'Donnell, A. M., & Levin, J. R. (2001). Educational psychology's health growing pains. *Educational Psychologist, 36*, 73–82.

Walberg, H. J., & Haertel, G. D. (1992). Educational psychology's first century. *Journal of Educational Psychology, 84*, 6–19.

Contributors

Lorin Anderson, University of South Carolina, Dept. of Educational Leadership and Policies, College of Education, Columbia, SC, 29208; voice: 803-777-7069; fax: 803-777-3050; e-mail: andregroup@aol.com

J. William Asher, Purdue University, Dept. of Educational Studies, 1446 Liberal Arts and Education Bldg., West Lafayette, IN 47907-1446; voice: 765-494-7295; fax: 765-496-1228; e-mail: asher@purdue.edu

David C. Berliner, Arizona State University, Psychology in Education Division, Tempe, AZ 85287; voice: 602-965-3291; fax: 602-965-6604; e-mail: berliner@asu.edu

Charles J. Brainerd, University of Arizona, Division of Learning, Technology, and Assessment, Tucson, AZ 85721; voice: 520-621-7831; fax: 520-577-7540; e-mail: brainerd@u.arizona.edu

Eric Bredo, University of Virginia, School of Education, Dept. of Educational Leadership, Foundations, and Policy, Charlottesville, VA 22903; voice: 434-924-0886; e-mail: erb7s@virginia.edu

Marcy P. Driscoll, Florida State University, Educational Research, Tallahassee, FL 32306-3030; e-mail: mdriscol@mailer.fsu.edu

Peggy A. Ertmer, 1413 Fairfax Drive, Lafayette, IN 47909; e-mail:
pertmer@purdue.edu

John F. Feldhusen, 1301 N. Tamiami Trail #205, Sarasota, FL 34236; voice:
941-366-4064; e-mail: feldhusenjf@aol.com

Patricia M. Greenfield, Dept. of Psychology, UCLA, 405 Hilgard Ave.,
Los Angeles, CA 90095; voice: 310-825-7526; fax: 310-206-5895;
e-mail: greenfield@psych.ucla.edu

Gerald L. Gutek, 437 South Edgewood Ave., La Grange, IL 60525; voice:
708-354-3805; fax: 708-354-3805; e-mail: ggutek@luc.edu.

Vernon C. Hall, Syracuse University, Dept. of Psychology, 150 Marshall St.,
Syracuse, NY 13210; voice: 315-443-2354; e-mail: vchall@psych.syr.edu

Linda Jarvin, PACE Center, Yale University, Box 208205, New Haven,
CT 06520-8205; voice: 203-432-4633; e-mail: linda.jarvin@yale.edu

Haggai Kupermintz, University of Colorado at Boulder, School of Education,
Campus Box 249, Boulder, CO 80309-0249; voice: 303-429-7090; fax:
303-492-7090; e-mail: kupermin@colorado.edu

Nancy C. Lutkehaus, University of Southern California, Dept. of Anthropology,
Los Angeles, CA 90089-0032; voice: 213-740-1917; fax: 213-747-8571; e-mail:
lutkehau@usc.edu

Richard E. Mayer, University of California Santa Barbara, Psychology Dept.,
Santa Barbara, CA 93106; voice: 805-893-2472; fax: 805-893-4303; e-mail:
mayer@psych.ucsb.edu

Edward K. Morris, University of Kansas, Dept. of Human Development and
Family Life, 1000 Sunnyside Ave., Lawrence, KS 66045-2133; voice:
785-864-4840; fax: 785-864-5202; e-mail: ekm@ku.edu

Frank Pajares, Emory University, Division of Educational Studies, Suite 240,
1784 North Decatur Road, Atlanta, GA 30322; voice: 404-727-6468; fax:
404-727-2799; e-mail: mpajare@emory.edu

Annamarie Sullivan Palincsar, 305 Sumac Lane, Ann Arbor, MI 49105; voice:
734-647-0622; e-mail: annemari@umich.edu

Michael Pressley, University of Notre Dame, Dept. of Psychology, Notre Dame,
IN 46556; voice: 574-631-3245; fax: 574-631-8883; e-mail:
gmpressley@aol.com

Alysia D. Roehrig, University of Notre Dame, Dept. of Psychology,
Notre Dame, IN 46556; voice: 574-631-3245; fax: 574-631-8883;
e-mail: roehrig.1@nd.edu

Dale H. Schunk, University of North Carolina at Greensboro, School of Education, 329 Curry Bldg. UNCG P. O. Box 26171, Greensboro, NC 27402-6171; voice: 336-334-3403; fax: 336-334-4120; e-mail: dhschunk@uncg.edu

Sheryl Scrimsher, Meredith College, Child Development Program, Raleigh, NC 27607-5298; voice: 919-760-2357; e-mail: slscrims@mindspring.com

Robert J. Sternberg, PACE Center, Yale University, Box 208205, New Haven, CT 06520-8205; voice: 203-432-4633; fax: 302-432-8317; e-mail: robert.sternberg@yale.edu

Jonathan R. H. Tudge, University of North Carolina at Greensboro, HDFS, P. O. Box 26170, Greensboro, NC 27412-5001; voice: 910-334-5307; e-mail: jonathan_tudge@.uncg.edu

Walter W. Wager, Florida State University, 4508 University Center, Bldg. C, Tallahassee, FL 32306-2550; e-mail: wwager@oddl.fsu.edu

Barry J. Zimmerman, City University of New York Graduate School and University Center, Educational Psychology Program, 365 Fifth Ave, New York, NY 10016-4309; voice: 212-817-8291; fax: 212-817-1516; e-mail: bzimmerman@gc.cuny.edu

I

The Founding Period:
1890 to 1920

1

Educational Psychology From 1890 to 1920

Vernon C. Hall
Syracuse University

The period between 1890 and 1920 was a golden era in educational psychology. Modern psychology was in its infancy and many of the most prominent psychologists of the time were identified with the area. This included six APA presidents (Cattell, Dewey, Hall, Judd, Seashore, and Thorndike) with several others (e.g., Bryan, James, Munsterberg, Warren, Woodworth, and Yerkes) making contributions. In addition, educational psychologists believed that the science of psychology would revolutionize education and many educators at all levels were willing to give the new science a chance. Before proceeding, it may be useful to be reminded of some of the events during this time that interacted with and affected educational psychology.

CONTEXTUAL FORCES INTERACTING WITH EDUCATIONAL PSYCHOLOGY

Immigration

Between 1840 and 1920 37 million people immigrated to the United States. This included 6 million Germans, 4.5 million Irish, 4.75 million Italians, and 4.2 million

3

from England, Scotland, and Wales. These people were either seeking a better life or fleeing from difficulties faced in their native lands. Many of them came through Ellis Island.

This immigration influenced educational psychology in at least two ways. First, these immigrants needed an education. America had always supported the idea of having literate citizens, and the expansion of elementary and secondary education at this time was rapid as many of the states passed compulsory attendance laws with Mississippi being the last in 1918 (Good, 1964, p. 376). For instance, the enrollment of Grades 9–12 in public and nonpublic schools increased from 359,949 in 1890 to 2,500,176 in 1920 (Good, 1964, p. 253). This meant the country needed elementary and secondary school teachers. Such teachers had in the past been prepared by high schools and normal schools. With the passage of the Morrill Acts of 1862 (which provided states with federal land to be used to found land grant colleges) and 1890 (which made additional annual funds available), new universities were founded or existing ones were made into land grant institutions. Although this money was made available to provide agricultural training, between 1890 and 1900 a number of these institutions established departments or schools of education that often included faculty and/or courses in educational psychology. R. B. Boon (cited in Good, p. 331) reported that in 1904, 250 colleges and universities out of 480 offered courses in education (see Charles, 1987 for a description of this development in a number of major universities). In addition, normal schools upgraded their programs to meet the challenge of new universities. One way of upgrading was to add courses in educational psychology. Many young educational psychologists acquired their first job at these normal schools.

The second way in which this immigration influenced educational psychology involved the nation's concern about having too many undesirable foreigners entering the country. Such concerns led the Immigration and Naturalization Service to begin screening immigrants on Ellis Island. This provided educational psychologists the opportunity to use their new intelligence tests to assess the abilities of the immigrants. The results of this assessment were used by some as additional justification for placing limits on new immigration.

Rapid Expansion of Science and Technology

Between 1890 and 1920 Americans experienced great changes in all aspects of their lives. Popcorn, peanut butter, and tea bags made their first appearance, while hot dogs and hamburgers were first served on buns, and America's first pizzeria was opened. On a more serious note, the automobile replaced the horse as the chief mode of transportation, airplanes first flew, X-ray photography and zippers were invented, radio signals and phone calls were sent across the Atlantic Ocean and Einstein published his theory of relativity. The world learned what could be accomplished if we placed resources in science and technology.

Science, however, was not automatically welcomed by educators. Immediately after the Civil War universities were concerned with discipline and piety. Science appeared to reduce the place of man in the universe, and some felt it was too easy to be in the curriculum (see Veysey, 1965). At the same time German universities were producing scientists, and Americans acquiring their education there were returning convinced that American universities should do the same. In addition, the fruits of science were difficult to reject and universities were identified as the place for scientific research. Just prior to and during this period, several universities were founded that provided much scientific research in general and psychological research in particular. Cornell in 1869 and Johns Hopkins in 1876 were both founded by wealthy Quakers. Johns Hopkins is often identified as the first research university in America built from the ground up. Clark followed in 1889, Stanford in 1891, and Chicago in 1892. Teachers College became associated with Columbia in 1898. These universities, along with Harvard and Yale, were crucial to the development of educational psychology. They were also where graduate students became the scientist's helper and thus future scientists. This does not mean that there were huge numbers of graduate students. In 1900 there were only 5,668 graduate students in the United States (Veysey, p. 269). On the other hand, these students were a dedicated group. Virtually all of the present American educational psychologists can trace their academic heritage directly to professors trained during this period.

Psychologists saw scientists in other areas making giant strides, and the applications of their findings were changing the world. They felt they could do the same. The educational system was a natural place where they could contribute, and educational psychology was a vehicle they used. Indeed, there was a strong belief that science would make a real difference in the field of education. The nature and degree to which education can be a science and psychology can make a contribution to education is still being debated.

The Progressive Movement

Beginning in about 1900 a Progressive Movement emerged that influenced all phases of American life. This movement was led by a combination of labor and urban middle class citizens. After the Civil War, Americans supported a minimum of government and counted on the law of competition to let successful and honest men supply the leadership while the socially misfit would sink to the bottom. Unfortunately, this led to domination by the very rich and often dishonest owners of big business. Many city governments were corrupted by politicians like the Tammany machine in New York City. Most of the gas, electricity, and water facilities were privately owned and extremely profitable. This led to large-scale corruption and calls for municipal and state reform. Citizens were made aware of these problems by a group of journalists known as muckrakers.

Results of the Progressive Movement include direct election of senators, labor legislation that included workmen's compensation, direct primaries for the major political parties, referendums for the recall of elected officials, prohibition, and women's suffrage. The Progressive Movement did not leave out education, and John Dewey, one of the founders of Progressive Education, was involved in both educational and social reform.

The Great War

The First World War, which began in 1914 and America entered in 1916, led to a rejection of the German language and history in the schools, but the migration of Americans to German institutions of higher education had ceased well before the war. The major influence of the war on educational psychology was the opportunity to develop and administer the Alpha and Beta tests. It is doubtful that this made a big difference in the war effort, but it certainly made testing more acceptable to the public, and copies of these tests left over from the war were made available for distribution to the public schools.

Darwinism

The Theory of Evolution published by Charles Darwin (1809–1882) in 1859 and its acceptance "is considered by many as the greatest scientific achievement of the century" (Boring, 1957, p. 470). While the idea was not new, the amount of new data Darwin presented was persuasive. The theory challenged the account of creation contained in Genesis, which was widely accepted in the western world. Darwin maintained that man was really an animal with considerable intellectual capacities, but in other ways no different from other animals. This led to the study of lower animals as a way to understand human behavior. It has been suggested by Gardner Murphy that "The influence of Darwinism upon psychology during the last quarter of the nineteenth century probably did as much as any single factor to shape the science as it exists today" (Murphy, 1949, p. 116). With regard to educational psychology, all of the prominent players during this period were Darwinian, and the theory had a major influence on the way they viewed the world.

THE AREAS OF EDUCATIONAL
PSYCHOLOGY

Psychology is one of the broader fields in science as there are presently more than 50 independent divisions in The American Psychological Association. Educational psychology, as an applied area, has generally been identified with the more basic areas of learning, measurement, and development. This does not mean that these are the only areas in which psychology made contributions to education, but these are the ones that educational psychologists focused on during this period. While these areas were not independent and certainly psychologists were active in more than one area, they do have relatively independent histories as presented in the following.

Learning

Educators. When historians discuss those who have influenced classroom learning, they generally list a number of people who have been influential in both education and psychology. These include Juan Vives (1492–1540) who, among other things, supported the education of women, recommended the study of nature, and advocated induction as a method of study and Johann Heinrich Pestalozzi (1746–1827), who advocated proceeding gradually and cumulatively from the immediate, easy, and concrete to the distant, complex, and abstract. He also developed what became known as "object teaching," which involved beginning with a concrete object and proceeding from naming the object and its concrete characteristics to more abstract learning such as reading and mathematics. Finally, there is Frederich Froebel (1782–1853) who is credited with being the founding father of the kindergarten movement. There were disciples of each of these men who were involved in American education in the late 1800s. For instance Pestalozzi's ideas were introduced in the United States by the first commissioner of education, Henry Bernard. Austin Sheldon (1823–1897) who was the leader in founding the public schools and normal school in Oswego, New York, acquired educational materials in Canada that had come from an English Pestalozzian group. Sheldon also hired the son of Pestalozzi's first assistant to train his teachers.

Francis W. Parker (1837–1902) also borrowed from the ideas of Pestalozzi and Froebel. Parker was a colonel in the Civil War before devoting the remainder of his life to education. After traveling in Europe and becoming familiar with the educational theories of the day, he developed a reputation of positively changing the school system in Quincy, Massachusetts. He then proceeded to found the Cook County Normal School, which trained teachers. He was given money from a McCormick family to found a teacher training facility and a private school. The Francis W. Parker School, which he founded, is still in existence. He encouraged the use of concrete materials and combining several subjects into one lesson. Dewey sent his children to Parker's school while at the University of Chicago and referred to Parker as the father of Progressive Education.

During the mid and late 1800s schools were changing in ways that would eventually lead to the organization we now have. This included the administrative system of superintendents and principals who answer to elected school boards. One of the most influential educators during this period, who is often included in discussions of educational psychology, is William Torrie Harris (1835–1909). At 33 years of age Harris became the superintendent of schools in St Louis. This was not an easy job as the city had many problems. Many immigrants settled here, including 60,000 Germans who wanted classes conducted in their native tongue.

There was also a large contingent of transients who posed educational difficulties, and tensions still existed in this border city between northerners and southerners stemming from the Civil War.

Harris was a man of tremendous energy, and he had a number of innovative ideas. Although initiated by his predecessor, he continued a policy of flexible promotion. Students were evaluated every 10 weeks and could be promoted as a result of any of these evaluations. He instituted a system of supervision that included all administrators also teaching. He introduced kindergartens and provided them for black children; evening classes were instituted; music, gymnastics, and art were added to the curriculum; and he constructed a special alphabet to make initial reading easier. He also added a normal school, which became Harris Teachers College. After resigning from the superintendency, he became the second United States commissioner of education from 1889 until 1906.

More important for educational psychology in this period was the introduction of the ideas of Johann Fredrich Herbart (1776–1841). Some have labeled Herbart the father of educational psychology and/or scientific pedagogy because he believed in the development of a scientific psychology and had a strong interest in education. In addition, he is given credit for introducing the concepts of the unconscious and threshold of consciousness (the limit that an idea had to go beyond in order to become conscious), which found their way into the theorizing of Freud and Fechner. His use of the term "apperception" also influenced Wundt's thinking on that topic.

Several Americans had become aware of Herbart and enrolled in German universities to study his educational ideas. These included Charles De Garmo, who along with A. F. Lang translated Herbart's works into English. In 1896 De Garmo published *Herbart and the Herbatians*. Herbart's five steps for teacher preparation and presentation have a distinctly modern ring, and some have identified them as the antecedents to today's lesson plans. Teachers were advised to review old material and provide an overview of what is to follow before presenting new material. After presentation, this new material was to be related to what has been learned earlier and applications for the new material were then provided. He also emphasized the importance of interest in motivation, which was a major theme for both James and Dewey. Herbart's rejection of faculty psychology also found favor during this period. An indication of Herbart's influence was the formation of the Herbart Club in 1902, which subsequently became the National Herbart Society and eventually the National Society for the Study of Education. The annual volumes, still published by this society, have been quite influential and are sometimes required reading for graduate students in educational psychology.

Psychologists.   Within psychology there were several giants. First there was William James (1842–1910), whose *The Principles of Psychology* (1890) is arguably the most enduring psychology text ever written. James is one of the more interesting psychologists and philosophers in American history. He never earned a degree in either discipline but was president of both the American Psychological Association and the American Philosophical Association. He is known for only one minor experiment in psychology and was often critical of those doing experimental work in the area, but is universally recognized as one of the most influential psychologists of all time (e.g., Korn, Davis, & Davis, 1991).

James' father was independently wealthy and the family spent much time traveling while the children attended private schools in such places as New York, Boulogne, and Geneva. Both William and his famous brother Henry avoided service during the Civil War while their two younger brothers enlisted. In 1860 William briefly studied art before enrolling at Harvard as a chemistry student in 1861. He then switched to physiology after deciding to acquire a degree in medicine. In 1864 he entered medical school but before completing his degree, he traveled to the Amazon to work with a Harvard biologist, Louis Agassiz. After a short time he became ill and returned to America. Instead of immediately finishing his medical degree, James entered a period of depression and poor health but continued to study. While in Europe to receive treatment for his back, he became acquainted with many prominent figures including Wilhelm Wundt. In 1869, he finally received his medical degree. He then entered into a period of more depression and experienced a psychological crisis. In 1872 James received an offer to teach physiology at Harvard and did so for a year. After a tour of Europe the following year, he returned to Harvard to teach courses in physiology and psychology. In 1875 he opened a demonstration laboratory in psychology and in 1878 he signed a contract to write his famous psychology book.

James was optimistic and positive yet went through severe bouts of depression. During these times he was considered suicidal. He was an excellent teacher, he had a tremendous influence on other people, and he was the type of person others sought out. He was certainly the type of person a student would want as his or her major professor.

> His simplicity and modest and ardent sincerity won him friends wherever his name was known; his freedom from dogmatism and prejudice and his love for truth and fair play brought him in closest touch with the greater scientists and philosophers, and his approachable, friendly, happy manner, together with his desire to see the good in a fellow, caused him to be loved by all his students, as hundreds will testify. It has been said that he helped more young men find themselves than any other philosopher or educator in this country. (Baldwin, 1911, p. 370)

James was a Darwinian who helped introduce the theory into psychology. As a functionalist and pragmatist, he was a strong advocate for applied psychology. He is particularly remembered in educational psychology for his *Talks to Teachers on Psychology: And to Students on Some of Life's Ideals* (1912). This book is a collection of lectures originally given weekly to Cambridge teachers along with three concluding chapters of lectures given to students at women's colleges.

As a Darwinian, he believed that man had inherited many instincts (more than other animals). Thus, it should not be surprising that there is a lecture on instincts. He includes as instincts crying modesty, fear, love, curiosity, imitation, and ownership. In reference to the latter he makes the interesting comment that, "The depth and primitiveness of this instinct would seem to cast some sort of psychological discredit in advance upon all radial forms of communist utopia. Private proprietorship cannot be practically abolished until human nature is changed" (James, 1912, p. 56). Several of these instincts follow the "law of transitoriness of instincts," which means that they reach their zenith and then decline rather rapidly. He provides the example of birds following their mothers for a short period after birth (we now call this imprinting). While these brief instincts also occur in children, "for many an infant prodigy, artistic or mathematical, has a flowering epic of but a few months" (p. 61), he admits that observing parents are in a much better position to take advantage of them than teachers. The teacher still must recognize and use his or her knowledge of longer lasting instincts to develop useful habits because, "Education is for behavior and habits are the stuff of which behavior consists" (p. 66). One of his most cited chapters in the longer book on psychology is on habits, and he gives a similar lecture to the teachers.

While the entire book is interesting, his treatment of memory and faculty psychology is quite creative and has a modern ring. His contention is that memory is enhanced when it is organized. "Briefly, then, of two men with the same outward experiences, *the one who thinks over his experiences most*, and weaves them into the most systematic relations with each other, will be the one with the best memory" (James, 1912, p. 123). Thus, instead of a single memory faculty, we have many independent memory faculties organized around knowledge domains like history and chemistry. The following example is particularly appropriate when we consider the recent research using sports scripts (e.g., baseball) that has found domain knowledge to be more important than aptitude in recall (e.g., Walker, 1987). "A college athlete, who remains a dunce at his books, may amaze you by his knowledge of the 'records' at various feats and games, and prove himself a walking dictionary of sporting subjects" (p. 128). While James points out that mnemonics are "an excessively poor, trivial, and silly way of 'thinking' about dates" (p. 128) as opposed to how historians think about them, and cramming is a poor strategy because we can make so few connections in such a short time, he does think there is some merit to memorizing some things using efficient methods.

Another way that James contributed to educational psychology was through his influence on other psychologists of the day such as Thorndike and Dewey. These men were among the most influential in educational psychology during this period. His closest relationship may have been with Thorndike (1874–1949). Although James did not engage in much experimentation, he allowed Thorndike to use his basement to continue his famous research with chickens. He also encouraged Thorndike to forgo study in Europe and continue his studies at Johns Hopkins with James McKee Cattell. Thorndike always acknowledged James' influence and even discussed James' one well-known study, which concerned whether memorizing in one area will improve memory in general, in the report of his initial transfer studies (Thorndike & Woodworth, 1901a) and later in his widely cited educational psychology text (Thorndike, 1913).

Thorndike was the giant in learning during this era. His accomplishments and the accounts of his life make it clear that he was a workaholic and loved his job. Besides reading mysteries and playing bridge, his work was his hobby (see Joncich, 1968). Accounts by his son of him reading the encyclopedia in bed in order to acquire readings for tests (Thorndike, 1991) and of colleagues recounting how he needed to compute just one more correlation (Veysey, 1965), speak to his love for his work. His mission in educational psychology was to use scientific experimentation and theory to improve education.

Like many other psychologists, Thorndike came from a minister's family and after having an outstanding undergraduate record at Wesleyan from 1891 to 1895, he proceeded to Harvard where he encountered James and earned his master's degree in 1897. He then enrolled at Columbia to study with Cattell and received his Ph.D. in 1898. After a brief time at Western Reserve College For Women, he returned to Columbia where he remained until his retirement at the age of 65. Besides publishing an average of one article a week, a number of psychology books, a series of primers in reading and math, and devising several tests, he raised four children who all obtained advanced degrees including one who became a prominent psychologist.

His place in psychology and education was secured with the series of studies coauthored by R. S. Woodworth concerning transfer and faculty psychology (Thorndike & Woodworth, 1901a, b, c). It was the contention of faculty psychologists that training in certain subjects was special because such training would lead to transfer to many other areas. "One of the quarrels of the educational theorists concerns the extent to which special forms of training improve the general capacities of the mind. Does the study of Latin or of mathematics improve one's general reasoning powers? Does laboratory work in science train the power of observation for all sorts of facts? Does matching colored sticks educate the senses for all sorts of discriminations" (Thorndike, 1913, p. 358)? The Thorndike and Woodward studies, were designed to empirically test the extent of the transfer.

The actual studies are interesting reading. The tasks were carefully chosen to test transfer in important areas. The estimation of magnitudes was selected because it resembled tasks used by "a tea-tester, tobacco-buyer, wheat-taster or carpenter, who attains high proficiency in judging magnitudes or, as we ambiguously say, in delicacy of discriminating certain sense data. It is thus like common cases of sense training in actual life" (Thorndike & Woodworth 1901a, p. 249). They also used training in the observation of words containing certain combinations of letters that was designed to correspond to "learning to attend to any small details" and training in memorizing "on the general ability to memorize." In essence the task "samples were chosen because of their character as representative mental functions, because of their adaptability to quantitative interpretations and partly because of their convenience" (p. 250).

The general method was to pretest on two tasks, provide training on one, and then posttest on the two tasks. The studies used relatively small samples (4–6) and reported individual performance before training, after training, and on transfer tasks. There were no tests of significance but observation of individual performance on pre and posttests would lead to the conclusion that there were no large transfer effects. Thorndike concluded that transfer between two tasks was determined by identical elements shared by the two tasks.

This does not mean that all psychologists of the time accepted these results. There were a number of further studies that addressed the problem and found evidence for broader positive transfer. For instance, in 1907 Coover and Angell were quite critical of the Thorndike and Woodworth studies and cited a number of other experiments that had found positive transfer effects supporting faculty psychology. In their own work, they attempted to select training tasks that were different enough from each other that the explanation of identical elements could not be invoked as an explanation for improvement. In the first study, they trained students in sound discrimination and tested on light discrimination. In the second study, they trained on card sorting and tested on "typewriter reaction," which translated into measuring reaction time and errors to typing letters a, t, e, and n as they appeared on a screen. There were two additional features of these studies. First, they included control subjects who only took the pre and posttests. While Thorndike and Woodworth had included controls in their last study and had been given credit by Boring (1953) for being the first to use them, Dehue (2000) has noted that Coover and Angell were the first to emphasize the importance of such controls in psychological studies. Second, Coover and Angell believed that introspection should be used to better understand the nature of transfer. They found clear evidence of transfer in their first study but had to rely on introspective reports in the second. Thorndike subsequently reported in detail the results of the second study in his text (Thorndike, 1913, p. 407) to show the lack of transfer in reaction time and errors.

W. H. Winch also performed a number of transfer studies, which were widely reported. For instance, in the *Psychological Bulletin* in 1909 it is reported that he performed a series of studies in memory practice on poetry and school subjects (the studies were originally contained in the *British Journal of Psychology* and he found considerable transfer). Later he reported failing to find transfer from improvement in numerical computation to improvement in arithmetical reasoning (Winch, 1911).

In 1914, Dr. Nellie Hewins reported a fairly sophisticated study in which high school students were pre and posttested on the observation and descriptions of biological and nonbiological material. Training for the experimental group consisted of 2 weeks of observing and describing biological material. Three classes of students were individually assigned to experimental and control groups on the basis of their ranking on the pretests (beginning with the highest average being assigned to the control and the next to the experimental, etc.). While there was no significance testing, it is clear from the posttest results that the experimental group outperformed the control group on accuracy of descriptions of both biological and nonbiological material.

Be that as it may, subsequent educational psychology books (e.g., Stroud, 1946; Trow, 1950) cited the Thorndike and Woodworth articles when discussing transfer of training and gave them credit for the rejection of the faculty psychology position on transfer. This remains true of history of psychology (e.g., Hergenhahn, 1997; Thorne & Henley, 1997) and history of education (e.g., Good, 1964) texts. These studies were also cited in the 50th anniversary issue as among the most influential articles to appear in *Psychological Review* (Langfeld, 1943).

Thorndike's best known book in the area of educational psychology was really three books in one "which together give the main facts of educational psychology" (Thorndike, 1913, p. vii). Published in 1913, the year after he served as president of APA, it was dedicated to William James, James McKeen Cattell, and "to that intrepid devotee to concrete human nature, Stanley Hall, whose doctrines I often attack, but whose genius I always admire" (p. vii). This is interesting because the first book that "describes man's original equipment" (p. vii) systematically refutes Hall's theory of recapitulation.

The second book "treats the laws of learning in general, the improvement of mental functions by practice and their deterioration by fatigue" (Thorndike, 1913, p. vii). The final volume deals with individual differences and their causes. This latter would be the most controversial today because it treats the "influence of sex, race, immediate ancestry, maturity and training in producing these variations" (p. vii). Here Thorndike contends that men exhibit more variability than women in most tasks. In addition, he addresses racial differences under the general heading "The influence of remote ancestry" (p. 206). The racial distributions for intelligence displayed (from Galton) are remarkably similar to the same distributions included in the more recent *Bell Curve* (Herrnstein & Murray, 1994).

It is clearly Thorndike's book as he often uses the first person and is filled with enthusiasm and certainty. The book contains much research, always interpreted to support his major contentions. It is not a book that can be read casually, and one wonders how many teachers actually spent time attempting to connect and strengthen bonds when teaching literature or even educational psychology.

The section describing his theory of transfer begins by describing faculty psychology and quotes a number of contemporary psychologists and educational administrators who support the theory including Woodrow Wilson. (This was when Wilson was president of Princeton. According to some, Woodrow Wilson discussed becoming a psychologist with G. Stanley Hall while they were both at Johns Hopkins.) His general statement concerning the teaching of Latin to promote desirable habits in adulthood is a good example of his writing.

The notion that doing what is irksome and distasteful in school gives one power and willingness to work for truth and justice in the world is a sample of naive verbal thinking that still too often pervades education. In the first place, the habit formed is often that of *not* doing it. Latin in American high schools, for example, may well drive two pupils away for every one that it attracts to scholarly habits. In the second place, the habit formed is sometimes that of doing the disagreeable with blind confidence- a superstitious puritanism which expects that out of aimless subjection of oneself to the disagreeable, good will come by magic. It will not. In the third place the habit is formed of doing the disagreeable to avoid a greater misery, such as repeating the misery another year, or failing to graduate. Here the value obtains that comes from any subjection of present impulse to a remote end, but the value could be far greater if the remote end were not so cheap a one, and the subjection of present impulses were the means of creating some worthy permanent interest. (p. 423)

In a survey of educational psychology texts being used, Alfred Hall-Quest reported in 1915 that these three books combined made Thorndike the most popular author. The single most popular book was S. S. Colvin's *The Learning Process* (1911), which was more of a survey and less of a dogmatic presentation than Thorndike's books. Authors of other books in use included Bagley, James, Judd, and Kilpatrick.

It is interesting that contemporary educators and psychologists have differing views of Thorndike's accomplishments and legacy. Educational critics see a person who used findings with animals to develop an inadequate learning theory for humans. Others see him as a victor over a more socially responsible educational system proposed by Dewey (Church, 1971). Many psychologists, on the other hand, view him as a dedicated, extraordinarily productive psychologist, who made many positive, lasting contributions in a variety of areas.

Also important was his influence on the lives of Naomi Norsworthy and Leta Hollingworth. As his primary biographer points out, "Thorndike lacks the academic prejudice against women as students and colleagues" (Joncich, 1968, p. 221). Norsworthy (1877–1916) completed her Ph.D. in 1904 and was the first female Ph.D. in psychology at Columbia. As a faculty member at Columbia, she had a reputation as an excellent teacher and was also a promising researcher. In the first Thorndike and Woodworth article, a study by Norsworthy is cited in which she failed to find transfer between accuracy and speed on several tasks.

Thorndike championed her promotion to Associate Professor in 1908, overriding Cattell's opposition (Joncich, 1968). Norsworthy spent the last part of her life taking care of her mother, who had cancer, and shortly thereafter Naomi also contracted cancer and died on Christmas day, 1916. Cattell was among those who memorialized her by indicating she was "skilled in research, a truly great teacher, a noble woman" (Joncich, 1968, p. 222).

Letta Stetter Hollingworth (1886–1939) was a remarkable women. Born and raised in western Nebraska by grandparents and an alcoholic father, she always aspired to be a writer. After graduating from high school in a class of eight students, she proceeded to the University of Nebraska. She had an outstanding undergraduate career being elected to Phi Beta Kappa and becoming the class poet. Upon graduation she taught for 2 years in small Nebraska towns before marrying her college boyfriend and moving to New York where her husband was an assistant at Columbia University. He eventually became president of APA and also wrote a biography of his wife.

When Leta arrived in New York, she expected to teach but found that the schools did not hire married women as teachers. She subsequently took classes at Teachers College and after two courses with Thorndike, was hooked on psychology. Thorndike did not impress her as a teacher, but she found his ideas exciting. She was surprised that Thorndike would advise her dissertation, which was on the topic of the effects of the menstrual cycle on mental performance. Later she questioned Thorndike's acceptance of the doctrine that men exhibited greater variability than women. The reasoning was couched in the usual Darwinian terms. While women maintained the status quo, males through their greater variability would provide evolutionary progress. Hollingworth believed the evidence provided (that there were more men than women in feeble minded institutions and in places of prominence) was weak and set out to provide careful empirical tests. Her subsequent research produced considerable evidence against the doctrine, which she believed that Thorndike accepted (they subsequently became close friends). She replaced Norsworthy at Columbia and went on to an outstanding career in the area of exceptional children (see Hollingworth, 1990 and Shields, 1991).

Another major figure during this period was John Dewey (1859–1952). Dewey, like Thorndike, never studied abroad. He earned his undergraduate degree at the University of Vermont in 1879 and his Ph.D. from Johns Hopkins University in 1884. He spent his first 10 years thereafter at the University of Michigan before becoming chair of the Department of Philosophy, Psychology, and Pedagogy at the University of Chicago in 1894. In 1904 he moved to Columbia, where he spent the remainder of his academic career. His article "The Reflex Arc Concept in Psychology" published in 1896, is still cited as the initial functionalist statement. In it he indicated that breaking things down into small units was not the way to understand the human mind. In 1899 he was elected president of the American Psychological Association.

Dewey's major impact on education was through his participation in the progressive education movement while he was at the University of Chicago. Dewey, who was also a political activist, believed that changes that had occurred in the culture necessitated changes in the classroom. Classrooms should prepare students to be good citizens in the modern world. Thus, classrooms should be democracies and provide freedom for children to make decisions and learn by doing. Any type of drill or lecture was frowned on.

In 1896 he opened the University Elementary School at the University of Chicago with his wife as principal and in 1900 he published a book describing the school titled, *School and Society*. This book was reprinted a number of times and circulated among the nation's teachers and eventually throughout the world. It is still assigned in many education and educational psychology courses. The book consists of three lectures and a description of his school after it had been operating for 3 years. It includes his view of the place of the school in the social order and the nature of children. He believed children were curious and active and would learn best when provided freedom to explore their interests. In the first lecture he describes how the changes in society from agrarian to industrial necessitates a change in the school system and suggests that the classroom should be a small community that will train students to live in the larger society.

> When the school introduces and trains each child of society into membership within such a little community, saturating him with the spirit of service, and providing him with the instruments of effective self-direction, we shall have the deepest and best guarantee of a larger society which is worthy, lovely, and harmonious. (p. 44)

The second lecture titled, "The School and the Life of the Child" provides examples of excited children learning through cooking and determining the difference between cotton and wool as they attempt to create thread and hence cloth. A reader immediately wants his or her child to attend such a school. The final chapter, "Waste in Education" describes how the different parts of education (kindergarten, elementary school, grammar school, normal school, university) have separate histories and purposes. In addition, education has been separated from life outside the school. His school was designed to unite all of these elements so they have a common purpose and help the child understand the relationship between education and society at large.

> The child can carry over what he learns in the home and utilize it in the school; and the things learned in the school he applies at home. These are the two great things in breaking down isolation, in getting connection—to have the child come to school with all the experience he has got outside the school, and to leave it with something to be immediately used in his every day life. The child comes to the traditional school with a healthy body and a more or less unwilling mind, though, in fact, he does not bring both his body and mind with him; he has to leave his mind behind, because there is no way to use it in the school. (p. 97)

He concludes the chapter by indicating that his is a demonstration school and he does not expect all schools to be exactly like his but rather to use it as a model.

> A working model is not something to be copied; it is to afford a demonstration of the feasibility of the principle, and of the methods which make it feasible. So (to come back to our own point) we want here to work out the problem of the unity, the organization of the school system in itself, and to do this by relating it so intimately to life as to demonstrate the possibility and necessity of such organization for all education. (p. 110)

Several schools were indeed founded throughout the country as progressive schools with various titles and philosophies. These included the The School of Organic Education in Fairhope, Alabama established in 1907 by Marietta Johnson; the experimental elementary school founded by Junius Meriam in 1904 at the University of Missouri; the Gary Plan developed by William Wirt and instituted in Gary, Indiana in 1908; and the Winnetka Plan begun in 1919 by Carleton Washburn. In 1915 Dewey published, with his daughter, *Schools of Tomorrow*. This book, which also received wide circulation, described several of these schools. The Progressive Education Association was formed in 1919 and continued through 1955.

Probably the most well known of the innovative schools was the Gary Plan, which at its height spread to over 1,000 schools and was considered for adoption in New York City. This plan described as a work–study–play plan, was developed by William Wirt, who was brought to Gary to put his plan into practice. A rather detailed description of this plan may be found in Travers (1983). Special features included an 8-hour school day (because otherwise children would waste out-of-school hours), having children of all ages in the same school building (which provided a good deal of peer tutoring), children taking part in all phases of the school operation including preparation of the meals and building maintenance, teachers making home visits, teaching all courses for application in the real world, instituting science classes in the elementary schools, and offering adult classes. According to Travers (1983), the most appealing part of the plan seemed to be its economy. Having the children help with maintenance, bookkeeping, and meal preparation reduced costs while providing a superior education. In 1915 the superintendent was so confident of the school's superiority that he called for an evaluation. This evaluation led to the program's downfall.

Adam Flexner, who had founded a traditional school of his own, was hired to complete the evaluation. His procedure was to acquire measurements of Gary students and compare them with various normative groups. The problem revolved around these comparison groups and the actual measures used. Gary had a rather unique student population with a large percentage born abroad and thus behind in English. When the Gary children were compared to children not having foreign-born parents, they were at a disadvantage. In addition, the tests used measured skills taught in standard curricula and not those unique skills and abilities that the Gary school fostered. At any rate, the evaluation was a large-scale event that resulted in seven volumes of material. The conclusion was that the Gary children were performing worse than the comparison groups in nearly all areas measured and this led to the eventual demise of the Gary system.

It should be noted that Dewey did not engage in research, and his 1915 book contained only descriptions of the schools. There were, however, occasional articles in journals attempting to compare progressive schools with traditional approaches. For instance, J. L. Meriam, director of the progressive school at the University of Missouri (Meriam, 1915), published an article in the *Journal of Educational*

Psychology, which pointed out that while traditional elementary schools were designed to prepare students for high school, most students did not go to high school and a more appropriate approach would be to prepare elementary students for the "more immediate needs of the pupils." Thus, in his school the students engaged in the following four studies:

1. Observation of nature and industrial activities.
2. Playing games of present interest.
3. Handiwork: making things of immediate usefulness.
4. Enjoyment of stories, pictures, music (p. 361).

There was no formal training in the traditional subjects. Meriam presented comparisons of students who had attended this school with students who had attended traditional elementary schools on high school performance. The differences were negligible with the students in the progressive school doing slightly better.

In spite of the efforts of these progressive educators, education did not change in the ways that Dewey had advocated and foreseen. There have been a number of speculations concerning why the schools did not change. Some have blamed Thorndike or mainstream educational psychologists for not taking up the progressive cause (Church, 1971). They suggest that educational psychologists were too committed to hard science or studying the limitations rather than the potentials of children. Church looked at the educational psychology literature between 1910 and 1920 and found a "surprising lack of concern for education's social role and a dearth of programmatic statements about what social service education was to perform and what ends it was to serve" (p. 391). I suppose one could come to the same conclusion reading current issues of the *Journal of Educational Psychology* and failing to find articles on school violence or drug use in schools.

There were other possible reasons for the failure of progressive education to become universal. First, Dewey did not seem interested in experimental validation. He published descriptions of schools, not empirical data. Second, being a teacher in such schools is more difficult than one imagines. It is much easier to present material and give tests than to get students to make intelligent choices and learn by doing in an excited manner. To train such teachers the normal schools and universities would have needed to revamp their teacher training curricula. Dewey was not interested in training teachers and in fact one of the reasons he left Chicago was because the faculty voted to have his school merged with the Teacher Training Institute (Thorne & Henley, 1997). It should be mentioned that Dewey was not a particularly good teacher and Joncich (1968) quotes students as saying, "that he is at his best when he forgets to come to class" (p. 217).

Dewey and Thorndike while at Columbia together saw things quite differently. Thorndike maintained that he did not understand Dewey (Joncich, 1968). It is certainly true that their writing styles were quite different. A good way to compare these styles and approaches to education is to read Dewey's APA presidential address (Dewey, 1900a) and Thorndike's article in the initial issue of the *Journal of Educational Psychology* (Thorndike, 1910). Nevertheless, they respected each other, and Thorndike reacted positively to Dewey's doctrine of interest in his 1913 text:

> The doctrine so brilliantly and earnestly defended by Dewey, that school work must be so arranged as to arouse the problem-attitude—to make the pupil feel needs and work definitely to satisfy these—would probably be accepted by all, at least to the extent of agreement that pupils will progress much faster if they do approach work with needs which its accomplishment satisfies, and with problems whose solutions its accomplishment provides. (Thorndike, 1913, p. 225)

As all graduate students in psychology know, many American students and psychologists during this time migrated to Germany for graduate training. The migration was rather short lived and only lasted from 1881 to 1895. German universities were known for providing faculty freedom to lecture and study what they felt was important in their field. This support for research seems to have been unique in the world. The faculty in these institutions came from a privileged segment of society sometimes referred to as the Mandarian Class. The education was cheap (it was estimated by Veysey [1965] that the cost of studying a year in Germany was one third the cost of a year at Johns Hopkins), and there was considerable prestige attached to receiving a German degree.

Many of the students who migrated from the United States were interested in the new science of psychology that was being pursued in Leipzig by Wundt. The subject matter of Wundt's psychology is often represented or misrepresented (see Blumenthal, 1975), as quite narrow and nonapplied. The major interest consisted of determining the structure of the mind, but Wundt also wrote extensively on language and social psychology. Training received by students could be quite broad. Students had to study psychology and two other areas of interest on which they were subsequently tested. In addition, the psychology that Americans studied in Germany was not the psychology they brought back to the United States. Even Titchener, who is often described as Wundt's disciple in the United States, has subsequently been represented as studying a different psychology than Wundt (Leahey, 1981).

A number of the returning Americans became pioneers in educational psychology. These included James McKeen Cattell, who used his German dissertation to begin a long-term interest in individual differences; Lightner Witmer (1867–1956); George Frederick Arps (1874–1939); Edmund Burke Huey (1870–1917); G. Stanley Hall (1844–1924); and Charles Hubbard Judd (1873–1946). Two other students of Wundt, Titchener and Munsterberg, who were not American, were recruited by American universities and made contributions to educational psychology through their work and/or their students (Benjamin, Durkin, Link, Vestal, & Acord, 1992, provide a list of American students of Wundt).

One of the most prominent of those trained in Germany was Charles Judd (1873–1946). Judd began college expecting to become a minister and actually attended Wesleyan University at the same time as Thorndike. (They never mentioned meeting each other at that time but must have crossed paths. For instance, Thorndike succeeded Judd as president of the Football Association.) Both seemed to have acquired an interest in psychology from Professor A. C. Armstrong. Judd also gave Armstrong credit for taking him to an early meeting of the American Psychological Association where he met James and Dewey and visited Cattell's laboratory. After graduating from Wesleyan, he was able to borrow money from a minister friend and went to Europe for graduate work at Leipzig. Judd chose as his two minor areas anatomy and pedagogy. Judd, more than most, seems to have been influenced by Wundt's personality and modeled his later behavior after Wundt. In addition, while in Germany, he undertook the translation of Wundt's *Grundriss der Psychologie* into English.

After returning to America, he taught 2 years at Wesleyan University, being selected over Thorndike. He then went to NYU for 2 years where he got into trouble for demanding that the standards set for education students be raised. In his autobiography (Judd, 1918b), he indicates that he learned from this incident that change in such institutions must be gradual. After a year at the University of Cincinnati, he obtained a full professorship at Yale. While at Yale he published *Genetic Psychology for Teachers* and his famous transfer study (Judd, 1908). In 1909 he was elected president of APA and moved to the University of Chicago to take the position that had been vacated by Dewey.

Judd was a prolific researcher and champion of high standards for those institutions training educators. At Chicago he was initially head of the school of education, which later became a department. He made admission and graduate requirements in education meet the same standards as the remainder of the university. He found that there were no qualified candidates for the positions he had to fill so he set out to identify qualified graduate students whom he trained for the positions. At the end of his career at Chicago, 10 of 15 professors in his department had been trained by him. He also raised the standards of the three journals published by the department and became editor of *The Elementary School Journal*. Those wishing to read original Judd can consult the editorials in this journal, which he wrote for every issue until 1914.

Judd's view of educational psychology was unique in several ways. First, he emphasized the importance of education as a social phenomena. Second, he related specific subject matter to psychological processes and in 1915 authored *Psychology of School Subjects*. Third, Judd was less impressed with the importance of instincts than James and other psychologists of his day. He felt that we should place more emphasis on man's superior intelligence, which was the important product of evolution. Fourth, Judd disagreed with Thorndike's views on transfer and the theory of connectionism. He felt transfer was far more complicated than what could be accounted for by identical elements and that connectionist learning only occurred in specific types of situations (e.g., spelling). He suggested that transfer really depended on how instruction was carried out. If the instructor taught for transfer then it would occur. His classic article on transfer was often required reading in graduate courses in educational psychology. He found that students taught the principle of refraction would use that principle later in a task requiring the application of that principle. The study was replicated some years later using an air gun rather than throwing darts as Judd had employed (Hendrickson and Schroeder, 1941). Finally, he was also a developmentalist and believed, in contrast to Thorndike, that cognitive developmental periods did exist.

Judd's views were far closer to current cognitive views of learning than those of Thorndike. Thus, one wonders why he is far less prominent in history books than Thorndike. Certainly it is not due to his lack of productivity as he is said to have authored 685 articles or books.

Other Learning Research. During this period there was considerable research on learning. For instance, the classic studies of telegraph operators were carried out at the University of Indiana (Bryan & Harter, 1899). Harter had been a telegraph operator on the railroad and noticed changes in proficiency as learning progressed. These studies, which documented the changes, were cited in educational psychology texts for many years to illustrate the learning curve (e.g., Stroud, 1946; Trow, 1950) and are still cited as an example of automaticity (Sternberg, 1999). Bryan, a Clark student, was president of APA in 1904 and later became president of Indiana University.

Once it was founded in 1910, the *Journal of Educational Psychology* reported much of the learning research. It was published monthly from September to June and cost $3.00 per year. The board of four editors included Bell, Seashore, Bagley, and Whipple. Bell was the managing editor and attended both the Universities of Berlin and Leipzig before acquiring his Ph.D. at Harvard. Seashore received his Ph.D. at Yale and spent his academic career at Iowa. He preceded Thorndike as president of APA and is best known for the development of several tests including the *Seashore Measure of Musical Talent*. Both Whipple and Bagley were students of Titchener and received their Ph.D.s from Cornell.

During those years the *Journal of Educational Psychology* was unique in that it provided applied information and a publication outlet for psychologists and educators at all levels. Instead of listing an editorial board, the journal listed 40 collaborators. While this list included many of the most prominent psychologists of the day, it also included three school superintendents and one school principal (Anna J. McKeag was the only female listed). In the first 10 volumes there were 296 authors and coauthors of articles. Forty of these were at normal schools and 34 were employed at elementary or secondary schools (teachers and principals) or were actively engaged in educational professions (superintendents, members of boards of education, employed by bureaus of education, etc.).

Besides research articles, there were book reviews, instructional suggestions (e.g., it is better to lecture without looking at notes), editorials on contemporary issues (e.g., the importance of establishing bureaus of education), reports on class demonstrations (Naomi Norsworthy reported a demonstration to show that students who learn the most rapidly also retain the most information), and letters commenting on findings. For example, in a 1919 letter that has a contemporary ring, A.W. Kallom of the Boston Department of Educational Investigation and Measurement reported that his findings agreed with those of M. Garfinkel from Public School 9 that student test scores fall over the summer.

One gets the sense from the articles that authors believed psychological learning research would make major contributions to education and with sufficient research, general learning principles would become apparent. The application of these principles would then lead to improvements in education.

Measurement

During this period immense interest was shown in measurement. This included the development of intelligence and achievement tests that led to new statistical techniques. In addition, new item types and methods of scoring were first presented. Americans were interested in individual differences and school administrators wanted to know how well their students were doing. It should be no surprise that measurement has been a major topic in the *Journal of Educational Psychology* since its inception (see Ball, 1984).

Development of Intelligence Tests.   As Jensen (1987) has pointed out,

> The concept of mental ability, as we conceive of it today, is of surprisingly recent origin in the history of human thought. There is little evidence of association between the concept of *mind* and the concept of *ability* in the literature of theology and philosophy prior to the latter half of the 19th century. It is the ability aspect of mental ability that was so delayed in making its appearance. The notion of individual differences in mental ability is even more scarce in philosophical thought prior to the 19th century. The leading theologians, philosophers, and political and social thinkers before that time apparently did not concern themselves with the subject of individual differences in mental abilities. (p. 63)

Even more surprising is the fact that the concept of intelligence was so readily accepted in America and England in contrast to France, where the most successful test originated, and the remainder of Europe. Travers (1983) suggests this is because it fit in so well with Social Darwinism presented by Herbert Spencer. Social Darwinism was accepted because it justified the social strata as it existed in America at that time. Naturally, smart people became wealthy and dumb people should not be helped. To some extent, it was the results of this view that the progressives were reacting against.

Nearly every psychology text presents an account of the development of intelligence tests. It usually begins with a description of the contributions of Francis

Galton (1833–1911), cousin of Charles Darwin. Galton was clearly a genius who never worked for money and spent his life investigating things that interested him (see Forrest, 1991). His many contributions in a variety of areas are truly amazing. He produced the first weather maps, found that finger prints were suitable for identification and convinced Scotland Yard to use them, discovered the correlation coefficient, and invented several types of engines and the Galton Whistle (which was used in early psychological laboratories). He actually devoted less than half of his time on problems of interest to psychology.

Galton's psychological work seems to have begun during the writing of *Hereditary Genius*, published in 1869. In that book, he maintained that talent was more the result of genetics than environment. Using published obituaries as an operational definition of talent, he was able to show that the closer the genetic relationship to eminent people the greater the likelihood that a person would be talented. He believed that the three inherited characteristics that would lead to eminence were intelligence, zeal, and the ability to engage in hard work. Although he did not attempt to directly measure these abilities, he suggested that they could be arranged in a distribution resembling the normal curve. Galton was convinced that the implication of his genetic work was that societies should foster the mating of talented individuals. This emphasis on eugenics remained important to him throughout his life.

In 1884 he opened a personally financed anthropometric laboratory and began collecting data that included measures of strength, reaction time, sensory discrimination, height, and weight. Soon others were founding similar labs and collecting data.

James McKeen Cattell (1860–1944) visited Galton in 1888 after completing his degree with Wundt in 1886. After graduating from Lafayette College Cattell journeyed to Europe where he sought to become proficient in French and German as well as learn about the new psychology. While at Leipzig, he wrote an essay that resulted in a fellowship at Johns Hopkins. When his fellowship was not renewed, he returned to Germany and earned his Ph.D. from Wundt.

Cattell was the perfect person to carry on Galton's investigations elsewhere. He had adopted the view that it was important to gather data and that the importance of the data would become apparent later. Michael Sokal, who is a leading expert on the life of Cattell, has written a brief and very readable description of Cattell's career in measurement (Sokal, 1987b). Sokal traces the belief in the importance of collecting data without a well thought out theory to Cattell's undergraduate days at Lafayette where he fell under the spell of a Baconian philosopher. The idea is that the usefulness of good data will eventually make itself known. Thus, Cattell collected a tremendous amount of data, and it was widely publicized that these data would eventually be of use. Teachers who were looking for help paid attention to Cattell's publications.

Cattell began his academic affiliation at the University of Pennsylvania in 1889 and founded a psychological laboratory designed for undergraduates. In 1891 he moved to Columbia University where he spent the first 3 years developing a laboratory. There he spent much time collecting data, and convincing the president of Columbia that his tests should be given to students. In 1895 he was elected president of APA. While president, he appointed a committee "to consider the feasibility of cooperation among the various psychological laboratories in the collection of mental and physical characteristics" (cited in Sokal, p. 34). This committee issued a final report in 1897 supporting the collection of mental anthropometry, but other events interceded. Sokal reports that several of those originally interested in the testing abandoned their programs. Then the crucial test of Cattell's approach occurred.

The story begins with Clark Wissler, who graduated from Indiana in 1887 and went to Columbia to work with Cattell. While at Columbia, Wissler learned how to calculate correlations and correlated Cattell's different measures with each other and with grades. He found that the Cattell measures did not correlate significantly with anything including themselves, but that grades correlated very well with each other (Wissler, 1901). This ended the anthropometric mental testing movement. Cattell left experimental psychology but continued as an influential force in psychology. Before proceeding to Binet, it should be pointed out that the failure of several of the measures to correlate may have been more the function of factors other than invalid measures. We will return to this point when Spearman is discussed. However, there has been a recent revival of interest in reaction time as a correlate of intelligence (Deary & Stough, 1996, Jensen, 1982) and other information processing skills (e.g., Hunt, 1978). In addition, some of Cattell's other measures have been used in specialized tests (e.g., Seashore used tonal accuracy in his measure of musical ability), and some of the phenomena he discovered (e.g., the fact that letters when included in words can be identified faster than when displayed by themselves) have been of interest to current cognitive psychologists trying to understand perception and reading phenomena.

Alfred Binet (1857–1911) was a physician's son. He pursued law and medicine before developing an interest in abnormal psychology and eventually mental retardation. In 1895, he was the director of the Laboratory of Physiological Psychology when he founded the *L'Annee Psychologique* in which he published most of his work. In the search for measures of intelligence, he pursued dot counting, reaction time, head measurements, palmistry, and speech fluency without much success. In 1904, a commission appointed by The French Minister of Public Instruction to study ways of educating students with mental retardation in Paris public schools decided to segregate such students in special classes. Unfortunately, they had no good way to classify students with normal mental abilities and students with mental retardation so they asked Binet and Theodore Simon, a physician, to devise a reliable classification system. In 1905 Binet reported that in his quest for an appropriate method, he located a short article by a Dr. Blinn (a physician at Vaucluse Asylum) and his pupil, Dr. M. Damaye, in what he felt was "a first attempt to apply a scientific method to the diagnosis of mental debility" (Binet & Simon, 1916, p. 28). This method consisted of asking questions, in a standardized fashion, about

20 topics. Although he points out some defects (all items are given the same weight and there are no cut off scores for classification), Binet adopted this technique and some of the items for his measure. Blinn's name seems to have disappeared from most descriptions of Binet's work and later in the year, Binet published items in his initial test. One of Binet's major contributions was the demonstration that items could be categorized by age at which they could be passed. In 1908 the first scale with grading was published and in 1911 he published his final scale (the year in which Binet and Galton died).

It is here that Charles Goddard (1866–1957) entered the scene. Goddard was a Quaker (thus socially concerned) who acquired his first two degrees from Haverford College. After being a teacher and principal, he entered the doctoral program at Clark University. Upon acquiring his Ph.D. in 1899 under G. Stanley Hall, Goddard became a professor at West Chester State Teachers College. In 1906 he became the director of research at the Training School for the Feebleminded in Vineland, New Jersey. In search of ideas, Goddard went to Europe in the spring of 1908 and visited a number of institutions similar to Vineland. It was in Brussels, where a Dr. Decroly and Mlle. Degard were using Binet's items, that Goddard first encountered Binet's test of intelligence and realized its importance. As Zenderland (1987) points out, Binet and Goddard had several things in common. Both were outside of academic psychology, had been involved in child study movements where they had worked with teachers of the handicapped, and were familiar with medical personnel and medical ideas. When Goddard returned from Europe, he immediately began to gather data using the new items at Vineland and was very excited about the results. The test scores corresponded quite closely with the informal diagnoses that had been arrived at by the professional staff. In addition, the test yielded a specific score for each child that provided a basis for classification. Subsequently, Goddard was able to have the medical association adopt a classification system for children (e.g., moron) that still survives. Goddard also began translating Binet's work and circulating it in America.

Goddard was an avowed Darwinian and felt that the major antecedent to intelligence was genetic. At about that time Mendel's work was circulating and Goddard felt that Mendel's findings supported his position. In probably his most famous publication, Goddard (1913) traced the descendants of two families of a specific person. In his early days, Martin Kallikak, Sr. had fathered a child with a barmaid. Later, Kallilkak had married a more well-to-do woman. Goddard traced the descendants of the two women and found that the barmaid's descendants included a number of social misfits while the wife's descendants included mainly highly successful people. It should be mentioned that there had been other similar studies with similar findings (e.g., the Jukes, the Hill folk, the Nam family).

Because Goddard, along with many others at that time, believed that low intelligence could mean inability to tell right from wrong, he advocated eugenics and voluntary (with incentives) sterilization. He also supported segregating persons with mental retardation. Among other things, Goddard acted as a consultant for the New York Public Schools and advocated using his form of the Binet test to classify children into special classes. This could have both positive and negative effects. Many children, particularly those with physical disabilities, were mistakenly placed in these special classes. In addition, these classes could be used as places teachers could send able children they found undesirable. By using Goddard's test, such children would be allowed to leave these classes for a more appropriate placement. On the other hand, once children were placed in such classes on the basis of Goddard's test, little would be expected of them. Extending his philosophy even further, those scoring high on the test did not need to be trained on problem solving because that was part of their inherited ability.

In the June 1914 issue of the *Journal of Educational Psychology*, J. Carleton Bell reports on the case of Jean Gianini, who murdered his teacher. The trial "offered the first instance of the acceptance by the courts as expert testimony the evidence of a non-medical specialist in feeble-mindedness (Dr. H. Goddard), and the general consideration of the legal status of the feeble-minded" (Bell, 1914b, p. 362). Goddard determined, via the Binet test, that Gianini had a mental age of 10 and thus was clearly feeble-minded. Gianini was found not guilty "because of insanity."

While some have tended to leave Goddard out of the history of educational psychology, (e.g., Hilgard, 1996) and many may find actions and views he took as distasteful, he was merely reflecting the attitudes of his time, and the fact remains that he was the first to translate and circulate Binet's scales in America.

Louis Terman (1877–1956) was also a staunch Darwinian and graduate of Clark University. Terman was the 12th of 14 children in an Indiana farm family. He attended Central Normal College in Danville, Indiana before becoming a rural school teacher and high school principal. After acquiring his bachelor's and master's degree from Indiana University, Terman accepted a fellowship at Clark University. He received his Ph.D. in 1905 with Sanford as his advisor (Hall was not interested in individual differences). From there he spent time as a high school principal and then accepted a position at Los Angeles State Normal school. In 1910 he began his long tenure at Stanford University where he became chairman of the psychology department in 1922, a position he retained until his retirement in 1942. (He received the job after E. B. Huey, who wrote a classic book on reading (Huey, 1908), had turned it down. A promising educational psychologist, Huey died at an early age.) Thus, in educational background, experience, and viewpoint Goddard and Terman were quite similar. The difference was that Terman was initially interested in both ends of the spectrum and eventually became interested in genius. (His dissertation was titled "Genius and Stupidity: A Study of Some of the Intellectual Processes of Seven Bright and Seven Stupid Boys." In the study he used some of the items Binet had used in earlier testing efforts.) We know that they communicated and that Goddard gave Terman a book of translations of Binet's works in 1916 (which was republished in a limited edition with Terman's notations in 1980). Terman's contribution was to revise and standardize the test. He and Childs tested 396 students using a revision of the 1908 scale in 1910 and published the results in 1912

(Terman & Childs, 1912). Terman published the best known scale before 1920, in 1916.

In the development of a scoring system for intelligence tests, there were at least three approaches advocated. Binet reported norms for particular ages while Yerkes advocated a universal point scale where performance could be evaluated by comparison with several norms. Terman in the 1916 revision of the Binet–Simon scale adopted a procedure advocated by William Stern of using an intelligence quotient that was the ratio between mental and chronological age. This system remained in effect until the standard score was introduced some years later.

If one reads Terman's book, *The Measurement of Intelligence* (1916), there is little to distinguish him from Goddard. He cites Goddard's studies and stand on the potential immorality of those scoring low on IQ tests. He also cites the low IQ scores of prostitutes, delinquents, reformatory residents, and studies of degenerate families. He acknowledges that not all criminals are of low intelligence but believes that all low intelligence people are potential criminals because morality requires judgment. Here he presents a theory of development in which all children are immoral until they acquire sufficient intelligence to understand moral principles. When we turn to the uses of the intelligence test for other groups, Terman makes his case for the use of the intelligence test for placing children in the correct grade, for ascertaining vocational fitness, and determining racial differences. It was after 1920 that Terman engaged in his famous debates with Walter Lippman.

It is interesting that the development of the most useful and most used intelligence test was largely nontheoretical. While Binet believed that assessment of higher mental skills was necessary to acquire an index of intelligence, he did not explicitly develop a theory. Both Goddard and Terman were interested in the practical applications of the intelligence test and did not provide theoretical analyses of intelligence. The two initial theories of intelligence tests came from Spearman and Thorndike. While Thorndike's theory was presented after 1920, Spearman published his initial article in 1904.

At about the same time Binet was trying out his new tests, Charles Spearman (1863–1945) was engaged in another endeavor. After a career in the English army he decided to pursue a new career in psychology. He studied in Leipzig with Wundt and received his Ph.D. in 1904. During that same year he published his classic study, "General Intelligence, Objectively Determined and Measured" (Spearman, 1904).

The article began by indicating that while there had been considerable experimental activity in psychology, there had been few usable results.

> Take for example education. This is a line of practical inquiry that more than all others has absorbed the energy and talent of younger workers and that appears to offer a peculiarly favorable field for such methods. Yet at this moment, not withstanding all the laborious experiments and profuse literature on the subject, few competent and unprejudiced judges will venture to assert that much of unequivocal information of capital importance has hitherto come to light. (Spearman, 1904, p. 203)

What he wanted to do is show that results from laboratory studies were relevant to real life by using correlations "for the purpose of positively determining all psychical tendencies, and in particular those which connect together the so-called 'mental tests' with psychical activities of greater generality and interest" (p. 205). In this case he was following up an observation of Galton's that "men of marked ability" also have "an unusually fine discrimination of minute differences in weight" (p. 207).

In the article, Spearman provided an excellent review of previous attempts to determine the relationship among mental abilities. He found considerable research, carried out by many of the more prominent psychologists including Bagley, Binet, Seashore, and of course Thorndike, and Woodworth as well as Wissler. Spearman's conclusion from this review was that the past research seemed to "absolutely deny any such correlation at all" (Spearman, 1904, p. 219). This did not deter Spearman because he had critically examined the research and found four primary deficiencies. First, only Wissler had "attained to the first fundamental requisite of correlation, namely, *a precise quantitative expression*" (p. 223). Second, no one had calculated "probable error" (p. 223). Third, no one had explicitly stated the problem they were attempting to resolve and finally, no one had taken into account errors of observation. Spearman then proceeded to acquire and correlate measures of sound, light, and weight discrimination with three measures of real world ability (ranking in grades, ratings of brightness by teachers, and rating by peers on common sense).

After correcting for a number of errors (e.g., attenuation) Spearman concluded "there is found to actually occur a correspondence—continually varying in size according to the experimental conditions—between all the forms of Sensory Discrimination and the more complicated Intellectual Activities of practical life" (1904, p. 234). In accounting for the different findings of Wissler (who had included perceptions of weight and pitch), Spearman suggested there had been errors of measurement (three people had been measured at once and only 45 minutes had been used to acquire a multitude of measures) and Wissler's subject population was too homogeneous. Spearman felt his findings justified the conclusion "*that all branches of intellectual activity have in common one fundamental function (or group of functions), whereas the remaining or specific elements of the activity seem in every case to be wholly different from that in all the others*" (p. 284). Thus, we have an initial statement of Spearman's two factor theory of intelligence.

These findings had several consequences. First, there was now a theory of intelligence that was based on empirical findings. This theory is still being debated. Second, we now had a statistical procedure that became factor analysis and has been developed as a primary statistical tool for trait and factor theories (which are not far removed from some tenets of faculty psychology). Third, we could explain why Binet's test seemed to predict school performance so well. It was because Binet's tasks and school performance both were heavily loaded on "g".

There were, of course, those who criticized Spearman's approach and other results were presented. Thorndike (1913) discussed traits at length and in discussing Spearman's two factor theory he says, "The doctrine requires not only that all branches of intellectual activity be positively correlated, which is substantially true, but also that they be bound to each other in all cases by one common factor, which is false" (p. 364). Thus, as Hilgard (1987) points out, "So there was Spearman on the side of 'g' with special abilities and Thorndike on the side of special abilities without 'g'" (p. 475). Thorndike's theory of intelligence, which was contained in a measurement book published in 1927, suggested that intelligence was based on the number of S-R bonds developed. That theory has disappeared while factor analysis and trait and factor theory continue to flourish.

Testing and the War. As mentioned earlier, the First World War provided the opportunity for American psychologists to advocate the use of their tests for practical purposes. Accounts of the importance of these tests in the war effort have varied widely but it appears that they were not very influential (Sokal, 1987a). At an early meeting of psychologists interested in contributing to the war effort, von Mayrhauser (1987) has documented a crucial split between the best known industrial psychologist of the day, Walter Dill Scott, and the president of APA, Robert Mearns Yerkes. Scott had spent many years as an applied psychologist serving industry, while Yerkes was an experimental psychologist investigating the hierarchy of intelligence among the various species including man. After the two went their separate ways, Yerkes proposed that those recruits suspected of being incompetent be given individual intelligence tests. This was obviously undoable and after some effort Yerkes was talked out of the individual intelligence test for military use. At a meeting of the APA Committee on Methods of Psychological Examining of Recruits at Vineland, New Jersey (under the leadership of Yerkes, and including Goddard, Terman, Whipple, and Woodworth) a new method for mass testing was introduced. The method was group presentation with a newly developed multiple choice format. Arthur Otis (1884–1963), a graduate student of Terman's, had developed a group test that Terman took to Vineland. (According to Travers [1983] the origin of the group method of presentation was an attempt by Otis to complete an assignment to give the test individually to a number of students by instead giving the items on a group basis and reporting the results as if they had been obtained individually.) The group test developed at the Vineland meeting became the Army Alpha test that was given to over 1,700,000 recruits. The results of this massive undertaking were published in 1921 and included the relative performance of recruits from different national origins. There was an entire chapter on the "Intelligence of the Negro," which failed to mention the many disadvantages of being black in America, and views derived from these tests were not really questioned until the 1930s.

While there has been some speculation concerning the origin of the multiple choice item, Samelson (1987) has identified Frederick J. Kelly as the originator and listed what he believes to be the first item. It appeared in The Kansas Silent Reading Test in 1914–1915, while Kelly was director of the Training School at the State Normal School in Emporia, Kansas. He had written his dissertation at Teachers College on "the unreliability of teachers marks" (Samelson, 1987, p. 118) and was looking for a test format that required only one correct answer and would reduce "the time and effort in the test's administration and scoring" (p. 119). Kelly later became dean of the College of Education at the University of Kansas, dean at the University of Minnesota, and finally chief of the Higher Education Division at the Office of Education. The sequence then seems to be Kelly to Otis to Terman for the Army Alpha. The appearance of the multiple choice item in America may have had a greater impact on teaching and testing than any other single invention during this period. From the very beginning, people were noting its weakness of often measuring only superficial knowledge, but the advantages have kept it popular throughout the years.

It should be mentioned that in the first issue of the *Journal of Educational Research*, W. A. McCall (1920) wrote an article in praise of the new true–false item. Among the many advantages of this format were that it was easy to give, teachers liked it, students liked it, it is a "genuine honesty test and shows the beginnings of a technic for measuring in satisfactory fashion this valuable character trait," (McCall, 1920, p. 45).

Measurement and Educational Research. In addition to the development of intelligence tests, there was considerable activity in their use, the development of other measures, and educational research in general during this period. Although rarely mentioned in educational psychology literature, Joseph Mayer Rice (1857–1934) was an initiator of educational research in the United States. Rice was a pediatrician who in 1888 traveled to Germany to study psychology and education at Jena and Leipzig. During that time, he visited a number of German classrooms. When he returned to the United States, he personally observed and compared American classrooms in 36 American cities with what he had seen in Germany. He published his observations in the *Forum* and a book. In general, Rice found "the teaching mechanical in most schools, the curriculum narrow and based upon test books alone, and the discipline repressive" (Good, 1964, p. 397). When these publications failed to produce a public outcry, he proceeded to collect his own achievement data. In fact, he collected a considerable amount of achievement data from 1895 to 1903 that he also published. In 1903, he attempted to organize a Society of Educational Research but did not succeed because he received no backing from the more legitimate educational researchers of the time. Rice's efforts are detailed in Travers (1983).

Support for educational research also began to appear from such agencies as the Russell Sage Foundation, the General Educational Board, and the Carnegie Foundation. Most of the projects funded were surveys or tests designed to assess and improve education. There was also a general movement to encourage school systems, state agencies, and universities to establish their own research bureaus. A number of articles were published by directors of such bureaus and even teachers in the *Journal of Educational Psychology*. In an editorial in the *Journal of Educational Psychology*, J. Carleton Bell (1914a) described the activities of such a department in New Orleans and indicated that

> "Today the people themselves are beginning to show doubt and unrest at traditional procedures and are insisting on school inquiries, school surveys and objective standards of efficiency in all lines of school activity. The progressive superintendent is quick to take advantage of this change of attitude and seizes every opportunity to organize the resources of his community for the benefit of the schools, and to get more light upon the various aspects of school work". (pp. 107–109)

Such activities have also been identified with the general efficiency movement made popular by Frederick W. Taylor. Taylor had published *The Principles of Scientific Management* in 1911 describing his approach to management, and there was interest in adapting some of these ideas in the schools.

School systems were also being evaluated by outside agencies or psychologists, and people (such as Judd) were earning extra money for such evaluations. The Department of Education was also undertaking statewide surveys and there was talk of national educational standards. The *Journal of Educational Psychology* contained a number of tests and editorials that would lead one to believe that the results of such tests would result in the improvement of education. For instance, in the January 1920 issue, Bell describes the concept of an EQ (Educational Quotient).

> The development of standard tests to furnish a measure of E.Q., the combination of those tests into an educational scale, the determinations of educational norms for different ages and environmental conditions, the amount of educational change that can be produced in a given time by given means, the correlations between the I.Q. and E. Q., are among the interesting problems with which educational investigators are now grappling. (p. 47)

Unfortunately, the promises of better education through research did not materialize as rapidly as everyone hoped and some became disenchanted—but that came later. Johanningmeir (1969) has chronicled this disenchantment in William Bagley.

Developmental Psychology

Even though the first issue of the *Journal of Educational Psychology* contained an article by Earnest Jones (1910) titled, "Psycho-analysis and Education" the early years of educational psychology were not dominated by developmental psychologists. The foremost player in educational psychology, who was interested in developmental issues was G. Stanley Hall (1829–1944). Hall was raised on a farm in rural Massachusetts. His mother wanted him to go to college, and he agreed even though attending college was not a popular choice where he lived and he did not let his friends know his plans (see Veysey, 1965). Upon graduating from Union Theological Seminary, where he enjoyed exploring New York City, attending the theater, churches, and courts, he was advised to seek additional education abroad. He was able to acquire a small loan and studied theology, philosophy, and physics in Bonn and Berlin. Returning to America in 1871, he first acquired employment as a private tutor and then as a language instructor at Antioch College. He then proceeded to Harvard where he worked with James and received his doctorate in psychology (some argue this was the first doctorate in psychology while others note it was given on the recommendation of the philosophy department and does not qualify as a psychology degree). Next he proceeded to Europe for a second time and studied with Helmholtz and then with Wundt as his first American student.

When he returned to America, Hall was married and without a job until the president of Harvard asked that he give some talks on education. In 1882 Hall was invited to Johns Hopkins and in 1884 he was given an appointment as professor of psychology and pedagogics. He had already set up a psychology laboratory in a private house. His students at Hopkins included Joseph Jastrow, Edmund Sanford (whom he took to Clark University), and James McKeen Cattell. He also established the *American Journal of Psychology* when a stranger offered him $500 to found a journal (the stranger thought he was supporting a journal dedicated to psychical research).

Joseph Gilman Clark approached Hall in 1888 and asked him to head a new institution in higher learning that he was endowing. Hall accepted and traveled to Europe for a year where he gathered ideas for the new school and had a good time. Hall founded Clark University in 1889 where he spent the remainder of his academic years. These years were filled with financial difficulties caused by disagreements with Mr. Clark and Hall subsequently lost many of his initial faculty to the University of Chicago (see Veysey, 1965 and Watson, 1971). However, Clark provided what many thought was a good learning environment that included much freedom to study and learn. The seminars that Hall hosted where students presented and Hall critiqued are often mentioned as a high point in this environment.

Hall was more of an initiator, mentor, and founder than a scientist. In 1891 he founded the *Pedagogical Seminary* (presently the *Journal of Genetic Psychology*). The centennial issue of this journal, published in 1991, includes several of the studies published during this time. In 1892 he organized and became the first president of the American Psychological Association. In 1893 Hall published "The Contents of Children's Minds" in the *Princeton Review*, which signaled the beginning of the child study movement. The history of this movement and its demise has been chronicled by Davidson and Benjamin (1987). They describe this movement as the " 'pop psychology' of its day" (p. 54).

Hall championed the questionnaire method of acquiring information from children. He had observed the use of questionnaires with children in Germany and transported the method to America. He collected information from thousands of children on a number of topics. The data resulting from these questionnaires was widely criticized on methodological grounds. As it was used, children were often interrogated in small groups, the procedure and the questions were not standardized, and leading questions were asked. Nevertheless, much of the information gathered was interesting and documented that children were more ignorant than expected. It was clear that teachers should learn more about what children knew. Hall also conducted research concerning morality, when it was developed, and who was important in its development (conscience developed rather late with teachers, parents, and friends being influential).

Hall is remembered for his classic book on adolescence (Hall, 1904). The theory of recapitulation presented in this book, which he derived from Darwin, was quite controversial. This theory suggested that "every child from the moment of conception to maturity, recapitulates, very rapidly at first, and then more slowly every stage of development through which the human race from its lowest beginnings has passed" (Hall, 1923, p. 380). Thus, children pass through the three phases that correspond to the behavior of subhuman primates (preschool), pre-civilization (elementary school), and early civilization (adolescence).

Later, he published a two-volume book addressing education (Hall, 1910). Obviously, his views did not correspond with those of Dewey. Elementary school should consist of short periods of drill administered by a strict teacher. The child was assumed to lack reasoning ability and thus needed to acquire the basics through memory. As an extension of the recapitulation theory, Hall maintained that children often exhibit the negative instinctual behaviors of animals lower on the phylogenetic scale, and these behaviors must be expressed or they will appear in adulthood. This makes childhood and adolescence an excellent time to study instinctual behaviors. He also advocated that the sexes should be educated separately.

It is difficult to determine how much influence Hall's theorizing and recommendations had on education and educational psychology. Both Thorndike and Judd tended to ignore his positions, and Hall did not publish in the *Journal of Educational Psychology*. Still his views were represented in educational psychology texts of the day. For instance, Colvin and Bagley, when discussing negative behaviors in play, indicate,

> Some of these, like teasing and bullying and fighting, may, perhaps be worse than useless at present. They are survivals of the brute stage of human life, like the vermiform appendix, they are troublesome, but must be reckoned with. Dr. Hall holds that such barbarous behavior should not be too suddenly repressed. By giving vent in play to these savage impulses, the child frees himself from them in a relatively harmless manner. If, however, these tendencies are too rigorously and suddenly checked, the instincts behind them may, Dr. Hall says, break out in later childhood or in adult life, with serious results. Free play, therefore, even though it be crude and perhaps, somewhat savage in character, should be permitted within certain bounds. (Colvin & Bagley, 1913, p. 43)

A major innovation in early childhood education during this period was developed by the first female physician in Italy, Marie Montessori. In 1906

Dr. Montessori was asked to develop an educational program for young children in a government-owned tenement and apartment house area. Montessori had been connected with the Psychiatric Clinic in Rome and had specialized in feeble-minded children. She had based her work on Sequin but included modifications of her own developed while studying experimental psychology at the University of Rome and working in primary schools. Word of her success spread quite rapidly and soon people were visiting from other countries.

Montessori visited the United States in 1912, was given a reception at the White House, and her first lecture was presented at Carnegie Hall. A Montessori Association was formed in America with Mrs. Alexander Graham Bell as the first president and President Wilson's daughter as secretary. Schools were set up throughout the country with one being at the Alexander Graham Bell residence. Montessori returned to America in 1915 and presented at the San Francisco World's Fair. Many positive articles appeared about the Montessori method. For instance, in 1912 Howard C. Warren (then president of APA) published a positive article in the *The Journal of Educational Psychology*. He carefully described the Montessori program and praised its successes. The positive features he emphasizes sound similar to those supported by Dewey. "The aim of the school is practical training, every step of which is of real value for the future" (Warren, 1912, p. 124). He goes on to indicate that "the children are subject to no drill. They sit on low chairs at small tables which they often move to another position. They come and go at will" (p. 124). He also mentions that there is no reward or punishment. "The pleasure of accomplishment is deemed a sufficient reward" (p. 124). Social relevance is emphasized. "A second point of special interest to the sociologist, is the influence of the schools on the social community. Especially in the poorer dwellings the lessons of politeness, self-control, and individual initiative react upon the parents, and count as an uplifting factor in the social life" (p. 123).

Warren likes the sensory training and indicates that "Montessori insists that the aim of education, especially at the start, is to train the child's energies along natural lines—to improve the motor and perceptual powers already present rather than start abruptly upon something new" (p. 126). He also notes the self reliance of the children. "At the Case dei Bambinos every effort is made to have the children work out their own education. Self-reliance, initiative, self-control, are fostered, and as a consequence the pupils have a poise and determination not often found at a much more advanced age" (p. 131).

Warren is particularly impressed with progress in reading and arithmetic. "I should not have expected to find reading and writing within the capacity of the average child of 4 or 5 years old. And yet, when we examine the progressive development of studies at these schools, we see that these attainments are reached naturally and easily" (p. 132). He concludes by wondering how these children would score on the Binet-Simon scales.

Two years later a monograph appeared in America that some (e.g., Lilliard, 1972) believe to be responsible for the demise of Montessori schools in America for the next 40 years. Dr. William Heard Kilpatrick (1871–1965) was a well known educator who published widely. He came from White Plains, Georgia, and received his first two degrees from Mercer College and a Ph.D. from Columbia University. In 1901 he accepted an appointment at Teachers College and remained there until retirement. He was known as an outstanding teacher and in 1918 published an important paper describing the project method (Kilpatrick, 1918). This method was designed to engage students in an act of social, purposeful learning. It included the four phases of purposing, planning, executing, and judging with students independently completing all four. The project method was widely adopted by progressive educators and has staged a recent comeback with constructionist educators. As a leading progressive who served on the board of the Progressive Education Association, Kilpatrick was a founder of Bennington (a progressive college), and a lifelong admirer of John Dewey. In fact, he acknowledges John Dewey (and Naomi Norsworthy) for reviewing the manuscript of his book. Who better to visit Italy and write about Montessori?

It is difficult to believe that Warren and Kilpatrick visited the same school. Although Kilpatrick liked the freedom given to the children and seemed impressed with the reading training, he clearly did not like the school or Dr. Montessori. He believed that the lack of social interaction shown in the children's independent behavior was not preparing them for later social success. In addition, he thought the type of sensory training provided presupposed a belief in the rejected faculty psychology. He doubted that she had even heard of the controversy and rejection of faculty psychology. "Here we have most of the ear marks of the old theory of general discipline. 'Not that the child shall know colors forms . . . but that he refine his senses, intellectual gymnastics,' and the same old analogy of mind and body" (Kilpatrick, 1914, p. 46). He felt that Montessori acquired her ideas from "Seguin whose ideas were first published in 1846; when we consider in particular, that Madam Montessori still holds to the discarded doctrine, she belongs essentially to the mid-nineteenth century, some fifty years behind the present development of educational theory" (p. 63).

Kilpatrick compares Montessori unfavorably with Dewey and finds that while they share the idea of freedom, Dewey's ideas are much better. For instance, in discussing her educational devices, he indicates,

> A simple procedure embodied in definite, tangible apparatus is a powerful incentive to popular interest. Professor Dewey could not secure the education which he sought in so simple a fashion. Madam Montessori was able to do so only because she had a much narrower conception of education, and because she could hold to an untenable theory as to the value of formal and systematic sense-training. (p. 64)

Because the monograph was written for educators and Kilpatrick was a respected educator, it is easy to understand why Montessori schools disappeared from America.

Hunt, (Montessori, 1964) speculated on other possible reasons for the demise of Montessori schools in America. He suggests that her ideas were essentially against the Zeitgeist of the time.

EDUCATIONAL PSYCHOLOGY IN 1920

In 1920 educational psychology was still a developing area in the field of psychology. Many of the original giants were alive and still active (e.g., Dewey, Goddard, Hall, Spearman, Terman, Thorndike). In addition, a new set of psychologists was about to take the field. Progress was being made on new measurement instruments, the first of several learning theories had been developed and progressive education was active and advocates hopeful. The *Journal of Educational Psychology* was healthy and new journals were appearing. Even though teachers were receiving mixed messages and becoming skeptical of the promise of the new science, there was still a feeling of optimism among educational psychologists that the applied science of psychology would lead to better, more efficient schools. It was still a good time to be an educational psychologist.

REFERENCES

Baldwin, B. T. (1911). William James' contributions to education, *Journal of Educational Psychology, 2*, 369–382.

Ball, S. (1984). Educational psychology as an academic chameleon: An editorial assessment after 75 years. *Journal of Educational Psychology, 76*, 993–999.

Bell, J. C. (1914a). Research in public schools. *Journal of Educational Psychology, 5*, 106–108.

Bell, J. C. (1914b). Feeble-mindedness in the courts. *Journal of Educational Psychology, 6*, 361–362.

Bell, J. C. (1920). The educational quotient. *Journal of Educational Psychology, 9*, 45–47.

Benjamin, L. T., Durkin, M., Link, M., Vestal, M., & Acord, J. (1992). Wundt's American doctoral students. *American Psychologist, 47*, 123–131.

Binet, A., & Simon, T. (1916). *The development of intelligence in children*. The Training School at Vineland, NJ.

Blumenthal, A. L. (1975). A reappraisal of Wilhelm Wundt. *American Psychologist, 30*, 1081–1088.

Boring, E. G. (1953). The nature and history of experimental control. *American Journal of Psychology, 67*, 573–589.

Boring, E. G. (1957). *A history of experimental psychology* (2nd ed.). New York: Appleton-Century-Crofts.

Bryan, W. L., & Harter, N. (1899). Studies on the telegraphic language. The acquisition of a hierarchy of habits. *The Psychological Review, VI*, 346–375.

Charles, D. C. (1987). The emergence of educational psychology. In J. A. Glover & R. R. Ronning (Eds.), *Historical foundations of educational psychology* (pp. 17–38). New York: Plenum.

Church, R. L. (1971). Educational psychology and social reform in the progressive era. *History of Education Quarterly*, 390–403.

Colvin, S. S. (1911). *The learning process*. New York: Macmillan.

Colvin, S. S., & Bagley, W. C. (1913). *Human Behavior: A first book in psychology for teachers*. New York: Macmillan.

Coover, J. E., & Angell, F. (1907). General practice effect of special exercise. *American Journal of Psychology, 18*, 328–340.

Costa, P. T., & McCrae, R. R. (1992). 4 ways 5 factors are basic. *Personality and Individual Differences, 13*, 653–665.

Davidson, E. S., & Benjamin, L. T. (1987). A history of the child study movement in America. In J. A. Glover & R. R. Ronning (Eds.), *Historical foundations of educational psychology* (pp. 41–59). New York: Plenum.

Deary, I. J., & Stough, C. (1996). Intelligence and inspection time. *American Psychologist, 51*, 599–608.

DeGarmo, C. (1920). [Review of the book Psychology and the teacher]. *Journal of Educational Psychology, 11*, 1142–1144.

Dehue, (2000). From deception trials to control reagents. *American Psychologist, 55*, 264–268.

Dewey, J. (1896). The reflex arc concept in psychology. *Psychological Review, 3*, 357–370.

Dewey, J. (1900a). Psychology and social practice. *Psychological Review, 7*, 105–124.

Dewey, J. (1900b). *School and society*. Chicago: University of Chicago Press.

Dewey, J., & Dewey, E. (1915). *Schools of tomorrow*. New York: Dutton.

Forrest, D. W. (1991). Francis Galton. In G. A. Kimble, M. L. Wertheimer, & C. L. White (Eds.), *Portraits of pioneers in psychology* (pp. 1–18). Hillsdale, NJ: Lawrence Erlbaum Associates.

Goddard, H. H. (1913). *The Kallikak family, A study of heredity and feeblemindedness*. New York: Macmillan.

Good, H. G. (1964). *A history of American education*. New York: Macmillan.

Hall, G. S. (1904). *Adolescence: Its psychology and its relations to physiology, anthropology, sociology, sex, crime, religion, and education* (Vols. 1–2). New York: Appleton.

Hall, G. S. (1910). *Educational Problems*. New York: Appleton.

Hall, G. S. (1923). *Life and confessions of a psychologist*. New York: Appleton-Century-Crofts.

Hall-Quest, A. L. (1915). Present tendencies in educational psychology. *Journal of Educational Psychology, 6*, 601–14.

Hendrickson, G., & Schroeder, W. H. (1941). Transfer of training in learning to hit a submerged target. *Journal of Educational Psychology, 32*, 205–213.

Herrnstein, R. J., & Murray, C. (1994). *The bell curve*. New York: The Free Press.

Hergenhahn, B. R. (1997). *An introduction to the history of psychology* (3rd ed.). Monterey, CA: Brooks/Cole.

Hewins, N. P. (1914). The doctrine of formal discipline in the light of experimental investigation. *Journal of Educational Psychology, 5*, 168–174.

Hilgard, E. R. (1987). *Psychology in America*. Orlando, FL: Harcourt Brace Jovanovich.

Hilgard, E. R. (1996). History of educational psychology. In E. C. Berliner & R. C. Calfee (Eds.), *Handbook of Educational Psychology* (pp. 990–1004). New York: Macmillan.

Hollingworth, H. L. (1990). *Leta Stetter Hollingworth*. Boston, MA: Anger Publishing.

Huey, E. B. (1908). *The psychology and study of reading*. New York: Macmillan.

Hunt, E. B. (1978). Mechanics of verbal ability. *Psychological Review, 85*, 109–130.

James, W. (1890). *The principles of psychology* (Vols. 1 & 2). New York: Holt, Rinehart & Winston.

James, W. (1912). *Talks to teachers on psychology: And to students on some of life's ideals*. New York: Holt, Rinehart & Winston.

Jensen, A. R. (1982). The chronomety of intelligence. In R. J. Sternberg (Ed.), *Advances in the psychology of human intelligence* (Vol. 1) (pp. 255–310). Hillsdale, NJ: Lawrence Erlbaum Associates.

Jensen, A. R. (1987). Individual differences in mental ability. In J. A. Glover & R. R. Ronning (Eds.), *Historical foundations of educational psychology* (pp. 61–88). New York: Plenum.

Johanningmeir, E. V. (1969). William Chandler Bagley's changing views on the relationship between psychology and education. *History of Education Quarterly*, 3–23.

Joncich, G. (1968). *The sane positivist: A biography of E. L. Thorndike*. Middletown, CT: Wesleyan University Press.

Judd, C. H. (1908). The relation of special training to general intelligence. *Educational Review, 36,* 28–42.

Judd, C. H. (1918b). In C. Murchinson (Ed.), *A history of psychology in autobiography* (Vol. 3) (pp. 207–236). New York: Russell & Russell.

Kilpatrick, W. H. (1914). *The Montessori system examined.* Boston: Houghton Mifflin.

Kilpatrick, W. H. (1918). The project method. *Teachers College Record, 19*(4), 319–335.

Korn, J. H., Davis, R., & Davis, S. F. (1991). Historians' and chairpersons' judgments eminence among psychologists. *American Psychologist, 46,* 789–792.

Langfeld, H. S. (1943). Jubilee of the Psychological Review: Fifty volumes of the Psychological Review. *Psychological Review, 50,* 143–155.

Leahey,T. H. (1981). The mistaken mirror: On Wundt's and Titchener's psychologies. *Journal of the History of the Behavioral Sciences, 17,* 173–182.

Lillard, P. P. (1972). *Montessori: A modern approach.* New York: Schocken.

McCall, W. A. (1920). A new kind of school examination. *Journal of Educational Research, 1,* 33–46.

Meriam, J. L. (1915). How well may pupils be prepared for high school work without studying arithmetic, grammar, etc.? *Journal of Educational Psychology, 6,* 361–364.

Montessori, M. (1964). *The Montessori method.* New York: Schocken.

Munsterberg, H. (1909). *Psychology and the teacher.* New York: Appleton.

Murphy, G. (1949). *Historical introduction to modern psychology* (Rev. ed.). New York: Harcourt, Brace.

Ross, B. (1991). William James: Spoiled child of American psychology. In G. A. Kimble, M. L. Wertheimer, & C. L. White (Eds.), *Portraits of pioneers in psychology* (pp. 13–25). Hillsdale, NJ: Lawrence Erlbaum Associates.

Samelson, F. (1987). Was early mental testing: (a) racist inspired, (b) objective science, (c) a technology for democracy, (d) the origin of the multiple-choice exams, (mark the right answer). In Michael Sokal (Ed.), *Psychological testing and American society* (pp. 113–127). New Brunswick, NJ: Rutgers University Press.

Shields, S. A. (1991). Leta Stetter Hollingworth: "Literature of Opinion" and the study of individual differences. In G. A. Kimble, M. L. Wertheimer, & C. L. White (Eds.), *Portraits of pioneers in psychology* (pp. 243–256). Hillsdale, NJ: Lawrence Erlbaum Assoociates.

Sokal, M. (1987a). Introduction: Psychological testing and historical scholarship—questions, contrasts and context. In Michael Sokal (Ed.), *Psychological testing and American society* (pp. 1–20). New Brunswick, NJ: Rutgers University Press.

Sokal, M. (1987b). James McKeen Cattell and mental anthropometry. In Michael Sokal (Ed.), *Psychological testing and American society* (pp. 21–45). New Brunswick, NJ: Rutgers University Press.

Spearman, C. E. (1904). General intelligence: Objectively determined and measured. *American Journal of Psychology, 15,* 201–293.

Sternberg, R. J. (1999). *Cognitive psychology* (2nd ed.). Fort Worth, TX: Harcourt Brace.

Stroud, J. B. (1946). *Psychology in education.* New York: Longmans, Green.

Terman, L. M., & Childs, H. G. (1912). A tentative revision and extension of the Binet-Simon measuring scale of intelligence. *Journal of Educational Psychology, 3,* 61–74, 133–143, 198–208, 277–289.

Terman, L. M. (1916). *The measurement of intelligence.* Boston: Houghton Mifflin.

Thorndike, E. L., & Woodworth, R. S. (1901a). The influence of improvement in one mental function upon the efficiency of other functions. *Psychological Review, 8,* 247–261.

Thorndike, E. L., & Woodworth, R. S. (1901b). The influence of improvement in one mental function upon the efficiency of other functions. *Psychological Review, 8,* 384–395.

Thorndike, E. L., & Woodworth, R. S. (1901c). The influence of improvement in one mental function upon the efficiency of other functions. *Psychological Review, 8,* 553–564.

Thorndike, E. L. (1910). The contribution of psychology to education. *Journal of Educational Psychology, 1,* 5–12.

Thorndike, E. L. (1913). *Educational psychology* (Vols. 1–3). New York: Mason.

Thorndike, R. L. (1991). Edward L. Thorndike: A professional and personal appreciation. In G. A. Kimble, M. L. Wertheimer, & C. L. White (Eds.), *Portraits of pioneers in psychology* (pp. 138–152). Hillsdale, NJ: Lawrence Erlbaum Associates.

Thorne, B. M., & Henley, T. B. (1997). *Connections in the history of psychology*. Boston: Houghton Mifflin.

Travers, R. M. W. (1983). How research has changed American schools: A history from 1840 to the present. Kalamazoo, MI: Mythos.

Trow, W. C. (1950). *Educational psychology* (2nd ed.). Boston: Houghton Mifflin.

Veysey, L. R. (1965). *The emergence of the American university*. Chicago: The University of Chicago Press.

von Mayrhauser, R. (1987). The manager, the medic, and the mediator: The clash of professional psychological styles and the wartime origins of group mental testing. In M. Sokal (Ed.), *Psychological testing and American society* (pp. 128–157). New Brunswick, NJ: Rutgers University Press.

Walker, C. H. (1987). Relative importance of domain knowledge and overall aptitude on acquisitions of domain related information. *Cognition and Instruction, 1*, 25–42.

Warren, H. C. (1912). The "house of childhood": A new primary system. *Journal of Educational Psychology, 3*, 121–132.

Watson, R. I. (1971). *The great psychologists* (3rd ed.). Philadelphia: Lippincott.

Winch, W. H. (1911). Further work on numerical accuracy in school children. Does improvement in numerical accuracy transfer? *Journal of Educational Psychology, 2*, 262–271.

Wissler, C. (1901). The correlation of mental and physical tests. *Psychological Review Monographs* (Suppl. 3, No. 6).

Woody, C. (1920). The administration of the psychology prerequisite to courses in education. *Journal of Educational Psychology, XI*, 61–77.

Woolfolk, A. E. (1998). *Educational Psychology* (7th ed.). Boston: Allyn & Bacon.

Zenderland, L. (1987). The debate over diagnosis: Henry Herbert Goddard and the medical acceptance of intelligence testing. In M. Sokal (Ed.), *Psychological testing and American society* (pp. 46–75). New Brunswick, NJ: Rutgers University Press.

2

William James: Our Father Who Begat Us

Frank Pajares

Emory University

More than half a century ago one of his former students began a tribute to William James by confessing that "it is hardly possible to say briefly anything newly significant about Professor James" (Delabarre, 1943, p. 125). If that was true for someone both intimately familiar with James' work and with James himself, imagine my predicament. So let me confess from the outset that I too believe I can say nothing that is newly significant about William James. But I am fortunate on one account. Familiar though most readers will be with his name and honorary title as the Father of American psychology, perhaps even familiar with some of his humorous anecdotes or clever aphorisms, few will have actually read much of James' work or will be acquainted with even the more general facts of his life (Allport, 1943). As such, perhaps I need not reach for significance, if that be unavailable. Perhaps my more modest aim should be simply to familiarize readers of this volume with this most remarkable of men.

The editors would not be satisfied with mere familiarization, however. This is a volume about one hundred years of contributions to educational psychology, and so I have quite reasonably been instructed to outline and evaluate the legacy left by James to present-day education and educational psychology. Again I am fortunate, for I have what at least can be described as some scattered thoughts on this. The editors also asked that I present James' perspective on four issues of critical importance to educators—the nature of the learner, the nature of learning, the optimal conditions of instruction, and the nature of important learning–instructional outcomes. And fortune smiles on me yet again, for James left rather a clear blueprint of these perspectives. Before I begin, however, let me put my bias clearly on the table. I can claim no sense of objectivity about this man or about his work. For over 30 years, I have been smitten with William James. I read him for work and for play. I read him for guidance. I read him for inspiration. I read him when my spirits are low. I read him to discover what I really think. I read him to learn. I am never disappointed. My admiration borders on adulation. How could anyone fail to see the profundity of this man's wisdom, the elegance of his thought, or the simplicity of his uncommon common sense. *Caveat emptor*. Let me begin with a biographical sketch.

A LIFE OF LOVE AND WORK[1]

William James was born in New York City on January 11, 1842, to an affluent, cosmopolitan, and deeply religious family. His father Henry dabbled in theology, doted on his five children, was well connected to literary and philosophical luminaries of the day, and often took the family for extended stays in Europe. His journeys to the Continent were primarily theological and philosophical odysseys intended to resolve his conflicting spiritual bouts. His right leg had been amputated after burns suffered in a boyhood accident failed to heal. His spirit never quite recovered. A devoted father, he sought to provide his children with the sort of education that would enable them some day to outdistance their countrymen both in erudition and in breadth of knowledge. To this end, he enrolled them in fine schools, obtained for them gifted tutors, and saw to it that they frequented museums and attended lectures and the theater with regularity. William and two of his siblings would give fruit to their father's liberal educational efforts. Brother Henry became one of America's most famed novelists, and sister Alice acquired a literary reputation of her own after her diaries were posthumously published.

When William was but 1 year old, the family went for a two-year stay to Europe. At the dawn of his adolescence, the family made a second journey. William attended schools and had a succession of private tutors in England and France. When he returned home at the age of 16, he spoke, read, and wrote French fluently. A year later, while he was attending school in Newport, Rhode Island, Darwin's *The Origin of Species* was published. It was back to Europe two years later, to more schools and private tutors, this time in Germany and Switzerland, where he first enrolled at the Geneva Academy as a university student. By this time William had added German to his repertoire of foreign languages.

Before William James entered the Lawrence Scientific School at Harvard University to begin medical school at the age of 19, he was familiar with nearly every major museum on the continent, was fluent in five languages, and had met various major figures who frequented the family home. These included Carlyle, Greeley, John Stuart Mill, Tennyson, Thoreau, and James' godfather, Ralph Waldo Emerson. He had first wanted to be a painter and had studied with famed artist William Morris Hunt, but he came to believe that he was not touched with genius in this area and decided to look elsewhere. He was also acceding to his father's urging that he seek a more traditional career path. He enrolled in Harvard and began to study comparative anatomy.

James began his studies at Harvard at the same time that the American Civil War began to rage. Although his brothers Wilky and Bob enlisted, William and Henry Jr. did not, pleading health issues—William suffered from neurasthenia and a host of ailments, including weak vision, digestive disorders, and a severe depression that brought about thoughts of suicide. He was well enough by 1865 to interrupt his studies and join an expedition to the Amazon with naturalist Louis Agassiz. But there, too, James was beset by medical maladies. Two years later he traveled to France and Germany, where he remained for 18 months "taking the baths" to alleviate crippling back aches. He also used the opportunity to read widely in philosophy—particularly Kant, Schiller, Goethe, and Herder—and to study under Hermann von Helmholtz and other leading European experimental psychologists. He returned home to complete his course work and received his degree from the Harvard Medical School in 1869. The MD was the only degree William James ever received.

For almost three years after graduation, James lived in the family home. His bouts of depression increased after a young woman whom he had befriended died following a prolonged illness. He would later describe his depression as a descent into a profound crisis—of spirituality, of being, of meaning, of will (James, 1902/1990, p. 136). He suffered panic attacks and hallucinations that left him mentally crippled. His father had suffered similar attacks and had sought refuge from them in spiritual quests. William feared that his infirmity was rooted in a biological destiny he would be unable to overcome. He shrouded his angst with secrecy and used only his reading and journal writing to deal with the mental anguish. One April evening in 1870, the psychological fever began to break. He recorded in his journal that, after reading an essay on rational psychology by Charles Renouvier, he had come to believe that free will was no illusion and that he could use his will to alter his mental state. He need not be a slave to a presumed biological destiny. "My first act of free will," he wrote, "shall be to believe in free will."

James was now 30, three years out of medical school, and with no career prospects or plans except for a vague desire to devote himself to philosophy in some fashion. It was at this propitious time that Harvard president Charles Eliot, a neighbor and former teacher of James, offered him a post at Harvard teaching physiology for the modest sum of $600 per year. His acceptance signaled the start of a prestigious career, for James was to become a gifted teacher, a skilled orator, and, of course, a prodigious thinker and writer. It signaled also the renewal of his spirit. James took to teaching. His students described him as a rigorous instructor, a lively and humorous lecturer, and a caring soul mate—"To see him," one wrote, "was never to forget what it means to be alive."

As it does to most new teachers, however, the first year left James utterly exhausted. To recharge his batteries, he traveled with his brother Henry through Italy, returning home in the fall of 1874 to resume his teaching duties. The following year he offered a graduate course on the relations between physiology and psychology and established the first laboratory of experimental psychology in the United States. In 1876 he became the country's first assistant professor of psychology. "The first lecture in psychology that I ever heard," he wrote, "was the first I ever gave." Two years later he began writing *The Principles of Psychology*, a task which was to take him a dozen years to complete. He also became engaged to Alice Howe Gibbens.

James had warned Alice that, should she deign to accept his proposal of marriage, she should be well aware of his mental condition. He confessed to her his neurasthenia, his bouts of deep depression, his thoughts of suicide, his lingering spiritual crisis. He cautioned her that he could as easily get worse as better. Alice threw caution to the wind and married William on July 20 of 1878. His neurasthenia got better very quickly.

No academic field could easily contain James' interests. He had switched from teaching physiology to psychology and, in 1879, he shifted to philosophy. The following year he was made assistant professor of philosophy. He saw the new decade in with the birth of the first of his five children. It was a decade devoted to teaching, writing numerous articles for the best journals, and meeting with the finest minds at home and in Europe. But it was also a decade marked by personal tragedy. He lost his mother early in 1882 and his father before that year was out. Three years later, his third child Herman, less than a year old, died of bronchial pneumonia. At decade's end, the family moved to a new home in Cambridge. On September 25 of 1890, Holt began distribution of *The Principles of Psychology* at $6 for the 2-volume set ($5 after dealer discount).

In many ways, the two-volume work was as much philosophy as it was psychology. It was also literature, autobiography, self-help manual, and confessional tale. It was widely admired and for the most part positively reviewed, although a number of readers found it too personal in tone and substance. Although James would self-effacingly claim that "I have no facility for writing, as some people have," the lucid style and rich literary tone he used in this and future works earned for him the accolade that he was actually the real novelist of the James brothers, a novelist who wrote about psychology. Henry, on the other hand, was the real psychologist who wrote novels. But it was not an accolade typically given by members of his discipline. "It is literature," the renowned psychologist Wilhelm Wundt said of the *Principles*, "it is beautiful, but it is not psychology." At the urging of his publisher to create a more digestible book with greater classroom appeal, James later condensed the two volumes into one, *Psychology: The Briefer Course*. Soon the complete work came to be known as *The James*, and the abridged tome as *The Jimmy*. For years, the two would become the standard texts for generations of American university students.

The year 1892 should be an auspicious one to students of education and educational psychology because it was in July of that year that William James delivered the first of a series of twelve lectures on psychology to teachers at Cambridge.[2] His speaker's fee was $50. Such was his eloquence and appeal that the size of his audiences increased after each lecture. After the success of *Principles* and of the lectures, James was exhilarated but exhausted, and an exhausted James always turned to travel. He obtained a year's sabbatical from Harvard, turned his laboratory over to Hugo Münsterberg, and, as had his father before him, he took the entire family to Europe, where he enrolled his boys in an English school in Florence.

When the family returned, James found an America ravaged by a financial depression that had severely depleted his savings. Moreover, he feared he was losing touch with his own national identity. "One should not be a cosmopolitan," he wrote, "one's soul becomes 'disaggregated' " and "one's land seems foreign." He determined to reclaim his cultural identity and began a period of intense activity in social and political causes. The increase in political activism was also marked by decreased interest in psychology—"I wish to get relieved of psychology as soon as possible," he wrote to a friend. European experimentalism, spearheaded by Wundt, was now in full bloom in American psychology. It emphasized an objectivist view of human functioning in which only observable experience merited scientific interest. James found it trivial, mindless, and intellectually indigestible. Though disheartened by the growing success of the behaviorist movement, he continued throughout his life to fight for his introspective view of psychology, and he remained an active member both of the American Philosophical Association and of the American Psychological Association, even serving as President of each organization.

During the closing years of the century, James lectured widely, remained politically active, and published *The Will to Believe and Other Essays in Popular Philosophy*, a book more in keeping with his growing spiritual and philosophical concerns. His lectures to teachers were collected and published in *Talks to Teachers on Psychology: And to Students on Some of Life's Ideals*. At a lecture delivered at the University of California, Berkeley, entitled "Philosophical Conceptions and Practical Results," he put forth his first explanation of the method of pragmatism, an idea that he credited to Charles Sanders Peirce but which James appropriated and transformed.

Ill health once again beset James in the form of a heart condition, and he welcomed the new century convalescing in Europe, where he remained for two years. Proclaiming himself a "piecemeal supernaturalist," James deepened his interest in spirituality and religion during this time, and his Gifford lectures delivered in Scotland formed the basis for a new book entitled *The Varieties of Religious Experience*. Back on home soil, his social activism continued, and he wrote a series of pieces against what he perceived to be America's growing aggression and imperialism. He was delighted when in 1903 Harvard conferred on him an honorary doctorate, but soon after that he was back on a European sabbatical with brother Henry.

In 1906, James accepted an invitation to spend a term at Stanford University and, while there, experienced the earthquake that very nearly destroyed San Francisco. James and Alice survived unscathed, losing only some pottery to the calamity. Later that year he delivered the Lowell Lectures in Boston—lectures that subsequently served as the foundation for *Pragmatism: A New Name for Old Ways of Thinking*. James was now at the height of his eminence both in philosophy and psychology. Although pragmatism had more than its share of detractors, it was also promoted by powerful allies such as the up-and-coming English philosopher Canning Schiller and the American educator, philosopher, and psychologist John Dewey. But James was the preeminent voice.

William James taught his last class at Harvard on Tuesday, January 22, 1907. On that day his classroom overflowed with his own students, former students, colleagues, and Harvard administrators. Even Alice snuck in to view the proceedings. A committee of his graduate students and teaching assistants presented him with a silver-mounted inkwell. His undergraduates gave him a loving cup. The gifts represented an acknowledgment by his students of the quality of their professor's work and the appreciation for his love. If Sigmund Freud was correct that love and work are the cornerstones of humanness, James' students were deeply aware that they had been touched by one of the most human of men. James was genuinely touched and surprised, remarking on "how warm-hearted the world around one is."

He had hoped of course to relax during his retirement, but he was in constant demand for lectures. The few that he now gave played to overflow halls. The Hibbert lectures given at Oxford resulted in the publication of *A Pluralistic Universe* in 1909, the same year that *The Meaning of Truth* came out. In September of that year he attended a celebration at Clark University where he met Sigmund Freud and Carl Jung. He liked Jung well enough; he found Freud "a man obsessed by fixed ideas." The three men took part in a historic photograph.

But James was not well, and his health was deteriorating. He made one final, brief trip to Europe to look in on an ailing Henry and take the baths at Nauheim before he returned to his country home in Chocoura, New Hampshire. There, just before 2:30 in the afternoon of August 26 of 1910, William James passed away cradled in the arms of his wife Alice. He was 68. An autopsy revealed that he had died of an enlarged heart. Two years after his death, a number of his articles were collected and posthumously published as *Essays in Radical Empiricism*.

CONTRIBUTIONS TO PSYCHOLOGY

By the time that William James had published *The Principles of Psychology* in 1890, Rousseau's doctrine of innate ideas was under attack in the field of psychology from associationists who favored Locke's model of the human mind as a *tabula rasa*. The Russian school of reflexology, known today to psychology students primarily through the work of Ivan Pavlov and his discovery of the principle of conditioned reflexes, was having a profound influence on European elementist psychologists. Theirs was an antimentalist view of human functioning in which only observable experience was deemed worthy of scientific scrutiny. This positivist perspective would travel to the United States by way of structuralist Edward Titchener and others. The intellectual precursors of John Watson's and B. F. Skinner's brand of radical behaviorism were well on their way to capturing the discipline, and they wanted a discipline in which self-perceptions and other internal mental states played no meaningful role in a scientific psychology. Moreover, notions of mind–body dualism were still well entrenched within the discipline.

These were not ideas that sat well with James, a man who had come to psychology by way of art and philosophy and who believed that a psychology without introspection could not aspire to explain the complexities of human functioning. It was by looking into his own conscious mind that he made sense of his own psychology, and it was primarily through this method that he developed what he believed were sound principles of psychology. After all, James (1890/1981a) would argue, "introspective observation is what we have to rely on first and foremost and always" (p. 185).

There is general agreement regarding the major ideas with which James imbued his psychology and which he used to ward off the emerging positivist influence. There are, of course, the foundational ideas of functionalism, radical empiricism, and pluralism. James also emphasized self-processes and expressed a profound belief in free will, and he argued strongly for the critical role that mental associations play in the development of human functioning. There is, as well, pragmatism, a method by which ideas can be appraised.

As the 19th century came to a close, it was primarily James' functionalism that stood in opposition to prevailing notions of mind–body dualism and to the growing positivist theories that would rule American psychology during the better part of the 20th century. Initially influenced by Darwin's evolutionary thought that established a connection between structure and function, functionalism emphasized the interactive nature of mind and body and the unity and dynamic nature of what James would describe as "the stream of consciousness." According to James (1899/1958), mental processes are functional in the sense that they aid individuals in their attempts to adapt themselves to their world and their environments—"Man, whatever else he may be, is primarily a practical being, whose mind is given him to aid in adapting him to this world's life" (p. 34).

Perhaps the most identifiable feature of functionalism is its claim that mental states are characterized by their interactions with and causal relations to other mental states. Moreover, because mental events must be understood in terms of their relation to the sensory inputs from which they emanate and to the behavioral outputs that they produce, functionalists argued that elements of mental functioning and rules for the association of ideas cannot be investigated in isolation. These elements are but a function of a continuous stream of thought that can only be understood in relation to the conscious actions of human beings as they go about the business of day-to-day living. Consciousness itself, argued James, is adaptive and functional and makes it possible for individuals to engage in self-regulation.

As had John Locke's empiricism, James' radical empiricism represented a break with Cartesian dualist notions that the real world is an extension of a larger world that exists within the mind. Whereas Locke's empiricism became foundational to positivist views that would focus exclusively on an individual's experienced reality as the *fons et origo* of their psychologies, James' "radical" view of reality had a pronounced phenomenological bent (Allport, 1943; Hilgard, 1987; Wilshire, 1968). For James, mental events stand on an equal footing with observable events as representations of reality. In fact, James made little distinction between experience and reality (Boller, 1979). Whether mental events are or are not simply a function of the external world, they can influence human functioning independently of that world. Consequently, "ideas, feelings, sensations, perceptions, concepts, art, science, faith, conscious, unconscious, objects, and so-called illusions" each merit attention and investigation (Barzun, 1983, p. 111). James believed that an individual's immediate experience represents the essence of psychological truth (Allport, 1943). As for truth itself, that also is a hypothesis. After all, "the universe is still pursuing its adventures" (James, 1907/1975, p. 123). Moreover, the mental and physical events—the immediate experiences—that an individual uses both for self-understanding and to understand others are selected and interpreted by the individual.

Although the dominance of positivist psychology throughout many of the decades that followed James resulted in a large part of the discipline eschewing his brand of radical empiricism (Allport, 1943; Barzun, 1983; Perry, 1958), James' argument that mental states were appropriate subjects of investigation won the day in a number of areas within psychology. It was, of course, a basic staple in Freud's psychodynamic theories, and it gathered adherents in personality research; social, clinical, and child psychology; abnormal psychology; and educational and school psychology.

It is consistent with James' interdisciplinary mind, his "catholicity of spirit" (Taylor, 1996), that he should view the solution to each question in psychology from a variety of perspectives and that he should urge others to do likewise. He had early on dismissed dualism, the notion that reality is reducible to two, independent, mutually irreducible elements. He also wrestled with the problem of monism, the view that reality represents a unified whole, and found it deficient for a number of reasons: It violated the dynamic nature of personal experience, constrained the character and expression of reality, and resulted in mechanistic and absolute conceptions of the world (Viney, King, & King, 1992). This was for James (1907/1975) "the most central of all philosophical problems" and one he had resolved by proposing a pluralistic view of the universe—"the world of concrete personal experiences . . . is multitudinous beyond imagination, tangled, muddy, painful, and perplexed" (p. 18). How could understandings of these experiences be otherwise? Pluralism represented for James a belief in concert with his brand of radical empiricism and with the pragmatist philosophy he would adopt. It represented also his conviction that the facts of the world can be understood only when they are embedded in their local conditions.

There were no boundaries to James' interest in psychological processes, and no areas to which his mind would not travel. He was criticized broadly for his interest in psychical research, and he was known to have attended seances. In the *Principles*, he devoted chapters to habit, attention, perception, association, memory, reasoning, instinct, emotion, imagination, psychological methods, and even hypnotism. Of all psychological processes, however, one was clearly central to a Jamesian psychology—the *self*.

It bears noting that "The Consciousness of Self" is the longest chapter in the two volumes of the *Principles*. In it, James (1890/1981b) described an individual's sense of self as "duplex," composed of objective and subjective selves. He differentiated between the self as knower, or the *I*, and the self as known, or *me*. The *I* is pure ego, consciousness itself. The *me* is one of the many things that the *I* may be conscious of, and it consists of three components, one physical or material, one social, and one spiritual. James was careful to point out that the two selves are discriminated aspects of self rather than "separate things." The self is also purposive, dynamic, and active. James was also one of the first writers to use the term self-esteem, which he described as a self-feeling that depends on what one decides to be and to accomplish. Self-esteem may be raised, James argued, either by succeeding in our endeavors or, in the face of incessant disappointments, by lowering our sights and surrendering certain pretensions. James' belief in God permeates his psychology and plays an important role in his understanding of self (particularly of the *I*). For example, his discussion of the soul as a combining medium of thought or consciousness is permeated with references to a spiritual being and the role that such a being may play in understanding an individual's self. He argued that psychology must "admit" the Soul.

All of which leads to the manner in which James himself evaluated philosophical and psychological ideas. Just as he is acknowledged as the father of American psychology, William James is also recognized as the father of American pragmatism, an idea that he credited to Charles Sanders Peirce but which, in James' hands, became one of the prevailing philosophical movements of the 20th century. It became also one of the most criticized, misinterpreted, and ill-used philosophical movements of the 20th century to the point where, in modern parlance, being "pragmatic" has become synonymous with being practical, expedient, and relativistic, each independent of moral and ethical ramifications.

Of course, that is not how James viewed or expounded pragmatism, which was for him more method than philosophy, a method for resolving philosophical disputes, for arriving at the meaning and truth of ideas. Originally expounded by Peirce in 1878 in an article entitled "How to Make Our Ideas Clear," the pragmatic method, as James (1907/1975) came to define it, aimed to discover the truth of an idea. "Truth," argued James, "*happens* to an idea," and it happens when "we can assimilate, validate, corroborate, and verify" its agreement with reality (p. 97), "be such realities concrete or abstract" (p. 101). Pragmatism asks its practitioners to consider the value of truth in terms of its utility—"Grant an idea or belief to be true, it says, what concrete difference will its being true make in anyone's actual life? How will the truth be realized? What experiences will be different from those which would obtain if the belief were false? What, in short, is truth's *cash-value* in experiential terms" (p. 97)? Criticisms of pragmatism are typically predicated on the assumed effectiveness of questionable short-term actions, but determining the cash value of an idea requires determining the practical, ethical/moral, and intellectual long-term *consequences* that will emanate from the actions the idea will generate. Moreover, although for pragmatists such as James and Dewey truth is indeed provisional, the moral standards that undergird the cash value of an idea must be founded on democratic, progressive, and pluralist principles (Rorty, 1991).

When Jamesian passages are lifted out of their contextual moorings, they can be used to illustrate and defend the view that pragmatism asks nothing of truth but that it be practical, useful, and personally self-serving. James (1907/1975) wrote that "truth in our ideas means their power to work" (p. 34); "A new opinion counts as 'true' just in proportion as it gratifies the individual's desire to assimilate the novel in his experience to his beliefs in stock" (p. 36); "The true is the name of whatever proves itself to be good in the way of belief, and good, too, for definite, assignable reasons"; "'What would be better for us to believe!' This sounds very like a definition of truth" (p. 42).

James (1907/1975) himself was aware of "how odd it must seem to some of you to hear me say that an idea is 'true' so long as to believe it is profitable to our lives" (p. 42), and he worked both to clarify his definition of pragmatism and to emphasize the moral element that accompanies it. But it was not James' pragmatism that caught the fancy of America as it turned into a new century. The land of the individual, of the entrepreneur, and of the competitive marketplace preferred the wrongly understood, self-oriented, practical, expedient approach. James would struggle through his remaining years both against critics whom he believed misinterpreted his pragmatism and against admirers who sang its praises and used a mutated form to defend and promulgate their political or philosophical agendas.

He would also struggle against the growing atomistic and mechanistic tendencies in psychology. He dreaded the encroachment of this "microscopic psychology" that was "carried on by experimental methods, asking of course every moment for introspective data, but eliminating their uncertainty by operating on a large scale and taking statistical means. This method taxes patience at the utmost, and could hardly have arisen in a country whose natives could be *bored*" (Perry, 1935b, p. 114). Nonetheless, the growing successes of behaviorist psychology, which was turning the new experimental laboratories into laboratories geared at discovering the roots of animal learning, isolated James from many of his colleagues and from the discipline. Not long after the publication of the *Principles*, he began to lose interest in formal psychology and turned his attention to philosophical pursuits.

He developed as well a curiosity for unusual states of consciousness, psychic phenomena, and religious experience. He began also to apply the principles of his psychology and the fruits of his philosophical thinking to other areas of human endeavor. One of these areas was education.

WILLIAM JAMES
AND EDUCATIONAL PSYCHOLOGY[3]

With the appointment of Paul Henry Hanus as assistant professor of the History and Art of Teaching in 1891, only a year after the debut of the *Principles*, Harvard University began a process that culminated in the creation of a Division of Education in 1906 and a Graduate School of Education in 1920. At the time of the appointment, the Harvard administration also proposed to its instructors that they address issues of concern to teaching from the perspectives of their own disciplines. James did so and incorporated the fruits of his labors into his own teaching (James was perhaps the first university professor ever to elicit evaluations of his teaching from his students). I believe it safe to say that William James was the first American psychologist to directly address educational issues.

When Harvard also suggested to James that a series of lectures to classroom teachers on the relationship between psychology and teaching would be well received, James saw the opportunity to promote attention to his newly published *Principles* and to increase his university income. On July of 1892,[2] he delivered the first lecture to a group of Cambridge teachers under the title of "Talks on Psychology of Interest to Teachers." According to Harvard's university calendar, the first lecture was delivered on a Tuesday evening; lectures then followed every Thursday (Baldwin, 1911). He would subsequently deliver the lectures throughout the country. After being published in installments in the *Atlantic Monthly*, they were collected and published in 1899 as *Talks to Teachers on Psychology and to Students on Some of Life's Ideals*. *Talks* became popular with teacher educators, who used it prominently in teacher training programs throughout the nation for the next thirty years. By 1929 it had been reprinted 23 times.

Most readers familiar with the *Principles* quickly realize that, had William James had access to a personal computer, he would have made frequent use of the cut and paste feature to compose the lectures. As he had done for the *Jimmy*, James used scissors and paste to produce the bulk of the text, adding where appropriate exemplars, aphorisms, and instructive maxims relevant to education. Some have argued that both the lectures and book may have been prompted more by financial considerations than by an abiding interest in teaching and in education (e.g., Hilgard, 1987; Simon, 1998). Indeed, in his private correspondence James revealed that he had little patience with or admiration for teachers as a whole, and he could be dismissive both of the lectures and the subsequent book—"Pray do not wade through the Teacher part, which is incarnate boredom," he wrote to a friend about *Talks*. Others contend that James was genuinely interested in the work of teachers and in the workings of education (Perry, 1935b). His essays related to university education (e.g., "The Ph.D. Octopus") attest to the fact that he was interested in how American students were educated, at least at the university level.

James (1899/1958) began his talks by declaring to the teachers in his audience that they held the future of the country in their hands. Shrewdly, he went on to lower their expectations of what they could hope to take from his lectures. He cautioned them that knowledge of psychology does not ensure effective teaching. Indeed, they would make a "great, very great" mistake if they believed that scientific psychology could offer them teaching strategies or instructional methods they could readily incorporate into their teaching. After all, "psychology is a science, and teaching is an art; and sciences never generate arts directly out of themselves" (p. 23). Moreover, knowledge of psychology cannot help anyone develop ingenuity or tact, and these are skills central to the art of teaching. He went even further: The amount of psychology necessary to effective teaching "might almost be written on the palm of one's hand" (p. 26). What psychology can do is to "save us from mistakes. It makes us, moreover, more clear as to what we are about. We gain confidence in respect to any method which we are using as soon as we believe that it has theory as well as practice" (p. 25).

If psychology could provide teachers with but modest help, what did James find to lecture them about? And, in keeping with the aims of this chapter, what were James' views on four issues of critical importance to educators—the nature of the learner, the nature of learning, the optimal conditions of instruction, and the nature of important learning–instructional outcomes? Where possible, let me try to make use of James' own words to answer these questions.

Perhaps the most often quoted Jamesian phrase that provides insight into his view of the nature of the learner is that a student is "a little sensitive, impulsive, associative, and reactive organism, partly fated and partly free" (p. 131). In coming to understand the basic nature of a child, James was influenced by his physiological training. He viewed the pupil as a "subtle little piece of machinery" that possesses a number of native reactions that are present from birth—"We are by this time fully launched upon the biological conception" (p. 42). These instinctive reactions include fear, love, curiosity (which is "the impulse toward better cognition"), ownership, and constructiveness. Children are also imbued with "ambitious impulses" that include imitation, ambition, pugnacity, and pride.

There is always a tension in James's description of the source of human activity. Not averse to resorting to overstatement to drive home a point, James proposed that "ninety-nine hundredths or, possibly, nine hundred and ninety-nine thousandths of our activity is purely automatic and habitual, from our rising in the morning to our lying down each night" (p. 56). We are all "mere bundles of habit . . . stereotyped creatures, imitators and copiers of our past selves" (p. 58). As an empiricist, James believed that individuals learn and behave by reacting to impressions. A child's mind is there to help determine those reactions, and a critical essence of learning is a child's success in making reactions numerous and perfect.

James' insights regarding how information is best learned surely resounded with experienced teachers. Associationist to the core, he argued that a teacher should begin with the child's native reactions and, by connecting them to novel information and academic material, help the child to acquire new reactions—"Every acquired reaction is, as a rule, either a complication grafted on a native reaction, or a substitute for a native reaction which the same object originally tended to provoke. The teacher's art consists in bringing about the substitution or complication; and success in the art presupposes a sympathetic acquaintance with the reactive tendencies natively there" (p. 42). Even interest in academic material could be generated through the process of association. Material not interesting in itself could be made interesting by being associated with material that a child already finds interesting—"thus things not interesting in their own right borrow an interest which becomes as real and as strong as that of any natively interesting thing" (p. 74). The teacher's task is to discover what the child finds inherently interesting and make the appropriate connections to the novel task or activity. And what do children find inherently interesting? All things wed to their own personal selves. Connect that to be taught to personal relevance, and the teacher is nearly home.

An experienced and dedicated teacher, James did not imagine that the teacher's task was anything but challenging and arduous. The blueprint for effective teaching, however, was simple enough: Be aware of the child's native interests, bring forth the child's existing knowledge regarding the material to be presented, present material in a straightforward and clear manner, and carefully connect the new knowledge to the existing knowledge and to the native interests in a natural, logical, systematic, and telling way. Though the blueprint is clear enough, however, James acknowledged that "the accomplishment is difficult in the extreme" (p. 82), and he took seriously his responsibility to provide as many practical suggestions as possible regarding how these connections could be made, as well as how teachers should practice their craft. He urged them to become familiar with their students' native tendencies if they wished to enlarge their pupils' worlds. It was also important that teachers not attempt to make their students do that which the teacher could not do, for "the deepest spring of action in us is the sight of action in another" (p. 51). They should also take care not to "preach" to their charges or present information in abstract terms. *Talks* abounds with passages that exemplify the manner in which James sought to stimulate a teacher's instructional strategies:

> If the topic be highly abstract, show its nature by concrete examples; if it be unfamiliar, make it figure as part of a story; if it be difficult, couple its acquisition with some prospect of personal gain. Above all things, make sure that it shall run through certain inner changes, since no unvarying object can possibly hold the mental field for long. Let your pupil wander from one aspect to another of your subject, if you do not wish him to wander from it altogether to something else, variety in unity being the secret of all interesting talk and thought. (p. 84)

The difference between interesting and dull teachers, according to James, is simply the inventiveness with which they go about the process of mediating the associations and connections necessary to learning. On the argument of whether an effective teacher is made or born, however, James again landed on the side of biology—"When all is said and done, the fact remains that some teachers have a naturally inspiring presence and can make their exercises interesting, whilst others simply cannot. And psychology and general padagogy here confess their failure, and hand things over to the deeper spring of human personality to conduct the task" (pp. 80–81).

It is not difficult to credit James' educational philosophy as contributing to the child-centered movement that progressive education would launch or to the self-oriented, child-centered approach that humanistic educators would subsequently propose. But it is important to remember that he was rather more of a traditional at heart. In fact, James was more progressive regarding how children should be taught than he was regarding the aims of their education. He had no patience for those who preached permissiveness in educational practices, and there is little doubt but that he would have viewed the excesses of the humanistic movement with some distress. When a teacher who attended one of his lectures wrote him to complain that his emphasis on the critical importance of interest and perceived relevance had sounded to her like a suggestion that rigorous, uninteresting material should be abandoned, he made a point to alter his text to be clear than he was suggesting no such thing. "Soft pedagogics," he cautioned his listeners, "have taken the place of the old steep and rocky path to learning. But from this lukewarm air the bracing oxygen of effort is left out. It is nonsense to suppose that every step in education *can* be interesting. The fighting impulse must often be appealed to" (p. 51). James was also forthright in declaring that competitive classroom environments best foster learning—"The feeling of rivalry lies at the very basis of our being . . . no runner running all alone on a race-track will find in his own will the power of stimulation which his rivalry with other runners incites, when he feels them at his heels, about to pass" (pp. 50–51).

Although James emphasized continuously that habit and automatic responding were responsible for nine hundred and ninety-nine thousandths of an individual's daily activity, the one-thousandth remaining was critical to him, for it is here that individuals exercise free will. James' brand of associationism was not the passive compounding of the British associationists (Hilgard, 1987) or of the early proponents of conditioning in learning. For James, proactive processes such as interest and will, as well as reactive processes such as self-reflection and self-evaluation, could determine the actions that result from the associations created, just as they could determine the "prepotency" of the things associated. His emphasis on the importance of these processes notwithstanding, however, James was often criticized for emphasizing that individuals possess free will while simultaneously contending that they are, essentially, creatures of the habits they have created.

The purpose of education, and the teacher's primary concern, should be to "ingrain into the pupil that assortment of habits that shall be most useful to him throughout life. Education is for behavior, and habits are the stuff of which behavior consists" (p. 58). But the purpose of inculcating habits is to help create thoughtful, independent, generous, and energetic citizens who can guide the democracy that will soon be in their charge (Miller, 1997). The central aim of education, thus, is not to serve as a vehicle for transmitting information but rather to help students learn how to evaluate the information available to them, and this evaluation is accompanied by a moral imperative—"See to it now, I beg you," he pleaded with his audiences, "that you make freemen of your pupils by habituating them to act, whenever possible, under the notion of a good. Get them habitually to tell the truth, not so much through showing them the wickedness of lying as by arousing their enthusiasm for honor and veracity" (p. 113). As it would be for Dewey, the school was for James especially suited to build a student's character and impart democratic values—"only by sharing our individual experiences and pooling our knowledge [is] it possible to gain a better grasp of things, devise betters ways of living together, and move toward a more democratic, tolerant, and humane world" (p. 164).

In all, James put forth a psychology of education consistent with his functionalist, pluralist, and pragmatic positions. It is a child-centered psychology primarily in the sense that James urged educators to familiarize themselves with the needs and interests of their students so that teaching practices can be geared at making the associations and connections necessary to ensure effective learning. But James never confused acquaintance with the needs of students with acquiescence to their whims. Although certainly progressive and nontraditional for its day, James' educational psychology today would be described as a traditional, almost old-fashioned, no-nonsense view of teaching and learning in which freedom and compulsion each play its appropriate role (Barzun, 1983). It is an educational psychology that abounds with references to rigor, effort, ambition, competition, pugnacity, and pride. It is in many ways a combative view of teaching and learning, as James exhorts his teachers to struggle for their students' attention, to rouse in them "the fighting impulse." James' commonsense psychology appealed to the teachers in his audience. It is likely that it would appeal also to modern audiences. James said the sorts of things that parents want to hear from their child's teacher during a teacher conference.

But James' educational psychology also abounds with references to character, civility, patience, democracy, wisdom, self-appreciation, the cultivation of sensitivity, volition, and even love. *Talks to Teachers* ends with James' observation that "I cannot but think that to apperceive your pupil as a little sensitive, impulsive, associative, and reactive organism, partly fated and partly free, will lead to a better intelligence of all his ways. Understand him, then, as such a subtle little piece of machinery. And if, in addition, you can also see him *sub specie boni*, and love him as well, you will be in the best possible position for becoming perfect teachers" (p. 131). One need only cast a casual glance at the current American landscape to see that attending to the personal concerns and character of students is both a noble and necessary enterprise.

THE JAMESIAN TRADITION

Few would argue that James' ideas have had a pronounced influence on philosophy, politics, sociology, religion and theology, literature, and, through the pragmatic philosophies of Supreme Court justices Oliver Wendell Holmes and Louis Brandais, even jurisprudence (see Morris, 1950; Posnock, 1997). In each of these areas James was and continues to be widely read and studied. Many prominent figures have expressed their admiration for James and acknowledged their intellectual debt. Most prominent among these have been John Dewey, George Herbert Mead, Charles Cooley, Josiah Royce, Charles Peirce, Gordon Allport, Reinhold Niebuhr, Gardner Murphy, and Henry Murray, as well as a number of James' students, including E. L. Thorndike (an admirer but not a follower), Dickenson Miller, E. B. Holt, Robert Frost, Gertrude Stein, James Angell, Walter Lippmann, and W. E. Dubois, who once said that "my two best friends in life have been my mother and William James" (Taylor, 1992). But what can be said of his lasting influence, of his legacy, on psychology? Is the Jamesian tradition alive and well in the field as it enters a new century?

When the American Psychological Association celebrated its 75th anniversary in 1977, David Kreech described William James as "our father who begat us" (Barzun, 1983, p. 298). But it is easier to recognize James' contribution to the origin of the discipline than it is to evaluate the lasting contribution of his ideas. In mainstream psychology, the first three decades of the 20th century were dominated by John Watson's experimentalist views, characterized by fierce polemics against introspective, mentalist psychologists such as James. Until a scant two decades ago, B. F. Skinner's operant conditioning theory vied for supremacy with Freud's psychodynamic views. Clearly, neither Watson's experimentalism, Skinnerian behaviorism, nor Freud's psychoanalysis were in concert with a Jamesian view of human functioning, and so it cannot be said that James' views held any real sway in American psychology during the decades when these movements were prominent. More recently, cognitive psychology, influenced by technological advances and by the advent of the computer, which became the movement's signature metaphor, has become the dominant force in American psychology.

Because the current wave of cognitive theorists and researchers emphasize internal, mental events, one might well think that the Jamesian tradition has resurfaced after the dominance of behaviorism. Indeed, some of the questions of cognitive psychology are questions that would surely have interested James—questions about automaticity, encoding and decoding of human thinking, information processing strategies, higher-order thinking, and problem-solving. But this new psychology, part artificial intelligence, part linguistics, and part logic and philosophy of science (Myers, 1992), has itself developed a mechanistic mind set and shied away from exploring the issues that were of primary concern to James—issues related to self and self-belief, to will, to introspection (Bruner, 1990, 1996). Some have argued that the new cognitive psychology has nothing of a Jamesian character at all (Robinson, 1993).

It is difficult to gauge how the Jamesian tradition has fared in American psychology. Perhaps Hunt (1993) summed it up well when he concluded that "James's influence on psychology, though great, was fragmented; though pervasive, was never dominant. James avoided creating a system, founded no school, trained few graduate students, and had no band of followers" (p. 164). Taylor (1996) similarly concluded that James paved a road that most psychologists have not taken. As for pragmatism, the Jamesian type has long disappeared from mainstream psychology (Robinson, 1993).

If these appraisals are correct, James bears a measure of responsibility for his lack of concentrated influence on the discipline. There is little disagreement that he often expounded ideas in ways that appeared either inconsistent or out-and-out contradictory, and much ink has been spilled on what Allport (1943) called the "productive paradoxes" of William James. For example, in the *Principles* he argued against unconscious mental states whereas later, in the *Varieties*, he argued for "subliminal consciousness." His description of the role of habit seems often at odds with his views on self and personal volition. When he was criticized for putting forth arguments both for determinism and free-will, he explained that the science of psychology could quite safely adopt a posture of determinism despite the fact that free will was true. James' associationist tendencies may easily be viewed as inconsistent with his view of self as purposive and selectively conscious, not to mention with his insistence that individuals are endowed with free will (Allport, 1943; Boring, 1942). In fact, depending on the interpretation of his words and meanings, he can as easily be described a committed phenomenologist (Boring, 1942) or as a staunch supporter of behaviorist thinking (Dewey, 1940). Many have long claimed that James was instrumental in the success of the behaviorist movement by promulgating some of the basic tenets of associationist thinking. Indeed, some of the origins of stimulus–response can be traced to James' description of "impression" and "expression" (Bolton, 1930). When one scholar went in search of James to gain support for one of his contentions, he found ample evidence with which to buttress his position but found also ample evidence to contradict it. "Could anything," he vented with frustration, "be more perverse!" (James, 1892/1961, p. *xx*).

James responded to the charge that he was inconsistent by arguing that no author could be understood if pieces of his thinking were carelessly considered in isolation or taken out of context. After reading a dissertation in which one of his students pointed out a number of inconsistencies in some of the arguments that James put forth, he testily responded that "you take utterances of mine written at different dates, for different audiences, belonging to different universes of discourse and string them together as the abstract elements of a total philosophy which you then show to be inwardly incoherent" (Simon, 1998, p. *xvi*). For James, "a man's vision is the great fact about him" (James, 1909/1977, p. 20), and capturing the "center" of that vision could only be accomplished through "an act of imagination" (Bjork, 1997, p. *xiii*).

Allport (1943) put the issue of inconsistency in perspective when he observed that one major reason for the Jamesian paradoxes is that, unlike most psychologists, James was willing to take the persistent "riddles of psychology" head on. Moreover, in James, wrote Allport, "we are not dealing with smart rhetorical paradoxes, each of which seems true enough in separate contexts but irreconcilable when juxtaposed" (p. 115). We are dealing instead with a pragmatic thinker attempting to piece together the fragments of a loosely joined universe. In truth, of course, we also have in James a man "hankering for the good things on both sides of the road" (James, 1907/1975, p. 14). It bears recalling that Emerson, who had crafted his own position statement on the issue of foolish consistency, was William James' godfather.

In addition to being perverse regarding consistency, there is little doubt James suffered from what Dewey (1933) would describe as lack of "whole-heartedness" about psychology. Quite simply, psychology could not contain William James, and its questions could not maintain his interest for very long. His interdisciplinary mind could not prevent the divided interest with which he approached the discipline. This given the fact that James did not deliberately try to be interdisciplinary; "he could think no other way" (Bjork, 1997). For this reason, James seems to be everywhere in psychology, but in no particular or concentrated place (Taylor, 1992). Given the richness of his thinking, not to mention what he did accomplish, one wonders what else he might have accomplished had this "unsystematic psychologist" (Hilgard, 1987) but lingered a while longer on one line of thought.

Although James' psychology has not persisted in America in anything like its original form, it is remarkable to note the almost hypnotic lure he continues to exercise on individual members of the discipline and the attention he regularly receives. During the past two decades it seems that no year goes by without a new book on James or a retrospective of some sort. And it seems that James is always there when a movement requires an advocate, even if that advocacy is typically discovered only in retrospect. He influenced the behaviorist onslaught on psychology, but when the humanists looked around in search of an antidote for behaviorism, they too stumbled on to William James and his plea for a psychology centered on the individual, a psychology receptive to the importance of self-processes and introspection. Current social cognitive ideas regarding the reciprocal nature of determinism (Bandura, 1986) also owe to the Jamesian view of human functioning in which individuals and environments influence each other reciprocally.

If the influence that William James has had on the general field of psychology can be described as foundational but uneven, what of his influence on education and on the psychology of education? In 1903 John Dewey referred to James' *Principles* as the "spiritual progenitor" of the progressive education movement that

Dewey was launching at the University of Chicago (Morris, 1950). Educational reforms inspired by Dewey were influenced by James' functional and pluralistic psychology, and James' "democratic temperament," as well as his argument that education should serve the aims of democracy, also found its way into Dewey's movement. James' ideas also served as foundational for the scientific pedagogy that G. Stanley Hall and Edward L. Thorndike would later promulgate.

Psychological theories have always had an influence on education, and there is evidence that James' educational ideas were embraced by the educational community of his day. Writing a year after James' death, Baldwin (1911) observed that James' educational theory had served as the prevailing influence on most educators during the last two decades of James' life, particularly as regarding James' call for attention to self-processes and to the needs and dispositions of the child. Baldwin contended also that James was primarily, though not exclusively, an educational psychologist. This bit of overstatement was no doubt due to the fact that Baldwin was writing what amounted to a combination tribute article and eulogy for the new *Journal of Educational Psychology*.

What are we to make, then, of the influence on modern educational psychology of James' propositions related to the psychological constructs that he believed important? Some have fared well and are thriving. For example, reviewing the current state of knowledge related to theories and principles of motivation for the 1996 *Handbook of Educational Psychology*, Graham and Weiner observed that current research in educational psychology "reflects what is probably the main new direction in the field of motivation—the study of the self" (p. 77). Self-constructs are so pervasive in research on academic motivation that Graham and Weiner concluded that the self is on the verge of dominating the field. Interest and research on habit also continues to thrive, although the construct now travels under the guise of automaticity. Motivation researchers are also active in their study of interest, perceived value, attention, memory processes, modeling and imitation, and transfer. And of course, Vygotsky's (1978) social constructivism, a view of meaning construction in line with James' own theory of knowledge, seems today to have caught the imagination of many teachers, teacher educators, and researchers.

The renewed attention to a student's sense of self and its relationship to competence focuses on the critical aspects of self-awareness and personal cognition that James believed vital to a study of psychology and which he so strongly expounded (see Markus, 1990; Smith, 1992; Strube, Yost, & Bailey, 1992). It focuses, also, on the powerful influence of self-beliefs in academic functioning, self-beliefs such as self-concept, self-efficacy, self-schemas, and possible selves. Similarly, the current interest in conceptual change can be traced to James' vivid description of this process. In fact, I believe that no account of the process of conceptual change and allegiance to ideas is as clear and compelling as James' account of belief alteration, of how an individual settles into a new opinion (James, 1907/1975). Moreover, there is renewed appreciation in some quarters of educational psychology for the role of context in psychological descriptions and prescriptions.

On the whole, however, I am uncertain as to whether James would look kindly either on the major questions with which educational psychology typically concerns itself or with the manner in which it goes about seeking the answers to the questions that would interest him. Current fascination with self constructs, constructivism, and social cognition notwithstanding, the core of educational psychological research continues embedded in the mechanistic aims of positivist science (Bruner, 1990, 1996; House, 1991). The aim of researchers is typically to "discover a set of transcendent human universals—even if those universals are hedged by specifications about 'cross-cultural' variations" (Bruner, 1990, p. 20). For all that educators and educational psychologists deplore decontextualism, the quest for universal truths is not only prevalent but deeply entrenched in educational psychology classes and teacher education programs. Although in these constructivist times no one disputes Austin's (1962) premise that it takes a meaning to catch a meaning, more than a fair amount of what is taught in educational psychology courses consists of learning how to decontextualize—how to categorize behavior, personality, thinking styles, environmental events, and even self-beliefs in the abstract terms that theoretical formulations employ and that educational research thrives on. It goes without saying that these tendencies toward universal absolutes and nomothetic practices would strike at the very core of James' pluralistic and idiographic sensibilities.

Following the habits of its parent discipline, educational psychology continues to show impatience with modes of inquiry and analysis not reducible to quantities and not assessable statistically. Too often, the "neat little studies" (Bruner, 1996) populating the field's journals seem to amount to little more than methods in search of a problem (Robinson, 1993). Had the zest for statistical analysis been as prevalent in his day as it is in ours, no doubt James would have aimed his verbal darts at those of us who traffic nearly exclusively in numbers—"I for my part cannot but consider the talk of the contemporary sociological school about averages and general laws and predetermined tendencies, with its obligatory undervaluing of the importance of individual differences, as the most pernicious and immoral of fatalisms" (James, 1897/1956, p. 262). As Robinson (1993) observed, pluralism requires an ideographic psychology skeptical, if not scornful, of "every form of statistical lumping and clumping" (p. 642).

It is not incongruous to suggest that the man who provided "principles" of psychology, presented psychology as a science, and populated his lectures to teachers with maxims would reject universal prescriptions, nomothetic theorizing, and over reliance on statistical findings. James (1909/1978) always underscored the point that "to consider hypotheses is surely always better than to dogmatize" (p. 47), and he would heartily agree with Cronbach's (1975) caution that "when we give proper weight to local conditions, any generalization is a working hypothesis, not a conclusion" (p. 125). James (1907/1975) proffered his principles with frequent warnings about the need for situated and contextual understandings of phenomena—"what we say about reality depends on the perspective into which we throw it" (p. 118).

He knew also that scientific principles are never derived through statistical analysis and that the ideology of accumulated observations and generalizations drawn from statistical results is incompatible with nomothetic theorizing (see Hammond, 1966; Lewin, 1935). He would argue that what characterizes good science is that it tries to elucidate something particular about a phenomenon, something related to other phenomena that also have to do with particulars.

What, then, would be the aspirations of an educational psychology grounded on the Jamesian tradition? One need not look far to imagine it—deeply contextual, pragmatic, individualistic, functionalist, phenomenological, pluralistic, interdisciplinary and multifaceted, unapologetically eclectic. My time is nearly up, and so I will briefly touch on only one of those aspirations. A Jamesian educational psychology would be in constant dialogue with other social sciences, with the arts and humanities, and even with the "hard" sciences. Interest in and attention to interdisciplinary scholarship has of late soared in Academe. Many have contended, however, that the interdisciplinary dialogue that takes place between most psychology departments and other departments of a university takes place primarily in the other departments (Bruner, 1996; Derry, 1992; Gardner, 1992, Taylor, 1996). It is not unusual for professors of language arts, philosophy, anthropology, sociology, history, or law to profess on psychological interpretations of the people or texts relevant to their discipline, but it is unusual for psychology professors to profess on matters and problems beyond their own discipline. Classes on the psychology of ethics or religion are more likely to be found in departments of religion or colleges of theology than in departments of psychology (Taylor, 1996). Gardner (1992) has argued that cognitive psychology has itself been appropriated by other disciplines. In educational psychology, being interdisciplinary too often means including a variable from a competing theoretical perspective into one's own statistical model. More important, perhaps, a Jamesian educational psychology would be in constant dialogue with schools and with students, and it would endeavor to convey its theoretical insights and research findings directly and unequivocally to teachers, school administrators, and makers of educational policy.

Let me complete this transparent tribute to William James by ending it as he ended his essay, "The Will to Believe," with a portion of a passage from Fitz James Stephen that he deeply admired. For James to close such a personal essay with the words of another, he must have believed them to have special import.

> What do you think of yourself? What do you think of the world? These are questions with which all must deal as it seems good to them. They are riddles of the Sphinx, and in some way or other we must deal with them . . . In all important transactions of life we have to take a leap in the dark . . . if we decide to leave the riddles unanswered, that is a choice; if we waver in our answer, that too, is a choice: but whatever choice we make, we make it at our peril.

Will educational psychology aspire to embrace a Jamesian tradition—to reformulate the manner in which it construes meaning, rethink the questions it finds significant, expand the methods through which it seeks answers to the questions it has selected, and reexamine the way it looks at itself and the way it looks at the world? Such redefinition and altering of purpose would require long and thoughtful introspection. It would require pragmatically assessing the cash value that the broader world of education places on the fruits of its labors. It would require the breaking of well-established mental habits and settling into new opinions. It would require talking to teachers again.

ACKNOWLEDGMENT

The author would like to express his appreciation to Barry Zimmerman for his invaluable suggestions and thoughtful commentary of the manuscript.

NOTES

1. Biographical sources include Barzun (1983), Bjork (1997), Hunt (1993), Lewis (1991), King (1992), Mathiesen (1947), Miller (1997), Moore (1965), Perry (1935a, 1935b, 1958), and Simon (1998).
2. The actual date is difficult to pin down. Some sources list the date as 1891 (e.g., Simon, 1998). Bird Baldwin (1911), writing but a year after James's death, provided the specific date of October 27, 1891, for the first lecture. Other authoritative sources give the date of 1892 (e.g., Barzun, 1983; Bolton, 1930; Perry, 1935b; Paul Woodring in his introduction to James' *Talks to Teachers*, 1958). James himself writes in the preface to the book that "In 1892 I was asked by the Harvard Corporation to give a few public lectures on psychology to the Cambridge teachers." Subsequently, I have selected 1892. Of course, one should not take James' memory as authoritative—"I myself 'founded' the instruction in experimental psychology at Harvard in 1874–75, or 1876, I forget which," James once wrote (Bolton, 1930, p. 85).
3. Unless otherwise noted, page numbers provided are from James' (1899/1958) *Talks to Teachers*.

REFERENCES

Allport, G. W. (1943). Productive paradoxes of William James. *Psychological Review, 50*, 95–120.
Austin, J. L. (1962). *How to do things with words*. Cambridge, MA: Harvard University Press.
Baldwin, B. T. (1911). William James' contribution to education. *Journal of Educational Psychology, 2*, 369–382.
Bandura, A. (1986). *Social foundations of thought and action: A social cognitive theory*. Englewood Cliffs, NJ: Prentice Hall.
Barzun, J. (1983). *A stroll with William James*. Chicago: University of Chicago Press.
Bjork, D. W. (1997). *William James: The center of his vision*. Washington, DC: American Psychological Association.
Boller, P. F. (1979). William James as an educator: Individualism and democracy. *Teachers College Record, 80*, 587–601.
Bolton, F. E. (1930). Great contributors to education: William James. *Progressive Education, 7*(2), 82–88.

Boring, E. G. (1942). Human nature vs. sensation: William James and the psychology of the present. *American Journal of Psychology, 55*, 310–327.

Bruner, J. (1990). *Acts of meaning*. Cambridge, MA: Harvard University Press.

Bruner, J. (1996). *The culture of education*. Cambridge, MA: Harvard University Press.

Brunswik, E. (1943). Organismic achievement and environmental probability. *Psychological Review, 50*, 265–266.

Cronbach, L. (1975). Beyond the two disciplines of psychology. *American Psychologist, 30*, 116–127

Delabarre, E. B. (1943). A student's impression of James in the late '80's. *Psychological Review, 50*, 125–127.

Derry, S. J. (1992). Beyond symbolic processing: Expanding horizons for educational psychology. *Journal of Educational Psychology, 84*, 413–418.

Dewey, J. (1933). *How we think*. Lexington, MA: Heath.

Dewey, J. (1940). The vanishing subject in the psychology of James. *Journal of Philosophy, 37*, 580–599.

Donnelly, M. E. (Ed.). (1992). *Reinterpreting the legacy of William James*. Washington, DC: American Psychological Association.

Gardner, H. (1992). Scientific psychology: Should we bury it or praise it? *New Ideas in Psychology, 10*, 179–190.

Glover, J. A., & Ronning, R. R. (Eds.). (1987). *Historical foundations of educational psychology*. New York: Plenum.

Graham, S., & Weiner, B. (1996). Theories and principles of motivation. In D. C. Berliner & R. C. Calfee (Eds.), *Handbook of educational psychology* (pp. 63–84). New York: Simon & Schuster Macmillan.

Hammond, K. R. (Ed.). (1966). *The psychology of Egon Brunswik*. New York: Holt, Rinehart & Winston.

Hilgard, E. R. (1987). *Psychology in America: A historical survey*. San Diego, CA: Harcourt Brace Jovanovich.

House, E. (1991). Realism in research. *Educational Researcher, 20*, 2–9, 25.

Howard, G. S. (1993). Why William James might be considered the founder of the scientist–practitioner model. *The Counseling Psychologist, 21*, 118–135.

Hunt, N. (1993). *The story of psychology*. New York: Anchor.

James, W. (1956). *The will to believe and other essays in popular philosophy*. New York: Dover. (Original work published in 1897)

James, W. (1958). *Talks to teachers on psychology: And to students on some of life's ideals*. New York: Norton. (Original work published in 1899)

James, W. (1961). *Psychology: The briefer course*. Notre Dame, IN: University of Notre Dame Press. (Original work published in 1892)

James, W. (1975). *Pragmatism: A new name for old ways of thinking*. Cambridge, MA: Harvard University Press. (Original work published in 1907)

James, W. (1976). *Essays in radical empiricism*. Cambridge, MA: Harvard University Press. (Original work published in 1912)

James, W. (1977). *A pluralistic universe*. Cambridge, MA: Harvard University Press. (Original work published in 1909)

James, W. (1978). *The meaning of truth*. Cambridge, MA: Harvard University Press. (Original work published in 1909)

James, W. (1981a). *The principles of psychology*, Vol. 1. Cambridge, MA: Harvard University Press.

James, W. (1981b). *The principles of psychology*, Vol. 2. Cambridge, MA: Harvard University Press. (Original work published in 1890)

James, W. (1990). *The varieties of religious experience*. New York: Vintage Books. (Original work published in 1902)

King, D. B. (1992). Evolution and revision of the Principles. In M. E. Donnelly (Ed.), *Reinterpreting the legacy of William James* (pp. 67–76). Washington, DC: American Psychological Association.

Lewin, K. (1935). *Dynamic theory of personality.* New York: McGraw-Hill.

Lewis, R. W. B. (1991). *The Jameses: A family narrative.* New York: Farrar, Straus & Giroux.

Markus, H. (1990). On splitting the universe. *Psychological Science, 1,* 181–185.

Mathiessen, F. O. (1947). *The James family: A group biography.* New York: Knopf.

Miller, J. L. (1997). *Democratic temperament: The legacy of William James.* Lawrence, KA: University Press of Kansas.

Moore, E. C. (1965). *William James.* New York: Washington Square Press.

Morris, L. (1950). *William James: The message of a modern mind.* New York: Scribner's.

Myers, G. E. (1992). William James and contemporary psychology. In M. E. Donnelly (Ed.), *Reinterpreting the legacy of William James* (pp. 49–64). Washington, DC: American Psychological Association.

Perry, R. B. (1935a). *The thought and character of William James,* Vol. 1. Boston: Little, Brown.

Perry, R. B. (1935b). *The thought and character of William James,* Vol. 2. Boston: Little, Brown.

Perry, R. B. (1958). *In the spirit of William James.* Bloomington, IN: Indiana University Press.

Posnock, R. (1997). The influence of William James on American culture. In R. A. Putnam (Ed.), *The Cambridge companion to William James* (pp. 322–342). Cambridge, England: Cambridge University Press.

Robinson, D. N. (1993). Is there a Jamesian tradition in psychology. *American Psychologist, 48,* 638–643.

Rorty, R. (1991). *Objectivity, relativism, and truth.* Cambridge, MA: Cambridge University Press.

Simon, L. (1998). *Genuine reality: A life of William James.* New York: Harcourt Brace.

Smith, M. B. (1992). William James and the psychology of self. In M. E. Donnelly (Ed.), *Reinterpreting the legacy of William James* (pp. 173–188). Washington, DC: American Psychological Association.

Strube, M. J., Yost, J. H., & Bailey, J. R. (1992). William James and contemporary research on the self: The influence of pragmatism, reality, and truth. In M. E. Donnelly (Ed.), *Reinterpreting the legacy of William James* (pp. 189–208). Washington, DC: American Psychological Association.

Taylor, E. (1992). The case for a uniquely American Jamesian tradition in psychology. In M. E. Donnelly (Ed.), *Reinterpreting the legacy of William James* (pp. 3–28). Washington, DC: American Psychological Association.

Taylor, E. (1996). *William James on consciousness beyond the margin.* Princeton, NJ: Princeton University Press.

Viney, W., King, C. L., & King, D. B. (1992). William James on the advantages of a pluralistic psychology. In M. E. Donnelly (Ed.), *Reinterpreting the legacy of William James* (pp. 91–100). Washington, DC: American Psychological Association.

Vygotsky, L. S. (1978). *Mind in society: The development of higher psychological processes.* Cambridge, MA: Harvard University Press.

Wilshire, B. W. (1968). *William James and phenomenology: A study of The Principles of Psychology.* Bloomington, IN: Indiana University Press.

Woodward, W. R. (1992), James's evolutionary epistemology: "Necessary truths and the effects of experience." In M. E. Donnelly (Ed.), *Reinterpreting the legacy of William James* (pp. 153–170). Washington, DC: American Psychological Association.

3

Alfred Binet's Contributions to Educational Psychology

Linda Jarvin
Robert J. Sternberg
Yale University

Alfred Binet was born in the French town of Nice on July 11, 1857. According to his daughter Madeleine (Avanzini, 1974), Alfred was a bright child who succeeded so well in school that his mother decided to send him away to the capital when he was barely 12 years old, in order that he might study at one of the best schools of the country. Binet is remembered by his daughter as a joyful and agreeable person, who could be timid and very modest. He also knew how to be authoritative and firm, however. In his own words, Alfred Binet was born to work, and he increased his efficiency by maintaining many fruitful, and often inter-disciplinary, professional collaborations. Upon graduation from high school, he completed a law degree in 1877,[1] but then decided to pursue studies in medicine and biology. Under the supervision of Balbiani, who was later to become his father-in-law, he started writing a dissertation on "The sub-intestinal nervous system of insects." At the same time he wrote plays for the theater. Throughout his career, Binet's prolific scientific production was complemented with more literary work on famous writers and artists, as well as with the creation of nine plays, written in collaboration with André de Lorde.

Binet studied a large number of diverse topics, some largely unnoticed (Siegler, 1992), and a chronological account of his bibliography shows that his research interests included, but were not limited to, perception, hallucinations, reasoning,

65

animal magnetism, hysteria, mental images, fetishism in love, moral responsibility, court witnessing, double consciousness, movement, inhibition, language, audition, chess players, memory, physiology, anatomy, graphology, intellectual exhaustion, craniometry, suggestibility, pedagogy, intelligence, literary creation, retardation and academic underachievement, the soul, abnormality, mental alienation, and measurement of intelligence. A complete bibliography can be found in Avanzini's (1974) collection of Binet writings, or in Zuza (1948). Though at first glance these topics may seem unrelated, a general theme can be perceived throughout Binet's life and work. Binet's ultimate goal was to understand the complexities of the human mind, and this understanding entailed reaching beyond general psychology and studying individual differences. His aim was to establish what he called "an individual psychology" (Binet, 1898). This passion for understanding the complexities and singularities of the human mind also showed itself in the characters he created in his plays. To simplify, one can distinguish three phases in his career as a psychologist, although his publications prove that they were overlapping rather than strictly separate (Delay, 1958): psychopathology, experimental psychology, and child psychology.

French psychology in the second half of the 19th century was mainly focused on psychopathology, and Binet's early interests were not an exception. During this first period, his main influences were Théodule-Armand Ribot[2] and Jean-Martin Charcot[3]. His first major writings explored the domains of sensations, hysteria, hypnotism, and personality disorders (Binet, 1886; Binet & Féré, 1887; Binet, 1892). Binet worked closely with Ribot between 1880 and 1907, and published over 40 articles in Ribots's *Revue Philosophique*. During this period, he also began to study hypnosis under the famous neurologist Charcot at the Salpetrière Hospital in Paris.

In 1891 Binet obtained a position at the Physiological Psychology Laboratory at the Sorbonne University in Paris, where his research focus switched from clinical to physiological and experimental psychology (Robinson, 1977–78). The main contemporary influences in psychophysiology and experimental psychology were German, namely Wundt, whose laboratory in Leipzig served as a model for the one created in Paris. Binet completed his thesis in biology in 1895, the same year in which he became the head of the Physiological Psychology Laboratory and published an *Introduction to Experimental Psychology*. This was also the year in which he founded a journal that is still published today, *L'Année Psychologique*. In 1899 Binet met Théodore Simon, who was to become his closest and most constant collaborator, and that same year he joined the Free Society for Psychological Child Studies[4], of which he became the President in 1902. Like many researchers of his time, Binet decided to follow in the footsteps of the neurologist Paul Broca, and explored intelligence through phrenology, believing that there is a direct relation between the size of the cranium and a person's level of intelligence (see for example, Binet, 1901a, or Gould, 1981). His empirical investigations, measuring the crania of school children considered by their teachers to be bright and comparing them with the measures obtained from low-achieving children, showed that there are noticeable differences in the cranium size and shape of children from contrasted groups. Very bright students ("the elite") have larger skulls than very low-achieving students (Binet, 1901a). However, in 1901, he conceded that "the idea of measuring intelligence by measuring the head . . . seemed ridiculous" (Binet, 1901b, p. 403). In the same 1901 volume, he explained that the initial measures showing a cranium size difference between low- and high-achieving students were probably due in part to his own suggestibility. With a rare sense of honesty, he admitted that, having looked for differences, he found them where he expected them. He also abandoned hypnosis, and pursued the exploration of the human psyche through new tests and puzzles that he initially developed for, and tested on, his two daughters (Binet, 1890, Binet, 1903). As was the case with Piaget several years later, most of his theoretical ideas on cognitive development sprung from the observation of his own children.

After a first period devoted to psychopathology, and a second centered on experimental psychology, a third period can be distinguished in Binet's professional life, mainly dedicated to child psychology. The starting of this period can be dated to 1905, the year in which Binet and Simon published an article on the diagnosis of abnormality, and the year of the opening of a laboratory of experimental pedagogy, where Binet worked closely with teachers. The *Laboratoire de la rue Grange-aux-Belles* was opened in a school, thanks to a close collaboration with its principal, Mr. Vaney, and several representatives from the equivalent of the Board of Education. It was during this period that Binet made his major contributions to the study of academic underachievement, and also to psychometrics. In addition to these contributions, a further major contribution of Binet to child psychology was the view that children are not, as previously thought, miniature adults, but rather, obey different rules of cognitive functioning (Zazzo, 1958). On October 30, 1911, Alfred Binet passed away unexpectedly, at the age of 54. The rest of this chapter will focus on the enormous important contributions Alfred Binet made to educational psychology, as applied to both normal and low-functioning students.

THEORY AND RESEARCH: MAIN CONTRIBUTIONS TO THE FIELD OF EDUCATION

Binet's first writing on pedagogy appeared in 1899, in a volume entitled *Mental Fatigue*. Among Binet's contributions to educational psychology, *Mental Fatigue* (Binet & Henri, 1898) can be seen as a manifesto, and *Modern Ideas about Children* (1909) as his testament. In these volumes, he criticized the widespread lack of a rigorous experimental method, and stressed the fact that pedagogical choices were all too often arbitrary or based on hastily collected empirical results without

any theoretical framework (Reuchlin, 1957–58). We will focus our description
of Binet's research on two main topics: the use of an experimental method to
investigate learning related issues, and the development of a cognitive assessment
tool, the Metric Intelligence Scale.

Applying the Experimental Method to Educational Psychology

Binet's contribution to educational psychology was not so much a new theory of
pedagogy as it was the use of new, experimental methods in the field of educational research. Whereas much work at the time focused on the "moral effects"
of teaching, Binet, deeming it more appropriate for rigorous scientific study, focused on instruction, that is, on all that would be taught by the teacher and learned
by the student. In pedagogy as well as in psychology, it is imperative to observe and experiment. For his collaborator Simon, "experimental pedagogy is
the study of students' reactions to teaching," with these reactions resulting from
instruction (Simon, 1930, p. 18). Or, in Binet's own words, "Psychological, pedagogical, or educational issues will not be resolved with literary theories, but by the
slow, patient, and minute investigation of facts" (Binet, 1904, in Avanzini, 1974,
p. 17).

In 1898, Binet and Henri published *Mental Fatigue*, the first volume in a collection of books entitled *Bibliothèque de Pédagogie et de Psychologie* [Pedagogy and
Psychology Collection], created to promote recent research in psychology relevant
to educators. Their aim was not to "reform the old pedagogy," but, rather, to "create
a new pedagogy" (p. 1). This new pedagogy must be "based on observation and
experimentation," it must, above all, "be experimental" (p. 1). In *Mental Fatigue*,
Binet and Henri gave a first description of the experimental method as applied
to education. Let us look at their description of the method, and an illustrative
example of its application. The authors distinguished two types of educational experimentation: experiments conducted in the laboratory and experiments carried
out in the classroom. They felt that the researcher ought to start with experiments
of the first kind, studying processes in detail and at length with volunteer subjects. Most methodological problems could be solved that way, and the important
research questions established. Based on these first results, a practical plan for continuing experimentation in school settings could be elaborated. The plan was that
experimentation in schools should not disrupt the class for more than 15 minutes,
and a given classroom not visited more than twice a month. If one respects these
two conditions, the authors saw little reason for teachers not to cooperate, and data
could thus be collectively gathered and subsequently analyzed on the researcher's
return to the laboratory. An illustration of an experimental investigation by Binet
and his collaborators is that of mental fatigue (Binet & Henri, 1898). The question
of mental fatigue, of whether the workload imposed on children in school was

too heavy and exhausting for students, was first raised in the French Academy of Medicine in 1886. At around the same time, politicians in Germany debated the same issue, and commissioned a psychologist to investigate the phenomenon. The phenomenon of mental fatigue had important potential consequences on several educational choices, such as the length of instructional programs and exams, the age limit for certain programs and exams, or the way time was divided between instruction, free periods, physical education, and sleep. In *Mental Fatigue*, Binet and Henri (1898) described in what manner the issue was debated in the Academy of Medicine: The questions were raised in very general terms, and doctors expressed their opinions without providing any evidence or even referring to relevant experimental results. Binet and Henri point out that the only means to establish that mental fatigue is widespread and that measures to reduce the phenomenon should be taken, is through experimental investigation. Binet and his collaborators thus proceeded to measure the impact of intellectual activity (i.e., an activity involving mainly concentration, attention, and intelligence—as opposed to a physical activity involving mainly muscular effort) on various physiological and psychological characteristics. Physiological measures included heart rate and heart rhythm, blood circulation, quantity of blood in the brain, blood pressure, body temperature, breathing rhythms, muscular strength, and digestive functions. The psychological effects of mental fatigue were explored in two settings, first in the laboratory, and then in the classroom. The main experimental results showed that mental fatigue decreased mental activity, and reduced mnemonic capacities. This effect however varied depending on the duration of the sustained effort and on the number and the length of pauses during the activity. Indeed, research studies conducted in school settings showed that the moment of the day during which students were assessed had an effect on their performance (performance levels decrease as the day goes on), and that a break for physical activities did not, contrary to what was generally thought, restore performance levels. These results were obtained with both language- and math-based assessments, by both Binet and colleagues working in other countries. Binet and Henri (1898) drew three main conclusions from this body of research: (a) no intellectual effort can be undertaken without affecting the organism; (b) during the first 30 minutes of the effort there is an increase (in heart beat, rhythm, blood pressure, concentration, speed of execution, etc.), but when the effort is sustained for more than an hour a general decrease can be noted; and (c) the distinctive trait that differentiates mental fatigue from nonpathological weariness is the amount of rest needed to repair it. Whereas "normal" weariness will be overcome with sleep and rest, mental fatigue will not be restored as easily. In today's language, Binet's mental fatigue can be equated to the phenomenon of burn-out. This account serves to illustrate what Binet defined as experimental psychology.

Binet's will to apply a scientifically sound study method to pedagogical issues also brought him to develop new statistical tools and to make a systematic use of control groups. Among the statistical inventions were the use of rank correlation coefficients to investigate the relations between academic results and social–economic background. His attempt to use established control groups was not always well met by teachers, though.

Most of Binet's research was conducted with primary school students or children with mental retardation. Binet was the first in France to promote the use of an experimental method in educational research. In a 1920 *Journal of Educational Psychology* review of contemporary research in France, Binet's was the only research cited (Vattier, 1910). Binet used different terms to refer to this field of inquiry (experimental, scientific), but "experimental pedagogy" was the one he favored. The concept of experimental pedagogy encompasses two notions: that of experimentation and that of pedagogy. Experimentation refers to the methodological means by which one can approach pedagogical problems, as previously described. Pedagogy is the object of study. The object of study is a collection of facts (actions and events in the learning situation) rather than a collection of opinions or theories (about what constitutes good education). According to Binet, the ideal for scientific method must be "a collaboration between theory and experimentation," that is, a sustained effort to collect facts first-hand rather than gather them from readings (Binet & Simon, 1908, p. 1). Modern pedagogy is a positive science insofar as it seeks to furnish proofs of what it advocates. According to Binet, all experimental research in education should follow four steps: statement of a hypothesis, collection of facts, interpretation of data, and replication. The hypotheses are often provided by "old pedagogy." For the data gathering, Binet stressed that the use of complicated instruments should be avoided. The best collection tool is the one that requires the least knowledge on behalf of the person administering the instrument. Binet also stressed that the quality and depth of the investigation count more than the number of investigations. Quantitative data must be gathered with care, preferably using statistics such as rank or majority. The last step of a study should always be a replication of one's findings.

Cognitive Assessment

Binet's main research contribution to the field of educational psychology was arguably in the area of cognitive assessment.

Starting at the beginning of the 20th century, Binet showed great interest in the study of "abnormal children" (Binet & Simon, 1907) and his Free Society for the Psychological Study of Children pushed the French government to start evaluating students with the aim of early identification of abnormal children and the provision to them of special education. In 1904, Binet was officially appointed by the Minister of Public Education in France to a commission charged with devising a means of identifying school children with mental retardation. It was based on this interest in abnormal children that the Metric Intelligence Scale was devised during the first 6 months of 1905 (Avanzini, 1974), with the help of his doctoral student Theodore Simon (Minton, 1998). By means of this scale, children with learning impairments, who nevertheless were thought to be able to profit from education, were selected and put into special education classes. The first "perfectioning class" was opened in 1907, and two more followed that year. Although he himself was convinced that abnormality could to some extent be overcome, Binet always stressed the importance of empirically assessing the correctness of his ideas and, though mainly working on applied problems, he never forgot strict experimental methodology. Binet insisted that, before any legislative measures are taken to make these special education classes available for all children with mental retardation, their positive impact must be assessed experimentally.

Before further describing the Metric Intelligence Scale and its most widespread American adaptation, known as the Stanford-Binet Scale of Intelligence, let us first go back to Binet's theory of abnormal children and the need for special education classes, which in turn led to the need for psychometric assessment.

In their 1907 publication *Abnormal Children*, Binet and Simon developed a theory of mental retardation, taking a stand different from the two most widespread stands at the time. The first stand was based on Esquirol's distinction between the idiot and the demented person. The idiot is wholly unable to acquire any new knowledge, and mental development thus essentially is impossible. The second stand is that the abnormal child suffers from mental retardation, with a level of functioning of a normal, but much younger, individual. Binet rejected the first stand because he believed in the perfectibility of the human mind. He rejected the latter stand because it was based on superficial and only partly accurate observations. Binet believed that the implications and impact of an acquisition are linked to the age at which the acquisition is made. Thus, learning to read at age 6 does not have the same implications as learning to read at age 12. What characterizes the abnormal child is notable imbalance, for even though there might be an important delay in the acquisition of certain aptitudes, the development of other aptitudes (cognitive and somatic) may be normal. The abnormal child who learns to read at 12, for example, has a wider vocabulary and more extrascholastic interests than does the normal 6-year old. According to Binet and Simon, the abnormal child is not a normal child that has either stopped developing or who has slowed down in development, but rather, a child with a different developmental pattern. This pattern is unbalanced, with some aspects identical to those of normal children, and others, different. It is this lack of balance between the different developmental aspects that constitutes the abnormality. Abnormality can be characterized by three major components: a global developmental delay, the inequality of this delay depending on the aspects measured, and the resulting lack of coordination in the functioning of the mind. It is precisely because abnormality is seen as a different developmental pattern, and not as mere retardation, that special education is possible and also is needed.

The rationale for the Metric Intelligence Scale devised by Binet and Simon, as well as the scale itself and the guidelines for its administration, were published in 1905. The scale was based on the principle that by sampling a large number of heterogeneous situations or examples of cognitive functioning, one will obtain a better picture of a person's general level of intelligence than by studying a smaller number of mental operations in depth. This notion of sampling justifies why several measures can be added. One must keep in mind that Binet's conception of intelligence as higher order processes was novel, and almost provocative, at the time. Before Binet, most experimental psychologists, following Wundt's example, thought that intelligence was best explored by studying lower order, very simple, processes. Binet not only decided to explore higher order cognitive functions, but to do so with the same experimental rigor that had previously been applied to simpler processes. Binet was also a pioneer in postulating the existence of a unified general intelligence, when most of his predecessors and contemporaries believed in separate mental functions. The Metric Intelligence Scale contained 30 tests, some of them expressly created for the scale, and some adaptations of existing cognitive tests, namely those developed by the French physicists Blin and Damaye (Minton, 1998). Binet defined tests as "quick experiments aimed at assessing children's faculties" (Binet & Simon, 1905, pp. 195–196). All tests had been piloted on samples of "normal" and "retarded" population samples ages 2 to 12. The different tests measured everything from such basic tasks as movement coordination, or imitation, to complex processes such as comprehension, judgment, or abstract reasoning. Among the tests, Binet distinguished between tests of results, that is, those tests aiming to assess the level attained by the student (what are today referred to as achievement tests), and tests of analysis, that is, those tests aiming to understand underlying cognitive constructs (what are today referred to as ability tests). The tests were presented in order of increasing difficulty and at different levels distinctions could be established between normal and retarded children on the one hand, and between younger and older normal children on the other. The easiest tests distinguished severely and profoundly mentally retarded children (at the time labeled as "idiots") from the rest; tests of intermediate difficulty distinguished between severely retarded and moderately retarded (then labeled as "imbeciles"); and higher level tests distinguished between mildly retarded (those corresponding to Goddard's category of "morons", Minton, 1998) and normal children of the same age, as well as between younger and older children. As a member of the ministerial committee on education, Binet's main purpose was to identify the children with mild retardation in order to provide them with the special education that was thought to be able to increase their cognitive functioning.

In the first 1905 publication of the Assessment Scale, Binet and Simon emphasized that the Scale should only be used as an indication of the child's cognitive level at the time of administration, and that this performance level could be subject to change through an appropriate education. The 1905 Scale was administered to a broad sample of children and the tests then were rearranged by age level. A revised version of the Scale was published in 1908, and offered the possibility of establishing a child's "mental age," a notion first introduced by Chaillé in 1887. If 65 to 75% of the children from a given age group, 6 years, for example, succeeded on a test, the test was classified as corresponding to that age level. A child could thus succeed on tests at a "mental age" level that was either lower, equal to, or higher than the level corresponding to the child's biological age. This mental age simply corresponds to the performance norm of a given age group, and does not, as was thought in the American adaptation of the Scale, give an indication of the stage of developmental progression reached by the child. Having a given mental age does not imply functioning as a child of that age; it only implies that the performance on the test corresponds to what the majority of children at a given age will achieve. Binet explicitly warned against the use of performance on an IQ test as a fixed measure of intelligence. It must be noted that, due to the manner in which these tests were constructed, many children of a given age would not succeed on a test intended for their age (Lippmann, 1922).

To facilitate the selection of children eligible for special education, Binet introduced "pedagogical distinctions" among idiocy, imbecility, and debility. The categorization of an individual was not viewed as a mere judgment, but rather as founded on a psychological examination that minimized the risk of an erroneous diagnosis. First, the schoolteacher needed to make a list of "possibly retarded" pupils, based not on personal impression but on weak performance in their studies. This first impression, however, needed to be corroborated by the administration of instructional-level achievement tests, chosen by the principal or regional inspector. But a possible confusion between normal but ignorant, and abnormal children is still possible. The last step must therefore be a psychological examination. Binet also made it clear that the scale was just one assessment tool, and that the observation of the "global person" and the test taker's reaction to the situation are as important as the quantitative test results per se. More than the end results, it is the paths by which they are reached that interested Binet. Binet also insisted on the importance of not knowing the prior diagnosis of the child being examined. Otherwise, one risked a kind of confirmation bias whereby one would confirm the diagnosis already made.

Although Binet's aim was to detect abnormality in children, it was not to segregate them. Binet was convinced that children with mental retardation could and would profit from special education and also that they would be at a loss within the regular school system. His aim was to prevent further rejection of these children by supplying them with special education that would eventually enable them to return to the regular school system. Unfortunately, the American developers of his work believed in fixed IQ and substantially modified Binet's original ideas and intentions. As opposed to most of his contemporaries, Binet believed that "abnormality" could be cured and his faith in education seemed to have practically no limits.

Once again, it is important to remember that Binet did not view intelligence as an entity fixed at birth, but rather, as incremental. It is precisely because of the elastic nature of intelligence and the possibility of developing it through education that children with specific needs, who were not totally benefiting from the regular school system, needed to be identified and to be given the special education that would help them develop their intellectual abilities. This, however, was not the belief of the "Galtonian" researchers who imported Binet's instrument to the United States and Great Britain. Lewis Terman, who in 1916 introduced a U.S. version of the Metric Intelligence Scale known as the Stanford-Binet Intelligence Scale, stressed the importance of hereditary factors in explaining IQ performance. Terman considered this genetic influence to be so strong that it could not possibly be altered through education. Terman advocated placing children with low IQ scores in special classes, not in order that they get the special attention they needed to progress, but because there was no hope of their being able to integrate into and profit from normal schooling. The Metric Intelligence Scale proved to be powerful in distinguishing even "high-grade defectives," that is, those children closest to normal functioning. For Terman, there was no doubt that the identification of these children would

> ultimately result in curtailing the reproduction of feeble-mindedness and in the elim-
> ination of an enormous amount of crime, pauperism, and industrial inefficiency. It
> is hardly necessary to emphasize that the high-grade cases, of the type now so fre-
> quently overlooked, are precisely the ones whose guardianship it is most important
> for the State to assume. (Terman, 1916, p. 545)

The importance of psychometrically sound assessment scales to measure the level of cognitive development was soon generalized beyond the population of abnormal children and constitutes one of Binet's most important legacies to the field. The high positive correlation between children's scores on the Binet-Simon Metric Intelligence Scale and the children's school performance, which is due in part to the scholastic nature of the test items, was seen as a proof that the scale was indeed measuring intelligence, and contributed to its widespread success (Eysenck & Kamin, 1981).

IMPACT ON THE FIELD
OF EDUCATIONAL PSYCHOLOGY

We will now examine Binet's view on four specific learning-related issues: the nature of the learner, the nature of the learning process, optimal conditions of instruction, and the nature of important learning–instructional outcomes.

The Nature of the Learner

The nature of the learner is a question mainly addressed in Binet's *Modern Ideas on Children* (1909)[5]. In the early 20th century, children were often considered to be miniature adults, "homonculi" (Binet, 1909, p. 7), that were only quantitatively, rather than qualitatively, different from adults in everything from physical attributes such as size to cognitive skills. Binet insisted on the importance of studying individual differences, not only between age groups but also between children of a given age, in order to better address the needs of different learners. A teacher should not teach in abstracto, without taking into consideration differences in memory ability, preferred learning strategy, or even age (it was not uncommon practice in Binet's time to group children of various ages in the same classroom), and visual or auditory capacities. Binet and his team were the first, in the Paris school district, to impose annual tests of vision and audition for all children attending school. In a study of apprentice teachers, that Binet conducted with Victor Henri (Binet, 1909), he showed that on all the tests related to scholastic aptitudes (close to the knowledge taught in school) the teachers designated as bright by their instructor excelled. On other tasks, requiring practical or sensitive skills, the subjects defined as less bright, however, performed as well as, or better than, those belonging to the top group of the class. From this, Binet and Henri concluded on the importance of (a) assessing a broad range of skills in order to increase all students' chances of showing their strengths, and (b) teaching in ways that correspond to different children's patterns of abilities (1909, pp.10–11). Taking individual differences into account should not, however, mean that each child is taught individually with a method suited only for her or him. Rather, it means that teachers should strive to find a balance between individual strengths and the requirements of the collective learning environment. Practically, this could, for example, mean that, in larger schools, students of a given grade level be regrouped in different classrooms according to their pattern of abilities.

The Nature of the Learning Process

Repetition and training were the key to learning for Binet (Binet, 1909). According to Binet, whatever the domain, be it typewriting or learning to cross out specific letters on a sheet of paper, the precision and speed of execution would increase with repeated training until they reached a given level, at which performance is stabilized. This growth curve was similar across domains, and the role of education was to help children reach their highest level of performance. Because learning follows a curve, it was important to assess which point of the learning curve a given child has reached, in order to adapt the level of teaching to the child's level. In Binet's words, "Suppose that we are being given a lecture on geometry, and that the 100th theorem is being taught, even if we had the mind of a Pascal[6], we would be unable to understand had we not been taught the previous 99 theorems" (Binet, 1909, pp.147–148). Binet pointed out that, while some difficulty is beneficial and would bring the child to grow, all too often it was the case in the classroom that children were taught things that were out of their reach. The ideas developed by Binet in *Modern Ideas on Children* (1909) and discussed in very broad terms were to be much more systematically explored by Vygotsky and his work on the notion of "zone of proximal development." Once a child's level of functioning had been determined, learning would increase through repeated exercises and a gradual increase of the level of difficulty. According to Binet, learning came with practice, and the student must not only be lectured to, but also be given frequent opportunities to practice his or her knowledge. Such activities as manipulation, practical applications, visits to businesses, or walks in the forest should be promoted. "Above all, the student must be active," said Binet (1909, p. 156), and referred to American researchers' and Spencer's[7] notion of "learning by doing" (1909, p. 159). Again without theorizing or explicitly naming it, Binet's conception was close to what was later to be defined as "constructivism."

Optimal Conditions of Instruction

Binet (1909) considered the key to good instruction to be in teacher training, and he stressed the importance of teaching future teachers to observe. By learning to observe, teachers would become aware of individual differences, and it would help them to adapt the level of teaching to the child's level of knowledge, as just described. According to Binet, the most frequent error in education was to forget that one must "proceed from the simple to the complex" (Binet, 1909, p. 148). Developing teachers' observational skills could be achieved by an increased focus on practical, case-based, exercises during preservice, and by making pedagogical consultations by specialists readily available to all classroom instructors.

The Nature of Important
Learning–Instructional Outcomes

Binet was convinced that, within a certain limit, children's cognitive functioning and abilities could improve when placed in optimal conditions for learning. He was also of the opinion that cognitive functioning cannot be separated from emotions, and that a multitude of factors must be taken into account when studying the complexities of human functioning. This broad interest in the child's development and well-being is exemplified by the studies Binet conducted on the relation between eating habits and intellectual achievement (Binet, 1899). In Wolf's (1973) translation, Binet stated that "intelligence is susceptible to development. With practice and training, and especially with appropriate methods (of teaching) we can augment a child's attention, his memory, his judgment—helping him literally to become more intelligent than he was before . . . right up to the moment when he arrives at his limit." (Wolf, 1973, p. 207). This is illustrated by the instructional methods Binet advocated for abnormal children. Once these abnormal children had been recognized and put into special education classes, what tools were used to favor their development? Binet did not consider abnormality to be a kind of retardation. He gave specific guidelines on the didactics to be used with abnormal children (Binet & Simon, 1907). Binet and Simon stressed the importance of capitalizing on the children's strengths, diminishing the number of pure analytical activities in favor of more practical exercises. More instruction should be carried out in the workshop instead of the classroom, and teachers were encouraged to spend time on "everyday activity exercises," such as putting on one's shoes or sending a letter. New disciplines, such as "Mental Orthopedics," were also introduced, with the aim of re-educating psychological functions and attaining increased developmental synchrony. One example is the "statue game," in which all the students must freeze and keep immobile. This exercise proved beneficial to increase children's concentration and focus, and considerably calmed down the classroom atmosphere. Many of these "orthopedic" exercises are still used in special education classes today. The importance of individually adapted teaching was also underscored.

BINET: A PIONEER AHEAD OF HIS TIME

In retrospect, Binet's most well recognized contribution to the fields of psychology and education is, quite ironically, the Stanford-Binet Intelligence Scale, which owes its popularity largely to the work of L. M. Terman rather than to Binet himself. The intelligence scale became the tree hiding the forest, for at the same time, much of Binet's outstanding, and often revolutionary, research is largely ignored, a paradox that has been pointed out before (Piéron, 1958, Reuchlin, 1957–58, Siegler, 1992). This work includes research in the fields of perception, language development, memory, conceptual development, and other aspects of cognition. Binet was also a pioneer in his methods of investigation, resolutely turning his back to philosophical speculations, and insisting instead on the necessity of empirical investigations (Fraisse, 1958; Reuchlin, 1957–58).

To paraphrase the title of Sarason's article (1976), the fate of Alfred Binet and school psychology was unfortunate. As described, Binet's aim with the Metric Intelligence Scale was to develop an instrument that would contribute to the identification of those children who needed special help in order to make the most of their potential. But this second aspect of optimizing on potential was all too often forgotten and Binet's scale was used to weed out rather than to select children for special programs. Though Binet can be seen as a school psychologist, there are important differences between what Binet did in his day and what much of school psychology has become. As pointed out by Sarason (1976) and Wolf (1973), whereas for Binet the assessment scale was just a means to adapt and enrich education, the role of school psychologists today is all too often limited to evaluation without the psychologists' making the essential link to education. The school psychologist has become a test administrator without a broader perspective or influence on what happens to the child after she or he has been "labeled."

Binet's contributions, therefore, has been misdirected in a way that might well have Binet turning over in his grave!

NOTES

1. The dating of several events, such as Binet's completion of his law degree, or that of his doctoral dissertation, vary according to sources. When several dates are available, we have chosen to use those present in Henri Piéron's 1958 article. This choice is based on Piéron's actual collaboration with Binet, but is not a guarantee of historical veracity.
2. 1839–1916. French philosopher and later Professor of experimental and comparative psychology. Founder of *La Revue Philosophique*.
3. 1825–1893. French physician and professor of nervous disorders. Best known for his clinical work on hysteria and hypnotism.
4. Société Libre pour l'Etude Psychologique de l'Enfant.
5. Its title nonwithstanding, *Modern Ideas on Children* was written almost a century ago, and although the content is still relevant, the style is dated. Binet addresses his *readers* as fathers, teachers or sociologists the latter two in the masculine form of the French word (Binet, 1909, p. 2).
6. Blaise Pascal, French philosopher and mathematician.
7. In *Modern Ideas on Children* (1909), Binet refers his readers to Herbert Spencer's *On Education*, Gustave Le Bon's *Psychology of Education*, and Buyse's *American Methods of Education*. In general, Binet was very inspired by American educational research.

REFERENCES

Avanzini, G. (1974). *A. Binet: Ecrits psychologiques et pédagogiques* [Writings on Psycholgy and Pedagogy]. Toulouse, France: Privat.

Binet, A. (1886). *La psychologie du raisonnement, recherches sur l'hypnotisme* [Psychology of Reasoning, research on hypnotism]. Paris: Alcan.

Binet, A. (1890). Recherches sur les mouvements de quelques jeunes enfants [Research on the movements of some young children.]. *Revue Philosophique, 29*, 297–309.

Binet, A. (1892). *Les altérations de la personnalité* [Personality changes]. Paris: Alcan.

Binet, A. (1898). La mesure en psychologie individuelle [Measurement in Individual Psychology]. *Revue Philosophique, 46*, 113–123.

Binet, A. (1899). Note relative à l'influence du travail intellectuel sur la consommation du pain dans les écoles [A commentary on the influence of intellectual work on the consumption of bread in schools]. *L'Année Psychologique, 5*, 332–335.

Binet, A. (1901a). Recherches sur la technique de la mensuration de la tête vivante [Research on the technique of measuring a living head]. *L'Année Psychologique, 7*, 314–368.

Binet, A. (1901b). Etudes préliminaires de céphalométrie sur 59 enfants d'intelligence inégale, choisis dans les écoles primaires de Paris [Preliminary studies of cephalometry on 59 children of varying levels of intelligence, sampled from primary schools in Paris]. *L'Année Psychologique, 7*, 369–374.

Binet, A. (1903). *L'étude expérimentale de l'intelligence* [Experimental Study of Intelligence]. Paris: Schleicher Frères.

Binet, A. (1909). *Les idées modernes sur les enfants* [Modern ideas on children]. Paris: Flammarion.

Binet, A., & Féré, C. (1887). *Le magnétisme animal* [Animal Magnetism]. Paris: Alcan.

Binet, A., & Henri, V. (1898). *La fatigue intellectuelle* [Intellectual Fatigue]. Paris: Schleicher Frères.

Binet, A., & Simon, T. (1905). Méthodes nouvelles pour le diagnostic du niveau intellectuel des anormaux [New methods for diagnosing intellectual performance in abnormal persons]. *L'Année Psychologique, 11*, 191–244.

Binet, A., & Simon, T. (1907). *Les enfants anormaux* [Abnormal children]. Présentation par Guy Avanzini (1978). Paris: Privat.

Binet, A., & Simon, T. (1908). Le développement de l'intelligence chez les enfants [The development of intelligence in children]. *L'Année Psychologique, 15*, 1–94.

Delay, J. (1958). La vie et l'oeuvre d'Alfred Binet [The life and work of Alfred Binet]. *Psychologie Française, 3*, 85–95.

Eysenck, H. J., & Kamin, L. (1981). *The intelligence controversy*. New York: Wiley.

Fraisse, P. (1958). L'oeuvre d'Alfred Binet en psychologie expérimentale [Alfred Binet's work in experimental psychology]. *Psychologie Française, 3*, 105–112.

Gould, S. J. (1981). *The mismeasure of man*. New York: Norton.

Jacoby, R., & Glauberman, N. (Eds.). (1995). *The bell curve debate: History, documents, opinions*. New York: Random House.

Lippmann, W. (1995). The mental age of Americans. In R. Jacoby & N. Glauberman, (Eds.), *The bell curve debate: History, documents, opinions*. New York: Random House. (Original work published 1922)

Minton, H. L. (1998). Introduction to "New methods for the diagnosis of the intellectual level of subnormals: Alfred Binet and Theodore Simon, 1905." http://psychclassics.yorku.ca/Binet/intro.htm

Piéron, H. (1958). Quelques souvenirs personnels [A few personal memories]. *Psychologie Française, 3*, 89–95.

Reuchlin, M. (1957–58). La mesure de l'intelligence, œuvre paradoxale d'Alfred Binet [The measurement of intelligence—Alfred Binet's paradoxical work]. *Bulletin de Psychologie, 11*, 306–320.

Robinson, D. N. (Ed.). (1977–78). Preface to Binet's "Alterations of personality" and "On double Consciousness". In *Significant contributions to the history of psychology, 1750–1920. Series C. Medical Psychology. Volume V.* Washington, DC: University Publications of America.

Sarason, S. B. (1976). The unfortunate fate of Alfred Binet and school psychology. *Teachers College Record, 77*(4), 579–592.

Siegler, R. S. (1992). The other Alfred Binet. *Developmental Psychology, 28*(2), 179–190.

Simon, T. (1930). *Pédagogie expérimentale* (Ecriture – Lecture – Orthographe) [Experimental psychology (Writing – Reading – spelling)]. (2nd ed.). Paris: Colin.

Terman, L. (1995). The measurement of intelligence. In R. Jacoby & N. Glauberman, (Eds.), *The bell curve debate: History, documents, opinions*. New York: Random House. (Original work published 1916)

Vattier, G. (1910). Experimental pedagogy in France. *Journal of Educational Psychology, 1*, 389–403.

Wolf, T. H. (1973). *Alfred Binet*. Chicago: University Press of Chicago.

Zazzo, R. (1958). Alfred Binet et la psychologie de l'enfant [Alfred Binet and Child Psychology]. *Psychologie Française, 3*, 113–121.

Zuza, F. (1948). *Alfred Binet et la pédagogie expérimentale* [Alfred Binet and Experimental Psychology]. Paris: J. Vrin Editeur.

4

The Development
of Dewey's Psychology

Eric Bredo
University of Virginia

While John Dewey is usually remembered as one of America's most influential philosophers and educational thinkers, he is not generally thought of as a psychologist. This is perhaps not surprising, since Dewey did not think of himself as a psychologist, either, at least for much of his career. Nevertheless, Dewey had considerable influence on the field of psychology during its formative years. He was one of the founders of functional psychology, the first American school of psychology (Sahakian 1975). He also served as an early president of the American Psychological Association and influenced many important psychologists, from Allport to Vygotsky. To properly understand the development of educational psychology in the 20th century it is essential to consider Dewey's contribution.

There are also less purely scholarly and antiquarian reasons for reconsidering Dewey's psychology. Psychology today is often quite fragmented. Cognitive and behavioristic psychology have developed in some isolation and have even been depicted at times as two separate fields. Theories of cognition and emotion have also developed separately, attention being commonly being given to cognition independent of its emotional significance or emotion without reference to its objects. Compounding the difficulty, individual and social psychology have often been isolated as well, as have biological and cultural psychology. Each facet of psychology seems to become a separate industry that develops without much regard for the others, making it hard to develop a more theoretically integrated discipline. Perhaps more importantly, it also creates practical and ethical problems, since treating facets of people's behavior in isolation is all too likely to result in mistreatment, like a liver specialist who regards a patient as a walking liver rather than a whole person. Dewey's psychology can be helpful in this context because it emphasized the relationships between these aspects of psychic life, making it a useful corrective to today's fragmented specialization.

Dewey's work in psychology can also be helpful in another way, by better relating psychology to its own social and political implications. While the point is often overlooked, the concepts on which a psychological theory is built involve value-laden assumptions. As William James put it, "conceptions, 'kinds,' are teleological instruments. No abstract concept can be a valid substitute for a concrete reality except with reference to a particular interest in the conceiver" (James, 1897/1956, p. 70).[1] Unfortunately, many of the best-known theories in educational psychology have incorporated assumptions characterizing people as passive and conformist. Studying behavior on well-structured tasks or in highly controlled laboratory environments was viewed as essential to developing a science of psychology. In doing so, however, there has been a tendency to ignore the way people alter, restructure, and renegotiate their environments (Newman et al., 1989). As McDermott and Hood put it:

> Experimental procedures create constraints independent of the involvements and concerns of the people under analysis, and rob them of many of the normally available resources for organizing their own behavior. . . . Whereas participants in everyday life use a wide range of procedures to simplify, alter, and negotiate tasks . . . laboratory analysts achieve purity by the single simplifying assumption that subjects are responding to tasks predefined by the experimenter. (1982, p. 234)

The all too often result has been a psychology that is better suited to managing controlled or conforming subjects than dealing with more freely interacting people in naturalistic settings. In contrast, Dewey's psychology emphasized the way people can intelligently alter and restructure their environments. Viewing person and environment relationally, he emphasized the cooperative dynamics of person and environment in the successful act, rather than the conformity of one to the other. One of the benefits of such a psychology is that it is more consistent with a democratic way of life, rather than a merely technically managed one, giving another important reason for reconsidering Dewey's psychology today.

Gaining a good sense of Dewey's psychology does present challenges, however. As John Watson, one of the founders of behaviorism, put it, "I got something out of the British School of Philosophers—mainly out of Hume, a little out of Locke, a bit out of Hartley, nothing out of Kant, and strange to say, least of all out of John Dewey. I never knew what he was talking about then, and unfortunately for me, I still don't know" (Watson, 1961, p. 274). While one may wonder whether

Watson's failure was willful, Dewey's thought can at times be hard to understand. One difficulty comes from the fact that Dewey's work evolved over a 70-year career and often presupposed that the reader was familiar with earlier work. Without such familiarity one often gets an exaggerated view of Dewey's emphasis at a given time, failing to see how it as a mere part of the overall story. Given this long evolution, and Dewey's own emphasis on "growth," it seems appropriate to consider Dewey's thinking developmentally.

In what follows I describe the development of Dewey's psychological thought over time, beginning with a biographical overview, focusing primarily on the period from 1884 to 1916. I trace his work through three phases of development, which should be regarded more as ways to highlight shifts in relative focus and emphasis than as structurally distinct stages. The first, when Dewey was still strongly influenced by neo-Hegelian Idealism, might be called his "idealistic" phase. This was followed by a more naturalistic "functional" phase, influenced by his reading of James's *Principles of Psychology* (James, 1890). The third "democratic" phase, culminating in *Democracy and Education* (Dewey, 1916), more explicitly linked his psychology to his emerging social philosophy. By considering Dewey's psychology developmentally in this way I hope to clarify the connections between facets of his work that are often taken in isolation, such as his work on thinking and emotion, or the link between his psychology and his social thought.

BIOGRAPHICAL BACKGROUND

John Dewey was born in 1859 near Burlington, Vermont, to Archibald and Lucinda Rich Dewey. His father, who came from a farming family, was a grocer and then a cigar store owner. His mother, 20 years younger, came from a more prosperous and socially prominent farming family. John was the third of four boys, the first of whom died young. His relations with his tolerant and easygoing father were "cordial," while his mother, although kindly, was more "narrow and strict in her view of morals and religion" (Dykhuizen, 1973, p. 6). She became an intense evangelical, and, to Dewey's apparent dislike, used to ask the young Dewey frequently whether he was "right with Jesus" (Walker, 1997, p. 2). Dewey later attributed his desire for unification to the divisions of life in Calvinist New England (Dewey, 1960), but one might suspect that some of them also arose between loving but quite different parents. Whatever the source, Dewey's work virtually always involved adopting a mediating role between polarized positions.

Dewey's early education was in a Burlington elementary class of 54 pupils, aged 7 to 19, an example of the prevailing low standards of educational provision. When he went on to high school his classes were oriented toward classical subjects suitable for college preparation, including several years of Latin and Greek, French and English grammar, English literature, and mathematics (Dykhuizen, 1973, p. 4–5). After graduating at 16, he went to the University of Vermont, where several of the eight faculty, as well as an earlier president, were friends of the family. There he continued in a largely classical curriculum with special interest in political and social philosophy. H. A. P. Torrey, the professor of mental and moral philosophy, helped introduce him to Kantian and Scottish commonsense philosophy. However, Dewey later recalled that a "distinctive philosophical interest" was first aroused by a physiology course with a text by T. H. Huxley.[2] This inspired Dewey with a "sense of interdependence and interrelated unity . . . to which material in any field ought to conform." It also led him to subconsciously "desire a world and a life that would have the same properties as had the human organism in the picture of it derived from study of Huxley's treatment" (Dewey, 1960, p. 4).[3] Dewey's first philosophical impulse was, thus, to view the universe in living, organic terms (Phillips, 1971).

After graduating from the university at 20, Dewey taught high school in Oil City, Pennsylvania, for 2 years (1879–1881) and then for a year at a private seminary in Charlotte, Vermont. He seems to have gotten on well with the students in Oil City, but had trouble maintaining control of those in Charlotte. During the latter period he returned for private tutoring with Torrey in the history of philosophy, and decided to make philosophy his life's work.

In 1882, at the age of 23, Dewey went on for that "new thing," graduate work, at Johns Hopkins University. In support of his application for a fellowship, the President of the University of Vermont wrote, "John Dewey has a logical, thorough-going, absolutely independent mind. He is sound and sweet all through—is true and loyal in matters of religion, and without any crotchets, or drawbacks of any kind, so far as I know. He is very reticent, as you see. . . . This is the only question that would arise in the minds of those who know him . . ." (Dykhuizen, 1973, p. xxi). At Hopkins, Dewey worked with G. Sylvester Morris, a neo-Hegelian philosopher who also taught at the University of Michigan. Morris, Dewey's favorite instructor, lectured on the "demonstrated truth" of German Idealism, converting Dewey for a time to neo-Hegelianism. In this view, reality was seen "as an organic unity whose parts are interrelated like those of a biological organism." It was, in effect, "a single . . . Life or Mind that differentiates itself into countless lives or minds, realizing its own higher Life in and through these finite ones" (Dykhuizen, 1973, p. 34). Dewey later wrote that Hegel's thinking satisfied "a demand for unification that was doubtless an intense emotional craving." Hegel's work also involved an attempt to synthesize various opposing positions by showing how they make sense together when considered developmentally. As Dewey put it, his synthesis of "subject and object, matter and spirit, the divine and the human, was . . . no mere intellectual formula; it operated as an immense release, a liberation" (Dewey, 1960, p. 10).

Dewey also studied with G. Stanley Hall, the first American Ph.D. in psychology (under William James at Harvard following work with Wilhelm Wundt in Germany). Hall had an expansive vision of an evolutionary approach to psychology that would help integrate the field and guide educational and social reform

(Hall, 1885; Hall, 1909; Hall, 1916). Dewey took classes with Hall in physiological and experimental psychology, psychological and ethical theories, and "scientific pedagogics" (Dykhuizen, 1973, p. 31). While he did not initially see any close relation between the "new psychology" taught by Hall and the philosophy he was learning from Morris, during his last year he became very excited about psychology. He nevertheless found Hall too "narrowly scientific" and "contemptuous of philosophy," a criticism that was later returned in inverted form by Hall (Clifford, 1968, p. 241). Dewey also took a course on logic from Charles Saunders Peirce, the founder of pragmatism, but found it disappointing due to its heavily mathematical and scientific orientation. Only 20 years later did he realize the importance of Peirce's work for his own (Dykhuizen, 1973, pp. 30–31).

After completing his Ph.D. in 1884, Dewey was hired by Morris to teach at the University of Michigan. There he taught many courses in psychology, including Empirical Psychology, Experimental Psychology, Speculative Psychology, History of Psychology, and Psychology and Philosophy. He also taught courses on Kant, Spencer, logic, and other subjects (Dykhuizen, 1973, p. 46; Coughlan, 1975, p. 54). Dewey began his active involvement in education in this period, serving on a school investigating committee. He also gave a first lecture at Jane Addams' Hull House in Chicago. Aside from these intellectual involvements in social reform, however, Dewey "did not join any social reform movement or enlist in any cause" during this time (Dykhuizen, 1973, p. 51). In his second year at Michigan he met and married Alice Chipman, a student and fellow boarder in his rooming house. As their daughter, Jane, wrote, "she had a brilliant mind which cut through sham and pretense . . . (and) a sensitive nature combined with indomitable courage" (Dykhuizen, 1973, p. 53). Jane Dewey went on to suggest that "she was undoubtedly largely responsible for the early widening of Dewey's philosophic interests above the commentative and classical to the field of contemporary life. Above all, things which had previously been matters of theory acquired through his contact with her vital and direct human significance" (Dykhuizen, 1973, p. 54).

A number of others at Michigan also became important colleagues. Dewey hired James Hayden Tufts to teach the introductory psychology and philosophy courses. Tufts stayed a year before going on to Germany for further study and then to a position at the University of Chicago, where he was later instrumental in Dewey's hiring. George Herbert Mead replaced Tufts at Michigan, having just completed his dissertation with Josiah Royce at Harvard. Writing about their relationship later on, Jane Dewey noted that "from the nineties on, the influence of Mead ranked with that of James" (Dykhuizen, 1973, p. 68). The sociologist Charles Horton Cooley, author of the "looking glass" (reflective) theory of the self, was also a colleague. During 10 years at Michigan, interrupted by a year at Minnesota, Dewey published his first book, *Psychology* (Dewey, 1887). This, along with early articles on the relation between psychology and philosophy, helped give Dewey an "international scholarly audience and reputation" (Coughlan, 1975, p. 61). He also published a book on Leibniz's philosophy (Dewey, 1888) and two books on ethics. Another book, *Applied Psychology* (McLellan & Dewey, 1889), primarily written by McLellan, provided a helpful introduction to Dewey's psychology and its educational implications.

In 1894 Dewey moved to the University of Chicago. The president of the new, Rockefeller-funded university, William Rainey Harper, had offered the position to two more senior philosophers, but after they turned him down, hired Dewey, on Tufts' recommendation (Rucker, 1969, p. 4). Dewey was appointed chairman of the Department of Philosophy, which included psychology and pedagogy, providing a rare opportunity to relate thinking across these three fields. Being able to work in psychology and education, as well as in philosophy, was one of the principal reasons Dewey was attracted to the job, although he complained of being underpaid (Rucker, 1969, p. 7). He also had the opportunity to hire a number of colleagues, bringing in George Herbert Mead from Michigan, and hiring J. R. Angell, a former student at Michigan who had completed graduate work with William James at Harvard. Mead became important in the development of the social–interactional aspects of pragmatism, which was very influential in interactional sociology. Angell became important for his work in the development of functional psychology (Angell, 1904; Angell, 1907; Angell, 1961). These four colleagues, Dewey, Mead, Angell, and Tufts, "were the nucleus of the Chicago School in the decade from 1894 to 1904, when the foundations of the new philosophy were being laid" (Rucker, 1969, p. 4). As a result of Dewey's opportunity to hire congenial and excellent colleagues, the Chicago group was unusually tight-knit. As William James wrote after the publication of *Studies in Logical Theory* (Dewey, 1903), "Chicago University has during the past six months given birth to the fruit of its ten years of gestation under John Dewey. The result is wonderful—a real school, and real Thought. Important thought, too! Did you ever hear of such a city or such a University? Here (at Harvard) we have thought, but no school. At Yale a school but no thought. Chicago has both" (Rucker, 1969, p. 3).

Many of those at the University of Chicago, from the president on down, were at the time involved in social and educational reform. Dewey became a trustee and active participant in Jane Addams' Hull House, a settlement house in the city's slums (Addams, 1990). As Dykhuizen commented, "Dewey owed much to the influences he encountered at Hull House. His contacts with people with more radical and extreme views than his deepened and sharpened his own ideas. Jane Addams's faith in the common man and her conviction 'that the simple humble peoples of the earth are those...(whose) friendly affections are least spoiled' reinforced Dewey's own 'faith in democracy as a guiding force in education'" (Dykhuizen, 1973, p. 105). He was involved with the reform of the Chicago public schools, and Ella Flagg Young, a superintendent and important educational thinker in her own right, became a valued colleague at the university. Dewey also started the University Laboratory School as a way of testing the new psychological and pedagogical theories in practice. This later merged with Colonel Parker's school, with Alice Chipman Dewey as its principal. Despite this practical involvement in social and educational reform, Dykhuizen (1973, p. 104) notes that in his published articles Dewey "did not . . . touch upon any of the explosive issues of the day."

At Chicago, Dewey taught many courses on education in addition to those in philosophy. These included Educational Psychology, Philosophy of Education, Educational Methodology, Evolution of Educational Theory, Elementary Education, Logical Methods in Relation to Education, and Evolution of the Curriculum in the Fifteenth to Seventeenth Centuries (Dykhuizen, 1973, p. 87). Some of his most widely read educational works were published in this period, including *School and Society* (Dewey, 1900/1956) and *The Child and the Curriculum* (Dewey, 1902/1956), as well as the largely forgotten, *The Psychology of Number and Its Applications to Methods of Teaching Arithmetic* (McLellan & Dewey, 1895/1905). The Chicago years saw the publication of some of Dewey's most important psychological essays, as well, including his very influential critique of the reflex arc concept in psychology (Dewey, 1896), his papers on the theory of emotion (Dewey, 1894; Dewey, 1895) and "Interest in Relation to Training of the Will." These contributions were given formal recognition by his election as president of the American Psychological Association in 1899. The more general philosophical implications of his approach to pragmatism, which he termed "instrumentalism," were presented in *Studies in Logical Theory* (Dewey, 1903).[4]

Dewey left the University of Chicago in 1904, following continuing differences with its president, William Rainey Harper, and a dispute over his wife's being replaced as principal of the Laboratory School. Columbia University immediately hired him, giving him a position at Teachers College as well. At Columbia he came into contact with a wider group of philosophers, helping to challenge and sharpen his approach. He also came into contact with anthropologists, such as Franz Boas, who helped extend the social and cultural aspects of his work. Dewey's psychologically oriented publications from his early years at Columbia include *How We Think* (Dewey, 1910) and *Interest and Effort in Education* (Dewey, 1913). *Schools of Tomorrow*, a description of progressive schools written with his daughter Evelyn (Dewey & Dewey, 1915), was also published along with a revision of the *Ethics* he had earlier written with Tufts (Dewey & Tufts, 1908/1932). The social and psychological aspects of Dewey's work were more fully integrated with one another during this period and applied to education in *Democracy and Education* (Dewey, 1916a), which Dewey felt was for many years the place where his philosophy was "most fully expounded" (Dewey, 1960). *Reconstruction in Philosophy* (Dewey, 1920), drawn from lectures given in Japan and China, helped summarize his reconceptualization of many traditional philosophical issues in short and easily accessible form. *Human Nature and Conduct* (Dewey, 1922) attempted to better relate the biological and social sides of his psychology to ethics. His most highly regarded work, *Experience and Nature* (Dewey, 1929/1958), elaborated his approach to metaphysics and the relation between mind and nature. Other work included *The Public and Its Problems* (Dewey, 1927), a theory of the evolution of the democratic state, and *The Quest for Certainty* (Dewey, 1929/1960), a criticism of traditional philosophy and religion.

During his years at Columbia, Dewey was involved in many issues, helping to found the American Association of University Professors, the American Civil Liberties Union, and the New School for Social Research (Dykhuizen, 1973, pp. 171–172). After retiring in 1930, he continued to do important work, of which the most relevant to psychology and education are *Art as Experience* (Dewey, 1934) and *Experience and Education* (Dewey, 1938/1963). The former helped relate his approach to aesthetics, something many had thought lacking in his "instrumentalism," while the latter criticized progressive educators for becoming too simplistically child-centered, as well as sharpening some of his own thoughts on the nature of educative experience. A fuller statement of his approach to logic was presented in *Logic: The Theory of Inquiry* (Dewey, 1938). He continued publishing significant work until his death in 1952, of which *Knowing and the Known* (Dewey & Bentley, 1949) is the most relevant to present-day psychology because of its situated approach to knowing.

THE NEW PSYCHOLOGY

Dewey's early work was part of the "new psychology" that was becoming influential in United States in the 1880s. This was inspired by German experimental research, on the one hand, and by Darwinian evolutionary theory, on the other. As Boring noted in his history of the field, "American psychology inherited its physical body from German experimentalism, but it got its mind from Darwin" (Boring, 1929, p. 494). Some sense of the new psychology can be gathered from a letter George Herbert Mead wrote to a friend: "What a contrast there is between the mental philosophers of 100 years ago and the busy student of idiots and the insane(,) the hunter after nerves and nerve ganglions(,) the discusser of methods of pedagogics (of today)" (Coughlan, 1975, p. 123).

The new psychology contrasted with the "old" psychology of Locke, Hume, Mill, Reid, and Bain, which was mechanistic and largely based on armchair speculation. The old psychology's underlying mechanical metaphor, drawn from Newtonian theory, contrasted with the new psychology's metaphor of the living organism, drawn from evolutionary theory. The latter metaphor helped conceive of people as living, growing, adapting beings rather than as machines, thereby furnishing the basis for a more *lively* and dynamic psychology. While evolutionary thinking was sweeping aside the older ideas (Miller, 1968, p. xi) there were different conceptions of evolution in play. On the naturalistic side, Spencer, Darwin, and Huxley were popular with scientists and those enthused with popular science, while on the idealistic side neo-Hegelian ideas were in vogue among more religiously inclined intellectuals. Darwinian naturalists and neo-Hegelian idealists differed substantially, but both emphasized the way form or structure emerges within an evolutionary or developmental process.

One of Dewey's first articles was a celebration of the new psychology (Dewey, 1884). In it he argued that the older associationistic psychologists had "emasculated experience" and "sheared it down till it would fit their logical boxes" (Dewey, 1963, pp. 49, 60). They had treated the person as "a neatly dovetailed psychical machine who may be taken as an isolated individual, laid on the dissecting table of analysis and duly anatomized" (Dewey, 1963, pp. 49–50). In contrast, the new psychology helped one see mental life as "an organic unitary process developing according to the laws of all life" (Dewey, 1963, p. 57). Rather than "considering psychical life as an individual isolated thing developing in a vacuum" (Dewey, 1963, p. 58), the new psychology would consider the individual in relation to the "organized social life into which he is born, from which he draws his mental and spiritual sustenance, and in which he must perform his proper function or become a mental and moral wreck" (Dewey, 1963, p. 58). Dewey's early psychology clearly emphasized individual development in the context of a social and cultural life that was itself developing.

Dewey's interpretation of the new psychology gave it a strongly Hegelian slant, as evident toward the end of the article. Here he suggested that the new psychology would view the evolution of intelligence as "an organism in which immanent ideas or purposes are realizing themselves through the development of experience" (Dewey, 1963, pp. 61–62). In effect, socio-cultural evolution would be viewed as part of the process of Absolute Spirit (i.e., God) realizing itself and becoming immanent in the world. The resulting approach would have "intensely ethical tendencies," making possible "a psychology of man's religious nature and experience," finding in the depths of man's nature "tendencies of devotion, sacrifice, faith, and idealism which are the eternal substructure of all of the struggles of the nations upon the altar stairs which slope up to God" (p. 62). As Dykhuizen, commented, "It is clear . . . that (at the time) Dewey saw an essential identity between the basic concepts of the new psychology—its organicism, its dynamism, its rejection of formalism . . . —and those of Neo-Hegelianism" (Dykhuizen, 1973, p. 38).

In this and other early articles (Dewey, 1963a; Dewey, 1963b), Dewey might be interpreted as attempting to work out the relationship between the evolutionary psychology of G. Stanley Hall and the neo-Hegelian philosophy of G. Sylvester Morris. Characteristically, he saw psychology and philosophy as interdependent aspects of a common endeavor, psychology providing a method for philosophy (seeing things in terms of their practical, psychological import) and philosophy the wider intellectual context for psychology. This unwillingness to separate psychology from philosophy accounts for some of the strengths of his approach, such as its strong links between psychology and logical, ethical, and aesthetic concerns, but it also flew in the face of the effort of psychologists to develop a science independent of philosophy.

SELF-REALIZATION: THE ROLES
OF COGNITION, AFFECT AND WILL

Dewey's first book, *Psychology* (Dewey, 1887), which came out after he joined the faculty at Michigan, was also the first textbook in the new psychology. It was quite popular and went through several printings before being thoroughly displaced by William James' *The Principles of Psychology* (James, 1890/1950). In his *Psychology*, Dewey attempted to organize the facts of the new, experimental psychology into neo-Hegelian categories. As Dykhuizen noted, its effect was to lead the reader "to believe that the facts of empirical psychology naturally and inevitably lead over into German metaphysical idealism" (Dykhuizen, 1973, p. 54). Despite the stultifying effect of attempting to pour all the new facts into old wineskins, it offered a conceptually rich approach that Dewey continued to elaborate and modify throughout his life.

Psychology was primarily an effort to show how cognition, affect, and will are related to one another, and how they function in human "self-realization."[5] Each of these three functions was taken as an *aspect* of "consciousness," not a separate thing. Cognition was the objective or universal aspect of a concrete thought or feeling. When we know about an object as a result of some stimulation, for example, this knowledge is universal because we know what anyone else may know about it. Affect is the subjective or particular aspect of consciousness. It involves how one is personally *affected* by the "tone" or manner of a stimulation. These two aspects are then "united" in the third aspect, will (Dewey, 1887). The latter point may be obscure, so an example may help. Consider what happens when one sees a bear approaching on a trail in the woods. The objective or cognitive aspect of this stimulation involves the perception that it is a bear and not some other object. The emotional or subjective aspect might include the sinking feeling in the pit of one's stomach and the feel of one's muscles tensed in fear. These aspects are "united" in the intention to act in a certain way, such as beginning to back away very carefully. This act unites the objective stimulus and the subjective emotional response in behavior that is consistent with some interpretation of each.

Dewey's early psychology is interesting today primarily because of the way it emphasized the interdependence of thinking, feeling, and willing. Rather than focusing on one of these functions independently of the others, Dewey insisted that each needs to be understood in relation to the others. Cognition depends on affect, for example, for without an interest in an issue, a person will simply not attend to it. Cognition also depends on will, because present directed activity affects the stimulus that is perceived. Affect depends similarly on cognition, because feelings change depending on their object: fear of an angry bear differs from fear of an angry Pekinese. Affect also depends on will, because feelings emerge as a result of threats to, or disruptions of, goal-directed activity. Will depends on cognition because controlled action depends on the objective qualities of the situation. Finally, will also depends on affect because emotional feelings indicate whether a given effort conflicts with other active aims. By indicating the way different functions affect one another, Dewey's analysis kept from "anatomizing" a live organism by attending only to a slice of its life while ignoring the functions with which it is coupled. It suggested, for example, that in education one needs to be sensitive to children's thinking in relation to their emotional feelings and practical intentions, and not to their thinking alone.

Dewey's *Psychology* also remains interesting because of its emphasis on "self-realization." As he put it, "It is evident . . . that ultimately there can be only one end to human action. . . . Each end is referable to a higher end, which stated in most general form, is self-realization" (Dewey, 1887, p. 370). This language may seem alien today, but is more comprehensible if one thinks of him as emphasizing "self-actualization," a concept familiar from the work of Carl Rogers and Abraham Maslow.[6] Consistent with Hegelian thought, Dewey suggested that one needs to consider a person as constantly growing or "becoming." One can see this as similar to Vygotsky's notion that the only good learning is that which is in advance of the present stage of development (Vygotsky, 1978). Dewey's early emphasis on self-realization as the end of human action was also the origin of his later emphasis on "growth" (Dewey, 1916a). His emphasis on the way cognition, affect, and will become differentiated and associated in complex ways with development would be similar to a contemporary focus on cognitive development, affective development, and moral development. But rather than isolating these aspects of development, Dewey focused on their relationships with one another. Since Dewey was still highly influenced by neo-Hegelianism, he tended to see individual self-realization as part of a larger process of unification with Absolute Spirit. As he put it, self-realization involves the "progressive appropriation of that self in which real and ideal are one; in which truth, happiness, and rightness are united in one Personality" (Dewey, 1887, p. 424). In other words, self-realization progressed toward unification with the Absolute.

Dewey's *Psychology* won high praise in some quarters, but was criticized by G. Stanley Hall and William James, the most prominent psychologists of the time. Hall grumbled that "the facts are never allowed to speak out plainly for themselves . . . but are always 'read into' the system" (Dykhuizen, 1973, p. 55). Indeed, "very few of them are satisfactory, and many we believe to be fundamentally wrong and misleading" (Coughlan, 1975, p. 58). James had hoped for something fresh but was sorely disappointed, feeling that Dewey took "all the edge and definiteness away from the particulars" when he interpreted individual mental lives in terms of the development of the larger Self (Dykhuizen, 1973, p. 55). Dewey's neo-Hegelianism was definitely too formulaic, but it did have the benefit of helping him see the interdependence of cognition, affect, and will. It also made him sensitive to the role of present functions in future self-realization, and helped him consider individual functioning in the context of an evolving socio-historical way of life.

The educational implications of Dewey's *Psychology* were elaborated in *Applied Psychology* (McLellan & Dewey, 1889), written with J. A. McLellan, the principal author. The overall maxim of the book was to "Learn to Do by Knowing and to Know by Doing," a theme consistent with Dewey's later thought. Various principles of instruction were suggested, including basing instruction on an activity, interest, or idea already enjoyed by the pupil. The goals of instruction were to be such that it would be significant, definite, and practical. The methods of instruction would involve teaching one thing at a time and in a connected manner (McLellan & Dewey, 1889, pp. 163–181).

THE INFLUENCE OF WILLIAM JAMES—AND DARWIN

Dewey's Idealistic (Hegelian) phase lasted "in full force for about seven years," from 1884 to 1891 (Dewey & Ratner, 1963, p. 13). It took William James' *Principles of Psychology* (James, 1890/1950) to loosen the hold of Hegelian thinking and push him in a more naturalistic direction (Dewey, 1960). James was deeply steeped in the work of Darwin and Huxley, having been near the center of the debate on evolution in the U.S. and having taught physiology at Harvard for 5 years (Bredo, 2002). His work helped Dewey see to develop an "organic" approach to psychology that was more concrete than that suggested by Hegelianism.

The most novel aspect of James' work was the fact that he based his psychology on Darwinian assumptions, viewing mind as a natural function evolved for the purpose of aiding adaptation. As he put it:

> (O)ur inner faculties are adapted in advance to the features of the world in which we dwell, adapted, I mean, so as to secure our safety and prosperity in its midst. . . . Mind and world . . . have been evolved together, and in consequence are something of a mutual fit. . . . The chief result of this more modern view is . . . that our various ways of feeling and thinking have grown to be what they are because of their utility in shaping our reactions on the outer world. (James, 1892, pp. 3–4)

This point may seem obvious, but James drew from it interesting implications that may still not have been fully absorbed. Foremost among these was the notion that thinking has evolved for purposes of practical action, since its primary purpose is to help an organism adapt to novel or contingent situations. Seen in this way, thinking is primarily for the sake of action, not merely for passively describing the way things are. As James put it, "My thinking is first and last and always for the sake of my doing, and I can only do one thing at a time" (James, 1892, p. 355). Since an organism has feelings and preferences that relate to the success of its actions, thinking was also closely related to emotion. Indeed, James saw thinking as largely driven by emotional interest. This active view of mind was central to pragmatism.

In James' account mind was also conceived as a dynamic function rather than a static thing. He reacted against all entitative conceptions, such as the associationistic view that complex ideas are formed out of elementary ideas of sense, because this conceived of elementary ideas as already discriminated static entities. He also opposed the view that thought is the result of the operations of a transcendental ego, since this posited another static entity, the ego, which would itself have to be explained. In James' view, thoughts are analogous to waves, and thinking is akin to the dynamics of interacting waveforms. Using this analogy one does not need to think of a complex idea as comprised of elementary parts because a waveform can have many patterns and sub-patterns within it. One also does not need a substantial ego to do the thinking because in a dynamic approach, "the thoughts themselves are the thinker" (James, 1892, p. 216). As Dewey noted, many had thought of mind in terms of static structures, but "It was reserved to James to think of life in terms of life in action" (Dewey, 1960, p. 16).

Whereas much of James' work was very dynamic, he structured his discussion around the notion of the sensory-motor reflex, which was thought to provide the basic unit for psychology. Sensory and motor nerves had been found to be separate from one another as they enter and exit the spinal cord (the Bell–Magendie law), making it seem as though psychology could be based on an input–output model.[7] As James put it, returning to a mechanical analogy, "the nervous system is well understood today to be nothing but a machine for receiving impressions and discharging reactions preservative to the individual and his kind" (James, 1892, p. 7). As a result, it seemed that behavior could be understood in terms a linear sequence of sensory input, central imagery or thought, and motor response.

During his later years at Michigan, Dewey grew very excited about the idea that the sensory–motor reflex provided the basic unit for psychology. If this was the basic unit of all behavior and thought, then in it "we have the universe expressed, and from its structure, therefore, we may read the main philosophic ideas. Every such action is representative of the whole because it is the whole in concentrated form, *not* because it is part of the whole" (Coughlan, 1975, pp. 136–137). Dewey was beginning to shift from the Hegelian notion that unification involves becoming identified with the Absolute to the more grounded notion that unification involves locally coordinated action, as evident when stimulus and response are well-coordinated in a developing act. Darwinian creatures only need to be in dynamic equilibrium with their local surroundings, not with everything. After 2 or 3 years, Dewey's enthusiasm became more tempered, however, as he began to be more critical of aspects of James' psychology for falling into some of the same dualisms as the old psychology (Dewey, 1946).

CRITIQUE OF THE REFLEX ARC CONCEPT

The most important of Dewey's articles in this "functional" period "The Reflex Arc Concept in Psychology" (Dewey, 1896) was a criticism of the reflex arc model and a position statement for the Chicago approach to psychology. This was considered the most influential article published in the first 50 years of the *Psychological Review* (See Bredo, 1998). As one commentator put it,

> The publication of "The Reflex Arc Concept in Psychology" probably marks one of the truly important turning points in the study of human behavior. It remained for decades one of the most influential works in the science of psychology and still retains that position among all students not dogmatically committed to some form, by whatever name, of the same mechanistic view that it attempts to correct. . . . Whenever the study of man rises above the concept of an organic robot as his model, the "Reflex Arc" is studied.[8] (McKenzie, 1971, pp. xiv–vx)

As noted above, the reflex idea suggested that behavior could be understood as the result of a serial connection between a stimulus and a response, which was viewed as equivalent to a connection between sensory and motor neurons. It suggested that psychology could be based a linear input–output model, like later stimulus–response (S-R) or stimulus–organism–response (S-O-R) theories.

Dewey believed that the reflex model retained many of the fragmenting assumptions of the older associationistic and ego theories, despite James' attempt to displace them: "The older dualism between sensation and idea is repeated in the current dualism of peripheral and central structures and functions; the older dualism of body and soul finds a distinct echo in the current dualism of stimulus and response" (Dewey, 1896, pp. 357–358). In other words, a psychology based on the reflex arc concept separated mind and body, and organism and environment, into separate *things*, much like the old psychology. It treated stimulus, central activity, and response as separate entities, thereby misunderstanding their more dynamic relationships. By focusing on sensory input and motor output as independent events, while ignoring the way they affect each other in parallel and are coupled through the environment, the reflex theory focused on a mere "arc" or fragmentary part of a complete *cycle* of behavior. As a result, "the reflex arc is not a comprehensive or organic unity, but a patchwork of disjointed parts" (p. 358). If organisms really behaved in this way, Dewey argued, their behavior would be "nothing but a series of jerks," the origin of each jerk being found either "outside of the process of experience" in the environment or in "some spontaneous variation within the organism" (p. 360). It would then become impossible to understand how an organism acts in a coordinated, flowing fashion. It is interesting to note that similar criticisms have been leveled today against conventional approaches to robotics that also involve separate sensory, reasoning, and motor components placed in sequence (Brooks, 1991).

Instead of basing psychology on separate sensory and motor events in linear sequence, Dewey argued that the basic unit of behavior is the goal-directed *act* in which an organism's response serves to alter its own stimulation. As Dewey put it, "the so-called response is not merely *to* the stimulus, it is *into* it" (Dewey, 1896, p. 359). Seen in this way, sensory and motor events are not linearly related, with sensation occurring first and then a motor response being triggered. Rather, sensory and motor events operate in cycles, motor events helping to alter sensory stimulation just as sensory stimulation helps regulate motor events. While Dewey did not have the modern concept of feedback, his conception was at least analogous to that of a system behaving so as to attain some targeted sensory state.

Dewey went on to argue that a stimulus cannot be reduced to mere sensation, nor can a response be reduced to mere motor reaction. Both perception and manipulation are functional acts, not mechanical impulses. In perception, for example, sensory input is altered by shifting one's body, orienting and focusing one's eyes. Motor activities alter sensory input until an object is recognized. Seen as acts rather than as entities, "stimulus" and "response" are perceptual and manipulatory sub-acts that work together to compose a larger act, like looking for one's coffee cup (stimulus) and reaching to pick it up (response), both of which are part of the act of taking a sip of coffee. As Dewey put it, "stimulus and response are not distinctions of existence, but teleological distinctions, that is, distinctions of function, or part played, with references to reaching or maintaining an end" (Dewey, 1896, p. 365). In a normal, well-coordinated act each function modifies the other as the act develops. It is only when the act breaks down that it indeed fragments into uncoordinated sensory and motor events, as assumed in the reflex arc model. As Dewey put it, "discrimination, not integration, is the real problem" (Dewey, 1895, p. 23). We would do better, then, to understand people as purposeful actors whose behavior is generally well adapted to achieving their goals, than as mechanical robots prodded to respond by external events.

One can see how Dewey's holism and search for unity informed this analysis. In effect, he was saying that the psychologist should start with what the organism is trying to do and then see how this act is broken up *by the organism* into sub-acts and sub-sub-acts, rather than imposing an external segmentation that is insensitive to the organism's purposive behavior. One of the reasons this approach may not have been adopted by many subsequent psychologists was that it suggested that psychology is always interpretive at base, since an organism's behavior must be understood in the light of its implicit aims or purposes as interpreted by an observer. This conflicted with the more positivistic attempt by those in the emerging profession of psychology to develop a psychology based on physical movements independent of interpretation in the light of aim or intention.

Dewey's analysis of stimulus and response, although abstract, had important practical implications. It suggested that an organism's behavior is not determined simply by external stimulation. As Dewey put it some years later, "every stimulus directs activity. It does not simply excite it or stir it up, but directs it toward an object. Put the other way around, a response is not just a re-action, a protest . . . against being disturbed; it is . . . an answer. . . . There is an adaptation of the stimulus and response to each other" (Dewey, 1916, p. 24). Because behavior is a result of what the organism is trying to do, along with whatever changes in the environment occur as result, "purely external direction is impossible" (Dewey, 1916, p. 25).

Thus, in attempting to educate a child, one needs to modify the environment in a way that goes *with* the child's tendencies rather than ignoring them. This analysis suggested a much more cooperative model of behavior, seeing an act as the result of an interaction between organism and environment rather than as determined by the environment. Dewey further elaborated on this cooperative approach to "direction" by showing the ways children are socialized into ways of thinking and valuing shared with others, helping them to become self-conscious partners in a joint act. Here, as elsewhere, Dewey sought to reframe a conventional analysis built on a division between person and environment in a more interactive way.

THE THEORY OF EMOTION

The psychology of the act that Dewey began to lay out in the reflex arc paper gave him a way of reconceiving the central concepts of his earlier *Psychology*, cognition, affect, and will, in more concrete behavioral form. The first concept Dewey reworked in behavioral terms was his conception of emotion (Dewey, 1894; Dewey, 1895). Because Dewey's theory of emotion was based on Darwin's and James' theories, it may be helpful to briefly consider these other theories before turning to Dewey's.

In *The Expression of the Emotions in Man and Animals* Darwin (1889/1904) argued that most emotionally expressive behaviors derive from functional parts of larger acts gain a new meaning. A dog's baring it's teeth in anger, for example, was originally simply the beginning of getting its lips out of the way to bite. Over time, such "serviceable associated habits" gained new functions in their own right, such as expressing anger. While Darwin thought that most expressive gestures had this origin, he noted that gestures that are already used to express emotion may also be reversed to express other emotions ("antithetical" expressions), such as submission being expressed by behavior that is the opposite of dominance. Other behaviors, such as trembling in pathological terror, are simply the products of "direct nervous discharge," having no distinctive functions of their own.

Darwin's analysis suggested that an animal first has an inner emotion, and then seeks to express it in external behavior. For example, a male dog might see another male in its territory, feel anger, and then expresses this anger in a tensed and snarling attitude. William James, thought this interpretation had the sequence backwards. In James' view an external stimulus causes a bodily response, such as an "angry" form of behavior, and this bodily response causes the inner emotional feeling rather than the reverse. As James wrote, "My theory, on the contrary, is that the bodily changes follow directly the perception of the exciting fact, and that our feeling of the same changes as they occur IS the emotion" (James, 1892, p. 375). In other words, in Darwin's theory the inner feeling causes the bodily response, while in James' theory the bodily response causes the inner feeling. As James put it, "we feel sorry because we cry, angry because we strike, afraid because we tremble, and not that we cry, strike, or tremble because we are sorry, angry, or fearful" (James 1892, p. 376).

Dewey thought James correct about the sequence of events, but believed both were wrong in identifying the feeling with the emotion. When we say an animal is "angry," Dewey argued, we do not mean that it has anger inside that it is trying to express, for this makes it out to be merely an actor simulating an emotion. A dog that stiffens and begins to snarl expresses anger to us as *observers*. Its being "angry" is a way of saying that it is likely to attack. Darwin confused the issue because he took the interpretation of the animal's behavior from an observer's point of view and made it an emotion inside of the head of the animal.[9] He was right, however, that expressive behavior generally performs useful functions. An emotional attitude or gesture is a preparatory phase of an act to come. As Dewey put it, "The reference to emotion in explaining the attitude (the expressive behavior) is wholly irrelevant; the attitude of emotion is explained positively by reference to useful movements" (Dewey, 1894, p. 556). The observer then uses these useful preparatory movements to anticipate what is coming.

Dewey thought James was more correct about the order of events, but believed both were wrong in identifying the feeling with the emotion. If Darwin confused having an emotion with expressing one, James confused feeling emotional with being emotional. When James wrote that "our feeling of the same changes as they occur IS the emotion" he was wrong, Dewey argued, because "I should not fear a man who has simply the 'feel' of anger, nor . . . sympathize with one having simply the 'feel' of grief" (Dewey, 1895, p. 17). Being angry or grief-stricken is not just a conscious feeling in the mind, but a whole-body response. The response or behavioral attitude *is* the emotion. This response then causes feelings of which we may or may not be aware, but these feelings are not the same as the whole-body response itself. Here one can see Dewey developing a behavioral theory of emotion to replace a traditional approach based on conscious inner feeling.

While every response has an emotional aspect, since it has to do with completing activities with which the organism is identified, a situation becomes particularly emotional when there is conflict within the act. In novel situations conflicting responses may be stimulated that inhibit one another when the organism has to respond promptly. A dog's snarl and stiffened posture is emotional because there is a conflict between the response of attacking and that of fleeing. If there were no conflict it would simply get about the business of biting its opponent in a relatively methodical and unemotional way, just as it would snap at an unthreatening fly. Emotionally excited responses occur when there is an impulse to act in a certain way, but no clear way to do so. As Dewey wrote, "The emotion is, psychologically, the adjustment or tension of habit and ideal and the organic changes in the body are the literal working out, in concrete terms, of the struggle of adjustment" (Dewey 1895, p. 30). Dewey certainly recognized that there are more complex instances where an emotion is consciously expressed as an actor or artist might, but in the first instance emotion was understood teleologically as a working out of conflicting bodily responses that prepared for one or another line of action, or a release of the inhibited responses when an action that involves struggle and uncertainty is successfully completed.

Dewey's new theory of emotion was more behavioral than his early view in *Psychology*, in which emotion was seen as an aspect of "consciousness." Nevertheless, it retained the connections between emotion, cognition and "will," now given more behavioral interpretations. Emotion was related to cognition because the emotionalized response depended on its stimulus object. The "struggle of adjustment" of stimulus and response was a matter of finding an interpretation of the stimulus that evokes a coherent response and finding a response that clarifies the stimulus. Emotion and "will" were also interrelated, with "will" reconceived as "habit" (Dewey, 1922) or as practical activity because emotional responses and feelings are intimately related to the "activity of which it is the consequence (Dewey, 1934, p. 49). Dewey later elaborated on his theory of emotion in *Art as Experience* 1934), giving it a central role in the production and appreciation of artistic objects (while recognizing that art may not be *about* emotion).

The practical implications of Dewey's theory derive from the fact that it placed emotional response within the context of activity involving a transaction between organism and environment. When one thinks of emotions as purely internal and subjective and goal-attainment as external and objective, then there is an implicit division between "interest" and "effort" or "interest" and "discipline" (Dewey 1897; Dewey 1913; Dewey 1916a). But if one sees emotions as emerging within activity there is no a priori split between intrinsic and extrinsic aspects of motivation. The educational implication is that one needs to introduce activities in the classroom that students value or in which they have a stake or interest. Participating in valued joint activities helps students learn to regulate their acts in cooperation with the activities of others, rather than experiencing a split between their own "internal" desires and "external" control by others. In this way Dewey also reconceived of motivation in a more cooperative and interactive way.

HOW WE THINK

By this point Dewey had revised two of the three main concepts of his earlier *Psychology*. He had reinterpreted emotion in terms of conflict within the act rather than as a subjective state of consciousness. He had also reinterpreted "will" as a process of intentional aiming during the controlled development of an act.[10] A final concept, cognition, remained to be reinterpreted in terms of action. Dewey began to elaborate a more naturalistic theory of cognition in *Studies in Logical Theory* (Dewey, 1903) but the psychological implications were more clearly revealed in *How We Think* (Dewey, 1910), published after his move to Columbia.

How We Think focused on "reflective" thinking and how it can be improved by "training" in school. Reflective thought involves "active, persistent, and careful consideration" of a belief "in the light of the grounds that support it, and the future conclusions to which it tends" (Dewey, 1910, p. 6). It contrasts with daydreaming, which involves undirected emotional associations, as well as with accepting a belief on the basis of authority. Having defined reflective thought, Dewey went on to describe the more or less distinctive stages of "a complete act of thought" (Dewey, 1910, pp. 68–78). Thinking begins in the first phase with a "felt difficulty." When the situation is uncertain and one does not know how to act, the emotional unsettlement stimulates thought. The second phase, "observation," involves attempting to find the nature and location of the difficulty, such as looking under the hood of a stalled car to see where the steam is coming from. In the third phase, "suggestion," the observed facts function inductively as stimuli, suggesting larger patterns or ideas in which they are parts. For example, the steam coming from the front of the car might suggest that the car is overheated. In the fourth phase, "reasoning," the further implications of the hypothesis are worked out deductively. If the overheating is due to loss of radiator fluid, for example, then the fluid should be low. Finally, the fifth phase involves the "experimental corroboration, or verification" of the idea (Dewey, 1910, p. 77). Here one might check to see if the fluid is indeed low or fill up the radiator and see if the problem resolves itself. If the initial difficulty is not resolved, then thinking begins again with a somewhat altered situation (an overheated car that now has a filled radiator) cycling through the same stages until a successful solution is found.

This description seems commonplace and is often given a conventional linear interpretation. However, there are distinctive features of Dewey's account that are easily overlooked. Most importantly, his analysis places thinking in the context of ongoing activity. Thinking does not begin with a well-defined problem that comes out of the blue. Rather, it begins with experienced trouble and uncertainty. The precise nature of the problem is, in fact, unknown until the difficulty is resolved. Seen in this way, thinking involves genuine uncertainty about how to behave, not mere pretense of doubt; it is not a case of "spontaneous combustion" that just occurs on "general principles" (Dewey, 1910, p. 12). Thought also has practical implications for action. Solving a problem "in one's head" may be fine as far as it goes, but it is not the same as actually trying the solution in practice. In other words, real thinking is situated and engaged. The implication for education is that children need to experience real uncertainty or conflict (within reason) and need to be able to try out their solutions in practice to see if they work. As recently suggested by scholars working on "situated cognition," they need to work on authentic problems arising in whole tasks where part of the problem is figuring out what the problem is (Brown et al., 1989). Once again, Dewey placed a psychological function, thinking, within the contex, of ongoing activity rather than approaching it in isolation.

Dewey's approach also conceived of thinking as an act rather than as a peculiarly inward process. Thinking is similar to any other activity, differing only in its function. Observation, for example, typically involves physical actions, such as opening the hood of the car and peering inside. The phase of generating possible alternative responses, suggestion, involves partially responding to a stimulus in terms of the larger act or sequence of events that it indicates is coming. Such partial responses to the meaning of a stimulus are what we mean by an idea, conceived behaviorally. Reasoning then involves a series of partial responses to the meanings suggested by a series of stimuli. It involves following a chain of "ideas" or suggestions until a satisfactory conclusion is reached. The final confirmatory phase involves acting on the basis of an idea, or hypothesis, and experiencing the consequences of acting in this way. Thinking thus involves tangible, physical activity. It involves an interaction of organism and environment that leaves behind an altered situation. As Dewey put it,

> the entire scientific history of humanity demonstrates that the conditions of complete mental activity will not be obtained til adequate provision is made for the carrying on of activities that actually modify physical conditions, and that books, pictures, and even objects that are passively observed but not manipulated do not further the provision required. (Dewey, 1910, p. 100)

Since Dewey conceived of minding as an activity, it was clearly trainable or educable, like any other habit. Observation may be improved, for example, by learning to use a magnifying glass, telescope, or other observational tool. Suggestion may be improved by more systematically considering different stimuli, such as first considering all instances of one class of stimuli, then all instances of another. Deductive reasoning may be improved by using the rules of formal logic to ensure that conclusions follow from premises. Corroboration may be improved by careful experimental design that ensures that one alters only one factor at a time while holding others constant. "Training" thought means teaching the use of such instruments in the context of real inquiry, that is, inquiry stimulated by genuine doubt whose conclusions are tested in action and evaluated in discussion with others. Seen in this way, "intelligence" relies on learning to use cultural tools in situationally appropriate ways, making it a feature of the interaction of organism and environment, and not something inside of the organism. Furthermore, intelligent behavior can be taught, much as Sternberg and others today teach people how to be "smart" in various situations. Dewey suggested, in addition, that authentic problem-solving, carefully carried out and tested by its consequences, fosters more general attitudes associated with good thinking, such as openness to a wide range of possible solutions ("open-mindedness"), willingness to follow the extended implications of a solution ("whole-heartedness"), and willingness to test ideas in practice ("responsibility").

DEMOCRACY AND EDUCATION

By this point Dewey had reworked all of the concepts of his early psychology— cognition, affect, and will. He had reinterpreted them as functions within activity rather than as aspects of consciousness, making each more concrete and behavioral. His earlier emphasis on relationships among these functions was retained, however, as well as the emphasis on their implications for self-realization (growth or development). What remained was to work out more fully the relationship between the self-realizing individual and the wider social life in which he or she participates. *Democracy and Education* (Dewey, 1916) attempted to do this.

Very often when philosophers try to identify education's role in better relating "individual" and "society," they have tended to take one or the other as fixed. Plato, for example, suggested that in the just society, people of different categories would be selected by the education system for the social positions to which they were best fitted. Men (and women) of brass, who were dominated by their appetites, were to become the merchants and artisans; those of silver, who were dominated by their emotions, would become the warriors; and those of gold, dominated by reason, would become the rulers. This approach emphasized the needs of society but, Dewey argued, treated people as types rather than as unique individuals (Dewey, 1916). Rousseau adopted the opposite approach, viewing the child as innately good and society as corrupt. The social constraints of the state were artificial and arbitrary in contrast to the nearly unchangeable constraints of human nature, with which they conflicted. Education should therefore be based on the child's natural development (Rousseau, 1762/1974). The difficulty with Rousseau's approach, however, was that it allowed for no way to institutionalize education or see how the child could be fitted into society without being corrupted. A third strategy, deriving from Hegel, was more sophisticated in the sense in viewing both individual and society as developing rather than as fixed. In this approach individual and state would be merged by fully incorporating the individual into the state and the state into the individual. Because culture had supposedly reached the highest level of development in Prussia, the individual in this naturalistic scheme who developed in such a way as to incorporate the rationality implicit in the state reached his or her own highest level of development as well.

Dewey rejected all of these schemes because all presupposed a fixed end. The Platonic view froze social life into a fixed pattern that did not allow for future adaptation. It also neglected the uniqueness of individuals, which is the great source of the variety required for social change. Rousseau's approach took individual nature as fixed, thereby failing to recognize that even the biological development of individuals, such as the growth of their muscles, skeletons, and brains, is influenced by the social activities in which they participate, and is thereby subject to change. Hegel's approach assumed that there was a fixed end to development while focusing within the nation and neglecting external relationships with other nations. Each adopted a fixed end and a one-sided view of what would be better understood as an interactive relationship from which new ends continue to change.

Democracy and Education was an attempt to reframe education in a more interactive and open-ended way. This involved rethinking the function of education, human nature, and society. Dewey conceived of education as having the function of

maintaining the continuity of social life, much as biological adaptation and speci-
ation maintain the continuity of biological life. Education helps to maintain continuity in social life when there are newcomers, such as children or immigrants,
entering and old-timer's gradually leaving, or when technological change has dis-
rupted existing relationships. Seen in this way, education has a mediating role
to play between generations or peoples, or those in different positions, helping
them to get in better step with one another. In some cases education may be very
traditional, but in societies like our own in which change itself has become institutionalized, education takes a more democratic form.

For this mediational view of education to make sense both human nature and
society had to be conceived in more varying and dynamic ways. Rather than seeing individual "nature" as opposed to "society," for example, Dewey suggested
that human nature is in fact well-adapted to social life. Children are born highly
dependent and plastic relative to other animals (Dewey, 1916, pp. 41–53).[11] Their
dependence and helplessness are the characteristics of social organisms in their infancy, rather than being "unsocial" in character. Properly understood, dependence
involves receptivity to social influence, while plasticity (or plurality of response)
implies that behavior is flexible enough to be shaped in socially contingent ways.
There is no inherent conflict between individual and society, then, because our individual nature is that of highly social beings. What we become, given our enormous
flexibility and social sensitivity, depends greatly on our interactions with others.

"Society" is also better understood interactively than as a static entity. As Dewey
put it, "society is one word, but many things" (Dewey, 1916, p. 82). People associate
in many different ways for different purposes and "within every larger social
organization there are numerous minor groups" (p. 82). A society is not a static
thing, but rather a way in which people behave in relation to one another. People
form a community (or communicative unity) when "all (are) cognizant of the
common end and all interested in it so that they regulated their specific activity in
view of it" (p. 5). In other words, community occurs when people modulate their
behavior with respect to the expected behavior of others so as to achieve common
ends. "Community" is like dancing gracefully together with others. It is more like
verb, such as communing or communicating, than a noun.

When conceived in this more pluralistic and dynamic way the real problem is
not how to integrate "individual" and "society," but how to enable people coming
from different prior experiences to become better able to act together for common
purposes. Viewed as a process that mediates between people (or generations),
helping to bring them into community with one another, education is social by its
very nature. Becoming educated means becoming able to modulate one's activity
in the light of its meaning for others. Education is not simply a matter of improving
task performance, like playing the notes of a tune in the correct order regardless
of their meaning for others. Education is also different from mere training, this
being what one gives an animal serving the ends of others rather than the way
one treats a partner in a mutually valued activity (Dewey, 1916, p. 13). Given this

interpretation of education, the primary way to become educated is to participate with others in mutually valued joint activities. If one attempts to accomplish ends in common with them, modulating one's actions to work with theirs, and investigating problems with others as they arise, education is a naturally occurring side effect.

This interactive interpretation of education left room for cases in which the older generation might impose itself heavily on the young, attempting to fit them into a relatively static social order, or where the young might be allowed to run wild and impose themselves on the old. The kind of education that Dewey emphasized, however, arises in democratic societies that attempt to have both change and intergenerational continuity. But what do we really mean by "democracy"? Dewey argued for a more active view of democracy as well, seeing it as "primarily a mode of associated living, of conjoint communicated experience" rather than a fixed set of institutions (Dewey, 1916, p. 87). A group or community tended to be more democratic, if its members had many interests in common (such as in a family—as opposed to a business, where monetary issues may predominate), and if its members interacted freely with other groups so there was an influx of new ideas, and their common interests were recognized as a factor in governance (Dewey, 1916, pp. 83–86). As Dewey also noted, "A society which makes provision for participation in its good of all of its members on equal terms and which secures flexible readjustment of institutions through interaction of the different forms of associated life is so far democratic" (Dewey, 1916, p. 99).

In such a democratic society it makes little sense to educate people according to fixed objectives because conditions are rapidly changing. Rather, individuals need to be educated to think for themselves and be as adaptable as possible. They have to be intelligently adapting in the present, using the results of past inquiries to help in their future adaptation. The end of education is then, continued "growth" rather than attaining some fixed end: "Since growth is the characteristic of life, education is all one with growing: it has no end beyond itself. The criterion of the value of school education is the extent in which it creates a desire for continued growth and supplies the means for making this desire effective in fact" (Dewey, 1916, p. 53). Many have found this obscure, but it is easy to understand when thinking of one's own children. Most of us do not want our children to become any one thing, as though we could dictate the aims of their lives. Rather, we want them to become increasingly competent to guide their own lives.

The teacher's role in this process is to create the conditions that enable students to become as capable as possible of finding the wider meaning of what they are doing and using these meanings to guide their own future activity. The way to do this is to participate in authentic problem-solving, addressing the problems emerging out of joint activity. As Dewey put it, "The essentials of method are . . . identical with the essentials of reflection" (Dewey, 1916, p. 163). In detailing what this meant, Dewey repeated the stages of the complete act of thought: First, it is important that the pupil have a genuine situation of experience—that there be a continuous activity in which he is interested for its own sake; secondly, . . . a genuine problem that develop(s) within this situation as a stimulus to thought; third, that he possess the information and make the observations needed to deal with it; fourth, that suggested solutions occur to him which he shall be responsible for developing in an orderly way; fifth, that he have opportunity and occasion to test his ideas by application, to make their meaning clear and to discover for himself their validity. (Dewey, 1916, p. 163)

In other words, the teacher's job is to provide an environment with engrossing joint activities from which genuine problems emerge that are full of potential for later use but still within the range of the student's ability to solve with assistance from the teacher or peers. Today we might say that the teacher should set up a properly scaffolded "zone of proximal development."[12] Students educated in this way would be more likely to continue to grow in the future because they would be solving problems that mattered to them and learning from their own experience in trying solutions and observing their effects. Having learned in this more active and varied way they would be more likely to enjoy future learning and more able to utilize the results of past learning to address future problems.[13] This was education as "growth."

One can see how this scheme retained some of Dewey's early emphasis on individual self-realization within a society that was progressing toward the ideals of Absolute Spirit. By this point, however, this had been given a more pluralistic and open-ended interpretation. Rather than attempting to find a synthesis of "individual" and "society" in some Hegelian end state, he sought unity in a better-coordinated and more continuously developing form of social life. The key to such a social life was education, broadly conceived.

CONCLUSIONS

Dewey's psychology attempted to interrelate many interests that often seem contradictory. It sought to interrelate mind and body, cognition and emotion, learning and development, individual and society, biology and culture. Approached in a functional and dynamic way, the apparent impossibility of integrating these contradictory psychological "things" was revealed to be an artificial and self-created problem. It was the result of static and polarized ways of thinking. The real problem is to achieve dynamic coordination and progressive continuity in interaction, not to fit one entity to the constraints of another.

When applied to education, the chief tendency of Dewey's psychology was to suggest ways in which a child's experience could be both integrative and progressive. By "integrative" Dewey meant as whole-hearted and unalienated as possible. If one is thinking, the problem should arise out of active life experience and genuine doubt rather than being externally posed. The solution should, similarly, be tested in practice. By "progressive" he meant that a child's life experience should build, so that what he or she learns in the family will be drawn on in school, just as school experiences build on one another and will be utilizable in later and wider life. He sought a form of education in which the child's tendencies could be coordinated in interaction with others while growing over time with them.

The resulting psychology could be extremely demanding for both educator and psychologist. It could be seen as offering no place to stand and a thousand ways to fall. It offered no fixed or general answers, no elixers or cure-alls. It also left the educator potentially open to criticism for falling into one or another of the many one sided approaches or "dualisms" that Dewey analyzed. For the psychologist, Dewey's approach could at times seem to make analysis itself impossible. As Boring put it "... Dewey went pretty far: he objected to the analysis of the reflex arc into stimulus and response, to the analysis of total acts into reflex arcs, and even at times to the isolation of total coordinations from their past and future. It is the totalities with which we must deal in psychology, he argued" (Boring, 1929, p. 540). This anti-analytic tone could make it hard to get a purchase for if any cut or distinction is the beginning of a fundamental error, then there is no way to begin.

Although Dewey's emphasis on unity in action could be inhibiting, a more sympathetic and correct interpretation is that he opposed boundaries and distinctions developed in one situation being imposed on another, rather than opposing all boundaries or distinctions, as Boring suggests. Distinctions drawn in one situation may clearly be helpful in another, but since each situation is unique one cannot simply impose distinctions drawn from outside of a given situation on that situation: interpretation and judgment are needed. For the psychologist studying an organism's behavior this means that one needs to understand what the organism is trying to do and the differences that make a difference to the organism, rather than imposing an external task definition on the situation. The resulting psychology will inevitably involve an interpretive aspect, conflicting with the aim of developing an interpretation-free science. Nevertheless, with today's videotape equipment and the like it is easy to provide repeatable and publicly available evidence, making a science of psychology possible, if not the mechanistic science dreamed of by positivists.

For the educator, Dewey's psychology offers valuable suggestions for achieving greater confluence among aims that are all too often in conflict. Helping to foster an environment where students can participate in joint activities in which they are invested, and where the problems that arise have future adult significance, can "unify" cognition, emotion, and disciplined action (will). If the activity is something one cares about then uncertainty within it is likely to motivate one to study the issue carefully, thereby closely relating emotion and cognition. With a valued activity in which one is allowed to play a responsible part self-discipline (will) is also more likely to develop without external coercion, since one will have to regulate oneself to succeed in or avoid disrupting the activity. The individual and social aspects of the activity can also be "unified" when the activity when individual differences in interest or skill are used for common purposes in a division of labor. When different people are doing different parts of something they care about in common the apparent logical contradiction between individual difference and social commonality disappears, although there may still be many practical difficulties in working together well. In these and other ways Dewey's dynamic, transactional psychology helped interrelate and soften considerations that are often taken as separate and opposed.

Looking at Dewey's psychology in retrospect we can see how it was intermediate between the earlier introspective psychology of consciousness that reached its high point with James, and the later behaviorism of Watson and Skinner. One can see many themes in his criticism of structuralism that were later picked up by the behaviorists, such as the criticism of mind as an entity. But where Dewey and the functional psychologists were critical of conceiving of mind as a thing, they still accorded "it" great importance. In contrast, many behaviorists took the criticism of mind to an extreme and eliminated it by reduction, in Watson's case reducing it to the operation of the glottis and vocal cords. With the rebirth of interest in cognition in the late 1950s, mind came back in, with many of the leaders, such as Bruner and Simon, citing James as an inspiration. However, most studied mind in isolation from situated and embodied action. They also studied cognition in isolation from emotion, which was either neglected or interpreted in highly truncated form (Simon, 1979). Cognitive psychology also shared, all too often, the individualistic bias of behavioristic psychology, studying cognition divorced from social interaction, as though symbolic reflective thought was simply a given inside of the organism. Dewey could come back from the grave, slightly modify his criticism of the reflex arc theory, and apply his criticism of a fragmented approach to all too much work in psychology (Bredo, 1994).

There are tendencies today that are much more in line with Dewey's approach, although often without much recognition of this fact. Work on situated cognition and situated robotics seeks to better relate thinking to activity, although often with little emphasis on emotion (Suchman, 1987; Lave, 1988; Brown et al., 1989; Clancey, 1992; Greeno & Moore, 1993). Work deriving from Vygotsky's theories, which were only introduced into the U.S. decades after his death, explores a social-interactive and social-evolutionary approach to learning and development that has some similarity to Dewey's, although again with little attention to emotion (Wertsch, 1985a; Wertsch, 1985b; Wertsch, 1991). Educators, such as Deborah Meier, are also actively using Deweyan conceptions to rework schooling (Meier, 1995). Nevertheless, there are aspects of Dewey's approach that continue to remain underappreciated. He had a better-elaborated behavioral conception of thinking than is evident in most current work on situated cognition, which is sometimes rather vague in its understanding of cognition. He also had a more developed theory of emotion and its relation to cognition and action than one commonly finds today. When Dewey's work is augmented with that of his colleague, George Herbert Mead, one gains, as well, a powerful approach to understanding the social formation of mind and self (Mead, 1934; Reck, 1964). Finally, Dewey linked psychology to ethics and aesthetics in ways that are often lost (and that I have not had opportunity to present here, although they are akin to the way he linked cognition, emotion, and action). While psychology has moved on, Dewey still has more to teach than is commonly recognized. Not least, his psychology suggests how we could better educate for a more democratic form of life.

NOTES

1. In a related point, Denis Phillips has recently argued that different approaches to psychology are based on different metaphors or models and that "educational psychologists ought to give explicit attention to the models of the phenomena that lie behind their research programs, not so that these models can be expunged but so that, like other aspects of research, they can become the objects of criticism and conscious investigation" (Phillips, 1996, p. 1013).
2. Presumably (Huxley, 1881).
3. The text was probably *Elementary Lessons in Physiology* (Huxley, 1881). Why Dewey would find this such an integrative experience is unclear given that it is more like an anatomist's manual than a treatise on evolutionary connectedness. However, it did have a very clear discussion of the structure and function of the brain and nervous system (See pp. 253–271).
4. Dewey's essays were reprinted in *Essays in Experimental Logic* (Dewey, 1916b).
5. This division of psychic life mirrors the classical division of the soul into thinking, feeling, and willing. It also relates to the classical division of philosophical interest into truth, beauty, and goodness.
6. Carl Rogers was influenced by Dewey when doing his doctoral work at Teachers College in the 1930s.
7. This "law," named after the Scottish physician Charles Bell (1774–1842) and the French physiologist Francois Magendie (1783–1855), states that "the ventral roots of the spinal cord contain only motor nerve fibers and that the dorsal roots contain only sensory fibers. The two kinds of fibers may be combined in a single nerve; they are separated only in their connections to the (spinal) cord" (Boring, 1929, pp. 35–36). As Boring noted, "Bell's work established the fundamental dichotomy of function which has remained the implicit assumption of almost all research upon the nervous system for a century" (p. 36).
8. The following comment gives a further indication of how the article was received by psychologists: "From the point of view of the modern psychologist, the greatest contribution of all emerges at this point, his very extraordinary paper on "The Reflex Arc Concept in Psychology." ... it is ... prophetic of Gestalt and organismic psychology, likewise prophetic of modern conceptions of the indissoluble unity of organism and environment, as taught by Kurt Lewin, prophetic of a social psychology which rejects the old dichotomies of person and social group, and above all I would say, as a student of perception, prophetic of the modern conception that the perceptual-cognitive life has its own complex unit, involving continuous modification, growth, together with learning" (Murphy, 1961, pp. 27, 29).
9. Making the mistake of confusing the observer's and the actor's points of view was what James termed the "psychologist's fallacy," a form of misplaced concreteness.
10. Dewy's terminology and emphasis sometimes changed over the years. As the wrote later on, "All habits are demands for certain kinds of activity.... In any intelligible sense of the word will, they *are* will" (Dewey, 1992, p. 26).
11. In *School and Society* Dewey noted other characteristics, such as a "social impulse" for conversation, personal intercourse and communication" and "constructive impulse" for making things.

A third impulse for "investigation" grew out of a combination of the constructive and communicative impulses, presumably with the constructive dominant. A fourth, the "art instinct," also grew out of the communicative and constructive impulses, presumably with the communicative dominant (Dewey, 1900/1956, pp. 43–44). Dewey's conception was similar to Vygotsky's (1978) notion that instrumental thinking and social speech are originally independent functions that merge later on to form more complex functions, such as "labor" (analogous to Dewey's "constructive" impulse).

12. Some years later, Dewey elaborated on these suggestions in *Experience and Education* (Dewey, 1938/1963), arguing that the criteria of an educative experience are "interaction" and "continuity." That is, an experience is truly "educative" if one can actively participate in it by doing and undergoing the consequences of one's actions and discussing its meaning with others (interaction), and if it builds so that present experiences contribute to future ones. One might summarize this by noting, again, that Dewey's approach was simultaneously interactional and developmental.

13. In Dewey's conception literal transfer of training was impossible, since each situation is unique when considered as a whole. When one has learned a concept or skill more actively, however, and under varied circumstances, one is more likely to be able to see its relevance to a new situation and/or modify the situation to make its use more possible.

REFERENCES

Addams, J. (1990). *Twenty years at Hull-House*. Urbana: University of Illinois.

Angell, J. R. (1904). *Psychology, An introductory study of the structure and function of human consciousness*. New York: Holt.

Angell, J. R. (1907). The province of functional psychology. *The Psychological Review, XIV*(2): 61–89.

Angell, J. R. (1961). *A history of psychology in autobiography: C. Murchison*. New York: Russell & Russell.

Boring, E. G. (1929). *A history of experimental psychology*. New York: Century.

Bredo, E. (1994). Reconstructing educational psychology: Situated cognition and Deweyian pragmatism. *Educational Psychologist, 29*(1), 23–35.

Bredo, E. (1997). The social construction of learning. In G. Phye (Ed.), *Handbook of academic learning: The construction of knowledge* (pp. 3–43). New York: Academic Press.

Bredo, E. (1998). *The Darwinian center to the vision of William James*. San Diego, CA: American Educational Research Association.

Bredo, E. (1998, May). Evolution, psychology, and John Dewey's critique of the reflex arc concept. *The Elementary School Journal, 98*(5), 447–466.

Bredo, E. (2002). The Darwinian Center to the Vision of William James. In J. Garrison, Ronald Podeschi, and E. Bredo (Eds.), *William James and Education*, (pp. 1–26) NY: Teachers College Press.

Brooks, R. A. (1991). New Approaches to Robotic. *Science*, v. 253, 1227–1232.

Brown, J. S., Collins, A. (1989). Situated cognition and the culture of learning. *Educational Researcher, 18*(1), 32–42.

Clancey, W. J. (1992). *"Situated" means coordinating without deliberation*. Santa Fe, NM: McDonnel Foundation.

Clark, A. (1999). *Being there: Putting brain, body, and world together again*. Cambridge, MA: MIT Press.

Clifford, G. J. (1968). *Edward L. Thorndike: The sane positivist*. Middleton, CT: Wesleyan University Press.

Cole, M. (1996). *Cultural psychology: A once and future discipline*. Cambridge, MA: Harvard University Press.

Cole, M., Engestrom, Y. (Eds). (1997). *Mind, culture, and activity: Seminal papers from The Laboratory of Comparative Human Cognition*. Cambridge, England: Cambridge University Press.

Coughlan, H. (1975). *The young John Dewey*. Chicago: University of Chicago Press.

Darwin, C. (1871/1981). *The descent of man and selection in relation to sex*. Princeton, NJ: Princeton University Press.

Darwin, C. (1889/1904). *The expression of the emotions in man and animals*. London: John Murray.

Dewey, J. (1884). The new psychology. In J. A. Boydston (Ed.), *John Dewey: The early works, 1882–1898* (pp. 48–60). Carbondale: Southern Illinois University Press.

Dewey, J. (1887). *Psychology*. New York: Harper & Brothers.

Dewey, J. (1888). *Leibniz's new essays concerning the human understanding*. Chicago: S. C. Griggs & Co.

Dewey, J. (1894, November). The theory of emotion: 1. Emotional attitudes. *Psychological Review, 1*, 553–569.

Dewey, J. (1895, January). The theory of emotion: 2. The significance of emotions. *Psychological, 1*, 13–32.

Dewey, J. (1896). The reflex arc concept in psychology. *The Psychological Review, 3*, 356–370.

Dewey, J. (1897, January). The psychology of effort. *Philosophical Review, VI*, 43–56.

Dewey, J. (1900/1956). *The school and society*. Chicago: University of Chicago Press.

Dewey, J. (1902/1956). *The child and the curriculum*. Chicago: University of Chicago Press.

Dewey, J. (1903). *Studies in logical theory*. Chicago: University of Chicago Press.

Dewey, J. (1910). *How we think*. Boston: Heath.

Dewey, J. (1913). *Interest and effort in education*. Boston: Houghton Mifflin.

Dewey, J. (1916a). *Democracy and education*. New York: Macmillan.

Dewey, J. (1916b). *Essays in experimental logic*. New York: Dover.

Dewey, J. (1920). *Reconstruction in philosophy*. New York: Holt.

Dewey, J. (1922). *Human nature and conduct*. New York: Random House.

Dewey, J. (1927). *The public and its problems*. Athens, OH: Swallow Press.

Dewey, J. (1929/1958). *Experience and nature*. New York: Dover.

Dewey, J. (1929/1960). *The quest for certainty: A study of the relation of knowledge and action*. New York: Putnam.

Dewey, J. (1934). *Art as experience*. New York: Putnam.

Dewey, J. (1938). *Logic: The theory of inquiry*. New York: Holt.

Dewey, J. (1938/1963). *Experience and education*. Toronto, Ontario, Canada: Collier.

Dewey, J. (1946). The vanishing subject in the psychology of James. In J. Dewey, *Problems of men*. New York: Philosophical Library.

Dewey, J. (1960). From absolutism to experimentalism. In Richard J. Bernstein, (Ed.), *John Dewey: On Experience, Nature and Freedom* (pp. 3–18). Indianapolis: Bobbs Merrill.

Dewey, J. (1963). The new psychology. In J. Ratner (Ed.), *John Dewey: Philosophy, psychology, and social practice* (pp. 49–62). New York: Putnam.

Dewey, J. (1963a). The psychological standpoint. In J. Ratner (Ed.), *John Dewey: Philosophy, psychology, and social practice* (pp. 87–108). New York: Putnam.

Dewey, J. (1963b). Psychology as philosophic method. In J. Ratner (Ed.), *John Dewey: Philosophy, psychology, and social practice* (pp. 109–133). New York: Putnam.

Dewey, J., & Ratner, E. J. (1963). *Philosophy, psychology and social practice*. New York: Putnam.

Dewey, J., & Bentley, A. (1949). *Knowing and the known*. Boston: Beacon Press.

Dewey, J., & Dewey, E. (1915). *Schools of tomorrow*. New York: Dutton.

Dewey, J., & Tufts, J. H. (1908/1932). *Ethics*. New York: Holt.

Dykhuizen, G. (1973). *The life and mind of John Dewey*. Carbondale, IL: Southern Illinois University Press.

Greeno, J. G., & Moore, J. L. (1993). Situativity and symbols: Response to Vera and Simon. *Cognitive Science, 17*(1), 49–59.

Hall, G. S. (1885, Feb.-Mar.). The new psychology. *Andover Review, 3*, 170–185.

Hall, G. S. (1909). Evolution and psychology. In *Fifty years of Darwinism: Modern aspects of evolution* (pp. 251–267). New York: Holt.

Hall, G. S. (1916). What we owe to the tree-life of our ape-like ancestors. *Pedagogical Seminary, 23*(1), 94–119.

Huxley, T. H. (1881). *Elementary lessons in physiology*. London: Macmillan.

James, W. (1890/1950). *The principles of psychology*. New York: Dover.

James, W. (1892). *Psychology: Briefer course*. New York: Holt.

James, W. (1897/1956). The sentiment of rationality. In *The Will to Believe* (p. 70), NY: Dover.

Langley, P., & Simon, H. A. (1981). The central role of learning in cognition. In J. R. Anderson, *Cognitive skills and their acquisition* (pp. __). Hillsdale, NJ: Lawrence Erlbaum Associates.

Lave, J. (1988). *Cognition in practice: Mind, mathematics and culture in everyday life*. Cambridge, England: Cambridge University Press.

McDermott, R. P., & Hood, L. (1982). Institutionalized psychology and the ethnography of schooling. In P. Gilmore and A. Gladthorn, Children in and out of school (pp. __). Washington, DC: Center for Applied Linguistics.

McKenzie, W. R. (1971). Introduction. In J. A. Boydston (Ed.), *John Dewey: The early works, 1882–1898* (pp. __). Carbondale: Southern Illinois University Press.

McLellan, J. A., & Dewey, J. (1889). *Applied psychology: An introduction to the principles and practice of education*. Boston: Educational Publishing Company.

McLellan, J. A., & Dewey, J. (1895/1905). *The psychology of number and its applications to methods of teaching arithmetic*. New York: Appleton.

Mead, G. H. (1934). *Mind, self, and society: From the standpoint of a social behaviorist*. Chicago: University of Chicago Press.

Meier, D. (1995). *The Power of Their Ideas*, Boston: Beacon Press.

Miller, P. (1968). *American thought: Civil War to World War I*. New York: Holt, Rinehart & Winston.

Murphy, G. (1961). Some Reflections on Dewey's Psychology. University of Colorado Studies in Philosophy, v. 2. (pp. 27, 29).

Newman, D., Griffin, P. (1989). *The construction zone: Working for cognitive change in Schools*. Cambridge, England: Cambridge University Press.

Phillips, D. C. (1971). John Dewey and the organismic archetype. In R. J. W. Selleck (Ed.), *Melbourne studies in education* (pp. 232–271). Melbourne, Australia: Melbourne University Press.

Phillips, D. C. (1996). Philosophical perspectives. In D. C. Berliner & R. C. Calfee (Eds.), *Handbook of educational psychology* (pp. __). New York: Simon & Schuster and Macmillan.

Reck, A. J. (Ed.). (1964). *Selected writings: George Herbert Mead*. New York: Bobbs-Merrill.

Rousseau, J. J. (1974). *Emile*. London: J. M. Dent and Sons.

Rucker, D. (1969). *The Chicago pragmatists*. Minneapolis: University of Minnesota.

Sahakian, W. S. (1975). *History and systems of psychology*. New York: Wiley.

Simon, H. A. (1979). Motivational and Emotional Controls on Cognition. In *Models of Thought* (pp. 29–38). New Haven: Yale University Press.

Suchman, L. A. (1987). *Plans and situated actions: The problem of human-machine communication*. Cambridge, England: Cambridge University Press.

Tiles, J. E. (1988). *Dewey*. London: Routledge.

Vygotsky, L. S. (1978). *Mind in Society: The Development of Higher Psychological Processes*. Cambridge, MA: Harvard University Press.

Walker, L. R. (1997, Summer). John Dewey at Michigan. *Michigan Today*, 2–5.

Watson, J. B. (1961). John Broadus Watson. In C. Murchison (Ed.), *A history of pschology in autobiography* (pp. __). New York: Russell & Russell.

Wertsch, J. V. (Ed.). (1985a). *Culture, communication, and cognition.* Cambridge, England: Cambridge University Press.

Wertsch, J. V. (1985b). *Vygotsky and the social formation of mind.* Cambridge, MA: Harvard University Press.

Wertsch, J. V. (1991). *Voices of the mind: A sociocultural approach to mediated action.* Cambridge, MA: Harvard University Press.

Wilson, E. O. (1978). *On human nature.* New York: Bantam.

5

E. L. Thorndike's Enduring Contributions to Educational Psychology

Richard E. Mayer
University of California, Santa Barbara

In the story of educational psychology, there is no more central character than
E. L. Thorndike. His pioneering work helped to establish educational psychology
as a scientific discipline, and his vision has shaped the character of educational
psychology for more than 100 years. The arrival of the new millennium provides an
opportunity to look back over the development of educational psychology during
the 20th century.

This chapter examines E. L. Thorndike's influence on educational psychology.
The first section introduces E. L. Thorndike and his contributons to educational
psychology. The second section contains a biographical sketch, which describes
major events in Thorndike's family life, personal life, professional life, and
publication life. Third, Thorndike's enduring contributions to ideas in educational
psychology, including his role in revolutionizing our conceptions of learning,
transfer, and individual differences are summarized. Fourth, Thorndike's enduring contributions to products in educational psychology, including his invention
of scientifically-based dictionaries, curricular materials, and tests are presented.
Fifth, I summarize Thorndike's enduring contributions to values in educational
psychology, including an unswerving faith in the scientific method, a preference
for quantitative data, and an interest in solving practical social problems. Sixth,
I offer a brief evaluation of Thorndike's major contributions. Finally, I conclude

with comments on what I consider to be the most valuable aspects of Thorndike's lasting legacy, with particular emphasis on how his values have guided the development of educational psychology.

WHO WAS E. L. THORNDIKE?

E. L. Thorndike is generally recognized as the main architect of the modern field of educational psychology. He achieved this status largely because of his highly successful efforts to transform the study of education from the realm of armchair speculation and moral philosophy into a science, based on empirical data gathered in methodologically sound experiments. In his historical review of educational psychology, Grinder (1989, p. 13) recognizes that "E. L. Thorndike was among the first in the 20th century . . . who sought to establish educational psychology as a compelling science." For 50 years Thorndike carried out his highly productive academic career at Teachers College, Columbia University, where he had been hired in 1899 to found the as-of-yet unnamed discipline of educational psychology. He leaves behind an astounding publication record consisting of approximately 250,000 pages in over 500 publications produced between 1898 and 1949. More importantly, 100 years after Thorndike burst onto the scene, he leaves behind the vibrant discipline of educational psychology that he, more than any other person, helped to shape. In keeping with his love of quantitative data, I list some quantitative facts about E. L. Thorndike in Table 5.1.

What Are Thorndike's Contributions to Educational Psychology?

Given the breadth and depth of Thorndike's work, it is no easy task to neatly summarize his major contributions. In a retrospective published on the occasion of Thorndike's death, his colleague Arthur Gates listed Thorndike's most important contributions as follows (in seeming chronological order):

TABLE 5.1
Selected Factoids About E. L. Thorndike

Number of publications: 507
Number of published pages (approximate): 250,000
Number of articles published in the *Journal of Educational Psychology*: 29
Number of cats tested in *Animal Intelligence*: 13
Number of courses taken in advanced mathematics: 0
Number of years as psychology major at undergraduate and graduate levels: 2
Number of years lived outside of New England before going to Columbia University: 0
Number of years at Columbia before earning doctorate degree: 1
Total number of years on faculty at Columbia University: 50
Number of siblings who became professors at Columbia University: 2
Number of children who became professors at Columbia University: 1

his methods of studying animal learning; his laws of learning; his attacks on formal discipline and his theory of transfer of training; his introduction of statistical methods to education and educational psychology; his development of achievement tests and scales; his detailed methods and materials for teaching arithmetic, algebra, reading, spelling, and other school subjects; his work on group intelligence tests, especially those for adults; his theory of intelligence; his analysis of work and play; his concept of the original nature of man; his investigations of the nature–nurture problem; his defense of the idea that mental "qualitative" differences can be explained as "quantitative"; his studies of vocabulary; his new pattern for the dictionary; his investigations of adult learning; and his theories of human nature in relation to society (Gates, 1949a, p. 241–242).

At the time of his death in 1949, obituaries appeared in prestigious journals in the United States and around the world (Gates, 1949a, 1949b; Goodenough, 1950; Humphrey, 1949; Thomson, 1949). In order to survey his peers' views of Thorndike's contributions, I noted each contribution that was cited in each of five major obituaries and categorized them into nine ideas in educational psychology (in Table 5.2) and five products in educational psychology (in Table 5.3). From these, I abstracted the three most commonly cited contributions to ideas—Thorndike's theoretical advances in learning, transfer, and individual differences—and the three most commonly cited contributions to products—Thorndike's dictionaries, curricular materials, and tests. In addition, the obituaries referred to Thorndike's underlying values, which included a commitment to scientific methods, quantitative measures, and practical issues.

In this chapter, I examine what I consider to be Thorndike's most important contributions to ideas, products, and values in educational psychology. These are summarized in Table 5.4. Considering his contributions to ideas, if he had only discovered the law of effect—psychology's first and most studied principle of learning—that would have been enough to give Thorndike an honored place in the history of educational psychology. Instead, this revolutionary discovery was his first publication and represented the beginning of what turned out to be psychology's first comprehensive theory of learning based on hundreds of careful experiments (Bower & Hilgard, 1981).

If he had only demolished the currently popular doctrine of formal discipline by conducting the first scientific studies of transfer of training, that would have been sufficient to place Thorndike's name in anyone's history of educational psychology. Instead, he built a comprehensive theory of how learning a new task depends on possessing knowledge that is specifically relevant to that task, producing psychology's first research-based theory of transfer (Singley & Anderson, 1989).

Finally, if he had only demolished the currently popular theory of faculty psychology—the view of the mind as consisting of general mental ability—with his theory of intelligence as being multicomponential, that alone would have been enough to entitle Thorndike to be recognized as a leading educational psychologist.

TABLE 5.2

Thorndike's Contributions to Ideas in Educational Psychology Based
on Five Obituaries

Learning

Laws of learning (1)

Development of his laws of learning which marked the beginning of the end of the
    [mental faculties] approach to psychology (2)

Formulation of the laws of readiness and effort, which provided a basis for a progressive
    education movement (2)

Thorndike's three laws of learning (3)

Thorndike's fundamental work on learning (4)

Well-known law of effect (5)

Transfer

Attacks on formal discipline and his theory of transfer of training (1)

Demolition of the faculty theory and the theory of formal discipline, an achievement
    which revolutionized education (2)

Development of his theory of transfer of training, which formed the basis of the
    personal and social utility approach to curriculum study (2)

Classic study of transfer (4)

Disciplinary value of certain school subjects and the more general question of transfer of
    training (5)

Demolishing the long-cherished belief of certain educators that the learning of Greek, Latin,
    and mathematics . . . would strengthen the mental powers (5)

Individual Differences

Theory of intelligence (1)

Defense of the idea that mental qualitative differences can be explained as quantitative (1)

Development of a comprehensive concept of individual differences and innumerable
    studies of their character and educational significance (2)

Development of a theory of intelligence (2)

Measurement of intelligence (4)

Theory of . . . the nature and organization of intellect (5)

Biological and Developmental Bases of Learning

Concept of the original nature of man (1)

Investigations of the nature-nurture problem (1)

Formulation of a theory . . . of the original nature of man, which gave new importance to the
    role of interest and readiness in education (2)

Extensive explorations of the reciprocal roles of heredity and environment (2) scientific
    studies of the genius and the trained exepert (2)

Study of twins (4)

Child development (5)

Relative effects of heredity and environment on human abilities (5)

Measurement of twins (5)

Psychology of Subject Areas

Studies of vocabularly (1)

Studies of vocabularies (2)

Psychology of arithmetic (4)

Handwriting (5)

Psychology of arithmetic and . . . psychology of algebra (5)

(Continued)

TABLE 5.2
(Continued)

Adult Learning
Investigations of adult learning (1)
Discoveries involving adult learning which form the foundation of adult education (2)
Pioneer work in adult education (4)
Adult education (5)

Social Issues
Theories of human nature in relation to society (1)
Development of theories of human nature in relation to society (2)
Study of many social institutions, such as . . . cities, business, industry (2)
Study of communities (3)
Measurement of the qualities of cities and states (5)

Animal Psychology
Methods of studying animal learning (1)
Making the first scientific study of animal intelligence and learning (his doctoral dissertation,
     which marked the beginning of animal psychology) (2)
First extended research on association in animals (4)
Transformed the study of animal behavior (5)

Other
Analysis of work and play (1)
Preaching a doctrine of work and play (2)
Studies in aesthetics, semantics, interests and attitudes, vocational guidance, bright children,
     minority groups, fatigue (2)
Effect of discussion on group decisions (4)
Psychology of wants, interests, and attitudes (4) (5)
Effect of ventilation and humidity on work decrement (5)
Studies in the field of language (5)

Note. (1) = Gates (1949a), (2) = Gates (1949b), (3) = Thompson (1949), (4) = Humphrey (1949), (5) = Goodenough (1950).

Instead, he was the first to offer a research-based conception of individual differences in intellectual ability that recognized the role of specific knowledge in intellectual performance (Sternberg, 1990).

In the realm of products, if he had only produced the world's first scientifically designed set of student dictionaries, the world's first quantitative tests of school achievement in subject areas, or the world's first scientifically based books for teaching school subjects, any one of these accomplishments would have placed him among the outstanding educational psychologists of all time. Instead, he can lay claim to all three products, as well as many others that revolutionized educational practice.

In the realm of values, if he had only demonstrated the role of experimental methods or the importance of quantitative data or the benefits of solving social problems, any one of these values would have been enough. Instead, by focusing so successfully on all three as well as others, he produced a highly productive vision for our field—which, one can hope, will continue to guide educational psychology into the 21st century.

TABLE 5.3
Thorndike's Contributions to Products in Educational Psychology
Based on Five Obituaries

Dictionaries
New pattern for the dictionary (1)
Development of an improved pattern for the dictionary (2)
Dictionaries for use by school children (5)

Tests
Development of achievement tests and scales (1)
Group intelligence tests, especially those for adults (1)
Invention of the scale for measuring quality of performance, as in handwriting or
    composition (2)
Launching of the achievement test movement (2)
Development of group intelligence tests, especially for superior adults (2)
Famous tests of intelligence (3)
Psychophysical methods [in] handwriting (4)
Scale for the general merit of children's drawings (4)
Intelligence tests and tests of educational achievement (5)
Standardized tests and scales (5)

Curricular Materials
Detailed methods and materials for teaching arithmetic, algebra, reading, spelling, and other
    school subjects (1)
Development of detailed methods and materials for teaching arithmetic, algebra, spelling,
    reading, language, and other school subjects (2)
Thorndike Arithmetics books (5)

Word List
The teacher's wordbook of 30,000 words (4)
Famous Teachers' Word Book . . . one of the most valuable research tools ever developed (5)

Statistical Methods
Introduction of statistical methods to education and educational psychology (1)
Introduction of statistical methods to education and psychology (2)
Simplified statistical devices and table for reducing the work of computation (5)

Note. (1) = Gates (1949a), (2) = Gates (1949b), (3) = Thompson (1949), (4) = Humphrey
(1949), (5) = Goodenough (1950).

TABLE 5.4
Thorndike's Major Ideas, Products, and Values in Educational Psychology

Ideas	*Products*	*Values*
Learning	Dictionaries	Scientific methods
Transfer	Curricular Materials	Quanitative data
Individual Differences	Tests	Practical issues

BIOGRAPHICAL SKETCH

There is a sense in which the magnitude of E. L. Thorndike's contributions are puzzling. How could someone with almost no mechanical skill (R. L. Thorndike, 1991), design and build an experimental apparatus—the puzzle box (Burnham, 1972)—that launched the modern scientific study of animal learning (Bitterman, 1969; Bower & Hilgard, 1981; Dewsbury, 1998)? How could someone who had never taken a course in higher mathematics (R. L. Thorndike, 1991), design and implement some of the first quantitative analyses of everything from how students learned to the livability of cities (Boldyreff, 1949)? How could someone whose major academic interest was English as an entering graduate student (Joncich, 1968a, 1968b) become a giant of psychology? The answer comes both from happenstance—the happy coincidence of events—and from Thorndike's quiet intensity—his drive to study just about anything that came his way. In this biographical sketch, I explore Thorndike's family life, his personal life, his academic life, and his publication record. Table 5.5 provides a timeline of Thorndike's major life events, books, and products.

Family Life

Edward Lee Thorndike was born on August 31, 1974, in Williamsburg, Massachusetts. His parents, Edward Roberts Thorndike and Abbie Ladd Thorndike, were New Englanders who grew up in an uncomplicated society of "nearly self-sufficient farms and unlocked doors" (Joncich, 1968a, p. 12). His father was a Methodist minister who served a succession of congregations in New England during Thorndike's childhood. The result of moving periodically and being under the scrutiny of a series of fundamentalist congregations was to ingrain a spirit of "self-reliance, and a tendency to limit dependence upon others to only a very few people outside the family itself" (Joncich, 1968a, p. 21). Thorndike spent his entire life in New England until moving to New York for his final year of graduate study in 1897. According to Geraldine Joncich, Thorndike's most prolific biographer, growing up in a "clergyman's household, combined with a New England setting, was the best predictor of a future career in science" for those of Thorndike's generation (Joncich, 1968b, p. 436).

Goodenough (1950, p. 291) notes that "Thorndike's family is a brilliant one." His two brothers became faculty members of Columbia University—his older brother, Ashley Horace Thorndike was in the English Department, where he served as Chair, and his younger brother, Lynn Thorndike was in the History Department. His sister, Mildred Thorndike, became a high school teacher.

In 1900, when he was 26 years old, he married Elizabeth Mouton of Boston. Their four children continued the family tradition of brilliance. The eldest, Elizabeth, taught mathematics for a time at Vassar; Edward became a professor of physics at Queens College; Robert, following in his father's footsteps, became

TABLE 5.5

Milestones in the Life of E. L. Thorndike

Year	Major Life Event	Major Book Publication	Major Product Publication
1874	Is born on August 31 in Williamsburg, MA into home of Methodist minister		
1895	Receives B.A. from Wesleyan University		
1896	Receives B.A. from Harvard University		
1897	Receives M.A. from Harvard University		
1898	Receives Ph.D. from Columbia University	*Animal Intelligence* (Thesis)	
1899	Joins faculty at Teachers College, Columbia University, remains for 50 years		
1900	Marries Elizabeth Mouton of Boston		
1901		*Notes on Child Study* (1st ed)	
		The Human Nature Club (1st & 2nd ed)	
1903		*Educational Psychology* (1st ed)	
		Notes on Child Study (2nd ed)	
1904		*Mental and Social Measurement* (1st ed)	
1905		*Elements of Psychology* (1st ed)	
1906		*Principles of Teaching Based on Psychology*	
1907		*Elements of Psychology* (2nd ed)	
1909			*Exercises in Arithmetic*
1910		*Educational Psychology* (2nd ed)	
1911		*Animal Intelligence* (Expanded ed)	*Scale for Measuring Writing*
		Individuality	
1912	Becomes president of the American Psychological Association	*Education: A First Book*	
1913		*Mental and Social Measurement* (2nd ed)	*Scale for Measuring Arithmetic*
		Educational Administration	*Scale for Measuring Drawing*
		Educational Psychology, Volume 1	
		Educational Psychology, Volume 2	

1914	Educational Psychology, Volume 3	Scale for Measuring Reading
1915	Educational Psychology: A Briefer Course	Scale for Measuring Arithmetic
		Scale for Measuring Handwriting
		Scale for Measuring Spelling
1916		Scale for Measuring Reading
		Scale for Measuring Aesthetic Appreciation
		The Thorndike Arithmetics
1917	Helps develop tests for the U.S. Army in World War I	
1918		
1919		Intelligence Examination for High School Graduates
1920	New Methods in Arithmetic	Thorndike Visual Vocabulary Scales
		Teacher's Word Book
1921	Co-founds Psychological Corporation	Thorndike-McCall Reading Scales
1922	The Psychology of Arithmetic	Thorndike Test of Word Knowledge
1923	The Psychology of Algebra	Scale for Measuring Drawings
		Arithmetic (School books)
1924		Intelligence Examination for High School Graduates (1925 ed)
		I. E. R. Intelligence Scale CAVD
1925	Measurement of Intelligence	
1926	Adult Learning	
1928	Elementary Principles of Education	
1929		Growth in Spelling
1931	Human Learning	Teacher's Word Book of 20,000 Words
		Intelligence Examination for High School Graduates (1931 ed)
1932	Fundamentals of Learning	
1934	Becomes President of the American Association for the Advancement of Science	
	Prediction of Vocational Success	

(Continued)

TABLE 5.5
(Continued)

Year	Major Life Event	Major Book Publication	Major Product Publication
1935		Psychology of Wants, Interests, and Attitudes	Thorndike–Century Junior Dictionary
		Adult Interests	The Thorndike Library
1939		Your City	
1940	Retires but continues working at Teachers College, Columbia University	Human Nature and the Social Order	
		144 Smaller Cities	
1941			Thorndike–Century Senior Dictionary
1942			Thorndike–Century Junior Dictionary (rev. ed.)
1943		Man and His Works	
1944			Teacher's Word Book of 30,000 Words
1945			Thorndike–Century Beginning Dictionary
1947			Thorndike Junior Dictionary (British ed.)
1949	Dies on August 9, 1949	Selected Writings from a Connectionist's Psychology	

a professor of educational psychology at Teachers College, Columbia University; and Alan, a Harvard Ph.D., became a research physicist working for the federal government (Goodenough, 1950).

In a recent biography, Thorndike's son, Robert L. Thorndike recalled him as "a gentle, retiring person who avoided contention and conflict and who felt that controversy was unproductive" (R. L. Thorndike, 1991, p. 139). Growing up as Thorndike's son, it became clear that "his work and his family were his life" (R. L. Thorndike, 1991, p. 151). E. L. Thorndike died on August 9, 1949. At the time of his death, his 7-year old grand-daughter remembered him as "someone who spent most of his time in his study with his feet up on the desk and a cigarette in his mouth, but who was always ready to blow smoke rings for her entertainment or make her a hat or paper boats out of a newspaper" (R. L. Thorndike, 1991, p. 151). This is a fitting image because it blends Thorndike's interests in work and family.

Personal Life

Thorndike is universally portrayed as brilliant, determined, and, hard working on the one hand and mechanically challenged and somewhat unsociable on the other hand. When he took Strong's Vocational Interest Test in 1927, he scored high in quantitative interests but low in social interests, high in interest in ideas but low in interest in objects (Joncich, 1968a).

Thorndike's brilliance, determination, and productivity are reflected in his amazingly influential career. His textbook on educational psychology, written when Thorndike was at the start of his career, for example made "the name of Thorndike practically synonymous with the field of educational psychology" (Humphrey, 1949, p. 56). The dean of his college recognized almost from the start that Thorndike was "destined to give mankind new knowledge of the workings of the human mind" and to "change the course of education" (Russell, 1949, p. 26).

In contrast to the ubiquitous presence of technology in today's educational psychology, it is interesting to note that the world's most influential educational psychologist never used even a calculator or a typewriter (R. L. Thorndike, 1991). His son reports that "I never saw him fix any device and if you look at pictures of the equipment he used in his original animal experiments you realize they would have shamed Rube Goldberg" (R. L. Thorndike, 1991, p. 145). In his own autobiography, Thorndike acknowledges his lack of mechanical skill—which he calls "an extreme ineptitude and distaste for using machinery and physical instruments"—as one of his major weaknesses (Thorndike, 1936, p. 267). Not surprisingly, he never learned to drive a car.

Moehlman (1944, p. 19) describes Thorndike as "reserved, almost shy . . . not an extroverted back slapper." He "avoided professional committees, inspirational speaking and platform hopping" (Moehlman, 1944, p. 19). His son notes that his father was "not a sociable person but he was reasonably successful in managing his institute and the committees that he served on" (R. L. Thorndike, 1991, p. 145).

The recollection of his dean at Columbia is that Thorndike "was impatient with committees, over-consultation with regard to decisions, and so-called democratic administration in general" (Russell, 1949, p. 28). He was not actively involved in politics, religion, or social life but "he would rather be getting or analyzing data than most anything else" (R. L. Thorndike, 1991, p. 151).

Professional Life

Being born in 1874, Thorndike grew up at a time when hopes were high that a newly developing reliance on science could eventually solve the problems of society. The most important scientific event in the years near his birth was the publication of Darwin's *The Origin of Species* in 1859, and the most important event for scientific psychology was Wundt's establishment of the world's first psychology laboratory in 1879.

In spite of these events, his early education did not emphasize science nor did his family provide encouragement for a career in science. He attended various Massachusetts public schools and spent 2 years at a classical Latin school. Ironically, in spite of his later research challenging the benefits of a classical education, he seems to have enjoyed his brief stay at the Roxbury Latin School as a high point in his early education. He entered Wesleyan University in Middletown, Connecticut, in 1891, earning a bachelor's degree that focused on English in 1895. Thorndike (1936, p. 263) states: "I have no memory of having heard or seen the word psychology until my junior year at Wesleyan University (1893–94), when I took a required course in it." Interestingly, the course did not win him over to psychology: "The textbook, Sully's *Psychology*, aroused no notable interest, nor did the excellent lectures of Professor A. C. Armstrong" (Thorndike, 1936, p. 263). Sully's book portrayed psychology as "chief of the moral sciences" (Sully, 1889, p. v) and as distinguished by its use of introspection as its chief method—views that are sharply at odds with the experiment-based science that Thorndike later helped to create (Joncich, 1966). Thorndike recalls that he was "stimulated . . . very little" (Thorndike, 1936, p. 263) by philosophical approaches to psychological issues based on fine discriminations and arguments rather than on experiment-based facts—a reaction he experienced both in his undergraduate courses at Wesleyan and later in his graduate courses with William James at Harvard. Although he performed well in courses in psychology while an undergraduate, he never "publicly committed himself to psychology" (Joncich, 1966, p. 44).

There was one event in his undergraduate career that forever altered Thorndike's academic life. As part of a prize examination—a sort of academic contest—he was required to read chapters from William James' *Principles of Psychology*. For the first time, he gained a vision of what psychology could become: an empirically based science. Foreshadowing Thorndike's contribution as an experimentalist, he appreciated that James devoted more than 200 pages of his textbook to reviews of experimental studies. He found James' textbook of psychology to be "stimulating, more so than any book that I had read before, and possibly more so than any read since" (Thorndike, 1936, p. 263). Based on this experience, Thorndike was eager to take a course from James at Harvard, although he did not plan a graduate career in psychology.

When Thorndike entered Harvard, he still did not see himself as a psychologist. His application requested English and French as his course of study (Joncich, 1966) and his first semester course of study turned out to be half English, one-fourth philosophy, and one-fourth psychology (Thorndike, 1936). However, during his first year in graduate school "work in English was dropped in favor of psychology . . . and by the Fall of 1897, I thought myself as a student of psychology and a candidate for the Ph.D. degree" (Thorndike, 1936, p. 264). Unfortunately by the time Thorndike was willing to commit himself to psychology, his main professor, William James, had already given up on conducting original research and was retreating back into philosophy. However, they both shared a rejection of complicated experimental apparatus and a "dislike of formal logical systems and prolonged intellectual analyses" (Joncich, 1966, p. 48).

Thorndike's graduate career demonstrates how choosing a research topic can sometimes be a matter a luck. University administrators thwarted Thorndike's efforts to study learning in children so he settled on studying learning in animals— namely, chickens. When his advisor, William James, was unable to secure a few square feet of lab space on campus for chicken research, the research project moved to the cellar of James' home. In a later autobiography, Thorndike attributed James' willingness to house the chickens in his cellar to his "habitual kindness and devotion to underdogs" and expressed the hope that "the nuisance to Mrs. James was . . . somewhat mitigated by the entertainment to the two youngest children" (Thorndike, 1936, p. 264).

After several years at Harvard, where he earned both a second bachelor's degree in 1896 and a master's in 1897, Thorndike moved to Columbia University. The move allowed him to take advantage of a fellowship, to escape the scene of a failed romance, and to work under the sponsorship of James McKeen Cattell. Thorndike brought a thesis proposal already approved at Harvard, and was allowed to continue this research at Columbia—this time working with cats and dogs in the attic of Schermerhorn Hall. Although Cattell was well known for his extensive research on individual differences, "Thorndike's research owes very little to Cattell in that initial period at least" (Joncich, 1966, p. 49). He was awarded a Ph.D. in 1898 for his thesis, *Animal Intelligence*, a landmark study in a field of research that interested none of his teachers. Though his thesis research eventually revolutionized the field of animal psychology, Thorndike focused on issues in human learning almost immediately after graduating. His thesis was a reflection of what can be done by a brilliant mind committed to a psychological science based on original experimentation.

Shortly after graduating in 1898, Thorndike accepted his first academic job as a teacher of education at the College for Women of Western Reserve University in

Cleveland. Interestingly, he had only two job offers upon graduating, and accepted the one with lower pay but higher academic status. After a year in Cleveland, he was offered a trial on the faculty of Teachers' College, Columbia University, in 1899. He remained at Teachers College throughout the next 50 years of his career, retiring in 1940 but staying on in emeritus status until his death in 1949. Reflecting back on his fateful decision to hire young Dr. Thorndike, the Dean of Teachers College, James Russell states:

> At the time neither the term nor the subject of educational psychology had been created; but I had a notion that a field of study so obviously fundamental to educational theory and practice should have both a name and a sponsor in the kind of teachers college which I was planning. After listening to one class exercise, I was satisfied that I had found the right man for the job. I promptly offered him an instructorship and he characteristically accepted it at once. Whether he has ever regretted such unseemly academic haste I do not know, but I do know that no hour of my life has been more profitably spent. (Russell, 1940, pp. 696–697)

Within a decade of joining the Teachers College faculty, Thorndike had already established himself as a titan of educational psychology. When the *Journal of Educational Psychology* was launched in 1910, E. L. Thorndike was given the honor of writing the lead article on "The Contribution of Psychology to Education," (Thorndike, 1910), because he "perhaps more than any other individual contributed to the definition and status of educational psychology" (Williams, 1978, pp. 290–291). He went on to publish more than two dozen articles in the *Journal* and serve on its editorial board for more than a decade. In reviewing the history of the *Journal of Educational Psychology*—educational psychology's premier research periodical since 1910—Williams (1978, p. 291) recognized Thorndike's overwhelming contribution: "Thorndike's basic work on learning and problem solving and on individual differences, his emphasis on the experimental method—all of his many contributions in fact—helped point the way toward acceptance of empirical research as a basis for educational planning and policy making. Thorndike's influence permeated the *Journal* for many years to come."

Thorndike did not come to Teachers College with a fully developed agenda for creating the discipline of educational psychology. Instead, his career reflects the same opportunistic events that were reflected in his seminal thesis work on animal learning—when challenges came his way, Thorndike went to work. In his autobiography, Thorndike (1936, p. 266) observes: "I have not 'carried out my career,' as the biographers say. Rather it has been a conglomerate, amassed under the pressure of varied opportunities and demands." His son, put it this way: "He took whatever came his way that seemed to need doing and devoted himself wholeheartedly to it" (R. L. Thorndike, 1991, p. 151).

In assessing the major holes in his education, Thorndike (1936) points to his lack of training in experimental instrumentation and quantitative methods—complaints not uncommon among psychology graduates of Thorndike's generation. In spite of his often-acknowledged lack of mechanical skill, Thorndike constructed a device—the puzzle box—which came to revolutionize research instrumentation in animal learning (Burnham, 1972). In spite of his lack of training in high-level mathematics, he managed to quantify everything from human intelligence to student handwriting to the quality of life in American cities. Instead, his greatest strength seems to have been an unwavering faith in the ultimate power of the scientific method and his genius in using experimentation to attack educationally relevant questions.

It is clear from the many accolades from Thorndike's colleagues at Teachers College that he was greatly respected (Gates, 1949b; Lorge, 1940, Rock, 1940; Russell, 1940; Woodworth, 1934), but it is equally clear that Thorndike took great comfort in their support of his work: "The good opinion of others, especially those whom I esteem, has been a very great stimulus, though I have come in later years to require also the approval of my own judgment" (Thorndike, 1936, p. 270). It is worthwhile to note that the remarkable 50-year career of the man who is today recognized as the father of educational psychology was grounded on only 2 years of education as a psychologist and on working under sponsors—James at Harvard and Cattell at Columbia—who were not particularly interested in his thesis research.

At the time of his death in 1949, he was recognized around the world not only as the world's leading educational psychologist but as one of the greatest scientists of his generation. The man who "never sought organizational honors" (Moehlman, 1944, p. 19) had served as president of the American Psychological Association and of the American Association for the Advancement of Science, as well as president of the New York Academy of Science, the American Association for Adult Education, and the Psychological Corporation. He was a member of the National Academy of Sciences and had earned honorary doctorate degrees from Athens, Chicago, Edinburgh, Harvard, Iowa, and Wesleyan.

Publication Life

During his lifetime, E. L. Thorndike produced more than 500 publications—dutifully listed in two issues of the *Teachers College Record* (1940; Lorge, 1949). In quantitative terms, Thorndike leaves behind more than 250,000 pages of original writing in approximately 500 publications covering virtually every major topic in educational psychology and beyond. While it is not possible to describe his publications in much detail, Thorndike's publication life can be analyzed into several major eras—each associated with seminal books.

Thorndike's publication career began with what has been aptly described as a "revolutionary document" (Goodenough, 1950, p. 293)—the publication of his thesis in 1898 as a monograph entitled, *Animal Intelligence* (Thorndike, 1898). This 100-page monograph—later expanded into a 300-page book (Thorndike, 1911)—

presented Thorndike's laws of learning based on his meticulous research with chickens, cats, and dogs. In terms of methodology, the monograph "transformed the study of animal behavior from imperfectly controlled observation to predesigned experimentation . . . in which the behavior could be described in quantitative terms" (Goodenough, 1950, p. 293). In terms of psychological theory, the monograph clearly articulated a theory of learning that "for nearly half a century . . . dominated all others in America" (Bower & Hilgard, 1981, p. 21) and continues to influence the field today. A major theoretical competitor recognized that the "psychology of animal learning . . . has been and still is primarily a matter of agreeing or disagreeing with Thorndike" (Tolman, 1938, p. 11) and even after his death learning researchers correctly acknowledge that "no comprehensive theory of human learning can afford to ignore the heritage left to us by Thorndike" (Postman, 1962, p. 397).

Between 1900 and 1905, Thorndike published a monograph on child development, entitled *Notes on Child Study* (1901); and a popular psychology book intended for the general public, entitled *The Human Nature Club* (1901); he also published his first textbook on educational psychology, entitled *Educational Psychology* (1903); his first textbook on measurement, entitled *Mental and Social Measurements* (1904); and his first textbook on general psychology, entitled *Elements of Psychology* (1905). Each book was later published in subsequent editions. His articles during this period included research on mental fatigue, learning in monkeys, measurements of cognitive abilities in twins, and his landmark series of three articles with Woodworth on transfer of learning published in the *Psychological Review* (e.g., Thorndike & Woodworth, 1901).

From 1906 to 1910 he produced important second editions of his textbooks, *Elements of Psychology* (1907) and *Educational Psychology* (1910), as well as a new book entitled *Principles of Teaching* (1906). His research articles covered topics ranging from college entrance examinations to handwriting to mental fatigue to mental retardation.

From 1911 to 1915 he produced expanded second editions of *Animal Intelligence* (1911) and *Mental and Social Measurement* (1913). Goodenough (1950, p. 295) notes that Thorndike's measurement textbook became "the standard textbook on educational measurements" because "for the first time the applications of statistical method to practical problems in education were clearly and simply shown." Perhaps the high point of his textbook writing career occurred with the publication of his three-volume *Educational Psychology* (1913, 1913, 1914) and its accompanying *Educational Psychology Briefer Course* (1914). Volume 1 focused on the biological bases of learning, volume 2 on the nature of learning, and volume 3 on an assortment of topics including individual differences. The books made "the name of Thorndike practically synonymous with the field of educational psychology for many years to come" (Goodenough, 1950, p. 295). In a 1944 review of Thorndike's contributions to teaching, Moehlman (1944, p. 19) states that "it is doubtful that any text has had greater influence on public school teachers" than these volumes. Thorndike's other publications focused on standardized testing of compositions, drawings, handwriting, as well as intelligence testing and his first study of the disciplinary value of school subjects. Also during this period, Thorndike became president of the American Psychological Association, following in the footsteps of his mentors, William James and James McKeen Cattell (Bulatao, Fulcher, & Evans, 1992).

Between 1916 and 1920, Thorndike's services were needed for the war effort, in which he was a central figure in designing and evaluating psychological tests for American military personnel. He published the first editions of *The Thorndike Arithmetics, Books 1, 2, and 3* (1917) and *Thorndike Intelligence Tests for High School Graduates* (1919) as well as many educational tests. Perhaps his most well-known research article of this period was his analysis of "reading as reasoning" published in the *Journal of Educational Psychology* in which he makes the argument that "understanding a paragraph is like solving a problem" (Thorndike, 1917, p. 431). In retrospective reviews of this landmark study, Stauffer (1971, p. 443) observes that it is "probably one of the most widely quoted studies in all of reading research" and Otto (1971, p. 435) concludes that "attempts to define reading are largely a matter of agreeing or disagreeing with Thorndike."

The period from 1921 to 1925 saw Thorndike publish the first edition of *The Teacher's Word Book* (1921) which was to become an often-used research tool and the basis for a revolutionizing the teaching of language arts. Thorndike's interest in school subjects was reflected in three books on mathematics education, *New Methods in Arithmetic* (1921), *The Psychology of Arithmetic* (1922), and *The Psychology of Algebra* (1923), as well a revised edition of his children's textbook, *Arithmetic, Books 1, 2, and 3* (1924). In this period he published more than a half dozen articles concerning transfer of training in which he provided overwhelming evidence against "the long-cherished belief of certain educators that the learning of Greek, Latin, and mathematics was worth while . . . because the mental exercise required for learning them would strengthen the mental powers" (Goodenough, 1950, p. 297). He also produced a set of articles on the nature and measurement of intellectual ability, clearly arguing for the existence of many small mental components rather a general factor of intelligence.

Between 1926 and 1930, he and his colleagues summarized the state of research on intelligence testing in *The Measurement of Intelligence* (1926), on whether adults learn like children in *Adult Learning* (1928), and on teaching methods in *Elementary Principles of Education* (1929). Writing toward the end of the psychometric glory days in 1950, Goodenough (1950, p. 298) characterized the intelligence testing book as "probably the most brilliant and closely knit discussion of intelligence and its measurement that has appeared up to the present time." Following up on his role in mental testing during World War I, Thorndike served on a committee that developed the widely used National Intelligence Test. However, his most cherished contribution to intelligence testing was his own CAVD test of intelligence, which was based on *The Measurement of Intelligence*. He also published two school books on spelling and a number of research articles dealing with topics such as how age and gender affect learning.

Between 1930 and his retirement in 1940, Thorndike summarized his long-time program of research on learning in two books, *Human Learning* (1931) and *Fundamentals of Learning* (1932). He also published a series of studies demonstrating that punishment was not as effective as reward, thus causing him to make the remarkable acknowledgment of the need to revise his law of effect. In the area of language arts, he published a revised edition of *Teacher's Word Book* (1931) and his first scientifically designed student dictionary, *Thorndike-Century Junior Dictionary* (1935). His research on the educational role of student interests, attitudes, and goals was summarized in *Psychology of Wants, Interests, and Attitudes* (1935). Also during this period he was elected president of the American Association for the Advancement of Science, a rare honor for psychology (Gates, 1934).

From shortly before his retirement in 1940 until his death in 1949, Thorndike added some new topics to his research agenda mainly involving social issues. Most notably, his work on measuring the quality of cities and states was summarized in *Your City* (1939) and *144 Smaller Cities* (1940). Based on quantitative measurements along 300 dimensions for each community—such as percentage of physicians, crime rates, and average levels of education—Thorndike devised three general scales that describe the quality of life. In *Human Nature and the Social Order* (1940), Thorndike sought to show how psychology could contribute to the study of broader social issues; in *Man and His Works* (1943) Thorndike showed how an understanding of heredity and environment can lead to the betterment of human life; and in *Selected Writings from a Connectionist's Psychology* (1949) he provided an anthology of 22 of his previously published works mainly in the field of learning. In the area of language arts, he and Lorge published yet another revised and enlarged edition of *The Teacher's Word Book* (1944) as well as the *Thorndike-Century Senior Dictionary* (1941) and the *Thorndike-Century Beginning Dictionary* (1945). He wrote essays on the contributions of his major mentors—William James and James McKeen Cattell—as well as an impressive array of research articles including the psychology of semantics, ability measurement, and racial inequalities. His final research paper in the *Journal of Educational Psychology* examined learning strategies for memorizing poems and vocabularies (Thorndike, 1948), demonstrating that even after 50 years, E. L. Thorndike was always ready to empirically study almost any hot topic in educational psychology.

A review of 50 years of writings must, of course, be selective, but it is clear that Thorndike's publications maintained the same themes from decade to decade— including the nature of learning and transfer, the nature and measurement of ability and learning outcomes, the effects of various instructional methods on learning school subjects, the creation of scientifically based tests and curricular materials for classroom use, and the role of psychology within the larger context of solving social problems.

THORNDIKE'S ENDURING
CONTRIBUTIONS TO IDEAS
IN EDUCATIONAL PSYCHOLOGY

A scientific revolution occurs when a dominant model or theoretical framework is overthrown and replaced with a new one (Kuhn, 1970; Leary, 1990). According to this view, Thorndike has been instrumental in revolutionizing basic psychological concepts concerning learning, transfer, and individual differences. Before Thorndike, the dominant view of animal learning was largely based on anecdotes about the supposedly human-like thinking by various animals, what Stam and Kalmanovich (1998, p. 1135) call "anthropomorphism and anecdotalism." This view was devastated by Thorndike's scientifically based laws of learning, and was replaced with a new conception of animal learning as the strengthening and weakening of stimulus–response connections. Before Thorndike, the dominant view of transfer was the doctrine of formal discipline—the idea that certain school subjects such as Latin and geometry improved students' minds in general. This view was devastated by research by Thorndike and his colleagues demonstrating that learning to perform one kind of cognitive task rarely had strong positive effects on learning other unrelated ones; it was replaced by a theory of transfer in which only identical elements of one task would positively transfer to learning a new task. Before Thorndike, the dominant view of ability was that humans possessed varying levels of each of certain basic faculties such as reasoning, memory, and perception. In contrast to the idea that intelligence consisted of general ability, Thorndike's research demonstrated that performance on intellectually demanding tasks required a constellation of smaller, more specific skills. In each example, Thorndike can be viewed as a revolutionary who helped demolish the existing views of the day based on massive empirical evidence, and who helped construct new views that have stood the test of time.

This section explores Thorndike's enduring contributions to ideas in educational psychology in three major areas: (1) the nature of learning, (2) the nature of transfer of training, and (3) the nature and measurement of individual differences in ability and achievement.

Learning

There is no more fundamental or pervasive principle in psychology than Thorndike's law of effect, the idea that a response that is followed by satisfaction is more likely to occur in the future under the same circumstances, and a response that is followed by dissatisfaction is less likely to occur. Thorndike (1911, pp. 244–45) stated the law of effect as follows:

> Of several responses made to the same situation, those which are accompanied or followed by satisfaction to the animal will, other things being equal, be more firmly

connected with the situation, so that when it recurs, they will be more likely to recur; those which are accompanied or closely followed by discomfort to the animal will, other things being equal, have their connections with that situation weakened, so that, when it recurs, they will be less likely to recur. The greater the satisfaction or discomfort, the greater the strengthening or weakening of the bond . . .

According to this view learning is a matter of strengthening and weakening of associations between a stimulus (S) and a response (R) through a process of reward and punishment.

The idea is based on a clever and exhaustive series of studies on chicks, cats, and dogs first reported in Thorndike's thesis (Thorndike, 1898) and later in an enlarged book (Thorndike, 1911). For example, a hungry cat was placed in a puzzle box—a closed wooden crate containing wooden slats and an escape door. In order to get out and eat some nearby food, the cat had to perform a simple act such as pulling a loop of string, which opened a trap door. Once the cat pulled the string, the door opened, the cat jumped out and ate the food. Then, the whole procedure could be repeated on another day.

Thorndike carefully observed the cats, recording both what they did and how long it took them to get out. Thorndike noticed that on average, the cats needed a long time to solve the problem on the first day, but required less time on each succeeding day. By graphing the time needed to get out of box (on the y-axis) as a function of the number of trials (on the x-axis) Thorndike produced the first quantitative analysis of animal learning—for each animal the curve showed a general downward pattern indicating that the animals were learning. In addition, Thorndike noticed that on the first trial the cats engaged repeatedly in irrelevant behaviors such as pushing their paws through the bars, meowing, and pouncing against the wall, before they eventually caught their paw on the loop of string and pulled it down. On subsequent trials, Thorndike noticed a decline in the number of irrelevant behaviors and an increase in the tendency to engage in the successful behavior. In this way, Thorndike concluded that the animal learned by trial and error and accidental success.

Thorndike's theoretical explanation for what he observed is as simple as it is profound. The cat began in the puzzle box with a preexisting set of responses associated with being in a confined area—responses such as hissing, meowing, putting paws through open spaces, pouncing, and wildly swinging a clawed paw around in the area. The cat exercised each preexisting response based on its strength of association. When the cat engaged in an irrelevant response such as putting paws through the bars, this resulted in an unpleasing effect (still being confined in the box) and therefore its connection with the situation was weakened. When all of the irrelevant responses had been sufficiently weakened, the cat might exercise the relevant response—swinging its clawed paw in the air by the loop of string. If the cat accidentally caught hold of the loop of string and opened the door, then the cat would escape and eat the food leading to a strengthening of the connection with that response. In this way, the connection between being in the puzzle box and making the unsuccessful responses became gradually weaker and the connection with the successful response became stronger. This strengthening and weakening of stimulus–response connections based on each response's consequences is the mechanism underlying the law of effect.

Thorndike's animal research program represented not just an important increment in our knowledge of learning, but rather a revolutionary change in the study of animal intelligence. Before Thorndike's study, the study of animal behavior was based on interpretations of anecdotes about human-like reasoning in animals as epitomized in Romanes' (1882) *Animal Intelligence*. Galef (1998, p. 1128) argues that "Thorndike's thesis can be considered the foundation document of comparative psychology" because "in it, Thorndike rejected earlier anecdotal, anthropomorphic, and introspectionist approaches to the study of animal behavior and provided novel methods for studying comparative psychology that, 100 years later, are still the basis for the field." Yet, my focus in this chapter is not on Thorndike's contributions to animal psychology, but rather on his amazing transition into the world of human learning in educational settings.

An important episode in the refinement of the law of effect occurred several decades after its debut. Based on a growing mass of research, including research on humans, Thorndike made the startling admission that his most well-revered contribution to psychology was wrong. Thirty years after proclaiming the law of effect, Thorndike offered the amendment that punishment was not as effective as reward, and in fact, punishment may not really lead to learning at all.

> In the earlier statements of the Law of Effect, the influence of satisfying consequences of a connection in the way of strengthening it was paralleled by the influence of annoying consequences in the way of weakening it. . . . I now consider that there is no such complete and exact parallelism. In particular, the strengthening of a connection by satisfying consequences seems, in view of our experiments, to be more universal, inevitable, and direct than the weakening of a connection by annoying consequences. The latter seems more specialized, contingent . . . and indirect. (Thorndike, 1932, p. 276)

The emphasis on reward over punishment had a widespread influence on educational practice, helping to end the practice of punishing students for giving incorrect answers. More importantly, this episode demonstrated the integrity of a scientist who valued the role of data so much that, when confronted with overwhelming evidence, he was willing to acknowledge that his most important discovery was wrong. For example, at an international psychology conference held in 1929, Thorndike began his address on his revision of the law of effect by confessing: "I am about to say three words you have seldom, if ever, heard from the lecture platform: I was wrong" (Rock, 1940, p. 752). There are few such incidents in the history of American psychology.

Along with the law of effect, Thorndike's research produced other laws of learning, such as the law of exercise and the law of readiness. The result was American psychology's first coherent theory of learning—which came to be called connectionism. Not only did connectionism form the basis for the behaviorist movement in American psychology, including Skinner's landmark work, but even today lives on in theories as diverse as connectionist models of cognition and to some extent in production system models of cognition. Although Thorndike's laws of learning no longer rule supreme, the saga of his experimental research still demonstrates how it is possible to create a scientifically based theory of learning.

The story of how Thorndike created psychology's first comprehensive theory of learning also highlights two important deficiencies in Thorndike's expertise. First, his experimental devices reflect a lack of mechanical skill. Photographs of his famous puzzle boxes show them to be flimsy contraptions made with uneven pieces of wood awkwardly hammered together. They were constructed from discarded packing crates containing labels such as "HEINZ'S BAKED BEANS" on their sides (Burnham, 1972, p. 161). In analyzing the largest published collection of photographs of the puzzle box, Burnham noted the "considerable contrast between this neat drawing (a line drawing of puzzle box in his original publication) and the crooked and uneven side pieces and bent nails seen in the photographs" (Burnham, 1972, p. 161). In contrast, later researchers such as Skinner (1938) were able to turn the clumsy puzzle box into a highly efficient instrument of gleaming metal and straight corners—the Skinner box. A review of photos of Thorndike's original puzzle boxes reveals that Thorndike lacked the mechanical skill to produce good-looking devices (Burnham, 1972), but they certainly functioned well enough to earn him a doctorate and a place in history as the founder of modern animal psychology (Dewsbury, 1998; Galef, 1998; Stam & Kalmanovich, 1998).

Second, Thorndike's theoretical account of the strengthening and weakening of connections reflected a lack of mathematical sophistication. *Animal Intelligence* (Thorndike, 1898) contains many numbers to describe the animals' behaviors—such as the time it took for cats to escape—but the underlying theory is not presented in mathematical terms. In contrast, later researchers were able to convert the laws of learning into a set of precise formulas, perhaps reaching their heights with Hull's (1943) comprehensive mathematization of learning theory. Again, although Thorndike's account of learning lacked the mathematical sophistication of Hull's, it represented a true conceptual and methodological breakthrough.

From the vantage point of the new millennium, it is not difficult to ascertain which of the following represents the most important contribution to psychology: Thorndike's building of psychology's first conception of learning, Skinner's improving of the underlying instrumentation for testing this conception, or Hull's mathematizing of this conception. Although all three represent important achievements, it is Thorndike's fundamental conception of learning as response strengthening that has stood the test of time—in spite of Thorndike's less-than-perfect instrumentation and mathematical expertise.

Transfer

Thorndike's research on transfer of training represents a case study in how scientific research can address important educational issues, and how this process depends on a reciprocity between theory and practice. At the opening of the 20th century, the dominant theory of transfer was the doctrine of formal discipline—the idea that certain school subjects help to improve students' minds in general. This view is the impetus for the Latin school movement, which has been a part of American education for centuries. For example, according to the doctrine of formal discipline, learning languages such Latin (as well as some Greek and Hebrew) and mathematical topics such as geometry and logic would produce "proper habits of mind" (Rippa, 1980). The disciplinary value of Latin and other classical subjects rested in their helping students improve their mental discipline, their systematic thinking, and so forth. The notion of formal discipline is rooted in faculty theory, the idea that the mind consists of mental faculties—such as reasoning and memory—which can be improved through proper exercise.

By the late 1800s, educators increasingly questioned the role of a classical education in light of the widespread implementation of compulsory public education coupled with the needs of an industrialized society. Thorndike and his colleagues were the first to use scientific methods to examine this explosive issue (Thorndike & Woodworth, 1901; Thorndike, 1906). For example, in well-controlled studies, learning to perform one kind of task (e.g., estimating the length of lines .5 to 1.5 inches long) rarely had a strong effect on learning to perform another kind of task (e.g., estimating the length of lines 6 to 12 inches long). In school-based studies, learning of one school subject was not highly related to learning other, unrelated subjects, and learning Latin produced no more positive transfer than other more mundane subjects. Overall, Thorndike found that improving one cognitive skill resulted in improvements in a different cognitive skill, only to the extent that the two skills shared many elements in common. Based on these results, Thorndike proposed a theory of transfer based on identical elements: "One mental function or activity improves others in so far as and because they are in part identical with it, because it contains elements common to them" (Thorndike, 1906, p. 243). For example, "knowledge of Latin gives increased ability to learn French because many of the facts learned in the one case are needed in the other" (p. 243).

Thorndike's research—both in the classroom and in the laboratory—repeatedly demonstrated that transfer was specific rather than general. His relentless search for research data put an end to the idea that learning Latin would affect other kinds of learning, and forever demolished the doctrine of formal discipline. "Certainly nobody can now believe it in the face of these experiments," he proclaimed (Thorndike, 1913, p. 417). Modern researchers have continued to have difficulty in finding evidence of transfer, but the search of transfer continues (Detterman & Sternberg, 1993; Mayer & Wittrock, 1996; McKeough, Lupart, & Marini, 1995).

"Improvements in any single mental function need not improve the ability in functions commonly called by the same name" (Thorndike, 1903, p. 91) because faculties such as "memory" or "reasoning" do not exist. Instead, "the mind is a host of highly particularized and independent abilities" (p. 39). Thorndike's research helped end faculty psychology and replace it with a kind of domain-specific componential analysis of cognition that is still developing today.

Individual Differences

Thorndike's third major contribution involved a change from viewing intellectual ability as based on mental factors to based on knowledge acquisition. The dominant theory of intelligence in Thorndike's era held that individual differences on cognitive tasks depended on the individual's level of general intellectual ability such as, the overall speed of mental activity (Galton, 1883) or the amount of mental energy (Spearman, 1927). In short, there was a mental factor called intelligence and each person possessed a certain amount of it. In addition, there may be other more specialized factors such as memory ability or perceptual ability or reasoning ability but for each factor an individual possessed a certain amount.

In contrast to factor theories, Thorndike was among the first to propose that individual differences on cognitive tasks depended on knowledge—in particular, on the number of S–R connections that the individual had acquired. On a variety of cognitive tasks, Thorndike found a strong relation between the amount of relevant knowledge that people possessed and their level of performance on cognitive tasks (Thorndike et al., 1926; Thorndike, 1913). Whereas Spearman interpreted the intercorrelation of tests as evidence for the existence of general intelligence, Thorndike interpreted correlations as evidence that the tasks required many of the same underlying pieces of knowledge—that is the tasks sampled many of the same S–R connections. Consistent with Binet's pioneering research in France, Thorndike proposed that intellectual ability can best be viewed as the ability to acquire knowledge from experience—that is, as the ability to learn.

Thorndike was the "first American to espouse a theory of intelligence" (Jensen, 1987, p. 77) and the first to show how research on learning was directly relevant to understanding the nature of intelligence. Thorndike's theory of intelligence, which became known as sampling theory, was popular during Thorndike's lifetime. Although his particular version of intelligence theory is no longer widely recognized, his basic vision of intelligence as the ability to learn is a major theme in modern theories of intelligence (Sternberg, 1990). Although today's componential analyses of intellectual ability now focus on information processing steps rather than S–R bonds, Thorndike's knowledge-based view of ability has won out over the mental factor view. In sum, although Thorndike's sampling theory is no longer widely recognized, modern theories of intellectual ability are consistent with Thorndike's idea that performance on intellectual tasks depends on many underlying pieces of knowledge rather than on the level of some general mental factor.

Other Ideas

Some of Thorndike's other major contributions to ideas in educational psychology include the biological bases of learning, psychology of subject areas, and adult learning. It is important to note that his landmark three-volume series on Educational Psychology began with a full volume devoted to the "original nature of man." His many line drawings of neurons in that volume reflect an emphasis on the cognitive neuroscience of his day—an emphasis largely ignored in the second half of the 20th century but one that is gaining increasing attention in the new millennium. It is also important to note that although he began with general laws of learning, he soon recognized the need to study learning within each school subject. His research revolutionized ideas and practice both in language arts, such as reading, and in mathematics, such as arithmetic. The focus on learning within specific domains is consistent with modern themes in cognitive science concerning the domain-specificity of cognition.

In the field of adult learning, Thorndike sought to understand the effects of aging on basic cognitive processes such as learning. His research clarified the nature of adult learning and paved the way for the improvements in the practice of adult education (Lorge, 1940). Again, his interest in adult learning is reflected in ongoing work in cognitive aging that represents one of the most intriguing and socially relevant topics of the new millennium.

Thorndike also contributed to ideas about child development, the role of play, interests and attitudes, special education, minority groups, mental fatigue, vocational guidance, aesthetics, semantics, and the role of humans in social institutions.

THORNDIKE'S ENDURING CONTRIBUTIONS TO PRODUCTS IN EDUCATIONAL PSYCHOLOGY

This section examines three of Thorndike's enduring contributions to products in educational psychology—in the area of dictionaries, curricular materials, and tests.

Dictionaries

The development of the world's first scientifically based student dictionaries epitomizes Thorndike's approach to educational psychology, namely, applying the rigorous methods of scientific research—with an emphasis on quantitative data—to the problems of education. The development of his dictionaries, *Junior* in 1935, *Senior* in 1941, *Revised Junior* in 1942, and *Beginning* in 1945, was no mere academic exercise. They immediately became "the most widely used school dictionary series" (Barnhart, 1949, p. 35) in the United States and have influenced the design of other student dictionaries ever since. Foreshadowing the modern interest

in user-friendly materials and consistent with the classic view of child-centered education, Thorndike's dictionaries were designed so that children could use them.
Barnhart (1949, p. 38) notes that Thorndike's dictionaries were "not written to
please scholars, certainly not to please pedants, but to help . . . pupils, especially
to help them to understand . . . and use English."

Like so many other fields that he entered, Thorndike revolutionized the field
of lexicography—the principles and practices of dictionary making. He is widely
recognized as the "first lexicographer to apply the principles of the psychology of
learning to, and use statistical methods in, the making of dictionaries" (Barnhart,
1949, p. 35). Thorndike's dictionaries were radically different from other school
dictionaries in the way that words were selected, the way the words were defined,
and in the order in which alternative definitions were listed.

First, consider word selection. Given that a student dictionary could contain
only a limited number of words, on what basis should the words be chosen?
Thorndike was the first to seek an answer to this question based on empirical,
quantitative data. He and his colleagues conducted a word count from a corpus
of 10 million running words sampled from 279 printed sources, including works
of adult literature, textbooks, commercial material, and children's readings. The
result was a list of the 20,000 most frequently used words along with the average
number of times per million words that they appeared—a frequency list that in an
enlarged form helped shape psychological research and the teaching of reading
for years to come. Using the frequency list, Thorndike was able, for example,
"to exclude rare adult words and technical terms such as *fabulist, fabaceous*, and
fauces, and devote more space to the explanation of *fabulous, faculty*, and *festivity*,
which should become a part of the working vocabulary of very person" (Barnhart,
1949, p. 37). In contrast to the commonly accepted practice of cramming as many
words as possible into school dictionaries, Thorndike devised a scientifically based
method for selecting basic words that everyone should understand.

Second, consider the specificity of the definitions. At what level of specificity
should words be defined? To solve this problem in a scientific, data-based way,
Thorndike devised straightforward principles based on his word counts. For example, according to the principle of probable use, simple words with high frequencies,
such as *spoon* or *little*, should be defined as simply as possible, because younger
children are most likely to look up such words. In contrast, harder words with
lower frequencies, such as *factitious* or *feminine*, could be defined more formally,
because older students are most likely to look up these kinds of words. A consideration of the probable knowledge by the student, suggested for example that the
following definition of cow would be difficult to understand for a fourth grader:
"the mature female of any bovine animal, or any other animal the male of which
is called bull." Instead, Thorndike's definition was presented in terms more familiar to a fourth grader: "1. the large animal that furnishes us with milk, butter, and
cheese. 2. the female of various animals, as, a buffalo cow, an elephant cow, a whale
cow." Another of Thorndike's principles for definitions was that no word should
be defined in terms of more difficult words. For example, his definition of *fable* is

"story that is not true." Yet another principle was to include an illustrative sentence to make the meaning clearer. For example, his definition of facilitate is "make easy; lessen the labor of; forward; assist. A vacuum-cleaner facilitates housework." In contrast to all other dictionaries before his, Thorndike's dictionaries were the first to adjust the level of detail of the definition based on the probable needs and maturity of the user, to control the difficulty of words used in the definitions, and to make widespread use of example sentences.

Third, consider the ordering of alternative definitions. When a word has several possible definitions, which alternative definitions should be included and how should they be ordered? Thorndike's answer to this question was to group similar meanings together so they appeared consecutively, and to order the meanings according to frequency of usage. For example, the entry for *club* begins with definitions based on a club as a kind of stick and ends with definitions based on a club as a group of members:

> 1. a heavy stick of wood, thicker at one end, used as a weapon. 2. beat with a club or something similar. 3. a stick or bat used for some games played with a ball, as golf clubs. 4. a group of people joined for some special purpose, as a social club, tennis club, yacht club, nature-study club. 5. the building or rooms used by a club. 6. join together for some purpose. The children clubbed together to buy their mother a plant for her birthday. (Thorndike, 1935, p. 150)

By grouping the definitions, reading one definition helps the student to understand subsequent ones.

When there are several possible meanings, Thorndike's dictionary presented only the most frequent ones and placed them in order of frequency. For example, the *Oxford English Dictionary* (*OED*) in use during Thorndike's time listed five definitions for *amenable*. The Lorge–Thorndike Semantic Count listed only 2 occurrences per million words for *amenable*, and only two of the possible five meanings occurred at all—"open to advice" (which was most common) and "accountable." Thus, the entry for amenable need contain only two definitions "open to advance" followed by "accountable." This technique was particularly useful in pruning the 29 definitions listed in the *OED* for *amend*, only 12 of which were used in the Lorge–Thorndike Semantic Count, or the 544 definitions of *set* of which only 27 had high frequency counts.

In addition to improving the selection of words, the appropriateness of the definitions, and the ordering of the definitions, Thorndike's dictionaries also contained more usable pronunciation guides, large type size, and graphics as an integral part of the definition. Thorndike's dictionaries represent an outstanding example of his unwavering faith that scientific methods could improve educational practice. The success of his approach is reflected in the fact that all subsequent school dictionaries have adopted aspects of Thorndike's techniques. In this way, without setting out to do so, Thorndike became "one of the foremost lexicographers of his time" (Barnhart, 1949, p. 35).

Curricular Materials

Complementing the contribution of Thorndike's dictionaries to instruction in language arts, Thorndike's arithmetic books—nicknamed *Thorndike Arithmetics*—represented an influential change in the teaching of mathematics. Joncich (1968a, p. 398) ranks the *Thorndike Arithmetics* along with his dictionaries as "the most widely seen evidence of Thorndike's direct influence upon education." At the time of their introduction in 1917, arithmetic instruction involved memorizing many facts that were not directly related to improvements in arithmetic skill. Thorndike sought to change mathematics instruction by focusing on learning of essential information in a more meaningful way.

Thorndike based the workbook series on a series of educational principles. First, all problems should be realistic. For example, consider the following problem: "Mary had just cut out 35 paper dolls, when the wind blew 16 away. How many were left?" According to Thorndike, this problem is not realistic because if wind blew some dolls away Mary would most likely count how many remained and then want to compute how many needed to be replaced. A corollary is that learning of arithmetic procedures should be contextualized within familiar situations. For example, learning the multiplication tables of threes should be based on converting yards to feet; learning the multiplication tables of twelves should be based on converting feet to inches; learning to add with decimals to the hundredths should be based on dollars and cents. Perhaps the most fundamental principle was that all topics—both easy and hard—were included for their intrinsic value rather than "merely for mental gymnastics" (Joncich, 1968a, p. 398). There were no exercises to improve reasoning for its own sake; all lessons were focused on content that was directly relevant to curricular objectives, such as knowing how to add, subtract, multiply, and divide.

On the surface, Thorndike's arithmetic books seem to contain elements that are both consistent and inconsistent with Thorndike's basic research on learning. On the one hand, Thorndike viewed learning as response strengthening so his books emphasized practice on basic arithmetic operations. Yet at the same time, he saw learning as more than the accumulation of isolated responses, and sought to help students see relations among facts and relations between arithmetic procedures and their everyday experiences. Joncich (1968a, p. 401) notes that Thorndike's arithmetic books emphasized "meaning, insight, and number relation" in learning arithmetic rather than "purely mechanical memorizations of the steps in arithmetic operations." The resolution of this seeming conflict between learning basic skills and learning with understanding is reflected in the idea that learning of basic arithmetic skills is more efficient when students learn general principles and connect them with realistic situations.

If adoption rate is the measure of success, then Thorndike's arithmetic books were highly successful—providing far more income for Thorndike than his salary from Columbia (Joncich, 1968a). Even more important is the idea that curricular materials can be based on scientific theories of how children learn. Today's books are brighter and more colorful than those of Thorndike's era, but the same debate about the relative place of basic skills and higher-order understanding still rages. Perhaps today's textbook writers could still benefit from Thorndike's realization that well-learned basic skills enable the learning of higher order skills—an idea that cognitive scientists refer to as automatization—and that lower-level skills are better learned within meaningful contexts than as isolated exercises—an idea that cognitive scientists refer to as situativity.

Tests

"Whatever exists at all exists in some amount." This famous quote from Thorndike (1918, p. 16) epitomizes his vision of educational measurement, and the revolutionary new measurement instruments that he helped produce. His contributions to educational testing include the following: He developed many standardized tests and scales for school-related performance, such as quantitative measures of English composition, drawing, and handwriting as well as reading ability and arithmetic ability. He was a member of a committee that devised and evaluated the Army Alpha and Army Beta tests as well as other psychological inventories, which were used in World War I for selection of military personal. He created the Thorndike IER Intelligence Examination for High School Graduates, which was used in college admissions at selective colleges until the appearance of the Scholastic Aptitude Test. He was a member of a committee that devised the National Intelligence Test, which was widely used in elementary schools. Together with his colleagues at Columbia, Cattell and Woodworth, he participated in founding the Psychological Corporation in 1921, which helped to professionalize educational testing.

Thorndike's single most visible testing instrument was the CAVD test of intelligence, one version of which was also used for college-entrance screening. It focused on four mental tasks: completion, arithmetic, vocabulary, and directions. Completion items involved asking students to determine a word that would complete a sentence. Arithmetic items asked students to solve arithmetic problems including arithmetic word problems. Vocabulary items asked about the meaning of words, such as "what is the opposite of ____?" Direction items test students' ability to comprehend printed directions. By using several different kinds of content areas, Thorndike was one of the first to emphasize the multidimensionality of intelligence. A unique feature of the test was the pairing of parallel content-based and content-free items so that it was possible to identify students who were bright (based on the content-free items) but not well-prepared (based on context-based items). Thus, Thorndike attempted to build distinguishable measures of ability and achievement into the same test. Finally, the test represented an advancement in measurement by expressing scores on a ratio scale (with true zero and equal units).

Thorndike held that one of psychology's major contributions for education was the ability to clearly specify the knowledge and skills of individual students

(Thorndike, 1910). It follows that the development of assessment instruments is one of psychology's most important achievements. The search for useful assessment techniques continues as a hot research area for the new millennium (Anderson et al., 2001).

Other Products

Other important products include the Thorndike–Lorge word list, which became "one of the most valuable research tools every developed" (Goodenough, 1950, p. 296), and Thorndike's applications of statistical methods to educational psychology (Gates, 1949b).

THORNDIKE'S ENDURING
CONTRIBUTIONS TO VALUES
IN EDUCATIONAL PSYCHOLOGY

Perhaps more important than Thorndike's ideas and products are the core values that he established for the new field of educational psychology—including a faith in scientific methods, a love of quantitative data, and a desire to improve education. In short, Thorndike's legacy of values helped create educational psychology as a science—based on experimental research, quantitative data, and practical issues.

Scientific Methods

The most salient value that Thorndike propagated was an unwavering faith in science. At the time of Thorndike's death, the President of Teachers College, William F. Russell, summarized:

> Thorndike was a scientist. He held no preconceived opinions. He did not believe one could learn the truth by idle speculation or random observation. He believed that the human mind could be studied and, given adequate experimentation and precise enough measuring instruments, there need be nothing secret.... What psychology needs is less speculation and more experimentation. (Russell, 1949, p. 27)

His colleague, Arthur Gates clearly recognized the overarching role that science played in Thorndike's career:

> Professor Thorndike's major life-purpose was not merely to establish "laws of learning" ... or even to found and father educational psychology. These and many similar achievements, any one of which would have given him lasting fame, were but means to a larger purpose, namely, to demonstrate the unrivaled fruitfulness of the scientific method in the solution of social problems ... Education, he judged, would be a highly suitable area in which to carry out this purpose.... He was magnificently

successful in his major purpose. Indeed, I am confident that the future will reveal the name of Edward L. Thorndike in the list of outstanding scientists of all time. (Gates, 1949b, p. 31)

Throughout his career, Thorndike was recognized as "one of the great pioneers in the scientific movement in education" (Moehlman, 1944, p. 19). He was elected president of the American Association for the Advancement of Science in 1934, being cited "as the man who gave most promise of employing scientific methods fruitfully in the study of education" (Gates, 1934, p. 88). His son recognized "though he appeared . . . as a connectionist, he was not by temperament a systematist but rather an empiricist, a conductor of investigations and an analyzer of data" (R. L Thorndike, 1991, p. 140). Indeed, Thorndike described himself as "an investigator rather than a scholar" (Joncich, 1962, p. 33).

Joncich (1968b, p. 434) notes: "Over his entire career Thorndike tried to guide his behavior by the scientist model, because this is what he wanted most to be, this is what he was convinced he could be, and this is what he thought he was." Furthermore, Joncich (1966, p. 45) concludes: "Thorndike saw himself as thus helping to build psychology into the only kind of science he thought worthwhile: one that is experimental, objective, quantitative, useful." A *New York Times* editorial of January 13, 1934, put it most succinctly: "But first and last, he is a scientist" (Joncich, 1968b, p. 445).

Thorndike's original vision of educational psychology as a science has defined our field for a century, and it is my hope that the science of educational psychology will continue to thrive. Although science is currently under attack in some educational researcher circles (Eisner, 1997), I share Thorndike's conviction that no value is more central to our field than the idea that arguments should be settled with scientifically sound data rather than speculation. Thorndike once reminded an educational conference that "sciences are built by research and not by proclamation" (Joncich, 1968b, p. 444). Perhaps this would be a worthwhile banner to carry into the new millennium.

Quantitative Data

Thorndike placed a high value on quantitative measurement. "To him, qualitative difference was merely a quantitative difference that man had not yet learned to measure" (Russell, 1949, p. 27). Jonich (1968a, p. 442) shows that Thorndike "was convinced . . . that psychology must attain the certainty and exactness of the physical sciences." His son notes that E. L. Thorndike "never had a course in calculus or advanced mathematics . . . but he undertook the measurement of everything from educational achievement through human wants and interests to the qualities of cities" (R. L. Thorndike, 1991, p. 141).

Thorndike viewed precise, quantitative measurements of learning outcomes as perhaps the greatest potential contribution of psychology to education. In his first educational psychology textbook, Thorndike (1903, p. 3) began by acknowledging the importance of quantitative measurements: "Commonly our measurements of mental conditions and so of the changes due to educational endeavor are crude, individual, and incomplete . . . An adequate measurement . . . will be one that is precise . . . objective . . . and complete. . . . " In the first issue of the *Journal of Educational Psychology*, Thorndike (1910, p. 5) observed that "psychology helps . . . by requiring us to put our notions of the aims of education into terms of the exact changes that education is to make, and by describing for us the changes which do actually occur in human beings." According to Thorndike, precise measurement is the key to educational improvement: "Psychology, which teaches us how to measure changes in human nature, teaches us how to decide just what the results of any method of teaching are" (Thorndike, 1910, p. 7). He emphasized quantitative measurements because he abhorred vagueness.

From the vantage point of the new millennium, it is clear that qualitative measures are taking their place alongside quantitative ones in educational psychology, helping to provide a richer and converging picture of human learning. Yet, a careful review of Thorndike's research reports shows that even he often provided qualitative descriptions, such as the following observation of a cat in his puzzle box (Thorndike, 1911, p. 35):

> When put into the box the cat would show evident signs of discomfort and of an impulse to escape confinement. It tries to squeeze through any opening; it claws and bites at the bars or wire; it thrusts its paws out through any opening and claws at everything it reaches; it continues its efforts when it strikes anything loose and shaky; it may claw at things within the box.

Similar descriptions, albeit very clear ones, were often included in his studies of human learning. However, his qualitative descriptions were supplemented, and usually overshadowed, by quantitative ones. A useful lesson for the new millennium may be to combine clear quantitative and qualitative measures to converge on answers to research questions, while keeping true to Thorndike's advice: "look to the evidence" (Goodenough, 1950, p. 301).

Practical Issues

With a scientific and quantitative orientation, Thorndike could have worked in many fields. It was his third major value—a determination to improve society— that predisposed him to direct his efforts toward educational psychology. Joncich (1968a, p. 368) observed: "To Thorndike science does not become less science when it investigates problems which have . . . obvious relevance for application . . . " Rock (1940, p. 761) noted that Thorndike had "almost equal interest in the theoretical and practical aspects of problems."

Thorndike recognized the reciprocal relation between education and psychology. In the inaugural issue of the *Journal of Educational Psychology*, Thorndike (1910, p. 12) wrote:

> The science of education can and will itself contribute abundantly to psychology. Not only do the laws derived by psychology from simple, specially arranged experiments help us to interpret and control mental action under the conditions of school life. School-room life itself is a vast laboratory in which are made thousands of experiments of the utmost interest to "pure" psychology.

He predicted that the journal would contain both "answers to psychological questions got from the facts of educational experience" and "answers to educational questions got from experiments of the laboratory" (Thorndike, 1910, p. 12).

The motivating issues for Thorndike were practical ones. In *The Principles of Teaching Based on Psychology*, Thorndike (1906, p. 1) summarized the challenge as follows:

> The word education is used with many meanings, but in all its usages it refers to changes. No one is educated who remains just as he was. We do not educate anybody if we do nothing that makes any difference or change in anybody. . . . In studying education, then, one studies always the existence, nature, causation, or value of change of some sort.

In short, Thorndike was interested in the practical and theoretical issue of how instructional manipulations foster change in learners.

In the preface to his first educational psychology textbook, Thorndike (1903, p. v) stated that educational psychology "attempts to apply to a number of educational problems the methods of exact science." May (1949, p. 34) credits Thorndike's genius with the "ability to relate the principle of pure science to practical problems." Yet to Thorndike, the distinction between theoretical and practical problems seemed somewhat misleading: interesting theoretical problems about learning and transfer and ability could best be tested within realistic settings that had practical implications whereas practical problems could best be solved by having a better understanding of the workings of the human mind. As educational psychology moves into the new millennium, Thorndike's way of balancing the theoretical and the practical still makes sense.

Other Values

Other values evident in Thorndike's life are productivity, originality, consistency, and pragmatism. Being able to produce roughly 10 publications per year for 50 years attests to the value that Thorndike placed in productivity. Thorndike's high valuation of originality is represented in his revolutionary contributions to theories of learning, transfer, ability, and child development, as well as his revolutionary educational inventions of dictionaries, workbooks, and texts. His consistency is reflected in his 50-year long tenure at Teachers College and his unending search for topics to be explored. Although he is sometimes portrayed as the founder of connectionism, his pragmatic values are reflected in his search for answers to scientific questions rather than a crusade to build a new "ism"—that is, he was more interested in finding answers than in preaching doctrine.

As educational psychology moves into the millennium, there is a resurgence of interest in "isms"—with many educational researchers actively searching for the perfect version of constructivism. Thorndike's steady and unwavering focus on creatively addressing practical and theoretical issues—rather than on building a doctrine—suggests an appropriate course for our field for the next millennium.

EVALUATION OF THORNDIKE'S ENDURING CONTRIBUTIONS

In this section, I provide a brief critique of Thorndike's major contributions to ideas about learning, transfer, and individual differences, as well as his contributions to products and values in educational psychology.

Critique of Thorndike's Ideas About Learning

Thorndike's laws of learning, particularly the law of effect, represent his single most important contribution to educational psychology (Rock, 1940). The law of effect is widely recognized as one of the most important and enduring principles of learning (Bower & Hilgard, 1981) and still today is a central pillar in textbook chapters on learning. However, in spite of its status as one of the most fundamental principles in psychology, Thorndike's law of effect can be criticized—justifiably I believe—on several grounds.

First, Thorndike's vision of learning as response strengthening has been soundly criticized, not for being wrong but rather for being incomplete. In contrast to Thorndike's claim that all learning involves building S–R connections, others have argued that building connections is only one type of learning. The Gestalt psychologist, Katona (1940, pp. 4–5) summarized the objection as follows: "The main objection to the prevailing theory, which makes one kind of connection the basis of all learning, is not that may be incorrect, but that in the course of psychological research it has prevented an unbiased study of other possible kinds of learning." Katona and his fellow Gestaltists argued that another important type of learning, which they called learning by understanding, involved mentally building a coherent structure. In spite of attempts at reconciliation (Brown & Feder, 1934), Gestalt and connectionist views of learning are fundamentally different (Mayer, 1995). According to Gestalt psychologists, Thorndike's conception of learning was adequate to explain rote learning but not to explain meaningful learning, that is, connectionism was concerned with the retention of a learned response but not with learning that promotes creative problem-solving transfer (Wertheimer, 1959).

Another way to state this objection is to say that Thorndike's conception of what is learned, namely S–R connections, is incomplete because in addition to forming associations, learners may also form coherent mental representations and create general strategies. For example, Tolman (1932) demonstrated that laboratory animals who were rewarded for various behaviors behaved as if they had formed cognitive maps and hypotheses rather than specific responses.

More recently, Mayer (1992, 1996) has shown how educational psychology's conception of learning has progressed during the 20th century from learning-as-response-strengthening in the first half of the century to learning-as-knowledge-acquisition during the information processing revolution of the 1960s and 1970s to learning-as-knowledge-construction during the constructivist revolution of the 1980s and 1990s. Placing Thorndike's vision of learning within the context of subsequent developments in the 20th century, it becomes clearer that he created educational psychology's first conception of learning—one that is still viable but one that has now been joined by several other viable conceptions of learning. In my opinion, the more recent conceptions—particularly constructivist views—have generated some of the most important advances in educational psychology.

Second, Thorndike's theoretical explanation for the law of effect has also been criticized for ignoring the role of cognition in learning. Although there is over-whelming evidence that rewards can affect behavior, there is not universal agree-ment with Thorndike's description of the underlying mechanism as automatic reinforcement. According to Thorndike, a reward automatically strengthens an S–R connection without the need for any cognitive activity on the part of the learner. In contrast, a review of subsequent research on reward is more consistent with the idea that learners sometimes use rewards and punishments as informa-tion with which to consciously guide their behavior (Mayer, 1987). For example, research on the hidden costs of reward has shown that under some circumstances rewards can actually weaken a response—depending on the learner's interpre-tation of the reward (Lepper & Greene, 1978). From the vantage point of the new millennium, it appears that the 100-year old law of effect works (at least under some circumstances) but not necessarily for the reasons that Thorndike proposed.

Critique of Thorndike's Ideas About Transfer

Thorndike's research on transfer stands as a model of how methodologically sound research can address issues of fundamental importance to education. His theory of transfer by identical elements makes as much sense today as it did 100 years ago—it is easier to learn a new task if you have already learned a task that contains many of the same elements. Yet, like his vision of learning, Thorndike's theory of transfer is not so much incorrect as it is incomplete—failing to account for situations in which general transfer occurs.

Thorndike's theory of transfer has been criticized on theoretical and empirical grounds. On the theoretical side, it seems extreme to claim that transfer occurs only when the same response is required in the same situation. For example, Meiklejohn (1908, p. 126) criticized this specificity of transfer as follows: "Think of learning to drive a nail with a yellow hammer, and realize your helplessness if, in time of need, you should borrow your neighbor's hammer and find it is painted red." Taken to its logical conclusion, Thorndike's theory allows only a rigid form of specific transfer and therefore seems to conflict with common experience. From the vantage point of the new millennium, it appears that Thorndike lacked the theoretical tools to clearly define what was meant by an identical element. Today's research on transfer of cognitive skills assumes that domain-specific principles, strategies, and solution methods can transfer from one situation to another (Mayer & Wittrock, 1996).

On the empirical side, one of Thorndike's early critics, Judd (1908), showed that students who learned a skill in one situation could transfer that skill to a new situation even when none of the responses were identical to the original situation but the general principle was identical. Wertheimer (1959) provided additional evidence for general transfer in cases where students learned by understanding a general principle. Perhaps even more striking, Thorndike and Woodworth's (1901) own results seemed to provide evidence for some modest forms of general transfer. For example, students who practiced in crossing out words that contained both the letters e and s in a passage performed better on a transfer task requiring different responses (e.g., crossing out words that contained two new letters) than did students who had not received the practice crossing out words with e and s. Singley and Anderson (1989, p. 5) note that "Thorndike observed more transfer than could be explained by common stimulus–response elements alone."

Overall, Thorndike's research on transfer stimulated a healthy research agenda that is very much alive today, challenging researchers to identify conditions that lead to general transfer (Detterman & Sternberg, 1993; Mayer & Wittrock, 1996; McKeough, Lupart, & Marini, 1995; Singley & Anderson, 1989). Clearly, there are situations in which only specific transfer occurs—as Thorndike proposed—but there is an increasing body of research documenting instructional treatments that lead to broader transfer (Mayer & Wittrock, 1996). In a way, throughout the 20th century, researchers have sought to clarify what Thorndike meant by identical elements. Singley and Anderson (1989, p. 6) provide the following evaluation: "Thorndike was successful in toppling a mistaken theory, the doctrine of formal discipline. In its place he put one that was largely vacuous. Despite these criticisms, Thorndike defined most of the issues that dominate discussions of transfer to the present day."

Critique of Thorndike's Ideas About Individual Differences

As with learning and transfer, Thorndike offered a revolutionary new view of individual differences in ability. While he was successful in overthrowing faculty psychology—the concept of general abilities such as reasoning, memory, perception—his particular theory of ability has not survived. Thorndike's conceptualization that ability depends on specific knowledge is amazingly consistent with modern theories of expertise (Chi, Glaser, & Farr, 1988) and intelligence (Sternberg, 1990) that emphasize the domain-specificity of cognitive ability. Yet, he can be criticized for having too limited a view of the components of ability—that is, by assuming that ability depended mainly on the number of specific S–R connections that a person possessed.

From today's vantage point it appears that Thorndike was essentially correct in his insistence that individual differences in performance on cognitive tasks were related to differences in knowledge—a view that was highly controversial in his day. Yet, he erred in having too limited a conception of the nature of knowledge—by focusing only on S–R connections. Again, his ideas seem incomplete rather than incorrect. Sternberg (1990, p. 91) points out that "perhaps because Thorndike's main body of work was in the learning theory tradition rather than the psychometric tradition, his contributions to theory and measurement of intelligence never caught on" However, it is interesting to note that ultimately the psychometric approach to ability differences largely has given way to a modern version of the learning-theory approach. Although Thorndike's specific theory has not survived well, his general approach now dominates the field.

Overall, the major limitation of Thorndike's theoretical contributions to educational psychology is a dependence solely on connectionism as the underlying framework. Although building a psychology based on connectionism is a major accomplishment, the 20th century has also produced several other major frameworks that enrich the field, including information processing and constructivism. Using the arsenal of new tools for analyzing human cognition, researchers working in the second half of the 20th century have complemented the work that Thorndike began.

Critique of Thorndike's Products

All of Thorndike's most popular products—his dictionaries, school books, and tests—are no longer widely available in their original forms, but subsequent developments in these areas have been forever influenced by Thorndike's original work. Thus, although the specific products are no longer used, the principles he used to create them are still a strong influence in the field. Yet, like his contributions to ideas, the principles he used to construct his products have been supplemented with a clearer vision of the nature of cognitive processing during learning, the analysis of what is learned, and the role of social contexts in learning.

Critique of Thorndike's Values

Finally, Thorndike's values—faith in the methodological rigor of science, his love of empirical data, and his interest in practical issues—continue to shape educational psychology. However, his values have been extended in some useful ways. In addition to the experimental methods that Thorndike so gloriously demonstrated, today's educational psychologists have added other scientific methodologies to their arsenal, including observational techniques and computer simulation techniques. Instead of relying only on quantitative data, today's educational psychologists value the appropriate use of qualitative measures as well. Instead of speaking mainly about how psychology can be applied to education, today's educational psychologists often see the relation as a two-way street in which educational issues also enrich psychology (Mayer, 1992). While retaining the solid values inherited from Thorndike, today's generation of educational psychologists have the opportunity to expand them in interesting new directions.

His later work on social issues (which was not as influencial as his earlier work in educational psychology) has been criticized for supporting questionable social recommendations such as implementing a program of eugenics and developing quantitative evaluations of people's character (Beatty, 1998). Like many other progressives of Thorndike's generation, a faith in science to solve social problems may have blinded him to the foreseeable consequences of his social recommendations. Ironically, the shortcomings of Thorndike's foray into sociology occurred when he abandoned his own values of basing practical recommendations on scientific methods and empirical data.

CONCLUSION

Reviewing the remarkable career of the world's first and foremost educational psychologist has been an enlightening and inspiring experience for me. Although I was born around the time that E. L. Thorndike died, I feel that I have somehow gotten a glimpse of him through researching this article. For the privilege of becoming better acquainted with this great man, I am grateful. It is a humbling experience to see that even at the close of educational psychology's first 100 years as a science, we are still grappling with some of the same issues that Thorndike addressed at the beginning.

It is clear that what Thorndike brought to our field was not technical expertise in instrumentation or quantitative methods nor even a rigorous training in science, but rather an endless curiosity about educational questions, an unfaltering faith that the methods of science could provide answers, and an unquestionable brilliance in creating methods and theories to assist him.

His ideas concerning learning, transfer, and individual differences have stood the test of time and have remained core themes in educational psychology for a century. His products reflect an optimism that the methods of science can be used in the service of helping students learn, and have been true success stories in the history of psychology's inventions. Yet, in my opinion, Thorndike's most important contributions to educational psychology concern the values he instilled in our field. These are the values that still shape our field today: favoring science over speculation, careful analysis and quantification over vague summaries, and understanding practical problems over purely theoretical ones.

At the start of the 20th century, Thorndike (1903, p. 3) eloquently summarized the challenge of educational psychology: "The work of education is to make changes in human minds and bodies. To control these changes we need knowledge of the causes which bring them to pass." To accomplish this goal, the new science of educational psychology would need to be based on clear data, gained through rigorous experiments that were related to educational issues. As educational psychology enters its second century as a science, the most important contribution of the world's first educational psychologist is his storehouse of values.

Ultimately, Thorndike's most fundamental legacy for educational psychology is his vision of the role of science in solving educational problems: "He made scientific method the hallmark of educational research and demonstrated its application in pedagogic practices" (Russell, 1949, p. 27). For 100 years, Thorndike's straightforward advice—gleaned from both his words and deeds—has been to base theories on clear data and plenty of it, to use scientific methods to gather data, and to study theoretically interesting issues that have practical implications. To the extent that educational psychology continues to follow this advice, there is reason for optimism in educational psychology's second century.

ACKNOWLEDGMENT

I appreciate the resources available at the Main Library of the University of California, Santa Barbara, as well as those available at Shields Library of the University of California, Davis. I also appreciate the helpful comments of Barry Zimmerman. Correspondence should be sent to: Richard E. Mayer, Department of Psychology, University of California, Santa Barbara, CA 93106.

REFERENCES

Anderson, L. W., Krathwohl, D. R., Airasian, P. W., Cruikshank, K., Mayer, R. E., Pintrich, P. R., & Raths, J. (2001). *A taxonomy of learning for teaching: A revision of Bloom's taxonomy of educational objectives*. New York: Addison-Wesley-Longman.

Barnhart, C. L. (1949). Contributions of Dr. Thorndike to lexicography. *Teachers College Record, 51,* 35–42.

Beatty, B. (1998). From laws of learning to a science of values: Efficiency and morality in Thorndike's educational psychology. *American Psychologist, 53,* 1145–1152.

Bitterman, M. E. (1969). Thorndike and the problem of animal intelligence. *American Psychologist, 24*, 444–453.

Boldyreff, J. W. (1949). Psychology and the social order. *Teachers College Record, 51*, 762–777.

Bower, G. H., & Hilgard, E. R. (1981). Thorndike's connectionism. In G. H. Bower & E. R. Hilgard, *Theories of learning* (5th ed, pp. 21–48). Englewood Cliffs, NJ: Prentice-Hall.

Bulatao, E. Q., Fulcher, R., & Evans, R. B. (1992). Statistical data on the American Psychological Association. In R. B. Evans, V. S. Sexton, & T. C. Cadwallader (Eds.), *The American Psychological Association: A historical perspective* (pp. 391–394). Washington, DC: American Psychological Association.

Burnham, J. C. (1972). Thorndike's puzzle boxes. *Journal of the History of the Behavioral Sciences, 8*, 159–167.

Brown, J. F., & Feder, D. D. (1934). Thorndike's theory of learning as Gestalt psychology. *Psychological Bulletin, 31*, 426–437.

Chi, M. T. H., Glaser, R., & Farr, M. J. (Eds.). (1988). *The nature of expertise*. Hillsdale, NJ: Lawrence Erlbaum Associates.

Detterman, D. K., & Sternberg, S. J. (Eds.). (1993). *Transfer on trial*. Norwood, NJ: Ablex.

Dewsbury, D. A. (1998). Celebrating E. L. Thorndike a century after *Animal Intelligence*. *American Psychologist, 53*, 1121–1124.

Eisner, E. (1997, August-September). The promise and perils of alternate forms of data representation. *Educational Researcher, 26*(6), 4–20.

Galef, B. G. (1998). Edward Thorndike: Revolutionary psychologist, ambiguous biologist. *American Psychologist, 53*, 1128–1134.

Galton, F. (1883). *Inquiry into human faculty and its development*. London: Macmillan.

Gates, A. I. (1934). Edward Lee Thorndike: President-elect of the American Association for the Advancement of Science. *Science, 79*, 88–89.

Gates, A. I. (1949a). Edward L. Thorndike 1874–1949. *Psychological Review, 56*, 241–243.

Gates, A. I. (1949b). The writings of Edward L. Thorndike. *Teachers College Record, 51*, 20–31.

Grinder, R. E. (1989). Educational psychology: The master science. In M. C. Wittrock & F. Farley (Eds.), *The future of educational psychology*. Hillsdale, NJ: Lawrence Erlbaum Associates.

Goodenough, F. L. (1950). Edward Lee Thorndike: 1874–1949. *American Journal of Psychology, 63*, 291–301.

Hull, C. L. (1943). *Principles of behavior*. New York: Appleton-Century-Crofts.

Humphrey, G. (1949). Edward Lee Thorndike, 1874–1949. *British Journal of Psychology, 40*, 55–56.

Jensen, A. R. (1987). Individual differences in mental ability. In J. A. Glover & R. R. Ronning (Eds.), *Historical foundations of educational psychology* (pp. 61–88). New York: Plenum.

Joncich, G. (1962). Science: Touchstone for a new age in education. In G. M. Joncich (Ed.), *Psychology and the science of education: Selected writings of Edward L. Thorndike* (pp. 1–26). New York: Teachers College Press.

Joncich, G. (1966). Complex forces and neglected acknowledgments in the making of a young psychologist. Edward L. Thorndike and his teachers. *Journal of the History of the Behavioral Sciences, 2*, 43–50.

Joncich, G. (1968a). *The sane positivist: A biography of Edward L. Thorndike*. Middletown, CT: Wesleyan University Press.

Joncich, G. (1968b). E. L. Thorndike: The psychologist as professional man of science. *American Psychologist, 23*, 434–446.

Judd, C. H. (1908). The relation of special training and general intelligence. *Educational Review, 36*, 28–42.

Katona, G. (1940). *Organizing and memorizing*. New York: Columbia University.

Kuhn, T. S. (1970). *The structure of scientific revolutions*. Chicago: Chicago University Press.

Leary, D. E. (Ed.). (1990). *Metaphors in the history of psychology*. Cambridge, UK: Cambridge University Press.

Lepper, M. R., & Greene, D. (1978). *The hidden costs of reward.* Hillsdale, NJ: Lawrence Erlbaum Associates.

Lorge, I. (1940). Thorndike's contribution to the psychology of learning of adults. *Teachers College Record, 41,* 778–788.

Lorge, I. (1949). Edward L. Thorndike's publications from 1940 to 1949. *Teachers College Record, 51,* 42–45.

May, M. A. (1949). Selected writings from a connectionist's psychology. *Teachers College Record, 51,* 31–34.

Mayer, R. E. (1987). *Educational psychology: A cognitive approach.* New York: HarperCollins.

Mayer, R. E. (1992). Cognition and instruction: On their historical meeting within educational psychology. *Journal of Educational Psychology, 84,* 405–412.

Mayer, R. E. (1995). The search for insight: Grappling with Gestalt psychology's unanswered questions. In R. J. Sternberg & J. E. Davidson (Eds.), *The nature of insight* (pp. 3–32). Cambridge, MA: MIT Press.

Mayer, R. E. (1996). Learners as information processors: Legacies and limitations of educational psychology's second metaphor. *Educational Psychologist, 31,* 151–162.

Mayer, R. E., & Wittrock, M. C. (1996). Problem-solving transfer. In D. C. Berliner & R. C. Calfee (Eds.), *Handbook of educational psychology* (pp. 47–62). New York: Macmillan.

McKeough, A., Lupart, J., & Marini, A. (Eds.). (1995). *Teaching for transfer.* Mahwah, NJ: Lawrence Erlbaum Associates.

Meiklejohn, A. (1908). Is mental training a myth? *Educational Review, 37,* 126–141.

Moehlman, A. B. (1944). Edward Lee Thorndike, master teacher. *Nation's Schools, 34,* 19.

Otto, W. (1971). Thorndike's reading as reasoning: Influence and impact. *Reading Research Quarterly, 6,* 435–442.

Postman, L. (1962). Rewards and punishments in human learning. In L. Postman (Ed.), *Psychology in the making* (pp. 331–401). New York: Knopf.

Rippa, S. A. (1980). *Education in a free society.* New York: Longman.

Rock, R. T., Jr. (1940). Thorndike's contribution to the psychology of learning. *Teachers College Record, 41,* 751–761.

Romanes, G. J. (1882). *Animal intelligence.* New York: Appleton.

Russell, J. E. (1940). An appreciation of E. L. Thorndike. *Teachers College Record, 41,* 696–698.

Russell, W. F. (1949). Edward L. Thorndike, 1874–1949. *Teachers College Record, 51,* 26–28.

Singley, M. K., & Anderson, J. A. (1989). *The transfer of cognitive skill.* Cambridge, MA: Harvard University Press.

Skinner, B. F. (1938). *The behavior of organisms.* Englewood Cliffs, NJ: Prentice-Hall.

Spearman, C. (1927). *The abilities of man.* New York: Macmillan.

Stam, H. J., & Kalmanovitch, T. (1998). E. L. Thorndike and the origins of animal psychology. *American Psychologist, 53,* 1135–1144.

Stauffer, R. G. (1971). Thorndike's reading as reasoning: A perspective. *Reading Research Quarterly, 6,* 443–448.

Sternberg, R. J. (1990). *Metaphors of mind.* Cambridge, England: Cambridge University Press.

Sully, J. (1889). *Outlines of psychology.* New York: Appleton.

Teachers College Record. (1940). Publications from 1898 to 1940 by E. L. Thorndike. *Teachers College Record, 41,* 699–725.

Thompson, G. (1949). Obituary: Prof. Edward L. Thorndike. *Nature, 164,* 474.

Thorndike, E. L. (1898). Animal intelligence: An experimental study of the associative processes in animals. *Psychological Monographs, 2*(4, Whole No. 8).

Thorndike, E. L. (1903). *Educational psychology.* New York: Lemcke and Buechner.

Thorndike, E. L. (1906). *Principles of teaching based on psychology.* New York: Seiler.

Thorndike, E. L. (1910). The contribution of psychology to education. *Journal of Educational Psychology, 1,* 5–12.

Thorndike, E. L. (1911). *Animal intelligence*. New York: Macmillan.

Thorndike, E. L. (1913). *Educational psychology. Volume II: The learning process*. New York: Teachers College Press.

Thorndike, E. L. (1917). Reading as reasoning: A study of mistakes in paragraph reading. *Journal of Educational Psychology, 8*, 323–332.

Thorndike, E. L. (1918). The nature, purposes, and general methods of measurement of educational products. *National Society for the Study of Education Yearbook 17*(2), 16–24.

Thorndike, E. L., Bregman, E. D., Cobb, M. V., & Woodyard, E. I. (1926). *The measurement of intelligence*. New York: Teachers College, Columbia University.

Thorndike, E. L. (1932). *Fundamentals of learning*. New York: Teachers College, Columbia University.

Thorndike, E. L. (1935). *Thorndike–Century Junior Dictionary*. Chicago: Scott, Foresman.

Thorndike, E. L. (1936). Edward Lee Thorndike. In C. Murchison (Ed.), *A history of psychology in autobiography* (Vol. 3, pp. 263–270). Worcester, MA: Clark University Press.

Thorndike, E. L. (1948). On methods of memorizing poems and vocabularies. *Journal of Educational Psychology, 39*, 488–490.

Thorndike, E. L., & Woodworth, R. S. (1901). The influence of improvement in one mental function upon the efficiency of other functions. *Psychological Review, 8*, 247–261.

Thorndike, R. L. (1991). Edward L. Thorndike: A professional and personal appreciation. In G. A. Kimble, M. Wertheimer, & C. White (Eds.), *Portraits of pioneers in psychology* (Vol. 1, pp. 139–151). Washington, DC: American Psychological Association.

Tolman, E. C. (1932). *Purposive behavior in animals and men*. New York: Appleton-Century-Crofts.

Tolman, E.C. (1938). The determiners of behavior at a choice point. *Psychological Review, 45*, 1–41.

Wertheimer, M. (1959). *Productive thinking*. New York: Harper & Row.

Williams, J. (1978). Analysis of the *Journal of Educational Psychology*: Toward a definition of educational psychology. *Educational Psychologist, 12*, 290–296.

Woodworth, R. S. (1934). Edward Lee Thorndike: President of the American Association for the Advancement of Science. *Scientific Monthly, 38*, 187–189.

period, he developed a new lifestyle that afforded much exposure to the outdoors, and he improved his lung health.

Two of his teachers at the Central Normal School at Danville had urged him to continue his studies at Indiana University (IU). In 1901 he enrolled in the graduate program in psychology at that institution, but because many of his normal school courses did not transfer, he had to enroll as an undergraduate junior. However, in the course of the next 2 years, he was able to complete both his A. B. and A. M. degrees. During this time, Terman came under the tutelage of W. L. Bryan, E. H. Lindley, and J. A. Bergstrom; all three psychologists had earned their doctorates in psychology at Clark University under G. Stanley Hall. Terman read the classical literature in philosophy and psychology and found his classes at IU to be intellectually inspiring. He was especially interested in his readings on mental deficiency, criminality, and genius, and these experiences sparked a lifelong interest in the gifted. His master's degree thesis research was an experimental study of leadership and suggestibility in children. In the conclusions to the study, he noted a strong link between leadership and intelligence, a relationship he would later pursue in his longitudinal research on gifted children.

Upon completion of his master's degree in 1903, Terman received a fellowship to study for a Ph.D. at Clark University. With money borrowed from his parents, Terman set off to Worcester, Massachusetts, with his wife Anna and their two children. Terman began work toward a doctorate in psychology with courses under the tutelage of G. Stanley Hall, E. C. Sanford, and W. H. Burnham, who were eminent psychologists in the field. In addition to the challenging faculty, Terman found his classmates, such as Arnold Gesell, Fred Kuhlmann, J. P. Porter, Charles Waddell, A. A. Cleveland, and E. B. Huey, to be very intellectually stimulating, and many of them would later become leaders in the emerging field of psychology. Terman's readings at Clark University included such leading theorists as Ebbinghaus, Stern, Spearman, Cattell, and Thorndike and led in his increasing interest in mental testing. Terman learned about the work of Alfred Binet through his classmate, E. B. Huey, who had spent a year in Europe.

A key research project of Terman's was a study of precocious development of children, which led him to focus his doctoral research in that area. His advisor, E. C. Sanford, offered little or no guidance, so Terman designed the project himself, developed tests and procedures, secured subjects from Worcester schools, carried out the testing procedures, analyzed the results, and wrote the dissertation. His subjects were seven very bright boys and seven boys of low ability. His dissertation title, "Genius and Stupidity: A Study of Some of the Intellectual Processes of Seven Bright and Seven Stupid Boys" (1906), incorporates terminology that would not be acceptable today. The subtests that he devised, included measures of inventiveness and creative imagination, logical processes, mathematical operations, mastery of language, insight, ease of learning to play chess, memory, and motoric ability. As expected, the bright boys were superior on all the intellectual tasks.

Although this dissertation experience led Terman to believe initially that intelligence was multifaceted (or multifactorial in the current vocabulary), Terman would later adopt the IQ as a single index of mental ability. He also concluded that intelligence was a product of natural endowment or genetic determination. In spite of misgivings by Hall about the statistical nature of Terman's dissertation, Terman passed his final orals in 1906. In the years to come, Hall eventually came to see mental testing as a valuable contribution to psychological understanding.

Terman's tubercular symptoms reappeared around the time of his graduation from Clark University, and this made the geographic location of his subsequent employment the primary selection criterion for him. Terman decided to relocate in California because of the climate, but he could not find a collegiate post. So he accepted instead a school principalship in San Bernardino, California, but his relocation eventually proved to be advantageous when a university faculty position opened in Los Angeles. He served as principal for a year before moving to the Los Angeles Normal School in 1907. When he joined the faculty at the Los Angeles Normal School, he renewed contacts with a former classmate from Clark University, Arnold Gessell, who became a lifelong friend as well as a prominent developmental psychologist. After 4 productive years at Los Angeles Normal School, Terman was offered an assistant professorship at Stanford University, which he accepted. The Terman family moved to Palo Alto in 1910, and Terman began his career as a scholar, researcher, teacher, writer, and leader in education and psychology.

HIGHLIGHTS OF TERMAN'S CAREER AT STANFORD

During his early years at Stanford, Terman's health continued to improve, and he was able to increase his personal and professional levels of activity. His professional productivity increased dramatically, and he began to enjoy considerable national visibility. In 1917, the United States Army decided to develop screening tests for new recruits coming into the Army and authorized Robert M. Yerkes to organize a committee of psychologists to work on the task. Yerkes invited Terman to work on the committee to develop tests for the Army. Terman reported to Yerkes that his (Terman's) graduate student, Arthur Otis, had developed a set of mental tests that could be administered to groups of people.

When the Yerkes' committee met at the Vineland Training School in New Jersey late May and early June of 1917, the tests that Otis had developed were used as a model for the new Army tests. After extensive trials, the *Army Examination Alpha* test was approved for administration by the U.S. Army on December 24, 1917. It was followed by another test, *Army Examination Beta* that was developed to test army recruits or personnel who could not read English well.

Terman worked with the committee for 2 years, 1 year as a civilian part-time worker and another year as a full time Army officer. Yerkes and Terman were appointed majors in the United States Army in 1917 and 1918 respectively. After receiving his commission, Terman took leave from Stanford and moved with his family to live in Washington, D.C. to work on the testing project. Terman was discharged from the Army in April 1919, and he returned to his position at Stanford University.

After the war, the use of group intelligence tests grew rapidly, especially for school and work applications. Although the Army testing program was severely criticized later for what we would now recognize were major psychometric shortcomings, it represented the first major application of psychological tests in the U.S. military.

Testing Children in School

Terman and Yerkes next made plans to develop intelligence tests for group administration to children and submitted a grant proposal for financial support for the project, which was ultimately funded. Edward Lee Thorndike of Columbia University joined them in this venture. A *National Intelligence Test* was designed for use in Grades 3 to 8. The subtests were derived from the Army tests, and the World Book Company published it.

Independently Terman began work on a high school group intelligence test for Grades 7 to 12, the *Terman Group Test of Mental Ability*, and it too would be published by the World Book Company. A short time later, Terman began work with Truman Kelley and Giles Ruch on what would become the first major, standardized test of academic achievement, the *Stanford Achievement Test*. The norming sample included 350,000 children, which was an enormous undertaking for that time period. The psychometric qualities of this new test far surpassed any previous test. Terman's development of this intelligence test and this achievement test led to widespread efforts in American and foreign schools to use these tests to evaluate and place students for academic purposes.

The Stanford Psychology Department

Terman was appointed as Head of the Department of Psychology in 1922. In his efforts to build a small department, he hired Edward K. Strong in 1923 in the area of vocational and industrial psychology. Strong achieved fame for his Strong Vocational Interest Blank and for the impressive research it generated. In the same year, Terman hired Truman Kelley as a specialist in statistical methods. When Kelley left for Harvard University later, Terman hired one of his own graduates, Quinn McNemar, who soon achieved national and international recognition as a psychologist–statistician.

As department head, Terman was active in Stanford University affairs and was instrumental in establishing advanced programs of study for gifted students in their junior and senior years. He continued to seek out and hire psychologists who were or would become leaders in their psychological specialties and thereby build the reputation of Stanford's Psychology Department to be one of the most prominent in the United States.

Longitudinal Study of Gifted Youth

Terman began gathering data on children who scored at high levels on mental tests in 1911, but he did not receive financial support for his effort for a decade. In 1921, the Commonwealth Foundation provided support for a major study of gifted youth. The first results of that research, published in 1925, dispelled many of the myths that were then prevalent about gifted youth. It was widely believed that the gifted individuals were an eccentric lot who displayed poor psychological and physical adjustment. Although Terman's sample of 1,500 12-year-olds with IQs above 135 was probably biased in favor of middle and upper middle class students, they were found to be superior in their mental and physical adjustment on a wide variety of measures. It is interesting to note that Terman took a personal interest in a number of his subjects in the longitudinal study, and he even counseled and financially supported some of them.

This longitudinal research continued throughout Terman's lifetime and culminated in five widely cited volumes that documented the lifelong achievements of the group. The most recent report (Holahan & Sears, 1995) focused on the Terman sample in old age and shows them to be intellectually dynamic and physically active.

Terman's research is still widely cited by researchers and school program developers (Subotnik & Arnold, 1995). The current Director of the Terman Study of the Gifted at Stanford University is Dr. Albert Hastorf. No further data gatherings are planned on surviving members of the sample, but a number of analyses of existing data are still being carried out. Dr. Hastorf summarized the results of the Terman research as follows:

> Terman's original goal was to describe both the social and physical characteristics of a group of intellectually talented children. They were identified at a relatively early age and Terman demonstrated, to his satisfaction, that intellectually gifted youngsters were happier and healthier than children in general. Furthermore, they were high achievers in school, prone to be accelerated by the school system, and seem to have responded positively to that. Their occupational success was considerable, both in terms of occupational status and monetary earnings. From Terman's standpoint the study supported his position that intellectual ability as tested was predictive of educational and occupational success. (1997, p. 7)

Terman's Graduate Students

Terman's graduate students admired him tremendously as a leading professional and research psychologist of his time and as a model scholar. He was known to set very high performance standards for all who worked with him, to be extremely supportive of students and colleagues, and to exhibit the highest levels of personal dedication and work.

All of these personal qualities were evident as he sought to place and guide his students. A particular problem at the time that Terman confronted was widespread anti-Semitism. Terman's level of resourcefulness in combating this discrimination was evident in the case of one of his most able graduate students, Harry Israel, who was Jewish. Terman feared that Israel's success in psychology would be impeded by his ancestry. Israel did, however, succeed in getting an offer from the Psychology Department at the University of Wisconsin, which he promptly accepted. When Terman met Israel a few days later, Terman urged Harry to change his last name if he wished to be successful academically. Harry Israel asked Terman to suggest another name, and Terman obliged with "Harlow" or "Crowell." Israel liked "Harlow" best and changed his name accordingly. At the University of Wisconsin, Harry Harlow established one of the leading primate labs of the world, published major research results on monkey mother–baby relationships, and was elected president of the American Psychological Association at the prime of his career. However, not all of Terman's efforts to assist his students met with similar success. Another student of Terman's, who was also of Jewish ancestry, became so discouraged by ethnic prejudice that he dropped out of the program before graduation.

The Presidency of the American Psychological Association

In 1923 Terman was elected president of the American Psychological Association. This achievement was a reflection of Terman's considerable national stature despite having pursued an applied career in psychology. In his presidential address, Terman argued that mental testing was an essential part of experimental psychology and that mental testing would prove invaluable in the study of individual differences. Terman envisioned the new testing movement that he had helped to launch as a door to a wide range of new research issues in psychology. Theoretically, Terman emphasized biological determinism and hereditary bases for individual differences, and he saw mental tests as a sound way of classifying individuals for different levels of employment or training.

Just before assuming the presidency, Terman became embroiled in a protracted nature–nurture debate. In 1922, William C. Bagley of Columbia University published an article in *School and Society* entitled, "Educational Determinism: Or Democracy and The IQ," in which he argued that too much emphasis was placed on heredity by proponents of IQ testing. Bagley felt that the IQ testing movement threatened democracy and diminished the role of education in the development of youth. The communications between Terman and Bagley about the roles of nature and nurture in education were filled with animosity.

The scope of the battle grew larger with the publication of a series of articles in the *New Republic* magazine by the famous columnist Walter Lippman. Lippman attacked intelligence tests and the testing movement in general by arguing that these tests surely could not measure general mental ability. He also argued that intelligence is not fixed or unchangeable, and test results might be used in ways that would be harmful to students.

Terman's reply was also published in the *New Republic* under the lengthy title "The, Great Conspiracy; or the Impulse Imperious of Intelligence Testers, Psychoanalyzed and Exposed by Mr. Lippman." Terman used a strong satirical style to suggest that Lippman really did not know or understand the phenomenon he was attacking. Terman disagreed with Lippman on several major psychometric issues, and Terman concluded that, although there was still little evidence concerning the impact of the environment on intelligence, many psychologists believed that heredity played a major role.

The nature–nurture question had not really been addressed empirically when the debate began, but it rapidly became a target of research after the debate was joined. In 1924, one of Terman's graduate students, Barbara Burks, completed a study of Frank and Lillian Gilbreth and their 11 children, all of whom were intellectually gifted. Burks concluded that the genealogy of the family gave rise to the consistent intellectual superiority of the offspring. Terman's interest in studying the inheritability of intelligence continued to grow during the following years. He supervised Barbara Burks' dissertation research on the intelligence of natural and foster parents and their children, and the results led her to conclude that the influence of heredity was greater than nurturing conditions. This strengthened Terman's belief that genetic factors were chief determinents of intelligence.

Continuation of the Terman Project at Stanford

Terman retired from Stanford in 1942 and embarked on a variety of professional activities including follow-ups of the participants in the longitudinal study. Volume Four of the *Genetic Studies of Genius* was published in 1947 under the title *The Gifted Child Grows Up* with Terman and Melita Oden as primary authors and Nancy Bayley, Helen Marshall, Quinn McNemar, and Ellen Sullivan as associated contributors. They concluded that gifted children often languished in school and that acceleration of these students by early admission, grade skipping, and early admission to college would be desirable to help them achieve their potential.

Volume Five of the *Genetic Studies of* Genius was published in 1959 with Terman and Melita Oden as authors (although Terman had died in 1956). The title of this volume was *The Gifted Group at Mid-Life*. It is interesting to read Terman's ultimate conclusion about the nature–nurture issue in this volume long after the debate with Lippman: "It should go without saying that neither this [the Concept Mastery Test] nor any other test of intelligence measures native ability uninfluenced by schooling and other environmental factors" (p. 53). Clearly Terman had concluded that nature and nurture were both involved in the development of intelligence. The extraordinary accomplishments of the gifted children in Terman's longitudinal study were well documented in this volume. Although none of these subjects achieved international fame or eminence, their attainment of high-level professional occupations was substantial and their salaries were far above the norm. These gifted subjects were also found to be active in societies, organizations, and political groups. Overall their achievements and successes far exceeded those of the general population.

This longitudinal study of gifted youth and adults was perhaps the most enduring of Terman's many contributions, and it continues to this day at Stanford University. In 1995, volume six, *Genetic Studies of Genius, The Gifted Group In Old Age* by Carole Holahan and Robert Sears was published. In this most recent follow-up study, the survivors of the Terman sample emerged as intellectually and physically active, productive, and living rich and engaging lives.

MAJOR PSYCHOLOGICAL ACHIEVEMENTS

Lewis Terman's primary achievements in his professional career were his development of intelligence testing, his international promotion of the testing movement, his pioneering longitudinal research on giftedness, his impact on school programs for the gifted, and his professional leadership in the field of psychology. Let me consider each of these seminal contributions in turn.

Development of Intelligence Tests

In 1912, Terman published an article entitled "A Tentative Revision and Extension of the Binet–Simon Measurement Scale of Intelligence" and in 1916 a full-scale version (Terman, 1916) of the *Stanford–Binet* (SB). Borrowing a procedure from William Stern (1914), Terman employed an individualized assessment format, and he interpreted the results using a single index—an intelligence quotient (IQ). The IQ measure is defined as the ratio of mental age to chronological age, multiplied by 100. Terman's test and index of intelligence would become recognized worldwide by psychologists and educators as a major measure of intellectual ability. Hundreds of research studies have showed that the Stanford–Binet IQ scores were highly predictive of school achievement and moderately predictive of vocational achievements.

The Testing Movement

The second great impact of Lewis Terman in psychology and education was his leading role in launching the pencil-and-paper testing movement. Following the model that guided the development of the *Army Alpha Intelligence Tests*, Terman worked with committees of psychologists to develop the *National Intelligence Test* in 1919. Terman also began to work independently on the *Terman Group Test of Mental Ability* for high school students in Grades 7 to 12. All of these tests were developed for use in schools, and Terman's goal was to help schools and teachers better understand and adapt instruction to meet the specific needs of individual students. Terman went on to develop the first major standardized school achievement test, the *Stanford Achievement Test* (Grades 2–8). The Stanford Achievement Test remains in use today and is a model of excellence in school achievement testing.

Testing of academic achievements and cognitive skills of students is a major activity of American schools. Current concerns about the lack of achievement of many American youth have led educators and parents to set higher standards at the state and national levels. These events have led state and federal leaders to appreciate anew the value of scientific instruments to determine students' academic success. The testing movement set in motion by Terman and others continues to play a major role in American education.

Longitudinal Study

Terman's next major accomplishment was the launching of the long-range study of 1,528 gifted children in 1920, which continues to the present day although some of the surviving subjects are more than 90 years of age. This study set the stage for a new understanding of precocious youth, most often called "gifted," but also labeled "genius" at the beginning of the 20th century (Fetterman, 2000). The early results of this research showed gifted and talented children and youth were physically healthy, socially well-adjusted, and were likely to go on to successful careers in the professions and the arts. At the same time, Terman discovered that intelligence was no guarantee of success; the professional attainments of some of these talented youngsters would be very modest. Terman's detailed study of these unsuccessful subjects showed that they lacked social skills, personality factors, and a drive to succeed (Fancher, 1985).

Periodic follow-ups of the Terman sample have shown the survivors to be physically and intellectually active in their old age (Holahan & Sears, 1995), as they had been in their youth and midlife. The continuing productivity of these gifted persons may be directly related to their superior physical and mental health in childhood.

School Programs for the Gifted

Terman's longitudinal study gave rise to the fourth great impact of Lewis Terman— the development of school programs for gifted and talented youth. Terman's pioneering influence was augmented substantially by the efforts of the National Association for Gifted Children. Although Terman himself did little in the way of defining programs for the gifted, his research was interpreted as calling for programs to meet the special needs of gifted youth. All of the states in the union now recognize and promote special services for gifted and talented youth. That same kind of program promotion and development is being extended throughout the world through the efforts of the World Council on Gifted and Talented Children. In addition there are now full-time, public residential schools for the gifted in 12 American states and several foreign countries. Numerous journals now publish research and development in the field of gifted education, such as: *Gifted Child Quarterly, Journal for the Education of the Gifted, Gifted and Talented International, Gifted Child Today, Journal for Secondary Gifted Education, and Gifted Education International*. The biennial meetings of the World Council on Gifted and Talented Children draw representatives from all over the globe.

Professional Leadership

After Terman's rise to the position of head of the Psychology Department at Stanford University, he led that department to world-class status. As president of the American Psychological Association, Terman brought test development, intelligence testing, and the study of gifted children to the forefront in psychology and education. Throughout his life Terman served on numerous professional committees, interacted with the great pioneering scholars of his time, and trained a host of graduate students who became leaders in psychology and education. Three of Terman's students became presidents of the American Psychological Association: Quinn McNemar, Harry Harlow, and Truman Kelly. Other students of Terman who achieved high-level recognition for their creative achievements in psychology were: Arthur Otis, Giles M. Ruch, Maud A. Merrill, Florence L. Goodenough, James C. DeVoss, Catherine M. Cox, and Robert G. Bernreuter. Finally, Terman's impact on the fields of psychology and education may be judged by his having served as editor or associate editor of 13 publications, his publication of 15 books and 5 monographs, 32 book chapters, and 139 articles and 39 critiques and reviews in professional journals. Ironically, this great leader in education and psychology noted in his autobiography (1961) that he had scored at the 90th percentile on the Bernreuter Introversion Scale. Clearly, Terman had to overcome a very reserved personality along with lung health problems in order to achieve eminence!

EVALUATIONS OF TERMAN IMPACT ON PSYCHOLOGY, EDUCATION, AND SCHOOLS

The *Stanford–Binet Intelligence Scale* has been a preeminent measure of cognitive ability since it was first published in 1916. Moreover, the nature and origins of intelligence remains at the forefront of current discourse, such as the controversy over the recent book entitled *The Bell Curve* (Herrnstein & Murray, 1994). The works of two leading educational psychologists of our time, Robert Sternberg and Howard Gardner, focus on issues of mental ability and intelligence. Although Sternberg's and Gardner's conceptual models of intelligence differ from Terman's, especially regarding their rejection of single indices of intelligence and their discounting of the role of inheritance, it is noteworthy that the *Stanford–Binet Intelligence Scale* and the *Wechsler Intelligence Scales for Children* continue to dominate the field of individual testing of intelligence. Through group testing of intelligence, which Terman helped to pioneer,educational and school psychologists have come to understand the differences among children, youth, and adults in their cognitive capacities for learning, thinking, and solving problems. These include tests such as the *Otis–Lennon Mental Ability Test* and the *Cognitive Abilities Test*.

Terman's efforts to get schools to recognize the academic precocity of high IQ children and accelerate the curriculum and instruction for them are especially noteworthy. He saw clearly from his research that gifted and talented students had special educational needs that could not be met by a standard mid-range curriculum at each grade level. His research revealed that the ultimate levels of success of these youth also depended on their personal, social, and motivational characteristics as well as their high IQ. Although there has always been much debate and controversy concerning the causes of cognitive and affective characteristics of students, the reality of these differences is abundantly clear to teachers, psychologists, and parents. Efforts to accommodate these differences have led to the "inclusion" movement of the 1990s, which rejects tracking by students' mental ability (Chapman, 1988). If Terman were alive today, he might argue that these inclusion efforts actually represent a new form of tracking, namely "tracking by age," which is based on the questionable assumption that students' age differences are more important for instruction than their cognitive differences.

In general, contemporary school leaders and teachers recognize that youth at the extreme ends of the mental ability curve do need special curricula and methods of instruction. As a result of Terman's emphasis on intelligence, many American and foreign schools offer special programs for youth of very high ability. In addition, there are governmentally sponsored special schools offering advanced educational programs at the secondary level for highly able youth. Many American states mandate and financially support special school programs for gifted children. Terman's influence is also evident in college courses on the gifted and talented, in the inservice training and certification of teachers of the gifted and talented, in the proliferation of books and journals about the gifted and talented, and in the many national and international organizations promoting services for the gifted and talented. To be sure, Terman mainly opened the territory of the gifted and talented for others, but the imprint of his work remains evident after nearly a century.

Perhaps a most notable sign of Terman's eminence was his lifelong professional association and friendship with leading psychologists and educators of his time. His contacts were sustained through professional meetings and conferences, cooperative projects, personal visits, and above all, correspondence. The dozens of boxes of copies of his letters, now housed in the library at Stanford University, represent a "who's who" of psychology and education from 1912 to 1956: E. L.

Thorndike, Arthur Otis, Leta Hollingsworth, Robert Yerkes, Arnold Gesell, Fred Kuhlmann, W. W. Charters, Elwood Cubberley, E. G. Boring, Robert Woodworth, Maud Merrill, Florence Goodenough, and Robert Bernreuther. As noted earlier, several of these people were his personal graduate students who went on to leadership roles in psychology and education.

Despite Terman's many academic achievements, he was self-critical about his failure to get advanced training in statistics and psychometrics at Clark University, but he seemed to gain competence in both areas later through his own self development and consultation with his many excellent colleagues at Stanford University. However, he was never known as a leading theorist or psychometician, and perhaps this paucity of statistical training proved to be a handicap.

Perhaps the most severe criticism of Terman dealt with his conclusions about the inheritability of intelligence and his acceptance of the tenets of the eugenics movement, especially its advocacy of selective breeding and sterilization of less able people (Minton, 1988). Although Terman was never active in furthering these goals of the Eugenics Society, he believed nevertheless that it was in the best interest of society to study the problem of high birth rates among less able people and low birth rates among professional and high IQ families. He served for a time on the Advisory Committee of the American Eugenics Society and was also a charter member of the Human Betterment Foundation, along with the president of Stanford University, David Starr Jordan (Minton, 1988). When the Nazis in Germany eagerly embraced enforced sterilization in the 1930s, Terman abandoned both eugenics groups. Throughout his years of involvement with the American Eugenics Society and the Human Betterment Foundation, Terman's major focus was on research rather than social interventions.

TERMAN'S ENDURING LEGACY

Through his research and development activities at Stanford University and through his inspiration of others, Terman help to found a field of research that eventually influenced psychology and education throughout the world (Terman, 1925; Cox, 1926; Burks, Jensen, & Terman, 1930; Terman & Oden, 1959; Terman & Oden, 1947). Building on the work of Binet and others, Terman developed the first major standardized test of school achievement that became a model for all later standardized achievement tests. His long-term longitudinal study of the gifted brought us new understanding of the assets, problems, and long-term predictability of gifted children. Finally, his many research publications fostered the field of gifted education and the development of school programs for gifted, talented, and precocious youth. The emergence of these school programs has also opened a new field of research on the impact of school and home environments on the gifted.

Terman's work influenced a legion of prominent psychologists such as: Arthur Otis, David Wechsler, Robert Yerkes, R. B. Cattell, Hans Eysenck, J. P. Guilford,

Lloyd G. Humphreys, Philip Vernon, Cyril Burt, John Horn, Arthur Jensen, John Ravens, Sandra Scarr, Richard Snow, John Carroll, Robert Sternberg, Howard Gardner, and a host of others. Their subsequent contributions define our current understanding of intelligence and related cognitive processes.

In educational psychology and education in general, the Terman legacy is evident in researchers and educators who focus on issues of identification of the gifted and talented, characteristics of the gifted in the school setting, grouping and teaching the gifted, educational problems of the gifted and their counseling needs, and long-term achievement of the gifted. These researchers and educators of the gifted include: Abraham Tannenbaum, A. H. Passow, James Gallagher, E. Paul Torrance, Dorothy Sisk, Julian Stanley, Camilla Benbow, Joseph Renzulli, Joyce VanTassel-Baska, Carolyn Callahan, Barbara Clark, Nicholas Colangelo, Sally Reis, Rena Subotnik, Kurt Heller, Roberta Milgram, Joan Freeman, Sidney Moon, Ann Robinson and a host of others. New work in the field of gifted education is published widely throughout the world in such foreign journals as *Gifted and Talented International, Gifted Education International*, and *High Ability Studies* and in such American journals as *Gifted Child Quarterly*, the *Journal of Gifted Education*, and the *Journal of Secondary Gifted Education*.

Terman's legacy is perhaps greatest in fostering deeper understandings of gifted and talented children (Fancher, 1985). He dispelled myths of gifted youngsters' abnormal personality and sought to provide greater understanding of their successes and failures. Although there may be some problems for the gifted and talented youth in their peer relationships and their response to a conventional school curriculum, we know now that most gifted and talented youth enjoy good physical and mental health. In midlife, their careers blossom in abundant professional successes— degrees, publications, and recognition of achievements. In later life they remain physically and intellectually active and productive (Holahan & Sears, 1995).

In closing, Terman said in his autobiography, "My favorite of all psychologists is Binet; not because of his intelligence test, which was only a by-product of his life's work, but because of his originality, insight, and open-mindedness, and because of his rare charm of personality that shines through all his writings." (Terman, 1961). The same can indeed be said of Lewis Terman. I have read his correspondence over the years with the greats and lesser stars in the fields of psychology and educational psychology, and I see a charm and gentleness of personality combined with creative insight that were the base of his great and original productivity. He was surely one of the major pioneers of our fields. I agree with Shurkin (1992) who, in her study of the Terman legacy concluded that "Terman's contributions to the social sciences and to society are historic whatever his flaws" (p. 296). We may now be well *Beyond Terman* (Subotnik & Arnold, 1995), but the research trail he pioneered leads on and continues to increase our understanding of gifted and talented youth.

REFERENCES

Bouchard, T. H. (1994). Genes, environment and personality. *Science, 264*, 1700.

Burks, B. D., Jensen, D. W., & Terman, L. M. (1930). *Genetic studies of genius: Vol. III, The promise of youth, follow-up studies of a thousand gifted Youth.* Stanford, CA: Stanford University Press.

Chapman, P. C. (1988). *Schools as sorters, Lewis M. Terman, applied psychology, and the intelligence testing movement.* New York: New York University Press.

Cox, C. M. (1926). *Genetic studies of genius: Vol. 1, The early mental traits of three hundred geniuses.* Stanford, CA: Stanford University Press.

Fancher, R. E. (1985). *The intelligence men: Makers of the IQ controversy.* New York: Norton.

Feldhusen, J. F. (2000). Terman. In R. E. Sternberg (Ed.), *Handbook of intelligence* (pp. 1063–1068). New York: Cambridge University Press.

Fetterman, D. M. (2000). Terman's giftedness study. In R. E. Sternberg (Ed.), *Handbook of intelligence* (pp. 1059–1063). New York: Cambridge University Press.

Gagne, F. (1999). *Tracking talents: Identifying multiple talents through peer, teacher, and self nomination.* Waco, TX: Prufrock Press.

Hastorf, A. H. (1997). Lewis Terman's longitudinal study of the intellectually gifted: Early research, recent investigations and the future. *Gifted and Talented International, 12*(3), 3–7.

Herrnstein, R. J., & Murray, C. (1994). *The bell curve: Intelligence and class structure in American Life.* New York: The Free Press.

Holahan, C. K., & Sears, R. R. (1995). *Genetic studies of genius: The gifted group in later maturity.* Stanford, CA: Stanford University Press.

Minton, H. L. (1988). *Lewis M. Terman, pioneer in psychological testing.* New York: New York University Press.

Plomin, R. (1994). *Genetics and experience: The interplay between nature and nurture.* Thousand Oaks, CA: Sage Publications.

Seagoe, M. V. (1975). *Terman and the gifted.* Los Altos, CA: Kaufmann.

Shurkin, J. N. (1992). *Terman's kids.* Boston: Little, Brown.

Snyderman, M., & Rothman, S. (1990). *The IQ controversy, the media and public policy.* New Brunswick, NJ: Transaction Publishers.

Stern, W. (1914). *The psychological methods of testing intelligence.* Baltimore, MD: Warwick & York.

Subotnik, R. E., & Arnold, K. D. (1995). *Beyond Terman: Contemporary longitudinal studies of giftedness and talent.* Norwood, NJ: Ablex.

Terman, L. M. (1916). *Measurement of intelligence: An explanation of and a complete guide for the use of the Stanford revision and extension of the Binet–Simon Intelligence Scale.* Boston: Houghton Mifflin.

Terman, L. M. (1922). The great conspiracy, or the impulse imperious of intelligence testers, psychoanalyzed and exposed by Mr. Lippman. *New Republic, 33*, 116–120.

Terman, L. M. (1925). *Genetic studies of genius: Vol. 1, Mental and physical traits of a thousand gifted children.* Stanford, CA: Stanford University Press.

Terman, L. M. (1961). Lewis M. Terman: Trails to psychology. In C. Murchison (Ed.), A *history of psychology in autobiography* (Volume 2, pp. 297–331). New York: Russell & Russell.

Terman, L. M., & Oden, M. H. (1947). *Genetic studies of genius: Vol. IV, The gifted child grows up.* Stanford, CA: Stanford University Press.

Terman, L. M., & Oden, M. H. (1959). *Genetic studies of genius: Vol. V, The gifted group at mid Life.* Stanford, CA: Stanford University Press.

Thorndike, E. L. (1903). *Educational psychology.* New York: Lemcke & Buechner.

7

Maria Montessori: Contributions to Educational Psychology

Gerald L. Gutek
Loyola University, Chicago

Maria Montessori (1870–1952) is recognized internationally for her philosophy of early childhood education that is undergirded by her distinctive ideas on educational psychology. In addition to her contributions to education, Montessori, a pioneer in the women's movement, successfully overcame many of the barriers that limited women's opportunities in the late 19th and early 20th centuries.

BIOGRAPHICAL OVERVIEW

Maria Montessori was born in 1870, just 10 years after Italy's unification under the House of Savoy. The "new Italy," a consequence of the "risorgimento" led by Cavour and Garibaldi, was experiencing gradual industrialization. Strong regional disparities persisted, especially between the industrializing north and the traditional agricultural south. Internal migration brought large numbers of former peasants, searching for better jobs, to cities such as Milan and Rome. In these cities, urban slums arose to house the new industrial underclass. In one of Rome's poverty-impacted districts, the San Lorenzo quarter, Montessori established her first Casa dei Bambini, or Children's House, where she initially implemented her method of early childhood education.

Though experiencing social change, the Italy in which Montessori was born was still very traditional and conservative. "La Famiglia," the family, remained the primary institution that gave individual Italians their identification and, in turn, demanded their loyalty. With family, socio-economic class was an key determinant of a person's future. Traditionally ascribed gender and class roles still fixed women's career expectations. As wives and mothers, Italian women were expected to be their family's maternal sustaining force. With their roles so narrowly prescribed, higher and professional education were generally inaccessible to women. Middle class women, like Maria Montessori, might become primary school teachers but other career options were closed. However, Maria Montessori would successfully challenge and conquer 19th century Italy's social and educational conventions.

When Montessori began to create her method of education, teachers still dominated classrooms as central pedagogical agents. Instruction in Italian schools accentuated memorization of textbooks, recitation, and dictation. Ruled by fixed routines, schools discouraged children's freedom of movement, spontaneous learning, and creativity. Just as she challenged the conventions that prescribed women's lives, Montessori devised a method of education that was a radical departure from traditional schooling.

Maria Montessori was born in Chiaravalle, a hill town overlooking the Adriatic Sea, on August 31, 1870. She was the only child of Alessandro Montessori, a civil servant in the Italian government's tobacco monopoly, and Renilde Stoppani. Signor Montessori, a decorated army veteran, personified the traditional values of a middle class gentleman. Maria's mother was a niece of Father Antonio Stoppani, a recognized scholar–priest, poet, and natural scientist. When Maria challenged the social and educational system, she also had to confront her father who wanted her to follow the customary role of middle class women.

In 1875, Signor Montessori was assigned to Rome. Maria attended the local primary school on the Via di San Nicolo da Tolentino. At age 12, when she was to enter secondary school, Maria revealed what would become her characteristic independence when she announced her intention of attending a technical school. With her father's reluctant acquiescence, 13-year-old Maria Montessori enrolled in the Regia Scuola Technica Michelangelo Buonarroti, a state technical school, in 1883. After completing her studies at the Scuola Tecnica, Maria Montessori entered the Regio Istituto Technico Leonardo da Vinci to study engineering. Technical and engineering studies departed from the conventional educational patterns of young Italian women.

In 1890, Montessori made still another highly significant career decision when she left engineering to apply to medical school. Overcoming faculty objections, she was the first woman to be admitted to the University of Rome's School of Medicine. Surmounting gender-based obstacles, she proved to be an academically talented student winning scholarships in surgery, pathology, and medicine.

During her last 2 years of medical school, Montessori was an intern in the Children's Pediatric Hospital, an experience that moved her in the direction of her lifelong preoccupation with early childhood education. In 1896, Maria Montessori became the first Italian woman to receive the Doctorate of Medicine. Montessori then affiliated with the University of Rome's Clinica Psichiatrica, where she researched children's mental illnesses. In her paper, "Moral Education," presented at the Pedagogical Congress of Turin in 1898, Montessori argued that mental deficiency was primarily a pedagogical rather than a medical problem. Sponsored by the Ministry of Education, Montessori delivered a lecture series to Italian educators on the education of "feeble-minded" children.

From 1898 to 1900, Montessori was codirector, with Dr. Giuseppe Montesano, at the State Orthophrenic School (Montessori, 1964, pp. 31–32). A mutual attraction, then an affair took place between them. She bore Montesano's son, Mario, but the two did not marry. Mario Montessori was first raised by others and then publicly presented as Maria Montessori's nephew. She later officially recognized him as her son. Mario Montessori would become a devoted and trusted assistant who directed international Montessori activities after his mother's death in 1952.

While at the Othrophrenic School, Montessori continued her research on children's mental retardation and psychological disorders. Her research interest led her to the works of Jean-Marc Gaspard Itard (1774–1838) and Edouard Seguin, (1812–1880), two French physicians and psychologists. Itard, a specialist in Otiatria, worked with severely hearing-impaired children. His most famous case was his well-publicized treatment of the "wild boy of Aveyron." Trained in clinical observation as a physician, Montessori enthusiastically called Itard's work "the first attempts at experimental psychology" (Montessori, 1964, pp. 33–34.)

Seguin was founder of a training school for children from the insane asylums of Paris. He developed several techniques Montessori would adopt such as basing instruction on developmental stages, using didactic training materials, and training children to perform practical skills to give them some degree of independence (Myers, 1913, pp. 538–41). Based on her research on Itard and Seguin, Montessori developed two principles that were foundational for her method: (1) mental deficiency requires a special method of instruction as well as medical treatment; and (2) special instruction is more effective when used with didactic materials and apparatus. She hypothesized that methods used in training mentally deficient children could be applied to normal children, especially at an early age. She found that the mentally deficient child who *"has not the force to develop"* and the very young child *"who is not yet developed* are in some ways alike," especially in motor coordination and sensory and language development (Montessori, 1964, p. 44).

Between 1904 and 1908, Montessori lectured at the University of Rome's Pedagogical School on the application of anthropology and biology to education. At that time, she was influenced by the work in physical anthropology of Giuseppe Sergi, founder of the Institute of Experimental Psychology at the University of Rome. Drawing inferences from physical anthropology, Montessori underscored the importance of the scientific study of children by using quantitative methods of anatomical and morphological measurement. She emphasized the importance of measuring and recording children's physical variations during key developmental periods (Kramer, 1988, pp. 68–69, 96–97). She stressed the need to take precise physical measurements of children—height and weight, size of head, pelvis, limbs, and types of malformation—and the systematic recording of them in an individualized record, a biographical chart. Her lectures were published as *L'Antropolgia Pedagogica, Pedagogical Anthropology* (Montessori, 1913).

In 1906, Eduardo Talamo, Director of the Roman Association for Good Building, a philanthropic society, asked Montessori to establish a school in the poverty-ridden San Lorenzo district. To improve living conditions among Rome's poor, the Association had remodeled some older buildings into model tenements but now faced a practical problem in that a large number of preschool-age children were left unattended while their mothers worked. The Casa dei Bambini, Montessori's first school, enrolling children between ages 3 and 7, opened on January 6, 1907, at 58 Via dei Masi. Montessori saw the school as having social and pedagogical purposes. By being located in the tenement, the school was socially connected to the children's families and community. Educationally, it provided a laboratory to test her hypotheses on scientific pedagogy.

Montessori's approach at the Casa dei Bambini blended both freedom and prescription. She required the children and their parents to follow explicit regulations. Children were to come to school with clean bodies and clothing. Believing schools were most effective when closely linked to the children's homes and families, she urged parents to be actively engaged and supportive of their children's education.

Montessori designed the school's physical environment according to children's needs. Stressing the educative power of the structured environment, she made sure the classroom setting did not hamper children's freedom of movement. Tables and chairs were sized according to children's heights and weights. Washstands were accessible to younger children. The classroom was lined with low cupboards where children could reach instructional materials and take responsibility for returning them to their proper location. The school setting was designed to encourage children's sensory sensitivity and manual dexterity, to allow choice within a structured environment, and to cultivate independence and self-assurance in skill performance.

Instruction rested on the principle of encouraging children's growth at crucial developmental times called "sensitive periods" that were particularly relevant to specific kinds of learning activities such as exercising motor skills, language learning, and social adaptation. During these sensitive periods, the children performed activities and used self-correcting didactic materials and apparatus. The use of self-correcting educational materials was based on Montessori's belief that children acquired self-discipline and self-reliance by becoming aware of their mistakes and repeating a particular task until it was done correctly.

Montessori's success at the initial Casa dei Bambini led to the establishment of three more schools in Rome, one of which was in a middle class area of the city. Her success gained the attention of the Societa Umanitaria, the Humanitarian Society of Italy, which popularized and supported the Montessori method. With the Society's backing, a Montessori school was established in Milan, Italy's leading industrial city.

By 1910, Montessori, who now enjoyed a reputation as a significant and innovative educator in her native Italy, was attracting attention in other European nations and in North America, especially in the United States where over 100 Montessori schools were functioning. American supporters formed a national organization, the Montessori Educational Association, to promote the cause. Under the Association's sponsorship, Montessori came to the United States in 1913 to undertake a national lecture tour. Although she received an enthusiastic response and complimentary comments from journalists, several American educators, including progressive professors of education, criticized the applicability of Montessori's method to American children. University of Omaha professor Walter Halsey disparaged Montessori's method as a mere "fad promoted and advertised by a shrewd commercial spirit" that appealed to the "novelty loving American public" (Halsey, 1913, p. 63). A very negative critique came from William Heard Kilpatrick, a distinguished disciple of Dewey at Columbia University's Teachers College, who relegating Montessori's ideas to the mid-19th century, dismissed them as 50 years behind the times. Kilpatrick faulted the Montessori method for insufficiently encouraging children's socialization and sense of experimentation (Kilpatrick, 1914, pp. 62–63). By Montessori's second visit to the United States in 1917, interest had ebbed in her ideas and method. It would not revive until the 1950s.

In Europe, the Montessori approach registered more impressive gains. Montessori accepted the invitation of Barcelona's municipal government to establish schools and a training institute. For much of the interwar period until the outbreak of the Spanish Civil War, Spain was an important location for Montessori's work. There was also a brief flirtation between Montessori and Mussolini's Fascist regime in Italy. In 1927, the Fascist government invited Montessori to establish schools and training centers. Although generally disinterested in politics, Montessori accepted Il Duce's invitation and returned to Italy. Mussolini wanted to showcase prominent Italians, such as Montessori, as supporters of his Fascist regime. Cooperation between Mussolini's Fascist government and Montessori was uneasy. While the regime sponsored a Montessori training college and publication, it also wanted to use Montessori as a public personage devoted to Fascism. Montessori, however, saw her role to be more international. In 1934, the Association Montessori Internationale, with representatives from a number of countries had been established to coordinate Montessori schools and activities. The Italian government, seeking to capture publicity, wanted to name Montessori as Italy's children's ambassador to the world. Montessori refused to accept the appointment unless the Italian government recognized her independence as the head of the Montessori Internationale. Mussolini, the Italian dictator, angered by having his orders questioned, responded quickly and ordered Montessori's schools closed. She, in turn, left Italy as an exile.

When World War II began in 1939, Montessori was lecturing in Madras, India. Although Italy and the United Kingdom were at war, British authorities permitted Montessori to carry on her educational activities. As a result, a large number of Montessori schools were established and several of her books were published in India.

In 1946 with the war's end, Montessori located in the Netherlands where an international headquarters was established to coordinate Montessori activities and disseminate her materials. She continued to write, teach, and lecture until her death on May 6, 1952. Before her death, she had entrusted administration of the international society to Mario Montessori.

Since the 1950s, the Montessori method has experienced a significant revival in the United States, where it was rediscovered by parents seeking a more academically oriented early childhood education than they believed was provided by public school kindergartens. A leading figure in the American Montessori revival was Nancy McCormick Rambusch, founder of Whitby School in Greenwich, Connecticut, who modernized the method to incorporate new developments in education. The revival of Montessorianism led to the organization of the American Montessori Society (Ahlfeld, 1970, pp. 75–80).

MONTESSORI'S PSYCHOLOGICAL CONTRIBUTIONS TO EDUCATION

Influenced by her medical training, Montessori saw herself as pioneering in a new field, "Scientific Pedagogy," which, like medicine, was moving away from philosophy and drawing greater insights from physiology and psychology. At the beginning of her educational research, Montessori asserted that "child psychology does not exist," but could be established only on a foundation based on the meticulous clinical observation of children. She believed that speculative philosophies such as those of Rousseau, Pestalozzi, and Froebel that rested on adult perceptions of children's psychological states should be questioned, revised, and, if need be, abandoned. Rejecting a priori first principles, Montessori sought to develop what she believed was a genuinely experimental psychology free of dogmatic preconceptions about child nature. She claimed to be using an "exact definition of the technique" that enabled educators to conduct clinical observations based on "the liberty of the pupils in their spontaneous manifestations" (Montessori, 1964, pp. 29, 72, 80). Her exaltation of the child's freedom, however, did not signify a romanticized Rousseauean absence of control but rather referred to children's freedom to act within a well-defined, structured, and prepared environment. Not an end in itself, child freedom was rather a necessary condition for the experimental study of children. Clinical observation, conducted under these guidelines, would fashion a genuine educational psychology that informed educators about children's developmental and learning processes.

Montessori's concept of a clinically based educational psychology revealed the continuing influence of her earlier medical training. She reasoned that the study of the relationship of motor skills and movement required investigators to possess a thorough and prior understanding of the human nervous system—the brain, sense organs, muscles, and the nerves. Metaphorically, she compared the nerves to cables that transmitted nervous energy to the muscles. Because of the functioning of these delicate physiological mechanisms, human beings were enabled to express themselves through movements and actions. The whole physiological apparatus— brain, senses, and muscles—enabled human beings to relate to and interact with their environment (Montessori, 1995, pp. 136–37).

Montessori believed that her projected scientific pedagogy required the methodical study of children, informed by pedagogical anthropology and experimental psychology. Her emphasis on human physiology as the starting point for clinical observation rested on her firm belief that educators needed a necessary foundation in physical anthropology as part of their training. She was especially interested in applying anthropometry, a subfield of physical anthropology that focused on measuring human physical characteristics, to children's growth and development. She believed that compiling a complete and scientifically accurate profile of an individual child required using a variety of apparatuses to measure children. Children were to be regularly measured and weighed, with special attention paid to the size and shape of head, face, pelvis, limbs and with the noting of any malformations or deviations from normal development. Then, the findings were to be recorded systematically in an individualized longitudinal record, a "biographical chart," which detailed the profile of the child's growth and development. Cooperatively maintained by the teacher, a pediatrician, and a psychologist, the chart was to be shared periodically with parents.

Montessori, who took a global view of child development, believed her method of scientific pedagogy was transcultural and not limited by particularities of socioeconomic class, ethnicity, or race. For her, there was only one scientifically sound educational method and that was based on the natural pattern of children's physiological and psychological development (Montessori, 1995, p. 75).

Sensory Education and Didactic Materials

In developing her method of sensory education, Montessori conducted pedagogical experiments in which children spontaneously selected and worked with didactic apparatus. Originally, the materials had been used in training children with mental deficiencies, and she readapted them for normal children. She noted that with the children with deficiencies the apparatus made education possible while with normal children it stimulated what she called "auto-education" (Montessori, 1964, p. 169). For normal children, the didactic apparatus controlled their responses, with the children correcting their errors until they mastered the task. After observing children working with the materials, she then readapted the apparatus. The prepared environment was itself a controlled one in that only certain materials, believed to have a special didactic potential, were located within it.

Like Froebel, the founder of the kindergarten, Montessori believed children possessed an interior spiritual force that stimulated their self-activity. This self-active learning, however, was not to be dissipated in chaotic activity for the mere sake of movement. It was a force to be used, in conjunction with the child's stages of development, to stimulate further motor, intellectual, and social growth.

Unlike conventional educators who believed children needed to be motivated, Montessori asserted that they naturally possessed a strong propensity for mental concentration. The key to exercising this self-activity came, however, from internal rather than external sources. If they were truly interested in their activity, children would concentrate their attention and energy on it.

Rather than being disorderly creatures, children actually desired order and strongly preferred a structured over an unstructured environment. Rather than diminishing freedom, Montessori believed that structure enhanced the child's freedom. In a structured learning environment, expectations were clearly known by the children. Furniture and other items were made for them and their size rather than being imposed on them according to adult designs. If didactic apparatus and materials were readily accessible to them, children, themselves, would make certain that they would enjoy this access in the future by carefully replacing the items so they could be used again. Further, children desired to learn and master new skills. On their own initiative, children would identify a task and persist in repeating it until they achieved mastery and could easily perform the task. Children realized that mastery of such practical skills as tying a shoe lace, buttoning a jacket, putting on gloves and overshoes without adult assistance gave them independence. Montessori concluded that children did not have to be forced to learn and if permitted to choose between work and play would choose the former. In such a learning climate, artificial rewards and punishments were not only unneeded but could distort the learning experience.

Montessori's method grew into a comprehensive educational theory; it embodied a general philosophy of education, a psychology of learning, and a method of instruction. Her educational method was guided by four principles: one, each child is to be respected as a person with individual needs and interests; two, all children, by their nature, have an innate drive, sensitivity, and intellectual capacity for absorbing information and for learning from the environment; three, the first 6 years of a child's life are crucial for both unconscious and conscious learning; four, children have a need for and enjoyment of work that comes from their nature and from the task being performed.

Developmental Stages

Montessori believed children progressed through a sequence of developmental stages, each of which required an appropriate and specifically designed kind of learning (Standing, 1962, pp. 108–18). She defined development as "a series of rebirths," a continuum, when one psychic personality has reached its full growth and leads to the beginning of another. The first of these periods, from birth to age 6, the stage of the "absorbent mind," was subdivided into two phases, from birth to 3 and from 3 to 6. The second period, from 6 to 12, was marked by important continuing growth rather than the profoundly formative developments associated with the preceding period of the absorbent mind. The third period from 12 to 18 was a time of great physical change with the body reaching its full maturity (Montessori, 1995, pp. 19–20). See Table 7.1 for a more detailed look at Montessori's three stages of development.

The primary emphasis in Montessori's work was devoted to the "sensitive periods," of the "absorbent mind." The term "absorbent" was coined from her postulate that children absorbed sensory impressions from stimuli in the environment. Since the quality of the impressions absorbed depended significantly on the kind of learning possibilities present in the environment, it was incumbent on the educator to carefully structure the environment to maximize the possibilities of absorption. The impulse for absorption is generated and driven by children's innate desire to know and to use knowledge for self-development. The earliest period of the absorbent mind occurs from birth to age 3, when children's minds function unconsciously, and they learn by interacting to and responding to the stimuli in the environment. In the next sensitive period, from 3 to 6, children become more aware that they can use their mind to direct and control their activities.

TABLE 7.1
Montessori's Stages of Development

Stage I: First period of childhood, the Absorbent Mind, from birth to 6 years

A. Phase 1: From birth to 3 years, initial development of cognitive and affective powers, characterized by unconscious absorption of stimuli from environment

B. Phase 2: From 3 to six years, further development of cognitive and affective powers and skills by self-instruction characterized by conscious absorption of stimuli from environment

Stage II: Second period of childhood, a cycle of continuing uniform growth, from age 6 to 12 years, characterized by refinement and exercise of mental and physical powers and skills, development of logical thought, and acquisition of social and cultural information and values related to group participation

Stage III: Period of transformation from childhood to adulthood, from 12 to 18 years

A. Phase 1: Puberty, from 12 to 15 years, characterized by profound physical, mental, and social change and adaptation and heightened personal and societal identification.

B. Phase 2: Adolescence, from 15 to 18 years, characterized by continuing physical, mental, and social change and adaptation and refinement of personal, social and economic skills

Montessori believed that the cognitive operations of the absorbent mind center around points of sensitivity that stimulate intense activity in the child. These sensitive points lead children to develop such important abilities as balancing, estimating distances, and developing language. Through interaction with the environment, children perform a series of actions that enable them to construct a psychic network of relationships, which in turn, builds the cognitive and affective integration of the healthy personality (Montessori, 1995, p. 51).

Montessori placed special emphasis on the period between ages 3 and 6, which she called the time of "constructive perfectionment" when the need for precision attracts and fully engages children. Children were now able to interact deliberately, consciously, and purposefully with the environment. These interactions were not simple random activities but constituted the necessary work to achieve greater independence. Children required the kind of activities that stimulated interest, and they needed to be shown how to perform them correctly. For example, correctly performing manipulative tasks satisfied children's need to coordinate and control their movements.

Children, engaged in a specific work activity, repeated the same series of movements again and again until mastery was achieved. Through such repetitious efforts, they were working to establish and perfect a new pattern of control in their nervous systems. Repetition fixes the power of correct performance that leads to independent performance and greater freedom of action.

Much as they absorb stimuli from their physical environment, Montessori believed children also absorbed impressions from their cultural environment. She believed the process of acculturation began much earlier in the child's life then generally assumed. As they developed language skills and acquisition, children were absorbing the beliefs, behaviors, and values of their social group. Montessori referred to these cultural patterns as the basic summarized past that is repeated in a group's habitual life. Children internalize these cultural patterns, making them a part of their psyches. In their later cultural development, the person, as an adult, will continue to build on the cultural patterns absorbed in early childhood (Montessori, 1995, p. 189).

Thus, the period from birth through 6, particularly 3 to 6, is a decisively significant stage of human physical, psychological, social, and cultural development. It is the time that children establish the basic strategies that they will use to deal with their environment in later life. While the refinement of these strategic abilities occurs as the person matures, this development takes place on the foundations established in early childhood (Kramer, 1988, pp. 180–81).

During the period of the absorbent mind, Montessori stressed that children have a need to give order and structure to the knowledge they construct through environmental interactions. As they order their unconsciously absorbed sensory information, they become increasingly aware that still more knowledge about their larger world is needed. Though children possess a tremendous innate capacity for acquiring and incorporating knowledge, the environment from which they acquire this knowledge needs to be structured so that it is rich in materials appropriate to their particular developmental stage. Montessori's prepared environment, with its specified learning episodes and self-correcting didactic apparatus, provided such an appropriately rich learning climate. Based on her theory of relating sensitive periods to the environment, Montessori constructed a curriculum that focused on three broad areas of learning: motor and sensory training, practical life skills, and literacy and computational skills.

Sensory exercises were designed to develop sensitivity to smell and sound and discernment of color and hue. Sensory boxes were filled with spices that have distinctive odors. Tone bells were used to cultivate the ability to recognize various sounds. Using color tablets, children learned to distinguish colors and shades. Working with the didactic materials, children learned to recognize, group, and compare similar objects and contrast them from dissimilar ones.

Practical exercises were designed to assist children in developing the skills of everyday life. Children first learned to perform "generic skills" such as tying, lacing, buckling, zipping, and buttoning that were performed daily and could be applied to related tasks. Among the range of practical activities were lacing and tying shoes, buttoning smocks and coats, setting a table with dishes and silverware, serving meals, and washing dishes. The children then progressed to learning more formal skills such as reading, writing, and computing. In this area, Montessori attracted considerable attention by claiming that children of ages 4 and 5 "burst spontaneously into writing (Standing, 1962, p. 47)." To encourage readiness for writing and reading, two skills that Montessori believed developed in close relationship, she devised letters cut out of cardboard and covered with sandpaper. As the children touched and traced these letters, the directress voiced their sounds. Simultaneously with being prepared for writing the letter by tracing its shape, the children fix it in their minds and learn to recognize the sound it represents. Children burst into reading when they come to understand that the sounds of the letters they are tracing and writing form words. When the children know all of the vowels and some of the consonants, they are ready to form simple words. Using the vowels, the directress shows the children how to compose three-letter words and to pronounce them clearly. In the next step, the children write the words dictated by the directress. After sufficient practice, the children are able to compose words without assistance.

Children learn computation by counting objects and measuring by using rods of various lengths. They learn about the natural environment by planting and cultivating gardens. The presence of some small animals in the school introduces them to the animal kingdom. Gymnastics to develop physical dexterity and group games, songs, and stories for socialization are also part of the school day.

The Montessori method emphasizes the principle of freedom of choice within structure. Children are free to pursue their interests and activities at their own rate without facing peer group competition. They are free to observe the work of other children so that they can learn from it. No one is permitted to interfere with the work of others, to disrupt the order of the environment, or to damage or misuse equipment.

EVALUATION OF MONTESSORI'S IMPACT

Montessori's impact on educational psychology and early childhood education is examined in the following sections: the nature of the learner, the nature of the learning process, optimal conditions of instruction, and the nature of important learning–instructional outcomes.

Nature of the Learner

Montessori's conception of the nature of the learner was two-dimensional in that it included a physiological and an internal spiritual dimension, a psychic power. Together these dual dimensions acted to stimulate growth and development through the learner's interaction with the environment. However, the primal desire for action comes from the internal psychic power, the teacher within. The physiological and psychic dimensions are manifested in the child's free activity that, in turn, provides the educator with needed cues about the individual's readiness and interests (Montessori, 1964, pp. 104–05). Coming from the child and the focus of clinical observation, these cues provide the knowledge needed to structure Montessori's prepared learning environment. For Montessori, the educator collaborates with the child's nature by structuring appropriate activities and experiences within the prepared environment. The child, the active agent in the process, absorbs information and makes adaptations to situations encountered in the environment but ideally these are preplanned situations and not random happenings. Two key reference points for Montessori, then, are the individual child, with interior physiological and psychic powers and the prepared environment that allows freedom for development within a structure.

Montessori believed that because they possessed a universal human nature that children everywhere possessed these physiological and psychic powers. The phases of human development, therefore, were universal in that individuals experience the same stages in the development process regardless of their culture, race, or ethnicity. Because of this universality, the Montessori method, too, is global, transnational and transcultural. While its application may be conditioned by a given cultural context, the effectiveness of the method is not culturally dependent (Montessori, 1995, p. 80).

Based on her view of child nature, Montessori proclaimed the fundamental principle of scientific pedagogy to be the "liberty of the pupil; to permit the individual, spontaneous manifestations of the child's nature." (Montessori, 1964, p. 28). Scientifically based clinical observation was possible only when the child was free to act.

It is within the context of the learner's freedom of activity that the sense of discipline arises. A child's liberty to act is limited only to impede infringements on the collective interest of other children's freedom. All other activities must be permitted and clinically observed by the educator.

Montessori saw discipline as a self-generated process that leads to the development of continuing self-control. In becoming self-disciplined, children first acquire a "mental grasp" of the idea that is to be acted on. This "grasp" initiates repetition, the successive actions, needed to complete and accomplish the task. When children master a task through the necessary repeated actions, it reinforces their will power to attempt further challenges. Genuine discipline, Montessori argued, comes through activity directed to spontaneous work in which children, through their own repeated and sustained efforts, master a task. As they work to master external challenges, children are stimulated to exercise their interior spiritual power and, in turn, gain a sense of accomplishment and independence.

Nature of the Learning Process

Montessori defined education as a dynamic process in which children develop according to their "inner dictates" by their "voluntary work" in an environment prepared to give them freedom to express themselves (Kramer, 1988, p. 305). The aim of the learning process is to aid children in their own self-development, which provides self-empowerment or functional independence. Development is part of the drive, stemming from physiological and psychic urges, to independence. It is this "divine urge" that activates the child to perform those further actions that stimulate growth and subsequent development (Montessori, 1995, p. 83).

Education is not something a teacher does for children but rather is a spontaneous natural process that occurs in human beings. The Montessori directress, the name given to the teacher, is clinically skilled in observing children, like a scientist, but also is concerned with children's psychic spiritual nature. Empiricism is necessary to clinical observation but to it needs to be added sensitivity to children's inner spiritual or psychic powers. To carry out the requirement of trained scientific observation, the directress needs to be an objective observer, who respects the living, spiritual phenomenon being observed.

J. McV. Hunt credits Montessori with solving the "problem of the match." If the environmental circumstances children encounter are to be attractive and interesting and yet challenging enough to bring about the adaptations that constitute learning, they need to match those "standards" children have already achieved in their experience. Montessori solved this problem by encouraging individuals to follow their interests by self-selecting a particular didactic material from a variety of graded materials and to work with it at their own pace. The selection of the material reflected readiness to work with the particular item and to follow interests and to proceed from one level of complexity to a higher level. (Hunt, 1964, pp. xxviii–xxix).

Optimal Conditions of Instruction

A major optimal condition of instruction in the Montessori method is the freedom of children to follow their interests, select the task, and to work without interruption or interference from adults. Well-intentioned, overt, adult interference reduces the opportunity to develop self-reliance and self-discipline that comes from choosing, completing, and mastering a particular challenge.

Montessori considered her school to be a prepared environment in which children are able to develop freely at their own pace, unimpeded in the spontaneous unfolding of their natural capacities, through activities with a series of self-correcting didactic materials. She stated, "The school must permit the *free, natural manifestations of the child* if in the school scientific pedagogy is to be born" (Montessori, 1964, p. 15).

Based on her principles of "the liberty of the pupils in their spontaneous manifestations" and "liberty in activity," Montessori redesigned the classroom environment. In this prepared environment, children were empowered to regulate their own conduct and to perform correctly the communal acts of social life.

Instruction, in the prepared environment, is to be concise, simple, and objective so as not to interfere with the children's spontaneous activity.

The Nature of Important Learning–Instructional Outcomes

Two key learning outcomes are exercising children's continuing drive to self-development and creating of a sense of self-discipline. Both are necessary for independence, the freedom and competency to do and act for oneself without dependence on others. Children take pleasure in learning to master their environment; this mastery begins with the ability to manipulate objects, proceeds to acquiring life skills, and leads to a true sense of independence. Discipline relates to the will to carry out the task and to respect the rights of others by following the "principle of collective order." An outcome of this principle is to create an awareness of the kind of behaviors needed for individual expression within an orderly group. Montessori used the metaphor of players in an orchestra to illustrate the relationship of individual expression within an orderly group. The musicians must be individually competent in playing their instruments and as an orchestra, a collective orderly group, to follow the conductor's direction (Montessori, 1964, p. 117).

Montessori believed that a child's character and socialization developed spontaneously as did other skills and learning in the prepared environment. The first essential for children's moral and social development is the power of concentration, which to be exercised requires an environment containing objects on which to concentrate. Since there is only one specimen of each didactic object, children must wait until it is free to use it. By waiting, they learn to reign in their impulsiveness, take turns, and respect other's right to work.

CONCLUSION: MONTESSORI'S LEGACY TO THE FIELD

Montessori's major legacy to educational psychology was her recognition of the significance of early stimulation on later learning, especially its implications for the culturally disadvantaged child. An important related contribution was her emphasis on sensitive periods, phases of development appropriate to learning specific motor and cognitive skills. She anticipated and led what is now the current movement to provide more and earlier enrichment opportunities for children. Her early work with economically disadvantaged children in the slums of Rome has a special resonance for arguments for the enrichment of early childhood experiences for at-risk children.

In the United States, Montessori's greatest impact was on individuals who were outside of the public school and teacher education establishments. Her influence on educational psychology within this establishment was not pronounced. In the first period of Montessorianism in the United States (1910–1917), some prominent lay persons, generally associated with reform causes, were attracted initially to Montessori's educational ideas. Within the professional field of educational psychology however, Montessori was overshadowed by the functionalist, behaviorist, and psychoanalytic schools. For example, J. McV. Hunt concluded that Montessori, who accepted Itard's and Seguin's views on the effectiveness of pedagogical treatment for mental retardation, was "out of step" with the more generally accepted theories of fixed intelligence associated with J. McKeen Cattell and G. Stanley Hall and with Thorndike's and Watson's stimulus–response theory (Hunt, 1964, pp. xiv–xvii). The concept, advanced by Montessori, that intellectual development could be significantly influenced by deliberate stimulation in early childhood, was generally not a regnant idea among educational psychologists in the early 20th century. Additionally, Montessori's belief in the transfer of training had been largely abandoned within the field. Further, her emphasis on a clinical observation, derived from the medical field, was discounted as lacking the credibility of a true experimental science.

Sigmund Freud and Montessori had some correspondence but no real collaboration. Freud's daughter, Anna Freud, had an interest in Montessori education and for a time so did Erik Erikson. Montessori, herself, rejected Freud's ideas on infant sexuality and the impact of emotional conflict on later development.

Jean Piaget, trained in biology, found much of interest in Montessori's work, especially the "sensitive periods" as a developmental sequence in children's mental growth. He also gave credence to Montessori's emphasis on the role played by repetitive behavior in the development from motor to mental activities and in the need for the environment to stimulate interactive activities. Piaget, however, moved beyond Montessori to formulate his own developmental psychology (Kramer, 1988, p. 386).

While Montessori was generally "out of step" with mainstream thinking in educational psychology, she was also "out of step" with progressivism, the dominant theory in educational philosophy in the first half of the 20th century. Her work was attacked as being "50 years" behind the times by the prominent progressive educator William H. Kilpatrick, who criticized her for neglecting the importance of group project solving and concomitant learning. Despite the educational establishment's reluctance to take Montessori seriously, her ideas on early childhood education offered an alternative to mainstream thinking within the disciplines of educational psychology and philosophy.

Another reason that caused Montessorianism to lie at the periphery of educational psychology and teacher education can be attributed to Montessori herself. Exercising extremely close supervision over the diffusion of her method, Montessori distrusted those whom she had not personally trained to properly implement the method; nor, did she participate in the professional debates to which most educational theories are subjected.

Montessori was a somewhat doctrinaire leader who wanted her disciples to implement her method exactly as she designed it, without change or innovation. For her the scientific method meant the precise implementation and use of materials as she intended them to be used. She was advocating a precisely calibrated technique rather than an experimental method subject to further verification and revision.

Montessori was an independent woman, a theorist, who charted her own course. Her method of education was largely an independent one that stood on its own. Through the power of her personality and dedication to her cause, Montessori has prevailed as a force in education. Throughout the world are thousands of schools that bear her name. These schools are attended by children who continue on their path to independence and self-discipline.

REFERENCES

Ahlfeld, K. (1970). The Montessori revival: How far will it go? *Nation's Schools, 85,* 75–80.

Halsey, W. (1913). A valuation of the Montessori experiments. *Journal of Education, 77,* 63.

Hunt, J. M. (1964). Introduction. In M. Montessori, *The Montessori Method* (pp. xi–xxxv). New York: Schocken Books.

Kramer, R. (1988). *Maria Montessori: A biography*. Reading, MA: Perseus Books.

Kilpatrick, W. H. (1971). *The Montessori system examined*. Boston: Houghton Mifflin, 1914. Reprint, New York: Arno/New York Times, 1971.

Montessori, M. (1913). *Pedagogical anthropology*. New York: Frederick A. Stokes.

Montessori, M. (1964). *The Montessori method*. New York: Schocken Books.

Montessori, M. (1995). *The absorbent mind*. New York: Holt.

Myers, K. (1913). Seguin's principles of education as related to the Montessori method. *Journal of Education, 77,* 538–41.

Standing, E. M. (1962). *Maria Montessori: Her life and work*. New York: New American Library.

II

The Rise to Prominence: 1920 to 1960

8

The Rise to Prominence: Educational Psychology 1920–1960

J. William Asher
Purdue University

By 1920 educational psychology had nearly 30 years of development as a subarea of psychology. Researchers in this applied discipline had established an empirical base focusing on learning, human abilities, and educational achievement. They were also involved in research and theory in developmental psychology, individual differences, and psychological measurement. In short, they had the theories, tools of measurement, research design, and statistical analyses to make major scientific contributions to curriculum and instructional methods, and indeed they had already made a sizable impact in America.

In terms of measurement, standardized multiple-choice achievement tests were becoming available, such as the Iowa Test of Basic Skills and the Stanford Achievement Test. There was some recognition that research design and methods in education and psychology were somewhat different from the research methods used in the physical sciences, such as McCall's 1923 book entitled *How to Experiment in Education*. However, most researchers continued to emphasize controlling variables by matching subjects, by using nonsense syllables to eliminate prior meaning, or by using infrahuman subjects to eliminate effects of prior knowledge.

In terms of the curriculum and instruction, educational psychologists had begun to investigate teaching of reading, arithmetic, and spelling. Their investigations of learning were becoming influential in the development of curriculum in reading

189

and arithmetic. For example, Thorndike wrote an arithmetic textbook (1922), and its widespread adoption provided him with a considerable income. This allowed him to pursue his research interests with little financial restraint. Thus, at the dawn of the 1920s, educational psychologists were beginning to make substantial contributions to the scientific development of curriculum and instructional methods in American schools.

EDUCATIONAL PSYCHOLOGY
IN THE 1920s AND 1930s

Social History in the U.S.

With the end of World War I in 1918, American industry turned to mass-producing motor vehicles, electrical appliances, and labor-saving mechanical tools, and daily life throughout the country began to change. At the time, the U.S. labor force was primarily employed in farming, and sons and daughters began working on the family farm before they reached puberty. In these rural areas, the schools were often one-room buildings with stove heat and no electricity or running water, and teachers were trained in 2-year degree programs at normal schools. In urban areas, children often entered the workforce in factories or manual labor after completing elementary school to supplement the family income. Although most students acquired an eighth-grade education, only 10 to 15% attended high school and even fewer attended college. Public education received support primarily from local governments in cities and rural townships. The state governments were minimally involved except for teacher licensing standards and for supporting normal schools for teacher training. The federal government was so little involved that the primary mission of the U.S. Bureau of Education (later the Office of Education) was actuarial, such as counting the number of colleges and universities, college graduates and their majors, and primary and secondary curriculum practices.

There was little governmental support for educational research, which was particularly unfortunate because of the high dropout rate of students. Only about 50% of those students who started first grade in 1917 entered high school in 1925, and of those students who started high school, only 44% became seniors in 1928. African Americans rarely attended high school in the 1920s. Although they composed about 10% of the U.S. population, they composed only 1.5% of the high school students, and by 1930, their number had doubled to just 3% (H. M. Bond, 1952).

With the crash of the stock market in New York in 1929, the economic prosperity of the 1920s ended abruptly. The ensuing depression had a profound effect on all facets of society in the United States, including education. Unemployment reached 30%, and state and local charitable and welfare organizations were overwhelmed. This required the intervention of the federal government, which responded with numerous programs to cope with the widespread poverty. The gradual decline of employment in agriculture that had accompanied industrialization in the United States was reversed during the 1930s as people reverted to the farms to sustain themselves when they were laid off. The depression hit the youth of America particularly hard, with approximately 2 million unemployed during this period. To provide jobs for these adolescents, the Roosevelt Administration in 1933 started the Civilian Conservation Corps, a semi-military government organization to provide work on land and forest preservation projects. By February of 1934, nearly 1,500 camps were in operation at various sites throughout the United States.

Two little-remembered vehicles of support for educational research during the 1930s were the Works Progress Administration (WPA) and National Youth Administration (NYA) programs, both of which gave support to colleges to provide employment for students. Although the WPA program focused on clerical work and maintenance, there was also support for research assistants. The college and high school aid sections of the NYA helped students investigate delinquency, evaluate test items, study cultural cycles, and conduct surveys of community life, student life, traffic, and use of food products (Aubrey, September 24, 1937). Saul Sells, an educational psychologist, was Director of Educational Research in New York City for the WPA during this period.

During the 1930s, there was a dramatic increase in enrollment in high schools fueled mainly by the lack of employment for adolescents finishing elementary school. The percentage of students who enrolled in high school increased from about 15% in 1930 to about 65% by 1940 (Krug, 1972, p. 218). A 4-year college education became the norm for teacher training during this period, and elementary teachers were paid the same wage as high school teachers for the first time. Many teachers started their careers in small towns or rural areas and then moved to larger cities to secure higher paying jobs. Unfortunately, when women teachers married, they often were required to quit teaching so their job would be available for a man.

Social History Outside the U.S.

In Europe, monarchies that had governed before World War I were widely replaced by democracies after the war. The League of Nations was founded shortly after World War I to promote peace and cooperation among the nations of the world, but the international response to this bold initiative was disappointing. Even the United States Congress did not join the League despite President Woodrow Wilson's instrumental role in founding it. Russia, convulsed by a revolution in 1917, was not admitted until 1934, and Japan and Germany eventually withdrew as members due to increasing militancy.

The collapse of the New York stock market not only triggered a national economic crisis and depression but also an international one with profound political consequences. During the 1930s, this economic malaise led to the rise of Fascism in Germany, Spain, and Italy. In the Soviet Union, Stalin strengthened his grip on power by commandeering farmland, decimating his army's officer corps, and centrally planning the economy. In the Far East, imperialism took hold in Japan and led that country to invade Mongolia and coastal China in a quest for dominance of the Western Pacific Rim.

Because of their heavy World War I debt, citizens in Germany were especially impacted by inflation and depression, and they became very embittered. Hitler used the unrest as an opportunity to seize control of border territories, such as the Saar and Rhineland. Italy followed suit by attacking Ethiopia in 1935, and in 1936, the Spanish Civil War began. In 1938 Hitler annexed Austria, the Sudetenland, and finally the rest of Czechoslovakia. When he invaded Poland in 1939, the conflict escalated into a world-wide conflict—War World II had commenced.

During the 1930s, many African and Asian countries remained under colonial rule by European countries, such as England, France, Germany, Belgium, and the Netherlands. These countries brought their national institutions to their colonies, such as religion, language, currency, laws, administrative institutions, and school systems.

Theory and Practice

American Psychology. In the early 1920s, experimental psychologists, such as Guthrie, Tolman, and Hull, primarily investigated learning, transfer, and recall in laboratory settings. Their theories focused on strengthening connections or associations between stimuli and responses (S–R) through prompting (law of readiness), repetition (law of exercise), consequences (law of effect), as well as other variables. However, the link between these learning theories and educational practice in schools remained largely intuitive at the time. By contrast, Thorndike and many educational psychologists conducted research on instructional materials, which markedly improved the elementary and secondary curriculum in schools.

By 1922, John Dewey (1983) had largely abandoned a psychological description of his functionalist theory in favor of a philosophical account, which he called Pragmatism. These philosophical descriptions proved to be very popular, and they attracted the attention of an important group, Progressive educators. This reform group sought to expand the curriculum of the American public school by introducing practical courses, such as home economics, industrial arts, typing, and civics, and by supplanting teaching methods that emphasize repetition and memorization with methods that involve hands-on learning. As a reform movement, the Progressive educators made a substantial impact on curriculum and instruction in America. Unfortunately, Dewey's lack of operational definitions and demonstrative research led to many misinterpretations of his ideas, and these distortions eventually compelled him to distance himself from Progressive Education reforms.

By the 1930s, earlier explanations for learning based on simple associationism were being replaced with more elaborate S–R conditioning accounts (Hilgard, 1948; Stephens, 1956). These S–R accounts varied primarily in the their conception of how rewards impacted learning. For example, *E. L. Thorndike* reformulated his law of effect to include trial and error learning in 1932 (see earlier chapter by Mayer in this volume). He had discovered that his original conclusion that reward and punishment exerted equal and opposite effects on learning connections was wrong. Rewards did increase learning but punishments did not necessarily decrease it. During trial-and-error learning, many responses, which Thorndike labeled "errors," occur in somewhat random fashion and do not lead to a reward of any kind. However, if a response happens to lead to a reward of some kind, the response will be connected to the antecedent stimulus.

By contrast, *E. R. Guthrie* developed a S–R theory that emphasized the contiguity of stimulus and response instead of the impact of rewards. His law of contiguity stated "A combination stimuli which has accompanied a movement will on its recurrence tend to be followed by that movement" (Guthrie, 1935, p. 26). He later added a corollary to this law regarding the onset of learning (Guthrie, 1942, p. 30). "A stimulus pattern gains its full associative strength on the occasion of its first pairing with a response." He believed that so long as a response occurred, it becomes attached to any stimulus that is physically present. Although Guthrie agreed with Thorndike that rewards enhanced learning, he disagreed about the reason for their effectiveness. Instead Guthrie concluded that rewards served to cut off learning episodes and preserve the last response from the effects of subsequent learning.

The most elaborate S–R theory during the period was developed by *Clark Hull* (1943). Although he also recognized the role of rewards in learning, he concluded their impact was due to their effectiveness in reducing an underlying drive. Simply put, Hull believed that when a drive was at least partially reduced, the extant stimuli or conditions will be linked to the responses. Hull (1943) attempted to rigorously define and quantitatively measure drives as well as other related psychological variables, such as habit strength, so that they could be related mathematically and systematically tested in a laboratory.

A prominent American psychologist who sought to include a role for cognitive variables in S–R learning was *E. C. Tolman* (1932). He envisioned rewards as cognitive signs of a learner's effectiveness. He felt that learning involved acquisition of expectations and realizations rather than motor responses. He argued that subjects form cognitive maps of learning tasks, and he supported his claims with an impressive series of place learning studies. He believed that cognitive forms of learning are more fluid and transferable than behavioral forms.

European Psychology.   In contrast to the emphasis of American psychologists on learning as an overt S–R process, European theorists tended to emphasize covert processes such as perception, cognition, and language. For example, *Gestalt* psychologists viewed learning as a perceptual reaction to a complex pattern or organization. Their name stemmed from an interest in learners' holistic perceptions of meaning or "Gestalts." Among the most prominent of these German theorists were Kohler (1925), Wertheimer (1925), and Koffka (1924). Gestalt psychologists not only attempted to explain how humans perceived the world but also how humans discovered new things in problem solving fashion.

Gestalt researchers sought to identify the principles by which humans perceive simple patterns in complex, changing, or ambiguous stimuli. For these psychologists, learning was a matter of seeing underlying relationships in a problem to be solved. When a pattern is recognized, they believed that learning occurred suddenly rather than gradually as most American S–R psychologists had envisioned. Gestalt theorists were also called "field theorists" because of their emphasis on the importance of perceptual field in making figure–ground recognitions.

Another German psychologist who embraced field theory was *Kurt Lewin* (1936). He migrated to the United States during the 1930s, and he attracted the attention of educational psychologists because of his research on social processes and behavioral dynamics. For example, he studied the effectiveness of democratic, authoritarian, and laissez-faire leaders and discovered many advantages for a democratic approach (Lewin, Lippitt, & White, 1939). Lewin sought to depict human problem solving as the perceptual restructuring of a person's life spaces so that barriers to solutions are transformed into permeable paths, such as when a student who fears public speaking imagines the audience as close friends. Because of their Jewish heritage, Wertheimer, Koffka, and Kohler all emigrated from Germany to escape Hilter's discriminatory policies.

In contrast to the German Gestalt theorists' emphasis on human perception, a Swiss biologist, *Jean Piaget*, focused on cognitive development (see chapter by Brainerd in this volume). He became interested in children's cognitive development after working with Simon in the laboratory that Binet (who had died) had founded in Paris (See Jarvin and Sternberg's earlier chapter on Binet in this volume). In the early 1920s, Piaget left Paris to direct a research institute on children's development in Switzerland.

Piaget (1926, 1928) was a careful observer who kept detailed records of children's response to various stimuli in their natural environment. He sought to discover age-related differences, the size and direction of their conceptual errors. Unlike most biologists, Piaget did not limit himself to unobtrusive passive observation but instead intervened in ongoing experiences to see how a child would respond. But like many biologists, he formulated a stage theory. He concluded that children's cognitive functioning developed in four qualitative stages, beginning with simple sensory-motor stage reactions of infants and ending with formal mental operations stage of adolescents. Because of Piaget's unorthodox approach to psychological theory and research, he attracted little attention in the U.S. until the cognitive revolution of the early 1960s. However, since that time, Piaget's work has been read widely by educational psychologists, and he has had a major influence on educational practice.

In contrast to Gestalt theorists' emphasis on perception and Piaget's stress on cognition, a Russian psychologist, *Lev Vygotsky* (1978), focused on the role of language in human learning (see chapter by Tudge and Scrimsher in this volume). He theorized that the origins of higher mental functions were closely related to children's acquisition of language, which he envisioned as a uniquely human second signal system. He began his research and writing during the 1920s, and he had a particular interest in what is called "private speech," an area, which has intrigued educators interested in reading research for many years. Vygotsky believed that subvocal speech had a self-directive influence on children's learning and higher cognitive functioning.

Vygotsky also believed that children's cognitive development was the result of their social interaction with more cognitively advanced children and adults. During that revolutionary era in the Soviet history, he enjoyed the political support of Lenin's widow, N. K. Krupskava, and he was greatly influenced by Marxist theory with its emphasis on the causal role of social and historical forces on human development. He concluded that the higher cognitive functions such as problem solving, planning, self-control, concept formation, and attention originated in children's social interactions with others and were gradually internalized through covert speech. Unfortunately, by the time he died in 1934 at age 38, his ideas had been criticized on political grounds, and as a result, many of his writings were suppressed by Stalin, who viewed Krupskava and Vygotsky as a threat to his power. Thus, Vygotsky's ideas did not become available in the West for many decades.

Reading, Writing, and Language

From the founding of the discipline, educational psychologists have been highly involved in reading and language arts research in the schools. For example, Arthur Gates was very active in research in *reading* and wrote a widely received book, *The Improvement of Reading* (1947). Paul Witty also had a strong interest in research in reading and authored a prominent book, *Reading in Modern Education* (1949). The psychologist Guy Bond wrote several influential books, *Teaching the Child to Read* (with Eva Bond Wagner in 1950), and *Reading Difficulties: Their Diagnosis and Correction* (with Miles Tinker, 1967). Emmet Betts (1946) wrote an early book focusing on reading disabilities entitled, *Foundations of Reading Instruction*, and David Russell wrote a book, *Children Learn to Read* (1949), that incorporated his research on the language arts and children's thinking processes. Ruth Strang, a psychologist specializing in child and adolescent psychology, wrote extensively about reading at the high school and college levels (Strang, McCullough, & Traxler, 1955).

Spelling was another research interest of educational psychologists. David Russell (1955) and Arthur Gates (1937) focused on the characteristics of good and poor spellers and created lists of words that give them difficulty. Gertrude Hildreth (1955) also conducted research on spelling as well as reading, and Dorothea McCarthy wrote a chapter on language development in children that included research on spelling in the first edition of the *Manual of Child Psychology* (1954). Thorndike published a book on *handwriting* as early as 1910, and several decades later, Ernest Newland (1932) investigated handwriting, and Gertrude Hildreth (1949) also conducted research on the topic several years later. *Listening* is another aspect of the language arts. David and Elizabeth Russell wrote a book *Listening Aids Through the Grades* (1959), and Paul Witty and Robert Sizemore conducted a series of listening studies (1959a, 1959b, and 1959c).

Educational psychologists also investigated learning of *arithmetic* during the 1920s and 1930s. For example, Benezet (1935, 1936) found that children who had no formal arithmetic instruction until the sixth grade quickly became as competent as children who had had 5 years of arithmetic in Grades 1 through 5. He concluded that children's readiness for instruction increased with age. Somewhat later, William Brownell and Harold Moser at Duke (1949) studied meaningful versus mechanical learning and also were concerned about the development of readiness for meaningful learning of arithmetic. Brownell later became U.S. Commissioner of Education.

The Progressive Education Curriculum

As was noted earlier, the Progressive Education movement was widely embraced throughout America during the 1920s and 1930s. A major effort to evaluate this curriculum occurred in 1932 as part of an Eight-Year study under the direction of Ralph Tyler (1942), an educational psychologist. Thirty high schools were involved in an experiment to compare the effectiveness of a traditional, narrowly proscribed academic curriculum with a more flexible, progressive curriculum in preparing students for college. Students in experimental Progressive Education high schools were allowed to take any courses offered, including many new courses that were developed based on the principles of progressive education. A number of colleges agreed to admit the students from the experimental high schools without regard to their high school curriculum with only a recommendation from their principal. Over 1,400 students from the experimental schools eventually enrolled in 38 colleges, and these students were compared to students of equal ability from a control group of high schools who pursued a traditional curriculum.

Tyler discovered that the two groups achieved roughly the same grade point averages in college with small numerical advantages favoring the experimental group in all course areas except foreign language. When their collegiate instructors were asked to judge the students for their personal and intellectual qualities, the students in the Progressive Education experimental group were evaluated as superior in social awareness, participation in extracurricular activities, and interest in the arts. They were also judged as more intellectually curious, systematic, and resourceful. Furthermore, students from experimental high schools who deviated the most from the traditional curriculum did better than the students from experimental schools that were less innovative.

The study was large in its sample size and wide in its range of measures. Although the results generally favored the progressive education programs' approach to high school curriculum, they were largely ignored by subsequent educators. Contemporary high school educators, facing pressure from federal, state, and local governments to increase achievement standards, have tended to revert to extensions or revisions of the traditional curriculum in science, mathematics, literature, and history.

Another major research study examined the effectiveness of the Progressive Education curriculum. J. Wayne Wrightstone, a member of Teachers College Columbia Institute for School Experimentation, conducted an appraisal of newer school practices in selected public schools in 1935. He sought to improve on prior research methods by including measures designed to assess specific curricular objectives and instructional methods advocated by the Progressive educators. He discovered that Progressive Education practices were effective in enhancing students' personal and social development without impairing their academic achievement.

EDUCATIONAL PSYCHOLOGY IN THE 1940s

Social History

The ontset of World War II profoundly influenced American society during the decade of the 1940s. The depression finally ended, and economic activity accelerated as the nation prepared for war. The mobilization of young men and women for military service dramatically changed life at home as well as abroad. Manufacturing increased, unemployment dropped, and many women entered the workforce, often to hold jobs that had been exclusively men's. The movement of people from the cities to the farms during the 1930s reversed during the 1940s, and these shifts in population and modes of employment dramatically changed people's lives and educational needs.

Theory and Practice

The need for rapid learning of specific skills in the U.S. military, such as radio communication, telegraphy, artillery marksmanship, naval ship handling, radar screening, foreign languages translation, and navigation, presented a new challenge for educational psychologists. Because of the urgency of a war, the armed services needed to teach these vital military skills within months rather than years. A major concern of the services was the selection and training of crews for combat airplanes, such as pilots, navigators, and bombardiers. Initially, the failure rate of these crews during training was rather high.

John Flanagan, an educational psychologist with skill in measurement, was selected to improve this program, and he recruited many other educational psychologists to help him with this vital work, such as Robert Thorndike, David Tiedeman, Robert Glaser, J. P. Guilford, Chester Harris, Lloyd Humphries, Lyle Jones, and Benjamin Shimberg. Flanagan and his staff developed a number of tests, such as verbal, quantitative, spatial relations, and eye–hand coordination measures, and gave them to incoming trainees for air combat. They also developed many new forms of instruction for each combat skill that involved such technology as films, audiotapes, and detailed instructional manuals.

The educational psychologists followed these candidates through their various training regimens to see who was successful and who failed in each of three combat specialties (e.g., pilots, bombardiers, and navigators). They then used the tests that best discriminated between successful learners in order to select new trainees and assign them to one of the three air combat specialties. Flanagan and his colleagues also introduced the new forms of instructional technology into the soldiers' training regimen. As a result of these improved selection and instructional techniques, the learning times and failure rates of the trainees dropped markedly. It should be mentioned that Flanagan's staff also developed new methods for analyzing vast amounts of data on huge populations that were forerunners of contemporary multivariate methods of analysis.

Two educational psychologists, Phillip Rulon and Robert Thorndike, made major other contributions in psychological measurement during the 1940s. The phenomenon of regression-toward-the-mean is unusual in science generally and nearly unique to psychology. Very early in the 20th Century, Spearman (1910) and Brown (1910) separately demonstrated that measurement of psychological characteristics is not completely reliable. Very high and low scores on a psychological measure are more affected by chance, and as a result, these scores will move closer to the average of the population during retesting with the same measure. This well-known outcome is called "regression-to-the-mean."

The lack of knowledge about this regression phenomenon caused many mis-interpretations of educational and psychological data. From his research on this problem, Rulon (1941) located the source of the regression phenomenon, and Thorndike (1942) developed mathematical proofs documenting why it happens. Both Rulon and Thorndike's advances in statistical methodology were included in Gullickson's (1950) book, *Theory of Mental Tests*. During these eras, there were also improvements in research design, such as the inclusion of no treatment control groups for group data and the use of correction formulae when interpreting longitudinal data on individual subjects.

EDUCATIONAL PSYCHOLOGY
IN THE 1950s

Social History

As the war drew to an end, the U.S. Congress passed the G.I. Bill of Rights of 1944, which enabled millions of men and women to enter higher education during the post war years. Their numbers nearly overwhelmed the colleges and dramatically increased the education level of America. The end of the war also led to many marriages, which had been delayed during the Depression and war, and subsequently to a "baby boom," which had a major impact on the public schools during the 1950s and 1960s. These burgeoning educational needs led to the rapid construction of school buildings, which had slowed markedly during the Depression and stopped during World War II. There was also a need for many new teachers, and for more educational psychologists to enhance their training.

Prior to the 1950s, there was very little federal involvement in public education, but the onset of a "cold" war against communist countries and eruption of the "hot" war in Korea led to national concern about the importance of the country's international lead in science and mathematics. The first significant federal infusion of support came under the *National Science Foundation Act of 1950*. This act supported research and education in the mathematics, physical sciences, nonmedical biological sciences, and engineering.

In a second infusion of support, the U.S. Office of Education implemented the first extramural program of support for general educational research in 1956 under the auspices of the Cooperative Research Act of 1954. Many educational psychologists, such as Ralph Tyler, Dewey Stuit, H. H. Remmers, and Chester Harris, served on advisory committees appointed by the U.S. Commissioner of Education. Their superb research programs were instrumental in establishing a permanent research mission within schools of education at universities. A third infusion of federal aid for education occurred after the Soviet launching of a satellite in 1957, which implied to many leaders that the U.S. had fallen behind in the race for military dominance in space. This led to the Congressional passage of the National Defense Education Act of 1958, which supported education training in science, mathematics, and counseling and under Title VII, research in visual aids and instructional technology.

Another major event during the decade was the 1954 Supreme Court decision on school integration: *Brown versus the Board of Education of Topeka, Kansas*. Psychologists, notably Kenneth B. Clark and his wife, Mamie P. Clark (1950), produced much of the scientific data on the harmful effects of the existing doctrine of "separate but equal education" between the races. The court ended racially segregated schools throughout the southern part of the U.S. and raised the standard of equality of educational opportunity for racial groups throughout the country. Concern about the differential quality of schooling led to new research opportunities in the years to come.

Theory and Practice

After World War II, John Flanagan and other members of his team sought to employ their new methods in training and assessment in conventional instructional settings, such as public schools. Underlying Flanagan's success in conveying specific military skills were new scientific advances in the analysis, presentation, and measurement of human knowledge and skill. This scientific treatment of knowledge helped move the issue of cognition to the forefront of educational psychology. The credibility of Flanagan's approach grew among educational psychologists as a number of the members of his team made prominent methodological and research contributions and achieved important leadership positions in psychology, such as the election of Paul Guilford as president of the American Psychological Association.

Because of concern about military readiness during the 1950s, the armed services, especially the U.S. Navy's Special Devices Center, continued to support the development of instructional technology, such as the use of teaching machines, and new forms of instructional media, such as instructional television, simulators, overhead transparencies, and slides. The educational psychologist, Sidney Pressey, directed an impressive research and development program on teaching machines at Ohio State University and the psychologist, Ray Carpenter, developed a strong research program on new types of instructional media at Pennsylvania State University.

One of the most influential members of Flanagan's team on theory and practice in educational psychology was *Robert Gagne*, who specialized in instructional design (see chapter by Ertmer, Driscoll, and Wager in this volume). Gagne's research on simulators and other training devices in the Air Force Laboratories during the war led him to form an early information processing conception of human performance (Gagne, 1989). This framework led to his derivation of a taxonomy of learning outcomes, the concept of learning hierarchies, and related concepts of instructional events and conditions of learning (Briggs, 1980).

In his book *The Conditions of Learning* (1965), Gagne described how simple forms of S–R learning that interested researchers before the war were linked systematically to higher forms of learning that were studied during the war, such as rule learning and problem solving. The impact of his hierarchical formulation was to shift educational psychologists' attention from simple forms of learning to more complex ones and to understand the specific underlying conditions that underlie both forms of learning. Gagne sought to test the validity of his hierarchical model using programmed instruction designed to develop vertical transfer of intellectual skills (Gagne & Brown, 1961).

Another very different theorist who was also interested in programmed instruction was *B. F. Skinner* (1953) (see chapter by Morris in this volume). As a committed behaviorist, Skinner used behavior analysis to build better teaching machines using programmed methods of instruction. He sought to introduce information in smaller units, ensure mastery of each unit, and reinforce success more effectively than teachers did (Skinner, 1958). Skinner disavowed the use of the word "theory" to describe his approach because he believed that it was both unnecessary and unscientific to invoke inner mechanisms to explain behavior. He preferred to keep explanatory concepts to a minimum and simply report data and relationships.

As the result of Skinner's prolific research and writing, he had a major influence on educational psychology during the 1950s and beyond. His system of behavior analysis was widely implemented in schools, especially with children in special education programs and is still taught widely in schools of education. Behavior analysis and modification involved use of targeted behavioral objectives, token systems of reward, and carefully structured instruction. Skinner was also a leader in the development of time-series single subject research methodologies and was instrumental in establishing a series of journals, such as the *Journal of Applied Behavior Analysis* and *Journal of Experimental Analysis of Behavior*, which featured use of this methodology in a wide variety of formal and informal instructional settings.

Lee Cronbach had enormous influence on educational psychology (see chapter by Kupermintz this volume). He wrote a highly successful textbook entitled *Educational Psychology* (1954) and developed many important psychometric methods for assessing test reliability and validity. Kuder (also an educational psychologist) and Richardson (1939) overcame the limitations of split-half reliability with their KR-20 (and related formulas) for percentage data. Cronbach (1951) proposed a new alpha measure that could be used with all types of scores, observations, and interval scales. Later he expanded his thinking on reliability theory to generalizability theory (Cronbach, Gleser, Nanda, & Rajaratman, 1972).

During his 1957 presidential address to the American Psychological Association, Cronbach drew attention to a major division in theory and research methods between clinical and experimental psychologists. Clinical psychologists primarily developed individual difference measures of personality and abilities, such as anxiety or intelligence, and studied correlations between these measures and human functioning in natural contexts. By contrast, experimental psychologists primarily conducted training studies to test the effectiveness of a particular method of learning, such as programmed instruction. Cronbach (1957) suggested that these seemingly disparate traditions in theory and research could be integrated into a common methodology called Aptitude-Treatment-Interaction (ATI). He advocated studying students of varying aptitudes (e.g., high versus low anxiety) as they learned according to different training methods (e.g., programmed instruction versus text reading). Cronbach suggested that a statistically significant interaction in a two-factor analysis of variance model would reveal the best "match" between a student's aptitude and an optimal method of instruction. Although Cronbach's conceptualization seemed promising to many researchers, they did not discover many replicable ATIs (Bracht, 1970). However, Cronbach's psychometric advances continue to be widely taught in psychometric courses at the beginning of the 21st century.

There were other significant methodological advances in research during the 1950s. Ecological psychologists, Barker and Wright (1954), undertook an intensive study of students in the social-psychological habitat of a high school. Barker and Wright followed individual students and made extensive, detailed observations and notes in order to more deeply understand their behavior. They were interested in the influence of students' holding responsible positions in school and participation in curricular as well as extracurricular activities on their social, physical, and academic development. These adolescents played important roles in their school and town, which garnered them both status and power.

Using qualitative methodological techniques, Barker and Wright observed individual students and interviewed them, their cohorts, and associated adults, such as their mothers, fathers, teachers, and neighbors. Barker and Wright even counted naturally occurring environmental traces, such as the number of activities listed beneath students' pictures in the yearbook. To classify their results, they developed categories and definitions from observations based on Murray's (1951) theory. To conduct these interviews and observations reliably and validly, Barker and Wright gave their staff extensive training and emphasized to them the importance of alertness, concentration, and personal involvement.

Barker and Wright discovered that the high school days of the students involved extensive social-psychological interactions reflecting dominance, nurturance, resistance, appeal, compliance, aggression, submission, and avoidance. This information led them to the conclusion that the personal and social environments in smaller schools were superior. In such schools, every student is needed for multiple academic and social roles. For instance, a boy is needed to play on an athletic team as well as in the band at half time. He may practice for a part in a school play as well as participate in several after-school clubs. Similarly girls were involved in athletics, academic activities, and social clubs. In small high schools, both boys and girls were needed, personally encouraged, and recognized for participating in diverse activities.

The purpose of qualitative research methods is to understand a phenomenon in depth. Barker and Wright contrasted their qualitative approach with traditional, quantitative approaches by noting that qualitative researchers record what they see first-hand by using a great many words, but no numbers. Later the words are classified and often quantified. By contrast, quantitative researchers numerically count or rate what they see using predefined categories. Barker and Wright feel that both qualitative and quantitative methods are useful, but a qualitative approach is less constrained by preexisting assumptions.

Although Barker and Wright's research methods were lauded by educational psychologists, their results have been often ignored by school administrators who placed greater value on the greater curricular offerings and administrative economies of larger high schools despite their inferior personal and social environments.

SUMMARY

The 4 decades from 1920 to 1960 were a period of enormous change in America— with the nation shifting from a largely rural, agricultural nation into an urban, industrialized one. In 1920, only a small portion of the student population attained a high school or college education, but by 1960, a large percentage of students graduated from high school, and a substantial number of them enrolled in college. During this period, educational psychology grew from a promising subarea in psychology to an important discipline in its own right. Although educational psychologists had developed the use of standardized testing and the use of statistics procedures to answer educational questions by 1920, the connection between psychological theory and educational practice in schools was largely intuitive. However, by 1960, educational psychologists had convincingly demonstrated the effectiveness of their methods of research and training. The value of skill-based educational technology and assessment during World War II was widely recognized, and these military training methods were adapted later for use in public schools.

Because of national concern about improving education and special education generally, and science and mathematics education and instructional technology in particular, in the 1950s, the federal government expanded its financial commitment to education. The Cooperative Research Program in 1956 was the first extramural research program in the then U.S. Office of Education, and it was expanded greatly over the years to support general research in education. Educational psychologists were invited to serve on its advisory committees for selecting these research projects, and many other educational psychologists established and expanded programs of educational research at their universities. They developed new methods for scientifically assessing higher order forms of student cognition, such as strategies, rule learning, and problem solving. They also made advances in new research methodologies—both qualitative and quantitative. By 1960, large "mainframe" computers were being installed in Universities from coast to coast, and educational psychologists were able to undertake sophisticated statistical analyses of large bodies of data based on methods developed during earlier military research. Educational Psychology had risen to prominence as a scientific discipline.

REFERENCES

Aubrey, W. (1937, September 24). *The college and high school aid program of the youth administration.* F. D. Roosevelt Library, Hopkins papers, Box 13. Retrieved from http://newdeal.feri.org/texts/451.htm

Barker, R. G., & Wright, H. F. (1954). *Midwest and its children: The psychological ecology of an American town.* Evanston, IL: Row, Peterson.

Benezet, L. P. (1935). The story of an experiment, Part I. *Journal of the National Education Association, 24,* 241–244, 301–303.

Benezet, L. P. (1936). The story of an experiment, Part II. *Journal of the National Education Association, 25,* 7–8.

Betts, E. A. (1946). *Foundations of reading instruction.* New York: American Book Company.

Bond, G. L., & Wagner, E. B. (1950). *Teaching the child to read.* (Rev. ed.). New York: Macmillan.

Bond, G. L., & Tinker, M. (1967). *Reading difficulties: Their diagnosis and correction.* New York: Macmillan.

Bond, H. M. (1952). The present status of racial integration in the United States, with special reference to education. *Journal of Negro Education, 21,* 242–243.

Bracht, G. H. (1970). The relationship of treatment tasks, personalogical variables, and dependent variables to aptitude-treatment-interaction. *Review of Educational Research, 40,* 627–745.

Briggs, L. J. (1980, February). Thirty years of instructional design: One man's experience. *Educational Technology, 20,* 45–50.

Brown vs. Board of Education of Topeka 374 U.S. 483 (1954).

Brown, W. (1910). Some experimental results in the correlation of mental abilities. *British Journal of Psychology, 3,* 296–322.

Brownell, W. A., & Moser, H. E. (1949). *Meaningful vs. mechanical learning.* Durham, NC: Duke University Press.

Clark, K. B., & Clark, M. P. (1950). Emotional factors in racial identification and preference in Negro children. *Journal of Negro Education, 19,* 341–350.

Cronbach, L. J. (1951). The coefficient alpha and the internal structure of tests. *Psychometrika,* 297–334.

Cronbach, L. J. (1954). *Educational psychology.* New York: Harcourt Brace.

Cronbach, L. J. (1957). The two disciplines of scientific psychology. *American Psychologist, 12,* 671–684.

Cronbach, L. J., Gleser, G. C., Nanda, H., & Rajaratman, N. (1972). *The dependability of behavioral measurements: Theory of generalizability of scores and profiles.* New York: Wiley.

Dewey, J. (1983). Human nature and conduct. In J. A. Boydston (Ed.), *Middle Works, 1899–1924.* (Vol. 14, pp. 1–230). Carbondale, IL: Southern Illinois University.

Gagne, R. M. (1965). *The conditions of learning.* New York: Holt, Rinehart & Winston.

Gagne, R. M. (1989). *Studies of learning: Fifty years of research.* Tallahassee: Learning Systems Institute, Florida State University.

Gagne, R. M., & Brown, L. T. (1961). Some factors in the programming of conceptual learning. *Journal of Experimental Psychology, 62,* 313–321.

Gates, A. I. (1937). A list of spelling difficulties for children in grades II-VI. *Elementary School Journal, 53,* 221–28.

Gates, A. I. (1947). *The improvement of reading.* New York: Macmillan.

Gullickson, H. (1950). *Theory of mental tests.* New York: Wiley.

Guthrie, E. R. (1935). *A combination of the psychology of learning.* New York: Harper & Row.

Guthrie, E. R. (1942). Conditioning: A theory of learning in terms of stimulus, response, and association. In N. B. Henry (Ed.), *National Society for the Study of Education Yearbook,* Part II (pp. 17–60). Chicago, IL: University of Chicago Press.

Hildreth, G. (1949). The development and training of hand dominance. *Pedagogical Seminary and Journal of Genetic Psychology,* 197–275.

Hildreth, G. (1955). *Teaching spelling.* New York: Holt.

Hilgard, E. R. (1948). *Theories of learning.* New York: Appleton-Century-Crofts.

Hull, C. L. (1943). *The principles of behavior.* New York: Appleton-Century.

Koffka, K. (1924). *The growth of the mind.* London: Kegan, Paul, Trench, Trubner.

Kohler, W. (1925). *The mentality of apes.* Harmondsworth, England: Penguin.

Krug, E. A. (1972). *The shaping of the American high school, Vol. 2, 1940–41.* Madison, WI: The University of Wisconsin Press.

Lewin, K. L. (1936). *Field theory in social science.* New York: Harper & Row.

Lewin, K., Lippitt, T., & White, R. K. (1939). Patterns of aggressive behavior in experimentally created social climates. *Journal of Social Psychology, 10,* 271–299.

McCall, W. A. (1923). *How to experiment in education.* New York: Macmillan.

McCarthy, D. (1954). Language development in children. In L. Carmichael (Ed.), *Manual of Child Psychology* (pp. 492–630). New York: Wiley.

Murray, H. A. (1951). Toward a classification of interaction. In T. Parsons & E. A. Shils (Eds.), *Toward a general theory of action* (pp. 434–464). Cambridge, MA: Harvard University Press.

Newland, T. E. (1932). An analytical study of illegibilies in handwriting from the lower grades to adulthood. *Journal of Educational Research, 26,* 249–58.

Piaget, J. (1926). *The language and thought of the child.* London: Paul, Trench, Trubner.

Piaget, J. (1928). *Judgment and reasoning in the child.* New York: Harcourt, Brace.

Rulon, P. J. (1941). Problems of regression. *Harvard Educational Review, 11*, 213–223.

Russell, D. H. (1949). *Children learn to read*. Boston: Gunn.

Russell, D. H. (1955). A study of characteristics of good and poor spellers. *Journal of Educational Psychology, 46*, 129–41.

Russell, D. H., & Russell, E. F. (1959). *Listening aids through the grades*. New York: Teachers College, Columbia University.

Skinner, B. F. (1953). *Science and human behavior*. New York: Macmillan.

Skinner, B. F. (1958). Teaching machines. *Science, 128*, 969–977.

Spearman, C. (1910). Correlation calculated from faulty data. *British Journal of Psychology, 3*, 271–295.

Stephens, J. M. (1956). *Educational psychology*. New York: Holt, Rinehart & Winston.

Strang, R., McCullough, C. M., & Traxler, A. E. (1955). *Problems in the improvement of reading*. New York: McGraw-Hill.

Thorndike, E. L. (1910, March). Handwriting. *Teachers College Record, 11*, 79–80.

Thorndike, E. L. (1918). The nature, purposes and general methods of measurements of educational products. In G. M. Whipple (Ed.), *Measurement of educational products*, National Society for the Study of Education, 17 (Part 2, pp. 9–190). Bloomington, IL: Public School Publishing Co.

Thorndike, E. L. (1922). *The psychology of arithmetic*. New York: Macmillan.

Thordike, E. L. (1932). *The fundamentals of learning*. New York: Teachers College Press.

Thorndike, R. L. (1942). Regression fallacies in the matched group experiment, *Psychometrika, 7*, 85–102.

Tolman, E. C. (1932). *Purposive behavior in animals and men*. New York: Appleton-Century.

Tyler, R. W. (1942, October). Some techniques used in the follow-up study of college success of graduates of the thirty schools participating in the Eight-Year Study of the Progressive Education Association. *Journal of the American Association of Collegiate Registrars, 18*, 23–28.

Vygotsky, L. (1978). *Mind in society: The development of higher mental processes*. Cambridge, MA: Harvard University Press.

Wertheimer, M. (1923). Untersuchungen zur Lehre von der Gestalt II, *Psychol. Forsch [Laws of organization in perceptual forms]*, 4, 301–356.

Witty, P. A. (1949). *Reading in modern education*. Boston, MA: Heath.

Witty, P. A., & Sizemore, R. A. (1959a, 1959b, 1959c). Studies in listening: I, II, III, and A postscript. *Elementary English*, 297–301.

Wrightstone, J. W. (1935). *Appraisal of newer school practices in selected public schools*. New York: Teachers College.

9

Lev S. Vygotsky on Education: A Cultural-Historical, Interpersonal, and Individual Approach to Development

Jonathan Tudge
Sheryl Scrimsher
The University of North Carolina at Greensboro

This chapter focuses on Vygotsky's writings on education, placing them into the broader context of his theory. Our central argument is that understanding Vygotsky's views on education means examining the relations among individual, interpersonal, and socio-historical influences on human development. As we make that argument, we are going to rely heavily on quotations from Vygotsky's writings, primarily because as more and more scholars have come to invoke Vygotsky's name in support of their research, there seems to be limited attention paid to the corpus of his writings, even though they are now readily available to English speakers.

Vygotsky's thinking changed markedly over the course of his productive life. All theories develop over the lifetimes of the theorists, of course. Such change seems less remarkable for someone like Jean Piaget, however, whose productive life encompassed 6 decades than for Vygotsky, who died when he was only 37. In his early writings, Vygotsky displayed an approach that was heavily dependent on stimulus–response connections, reflexes, and reactions, and that was utterly unlike his thinking in the last 5 or 6 years of his life when he was developing his cultural-historical theory (Minick, 1987; van der Veer & Valsiner, 1994; Veresov, 1999). For that reason, quotations drawn from various stages of Vygotsky's life can provide a misleading account of his thinking. We have, therefore, consistently indicated the year of authorship or first publication of each quotation. We will first provide an overview of Vygotsky's life, followed by a discussion of his overall contributions to education. The third section, our evaluation of Vygotsky's impact on the field of education in North America, will include a discussion of Vygotsky's view of the role of the learner and the nature of learning.

OVERVIEW OF VYGOTSKY'S LIFE

If life illustrates science, Vygotsky's own life can best be understood with reference to the very things that he came to argue were essential to understanding development: the interrelations of the individual, the interpersonal, and the cultural-historical. (For fuller details of Vygotsky's life, see the sources from which the following was drawn: Blanck, 1990; Levitin, 1982; Luria, 1979; van der Veer & Valsiner, 1991; Veresov, 1999; Vygodskaia & Lifanova, 1999a, 1999b.)

Individual Characteristics

Lev Semenovich Vygotsky (then known as Vygodsky) was born in 1896 into a large, Jewish, intellectual family residing in Orsha, a small town near Minsk. Before Lev was a year old, the family moved, to Gomel'. Even though he showed intellectual potential early, he was still fortunate to be able to enter university in 1913 (a quota restricted the number of Jewish students who could attend). At the wishes of his parents, Vygotsky initially entered the Medical faculty of Moscow Imperial University, but a month later switched to the faculty of Law and, at the same time, enrolled in the History of Philosophy at the Shaniavskii University in Moscow. Here Vygotsky studied, among other things, literature; he wrote articles of literary criticism, as well as a major study of Hamlet.

Vygotsky returned to Gomel' in 1917, just prior to the Russian Revolution, and for the next few years had to deal with the problems of German occupation, Civil War, and famine. During this period, two of his brothers died from tuberculosis and typhoid. (Vygotsky himself, in 1920, also fell seriously ill with tuberculosis, the disease that would eventually kill him.) Only after 1919, when Gomel' was brought under Soviet control, did Vygotsky find work. He taught literature and psychology, and also edited a literary journal, wrote literary criticism, and published theater reviews. Out of this work grew his book entitled *The Psychology of Art* (completed, as his dissertation, in 1925, although not published until long after his death). If this were not enough, Vygotsky also worked at the Gomel' college for the training of teachers, where he organized a psychology laboratory and started work on his first book devoted exclusively to psychology, *Educational Psychology* (1926/1997a).

In 1924, Vygotsky presented three papers at the 2nd All-Russian Congress of Psychoneurology, including "The Methods of Reflexological and Psychological Investigation." At least one member of his audience, Alexander Romanovich

Luria, was so impressed that Vygotsky was invited to join Kornilov's Institute of Experimental Psychology in Moscow. Vygotsky participated in establishing the Institute of Defektology, an institute devoted to studying how mentally and physically handicapped children could be helped. He served as its "scientific leader" (van der Veer & Valsiner, 1991) and became its Director in 1929. By the end of his life Vygotsky was again focusing more on educational psychology; he died from tuberculosis in 1934, at the age of 37. Theoretically, Vygotsky gradually moved from a Sechenov- and Pavlov-based conditioning view of psychology (focusing on reflexes and reactions) to a cultural-historical theory that placed more significance on language, social interaction, and culture. However, even in his earlier writings on psychology, it is clear that Vygotsky was dissatisfied with reflexological views that separated mind and body and consistently attempted to create a new psychology that would overcome this dualism (Veresov, 1999).

Interpersonal Aspects

Discussion of what Vygotsky accomplished as an individual might lead one to suppose that he was a genius, a "Mozart" of his age (Levitin, 1982; Toulmin, 1978). However, it would be a mistake to view Vygotsky as a unique figure. To understand his development, one must consider his interpersonal interactions with others. He read voraciously and was well acquainted with the ideas of many scholars across Europe and in North America who are now viewed as being in the forefront of a "sociogenetic" approach to development (Tudge, Putnam, & Valsiner, 1996). Moreover, his own intellect was initially honed in many dinner-time discussions with his family (Vygodskaia & Lifanova, 1999a), and his later ideas benefited greatly from collaboration with the other major figures of early Soviet psychology, such as Luria and Leont'ev.

Historical Aspects

Vygotsky's development cannot be understood, however, without knowing the historical events that were taking place, specifically the post-Revolutionary zeal to create new ways of doing things, transform ideas on education, and develop a "new" psychology that would be based on Marxist–Leninist dialectical materialism. Although Vygotsky may well have been equally interested in the same issues regardless of what was occurring historically, the time was right in that the post-Revolutionary Soviet society supported his aim, at least for a while. But in the early years after the Revolution there was such a strong feeling of new possibilities to create new things in so many areas of life; Vygotsky's discussions with his colleagues and friends can only be understood against this backdrop. In summary, Vygotsky's development cannot be understood without taking into account his individual characteristics, his interactions with others, and the historical changes wrought by the Russian Revolution and its aftermath.

PSYCHOLOGICAL CONTRIBUTIONS
TO EDUCATION

The Russian Revolution and the formation of the Soviet Union were both a blessing and a curse for Vygotsky. On the one hand, they afforded him and his colleagues the opportunity to participate in the creation of a new society and to make a profound impact on psychology and education. On the other hand, Vygotsky's influence was short-lived, with his ideas being attacked on political grounds even before he died (Valsiner, 1988). It would be many years before his ideas were resurrected in the West. In his short life Vygotsky wrote widely about education. Before he moved to Moscow from Gomel' he wrote *Educational Psychology* (1926/1997a), the only complete book-length manuscript to be published during his lifetime (Jaroshevsky, 1994; Veresov, 1999).

Educational Psychology was Vygotsky's first attempt to write a book specifically about psychology, and it was designed as a textbook for students. It was one of the most ideology-related of his writings, seen not simply in the frequent citations of Marx, but in the apparent acceptance of the Marxist-Leninist perspective. As Vygotsky wrote in 1926: "Psychology is in need of its own Das Kapital—its own concepts of class, basis, value, etc." (1997a). *Educational Psychology* was written while Vygotsky was still very much influenced by stimulus–response approaches to psychology, and drew heavily on the concept of conditional reflexes, as developed by Pavlov and Bekhterev (Veresov, 1999). Even at this time, Vygotsky had already expressed concerns about intelligence testing of children, arguing that formal testing was unlikely to capture the ways in which children respond in real-world situations, an argument that foreshadowed Bronfenbrenner's (1989, 1995) subsequent concern with ecological validity.

During the 1920s and early 1930s Vygotsky was very interested in the development and teaching of children with mental and physical handicaps (a field known as *"Defektology"*), and edited a book on the topic (Vygotsky, 1924), as well as publishing numerous articles. As might be expected, given the ways in which his thinking changed over the course of his life, his views on the treatment of these children also underwent significant change. In keeping with the optimistic viewpoint of the early Soviet period, Vygotsky initially believed that speech could simply serve as the replacement that would allow blind or deaf children to compensate for their problem. This essentially reflexological approach changed in 1926 or 1927 under the influence of Adlerian psychology (van der Veer & Valsiner, 1991). The goal of these children, and of their teachers, was to develop "supercompensation" or a supporting "superstructure" that would allow alternative means not simply to replace the lack of hearing or sight but to bring about a restructuring of mind to reach these goals. By the end of the decade, however, Vygotsky was developing his cultural-historical theory, and his position on children who experienced mental and physical difficulties changed accordingly. The main difficulty that these children had was that they had not been enabled to experience the cultural development of normally developing children, and the answer was to mainstream the former into the collective of the latter.

Vygotsky by no means restricted himself to writing about disabled children, and from 1928 to 1934, the year he died, Vygotsky wrote extensively about "pedology" ("the science of child development" quoted in van der Veer & Valsiner, 1991, p. 308). By the time that Vygotsky was writing about pedology, he had moved far beyond the stimulus–response paradigm to the development of his cultural-historical theory. However, pedology was denounced in 1936 and all references to it, and to Vygotsky's theory, were banned in the Soviet Union until the 1980s. This is not to say that Vygotsky had no impact on the development of Soviet education, but rather that his impact, although fostered by his former colleagues and students, was rarely made explicit (Kozulin, 1990; Valsiner, 1988).

In the United States, despite the publication of several of Vygotsky's papers (Vygotsky, 1929, 1934, 1939) and the first version of one of his books in 1962 (incorrectly translated in abridged form as *Thought and Language*), there was little interest in his ideas until the late 1970s, with the publication of *Mind in Society* (1978). The role of various individuals, particularly Michael Cole, Jim Wertsch, Alex Kozulin, René van der Veer, and Jaan Valsiner, cannot be overestimated in this regard, as they made Vygotsky's ideas available to a far larger audience in the United States. However, in keeping with the theme of this chapter, cultural-historical factors also explain the rise in popularity of Vygotsky's work. As Piaget's theory came under increasing (though often misguided) attack, the time may have been ripe for educators and psychologists to look with some favor on a theorist who appeared to give more of a role to social factors in development.

Interpersonal, Cultural-Historical, and Individual Factors

As we have argued, Vygotsky's theory stresses the interrelatedness of these three factors in development. In North America, however, the complexity of Vygotsky's theory has been for the most part ignored in favor of a reliance on a single concept, *the zone of proximal development*. Moreover, the concept itself has too often been viewed in a rather limited way that emphasizes the interpersonal at the expense of the individual and cultural-historical levels and treats the concept in a unidirectional fashion. As if the concept were synonymous with "scaffolding," too many authors have focused on the role of the more competent other, particularly the teacher, whose role is to provide assistance just in advance of the child's current thinking (see, for example, Berk & Winsler, 1995; Brown & Ferrara, 1985; Bruner & Haste, 1987; Wood, 1999). The concept thus has become equated with what sensitive teachers might do with their children and has lost much of the complexity with which it was imbued by Vygotsky, missing both what the child brings to the interaction and the broader setting (cultural and historical) in which the interaction takes place (Griffin & Cole, 1999; Stone, 1993). For example, this interpretation misses entirely Vygotsky's position that developments in a child's life are akin to historical developments in societies (related to Marx's thesis that humans have an undeveloped potential that can only be released after the structural reorganization of society).

Translation Issues.   Before discussing the interpretation of Vygotskian concepts in more detail, however, it is necessary to raise the issue of translation, because some of the confusion about the apparently unidirectional flow from teacher to child stems from the way in which a key word has been translated. The Russian term *obuchenie* has been translated by different translators as instruction, teaching, or learning, whereas in fact the word connotes both teaching *and* learning (Bodrova & Leong, 1996; Valsiner, 1988; van der Veer & Valsiner, 1991; Wheeler, 1984). For example, the Plenum version of *Thinking and Speech* (1987) translated *obuchenie* as "instruction" throughout (see for example p. 212), whereas the *Mind in Society* (1978) translation of the same word in the same context is consistently "learning" (a totally different perspective on what Vygotsky meant). By contrast, the meaning of "teaching/learning" is subtly, but clearly, different from either of the words used alone. This means that those who have relied either on *Thinking and Speech* (1987) or on the older, less accurate, versions of *Thought and Language* (1962 or 1986) have been led to think of the concept as one that relates only to a teacher who provides the instruction to a child who learns.

A more appropriate translation of the term *obuchenie* infers a more bi-directional flow than is implied by "instruction" and allows us to make better sense of Vygotsky's position that "teaching/learning" occurs long before the child goes to school. The better translation also enables readers to understand that when a zone of proximal development is created in the course of interaction between a teacher and child, or between two or more peers, *all* participants participate both in the creation and in the subsequent development that may occur. Such a position nicely captures the view, beloved among many teachers, that one learns best when teaching! This more accurate and subtle translation should be borne in mind as we turn to a discussion of Vygotsky's treatment of the concept of the zone of proximal development.

Interpersonal Aspects.   The concept captures well the interpersonal aspect of Vygotsky's theory. Contrasting traditional (and, indeed, contemporary) measures of intellectual development (the *actual* level, as determined by tests of what the child can currently do independently) with the *proximal* level (what the child can do with assistance of someone more competent, whether adult or child), Vygotsky (1934/1987) argued that "the zone of proximal development has more significance for the dynamics of intellectual development and for the success of instruction than does the actual level of development" (p. 209). Therefore: "*[Teaching/learning] is only useful when it moves ahead of development. When it does, it impels or wakens a whole series of functions that are in a stage of maturation lying in the zone of proximal development*" (p. 212, italics in the original). The zone is not, therefore, some clear-cut space that exists independently of the process of joint activity itself. Rather, it is *created* in the course of collaboration:

> We propose that an essential feature of [teaching/learning] is that it creates the zone of proximal development; that is, [teaching/learning] awakens a variety of developmental processes that are able to operate only when the child is interacting with people in his environment and in collaboration with his peers. (Vygotsky, 1935/1978, p. 90)

The specific mechanisms that allow the child to construct higher psychological structures, according to Vygotsky, are internalization and externalization. Children internalize or interiorize the processes occurring in the course of the interaction with the more competent member of the culture—they "grow into the intellectual life of those around them" (Vygotsky, 1935/1978, p. 88). As Vygotsky argued:

> Every higher mental function was external because it was social before it became an internal, strictly mental function; it was formerly a social relation of two people.... We can formulate the general genetic law of cultural development as follows: Any function in the child's cultural development appears on the stage twice, or on two planes, first the social, then the psychological, first between people as an intermental category, then within the child as a[n] intramental category. (Vygotsky, 1931/1997c, pp. 105–106)

Internalization is not a matter of mere copying and is "far from being a purely mechanical operation" (Vygotsky & Luria, 1930/1994, p. 153), because this would preclude the emergence of novelty. Rather, children transform the internalized interaction on the basis of their own characteristics, experiences, and existing knowledge. Development is thus a process of reorganization of mental structures in relation to one another (Vygotsky, 1935/1994). In subsequent interactions with the social world, the transformed knowledge structures contribute to its reconstruction. Those who have already aided the child may assist in this process by encouraging externalization: "The teacher, working with the school child on a given question, explains, informs, inquires, corrects, and *forces the child himself to explain*" (Vygotsky, 1934/1987, pp. 215–216, italics added).

It would be a mistake, however, to think that Vygotsky conceptualized internalization, or even interactions creating a zone of proximal development, as processes that occur only in school contexts. Once the concept of zone of proximal development has been divorced from "instruction" it becomes much easier to understand how Vygotsky could discuss it in the context of children's play (see Nicolopoulou, 1993). In a 1933 lecture, Vygotsky (1978) argued that play is highly important in young children's development. One critical role for play is that it helps children in the use of symbolic forms: "In play thought is separated from objects and action arises from ideas rather than from things: a piece of wood begins to be a doll and a stick becomes a horse" (p. 97). Meanings of things are thus detached from their typical appearance and serve as mediating devices between objects and the things that the objects stand for, in just the same way that the written word will come to have that function for literate children. Vygotsky (1933/1978) concluded that "play creates a zone of proximal development of the child. In play a child always behaves beyond his average age, above his daily behavior" (p. 102). It is very difficult to fit this notion of play with the idea of instruction.

Cultural-Historical Aspects.   Having considered the interpersonal relations between children and others (people, objects, and symbols) in their environments, we will turn to the cultural-historical focus of Vygotsky's theory. We must emphasize the fact that Vygotsky's theory is appropriately termed a cultural-historical theory and that this is where the focus should be placed, even while acknowledging the important role played by individual activity in conjunction with others. As we will show, Vygotsky viewed the cultural world (instantiated as the ways in which people have become used to interacting with one another, their tools, and institutions) as the source of the development of higher mental functions. History can be viewed as relating to the development of the species and the cultural group but also as ontogenetic and microgenetic development (Scribner, 1985; Wertsch & Tulviste, 1992).

It is clear that, for Vygotsky, school and schooling play a critical role in determining the ways in which we think. However, school's importance is not so much as a context in which children are scaffolded but rather as the setting in which children are encouraged to become "consciously aware" of themselves, their language, and their place in the world. The issue of conscious awareness (or consciousness, as Vygotsky typically wrote) was central to his thinking; it is what makes us social beings or, in other words, human. It is in this sense that the links to history and culture become clear. What happens in the course of school teaching/learning is that children become more consciously aware of the meaning (not simply the sense) of concepts that earlier had been used in a nonconscious way. "Grandfather" is understood not only as a white-haired old man who tinkers in his workshop but also as a person occupying a role in a system of kinship. To extend the argument, we could say that the centrality of conscious awareness becomes evident as a child begins to think of the history of his relations with his grandfather and comes to realize that all grandfathers pass on cultural lessons to their grandchildren. Although Vygotsky was very interested in the distinction between sense (what a word connotes) and its meaning (what it denotes) (see, for example, chapter 7 of *Thinking and Speech*, Vygotsky 1933/1987), the issue of conscious awareness played a far more central role in his theory.

Through schooling, children learn new concepts ("scientific" concepts) in a way that is made conscious from the start. Vygotsky's example of the concept of "exploitation" illustrated the way that in learning/being taught scientific concepts, children become consciously aware not only of scientific concepts but also the everyday concepts that they have been accustomed to using nonconsciously. Using language as an example, Vygotsky pointed out that the preschool child "has already acquired the entire grammar of his native language. Nonetheless, while he declines and he conjugates, he does not know that he declines and conjugates" (1934/1987, p. 205). An example from Molière provides an apt illustration: M. Jourdain, the hero of *Le Bourgeois Gentilhomme*, was unaware of the fact that, while talking, he spoke prose. Still, the connection between scientific and everyday concepts is complex and mutually influencing for "both types of concepts are not encapsulated in the child's consciousness, are not separated from one another by an impermeable barrier, do not flow along two isolated channels, but are in the process of continual, unceasing interaction" (Vygotsky, 1935/1994, p. 365). In schooling, each subject has its own specific relation to the course of development that varies as the child advances his or her understanding of scientific concepts.

Although some have viewed Vygotsky as making a type of recapitulationist argument, his linking of what occurred when humans first used tools and what occurs when children go to school was not intended to imply that the child's ontogenetic development would go through the same processes as the species' phylogenetic development (Scribner, 1985). Instead, his position was that the participation of children in a world in which psychological tools (knots in handkerchiefs, gestures, linguistic or mathematical symbols) were used involves the creation of a zone of proximal development, drawing them into the cultural world of higher mental processes. As Wertsch and Tulviste (1992) pointed out, Vygotsky's position is quite clear; participation in a world of cultural tools does not simply facilitate processes that would have developed regardless, but utterly transforms mental functioning. "In the process of historical development, social man changes the methods and devices of his behavior, transforms natural instincts and functions, and develops and creates new forms of behavior—specifically cultural" (Vygotsky, 1931/1997c, p. 18). This approach "seeks to present the history of how the child in the process of education accomplishes what mankind accomplished in the course of the long history of labor" (1930/1997b, p. 88). In both cases the significance of the change is that one's relation with the external world becomes characterized by conscious (or self-conscious) awareness, that is, the ability to reflect on what one is doing or seeing, rather than simply reacting in a nonconscious way.

> This viewpoint is easily observed in phylogenesis, since the biological and historical formation of all function[s] are so sharply divided and so obviously belong to different types of evolution that both processes are evident in a pure and isolated form. In ontogenesis, however, both lines of development appear as an interwoven complex combination. (Vygotsky & Luria 1930/1994, p. 139)

Vygotsky drew connections between interactions within the zone of proximal development and an expanded context of social development. He defined the word "social" as "everything cultural, in the broadest sense of the word. Culture is the product of man's social life and his public activity" (1928/1993, p. 164). Involvement in the sociocultural world is what makes children human, by ensuring that they develop higher mental processes. "The higher functions of intellectual activity arise out of collective behavior, out of cooperation with the surrounding people, and from social experience" (1931/1993, p. 196). For example, spontaneous and impulsive actions, the hallmark of many preschoolers' activities, are transformed into the product of reflection in the course of playing with others, particularly playing rule-based games. Even the activities of a child playing alone must be studied as simultaneously an individual and a social phenomenon (Tudge et al., 1999). That is to say, the child at play brings to her activities those roles, rules, and reactions she has already seen enacted in her daily life (Vygotsky, 1933/1978). "The influence of play on development is enormous" (Vygotsky, 1933/1978, p. 96). Play liberates the child from constraints, excites new pathways of cognitive awareness and stimulates perception of the cultural world.

> Educators are beginning to understand that on entering a culture a child not only gets something from culture, assimilating it, inculcating something from the outside, but that culture itself reworks all the child's natural behavior and carves anew his entire course of development. The distinction between the two paths of development (natural and cultural) becomes the fulcrum for a new theory of education. (1928/1993, p. 166)

This view of social development makes clear that the zone of proximal development is not simply something that occurs in school contexts between teacher and child but deals with the development of new forms of awareness that are created as societies develop new social organizations, such as systems of schooling.

The Individual.   Because Vygotsky argued that the social world "is a source of development" (1935/1994, p. 351) many who have invoked Vygotsky have implied that his theory involves a view of culture and context that acts in a unidirectional fashion on the individual. This interpretation is far from accurate, and ignores the essentially Marxist-based dialectical nature of the theory (Elhammoumi, 2002; van der Veer & van IJzendoorn, 1985). It is clear that Vygotsky did not believe that social forces completely explained children's development. Although Vygotsky did not discuss the "natural" line of development in anywhere near as great a detail as he discussed historical, cultural, and social aspects of development, it cannot be ignored. Included within the natural line of development are all "inherited" factors.

> So, our first task consists in following the influence of heredity on child development through all its intermediate links, so that any developmental occurrences and any inherited factors are placed in genetically clear interrelationships. . . . Contemporary genetic research—which deals with both constitutional problems and with research on twins—offers a researcher an enormous amount of material for the deepest constitutional analysis of a child's personality with respect to heredity. (1931/1993, pp. 279–280)

Interestingly, in light of current debates involving behavior geneticists, Vygotsky's position was clear regarding the interrelations of genes and environment:

> Development is not a simple function which can be wholly determined by adding X units of heredity to Y units of environment. It is a historical complex which, at every stage, reveals the past which is a part of it.... Development, according to a well-known definition, is precisely the struggle of opposites. This view alone can support truly dialectical research on the process of children's development. (1931/1993, pp. 282–283)

Vygotsky's understanding of complexity means that the methods required to gather data on children's development must be truly developmental, using longitudinal ("etiological") rather than cross-sectional methods. In his words, researchers need to focus not on a single "slice" of development (one point in time), but on a series of slices that serve to "uncover the specific dynamic process" at work (p. 288).

> An etiological analysis must always show (1) how a given developmental stage is conditioned by the self-advancement of the whole, the internal logic of the development process itself, and (2) how one stage necessarily developed from the preceding stage of development, rather than being the mechanical sum of environmental and hereditary factors which are new to each stage. Lifting the etiological analysis of development to truly scientific heights means, above all, searching for the causes of the events which interest us in the developmental process itself, and uncovering its internal logic and its self-advancement. (1931/1993, p. 290)

Vygotsky discussed the interrelations of individual and environment in one of the last lectures he gave before his death, in which he argued that social influences can only be understood in relation to the child.

> The same environmental factors which may have one meaning and play a certain role during a given age, two years on begin to have a different meaning and to play a different role because the child has changed; in other words, the child's relation to these particular environmental factors has altered. (1935/1994, p. 338)

In the course of development, children change by virtue of the experiences that they previously had, as well as the meaning those experiences have had for them. Those experiences, though involving them in different social situations, have become "their personal property" (p. 352), influencing the ways in which they deal with other experiences. As a result, the meaning of any given social or environmental influence (such as a teacher trying to "scaffold" a group's understanding of some concept) will necessarily also be different for each child in that group. In other words, the impact of some social event is determined by "how a child becomes aware of, interprets, [and] emotionally relates to [that] certain event" (p. 341).

The event, by itself, is meaningless without consideration of the individuals involved in it. "This *dynamic and relative interpretation of environment* is the most important source of information for paedology when environment is under discussion" (p. 346, italics in the original).

The role of the individual in the group is also discussed in Vygotsky's writings on children with physical or mental disabilities (Vygotsky, 1993), in which he wrote about the problems that accrue when children are artificially prevented from participating in a social group. It is clear that Vygotsky believed that the education of children who had mental or physical difficulties (for example, deafness or blindness) is greatly enhanced by being mainstreamed, rather than having these children educated with others who suffer from a similar disability. When children with disabilities are able to interact with others who are less mentally disabled, or have more advanced hearing or better sight, they develop higher levels of functioning. In mainstreamed groups, "the personality of the severely retarded child truly finds a dynamic source of development, and . . . in the process of collective activity and cooperation, he is lifted to a higher level" (1931/1993, p. 201). The same is true with blind and deaf children (p. 205). Vygotsky ended his chapter with the following words:

> The basic principal and fulcrum for all our pedagogy for the abnormal child requires us now to be able to understand anew . . . the links between cooperation [collective activity] and the development of higher mental functions; between the development of the collective and the abnormal child's personality. Communist pedagogy is the pedagogy of the collective. (1931/1993, p. 208)

The essence of the process of cultural development is that "through others, we become ourselves" (Vygotsky, 1931/1997c, p. 105). The rules governing this process of becoming refer to each individual and to the history of each higher mental function. Presented earlier in this chapter as the "general genetic law," this expression of cultural development makes clear why everything internal was at first external (Vygotsky, 1931/1997c).

EVALUATION

The preceding section presented an overview of Vygotsky's contributions to education, focusing on an understanding of development that emerges through the interrelations of the individual, interpersonal, and cultural factors within an historical context. Bringing Vygotskian theory into contemporary discourse has been a complicated venture. The central problem is that Vygotsky's works are still not well understood, partly due to the fact that only during the past decade have there been any reasonable translations of much of his work. As Valsiner (1988) clearly demonstrated, scholars rely on one of two texts, one consisting of partial translations and a précis of writings from various periods of Vygotsky's life (*Mind in Society*, 1978) and, to a lesser extent, *Thinking and Speech* (1987). There is little evidence that the situation has changed greatly since then. Despite some excellent discussions of the issue (Minick, 1987; van der Veer & Valsiner, 1991; Veresov, 1999), people using Vygotsky's ideas have failed to appreciate the significance of the theoretical changes that he went through in his short life. This has led to compilations of quotations cobbled together from sources that are theoretically heterogeneous. A second major problem is that a single concept (the zone of proximal development) has been seized on as the essence of Vygotskian thought, with a failure to recognize either the limited role this concept plays in the theory as a whole or that, if the concept is to be used, it must be placed into its broader theoretical context. The focus on interpersonal aspects of the theory must be combined with simultaneous attention to culture and history and to the role played by the individual.

We now consider how writings of contemporary theorists and researchers might further illuminate our understanding of Vygotsky's contributions to education. Attention in North America focused immediately and almost exclusively on the zone of proximal development, which has fostered a great deal of interest both theoretically and empirically (Wells, 1999). The problem with much of this research, however, is that it has failed to put the concept into its broader theoretical framework. For example, in a review of research on children's collaboration that supposedly built on Vygotsky's theory, Hogan and Tudge (1999) found that although the studies dealt with the interpersonal world (typically what occurred between a more competent and less competent child), far fewer dealt with what either individual brought to the collaborative process, and even fewer considered the broader cultural and historical context within which the collaboration was situated.

The same is true of much of the research on teacher–child interaction that is supposedly related to Vygotsky's theory. Much of this work has appropriated Vygotsky's concept to that of scaffolding. This term was first used by Wood, Bruner, and Ross (1976) to capture the way in which an expert helped a novice to perform some task or skill in a more competent way than the novice could achieve without such assistance. Wood and his colleagues described the process as one in which "a child or novice [is enabled] to solve a problem, carry out a task or achieve a goal which would be beyond his unassisted efforts" (1976, p. 90). Although the authors do not cite Vygotsky, this sentence sounds highly Vygotskian. However, the authors continue: "This scaffolding consists essentially of the adult 'controlling' those elements of the task that are initially beyond the learner's capacity, thus permitting him to concentrate upon and complete only those elements that are within his range of competence" (p. 90). This may well be what many good teachers try to do, but it has little to do with Vygotsky's concept of the zone of proximal development[1] (Griffin & Cole, 1999; Stone, 1993).

The metaphor of scaffolding seriously downplays the fact that the more competent, as well as less competent, person can gain from the interaction. Whether the image that comes to mind is the scaffold that goes up to support a building being constructed or the scaffold from which someone is going to be hung, the image is that the person who provides the scaffold has clear control of the situation and is not expected to change in the process. Metaphors are, of course, powerful tools (as Vygotsky himself would argue), but they have their limitations. The limitation in this context is that Vygotsky's theory is conflated with one that stresses the teacher's role in providing the appropriate assistance to the child. For example, Berk and Winsler stated:

> A major goal of scaffolding, and education in general, is to keep children working on tasks in their ZPDs. This is usually achieved in two ways: (1) by structuring the task and the surrounding environment so that the demands on the child at any given time are at an appropriately challenging level, and (2) constantly adjusting the amount of adult intervention to the child's current needs and abilities. (1995, p. 29)

To be fair, Berk and Winsler went on to point out the danger of stressing the apparently teacher-dominated sense that can be taken from the concept of scaffolding and argued that interactions within the zone of proximal development are, of course, bi-directional. Ann Brown and her colleagues have made the same point, namely, that although scaffolding stresses the role of the expert, the process of learning is clearly reciprocal (Brown, Ash, Rutherford, Nakagawa, Gordon, & Campione, 1993; Brown & Palincsar, 1989). However, it is all too easy to treat the concept of scaffolding in a unidirectional fashion, focusing on child improvement as a simple function of teacher or parent assistance (Brown & Ferrara, 1985; Wood, 1999), as opposed to the dynamic process that Vygotsky intended. Giving *obuchenie* its meaning of teaching/learning encourages us to examine what happens to both partners in the interaction and to recognize that when a zone of proximal development is created in the course of interaction, both partners change. Treating the interacting partners as the unit of analysis, of course, creates statistical difficulties entirely avoided by treating the child as the only analytic unit of interest.

The more simplistic notion of scaffolding, said to be derived from Vygotsky, is being increasingly used as a tool to attack the notion that young children learn best simply by being allowed to play with objects, with the adult role primarily that of providing the objects and "supporting" what the children are doing. This view, supposedly (but erroneously) derived from Piaget, had an impact on elementary or primary education in the 1970s and is still relatively common in the discussions of "Developmentally Appropriate Practice" (Bredekamp, 1987; Bredekamp & Copple, 1997) in preschools and other child-care centers. Currently, there is greater discussion of adults' roles as scaffolders of young children, invoking the zone of proximal development, as a way of countering a view of preschool development that minimizes the teachers' role (McCollum & Blair, 1994).

One of the consequences of this lack of understanding is that there has yet to be a real debate about the value of the theory itself. Discussion has focused more on the Piaget versus Vygotsky debate, an argument that becomes sterile when it treats the two theorists as though they occupied entirely dichotomous positions

(Tryphon & Vonèche, 1996; Tudge & Rogoff, 1989; Tudge & Winterhoff, 1993). Areas that would warrant more serious debate include the implications for teaching and learning of a theory that argues for the interrelation of individual, interpersonal, and cultural-historical factors in development and that stresses a co-constructive relationship between teacher and pupil.

However, there are some areas in which Vygotsky's views have had an impact on education, albeit in limited settings. There is growing evidence that more appropriate uses of Vygotsky have been used to change the practice of preschool teaching and learning both in England (Pollard, 1993) and in the United States (Bodrova & Leong, 1996). Pollard is explicit in his view that teachers must consider intrapersonal, interpersonal, and socio-historical factors simultaneously. Bodrova and Leong go further, connecting their discussion of the zone of proximal development to the use, by teachers and children, of external mediators that link child, activity, and the social and cultural context. They describe, for example, the way one teacher uses a stuffed mouse to encourage the children to behave in socially acceptable ways. For Vygotsky, all human activity is mediated by tools, whether physical (a spade or computer) or psychological (words or other symbols), that serve as the links to the broader social and cultural context.

Similar changes can be seen with school-age children. For example, the work of Michael Cole and his colleagues has consistently stressed a Vygotsky-based approach to education that focuses on the historically and culturally mediated nature of learning. In the "construction zone" (Newman, Griffin, & Cole, 1989), for example, learning is accomplished as a dialectical combination of individual and social activity, making sense of materials that are provided, in conjunction with others both in the classroom (children and teachers) and outside (the broader culture). As Wertsch (1985) pointed out, cultural tools are the mediational means that serve as the "carriers" of sociocultural patterns, skills, and knowledge. Cole's views on the necessity of including the cultural context in any analysis of teaching are exemplified in the work he and his colleagues have since done with children (many of whom have been diagnosed as having learning difficulties by their teachers) in the "Fifth Dimension" (Cole, 1996, 1998). Children's activities, in conjunction with their peers and teachers, are explicitly linked to culture and history in what Cole has described as cultural-historical activity theory (or CHAT, Cole 1998), a theory that is based on Vygotsky and Leont'ev.

Luis Moll (2000; Moll & Greenberg, 1990), drawing on works by both Michael Cole and Sylvia Scribner, has also indicated the ways in which everyday practices, such as those that go on in schools, are necessarily cultural practices. As Moll (2000) indicated, Vygotsky's view of the zone of proximal development deals with "how human beings use social processes and cultural resources of all kinds in helping children to construct their futures" (p. 262).

Similarly, Gordon Wells has tried to move the discussion of Vygotsky's ideas of the teacher–child relationship from one of scaffolding to "dialogic inquiry" (Wells, 1999, 2000). The teacher must be viewed both as a co-inquirer and as a leader/organizer, ensuring that cultural mediators are used to link students to the cultural world of which they are a part. As he points out, however, "in most classrooms dialogic interaction is not evident . . . [and] there is a dearth of dialog throughout the years of schooling" (Wells, 2000, p. 67). Wells (1999) argued that an "expanded" view of Vygotsky's concept is needed, however, stressing the fact that teaching and learning are created in the course of this dialogue. We would argue, by contrast, that no such expansion is necessary; it is one of the key elements of Vygotsky's theory.

Tharp and Gallimore (1988) also illustrate the ways in which schools need to take into account the interactions of teachers and children, the activity settings in which those interactions take place, and the broader cultural-historical contexts that give sense to both the activity settings and the interactional processes themselves. "Schools are incorporated into the larger society and have that as their context, so that some of their activity settings are determined by this larger contextuality" (p. 274). The authors illustrate contextuality with reference to Hawaiian schools, but elsewhere Tharp (1989) demonstrates the completely different interactional styles that are associated with learning in Hawaiian, Anglo, and Navajo cultures. The type of setting that would benefit Hawaiian children, whose culture encourages joint work and "negative wait time" (children talking at the same time) would be inappropriate for Navajo children, who learn early on to wait for a long time to make sure that someone else has finished talking and who are less used to working in large groups.

CONCLUSION

By way of summarizing our argument, we will reflect on the nature of the learner and the nature of the learning process in Vygotsky's theory. We will then consider how Vygotsky's legacy might be extended in future theoretical explorations.

The Nature of the Learner

As in any systemic theory, and particularly any theory that stresses the interaction of individual and environment, it is difficult to point to the role played by the learner without reference to the context within which the learner is operating. Nonetheless, it is worth stressing the active nature of the individual in Vygotsky's theory, if for no other reason than to guard against the common view that this theory simply stresses the surrounding social context (see, for example, Miller, 1993).

As we have argued throughout, Vygotsky's theory is dialectical; social phenomena (both interpersonal and cultural-historical) and individual characteristics combine to affect development. For example, when discussing developmental changes, Vygotsky argued that, although "external conditions" determine the character of the changes themselves, "neither the presence nor the absence of some specific external conditions, but the internal logic of the process of development itself is responsible" for the disruptions brought about by becoming older (Vygotsky, 1932/1998, p. 192). For example, the "crisis" of moving from the preschool to school age manifests itself in problems for children and teachers alike:

> The seven-year-old differs from both the preschool child and from the school child and for this reason presents difficulties with respect to his teaching. The negative content of this age is apparent primarily in the disruption of mental equilibrium and in the instability of the will, mood, etc. . . . At turning points of development, the child becomes relatively difficult due to the fact that the change in the pedagogical system applied to the child does not keep up with the rapid changes in his personality. (1932/1998, pp. 193–194)

It is clearly necessary, then, for the social context (both at school and at home) to change as a result of the changes in the child's development:

> Toward the end of the given age, the child becomes a completely different being than he was at the beginning of the age. But this necessarily also means that the social situation of development which was established in basic traits toward the beginning of any age must also change since the social situation of development is nothing other than a system of relations between the child of a given age and social reality. And if the child changed in a radical way, it is inevitable that these relations must be reconstructed. (Vygotsky, 1932/1998, p. 199)

What does this mean for teaching? Teachers must be aware of what the child brings to the situation. "Determining the actual level of development is the most essential and indispensable task in resolving every practical problem of teaching and educating the child" (Vygotsky, 1932/1998, p. 200). But that, of course, is only the first step in the process. This understanding of the child's current developmental "symptoms" indicates only the current outcome of development, which is a necessary, but by no means sufficient, goal of teachers.

The Nature of the Learning Process

"A genuine diagnosis of development must be able to catch not only concluded cycles of development . . . but also those processes that are in the period of maturation" (Vygotsky, 1932/1998, p. 200). Vygotsky, as is well known, was highly critical of assessments of development that dealt purely with what children can accomplish independently. Vygotsky believed that one only knows what is maturing in the child's development by discovering what he or she can do with help. The contemporary view (both in Vygotsky's time and currently) is that data from a testing situation should be ignored if a child has been assisted in some way, as though the child who benefits from the assistance, or imitates the person who has helped, has done so in a purely mechanical fashion. For Vygotsky, by contrast, a child who is able to benefit from this type of help is actually revealing something highly important about his or her development. By "imitation" in this context Vygotsky meant anything that the child is able to achieve in cooperation with

someone else; this achievement, always more than what could be attained independently, is not "limitless" however, and is related to the child's current "actual"
level of development.

Vygotsky intended to provide a detailed discussion of the relevance of his conception of zones of proximal development to teaching; he made several references
to his intention (see, for example, 1932/1998, pp. 203–204, 330), but died before
he was able to do so. He restricted himself to the point that the optimal time for
teaching new skills or concepts should be when the relevant facilities are in the
process of maturing.

Vygotsky's Legacy

In relation to Vygotsky's legacy to the field, no answer can yet be provided given
that the theory is still not well understood, at least in North America. There is some
evidence, however, that in the field of North American early education at least,
Vygotsky has provided some theoretical support for the notion that preschool
teachers can play an effective role beyond the provision of the materials for children's play. Similarly, in elementary school, there is increased support for the role
of group work, though the extent to which this support derives explicitly (or even
implicitly) from Vygotsky is not clear. Perhaps most important, Vygotsky's use of
the concept of *obuchenie* has the potential of vastly enriching our understanding of
the relations of teaching and learning. We believe that effective teaching involves
learning from one's students, while at the same time learning from the very process
of teaching. At the core of Vygotsky's theory is the sense that children must be actively involved in teaching/learning relationships with more competent others who
both learn from children and draw them into fuller membership in their cultural
world. As the theory and practice of human development becomes increasingly
diverse, the concept of *obuchenie* may become the fulcrum for conversations in
education. For example, as European American theorists and practitioners observe
the ways in which adults from South American or African American cultures engage their children in cultural activities and welcome them into collective identities,
this may lead to transformations of more individualistic and competitive notions of
educational growth and success. In teaching/learning relationships, teachers must
be willing to build on and enhance the children's strengths in developmentally and
culturally appropriate ways. The theoretical support for this position is evident in
Vygotsky's writings. As yet, however, it is a promise that still has to be realized.

ACKNOWLEDGMENTS

We would like to thank Mohamed Elhamoumi, Nikolai Veresov, René van der Veer,
Mike Cole, and Jaan Valsiner for their helpful comments on earlier drafts of this
paper. For copies of this paper, please contact Jonathan Tudge, P.O. Box 26170,

Department of Human Development and Family Studies, The University of North Carolina at Greensboro, Greensboro, NC 27402-6170. Email: jrtudge@uncg.edu Web: http://www.uncg.edu/hdf/hdfs_faculty/jon_tudge/jon_tudge.htm

NOTE

1. Interestingly, Vygotsky did in fact use the term "scaffold" one time, to describe a child using a support to assist walking (van der Veer & Valsiner, 1991). Unfortunately, the translators confused the Russian term for "scaffolding" (*lesa*) with the same word (stressed differently) for "woods" and translated the key sentence as follows: "In short, his gait is not steady; it is still [linked], as it were, 'to the woods' of external tools that facilitate its development. Yet another month passes, and the child, having surpassed this 'woods,' discards it" (Vygotsky & Luria, 1930/1993, p. 207). The passage is striking not only as a demonstration of the pitfalls of translation but also as a clear illustration of the differences between the use of "scaffold" in the sense of simple assistance and the complexity that undergirds the concept of zone of proximal development.

REFERENCES

Berk, L. E., & Winsler, A. (1995). *Scaffolding children's learning: Vygotsky and early childhood education*. Washington, DC: National Association for the Education of Young Children.

Blanck, G. (1990). Vygotsky: The man and his cause. In L. C. Moll (Ed.), *Vygotsky and education: Instructional implications and applications of sociohistorical psychology* (pp. 31–58). New York: Cambridge University Press.

Bodrova, E., & Leong, D. J. (1996). *Tools of the mind: The Vygotskian approach to early childhood education*. Englewood Cliffs, NJ: Prentice-Hall.

Bredekamp, S. (1987). *Developmentally appropriate practice in early childhood programs serving children from birth through age five*. Washington, DC: The National Association for the Education of Young Children.

Bredekamp, S., & Copple, C. (Eds.). (1997). *Developmentally appropriate practice in early childhood programs* (Rev. ed.). Washington, DC: National Association for the Education of Young Children.

Bronfenbrenner, U. (1989). Ecological systems theory. In R. Vasta (Ed.), *Annals of child development, Vol. 6* (pp. 187–249). Greenwich, CT: JAI Press.

Bronfenbrenner, U. (1995). Developmental ecology through space and time: A future perspective. In P. Moen, G. H. Elder, Jr., & K. Lüscher (Eds.), *Examining lives in context: Perspectives on the ecology of human development* (pp. 619–647). Washington, DC: American Psychological Association.

Brown, A. L., Ash, D., Rutherford, M., Nakagawa, K., Gordon, A., & Campione, J. C. (1993). In G. Salomon (Ed.), *Distributed cognitions: Psychological and educational considerations* (pp. 188–228). New York: Cambridge University Press.

Brown, A. L., & Ferrara, R. A. (1985). Diagnozing zones of proximal development. In J. V. Wertsch (Ed.), *Culture, communication, and cognition: Vygotskian perspectives* (pp. 273–305). New York: Cambridge University Press.

Brown, A. L., & Palincsar, A. S. (1989). Guided, cooperative learning and individual knowledge acquisition. In L. B. Resnick (Ed.), *Knowing, learning, and instruction: Essays in honor of Robert Claser* (pp. 293–451). Hillsdale, NJ: Lawrence Erlbaum Associates.

Bruner, J., & Haste, H. (1987). Introduction. In J. Bruner & H. Haste (Eds.), *Making sense: The child's construction of the world* (pp. 1–25). London: Methuen.

Cole, M. (1985). The zone of proximal development: Where culture and cognition create each other. In J. V. Wertsch (Eds.), *Culture, communication, and cognition: Vygotskian perspectives* (pp. 146–161). New York: Cambridge University Press.

Cole, M. (1996). *Cultural psychology: A once and future discipline.* Cambridge, MA: Harvard University Press.

Cole, M. (1998). Can cultural psychology help us think about diversity? *Mind, Culture, and Activity, 5,* 291–304.

Elhammoumi, M. (2002). To create psychology's own Capital. *Journal for the Theory of Social Behavior, 32,* 89–104.

Fernyhough (Eds.), *Lev Vygotsky: Critical assessments* (pp. 276–295). London: Routledge.

Griffin, P., & Cole, M. (1999). Current activity for the future: The Zo-ped. In P. Lloyd & C. Fernyhough (Eds.), *Lev Vygotsky: Critical assessments* (pp. 276–295). London: Routledge.

Hogan, D. M., & Tudge, J. R. H. (1999). Implications of Vygotsky's theory for peer learning. In A. M. O'Donnell & A. King (Eds.), *Cognitive perspectives on peer learning* (pp. 39–65). Mahwah, NJ: Lawrence Erlbaum Associates.

Jaroshevsky, M. (1994). L. S. Vygotsky—victim of an "optical illusion." *Journal of Russian and East European Psychology, 32*(6), 35–43.

Kozulin, A. (1990). *Vygotsky's psychology: A biography of ideas.* Cambridge: Harvard University Press.

Levitin, K. (1982). *One is not born a personality: Profiles of Soviet education psychologists.* Moscow: Progress Publishers.

Luria, A. R. (1979). *The making of mind: A personal account of Soviet psychology.* Cambridge, MA: Harvard University Press.

McCollum, J. A., & Bair, H. (1994). In B. L. Mallory & R. S. New (Eds.), *Diversity and developmentally appropriate practices* (pp. 84–106). New York: Teachers College Press.

Miller, P. H. (1993). *Theories of human development* (3rd ed.) New York: Freeman & Co.

Minick, N. (1987). Introduction. In R. W. Rieber & A. S. Carton (Vol. Eds.); N. Minick (Trans.), *The collected works of L. S. Vygotsky: Vol. 1, Problems of general psychology* (pp. 17–36). New York: Plenum.

Moll, L. C. (2000). Inspired by Vygotsky: Ethnographic experiments in education. In C. D. Lee & P. Smagorinsky (Eds.), *Vygotskian perspectives on literary research: Constructing meaning through collaborative inquiry* (pp. 256–268). New York: Cambridge University Press.

Moll, L. C., & Greenberg, J. B. (1990). Creating zones of possibilities: Combining social contexts for instruction. In L. C. Moll (Ed.), *Vygotsky and education: Instrumental implications and applications of sociohistorical psychology* (pp. 319–348). New York: Cambridge University Press.

Newman, D., Griffin, P., & Cole, M. (1989). *The construction zone.* New York: Cambridge University Press.

Nicolopoulou, A. (1993). Play, cognitive development, and the social world: Piaget, Vygotsky, and beyond. *Human Development, 36,* 1–23.

Pollard, A. (1993). Learning in primary schools. In H. Daniels (Ed.), *Charting the agenda: Educational activity after Vygotsky* (pp. 171–189). London: Routledge.

Scribner, S. (1985). Vygotsky's uses of history. In J. V. Wertsch (Ed.), *Culture, communication, and cognition: Vygotskian perspectives* (pp. 119–145). Cambridge, England: Cambridge University Press.

Smagorinsky, P. (1995). The social construction of data: Methodological problems of investigating learning in the zone of proximal development. *Review of Educational Research, 65,* 191–216.

Stone, C. A. (1993). What is missing in the metaphor of scaffolding? In E. A. Forman, N. Minick, & C. A. Stone (Eds.), *Contexts for learning* (pp. 169–183). New York: Oxford University Press.

Tharp, R. G. (1989). Psychocultural variables and constants: Effects on teaching and learning in schools. *American Psychologist, 44,* 349–359.

Tharp, R. G., & Gallimore, R. (1988). *Rousing minds to life: Teaching, learning, and schooling in social context.* New York: Cambridge University Press.

Toulmin, S. (1978, September 28). The Mozart of psychology. *New York Review of Books.*

Tryphon, A., & Vonèche, J. (Eds.). (1996). *Piaget–Vygotsky: The social genesis of thought.* Hove, E. Sussex, England: Psychology Press.

Tudge, J. R. H., Hogan, D. M., Lee, S., Meltsas, M., Tammeveski, P., Kulakova, N. N., Snezhkova, I. A., & Putnam, S. A. (1999). Cultural heterogeneity: Parental values and beliefs and their preschoolers' activities in the United States, South Korea, Russia, and Estonia. In A. Göncü (Ed.), *Children's engagement in the world* (pp. 62–96). New York: Cambridge University Press.

Tudge, J. R. H., Putnam, S. A., & Valsiner, J. (1996). Culture and cognition in developmental perspective. In B. Cairns, G. H. Elder, Jr., & E. J. Costello (Eds.), *Developmental science* (pp. 190–222). New York: Cambridge University Press.

Tudge, J. R. H., & Rogoff, B. (1989). Peer influences on cognitive development: Piagetian and Vygotskian perspectives. In M. H. Bornstein & J. S. Bruner (Eds.), *Interaction in human development* (pp. 17–40). Hillsdale, NJ: Lawrence Erlbaum Associates.

Tudge, J. R. H., & Winterhoff, P. A. (1993). Vygotsky, Piaget, and Bandura: Perspectives on the relations between the social world and cognitive development. *Human Development, 36,* 61–81.

Valsiner, J. (1988). *Developmental psychology in the Soviet Union.* Brighton, England: Harvester Press.

van der Veer, R., & Valsiner, J. (1991). *Understanding Vygotsky: A quest for synthesis.* Oxford, England: Blackwell.

van der Veer, R., & Valsiner, J. (1994). *The Vygotsky reader.* Oxford, England: Blackwell.

van der Veer, R., & van IJzendoorn, M. H. (1985). Vygotsky's theory of the higher psychological processes: Some criticisms. *Human Development, 28,* 1–9.

Veresov, N. (1999). *Undiscovered Vygotsky: Etudes on the prehistory of cultural-historical psychology.* Frankfurt am Main, Germany: Peter Lang.

Vygodskaia, G. L., & Lifanova, T. M. (1999a). Lev Semenovich Vygotsky, Part 1. *Journal of Russian and East European Psychology, 37*(2), 23–90.

Vygodskaia, G. L., & Lifanova, T. M. (1999b). Lev Semenovich Vygotsky, Part 2. *Journal of Russian and East European Psychology, 37*(3), 3–90.

Vygotsky, L. S. (Ed.). (1924). *Voprosy vospitaniya slepykh glukhonemykh i umstvenno otstalykh detej [problems of upbringing of blind, deaf, and mentally retarded children].* Moscow, Russia: Izdatel'stvo SPON NKP.

Vygotsky, L. S. (1929). The problem of the cultural development of the child. *Journal of Genetic Psychology, 36,* 415–434.

Vygotsky, L. S. (1934). Thought in schizophrenia. *Archives of Neurology and Psychiatry, 31,* 1063–1077.

Vygotsky, L. S. (1939). Thought and speech. *Psychiatry, 2,* 29–54.

Vygotsky, L. S. (1962). *Thought and language.* Cambridge, MA: MIT press.

Vygotsky, L. S. (1978). *Mind in society.* Cambridge, MA: Harvard University Press. (Chapters originally written or published between 1930 and 1935)

Vygotsky, L. S. (1981). The genesis of higher mental functions. In J. V. Wertsch (Ed.), *The concept of activity in Soviet psychology* (pp. 144–188). Armonk, NY: Sharpe. (Originally published in 1931)

Vygotsky, L. S. (1987). *The collected works of L. S. Vygotsky: Vol. 1. Problems of general psychology* (R. W. Rieber & A. S. Carton, Vol. Eds.; N. Minick, Trans.). New York: Plenum. (Originally written or published between 1929 and 1935)

Vygotsky, L. S. (1993). *The collected works of L. S. Vygotsky: Vol. 2. The fundamentals of defectology (abnormal psychology and learning disabilities)* (R. W. Rieber & A. S. Carton, Vol. Eds.; J. E. Knox & C. B. Stevens, Trans.). New York: Plenum. (Chapters originally published or written between 1924 and 1935)

Vygotsky, L. S. (1994). The problem of the environment. In R. van der Veer & J. Valsiner (Eds.), *The Vygotsky reader* (pp. 338–354). Oxford, England: Blackwell. (Originally published in 1935)

Vygosky, L. S. (1997a). *Educational psychology*. Boca Raton, FL: St. Lucie Press. (Originally published in 1926)

Vygotsky, L. S. (1997b). *The collected works of L. S. Vygotsky: Vol. 3. Problems of the theory and history of psychology* (R. W. Rieber & J. Wollock, Vol. Eds.; R. van der Veer, Trans.). New York: Plenum. (Chapters originally written or published between 1924 and 1934)

Vygotsky, L. S. (1997c). *The collected works of L. S. Vygotsky: Vol. 4. The history of the development of higher mental functions* (R. W. Rieber, Vol. Ed.; M. J. Hall, Trans.). New York: Plenum. (Originally written in 1931)

Vygotsky, L. S. (1998). *The collected works of L. S. Vygotsky: Vol. 5. Child Psychology* (R. W. Rieber, Vol. Ed.; M. J. Hall, Trans.). New York: Plenum. (Chapters originally written between 1930 and 1934)

Vygotsky, L. S., & Luria, A. R. (1993). *Studies on the history of behavior: Ape, primitive, and child* (V. I. Golod & J. E. Knox, Eds. & Trans.). Hillsdale, NJ: Lawrence Erlbaum Associates. (Originally published in 1930)

Vygotsky, L. S., & Luria, A. R. (1994). Tool and symbol in child development. In R. van der Veer & J. Valsiner (Eds.), *The Vygotsky reader* (pp. 99–174). Oxford, England: Blackwell. (Originally written in 1930)

Wells, G. (1999). *Dialogic inquiry: Toward a sociocultural practice and theory of education.* New York: Cambridge University Press.

Wells, G. (2000). Dialogic inquiry in education: Building on the legacy of Vygotsky. In C. D. Lee & P. Smagorinsky (Eds.), *Vygotskian perspectives on literary research: Constructing meaning through collaborative inquiry* (pp. 51–85). New York: Cambridge University Press.

Wertsch, J. V. (1985). *Vygotsky and the social formation of mind.* Cambridge, MA: Harvard University Press.

Wertsch, J. V. (1989). A sociocultural approach to mind. In W. Damon (Ed.), *Child development today and tomorrow* (pp. 14–33). San Francisco: Jossey-Bass.

Wertsch, J. V. (1991). A sociocultural approach to socially shared cognition. In L. B. Resnick, J. M. Levine, & S. D. Teasley (Eds.), *Perspectives on socially shared cognition* (pp. 85–100). Washington, DC: American Psychological Association.

Wertsch, J. V. (2000). Vygotsky's two minds on the nature of meaning. In C. D. Lee & P. Smagorinsky (Eds.), *Vygotskian perspectives on literary research: Constructing meaning through collaborative inquiry* (pp. 19–30). New York: Cambridge University Press.

Wertsch, J. V., & Minick, N. (1990). Negotiating sense in the zone of proximal development. In M. Schwebel, C. A. Maher, & N. S. Fagley (Eds.), *Promoting cognitive growth over the life span* (pp. 71–88). Hillsdale, NJ: Lawrence Erlbaum Associates.

Wertsch, J. V., & Tulviste, P. (1992). L. S. Vygotsky and contemporary developmental psychology. *Developmental Psychology, 28,* 548–557.

Wheeler, M. (1984). *The Oxford Russian–English dictionary, 2nd Ed.* Oxford, England: Clarendon Press.

Wood, D. J. (1999). Teaching the young child: Some relationships between social interaction, language, and thought. In P. Lloyd & C. Fernyhough (Eds.), *Lev Vygotsky: Critical assessments* (pp. 259–275). London: Routledge.

Wood, D. J., Bruner, J. S., & Ross, G. (1976). The role of tutoring in problem solving. *Journal of Child Psychology and Psychiatry, 17,* 89–100.

10

B. F. Skinner: A Behavior Analyst in Educational Psychology

Edward K. Morris
University of Kansas

B. F. (Burrhus Frederic) Skinner was born in 1904, in the midst of the founding of educational psychology (1890–1920), less than 50 years after the enactment of the first statewide compulsory school attendance law in Massachusetts in 1856. William James (1904), author of *Talks to Teachers on Psychology* (James, 1899), was asking "Does 'Consciousness' Exist?," as he fashioned a functional concept of mind. G. Stanley Hall (1904), founder of developmental psychology in America, published *Adolescence*, much influenced by evolutionary biology. In France, a commission on the education of "subnormal children" was formed, for which Alfred Binet (1911) devised the first practical intelligence test, ensuring that psychology would be useful. Also that year, John Dewey moved from the University of Chicago to Columbia University, where he established himself further as the philosopher of Progressivism in America, especially in education (Dewey, 1916). Finally, Edward L. Thorndike (1904) published his *Introduction to the Theory of Mental and Social Measurements*, bringing methodological sophistication to educational testing, making educational psychology a science.

Fifty years later, as educational psychology was completing its rise to prominence (1920–1960), Skinner (1954) published the first of 15 articles that, along with 12 chapters, a technical report, programmed texts on handwriting and on the analysis of behavior, and a book, constituted the corpus of his direct contributions to educational psychology. Throughout that decade, Skinner's science made other advances in education through the work of his students and colleagues (e.g., in special education). Although his contributions reach back toward the founding of educational psychology, and forward into its modern period (1960–present), they arguably never achieved their full potential.

In this chapter, I describe the context in which Skinner's work emerged— intellectual (1600–1750), cultural (1890–1920), and personal (1904–1928)—and then his founding the field of *behavior analysis* (Michael, 1985), as organized by its subdisciplines (Morris, 1992): (a) the experimental analysis of behavior, in which Skinner analyzed basic behavioral processes (1930–1957), (b) the conceptual analysis of behavior, in which he was a systematist and a philosopher (1938–1974), and (c) applied behavior analysis, in which he addressed matters of social importance (1945–1990). I relate the foundational nature of Skinner's contributions to educational psychology in each subdiscipline, after which I devote a separate section to education. In my conclusion, I evaluate his legacy.

INTELLECTUAL, CULTURAL, AND INDIVIDUAL CONTEXT

Intellectual Context: Philosophy, Science, and Psychology

The modern history of science began with the Scientific Revolution (1600–1750), which dramatically changed the ways in which nature was understood and what was understood about it, and assumptions about the nature of nature. Religious and hermetic traditions gave way to observation and experiment, first in astronomy and physics, then in biology, and eventually in psychology. Nicholas Copernicus and Galileo Galilei challenged the assumption of a heliocentric universe; Charles Darwin and Alfred Russel Wallace challenged the discontinuity of species; John B. Watson challenged the concept of mind; Skinner was the most thoroughgoing of them all—he challenged the very idea of human agency.

With the Scientific Revolution came modern philosophy, begun in Rene Descartes' attempt to reconcile mind and body. In Cartesian dualism, the body operated according to mechanical principles, while humans alone possessed a soul. Accepting this, physicists and physiologists undertook an empirical analysis of body and behavior, while the empiricist and associationistic philosophers undertook a rational analysis of mind and consciousness. Bringing these programs together, Wilhelm Wundt founded "experimental psychology" in Germany in the late 1800s as the introspective study of the elements of consciousness under laboratory conditions. Transformed into *structuralism* in the United States, this was the psychology taught in American universities when Skinner was born.

Not every philosopher and scientist sought to harmonize mind and body. Some attempted to naturalize them, and science as well. In philosophy, Francis Bacon noted that science, then often abstract and contemplative, was intimately allied with craft and technology. Indeed, many scientific advances emerged in the context of solving technical problems (e.g., in navigation), making the goals of science both intellectual and practical. Knowledge was derived empirically from working directly with the subject matter, where nature was understood through its experimental analysis. Bacon also had a strongly reformist attitude: Scientific knowledge should be applied to problems of individual, social, and cultural importance. Skinner was Baconian in all these regards (Smith, 1986).

In science, the study of brain functioning and biological species was naturalized in two programs. First, Russian neuroscience materialized the mind into the brain and offered a reflex-based account of the latter. This was the tradition from which Ivan Pavlov's experimental analysis of involuntary behavior emerged—an approach Skinner took to voluntary behavior. Second, Darwin offered an evolutionary account of the continuity of species and proposed natural selection as the explanatory process. From this emerged comparative psychology and the psychology of adaptation. The former inquired into the evolutionary basis of mind and behavior with increasingly objective methods, while the latter sought mental and behavioral processes (e.g., association) by studying nonhuman species in laboratory settings (e.g., rats in mazes). Together, they were a catalyst for *functionalism*. Founded by Dewey and James, functionalism was concerned with the purpose—not the structure, form, or elements—of mind and behavior.

In philosophy, Ernst Mach reformulated Bacon's views in the context of evolutionary biology. Mach advanced a descriptive positivism, rejecting metaphysical entities; he analyzed the origins of scientific concepts, often finding metaphysical biases; and he saw science as economical adaptation—the discovery of functional relations, not the "Truth." This was a philosophy of science congenial to Skinner (Chiesa, 1992). A distinctly American philosophy also arose in this context—pragmatism—founded by Charles S. Peirce, William James, George Herbert Mead, and John Dewey. In this view, mind and behavior were acts-in-context, historically dependent, and so too was science. As science advanced, new findings often revealed the limitations of prior understanding, such that "effective action" in predicting and controlling functional relations became the criterion of truth. Philosophical pragmatism is deeply implicit in radical behaviorism (cf. contextualism; contra. mechanism; see Hayes, Hayes, & Reese, 1988; Morris, 1992, 1993).

Given these antecedents, *behaviorism* was almost inevitable. Within a decade after Skinner's birth, Watson (1913) had coined the term itself and founded the system: "Psychology as the behaviorist views it is a purely objective experimental branch of natural science" (p. 158). Its methods were objective; its subject matter was behavior. It would be the basis of the neobehaviorisms to follow, among them Skinner's (Malone, 1990). It was also resonant with a pragmatic American culture.

Cultural Context: The United States

The 1900s found the United States an emerging national power, but with internal conflicts between Enlightenment philosophy and religious values. Until the late 19th century, the latter were ascendant, but the nation was changing. Rural, agricultural communities and their religious traditions were giving way to urban, industrial centers and a faith in science and technology. Progressivism (1890–1920) emerged as a social movement that sought to resolve the strain of these changes through efficient professionalization in industry, business, government, and education. It promised progress: social progress through science and technology, and individual progress through self-improvement (O'Donnell, 1985). Skinner was distinctly American in this regard, maintaining a deep democratic optimism about social and individual change over the course of his career.

Individual Context: B. F. Skinner

This was the world into which Skinner was born on March 20, 1904, in Susquehanna, Pennsylvania, a small bustling railroad town (see Skinner, 1976). His family embodied the Progressive ethos, struggling toward self-improvement and middle-class respectability. His father sought to instill in him the Protestant ethic and civic "boosterism"; his mother sought to instill a concern with propriety (e.g., "What will people think?"). Skinner would challenge their aspirations and values, yet he was a dutiful son.

Skinner's childhood was typical of its time and place, yet distinguished on several accounts. He developed a strong penchant for ingenuity and engineering, both mechanical and intellectual. He constructed machines (e.g., scooters) and built models (e.g., airplanes); he invented (e.g., mechanical means for hanging up his pajamas) and experimented (e.g., whether faith could move mountains); and he found Bacon (e.g., "Nature to be commanded must be obeyed"). Although disposed in these ways toward science, he was drawn more to literature, encouraged by Mary Graves, a teacher to whom he would dedicate *The Technology of Teaching* (Skinner, 1968b). She broadened his intellectual and aesthetic horizons beyond those of his family and Susquehanna.

In 1922, Skinner matriculated into Hamilton College (Clinton, NY) with an intellectual independence that forever marked his psychology and his persona. He arrived a self-assured student, albeit somewhat socially self-conscious; he was encouraged by faculty and friends to engage the arts and criticize artifice; and he majored in English literature. His only encounter with a science that was related to his later psychology was in anatomy and physiology where he read Jacques Loeb's work on comparative psychology and the "organism as a whole." He graduated from Hamilton in 1926, the same year Sidney Pressey published the first account of a modern testing and teaching machine (Benjamin, 1988).

With encouragement from Robert Frost, Skinner undertook the life of a writer (1926–1928), but was unsuccessful—unsuccessful, but his life not unexamined:

"A writer might portray human behavior accurately, but he did not therefore understand it. I was to remain interested in human behavior, but the literary method had failed me. I would turn to the scientific" (Skinner, 1967, p. 395). Raised in a Progressive, modernist culture, where science and technology were valued, and having become intellectually independent, Skinner found himself interested in objective writing; he was influenced by Bertrand Russell's regard for Watson; he developed an anti-metaphysical bias; he read about Pavlov and Watson; and he displayed an inductive, Baconian aptitude. In seeking a useful profession, he entered Harvard University in 1928 to study scientific psychology. As his friend, the illustrator, Alf Evers said to him, "Science is the art of the twentieth century" (see Smith & Woodward, 1996).

THE EXPERIMENTAL ANALYSIS
OF BEHAVIOR

When Skinner arrived at Harvard, he found the psychology department more aligned with structuralism than with behaviorism. But, with access to the department's workshop and support from some students (e.g., Fred S. Keller) and faculty members (e.g., W. J. Crozier, Department of General Physiology), he began developing a natural science of behavior *qua* behavior—*the experimental analysis of behavior* (see Skinner, 1979).

Influenced by Pavlov's dictum, "Control the environment and you will see order in behavior," he invented and refined methods for controlling his independent and dependent variables (the "Skinner box"), measuring behavior in real time (the cumulative recorder), and experimentally analyzing the behavior of individual organisms (within-subject research designs), all emerging from Skinner's considerable efforts. His empirical work involved an analysis of the effects of drive (e.g., food deprivation) on behavior (i.e., eating food); his conceptual work involved an historical analysis of the reflex. From this, Skinner could see that the defining feature of behavior was neither mental (e.g., associations) nor physiological (e.g., muscle twitches), but rather a correlation between classes of responses and stimuli. His analysis was reminiscent of Dewey's (1896) reformulation of the associationists' reflex arc concept (i.e., the separable elements of stimulus, idea, and response) into an account of behavior-as-a-whole—an ever-adapting unit of action. Skinner's empirical and conceptual work became his doctoral thesis, for which he received his Ph.D. in psychology in 1931.

Supported on grants and fellowships, Skinner remained at Harvard for another 5½ years (1931–1936), further developing his science. His first academic appointment was in the Department of Psychology at the University of Minnesota (1936–1945), where he published his classic work, *The Behavior of Organisms: An Experimental Analysis* (Skinner, 1938). Next, as chairman of the Department of Psychology at Indiana University (1945–1947), he emphasized empirical-inductive theory-making over hypothetical-deductive theory-testing (e.g., he "studied nature not books"; Skinner, 1950). Finally, back at Harvard (1947–1974), he became the Edgar Pierce Professor of Psychology (1947–1964) and reached the "high point" of his research career (see Skinner, 1983).

Behavioral Processes

In the course of his research, Skinner made a crucial distinction between (a) involuntary or reflexive behavior, which *reacted to* the environment (i.e., respondent behavior; e.g., food elicits salivation) and (b) voluntary or instrumental behavior, which *acted on* the environment (i.e., operant behavior; e.g., bar pressing produces food). Whereas Pavlov provided a science of the former (i.e., responses elicited by antecedent stimuli), Skinner provided a science of the latter (i.e., responses reinforced by consequent stimuli). Skinner was thus not an S–R psychologist, but "selectionist" in his account of behavior. He studied the selection of instrumental or operant responses by their consequences, which for him was the process of education itself (e.g., teaching, learning).

While at Harvard in the 1930s, he analyzed operant conditioning (e.g., reinforcer immediacy), periodic reconditioning (i.e., schedules of reinforcement), discriminative stimulus control (i.e., occasions for reinforcement), conditioned reinforcement (e.g., by discriminative stimuli), and variables such as conditioning (i.e., learning history), drive (e.g., deprivation), and emotion (e.g., due to eliciting stimuli). At Minnesota, he analyzed the "three-term contingency" (i.e., the dynamic relations among discriminative stimuli, operant responding, and reinforcing stimuli) and made advances in the analysis of response differentiation through the reinforcement of successive approximations (i.e., shaping). At Indiana, he examined the differential reinforcement of response rates (e.g., low rates), stimulus discrimination (e.g., matching-to-sample), and responding on multiple operanda (e.g., concurrent responses). Back at Harvard, he studied noncontingent reinforcement and then reinforcement schedules, the latter of which became his last major empirical project—*Schedules of Reinforcement* with Charles B. Ferster, published in 1957.

Professional and Person Circa 1957

Skinner's research career was not over, however. He published seven more pertinent articles in the next several years and his laboratory remained active, for instance, in research on punishment by Nathan H. Azrin and on concurrent schedules of positive and negative reinforcement by William M. Baum, Richard J. Herrnstein, and Philip N. Hineline. Skinner also gained formal recognition for his research. In 1958, he received the Distinguished Scientific Award from the American Psychological Association (APA); a decade later, President Lyndon Johnson presented him with a National Medal of Science. These activities notwithstanding, Skinner turned increasingly toward theory and application, but this was not new. He often related his basic research to conceptual and applied issues, giving his contributions a coherence not usually found in the behavioral and social sciences. As for Skinner's personal life, in 1957, he and Yvonne (Eve) Blue celebrated their 20th wedding anniversary, by which time they were the proud parents of two beloved daughters, Julie (b. 1938) and Deborah (b. 1944). As we will see, Eve and Deborah had already played a role in Skinner's contributions to applied psychology, especially in education, while Julie would later contribute to education more directly, but not before Skinner made several conceptual advances.

THE CONCEPTUAL ANALYSIS OF BEHAVIOR

Skinner's *conceptual analyses of behavior* were many and varied, ranging from the meaning of terms and concepts (e.g., mind), to history and systems (e.g., psychological), to theory and philosophy (e.g., scientific). This section addresses his subject matter, his theory of behavior, and his philosophy of science.

The Subject Matter

Skinner's first conceptual contribution was his aforementioned analysis of the reflex, wherein he observed that behavioral concepts (e.g., reinforcement) described functional relations among responses (e.g., operants) and stimuli (e.g., reinforcers). Psychological concepts such as drive and emotion were likewise descriptive of functional relations (e.g., between response rate and either reinforcer deprivation or aversive stimuli). When he integrated these analyses with his empirical work, this became the first systematic statement of his science—*The Behavior of Organisms*.

Not until later did Skinner (1945) distinguish descriptive concepts from explanatory constructs. Descriptive concepts—whether found in ordinary language or operationally defined—identified psychology's subject matter (e.g., learning as *changes* in behavior), whereas, in the standard view, operational definitions were a means for inferring explanatory "hypothetical" constructs (e.g., changes in behavior as an *index* of learning). Skinner also first referred here to his philosophy as "radical behaviorism," in that both what he studied and his subject matter were behavior. In contrast, in the standard view he referred to as "methodological behaviorism," psychologists studied behavior, but their subject matter was the mind—an explanatory construct. Skinner did maintain, though, that psychology included both public and private events, where the latter were more respondent and operant behavior (e.g., toothaches, thinking "in one's head," dreaming), not independent explanatory constructs. In addition, observing and reporting one's public and private events was operant behavior acquired in social context, hence the social basis of consciousness in radical behaviorism.

Psychological Theory

Skinner's (1947, 1950) approach to theory was both conventional and unconventional. Conventionally, he wrote that "Behavior can only be satisfactorily understood by going beyond the facts themselves. What is needed is a theory of behavior" (Skinner, 1947, p. 26). Unconventionally, he did not mean a hypothetically deduced theory of physiological (e.g., neural traces), mental (e.g., self-efficacy), or conceptual constructs (e.g., knowledge) derived from between-subject analyses of hypothesized relations between situated organisms and environments, where statistical prediction from theory to behavior was the basis of explanation. Rather, he meant a more empirically induced theory, derived from within-subject analyses of generic responses and stimuli, wherein experimental control was the basis of explanation. On this view, theory meant the integration of known behavioral relations (e.g., about reinforcement; cf. evolutionary theory), not of hypothetical constructs based on a priori systems (e.g., cognitive maps; cf. intelligent design).

By theory, Skinner also meant "behavioral interpretation"—the analysis of behavior (e.g., education) in terms of, and constrained by, the basic behavioral processes (e.g., reinforcement), said interpretations often having practical implications (e.g., for teaching). Much of Skinner's work was theoretical in this sense, for instance, his 1957 book, *Verbal Behavior*, and his 1971 exploration of the socio-political implications of his science in *Beyond Freedom and Dignity*.

Philosophy of Science

Although Skinner initially adopted a strict cause-and-effect determinism, he developed an empirical epistemology in which ontology was contingent—selected for by success in science. He thereafter remained naturalistic, but his determinism was less mechanistic, evolving into a view of behavior as an "historic event," probabilistically dependent on contingencies (e.g., today's learning depends on yesterday's learning). Here, the content of knowledge is historically contingent (e.g., history), whereas the processes by which it is acquired are behaviorally generic (e.g., reinforcement). On this account, psychology is natural history—the product of behavioral processes in everyday context (e.g., self-esteem as the consequence, not the cause, of success)—while the experimental analysis of behavior is a natural science (e.g., behavioral processes).

Professional and Person Circa 1974

Although Skinner retired from Harvard in 1974 as professor emeritus, he continued making fundamental contributions in each subdiscipline of behavior analysis, the last overall treatment of which was his 1974 text, *About Behaviorism*. Just before this, in 1972, he had received the Humanist of the Year Award from the American Humanist Society, underscoring some shared social values. Afterward,

Skinner focused increasingly on those values and on the applied implications of his empirical and conceptual work. In his personal life, in 1974, he and Eve celebrated their 37th wedding anniversary; Eve was a docent at Boston's Museum of Fine Arts; and Julie and Deborah were established professionals—Julie, a professor of educational psychology at West Virginia University, and Deborah, an artist and restaurant critic in England. Both his daughters were married, Deborah to Barry Buzan and Julie to Ernest Vargas, the latter with children—Lisa (b. 1966) and Justine (b. 1970).

APPLIED BEHAVIOR ANALYSIS

Defined as "the process of applying . . . principles of behavior to the improvement of specific behaviors, and simultaneously evaluating whether or not any changes noted are indeed attributable to the process of application" (Baer, Wolf, & Risley, 1968, p. 91), *applied behavior analysis* is essentially the application of Skinner's science to problems of individual, social, and cultural importance. Although not himself technically an applied behavior analyst, Skinner did undertake notable applied work. Between the 1930s and 1950s, he invented a "verbal summator" for studying latent speech; published seminal research in behavioral pharmacology (e.g., caffeine), behavioral synthesis (e.g., anxiety), and human operant behavior (e.g., with mental patients); and offered interpretations of psychoses and psychotherapy. But, three other projects became more renown.

First, as part of the war effort, he devised methods for teaching pigeons to peck images on disks, behavior that could guide missiles to their destinations. Although not adopted by the military, this work was the basis for research on response shaping. Second, to assist Eve with Deborah's early rearing, Skinner constructed a "baby tender" as an alternative to playpens and cribs that offered no control of the environment. It was mobile; it had a clear Plexiglas front; and it had heating and humidity controls, and an air filter. As a result, Deborah interacted extensively with her family, and was active and healthy. Third, in response to "what young people should do" after the war, Skinner wrote *Walden Two*, a 1948 novel about a community that took behavior analysis to everyday life. He argued that young people should not accept pre-wartime verities, but instead should experiment. They should experiment with technologies for recycling waste, with work-share economies, and of course with education.

EDUCATION

In *Walden Two*, Skinner's prescriptions for education were prescient of his subsequent contributions: Learning was positively (not negatively) reinforced by its natural consequences (being right, not grades); teaching was empirically based (not just rationally designed); educational progress was graded by readiness (not age); and educational goals emphasized both content and process (e.g., thinking). Five years later, in *Science and Human Behavior*, Skinner (1953, pp. 402–412) offered a behavioral interpretation of education as a cultural practice whose purpose is to establish behavior that is "of advantage to the individual and to others at some time in the future" (p. 402). This behavior is mainly verbal, for instance, about history (e.g., "Sputnik I was launched on October 4, 1957").

Although the practical implications of Skinner's analysis and interpretation were clear, he was not impelled to action until he attended Deborah's fourth-grade math class on November 11, 1953—her class' "Father's Day." He came away distraught. Educational methods were inconsistent with what was known about behavior: "[Deborah's] teacher was violating two fundamental principles of teaching: The students were not being told at once whether their work was right or wrong . . . and they were all moving at the same pace regardless of preparation or ability" (Skinner, 1983, p. 64). For Skinner, an initial solution lay in technical assistance—assistance in the form of teaching machines and programmed instruction.

In a matter of days, he was constructing prototypes of these machines and their programs. Within a few months, he had demonstrated a machine that taught spelling and arithmetic at a national conference and presented his first paper on education, "The Science of Learning and the Art of Teaching" (Skinner, 1954). Within 4 years, he was conducting research on programming with his colleagues Lloyd Homme, Susan Meyer, and soon James Holland (see Holland & Skinner, 1961); he had secured research space from Harvard and funding from the Ford Foundation; and he was using programmed materials in his courses, enjoying great success as a teacher. In less than a decade, he was describing his progress in *Science* and *Scientific American*, and in education journals (e.g., Skinner, 1958, 1961a, 1961b, 1963). Societies were established; conferences were held; journals were founded; research was funded; books were published; companies were started; machines and programs were sold; and the culture took notice (Skinner, 1965b; see Lumsdaine & Glaser, 1960). In sum, Skinner had begun a movement in educational psychology and the culture at large (Benjamin, 1988; Vargas & Vargas, 1996; see Galanter, 1959; Smith & Moore, 1962). His main contributions to it were (a) a critique of standard educational practices, (b) a constructive alternative, and (c) considerations of some objections to his alternative.

A Critique of Standard Practices

Based on his science of behavior and his observations in Deborah's classroom, Skinner noted the following. Educational reinforcement was generally negative, not positive (e.g., criticism, failure). This aversive control generated by-products such as escape and avoidance (e.g., truancy, drop-outs), counter-control (e.g., aggression, vandalism), and neuroses (e.g., anxiety, apathy). Even when educational reinforcement was positive, it was often vaguely defined (e.g., the "utility" of an education) or, in the case of progressive education, too narrowly restricted to the natural consequences of but a small part of requisite learning. In addition, classroom conditions were far from optimal: Reinforcement was both infrequent (e.g., testing) and delayed (e.g., grading); academic curricula were poorly programmed (e.g., the steps between successive approximations to knowledge were too large); and classroom presentations and equipment (e.g., films) treated students as passive learners. Finally, the pedagogy of assign-and-test, tell-and-test, and trial-and-error learning did not teach. It merely held students responsible for learning and for learning to learn.

Parents and teachers attribute the resulting poor academic performances to explanatory constructs (e.g., a poor mind, poor information processing), while schools reduce the demands of the curriculum, emphasizing content having more inherent appeal. When educators seek reform, they are typically more concerned with philosophy (e.g., the free school, the whole child), schools (e.g., more schools, model schools), teaching standards (e.g., more learning, more hours), teachers (e.g., more teachers, more credentials), curricular materials (e.g., better texts, re-organized presentations), and materials and equipment (e.g., attractive texts, television), than they are with pedagogical methods—teaching defined in terms of learning (cf. Reese, 1986).

A Constructive Alternative

Skinner demurred. Educational reinforcement can be positive (e.g., the natural consequences of answering correctly); educational contingencies can be immediate (e.g., the "automatic" reinforcement of behaving competently); educational materials can be effectively programmed (e.g., in small steps); and reinforcement can be frequent (e.g., for the many small steps). The problem was technical, and Skinner had solved technical problems before. For instance, in the experimental analysis of behavior, he invented, arranged, delivered, and recorded contingencies of reinforcement with electro-mechanical devices. Classroom instruction was no less complex and no less in need of machines: "[A]s a mere reinforcing mechanism, the teacher is out of date . . . If the teacher is to take advantage of recent advances in the study of learning, she must have the help of mechanical devices" (Skinner, 1954, p. 95). The "recent advances in the study of learning" was the experimental analysis of behavior; the "mechanical devices" were teaching machines and programmed instruction.

The experimental analysis of behavior had made two notable advances in psychological science. It described basic behavioral processes that explained the production and maintenance of behavior. And, it provided a research methodology for within-subject experimental control that naturally yielded a technology for producing and maintaining the behavior. Skinner's science thus provided generalizable principles of learning and an effective technology of teaching. His direct contributions to the latter were teaching machines and programmed instruction.

Teaching Machines. "A teaching machine is simply any device which arranges contingencies of reinforcement" (Skinner, 1965a, p. 430). For Skinner, it became a device for delivering programmed instruction (i.e., hardware for software). Given that teaching was "the expediting of learning," teaching machines were a means for teaching "rapidly, thoroughly, and expeditiously a large part of what we now teach slowly, incompletely, and with wasted effort on the part of both student and teacher" (Skinner, 1961a, p. 92). In Skinner's inventive hands, their design evolved throughout the 1950s, from those that drilled and tested course content (e.g., manila envelopes with windows through which cards with questions and answers could slide) to those that shaped new behavior (e.g., covered disks that rotated to present questions, prompt responses, and display answers). Among the latter's design specifications were (a) that they introduce course content separately from answers to questions about it, (b) that they have students recall and construct their answers, not just recognize and select them, and (c) that they present answers as the immediate consequence of student responding (e.g., being correct). Any further design specifications were dictated by the means and ends of programmed instruction, for machines themselves do not teach. Programmed instruction was Skinner's critical contribution to the teaching machine movement.

Programmed Instruction. Among the ends of programmed instruction is individualized pacing: Students advance through instructional material at their own pace, not a rate prescribed for all students. As for the means of programmed instruction, these were both structural and functional. Structurally, instructional material is broken down into small steps and sequenced in "a plausible genetic order," that is, into a sequence of successive approximations to complex terminal performance. Skinner often noted the prescience of John Amos Comenius in this regard. Although necessary, successive approximations are not, however, sufficient for teaching. Each approximation has to be mastered before the next one is presented. This, Skinner recognized, was foreseen by Thorndike (1912): "If, by a miracle of mechanical ingenuity, a book could be so arranged that only to him who had done what was directed on page one would page two become visible, and so on, much that now requires personal instruction could be managed in print" (p. 175, as cited in Skinner, 1963). A teaching machine and its program constitute such a book.

Functionally, programmed instruction is based on the three-term contingency, in particular, the consequences and antecedents of responding. The consequences are the correct answers in each successive approximation to terminal performance which, when properly programmed, match the students' answers 95% of the time, and thus immediately reinforce responding on a rich schedule. Before reinforcement can be programmed, however, responding must occur first. This involves programming its antecedents, the techniques for which Skinner drew from *Verbal Behavior* (Skinner, 1957)—priming, prompting, and "vanishing." Priming evokes previously acquired responses or provides them (e.g., "The important parts of a flashlight are the battery and the bulb. When we 'turn on' a flashlight, we close a switch which connects the battery with the ___"). Formal and thematic prompting provides cues for partial responses in order to evoke complete or extended responses (e.g., "When we turn on a flashlight, an electric current flows through the fine wire in the ___ and causes it to grow hot"). Vanishing or fading gradually removes the prompts so that responses become independent of them (e.g., "When the hot wire glows brightly, we say that it gives off or sends out heat and ___"). When these techniques are systematically applied to a content domain (e.g., spelling, algebra, physics, neurology) in a sequence of successively mastered "frames," the result is a "program" of instruction that teaches (e.g., Sidman & Sidman, 1965). Table 10.1 presents the remainder of the program begun in the preceding parenthetical examples.

Programming is difficult. It involves complex and subtle interactions among programmers, programs, and students in reciprocal sets of contingencies at three different levels—cultural (education), interpersonal (teaching), and individual (learning). At the individual level, learning requires that students (a) master current material before moving forward; (b) be presented with new material only when they are ready; (c) emit answers without errors through the techniques described above, and (d) be motivated through immediate and frequent reinforcement. At the interpersonal level, teaching requires that programmers (a) define their content domain; (b) arrange it sequentially; (c) bring student responses under stimulus control (e.g., impart the "meaning" of terms); (d) transfer and multiply those controls (e.g., provide "instruction" about equivalent meanings); (e) integrate ("seed") prior material with new material to maintain behavior at strength; (f) program responding to be correct 95% of the time (e.g., sustain interest and motivation); and (g) take responsibility for anything less than 95% mastery (i.e., not blame the student). At the cultural level, education requires (a) that programmers bring students to the point where they too can be programmers and (b) that students bring programmers to the point where they become students of programming. This ensures that knowledge is retained in a culture for future selection (i.e., an evolutionary epistemology) and that knowledge is effectively analyzed (i.e., an empirical epistemology). As to the latter, Skinner (1961b) noted, "It is possible that we shall fully understand the nature of knowledge only after having solved the practical problems of imparting it" (p. 392).

Although these sets of contingencies are interlocking, one metacontingency ultimately maintains them—cultural survival (Skinner, 1984). Cultures in which learning, teaching, and education are established practices are more likely to survive than cultures in which they are not. What made Skinner distraught in 1954 was that these practices were more art than science, even though the experimental analysis of behavior already offered a science of learning and a technology of teaching. In the 1950s and 1960s, the teaching machine movement supplied and applied this science and technology (Benjamin, 1988); it significantly advanced

TABLE 10.1
A Sample of Programmed Instruction

Sentence to be Completed	Word to be Supplied
1. The important parts of a flashlight are the battery and the bulb. When we "turn on" a flashlight, we close a switch which connects switch which connects the battery with the _____.	bulb
2. When we turn on a flashlight, an electric current flows through the fine wire in the _____and causes it to grow hot.	bulb
3. When the hot wire glows brightly, we say the it gives off or sends out heat and _____.	light
4. The fine wire in the bulb is called a filament. The bulb "lights up" when the filament is heated by the passage of a (n)_____current.	electric
5. When a weak battery produces little current, the fine wire, or _____, does not get very hot.	filament
6. A filament which is *less* hot sends out or gives off _____light.	less
7. "Emit" means "send out." The amount of light sent out, or "emitted", by a filament depends on how _____the filament is.	hot
8. The higher the temperature of the filament the _____the light emitted by it.	brighter: stronger
9. If a flashlight battery is weak, the _____in the bulb may still glow, but with only a dull red color.	filament
10. The light from a very hot filament is colored yellow or white. The light from a filament which is not very hot is colored _____.	red
11. A blacksmith or other metal worker sometimes makes sure that a bar of iron is heated to a "cherry red" before hammering it into shape. He uses the _____of the light emitted by the bar to tell how hot it is.	color
12. Both the color and the amount of light depend on the _____of the emitting filament or bar.	temperature
13. An object which emits light because it is hot is called "incandescent." A flashlight bulb is an incandescent source of _____.	light
14. A neon tube emits light but remains cool. It is, therefore, not an incandescent _____of light.	source
15. A candle flame is hot. It is a (n) _____source of light.	incandescent
16. The hot wick of a candle gives off small pieces or particles of carbon which burn in the flame. Before or while burning, the hot particles send out, or _____light.	emit
17. A long candlewick produces a flame in which oxygen does not reach all the carbon particles. Without oxygen the particles cannot burn. Particles which do not burn rise above the flames as _____.	smoke
18. We can show that there are particles of carbon in a candle flame, even when it is not smoking, by holding a piece of metal in the flame. The metal cools some of the particles before they burn, and the unburned carbon _____collect on the metal as soot.	particles
19. The particles of carbon in soot or smoke no longer emit light because they are _____than when they were in the flame.	cooler, colder
20. The reddish part of a candle flame has the same color as the filament in a flashlight with a weak battery. We might guess that the yellow or white parts of a candle flame are _____than the reddish part.	hotter

(Continued)

TABLE 10.1

(Continued)

Sentence to be Completed	Word to be Supplied
21. "Putting out" an incandescent electric light means turning off the current so that the filament grows too _____to emit light.	cold, cool
22. Setting fire to the wick of an oil lamp is called _____the lamp.	lighting
23. The sun is our principal _____of light, as well as of heat.	source
24. The sun is not only very bright but very hot. It is a powerful _____source of light.	incandescent
25. Light is a form of energy. In "emitting light" an object changes, or "converts," one form of _____into another.	energy
26. The electrical energy supplied by the battery in a flashlight is converted to _____and _____.	heat, light; light, heat
27. If we leave a flashlight on, all the energy stored in the battery will finally be changed or _____into heat and light.	converted
28. The light from a candle flame comes from the _____released by chemical changes as the candle burns.	energy
29. A nearly "dead" battery may make a flashlight bulb warm to the touch, but the filament may still not be hot enough to emit light - in other words, the filament will not be _____at that temperature.	incandescent
30. Objects, such as filament, carbon particles, or iron bars, become incandescent when heat to about 800 degrees Celsius. At that temperature they begin to _____ _____.	emit light
31. When raised to any temperature above 800 degrees Celsius, an object such as an iron bar will emit light. Although the bar may not melt or vaporize, its particles will be _____not matter how hot they get.	incandescent
32. About 800 degrees Celsius is the lower limit of the temperature at which particles emit light. There is no upper limit of the _____at which emission of light occurs.	temperature
33. Sunlight is _____by very hot gases near the surface of the sun.	emitted
34. Complex changes similar to an atomic explosion generate the great heat which explains the _____ _____of light by the sun.	emission
35. Below about _____degrees Celsius an object is not an incandescent source of light.	800

Note. Part of a program in high-school physics. The Machine presents one item at a time. The student completes the item and then uncovers the corresponding word or phrase shown at the right.

From "Teaching Machines" by B. F. Skinner, 1958, *Science, 128*, p. 973. Reprinted with permission. Copyright 1958 American Association for the Advancement of Science.

our understanding of learning and teaching (Vargas & Vargas, 1996); and it notably improved academic achievement (e.g., Rushton, 1965).

Objections and Considerations

The teaching machine movement flourished, but was not uncontroversial. Indeed, objections to it arose years before Skinner built his first machine. Our enlightenment tradition notwithstanding, Western culture has never fully embraced a naturalistic worldview. The culture has always had misgivings about the purpose and purview of natural science (e.g., romantic, religious). Social critics and social constructionists have had disciplinary doubts about a science of psychology (e.g., dehumanization, scientism). And, individuals are wary of behavioral engineering (e.g., control). Skinner (1948, 1953) had previously considered these objections, some of them misunderstandings (cf. Sparzo, 1992; Todd & Morris, 1992). In the context of the teaching machine movement, he anticipated their more specific instantiations, among them the following.

The Nature of What is Learned.   Skinner's research was criticized for analyzing human knowledge and thought in "mechanistic" terms, reducing knowledge to responses and thinking to facts. His answer was three-fold. First, analyses such as these have historically proved effective in understanding many subject matters, reducing explanatory constructs (e.g., vitalism) to natural processes and products (e.g., biological). Second, knowledge and thought are not explanatory constructs, but descriptive concepts. For instance, "knowing how to solve algebraic equations" is not a mental process, but a behavioral repertoire of great subtlety and complexity. Third, independent of course content, programmed instruction can indeed teach thinking. For example, where thinking is a form of constructive self-management (e.g., problem solving), it can be analyzed, specified, and taught using what is known about logic, behavior, and the scientific method. Programmed instruction can also teach students to study, for instance, to attend selectively to texts and to reject irrelevant material. Reconceptualizing knowledge, thinking, and studying as behavioral repertoires sharpens the specification of educational objectives and outcomes.

The Nature of Learning and the Learner.   Another set of criticisms was that students would become dependent on teaching machines, individuality would be suppressed, and grades would be meaningless. For Skinner, student dependence on machines was an issue of generalization, and generalization could be programmed (e.g., students "weaned" from machines). Somewhat ironically, among the advantages of teaching machines is that they can be used independently of formal classroom settings, for example, in at-home instruction, correspondence courses, and distance learning. They are useful when and where teachers are unavailable.

As for individuality, Skinner maintained that "each of us is, I am sure, entirely unique [but] that does not mean that we have spontaneous capacities . . . We have to behave in a way that is determined by our genetic and personal history" (Houghton & Lapan, 1995, pp. 34–35). In programmed instruction, individuality is not a parameter of mastery, but instead of student pacing. It is observed in the number of programs mastered, not in how well they are mastered. Ironically again, programmed instruction has advantages. It can reduce motivational differences by having all students feel confident—eager for further learning. It can be constructed to take into account disabilities (e.g., sensory deficits) without sacrificing instruction (e.g., using Braille as a medium). And, it is self-paced and can include remedial branching, and thus be attuned to individual differences in the baseline, speed, and maintenance of learning (e.g., intelligence).

As for grades, they would not be meaningless, but would mean something different. They would not reflect levels of mastery normed or curved across students, where an A might mean 75% mastery of 100% of the material. Instead, grades would reflect differences within students in the amount of the material they mastered, where a C might mean 100% mastery of 75% of the course content.

The Nature of Teaching. Teaching machines were also criticized because they would undermine and jeopardize the teacher's position in the classroom. To the contrary, Skinner urged: Teaching machines no more eliminate teachers than research equipment eliminates researchers. What they eliminate are "tiresome labors" (e.g., grading) and duties (e.g., the disciplinarian), not classroom contact and responsibilities (e.g., refining instructional programs, recommending course content). Teachers would be better, not lesser, resources for cultural, intellectual, and emotional stimulation and support. In the end, they would also teach more material more thoroughly to more students, and thus could improve their professional and economic stature.

The Teaching Machine Movement

Skinner's responses to these objections notwithstanding, 10 years after he built his first teaching machine, the movement began to falter. Within 25 years, only a few machines remained in regular education classrooms; they were relegated to remedial education, private schools, business, industry, and the armed forces. The movement failed for internal and external reasons (Benjamin, 1988; Bjork, 1993, pp. 167–190). Internally, according to Skinner, American industry did not rise to the task he envisioned and few programmers understood programming. Inferior technology inundated the marketplace. Externally, the objections won out. The movement's philosophy was inconsistent with the norms of mind–body dualism, freedom and dignity, and personal responsibility. Its technology challenged traditions in which instructional objectives referred to the mind, not behavior; and in which instructional methods selected students who learned instead of teaching students to learn; and in which teaching was more personal and less mechanical.

Given that these norms and traditions are deeply ingrained in our national character, policy decisions regarding the application of science quite naturally come under their influence. Educational research, in particular, is strongly affected by cultural and institutional pressures, even to the extent that effectiveness does not guarantee use. As a case in point, a national Project Follow Through study (i.e., "follow through" on Head Start) in the late 1960s compared 22 educational models and found that those based in Skinner's technology of teaching—Direct Instruction and Behavior Analysis—produced superior outcomes compared to those based in more normative traditions (e.g., affective–cognitive; see Becker, 1978). However, those two programs were not afterwards differentially adopted, as was planned in the search for best practices. The Project was politicized (Watkins, 1997). Education still struggles no less today to assure that students receive scientifically validated instructional practices (Bushell & Baer, 1981).

Professional and Person: 1965–1990

For Skinner, the failure of the teaching machine movement was not a failure of the machines or their programming per se. He never lost his optimism about their potential. Moreover, he had only meant them as initial solutions to the teacher's dilemma, fearing their effectiveness would subvert the further analysis of educational practices. As a result, in the mid-1960s, he began advocating for teaching machines as part of the broader application of the experimental analysis of behavior to developmental disabilities, mental retardation, and mental illness (e.g., Wolf, Risley, & Mees, 1964; see Skinner, 1965a, 1968a, 1968b). In addition, he expanded his advocacy for the technology of teaching beyond instructional design, speaking to educational methods (e.g., behavioral objectives), classroom management (e.g., contingency management), and college teaching (e.g., personalized system of instruction; Keller, 1968; see Skinner, 1969, 1973, 1974). These efforts to improve the lives of atypically and typically developing individuals led to still more professional recognition—the 1971 International Award of the Joseph P. Kennedy Foundation for Mental Retardation and the 1978 Award for Distinguished Contributions to Educational Research from the American Educational Research Association.

In the years that followed, Skinner remained concerned about education, but his public advocacy of teaching machines and programmed instruction became more sporadic and his style more urgent, wistful, and utopian—and perhaps off-putting (Skinner, 1984, 1986, 1989). For instance, whereas in the 1970s, he urged that "Education is an important function of a culture—possibly in the long run its most important or only function" (Skinner, 1973, p. 448), in the 1980s, he chided: "A culture that is not willing to accept scientific advances in the understanding of human behavior, together with the technology [of teaching] that emerges from these advances, will eventually be replaced by a culture that is" (Skinner, 1984, p. 953). Skinner's public advocacy for education ebbed further as he turned his energies to other problems—the fate of psychology, politics and peace, and cultural evolution. In fact, he worked actively in every area of behavior analysis until the end of his life. Skinner died of leukemia on August 18, 1990, at the age of 86, the day after he completed the manuscript version of the address he had given 9 days earlier on the occasion of his receipt of APA's first Outstanding Lifetime Contribution Award (Skinner, 1990). He was survived by Eve, Julie, Deborah, Lisa, and Justine.

CONCLUSION

Skinner's legacy to educational psychology lies in a confluence of intellectual, cultural, and personal factors that made his contributions unique. At the same time, taken individually, these factors had shared effects on other psychologists. He was thus both ahead of his time and a man of his times.

Like William James, he was a functionalist, asking why mind and behavior existed, but he was not mentalistic. He fashioned a functional concept of mind as behavior. Like G. Stanley Hall, he was selectionist, but not teleological. He founded a science of "purposeful" behavior—behavior reinforced by its consequences. Like Alfred Binet and Edward Thorndike, he improved our means for measuring behavior, but he was not a psychometrician. He recorded behavior in real time and applied rigorous experimental control. Like John Dewey, he criticized the reflex arc concept, essentialist philosophy, and aversive control, and he offered workable alternatives. He offered the three-term contingency as a unit of analysis; he spoke both to historical contingency (e.g., reinforcement history) and ahistorical behavioral processes (e.g., reinforcement); and he demonstrated the efficacy of positive reinforcement.

As for the future, Skinner's philosophy, science, and technology retain their potential. His philosophy offers an alternative to mainstream logical positivism without being radically relativistic; it is anti-foundational, but grounded in nature; and its ontology and epistemology are evolutionary (Smith, 1986; Zuriff, 1980). His science offers basic behavioral processes ubiquitous throughout psychology (Catania, 1998). Although cognitive psychology and neuroscience may describe the structure of the repertoires called "knowledge" and how the nervous systems participates in "knowing," they supplement, not supplant, an independent science of behavior (Donahoe & Palmer, 1994). Finally, his technology of teaching is becoming part of the educational mainstream, albeit not always explicitly so (Sparzo, 1992). Behavioral objectives are "performance" objectives, fundamental to educational accountability (e.g., Education for All Handicapped Children Act of 1974, Pub. L. No. 94–142). Positive reinforcement is "feedback," widely acknowledged as best practice (Chance, 1992). Stimulus control is used in developing instructional materials and programs (Jensen, Sloane, & Young, 1988). And, behaviorally-based institutions, schools, and programs reflect all the foregoing (e.g., Direct Instruction, Precision Teaching; Bijou & Ruiz, 1981; Crandall, Jacobson, & Sloane, 1997; Frederick, Deitz, Bryceland, & Hummel, 2000; West & Hamerlynck, 1992).

Skinner's legacy arguably lies in the future, not in the past. He was ingenious in solving problems. Education was a problem to solve—and still is. He was Progressive in advancing technology. Education lacked a technology—and still does. He was naturalistic in his science. Education was a social and mental science—and remains so. Only empirical research will tell us whether these norms reflect natural limits in individual, social, and cultural practices or if the norms are historically contingent and subject to change. Skinner would not have wanted it otherwise. The experimental analysis of behavior is his legacy.

ACKNOWLEDGMENTS

Dedicated to the memory of Ellen P. Reese (1926–1997), teacher extraordinaire. I thank Montrose M. Wolf, who recommended to the editors that I write this chapter in his place, and Philip N. Hineline, Karen L. Mahon, and George B. Semb for their perspicacious comments on the manuscript proper.

REFERENCES

Baer, D. M., Wolf, M. M., & Risley, T. R. (1968). Some current dimensions of applied behavior analysis. *Journal of Applied Behavior Analysis, 1*, 91–97.

Becker, W. C. (1978). The national evaluation of Follow Through: Behavior theory-based programs come out on top. *Education and Urban Society, 10*(4), 431–458.

Benjamin, L. T. (1988). A history of teaching machines. *American Psychologist, 43*, 703–712.

Bijou, S. W., & Ruiz, R. (Eds.). (1981). *Behavior modification: Contributions to education*. Hillsdale, NJ: Lawrence Erlbaum Associates.

Binet, A. (1911). Nouvelles recherches sur la mesure du niveau intellectuel chez les enfants d'ecole [New investigations in the measurement of the intellectual level of school children]. *L'Annee Psychologique, 17*, 145–201.

Bjork, D. W. (1993). *B. F. Skinner: A life*. New York: Basic Books.

Bushell, D., & Baer, D. M. (1981). The future of behavior analysis in the schools? Consider its recent past, and then ask a different question. *School Psychology Review, 10*, 259–270.

Catania, A. C. (1998). *Learning* (4th ed.). Upper Saddle River, NJ: Prentice-Hall.

Chance, P. (1992, November). The rewards of learning. *Phi Delta Kappan,* 200–207.

Chiesa, M. (1992). Radical behaviorism and scientific frameworks: From mechanistic to relational accounts. *American Psychologist, 47*, 1287–1299.

Crandall, J., Jacobson, J., & Sloane, H. (Eds.). (2000). *What works in education* (2nd ed.). Cambridge, MA: Cambridge Center for Behavioral Studies.

Dewey, J. (1896). The reflex arc concept in psychology. *Psychological Review, 3*, 357–370.

Dewey, J. (1916). *Democracy and education: An introduction to the philosophy of education*. New York: Macmillan.

Donahoe, J. W., & Palmer, D. C. (1994). *Learning and complex behavior*. Boston: Allyn & Bacon.

Education for all Handicapped Children Act of 1975, Pub. L. No. 94–142, 20 U.S.C. 1401 et seq, 89 Stat, 773–796 (1977).

Frederick, L. D., Deitz, S. M., Bryceland, J. A., & Hummel, J. H. (1997). *Behavior analysis, education, and effective schooling*. Reno, NJ: Context Press.

Galanter, E. (Ed.). (1959). *Automatic teaching: The state of the art*. New York: McGraw-Hill.

Hall, G. S. (1904). *Adolescence* (Vol. 1–2). New York: Appleton.

Hayes, S. C., Hayes, L. J., & Reese, H. R. (1988). Finding the philosophical core: A review of Stephen C. Pepper's *World hypotheses: A study in evidence. Journal of the Experimental Analysis of Behavior, 50*, 97–111.

Holland, J. G., & Skinner, B. F. (1961). *The analysis of behavior*. New York: McGraw-Hill.

Houghton, R. W., & Lapan, M. T. (1995). *Learning and intelligence: Conversations with B. F. Skinner and R. H. Wheeler*. Dublin, Ireland: Irish Academic Press.

James, W. (1899). *Talks to teachers on psychology*. New York: Holt.

James, W. (1904). Does "consciousness" exist? *Journal of Philosophy, 1*, 477–491.

Jensen, W. R., Sloane, H. N., & Young, K. R. (1988). *Applied behavior analysis in education*. Englewood Cliffs, NJ: Prentice-Hall.

Keller, F. S. (1968). "Good-bye teacher..." *Journal of Applied Behavior Analysis, 1*, 79–84.

Lumdsdaine, A. A., & Glaser, R. (Eds.). (1960). *Teaching machines and programmed learning*. Washington, DC: National Educational Association.

Malone, J. C. (1990). *Theories of learning: A historical approach*. Belmont, CA: Wadsworth.

Michael, J. (1985). Behavior analysis: A radical perspective. In B. L. Hammonds (Ed.), *Psychology and learning* (pp. 99–121). Washington, DC: American Psychological Association.

Morris, E. K. (1992). The aim, progress, and evolution of behavior analysis. *The Behavior Analyst, 15*, 3–29.

Morris, E. K. (1993). Behavior analysis and mechanism: One is not the other. *The Behavior Analyst, 16*, 25–43.

O'Donnell, J. M. (1985). *The origins of behaviorism: American psychology, 1870–1920*. New York: New York University Press.

Reese, E. P. (1986). Learning about teaching about teaching about learning: Presenting behavior analysis in an introductory survey course. In V. P. Makosky (Ed.), *The G. Stanley Hall Lecture Series* (Vol. 6, pp. 65–127). Washington, DC: American Psychological Association.

Rushton, E. W. (1965). *The Roanoke experiment*. Chicago: Encyclopedia Britannica Press.

Sidman, R. L., & Sidman, M. (1965). *Neuroanatomy. Vol. I. A programmed text*. Boston: Little, Brown.

Skinner, B. F. (1938). *Behavior of organisms*. New York: Appleton-Century-Crofts.

Skinner, B. F. (1945). The operational analysis of psychological terms. *Psychological Review, 52*, 270–277, 291–294.

Skinner, B. F. (1947). Experimental psychology. In W. Dennis (Ed.), *Current trends in psychology* (pp. 16–49). Pittsburgh, PA: University of Pittsburgh Press.

Skinner, B. F. (1948). *Walden two*. New York: Macmillan.

Skinner, B. F. (1950). Are theories of learning necessary? *Psychological Review, 57*, 193–216.

Skinner, B. F. (1953). *Science and human behavior*. New York: Macmillan.

Skinner, B. F. (1954). The science of learning and the art of teaching. *Harvard Educational Review, 24*, 86–97.

Skinner, B. F. (1957). *Verbal behavior*. New York: Appleton-Century-Crofts.

Skinner, B. F. (1958). Teaching machines. *Science, 128*, 969–977.

Skinner, B. F. (1961a). Teaching machines. *Scientific American, 205*, 90–122.

Skinner, B. F. (1961b). Why we need teaching machines. *Harvard Educational Review, 31*, 377–398.

Skinner, B. F. (1963). Reflections on a decade of teaching machines. *Teacher's College Record, 65*, 168–177.

Skinner, B. F. (1965a). The technology of teaching. *Proceedings of the Royal Society, Series B, 162*, 427–443.

Skinner, B. F. (1965b, October 16). Why teachers fail. *Saturday Review*, 80–81, 98–102.

Skinner, B. F. (1967). B. F. Skinner. In E. G. Boring & G. Lindzey (Eds.), *A history of psychology in autobiography* (pp. 387–413). New York: Macmillan.

Skinner, B. F. (1968a). Teaching science in high school—What is wrong? *Science, 159*, 704–710.

Skinner, B. F. (1968b). *The technology of teaching*. New York: Appleton Century-Crofts.

Skinner, B. G. (1969). Contingency management in the classroom. *Education, 90*, 93–100.

Skinner, B. F. (1973). Some implications of making education more efficient. In C. E. Thorensen (Ed.), *Behavior modification in education* (pp. 446–456). Chicago: National Society for the Study of Education.

Skinner, B. F. (1974). Designing higher education. *Daedalus, 103*, 196–202.

Skinner, B. F. (1976). *Particulars of my life.* New York: Knopf.

Skinner, B. F. (1979). *The shaping of a behaviorist.* New York: Knopf.

Skinner, B. F. (1983). *A matter of consequences.* New York: Knopf.

Skinner, B. F. (1984). The shame of American education. *American Psychologist, 39,* 947–954.

Skinner, B. F. (1986). Programmed instruction revisited. *Phi Delta Kappan, 68,* 103–110.

Skinner, B. F. (1989). The school of the future. In B. F. Skinner (Ed.), *Recent issues in the analysis of behavior* (pp. 85–96). Columbus, OH: Merrill.

Skinner, B. F. (1990). Can psychology be a science of the mind? *American Psychologist, 45,* 1206–1210.

Smith, L. D. (1986). *Behaviorism and logical positivism: A revised account of the alliance.* Stanford, CA: Stanford University Press.

Smith, L. D., & Woodward, W. R. (Eds.). (1996). *B. F. Skinner and behaviorism in American culture.* Bethlehem, PA: Lehigh University Press.

Smith, W. I., & Moore, J. W. (Eds.). (1962). *Programmed learning.* New York: Van Nostrand.

Sparzo, F. J. (1992). B. F. Skinner's contribution to education: A retrospective appreciation. *Contemporary Education, 63,* 225–233.

Thorndike, E. L. (1904). *Introduction to the theory of mental and social measurements.* New York: Science Press.

Thorndike, E. L. (1912). *Education.* New York: Macmillan.

Todd, J. T., & Morris, E. K. (1992). Case studies in the great power of steady misrepresentation. *American Psychologist, 47,* 1441–1453.

Vargas, A. E., & Vargas, J. S. (1996). B. F. Skinner and the origins of teaching machines. In L. D. Smith & W. R. Woodward (Eds.), *B. F. Skinner and behaviorism in American culture* (pp. 237–253). Bethlehem, PA: Lehigh University Press.

Watkins, C. L. (1997). *Project Follow Through: A case study of contingencies influencing instructional practices of the educational establishment.* Cambridge, MA: Cambridge Center for Behavioral Studies.

Watson, J. B. (1913). Psychology as the behaviorist views it. *Psychological Review, 20,* 158–177.

West, R. P., & Hamerlynck, L. A. (1992). *Designs for excellence in education: The legacy of B. F. Skinner.* Longmont, CO: Sopris West.

Wolf, M. M., Risley, T. R., & Mees, H. (1964). Application of operant conditioning procedures to the behavior problems of an autistic child. *Behavior Research and Therapy, 1,* 305–312.

Zuriff, G. E. (1980). Radical behaviorist epistemology. *Psychological Bulletin, 87,* 337–350.

11

Jean Piaget, Learning Research, and American Education

C. J. Brainerd
University of Arizona

If nominations had been taken as the century turned to identify its most influential psychologists, the names of Sigmund Freud, B. F. Skinner, and Jean Piaget would surely have led the list. Although none was an educational psychologist by profession, two of them, Piaget and Skinner, had profound influences on American education. Skinner's work is considered elsewhere in this volume. The subject of the present chapter, Jean Piaget, was a researcher of catholic accomplishment, contributing prolifically to fields as diverse as biology, philosophy, and sociology. First and foremost, however, Piaget was a developmental psychologist—many would say *the* developmental psychologist of the 20th century and everyone would say *the* cognitive-developmental psychologist.

Unquestionably, it is for his work on the basic mechanisms of cognitive growth that Piaget is best eulogized and for which he would most wish to be remembered. His stage model of intellectual ontogenesis and his studies of the reasoning skills that figure in those stages (conservation, object permanence, perspective taking, proportionality, probability, and the like) have been the stuff of legend and freshman psychology textbooks for two generations. Although this is the core of Piaget's scientific legacy, his impact on education, especially American education, was also vast. Thirty years ago, his theory of cognitive development stimulated revolutionary changes in preschool and elementary school curriculum practices

251

(Lawton & Hooper, 1978), changes that went hand-in-glove with the political and social climate of the 1960s, though they ran counter to the then-dominant learning-theory perspective in educational psychology. In the ensuing decades, Piagetian thought has continued to foment major changes in American education, with the whole language approach to reading instruction being a recent illustration.

It is hardly remarkable, of course, that the work of *the* student of cognitive development should have had an enduring impact on educational psychology. After all, basic research on cognitive development is to educational psychology as physics is to engineering; it is the source of fundamental laws of children's learning, memory, and reasoning that supply the scientific foundation for curriculum research and for best instructional practice. (Perhaps I should say "ought to supply" as a way of acknowledging that anti-scientific philosophies of instruction have enjoyed considerable influence in some corners of professional education, with postmodernism being a recent example.) Consequently, university departments of educational psychology that do not place the study of cognitive development at the heart of graduate training are extremely limited. (Imagine a computer engineer attempting to design microprocessors without a thorough grasp of quantum physics!) Absent a deep conversance with the science of cognitive development, it is only by accident that its laws will be put into practice by educational psychologists. Piaget (1970b) put it more succinctly: Cognitive development *is* the science of educational psychology.

My aim in the present chapter is not to provide a comprehensive exegesis of Piaget's research program or of his grand theory of cognitive development. That would be impossible in so scant a space and would, in any case, go far beyond this volume's objectives. My aim is rather to focus attention on those aspects of Piaget's contributions that have proven to be of greatest significance for educational psychology. Because Piaget is an historical figure, the chapter begins with a biographical sketch. The rest of the chapter deals with Piaget's views on that most central of all educational topics, learning. This material is divided into two sections. The first section presents Piagetian ideas about the relation between cognitive development and learning, and it summarizes findings from classical experiments that tested those ideas. Interestingly, those experiments were conducted almost entirely by American educational psychologists, rather than by Piaget or his coworkers. The second section presents Piagetian ideas about instructional methodology, and it also summarizes findings from classical experiments that tested those ideas. Again, the experiments were conducted almost entirely by American educational psychologists. Thus, a factor of major historical significance emerges from the consideration of Piaget's view on learning: For the better part of 3 decades, there was a symbiotic relation between Piagetian theory and American educational psychology, with theoretical proposals about learning emanating from Piaget and his collaborators, but the research that was required to test those proposals emanating from the laboratories of American educational psychologists.

PIAGET'S (SCHOLARLY) LIFE

Bertrand Russell remarked in his *History of Western Philosophy* that since the 17th century, every serious advance in philosophy began with an attack on Aristotle. The reason is that by that time, Aristotle's ideas on just about every philosophical question had reigned supreme for a millennium, so that new views could only be justified by a close critique of Aristotle. There is a parallel phenomenon, though of smaller scale, in the recent history of cognitive development research. From the early 1960s to the early 1980s, Piagetian theory dominated cognitive development as thoroughly as Freudian theory dominated abnormal psychology decades before. The literature of those 2 decades was largely given over to articles that tested, extrapolated, or promulgated facets of Piaget's work. Although Piagetian hegemony has greatly dimished since then, in large measure because of research findings that will be discussed later, he remains our contemporary Aristotle: Progress in cognitive-developmental theory typically incorporates critical discussions of relevant aspects of Piaget's work.

It was not always so. Throughout most of his long and productive career, Piaget labored in splendid isolation, his research being only slightly known in American psychology and entirely unknown in American education. Actually, as Kessen (1996) pointed out, the situation is somewhat more complex. From the beginning of his career, owing to some investigations of language development in the 1920s (e.g., Piaget, 1926), Piaget had been regarded as one of the stars of European psychology. Carl Murchison invited him to contribute a chapter on children's philosophies to the first edition of the standard American reference work in child psychology, *The Manual of Child Psychology*, which was published in 1931. Piaget was also invited to Yale University in 1929 as a delegate to the first International Congress of Psychology. He was again invited to Yale in 1953 to speak on perception and to the Macy Foundation, in New York, to speak on consciousness. All this is on the one hand.

On the other hand, Kessen (1996) also documented that references to Piaget's research in the American psychological literature were virtually nonexistent before Piaget had reached normal retirement age. Indeed, the first two American Festschrifts for Piaget did not appear until after his 70th birthday (Bruner, 1966) and after his 73rd birthday (Elkind & Flavell, 1969). Kessen's documentation was drawn from a search of a standard reference source for the American psychological literature, the American Psychological Association's *Psychological Abstracts* for the years 1920 to 1980. In the years 1953 and 1954, for instance, Kessen located only two mentions of Piaget, a reference to an autobiographical chapter that he had written (Boring, Werner, Langfeld, & Yerkes, 1952) and a note on Piaget's invited address at the Macy Foundation (Abramson, 1954). The overall results of Kessen's search appear in Fig. 11.1, which plots total references to Piaget's work in the American psychological literature in 5-year blocks. The pattern is striking:

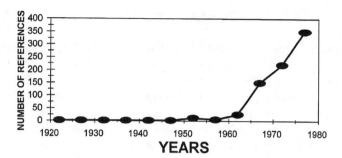

FIG. 11.1. References to Piaget's work in the American psychological literature (based on Kessen, 1996).

After 4 decades of utter obscurity, the curve turns upward after 1957 and reaches dizzying heights a decade and a half later.

What happened to transform American psychology and, later, American educational psychology into such fertile soil for Piaget's ideas? Two major events come to mind. First, the late 1950s and the 1960s were the years of the space race between the United States and the then-Soviet Union. Following the Soviet Union's launch of Sputnik in 1958, there was much public dissatisfaction with what was thought to be the substandard performance of American youth in mathematics and science. This provoked great interest in childhood cognitive development generally and, more particularly, in cognitive abilities that underlie the acquisition of mathematical and scientific knowledge. Because the learning-theory tradition of that era was focused on far simpler abilities, such as discrimination learning and transfer, it was not well equipped to respond to this challenge. However, the situation was tailor-made for a psychologist who had spent decades producing voluminous research findings on topics such as children's concepts of acceleration, cause–effect, equilibrium, geometry, mass, number, probability, proportionality, time, and weight. However, Piaget's writings, even when translated into English, were complex and, from the perspective of late-1950s psychology, theoretically impenetrable. The other major event removed this obstacle and ensured Piaget's apotheosis. A series of articles and volumes by American scholars appeared during the early 1960s that were devoted to explaining Piaget's work to their contemporaries (e.g., Kessen & Kuhlman, 1962; Ripple & Rockcastle, 1964). Far and away the most important of these explanatory efforts was *The Developmental Psychology of Jean Piaget* (Flavell, 1963).

Having rescued Piaget from his long years in the wilderness, it is time to go back and begin at the beginning. Piaget was born in August of 1896 and died in October of 1980. He began life in the Swiss university town of Neuchatel, which was famed in the 18th century as the redoubt of Jean Jacques Rousseau, and died in Geneva, having spent most of his career at the University of Geneva. Piaget had excellent intellectual bloodlines: His father taught medieval classics at the University of

Neuchatel and was something of an amateur historian. Piaget deeply respected his father and adopted his scientific perspective from an early age, focusing on intellectual pursuits even as a young boy. In contrast, he was little influenced by his mother, who suffered from maladies that, in later life, he variously described as "neurotic temperament" and "poor mental health" (Evans, 1973, p. 106) and that required periods of hospitalization. He also described his mother as a religious zealot who demanded close adherence to orthodox practices, especially in her son.

Piaget's first intellectual love was nature study, which he began at age 7. He developed a keen interest in birds and seashells, and the latter interest would lead ultimately to the topic of his Ph.D. dissertation. Piaget had submitted his first scientific paper for publication by age 10, and the article was published in a local Neuchatel natural history journal. At the time, no one was aware that the author was a 10-year-old. As Piaget continued to submit scientific papers, his age eventually became known, and some journal editors refused to publish the writings of a boy.

Between the ages of 10 and 14, Piaget concentrated on the study of natural history with the aid of the Director of Neuchatel's Museum of Natural History, Paul Godet. To train Piaget in natural history, Godet gave him the task of cataloguing a large personal collection of mollusk shells that he had acquired on field trips. This, in turn, gave Piaget access to the rest of the museum's collections, particularly its collections of fossils. Piaget continued this work, acquiring a shell collection on his own in the process, until he was 14, at which time Godet died.

During this period, Piaget wrote scientific papers on mollusks and submitted them to natural history journals. On the basis of these papers, his work had become well known to European malacologists by the time he was 14. Everyone assumed, of course, that he was an adult with postgraduate training in malacology. This misconception continued for some time because, at the turn of the century, telephones and travel to scientific conferences were uncommon. A humorous by-product of misconceptions of Piaget's age occurred when the director of Switzerland's leading natural history museum, in Geneva, wrote to him, offering to appoint him, purely on the basis of his published work, to the curatorship of the museum's mollusk collection. As high school and college still lay before him, Piaget gracefully declined.

During his early teenage years, Piaget developed an interest in philosophical questions, while continuing his work in natural history. Supervision of his philosophical studies was undertaken by his uncle. In 1915, Piaget suffered a nervous breakdown, which he attributed to intense philosophical reading and discussion. A year of recuperation was required, which slowed his academic progress somewhat. Nevertheless, he managed to finish his bachelor's degree by age 18 and complete his Ph.D. studies by age 21. Piaget's principal area of graduate study was biology, and his Ph.D. dissertation was in malacology. However, during the course of graduate study, Piaget concluded that the research career that most interested him was psychology rather than biology. Unfortunately, graduate studies in biology had not equipped him for such work.

To correct this deficiency, Piaget pursued the obvious remedy: postdoctoral studies in psychology. During 1918 and 1919, he undertook such studies at the University of Zurich, which was followed by further postdoctoral study at the Sorbonne (1919–1921). It was during this latter period that the first landmark event in Piaget's research career occurred. While learning psychiatric interviewing techniques at the Sorbonne, Piaget obtained what would now be called a graduate assistantship working in the laboratory of the developers of the modern intelligence test, Alfred Binet and Theodore Simon. Following the initial appearance of this test, a British psychologist had developed a parallel test that focused on syllogistic reasoning (e.g., All men are mortal. Socrates is a man. Is Socrates mortal?) Piaget was assigned the job of standardizing the British test, which had been translated into French, on Paris elementary school children. He did far more than the job description called for. When he administered the test to children, he also tried out his psychiatric interviewing techniques. As children responded to reasoning problems, Piaget recorded the numbers of correct and incorrect answers, which were the data that were required to standardize the test. But he followed up children's answers with probing questions that prompted them to explain the basis for their answers. The result was something of an epiphany. Piaget discovered that the explanations of children who gave *incorrect* answers were astonishing because the explanations showed that those children thought that the world works in unreal and magical ways. This methodology of posing reasoning problems to children and using psychiatric interviewing techniques to encourage children to explain their answers was implemented in Piaget's studies throughout the remainder of his life, and it ultimately came to be called the clinical method.

In 1921, after completing his studies at the Sorbonne, Piaget took up his first academic position, as Director of Research at the Rousseau Institute in Geneva, the position having been offered to him on the basis of three articles that he had published in 1921. There, he began the series of studies of the development of intelligence that were to occupy him for most of the rest of his life. The initial studies deal with language development and with children's philosophies of causation and morality. Of these, Piaget's work on language development, which was published in French in 1925 in a book entitled *The Language and Thought of the Child*, won him an international reputation. In that same year, Piaget returned to his home university in Neuchatel, where he assumed a chair in philosophy, but he maintained his research program at the Rosseau Institute. Between 1925 and 1931, his three children were born, and so Piaget and his wife studied the earliest beginnings of intelligence during this period. As a result of this work, Piaget realized that his clinical method was not completely adequate for investigating cognitive development because it could only be used with children who possess sophisticated language skills.

In 1929, Piaget returned to full-time employment in Geneva, where he became professor of The History of Science at the University of Geneva. During the decade that followed, he initiated his best known research, lines of investigation that focused on children's understanding of basic logical, mathematical, and scientific concepts, and he also began his collaboration with the most influential of his numerous coworkers, Barbel Inhelder. It was these lines of investigation that led to his well-known stage hypothesis (see the following subsection Theory: The Stage-Learning Hypothesis). This hypothesis eventually blossomed into Piaget's grand stage model, first published in 1947 in a book entitled *The Psychology of Intelligence*, in which the development of intelligence was said to progress through four qualitatively distinct periods: the *sensorimotor period* (birth to age 2), the *preoperational period* (2- to 7-years-old), the *concrete-operational period* (7- to 11-years-old), and the *formal-operational period* (age 11 and beyond). During the sensorimotor period, the central objective of cognitive development is to acquire the capacity for internalized thinking. Because this capacity is lacking at birth, intelligence is necessarily external and behavioral during this period. A prime example of such intelligence is the ability to search (visually or manually) for hidden objects. During the preoperational period, the central objective of cognitive development is to make intelligence less egocentric and more socialized. Prime examples are the acquisition of truly communicative (as opposed to self-stimulating) language, the acquisition of gender concepts, and the acquisition of rudimentary concepts of causality. During the concrete-operational period, the central objective of cognitive development is to bring intelligence into conformity with the fundamental laws of logic and mathematics, a form of intelligence that Piaget referred to generically as *operational*. It is during this period that children acquire the reasoning skills that constitute the most familiar examples of Piaget's work, such as the famed conservation concepts (see various sections that follow), transitive inference (John is taller than Jim. Jim is taller than Don. Who is taller, John or Don?), and class inclusion (Farmer Brown owns 7 cows and 3 horses. Does he own more cows or more animals?). Finally, during the formal-operational period, the central objective of cognitive development is to extend the forms of logical and mathematical reasoning that are acquired during the concrete-operational period to an abstract, symbolic level, with the aid of language. The hallmarks of this abstraction process are that reasoning becomes reflective and analytical.

Piaget first presented this stage theory of cognitive development in a series of lectures that he delivered to French scholars at the College de France in the midst of the Nazi occupation during Word War II. After the war, Piaget was intensely involved with the United Nations Educational, Cultural, and Scientific Organization. He served a 5-year term as president of the Swiss Commission of UNESCO, and several additional years as a member of that commission.

By the mid-1950s, Piaget's stage theory of cognitive development had been presented in many forms to many audiences, both scientific and lay, and his theory had become widely respected. From that time, until his death in 1980, Piaget turned his attention to the task of applying his theory to some classic topics in psychological research. His theory was what modern psychologists would call a grand theory in the tradition of the early schools of psychology, such as structuralism,

Gestalt psychology, behaviorism, and psychoanalysis. Although Piaget had spent most of his career investigating higher forms of intelligence, he was convinced that a theory as broad in scope as his stage model must have important implications for more basic psychological processes. To investigate this hypothesis, he initiated large-scale programs of research on such classic psychological topics as memory, perception, consciousness, and imagery. That research produced many interesting new phenomena, all of them inspired by the general idea that the operation of psychological processes other than intelligence are also governed by Piaget's stages of cognitive development. This work was so extensive that books and articles reporting new findings continued to appear under Piaget's authorship for several years following his death.

As this sketch of Piaget's scholarly life attests, his body of work was so vast that it is impossible to touch on most of it in a brief historical chapter such as the present one. The writer of such an historical chapter is therefore compelled to confine attention to one or two aspects of Piaget's work that are of overriding importance for the target audience. Because the audience for the present volume is educational, the choice is clear: It is Piaget's views on children's learning, and research related to those views, that are of primary interest. Therefore, the remainder of this chapter, which consists of two sections, is an historical review of Piaget's proposals about children's learning and of the body of learning experiments that put those proposals to the test. Although the selection of this material was dictated by the present volume's intended audience, it is important to note that, historically, learning research on Piaget's theory was the primary cause of the theory's decline from preeminence and for the rise of theoretical traditions that replaced it.

PIAGET ON CHILDREN'S LEARNING
I—THE LEARNING-DEVELOPMENT
RELATION

The most enduring impact of Piaget's theory of cognitive development on educational psychology was its perspective on children's learning, which was a classic readiness perspective coupled with Rosseauian assumptions about the nature of learning. Piaget's proposals about learning were quite different than those that had predominated in American learning theories up to the 1960s, though they were incorporated into subsequent learning theories. The core proposals can be conveniently grouped under two topic headings: (a) the learning-development relation and (b) instructional methodology.

This section begins with a precis of Piaget's ideas about the relation between children's levels of cognitive development and their ability to learn stage-related concepts, particularly the conservation concepts of his concrete-operational period, through deliberate training. This section concludes with a review of some illustrative American and Genevan learning experiments that tested two key predictions that followed from Piaget's proposals about the learning-development relation—namely, that children's ability to learn conservation concepts via deliberate training depends on their pretraining levels of cognitive development and that it is impossible for truly preoperational children to learn conservation concepts in this manner.

Theory: The Stage-Learning Hypothesis

The hallmark of Piaget's theory of cognitive development, of course, is that it is a stage model. That is, the ontogenesis of intelligence is treated on analogy to morphogenesis—different age levels are characterized by qualitatively distinct subspecies of intelligence. Piaget interpreted children's learning within the same morphogenetic framework, with learning being interpreted as a special case of stage-like cognitive development: "Learning is no more than a sector of cognitive development that is facilitated by experience" (Piaget, 1970b, p. 714). In early American discussions of Piagetian theory (e.g., Flavell, 1963; Wohlwill, 1959), this stance was thought to imply that stage-related concepts such as conservation, class inclusion, or transitive inference were thoroughly unteachable and that instead, they had to emerge spontaneously during the course of normal development. Piaget's coworkers soon pointed out that this interpretation was too extreme (e.g., Inhelder, Sinclair, & Bovet, 1974; Sinclair, 1973). They noted that rather than ruling out learning in an absolute sense, the thrust of the stage viewpoint was to place *developmental constraints* on learning.

These developmental constraints limit what and how much children can learn about a concept via explicit instruction (Brainerd, 1977a, 1978a). The precise nature of the constraints depends on children's current stage of cognitive development. During the elementary-school age range, some children (kindergartners and first graders) will be at the preoperational level, most children (second through fifth graders) will be at the concrete-operational level, and some children (sixth graders) will have reached the formal-operational level. Because concrete-operational children predominate during elementary school, Piagetian discussions of learning (e.g., Inhelder et al., 1974; Piaget, 1970b) revolved almost exclusively around children's ability to learn concrete-operational concepts, especially conservation concepts. In the end, virtually all research on Piaget's theory of learning dealt with the learning of conservation concepts (e.g., Brainerd, 1974; Brainerd, 1979b).

Piaget's developmental constraints perspective can be summarized in five principles. First and foremost, children's learning is limited by "the general constraints of the current developmental stage" (Piaget, 1970b, p. 713)—to know what is possible learning-wise, the current stage (preoperations? concrete operations? formal operations?) must be known. Second, the existence of stage constraints means that what children are able to learn about stage-related concepts will "vary very significantly as a function of the initial [pretraining] cognitive levels of the children" (Piaget, 1970b, p. 715). Cognitive levels (stages) are characterized by unique sets of cognitive structures, from which concepts such as conservation or class inclusion fall out as emergent properties. Therefore, third, the essence of learning is that it involves teaching children to apply cognitive structures *that have already developed* to new content. Fourth, because children obviously cannot learn to apply cognitive structures that they do not yet possess, they cannot be taught stage-related concepts from scratch, as it were—the basic cognitive architecture must first evolve on its own. Here, a morphogenetic analogy is helpful: No matter how much practice it receives, a butterfly cannot learn to fly while it is still a caterpillar because the necessary wing structures have not yet developed. Fifth, it follows that learning experiences that are designed to teach concepts that are clearly beyond the current stage of cognitive development (e.g., teaching conservation concepts to preoperational children) are a waste of both the teacher's time and the child's: "As for teaching children concepts that they have not already acquired in their spontaneous development, it is completely useless" (Piaget, 1970a, p. 30), and "operativity is malleable only within certain limits . . . children at the preoperational level do not acquire truly operational structures" (Inhelder & Sinclair, 1969, p. 19).

These principles could be used to generate many predictions about children's learning of stage-related concepts. There are two predictions, however, that everyone agreed would have to be confirmed if the principles were to be taken seriously. First, learning experiments with stage-related concepts should produce marked Aptitude × Treatment interactions. In learning research, Aptitude × Treatment interactions are variations in children's tendency to benefit from instruction ("treatment") as a function of variations in the abilities ("aptitude") that they bring into the instructional situation (e.g., Cronbach & Snow, 1977). In this instance, the aptitude component is children's level of cognitive structure, which defines their stage of cognitive development, and the treatment component is the learning procedure that is used to teach children, say, conservation concepts. Thus, the prediction is that the amount of learning that is measured in individual children will interact with measures of their stage of cognitive development (Inhelder et al., 1974). A second, even simpler, prediction is that it will be impossible to teach concrete-operational concepts to children who are functioning at the preoperational level (Inhelder & Sinclair, 1969).

During the 1960s and 1970s, extensive research was conducted on the learning of Piagetian concepts (for reviews, see Brainerd, 1973, 1977a; Brainerd & Allen, 1971), much of it concerned with the preceding two predictions. Most of these learning experiments were conducted by American educational psychologists, though some were conducted by Piaget's coworkers, and virtually all of them dealt with the learning of conservation concepts. On the whole, these experiments failed to verify either prediction, a fact that came to be regarded as challenging the Piagetian approach to learning and rendering it primarily of historical interest. Prominent examples of this research are summarized in the next subsection.

Research: Testing the Stage-Learning Hypothesis

Studies that bore on the Aptitude × Treatment interaction prediction involved somewhat different designs than studies that bore on the preoperational untrainability prediction. Therefore, research on the two predictions is covered in separate subsections.

Aptitude × Treatment Interactions

Measures of children's stage of cognitive development and measures of amounts of learning should produce Aptitude × Treatment interactions, with more learning being obtained for children who have reached more advanced stages of cognition. As I have noted in prior papers (Brainerd, 1977a, 1978b), unfortunately, Piaget did not supply investigators with the measurement tools that were necessary to detect such interactions. In his theory, stage and structure were explanatory concepts that were used to account for normal age variability in his familiar reasoning concepts. Neither Piaget nor his collaborators ever devised a standardized instrument that learning researchers could use to diagnose children's stages of cognitive development, and indeed, such instruments were anathema to Genevan investigators (Flavell, 1963). Thus, to evaluate the Aptitude × Treatment interaction prediction, learning researchers had to find some way to measure children's preinstructional stage of cognitive development.

In the end, this obstacle did not prove insuperable because such measures could be constructed from Piaget's own research reports. In his research, Piaget had described the development of individual concrete-operational concepts as three-stage sequences that corresponded to the preoperational level, the concrete-operational level, and a transition phase between them. Importantly, Piaget had provided descriptions of the types of behaviors that were characteristic of each stage. To illustrate, consider three familiar conservation concepts, which are shown in Fig. 11.2. The specific concepts are number conservation, quantity conservation, and length conservation. In each case, a three-step procedure is used to assess the concept. First, children are shown two objects (two rows of chips, two glasses of juice, two strands of string) that are obviously equal with respect to some target quantitative property (number of chips, amount of juice, length of string) because they are visually identical. Second, once children have agreed that the two objects are equal with respect to the quantitative property, one of the objects is deformed so that the perceptual identity is destroyed (one row of chips is lengthened, one quantity of juice is poured into a narrower glass, Muller-Lyer arrowheads are affixed to one of the strings). Third, children are asked whether the now different-looking objects are still equal with respect to the quantitative property. The correct answer is yes (conservation response), but younger children usually say no (nonconservation response).

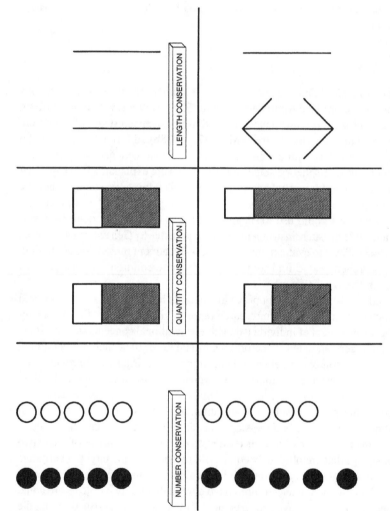

FIG. 11.2. Examples of three types of conservation problems: number conservation (left panels), liquid quantity conservation (center panels), and length conservation (right panels).

In his studies of individual conservation concepts, Piaget (e.g., 1952) described the three stages of development as follows. During Stage 1 (preoperational period), children consistently assert that the quantitative equivalence of the two objects is destroyed by the perceptual deformation, and quantitative relations are said to depend directly on perceptual similarity. For instance, the first row in the lower-left panel of Fig. 11.2 is said to contain more chips because it is longer, the narrower glass in the lower-middle panel is said to contain more juice because the juice is taller, and the line without the arrowheads in the lower-right panel is said to be longer because it looks longer. During Stage 2 (transition), children respond inconsistently. For each type of conservation in Fig. 11.2, Stage 2 children provide nonconserving answers on some problems but conserving answers on others. For instance, they provide conserving answers for number problems that involve small quantities of chips, but nonconserving answers for problems that involve large quantities of chips (Gelman, 1972). Or, they provide conserving answers for liquid problems that involve small quantities of juice, but nonconserving answers for problems involving large quantities (Brainerd & Brainerd, 1972). Finally, during Stage 3 (concrete operations) children consistently assert that the quantitative equivalence of the two objects is preserved by the perceptual deformation, and quantitative relations are said to be affected only if transformations involve adding or subtracting material.

These behavioral indexes were used by researchers to classify children according to their current stages of cognitive development prior to conducting a conservation learning experiment. Beginning with an article by Beilin (1965), several experiments were ultimately published by American researchers that made use of a design with four basic steps: (a) conservation pretests; (b) stage classification; (c) conservation training; and (d) conservation posttests. First, pretests for one or more varieties of conservation were administered to children whose age fell within the range in which children begin to acquire these concepts (kindergarten and first grade for most concepts). Pretesting was greatly facilitated by Goldschmid and Bentler's (1968) publication of a standardized instrument that assessed most types of conservation. Second, on the basis of their pretest responses, children were classified as Stage 1 (preoperational), Stage 2 (transitional), or Stage 3 (concrete operational). Only children who were classified as Stage 1 or Stage 2 continued to the training phase (because Stage 3 children were already performing perfectly). Third, children classified as Stage 1 or Stage 2 were assigned to either a control condition or a treatment condition (sometimes, to more than one treatment condition). Children in the treatment condition received training that was designed to improve their understanding of specific conservation concepts (e.g., number conservation), while children in the control condition participated in activities that did not involve deliberate training (e.g., merely responding to further conservation problems). Fourth, following the training phase, conservation posttests were administered to children in both conditions, with significant between-condition differences in performance providing evidence of learning. In most studies, two types of posttests were administered—posttests for the concepts that had been explicitly taught during training (e.g., number conservation) and posttests for related concepts that had not been explicitly taught (e.g., liquid quantity conservation, length conservation). To show that children in the treatment condition had learned general principles, rather than merely memorizing answers to specific problems, it was necessary to find between-condition differences in performance on both types of posttests. In a few studies, conservation posttests were also administered several days or weeks after training, on the ground that it is important to demonstrate that learning is durable.

The key prediction was that Stage 2 children should learn more than Stage 1 children. In other words, Stage 2 children, who already show some knowledge of conservation on the prestests, ought to derive more benefit from training than Stage 1 children, who show no knowledge of conservation on the pretests. Although this prediction followed from Piagetian theory, it also seemed intuitively obvious to most American researchers that concept learning would be easier if children possessed at least some knowledge of the concept (Brainerd, 1978b). As of 1977, 24 different data sets had been published in which the higher-stage-means-better-learning prediction had been tested. In a review (Brainerd, 1977a) of those data sets, it was found that the prediction had not been confirmed—that learning-induced improvements in conservation did not appear to depend on pretest levels of cognitive development. The pooled findings for Stage 1 and Stage 2 children in the learning conditions of those 24 data sets are shown in Fig. 11.3.

In the experiments on which Fig. 11.3 is based, the numbers and types of pretests and posttests that varied from experiment to experiment, and hence, the number of correct responses that children could make was different for different experiments. To simplify matters, the mean number of correct responses, pooled across all 24 data sets, is plotted for Stage 1 and Stage 2 children for both pre- and posttest

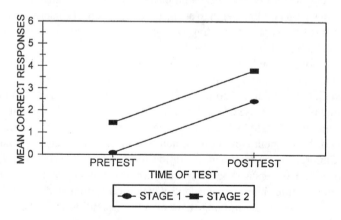

FIG. 11.3. Relation between children's pretest stage classifications and conservation learning (pooled data from experiments reviewed in Brainerd, 1977a).

performance. Naturally, the mean number of pretest correct responses must be higher for Stage 1 children than Stage 2 children because stage classification was based on this difference. The important feature of the graph is that the respective amounts of pre- to posttest improvement (learning) that were produced. The slope of the pretest–posttest line is the amount of improvement—the steeper the slope, the greater the improvement. The prediction is that improvement will be greater (i.e., the pre–post line will be steeper) for Stage 2 children that for Stage 1 children. However, as can be seen in Fig. 11.3, the amounts of pre–post improvement were the same for Stage 1 and Stage 2 children.

Clearly, theoretical proposals as important as Piaget's ideas about the learning-development relation should not be rejected on the basis of a single type of disconfirmatory finding, even if that finding is present in several experiments. There might be other explanations. For instance, the disconfirmatory finding in Fig. 11.3 is a null result, and null results can be due to low-power experimental designs. In particular, the procedure of classifying children according to their pretraining stage might be at fault. The number of children who participated in the various experiments was not large, and the pretesting on which those stage classifications were based was not extensive. Across the 24 data sets, 16 involved fewer than 30 Stage 1 children, 21 involved fewer than 30 Stage 2 children, and fewer than 3 conservation pretests were administered in 18 of the data sets. Because the rate of stage-classification error with conservation pretests is unknown, it is possible that substantial percentages of children classified as Stage 1 were actually Stage 2 and that substantial percentages of children classified as Stage 2 were actually Stage 1. If so, this would tend to mask the predicted stage–learning relation. American researchers dealt with this problem in later learning experiments, first by increasing statistical power (by increasing the number of participants and the number of pre- and posttests) and second by testing an equivalent prediction that avoided error-prone stage classification.

The equivalent prediction that avoided stage classification, which will be illustrated with the aid of Fig. 11.4, is "the more they know, the more they learn." Stage classifications are based on pretest performance, with children who display greater pretest knowledge receiving higher classifications that children who display less. As stage classification is merely a nominal scale transformation of pretest scores (i.e., all children with scores in a certain range are collapsed into a single category), this step can be eliminated because it does not add anything to those scores. Then, we can simply test the equivalent prediction that children with higher pretest scores will learn more than children with lower pretest scores. Because children in control groups do not receive training, the relation between their pre- and posttest scores is a measure of test–retest reliability, the relation being given by the familiar true score equation

$$Y_i \text{ (posttest score of child I)} = X_i \text{ (pretest score of child I)}$$
$$+ \text{ a (measurement error)}.$$

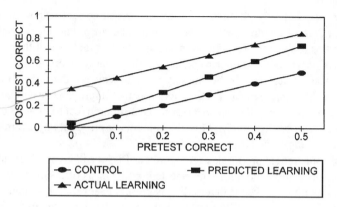

FIG. 11.4. Actual and predicted relations between children's pretest conservation performance and conservation learning (pooled data from five training methods in Brainerd, 1979a).

This relation plots as a straight line with slope = 1 (the lower line in Fig. 11.4). Because children in treatment groups receive training, an increment a ("learning") will be added to each of their pretest scores, the pretest–posttest relation being give by the equation

$$Y_i = X_i + L_i \text{ (amount of learning of subject I)} + a.$$

Under Piaget's conception of the learning–development relation, the size of L_i will depend on the child's pretest score with larger increments being added to children with larger pretest scores ("the more they know, the more they learn"). This situation is depicted in the middle line of Fig. 11.4, in which the increment that is added to any given pretest score is always slightly greater than the increment that is added to the previous score, which produces a pretest–posttest line whose slope is greater than one.

Later studies in which this more powerful approach was used concurred with the finding of earlier stage studies that children's learning was not constrained by their levels of cognitive development. For instance, I reported some experiments of this sort in which large numbers of children were trained on conservation concepts, and very extensive pre- and posttest batteries were administered (Brainerd, 1979a; Burns & Brainerd, 1979). For the sake of generality, five different training methods were used in the treatment conditions of these experiments (constructive play, corrective feedback, discrimination learning, dramatic play, and observational learning). None of the treatment conditions revealed a pretest–posttest relation with a slope greater than one. Instead, across the different training methods, the pretest–posttest relation plotted as a linear function with a slope of approximately one, like the line at the top of Fig. 11.4. That is, for children in the various treatment conditions, pretest–posttest increases did not vary as a function of children's pretest scores.

Preoperational Untrainability

The other, simpler developmental constraint prediction is that training will not produce learning of concrete-operational concepts in children who are still at the preoperational level. The key to testing this prediction, obviously, is to have strong evidence that children are preoperational. Researchers adopted two approaches to this diagnostic problem. One was to administer extensive pretests for several conservation concepts to kindergartners and first graders. Following such pretests, the only children who were permitted to continue to the learning phase were those who did not show the slightest knowledge of conservation. Because number is the first conservation concept to appear in most children (Figure 2, left panel), it was deemed crucial that the pretest battery include measures of this concept and that children show no evidence of it. The second approach was to conduct learning experiments with preschool children. As the average age range for the preoperational period is 2 to 7, preschoolers are still in the lower half of that range. Therefore, if subject samples are confined to preschoolers, it is only rare and precocious children who would not be truly preoperational.

The first approach (zero correct on pretest batteries that include number conservation) was eventually implemented in several experiments. Perhaps the best known was a dissertation study by Gelman (1969). Gelman pretested 5-year-olds on number conservation and three other conservation concepts (length, liquid quantity, and mass). Children who failed the pretests across the board were retained for training. During the learning phase, these children were trained on two of four pretested concepts (number and length). A posttest session, which consisted of readministrations of the pretests, occurred 2 to 3 weeks after each child's training session. Although all children had performed at floor prior to training, virtually all of them now performed perfectly on tests for the two concepts that were explicitly trained. In addition, good transfer to untrained concepts was observed: Approximately 60% of the responses to mass and liquid quantity tests were now correct as well. Finally, children were able to provide logically sound explanations of correct answers to posttest problems. In short, although Gelman's children exhibited consistent nonconservation on the pretest battery, the training procedure produced large learning effects that transferred to untrained concepts and that were durable up to 3 weeks after training.

Another example of experiments that used the first approach to identifying preoperational children was reported in an article by Rosenthal and Zimmerman (1972). These authors administered pretests for the six conservation concepts on Form A of Goldschmid and Bentler's (1968) instrument, which includes conservation of number, to 5- and 6-year-olds. Children who failed all of the pretests continued to the training phase. Posttests were administered immediately after training. Whereas the children had failed pretests for all six concepts, they now passed posttests for four of the six concepts, on average. Importantly, more than half their answers were correct on posttests for concepts that had not been specifically trained. Although other experiments that implemented the first approach could be mentioned, the basic outcome was the same throughout: Contrary to prediction, children who scored zero on extensive conservation pretests showed large improvements as a consequence of training, improvements that transferred to untrained concepts and that were stable over time.

The second approach (train preschool children) was also adopted in several experiments. Six examples—again, using a variety of training methods—are Brainerd (1974), Bucher and Schnieder (1973), Denney, Zeytinoglu, and Selzer (1977), Emrick (1968), Rosenthal and Zimmerman (1972; Experiment 4), and Zimmerman and Lanaro (1974). These experiments, too, failed to demonstrate that conservation learning is constrained by children's level of cognitive development. In the last-mentioned article, for example, 4-year-olds were administered pretests for length conservation and were then assigned to two learning conditions and a control condition. Immediately after the training phase, posttests for length conservation and area conservation (which was not trained) were administered to children in all three conditions. To measure durability of learning, these posttests were readministered 9 days later. Children in the two learning conditions showed large pre- to posttest improvements: 50% of their responses to length conservation problems were correct on the first posttest, and 63% of their responses were correct on the second posttest. In addition to being durable, learning transferred to untrained concepts: Approximately 36% of their responses to area conservation posttests were correct.

As another example, Denney et al. (1977) reported two conservation learning experiments with 4-year-olds. In the first experiment, pretests for number, length, and mass conservation were administered, and children were then assigned to three learning conditions and a control condition. In the three learning conditions, children received training on number and length conservation, but not on mass conservation. Posttests for all three concepts were administered 1 week later. The children in all three learning conditions performed at near-perfect levels on the number and length tests, but they did not perform better than controls on the mass tests. Thus, preschoolers showed durable learning, but their learning did not transfer to untrained concepts. This limitation was then addressed in Experiment 2. In this study, pretests for number, length, substance, and weight conservation were administered, and children were then assigned to one learning condition and a control condition. Children in the learning condition were trained on length and substance, but not on the other two concepts, and posttests for all four concepts were administered 1 week later. This time, learning was both durable and transferrable: One week after training, the correct-response percentages for children in the learning condition were 72% (length), 59% (substance), 61% (number), and 51% (weight).

Summary

As of the early 1980s, dozens of learning experiments had been conducted with Piaget's concrete-operational concepts, nearly all of them focusing on conservation concepts, and reviews of that literature had been published. The news was not good for Piaget's claims about the learning-development relation. Piaget had proposed strong developmental constraints on learning, such that children's ability to learn his stage-related concepts via explicit training would be limited by their level of cognitive development. Multiple experimental approaches to testing that prediction had been taken. Amounts of learning for children classified as Stage 1 or Stage 2 had been measured, the relation between quantitative scales of pre- and posttest performance had been studied, children who exhibited zero-correct performance on pretests had been trained, and children who were still in the first half of the age range for the preoperational period had been trained. Findings from all of these approaches converged on the same conclusion: Children's ability to learn conservation concepts as a result of training is not strongly constrained by their level of cognitive development.

PIAGET ON CHILDREN'S LEARNING II—INSTRUCTIONAL METHODOLOGY

Piaget and his collaborators also had many important things to say about the best methods of teaching concepts to children, given that they are prepared to learn them. Like the aforementioned ideas about developmental constraints, Piagetian proposals about instructional methodology were topics of much experimentation, for the better part of 3 decades. This work is discussed in the two subsections that follow. Theoretical proposals about instructional methodology are summarized first, and this is followed by descriptions of research that evaluated predictions that follow from those proposals.

Theory: Naturalism and Constructivism

Genevan writings on children's learning (e.g., Inhelder & Sinclair, 1969; Inhelder et al., 1974; Sinclair, 1973) stressed that all methods of teaching stage-related concepts to children were not equal. Claims about which methods were effective and which were not revolved around two theoretical principles, *naturalism* and *constructivism*.

Naturalism

This is what might be termed the "mother nature is always right" rule. Because the basic conceptual skills associated with Piaget's stages are known to appear spontaneously during the course of normal cognitive development, it is self-evidently true that everyday experience suffices to make them appear in children's thinking. It is these same everyday experiential processes that Piaget thought were the keys to effective instruction. Specifically, Piaget and his collaborators claimed that effective learning techniques were ones that closely emulated those everyday processes. To illustrate, Inhelder and Sinclair (1969) described the design of a series of Genevan learning experiments that were initiated in the late-1960s as follows: "The choice of exercise items [learning methods] has been dictated by what we know of spontaneous (that is, outside the laboratory) acquisition of the operations or concepts in question" (p. 5). Later, in the seminal Genevan volume on learning, the authors stated that "We started with the idea that under certain conditions an acceleration of cognitive development would be possible, but this could only occur if training resembled the kind of situation in which progress takes place outside the experimental set-up" (Inhelder et al., 1974, p. 5). Shortly before, one of the authors of this volume had remarked that "in learning—that is, in situations specifically constructed so that the subject has active encounters with the environment—the same mechanisms as in development are at work to make progress" (Sinclair, 1973, p. 58).

In reading these statements, it is especially important to separate empirical fact from theoretical speculation. On the one hand, it is a fact that children acquire concepts such as conservation, class inclusion, perspective taking, and the like in the course of their normal experience, without the need of explicit training by adults. On the other hand, it is an assumption that to be effective, explicit training procedures must embody those everyday experiential processes. To American educational audiences of the 1960s and 1970s, Piaget's notion that natural learning is the best learning seemed so intuitively reasonable that the idea was often uncritically accepted and implemented in curricula without bothering to determine its validity (see Lawton & Hooper, 1978). Because natural-learning-is-the-best-learning is so intuitively appealing, it is important to remind ourselves that intuitions can seriously mislead us when they are not confirmed by data. At bottom, this notion is merely a standard Rousseauean doctrine about education. Contrary to such a doctrine, there is no principle that has emerged from decades of learning research that establishes that the best learning methods are those that closely emulate everyday experience (Brainerd, 1978a). Moreover, no principle has emerged from such research that establishes that learning methods that depart radically from everyday experience are apt to be ineffective or, worse, harmful to children, as Piaget (e.g., 1970) sometimes suggested. Finally, no principle has emerged from such research that establishes that we cannot dramatically improve on the learning outcomes of everyday experience through imaginative laboratory techniques. Indeed, one might say that the history of American educational research on learning is a history of discovering how to improve on the biases, inaccuracies, and inefficiencies of everyday experience.

Constructivism

Late in life, Piaget was frequently asked to list his most significant intellectual contributions. The one that he mentioned most often was constructivism. Because social constructivism has been in vogue in American educational circles for the past few years, it is essential to distinguish Piaget's notion from the more contemporary concept. Piaget constructivism was the theoretical assumption that during cognitive development, children acquire their knowledge through a process of creative invention. Under this assumption, knowledge acquisition is not a process of "discovering" innate ideas (as rationalist epistemology would have it), nor is it a process of storing facts that are encoded from the environment (as empiricist philosophy would have it). Instead, Piaget thought that children literally create their knowledge as their biological predispositions interact with their experience. Construction, or creative invention, then, is the mechanism of interaction between heredity and experience that produces knowledge (Inhelder & Sinclair, 1969).

How does this mechanism operate in everyday life? Here, Piaget often related an anecdote that was told to him by a mathematician. As a young child, the mathematician, like other children of has age, believed that number was influenced by spatial arrangement. That is, he thought that the number of elements in a set of objects would be greater if they were spread out (e.g., the column of black chips in the lower left panel of Fig. 11.2) than if they were compressed (e.g., the column of white chips in the lower left panel of Fig. 11.2). One day, the mathematician was playing with a pile of pebbles, and he chanced to count them. He spread them out, expecting the number to increase, but when he counted them, the number had not changed. He clumped them together, and the number was still the same. The mathematician told Piaget that this discovery so astonished and fascinated him that it was the original impetus for his interest in mathematics.

This anecdote contains all the ingredients of a Piagetian constructive learning episode. At the beginning of the episode, the child possess come incorrect concept (e.g., number depends on spatial arrangement) that forecasts certain outcomes (e.g., more pebbles when they are spread out). Second, the child discovers on his own that actual outcomes are different than predicted outcomes (e.g., the number of pebbles does not change when they are rearranged). Third, this discovery induces surprise and causes the child to recognize the discrepancy between the incorrect concept (nonconservation) and actual outcomes. Fourth, recognition of the discrepancy causes the child to invent a new concept (conservation) that is able to encompass actual outcomes.

For Piaget, the key ingredient of construction episodes was the active self-discovery of discrepancies between current concepts and actual outcomes. He argued that it is absolutely essential for children to stumble across such discrepancies *on their own* if cognitive development is to occur. It is not productive, he thought, for teachers and other adults to spell out discrepancies for children or to correct children's erroneous ideas deliberately. This, he thought, circumvents the linchpin of cognitive development, the self-discovery process. These ideas were converted into recommendations about learning procedures as follows.

Genevan researchers drew a fundamental distinction between learning procedures that were constructive and learning procedures that they called *empiricist* or *tutorial*. The latter, which were said to be outgrowths of American learning theories, were described as procedures derived from "strictly empiricist epistemological tenets . . . whereby the subject has to accept a link between events (i.e., between expected outcomes and actual ones) because the link is imposed on him" (Sinclair, 1973, p. 57). These procedures were further said to "go counter to the developmental theory that is resolutely interactionist and constructionist" (p. 57). As a group, tutorial procedures were indicted as ineffective learning methods that "do not result in progress" (p. 57).

Two specific procedures that had been used in several prior experiments were singled out by Genevan investigators as concrete examples of ineffective tutorial methods. One was *prediction-outcome feedback*, and the other was *rule instruction*. Prediction-outcome feedback had first been investigated in a line of research by Smedslund that began in Geneva (e.g., Smedslund, 1959, 1961). In this method, nonconserving children are administered standard conservation problems with two added features. One is that children are asked to predict the effects of perceptual transformations on quantitative relations just before the experimenter performs them. The predictions will be wrong, naturally. The other added feature is that following each transformation, children receive feedback indicating that their prediction was wrong and that equivalence has been preserved. The other tutorial method, rule demonstration, which was developed by Wallach and Sprott (1964), was even simpler. Once again, nonconserving children are administered standard conservation problems. The only added feature occurs after children have responded to posttransformation questions (saying that the initial quantitative equivalence has been destroyed). The experimenter merely demonstrates the underlying logical rules to children (i.e., that spatial arrangement does not affect quantitative relations). Genevan researchers concluded, incorrectly it turns out, regarding prediction-outcome feedback and rule demonstration that "almost universally the results were negative" (Sinclair, 1973, p. 57).

Before turning to research on Piaget's claims about instructional methodology, it is important to mention a criticism of his construction principle that has long troubled American educational psychologists and that Piaget never satisfactorily resolved, as he admitted a few years before his death: "this idea of construction of novelty, this is the idea that is most difficult to make understood" (Evans, 1973, p. 39). The troubling point about constructivism is: How can this principle be reconciled with the fact that the basic elements of intelligence that it produces are apparently culturally universal? To put this question another way, a learning principle that is characterized as a process of creative invention of novelty would seem, on its face, to imply massive variability and individual differences in the cognitive outcomes that it produces (because children's everyday experience is so variable and individualized). However, the data show that at least as far as the preoperational and concrete-operational periods are concerned, the cognitive skills that Piaget regarded as outcomes of the construction process are acquired by all normal children. How can this be if construction is a truly creative, novelty producing mechanism? Piaget's answer was to append the qualification that the child's biological structures and the physical laws of nature limit the possible concepts that construction can produce. To take an example, Edison might have invented various illumination devices and Bell might have invented various devices for telephonic communication, but none of these devices could violate the basic laws of electrical transmission through inanimate matter. By and large, American educational psychologists were not satisfied by this qualification, the reason being that the limitations that are imposed by physical laws and biological structure are vague and general. They are so vague and general that it is difficult to fathom how they could constrain the construction process to the point that cognitive development produces culturally universal intellectual skills.

Research: Testing Naturalism and Constructivism

Because construction is the natural learning process, testing Piaget's views about the methodology of instruction came down to testing predictions that followed from the notion that effective learning procedures must involve construction. As with research that was designed to evaluate Piaget's views about developmental constraints, there are many predictions that might bear on his views about constructive learning. There are two obvious ones, however, that were centerpieces of research during the late-1960s, 1970s, and early-1980s: (a) tutorial procedures are ineffective in producing learning and (b) constructive learning procedures produce far better learning than tutorial procedures. Examples of research on both predictions is summarized in the following.

Are Tutorial Procedures Ineffective?

The era during which interest in Piaget's theory intensified was also the heyday of American learning theories. There were a number of theories within the American learning tradition that suggested specific instructional approaches to teaching concrete-operational concepts to children. Ultimately, four distinct approaches spawned substantial numbers of experiments: (a) perceptual training; (b) rule demonstration; (c) observation of skilled reasoners; and (d) corrective feedback. Each of these approaches was grounded in a particular learning theory of that era—attentional theory in the case of perceptual training (e.g., Trabasso & Bower, 1968), information-processing theory in the case of rule demonstration (e.g., Siegler, 1981), social learning theory in the case of observation of skilled reasoners (e.g., Zimmerman & Rosenthal, 1974), and discrimination theory in the case of corrective feedback (e.g., Kendler & Kendler, 1960). Importantly, all of these approaches were classified as tutorial by Genevan researchers because they taught concepts directly to children without allowing any room for the self-discovery process that Piaget deemed to be critical for successful learning. In fact, self-discovery was not explicitly mentioned in any of the parent theories. Therefore, these four approaches should not have been effective learning procedures because "empirical methods, whereby the subject has to accept a link between events because the link is imposed on him, do not result in progress." The results of many experiments proved otherwise.

1. Perceptual Training. The overriding error made by children who fail concrete-operational problems such as conservation, class inclusion, transitive inference, perspective taking, etc. is that they base their reasoning on visually salient features of task material, rather than less obvious (but logically correct) features. According to attentional theories of learning (e.g., Trabasso & Bower, 1968), children are merely paying attention to the wrong things; the limitation in reasoning cuts no deeper than that. If so, teaching concrete-operational concepts to children ought to be nothing more than a matter of inducing them to stop paying attention to the wrong information (e.g., in Fig. 11.2, the length and density of the rows in the left panel, the height and width of the liquid in the center panel) and shift attention to the correct information (e.g., in Fig. 11.2, the actual numbers of chips in the left panel, the actual amounts of liquid in the center panel). Training methodologies that were designed to reorient children's attention in this manner had already been developed to teach children other, simpler concepts (e.g., Zeaman & House, 1963). Consequently, researchers adopted those methodologies in perceptual training studies of concrete-operational concepts.

Two doctoral dissertations conducted under the supervision of a leading attentional learning theorist of the day, T. Trabasso, provided the first clear evidence that nonconserving children will learn conservation concepts as a result of perceptual training (Emrick, 1967; Gelman, 1969). The experiments reported in the two dissertations were quite similar, the chief difference being that Emrick's children were preschoolers and Gelman's were kindergartners. In both experiments, children who had been identified as nonconservers (of number, length, liquid quantity, and mass) on pretests participated in learning sessions that were focused on number and length conservation. During these sessions, a triad procedure was used to encourage children to shift their attention to the correct quantitative properties of stimuli. An example is shown in Fig. 11.5, two rows of chips are of the same length (but of different density and number), two rows have the same number (but are of different length and density), and two rows are of the same density (but of different length and number). The perceptual training procedure for number conservation consisted of presenting children with many triads of this sort, asking them to select the two rows that contained the same number, and when they chose incorrectly, pointing out the two correct rows for them. Triads that were similar to those in

FIG. 11.5. Example of the training triads that were used in the perceptual training studies of conservation (Emrick, 1967; Gelman, 1969).

Fig. 11.5, but that involved lines rather than rows of chips, were used in perceptual training of length conservation.

This attentional reorientation methodology proved to be highly effective in teaching conservation concepts to nonconservers. In Emrick's (1967) dissertation, approximately 75% of preschoolers' responses to number and length conservation problems were correct on problems that were administered 2 to 3 weeks after perceptual training, and approximately 40% of preschoolers' responses to liquid quantity and mass problems were also correct. Gelman's (1969) results for kindergartners were even more dramatic. Performance on number and length conservation problems was essentially perfect 2 to 3 weeks after perceptual training, and approximately 60% of kindergartners' responses to liquid and mass problems were also correct.

It should be added that later experiments by other investigators confirmed the power of perceptual training to turn nonconservers into conservers. For instance, replicating Gelman (1969), May and Tisshaw (1975) reported successful conservation learning in kindergartners with the triad procedure. Likewise, replicating Emrick (1967), Field (1981) reported successful conservation learning in preschoolers with the triad method. A final, fundamental question about perceptual training was answered by Boersma and Wilton (1974). As noted earlier, the underlying logic of perceptual training is that conservers and nonconservers are simply paying attention to different types of visual information. In a study in which children's eye movements were measured as they were administered conservation problems, Boersma and Wilton found that this was indeed the case. Specifically, they found that nonconservers' visual fixations centered on the wrong visual cues (e.g., length and density in number conservation), whereas conservers' visual fixations centered on the correct cues.

2. Rule Demonstration. In Piaget's studies of the development of concrete-operational concepts, he had used his famed clinical methods to elicit children's explanations of their reasoning. A key finding was that when children explained their reasoning, they annunciated principles that did not square with the underlying logic of the situation and, instead, focused on salient visual features of problem information. For instance, nonconservers of number would typically explain their wrong inferences with words to the effect that, "This row has more because it's longer" (Piaget, 1952), and nonconservers of liquid quantity would typically explain their responses with words to the effect that, "This glass has more because the juice is taller" (Piaget & Inhelder, 1941). Conservers, on the other hand, would typically explain their correct inferences by referring to more abstract principles that focused on underlying logical relations rather than visual features. Normative studies (e.g., Brainerd, 1977b) eventually showed that five such logical rules were cited in the explanations of conservers: (a) *qualitative identity* (e.g., number conservers: "the two rows are still the same, even though they look different"); (b) *quantitative identity* (e.g., number conservers: "the two rows still have the same number, even though they look different"); (c) *reversibility* (e.g., number conservers: "one row is longer now, but you could make both rows the same length again"); (d) *addition/subtraction* (e.g., number conservers: "no chips were added or taken away"); (e) *compensation* (e.g., number conservers: "this row is longer, but the chips are spread out more").

According to information-processing theory, erroneous reasoning is merely due to lack of understanding of these simple logical rules. If so, formal demonstration of the rules should transform conservers into nonconservers. The rule-demonstration approach was adopted in more published studies that any of the other three procedures. Rule demonstration was introduced in an experiment by Wallach and Sprott (1964, which was soon followed up in an experiment by Beilin (1965). Wallach and Sprott physically demonstrated a single rule, reversibility, to children who had been identified as nonconservers of number on pretests. During the learning phase, children were exposed to additional number conservation problems in which there were obvious functional connections between the two rows of objects. For example, one row was comprised of five dolls and the other row was comprised of five doll beds. The problem began with one doll in each bed, ensuring that the child would acknowledge that the numbers of dolls and beds were same. After the child had acknowledged the numerical equivalence, the dolls were removed from the beds and placed alongside each other in a row that was much longer (or shorter) than the row of beds. Of course, the child asserted that the longer row contained more things than the shorter row. The child was then instructed to return the dolls to the beds, placing one doll in each bed. Once this had been done, it was pointed out that the numbers of dolls and beds were again equal. This method of demonstrating the reversibility rule produced large improvements on conservation posttests.

Beilin's (1965) method of rule demonstration was even simpler. Rather than involving nonconservers in physical manipulations that demonstrated certain rules, he merely provided nonconservers with verbal explanations of the rules. As in Wallach and Sprott's (1964) experiment, children were administered further conservation problems during the learning phase. After the child responded incorrectly to a problem, the experimenter provided a statement of three logical rules that conservers give as explanations of correct responses (qualitative identity, quantitative identity, and reversibility). These rule explanations produced large improvements in conservation responses on posttests. Smith (1968) reported a very similar experiment, the key difference being that children were trained on weight conservation. During the learning phase, nonconservers of weight received the following rule explanation after giving incorrect responses: "If we start with an object like this one and we don't put any pieces of plasticine on it or take any pieces away from it (addition/subtraction rule), then it still weighs the same even though it looks different (quantitative identity rule). See, I can make it back into a . . . so it hasn't really changed (reversibility rule)" (p. 520). This explanation, like Beilin's, produced large improvements in conservation responses on posttests.

By the late-1970s, other rule-demonstration experiments had been published (e.g., Halford & Fullerton, 1970; Hamel & Riksen, 1973). Taken as a whole, these studies established that instructing nonconservers in one or more of the five rules that conservers use to justify correct responses did, indeed, transform nonconservers into conservers. Moreover, the learning effects that had been reported were ones that generalized from trained concepts to untrained concepts and that were stable for periods of weeks or months following learning sessions. Finally, these robust learning effects were obtained regardless of whether nonconservers were exposed to logical rules via physical demonstrations or via verbal explanations.

3. Observation of Skilled Reasoners. This procedure is grounded in social learning theory, which had evolved during the 1940s and 1950s as a means of accounting for the acquisition of human social behaviors, such as altruism, aggression, and gender roles. Without going into details, the basic idea was that inexperienced, developing organisms observe and imitate the social behavior of experienced, mature organisms—that the process is one of immature organisms matching the social behavior of mature organisms (e.g., Miller & Dollard, 1941). During the 1950s and 1960s, the notion of social learning through observation and imitation stimulated many studies of children's observational learning of pro- and antisocial behaviors, especially the work of Albert Bandura and his associates (e.g., Bandura & Walters, 1963). Eventually, two of Bandura's students, T. L. Rosenthal and B. J. Zimmerman, extended the purview of observational learning and imitation from the social sphere to the realms of children's acquisition of language and Piagetian concepts (e.g., Zimmerman & Rosenthal, 1974). It is the later work that is of interest here.

The first systematic research of this sort appeared in a series of four experiments by Rosenthal and Zimmerman (1972). Three of the experiments were concerned with conservation learning by first grade children, and the fourth was concerned with conservation learning by preschool children. The pretest phase was the same in all experiments: Children were administered the six conservation tests on Form A of Goldschmid and Bentler's (1968) standardized instrument, with only children who failed all the tests continuing to the learning phase. During the learning phase, children sat quietly and observed an adult who gave correct responses to the same series of six conservation problems. A 2 × 2 factorial design was used during learning, with the factors being feedback versus no-feedback (the adult's correct responses were verbally praised by the experimenter for half the child observers but no such praise was provided for the other half of the child observers) and rule versus no-rule (the adult explained each response for half the child observers but no explanations were provided for the other half of the child observers). Conservation posttests were administered following observation of the adult reasoner. Across the four conditions of the factorial design, roughly 75% of children's posttest responses to the six trained concepts were correct, and whereas these children had given incorrect, perceptually-oriented explanations of their incorrect responses to pretests, they gave correct, logical explanations of their correct responses to posttests. In their final experiment, with preschoolers, Rosenthal and Zimmerman used just one of the four observational learning procedures (no-feedback + no-rules). Following such training, preschoolers also showed large improvements in their performance on posttests for trained concepts.

Although these original experiments by Rosenthal and Zimmerman (1972) were unusually comprehensive by the standards of the times, two important points remained to be cleared up in later work. First, Rosenthal and Zimmerman's experiments did not establish that observational learning effects were durable over time because delayed posttests had not been included in their designs, and second, transfer of learning to untrained conservation concepts had not been demonstrated. Both points were successfully resolved. Retention of observational learning effects 1 to 3 weeks after training was soon reported (Charbonneau, Robert, Bourassa, & Gladu-Bissonette, 1976; Siegler & Liebert, 1972; Zimmerman & Rosenthal, 1974b), as was transfer to untrained concepts (e.g., Charbonneau et al., 1976; Zimmerman & Rosenthal, 1974b).

4. Corrective Feedback. Of the four approaches to training concrete-operational concepts, this last one involves instructional procedures that are the most passive and the furthest removed from the ideal of active self-discovery. From Piaget's point of view, therefore, such procedures should be the least likely ones to produce learning, a claim that was often advanced by his coworkers (e.g., Sinclair, 1973). The use of corrective feedback was inspired by research on children's discrimination learning, which was popular during the 1950s and 1960s (e.g., Kendler & Kendler, 1960). In a discrimination learning experiment, children are shown simple visual stimuli that have been compounded from familiar dimensions such as shape, color, and size. To illustrate, children might be shown pairs of stimuli

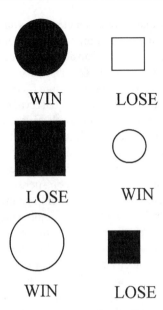

WIN   LOSE

LOSE   WIN

WIN   LOSE

FIG. 11.6. Examples of compound stimuli that were used in studies of children's discrimination learning. These stimuli were compounded from two values of the shape dimension (circle and square), two values of the size dimension (large and small), two values of the color dimension (black and white), and two values of the position dimension (left and right). The to-be-learned concept is "all circles are winners."

like those in Fig. 11.6, which have been compounded from two shapes (circle or square), two colors (black or white), two sizes (large or small), and two positions (left or right). The child's task is to learn a visual discrimination in which *one value of one dimension* is the "winner," and the other value of the same dimension is the "loser." Children learn these discriminations via corrective feedback: On each trial, they are shown a pair of compound stimuli, they are asked to choose the one they think is the winner, and following the choice, they receive feedback as to the correctness of their selection. In Fig. 11.6, for instance, three pairs of compound stimuli are shown, and the winner–loser classification of each stimulus appears just below it. This is the corrective feedback that children would receive if they selected that stimulus. The procedure of presenting pairs of compound stimuli, asking children to make a choice, and then providing corrective feedback about the choice continues until children are able to identify the specific concept (e.g., shape) that determines which stimuli are winners. In Fig. 11.6, it is easy to see that circle must be the winning concept. Even very young children readily learn such concepts via corrective feedback (for a review, see Stevenson, 1972).

In several experiments that were conducted in my laboratory, corrective feedback was also used in attempts to train concrete-operational concepts such as conservation (e.g., Brainerd, 1972), transitive inference (e.g., Brainerd, 1974), and class inclusion (e.g., Brainerd, 1982). The basic methodology can be illustrated with the usual three-step learning procedure for conservation concepts. After pretests had been administered for selected conservation concepts, children who were identified as nonconservers continued to learning sessions that provided corrective feedback. During these learning sessions, further conservation problems were administered, with a single addition to the testing procedure: Children were told "you're wrong" each time they gave an incorrect response, and they were told "you're right" each time they gave a correct response. For instance, returning to the problems in Fig. 11.2, children would be told "you're wrong" if they said that the longer row in the lower-left panel contains more chips, or if they said that the narrower glass in the lower-middle panel contains more juice, or if they said that the line without the arrowheads in the lower-right panel was longer. Because children had been identified as nonconservers on the pretests, the typical pattern in one of these feedback experiments was for children to give overwhelmingly incorrect answers to the first several training problems (and therefore to be told overwhelmingly "you're wrong"), to give mixtures of correct and incorrect answers to the next several training problems (and therefore to sometimes be told "you're wrong" and to sometimes be told "you're right"), and to give consistently correct answers to the final training problems (and therefore to be told consistently "you're right"). Following feedback training, children responded to a series of conservation posttests. As a rule, these immediate posttests included tests for untrained as well as trained concepts, and children's ability to provide sound explanations of their responses was also measured. In some studies, further posttests were administered several days or weeks after feedback training.

Although corrective feedback is extremely passive, from Piaget's standpoint, and provides children with no explicit conceptual information, it proved to be an effective learning procedure. In particular, it was found that children's posttest performance was virtually perfect for trained conservation concepts (e.g., Brainerd, 1972), that there were also large improvements in performance for untrained concepts (e.g., Brainerd, 1977b), and that children were able to provide acceptable explanations of correct posttest responses (e.g., Brainerd, 1972). These learning effects were also found to be stable on delayed posttests (e.g., Brainerd, 1974). Eventually, however, an important limitation of corrective feedback was identified that involved children's ages. As noted, it was found that preschool children could learn Piagetian concepts via perceptual training (Emrick, 1967), or rule demonstration (Field, 1981), or observational learning (Zimmerman & Lanaro, 1974). Corrective feedback experiments with preschoolers yielded much smaller learning effects than the other three methods had produced, presumably because these other methods provide children with conceptual information about the basis for correct responses.

Are Self-discovery Procedures More Effective Than Tutorial Procedures?

The other prediction of interest is that when the same concept is trained via self-discovery learning and some parallel form of tutorial learning, self-discovery should be palpably superior. Unfortunately, very little research was ever reported that was designed to compare specific self-discovery procedures to parallel tutorial procedures. Two factors that contributed to the lack of interest in such work were the high levels of success that had already been achieved by tutorial training and the inherently nonstandardized nature of self-discovery training. Regarding the first factor, recall from the previous section that, contrary to Piagetian predictions, tutorial learning procedures had proved to be very effective. For example, Gelman's (1969) perceptual training experiment had produced ceiling performance on trained concepts, high levels of transfer to untrained concepts, and learning effects that were stable over 2- to 3-week retention intervals. Similar results had been obtained with rule demonstration, observation, and corrective feedback. Such data made the question of the relative effectiveness of self-discovery and tutorial methods largely moot: Tutorial learning effects were so robust that there was little room left for self-discovery to produce learning that was better still. The other factor contributing to lack of interest in studies of self-discovery versus tutorial learning is that learning procedures that incorporate self-discovery are very difficult to standardize. Because when and how learning takes place must be under the control of individual children, one cannot, by definition, design uniform sequences of learning trials that are the same for all children. Consequently, although self-discovery learning procedures were developed and used by some of Piaget's collaborators (see especially, Inhelder et al., 1974), the fact that those procedures could not be standardized meant it was hard to replicate them in experiments that were designed to compare self-discovery learning to tutorial learning.

Despite these obstacles, some limited evidence was eventually reported that bears on relative effectiveness. Two findings are especially relevant. First, although Piaget's coworkers did not conduct studies of self-discovery versus tutorial learning, they did report a series of six experiments, five with conservation concepts and one with class inclusion concepts, in which self-discovery learning was used (Inhelder et al., 1974). Thus, it is possible to draw limited conclusions about relative effectiveness by comparing overall levels of learning in these studies to the overall levels that were obtained using the methods discussed in the preceding section. When detailed comparisons of this sort were made (see Brainerd, 1978a), the results were not favorable to self-discovery learning. On the whole, the magnitudes of the learning effects reported by Inhelder et al. were much smaller than the effects that I described for the four tutorial procedures. Instead of reporting percentages of correct responses and other average statistics of performance, these investigators used a three-category classification scheme, classifying children as no learning, partial learning, and complete learning following self-discovery training. Across the six experiments, 32% of the children showed no learning, 38% showed partial learning, and 30% showed complete learning. Crucially, only children who were able to pass at least some of the pretests show *any* learning (either partial or complete). For example, in the conservation training experiments, all of the children who showed either partial or complete learning had passed pretests for number conservation. Obviously, such findings stand in marked contrast to the data of tutorial experiments that produced virtually perfect posttest performance in children who failed pretests across the board (e.g., Gelman, 1969; Rosenthal & Zimmerman, 1972).

The second relevant finding comes from a single study that was reported by Sheppard (1974), which also failed to confirm the hypothesized superiority of self-discovery training. The significance of this experiment is that it used a procedure that was very similar to one that Inhelder et al. (1974) had devised to train liquid quantity conservation, except that training involved self-discovery for the children in the Inhelder et al. study but training tutorial learning for the children in Sheppard's. The Inhelder et al. procedure made use of pairs of liquid-containing glasses, such as those shown in the center panels of Fig. 11.2. Children were informed that liquid could be transferred from one pair of glasses to another. A training trial began with equal amounts of liquid in a pair of identical glasses (top-center panel, Fig. 11.2). Children were encouraged to transfer the liquid to other pairs of glasses that differed in diameter (bottom-center panel, Fig. 11.2) and to observe the changes that occurred. Children were also encouraged to transfer the liquid back to the pair of identical glasses and to observe the changes that occurred. The key element is that the experimenter never explained any of the changes to the children, and the experimenter carefully avoided telling the children that any of their reasoning was incorrect on the ground that "Such reasoning cannot, and for that matter should not, be eliminated by coercion" (Inhelder et al., 1974, p. 25). In contrast, Sheppard's procedure made use of the same materials and liquid transferrals, but his children were passive observers, and the experimenter corrected their erroneous reasoning. On each training trial, children were asked to describe what would happen if liquid were transferred from certain glasses to other glasses. After each prediction, the experimenter, not the children, performed the liquid transferral. Following this, the experimenter verbalized the results of the transferral, emphasizing whether children's predictions had been correct or incorrect.

Sheppard's (1974) tutorial version of Inhelder et al.'s (1974) self-discovery procedure yielded much better learning. In the first place, all of Sheppard's children had failed conservation pretests across the board, whereas many of Inhelder et al.'s children had passed some conservation pretests. On posttests, virtually all of Sheppard's trained children provided correct answers on at least some of the problems (partial learning by Inhelder et al.'s criteria), and more that 30% performed perfectly (complete learning by Inhelder et al.'s criteria). This may be contrasted with Inhelder et al.'s finding that only children who passed some of the pretests showed even partial learning as a result of self-discovery training.

Summary

By the early 1980s, several conservation-training experiments had been reported whose data were pertinent to Piagetian claims about naturalism and constructivism in children's learning. Like the previously discussed research on the stage-learning hypothesis, the news was not good for Piaget's views on instructional methodology. Piaget had proposed that the only effective learning procedures were ones that emulated the ways in which learning occurred in children's everyday experience and, more particularly, that effective learning procedures must incorporate active self-discovery of novel concepts. Two general lines of evidence ran counter to these proposals. First, four different classes of learning procedures that did not incorporate self-discovery and, in some cases, were downright passive, produced excellent learning. Second, self-discovery procedures were not found to be superior to nonself-discovery procedures. On the contrary, nonself-discovery procedures seemed to be superior. Among other things, such evidence argued strongly against the Rousseauean supposition that natural-learning-is-always-the-best-learning, which lay at the heart of the Piagetian perspective on learning.

PIAGETIAN THEORY AND LEARNING THEORY: A POSTSCRIPT

The American learning theories that dominated educational psychology until the late 1960s assigned little or no role to cognitive development. This is hardly surprising inasmuch as those theories evolved in the course of learning research with college students and animals. However, the adevelopmental nature of the theories meant that when they were applied to problems of classroom instruction, no definite, positive functions were assigned to developmental processes. By default, therefore, developmental differences had to be treated as noise.

Piaget's theory of children's learning changed all that. As we saw, he proposed that developmental processes contribute to children's learning in two fundamental ways. First, children's learning was said to be constrained by their current levels of cognitive development, which led to the stage-learning hypothesis. According to this hypothesis, children will be unable to learn concepts that are demonstrably below their current stage of cognitive development, and their ability to learn concepts will be positively related to their pretraining knowledge of those concepts. Second, assuming that children have reached the appropriate developmental level and are ready to learn the target concepts, only certain instructional procedures will be effective. More explicitly, effective instructional methods will be naturalistic ones that emulate informal learning processes in children's everyday lives. Piaget thought that the key element of informal learning processes is that they involve active self-discovery of new concepts, which he called construction.

As we also saw, however, learning experiments conducted by American educational psychologists failed to provide much confirmation for either of Piaget's principal claims. When the relation between level of cognitive development and children's learning was examined, the two variables were not found to be strongly related, as Piaget had postulated: Children who showed no evidence of concrete-operational concepts on pretests showed excellent learning, children who showed different amounts of pretest knowledge of concrete-operational concepts did not exhibit markedly different amounts of learning, and preschool children (whose ages place them in the first half of the preoperational period) were able to learn concrete-operational concepts. When Piaget's ideas about the necessity of naturalistic learning were investigated, the findings were similarly nonsupportive. Instructional procedures that were based on laboratory learning paradigms, rather than everyday learning mechanisms, were found to be highly effective learning methods. Further, the learning effects that Piaget's collaborators obtained in self-discovery experiments were noticeably smaller than those that American researchers obtained with laboratory paradigms.

To conclude, the historical relationship between Piagetian theory and traditional American-style learning theory might be summed up in three statements. First, American learning theories of the 1950s and 1960s assigned no definite role to developmental processes, treating them by default as noise factors in children's learning. Second, Piaget assigned a primary role to developmental processes, claiming that they constrained children's learning in two powerful ways. Third, research on children's learning repeatedly disconfirmed Piaget's proposed developmental constraints. Reflecting on these facts, it is not surprising that the influence of Piaget's perspective on learning on contemporary educational psychology is not as great as it formerly was. After all, it has been consistently established that as a result of rather brief instructional sessions (e.g., 10–20 minutes of perceptual training or rule demonstration or observation of skilled reasoners or corrective feedback), children readily learn concepts that they do not spontaneously acquire until some years later, concepts that Piaget thought could only emerge through a slow morphogenetic process. Thus, a large literature has established that developmental constraints on children's learning of Piaget's concrete-operational concepts are weak at best.

This is not to say, however, that regarding developmental differences merely as noise is appropriate or that there are no important developmental constraints on children's learning. Instead, a much more limited conclusion follows from the research record, the conclusion being that the particular developmental constraints that Piaget postulated (stages of cognitive development) do not appear to seriously restrict children's learning. Despite the lack of support for Piaget's particular constraints, the topic of developmental restrictions on children's learning remains a topic of continuing interest (e.g., Bjorklund, 1999).

REFERENCES

Abramson, H. A. (Ed.). (1954). *Problems of consciousness: Transactions of the fourth conference.* Princeton, NJ: Josiah Macy, Jr. Foundation.

Bandura, A., & Walters, R. H. (1963). *Social learning and personality development.* New York: Holt, Rinehart, & Winston.

Beilin, H. (1965). Learning and operational convergence in logical thought development. *Journal of Experimental Child Psychology, 2,* 317–339.

Bjorklund, D. F. (1999). *Children's thinking: Developmental function and individual differences* (3rd ed.). Belmont, CA: Wadsworth.

Boersma, F. J., & Wilton, K. M. (1974). Eye movements and conservation acceleration. *Journal of Experimental Child Psychology, 17,* 49–60.

Boring, E. G., Werner, H., Langfeld, H. S., & Yerkes, R. M. (Eds.). (1952). *A history of psychology in autobiography* (Vol. IV). Worcester, MA: Clark University Press.

Brainerd, C. J. (1972). Reinforcement and reversibility in quantity conservation acquisition. *Psychonomic Science, 27,* 114–116.

Brainerd, C. J. (1973). Neo-Piagetian training experiments revisited: Is there any support for the cognitive-developmental stage hypothesis? *Cognition, 2,* 349–370.

Brainerd, C. J. (1974). Training and transfer of transitivity, conservation, and class inclusion of length. *Child Development, 45,* 324–334.

Brainerd, C. J. (1977a). Cognitive development and concept learning: An interpretative review. *Psychological Bulletin, 84,* 919–939.

Brainerd, C. J. (1977b). Feedback, rule knowledge, and conservation learning. *Child Development, 48,* 404–411.

Brainerd, C. J. (1978a). Learning research and Piagetian theory. In L. S. Siegel and C. J. Brainerd (Eds.), *Alternatives to Piaget: Critical essays on the theory.* New York: Academic Press.

Brainerd, C. J. (1978b). The stage question in cognitive-developmental theory. *The Behavioral Brain Sciences, 1,* 173–182.

Brainerd, C. J. (1979a). Concept learning and developmental stage. In H. J. Klausmeier and associates (Eds.), *Concept learning and development: Piagetian and information processing perspectives.* Cambridge, MA: Ballinger.

Brainerd, C. J. (1979b). Markovian interpretations of conservation learning. *Psychological Review, 86,* 181–213

Brainerd, C. J. (1982). Children's concept learning as rule-sampling systems with Markovian properties. In. C. J. Brainerd (Ed.), *Children's logical and mathematical cognition.* New York: Springer-Verlag.

Brainerd, C. J., & Allen, T. W. (1971). Experimental inductions of the conservation of "first-order" quantitative invariants. *Psychological Bulletin, 75,* 128–144.

Brainerd, C. J., & Brainerd, S. H. (1972). Order of acquisition of number and quantity conservation. *Child Development, 43,* 1401–1406.

Bruner, J. S. (1966). *Studies in cognitive growth.* New York: Wiley.

Bucher, B., & Schneider, R. E. (1973). Acquisition and generalization of conservation by preschoolers using operant training. *Journal of Experimental Child Psychology, 16,* 187–204.

Burns, S. M., & Brainerd, C. J. (1979). Effects of constructive and dramatic play on perspective taking in very young children. *Developmental Psychology, 15,* 512–521.

Charbonneau, C., Robert, M., Bourassa, G., & Gladu-Bissonette, S. (1976). Observational learning of quantity conservation and Piagetian generalization tasks. *Developmental Psychology, 12,* 211–217.

Cronbach, L. J., & Snow, R. E. (1977). *Aptitudes and instructional methods: A handbook for research on interactions.* New York: Wiley.

Denney, N. W., Zeytinoglu, S., & Selzer, S. C. (1977). Conservation training in four-year-olds. *Journal of Experimental Child Psychology, 24,* 129–146.

Elkind, D., & Flavell, J. H. (Eds.). (1969). *Studies in cognitive development*. New York: Oxford University Press.

Emrick, J. A. (1968). *The acquisition and transfer of conservation skills by four-year-old children*. Unpublished doctoral dissertation, University of California at Los Angeles.

Evans, R. L. (1973). *Jean Piaget: The man and his ideas*. New York: Dutton.

Field, D. (1981). Can preschool children really learn to conserve? *Developmental Review, 2*, 326–334.

Flavell, J. H. (1963). *The developmental psychology of Jean Piaget*. Princeton, NJ: Van Nostrand.

Gelman, R. (1969). Conservation acquisition: A problem of learning to attend to relevant attributes. *Journal of Experimental Child Psychology, 7*, 167–187.

Gelman, R. (1972). The nature and development of early number concepts. In H. W. Reese (Ed.), *Advances in child development and behavior* (Vol. 3). New York: Academic Press.

Goldschmid, M., & Bentler, P. M. (1968). *Manual: Concept assessment kit, conservation*. San Diego, CA: Educational and Industrial Testing Service.

Halford, G. S., & Fullerton, T. J. (1970). A discrimination task that induces conservation of number. *Child Development, 41*, 205–213.

Hamel, B. R., & Riksen, B. O. M. (1973). Identity, reversibility, verbal rule instruction, and conservation. *Developmental Psychology, 9*, 66–72.

Inhelder, B., & Sinclair, H. (1969). Learning cognitive structures. In P. H. Mussen, J. Langer, & M. Covington (Eds.), *Trends and issues in developmental psychology*. New York: Holt, Rinehart, & Winston.

Inhelder, B., Sinclair, H., & Bovet, M. (1974). *Learning and the development of cognition*. Cambridge, MA: Harvard University Press.

Kendler, H. H., & Kendler, T. S. (1960). Vertical and horizontal processes in problem solving. *Psychological Review, 67*, 1–16.

Kessen, W. (1996). American psychology just before Piaget. *Psychological Science, 7*, 196–199.

Kessen, W., & Kuhlman, C. (Eds.). (1962). Thought in the young child: Report of a conference on intellective development with particular attention to the work of Jean Piaget. *Monographs of the Society for Research in Child Development, 27* (Serial No. 83).

Lawton, J. T., & Hooper, F. H. (1978). Piagetian theory and early childhood education: A critical analysis. In L. S. Siegel and C. J. Brainerd (Eds.), *Alternatives to Piaget: Critical essays on the theory*. New York: Academic Press.

May, R. B., & Tisshaw, S. K. (1975). Variations of learning-set training and quantity conservation. *Child Development, 48*, 661–667.

Miller, N. E., & Dollard, J. (1941). *Social learning and imitation*. New Haven, CT: Yale University Press.

Piaget, J. (1926). *The language and thought of the child*.

Piaget, J. (1952). *The child's conception of number*. New York: Humanities.

Piaget, J. (1970a). A conversation with Jean Piaget. *Psychology Today, 3*(12), 25–32.

Piaget, J. (1970b). Piaget's theory. In P. H. Mussen (Ed.), *Carmichael's manual of child psychology* (Vol. 1). New York: Wiley.

Piaget, J. (1970c). *Science of education and psychology of the child*. New York: Oxford University Press.

Piaget, J., & Inhelder, B. (1941). *Le developpement des quantites chez l'enfant* [English translation]. Neuchatel, Switzerland: Delachuax et Niestle.

Ripple, R. E., & Rockcastle, V. N. (Eds.). (1964). *Piaget rediscovered*. Ithaca, NY: Cornell University Press.

Rosenthal, T. L., & Zimmerman, B. J. (1972). Modeling by exemplification and instruction in training conservation. *Developmental Psychology, 6*, 392–401.

Sheppard, J. L. (1974). Compensation and combinatorial systems in the acquisition and generalization of conservation. *Child Development, 45*, 717–730.

Siegler, R. S. (1981). Developmental sequences within and between concepts. *Monographs of the Society for Research in Child Development, 46* (Serial No. 189).

Siegler, R. S., & Liebert, R. M. (1972). Effects of presenting relevant rules and complete feedback on the conservation of liquid quantity. *Developmental Psychology, 7,* 133–138.

Sinclair, H. (1973). Recent Piagetian research in learning studies. In M. Schwebel & J. Raph (Eds.), *Piaget in the classroom.* New York: Basic Books.

Smedslund, J. (1959). Apprentissage des notions de la conservation et de la transitivite du poids [English title]. *Etudes d'Epistemologie Genetique, 9,* 3–13.

Smedslund, J. (1961). The acquisition of conservation of substance and weight in children. II. External reinforcement of conservation of weight and the operations of addition and subtraction. *Scandinavian Journal of Psychology, 2,* 71–84.

Smith, I. D. (1968). The effects of training procedures on the acquisition of conservation of weight. *Child Development, 39,* 515–526.

Stevenson, H. W. (1972). *Children's learning.* New York: Appleton-Century-Crofts.

Trabasso, T., & Bower, G. H. (1968). *Attention in learning.* New York: Wiley.

Wallach, L., & Sprott, R. L. (1964). Inducing conservation in children. *Child Development, 35,* 71–84.

Wohlwill, J. F. (1959). Un essai d'apprentissage dans le domaine de la conservation du nombre [English]. *Etudes de'Epistemologie Genetique, 9,* 125–135.

Zeaman, D., & House, B. J. (1963). The role of attention in retardate discrimination learning. In N. R. Ellis (Ed.), *Handbook of mental deficiency.* New York: McGraw-Hill.

Zimmerman, B. J., & Lanaro, P. (1974). Acquiring and retaining conservation of length through modeling and reversibility cues. *Merrill–Palmer Quarterly, 20,* 145–161.

Zimmerman, B. J., & Rosenthal, T. L. (1974a). Conserving and retaining equalities and inequalities through observation and correction. *Developmental Psychology, 10,* 260–268.

Zimmerman, B. J., & Rosenthal, T. L. (1974b). Observational learning of rule-governed behavior by children. *Psychological Bulletin, 81,* 29–42.

12

Lee J. Cronbach's Contributions to Educational Psychology

Haggai Kupermintz
University of Colorado at Boulder

Lee J. Cronbach is one of the most prominent and influential educational psychologists of all time. His scholarship has had a profound impact on the discipline throughout a career that spanned over 5 decades, and his name has been associated with many phenomena in the fields of measurement, teaching and learning, and evaluation. Cronbach stated that his " . . . most sustained line of investigation, with publications extending over more than 40 years, has had to do with methods for appraising the accuracy of psychological or educational measurements and of inferences from them" (Cronbach, 1991, p. 385). Still, measurement issues were but one facet of a monumental intellectual enterprise, whose style Snow and Wiley (1991) so vividly captured:

> The Cronbach style is first to find the root problems, the hidden difficulties, the tacit assumptions, and the theoretical and methodological conventions that blind the investigator to limits and alternatives and thus impede progress in socially important fields of inquiry. He then learns how to think straight about the core issues by cutting away this excess and malconceived conceptual and methodological baggage to criticize the basic questions being pursued. Often this is accomplished by recasting existing data from some important study, reaching a new synthesis and pursuing implications that go well beyond those of the original investigator. His revision then

emerges as a carefully tutored central example for a field. He thus raises the level of conceptualization with which diverse investigators work by sharpening the questions that guide them and by reconfiguring the line of investigation, to clarify the meaning of evidence and to improve the opportunities for earlier solid payoff, both theoretical and practical. (p. 1)

This chapter examines Cronbach's legacy of scholarship to the field of educational psychology. I will not attempt the impossible task of providing a comprehensive review of Cronbach's work, nor will I tell a neat chronological story of an academic career. Rather, my aim in this chapter is to highlight several core themes that run through Cronbach's writings. Cronbach (1989, p. 79) cautioned: "My scholarly work must be discussed topically rather than chronologically, as I pursued interests simultaneously and discontinuously." Accordingly, this chapter is organized around three main themes: measurement issues, the interaction paradigm, and program evaluation. Within these topics, I will endeavor to show the lessons and insights from Cronbach's work that pertain to several core issues of interest to educational psychologists: the nature of the teaching–learning process, the measurement of variables describing instructional interactions, the evaluation of educational programs, and educational psychology's aspiration as an emerging social science discipline. But before moving on to the substantive issues, a brief biographical sketch outlining the major milestones in Cronbach's professional life will serve as historical context.

LEE J. CRONBACH: A SYNOPTIC BIOGRAPHY

Lee Cronbach was born in 1916 in Fresno, California. His first encounter with psychological measurement was taking the Stanford–Binet IQ test at the age of 5. A score of 200 earned him a place as a subject in Lewis Terman's landmark study of the intellectually gifted. The first mileposts in his incredible intellectual career were the completion of high school at the age of 14 and college at the age of 18. Recalling his teenage career as a debater, Cronbach (1989) professed: "I recall having defined, somewhere in those years, my goal in life as Being an Authority" (p. 64). A shift in interests from chemistry to education lead a B.A. degree from Fresno State's teacher's college, and a Master's from the University California, Berkeley in 1937. It was in Berkeley where Cronbach met his wife, Helen. Their five children were born between 1941 and 1956.

Thurstone's work on the measurement of attitudes provided an early impetus for Cronbach's lasting interest in educational and psychological measurement. Yet, during a fast-paced doctoral training in educational psychology at the University if Chicago (with Ph.D. earned in 1940, after only 2 years in the program), it had not occurred to Cronbach to elect courses with Thurstone, at the Psychology

Department next door. Nevertheless, working with Ralph Tyler and Karl Holzinger provided solid grounding in educational research, evaluation, and statistics. Cronbach joined the psychology faculty at Washington State College in 1940, teaching introductory, social, child, and industrial psychology in his first year there. Later he taught his first courses in evaluation and measurement, for which he wrote his *Essentials of Psychological Testing* (1949). (He also supervised Timothy Leary's master's degree work.) During WWII, Cronbach worked as a research psychologist at the Navy's sonar school in San Diego, gaining experience in instructional research as he developed a training course for sonar operators.

Cronbach returned to Chicago for 2 years in 1946, as Assistant Professor of Education, finally to profit from gatherings of the psychometric community hosted by the Thurstones. In addition to intensive psychometric work, he inherited Tyler's introductory course in education psychology, which led to a successful textbook on the subject (Cronbach, 1954). It was during that period that Cronbach established a professional identity that consistently avoided narrow specialization and a binding commitment to a particular content area: "Weaving strands into a tapestry was what I enjoyed, not spinning the thread" (Cronbach, 1989, p. 73). In 1948 he accepted, together with Nate Gage, a joint appointment in education and psychology at the University of Illinois, Urbana, whose measurement program later recruited Henry Kaiser, Lloyd Humphreys, and Ledyard Tucker. In Urbana Cronbach produced some of his most influential writings: the "Alpha" paper (Cronbah, 1951), the exposition, with Paul Meehl, of construct validity (Cronbach & Meehl, 1955), the "Two Disciplines" paper (Cronbach, 1957), early work on Generalizability theory (Cronbach, Rjaratnam, & Gleser, 1963), and a book on the use of psychological tests in personnel decisions (Cronbach & Gleser, 1957).

A realization emerged during that period: "By 1956 I had come to think . . . that I was serving primarily as a teacher of my profession" (Cronbach, 1989, p. 83). The profession's recognition is attested to by numerous honors. He was president of the American Educational Research Association, the American Psychological Association, and the Psychometric Society, and a member of the National Academy of Sciences, the National Academy of Education, the American Philosophical Society, and the American Academy of Arts and Sciences. He received many honorary degrees, including ones from Yeshiva University, the University of Gothenburg, Sweden, and the University of Chicago.

After a period of intensive professional committee and faculty governance work in the early 1960s, Cronbach returned to California in 1964 to join the faculty of Stanford's School of Education until his retirement in 1980. At Stanford he finished his seminal work on Generalizability theory (Cronbach, Gleser, Nanda, & Rajaratnam, 1972), collaborated with Richard Snow (Cronbach & Snow, 1977) to develop a conceptual and methodological framework for aptitude–treatment interactions (ATI) research, and advanced a reform in the field of program evaluation (Cronbach et al. 1980; Cronbach, 1982). His last major endeavor was completing a book, together with former students, on the concept of aptitude, extending the legacy of the late Richard Snow (Stanford Aptitude Seminar, 2002). The book was published 2 weeks before Cronbach passed away, on October 1, 2001, at the age of 85.

ISSUES IN MEASUREMENT

Since the turn of the 20th century, testing has been a defining feature of the American public education system. Countless educational decisions rely on test scores as a main source of information on educational attainment and potential: placement into alternative educational programs, retention and promotion, graduation, admission to higher education, and most recently, allocation of strong financial incentives and sanctions to teachers and schools. Measurement issues, then, are of paramount importance to educational psychologists. A rich psychometric tradition consistently provided mathematical models that helped educators and psychologists to analyze and interpret test score data. But the psychometric framework was lacking a deeper understanding of test takers as human beings rather than random variables. Cronbach's contributions included both improvements to the technology of psychometric modeling and reformulations that went beyond the mathematics to understand the psychology of test performance.

The pioneering work of Spearman and Brown laid the foundation for modern test theory and practice. Cronbach recognized the limitations of the classical psychometric model while analyzing test data from the Eight-Year Study at Chicago. Puzzlements registered during these analyses sparked a sustained effort to improve the way psychologists thought about and used test scores. The results included a major expansion of reliability theory, a conceptual framework for validating test scores, a decision-theoretic approach for evaluating decisions based on test scores, and the articulations of philosophical and empirical principles underlying various aspects of test theory. As with other Cronbach efforts, the scope was wide, the commitment eyed long-term goals, and the contributions address multiple aspects of the problems, both theoretical and practical.

An important motivation for moving beyond strictly psychometric formulations was the desire to examine more closely the conditions that affected performance on measures that purported to gauge what has been learned, and how well. Looking only at test content to draw inferences about the meaning of test performance as measures of academic achievement, Cronbach argued, was at best limited, and most likely to lead the analyst astray. Cronbach's attention to psychological dimensions that were important for drawing sound inferences from observed performance on learning tasks can be traced back to his Master's thesis at Berkeley (Cronbach, 1936) on student understanding of vocabulary in algebra. In that work, inspired by Dewey's *How We Think*, he explored the various ways students understood the concept of a *coefficient* in an effort to identify how and where learners had difficulties. Cronbach's subsequent work aimed to demonstrate and explain the psychological principles involved in test performance, and sought to provide intellectual and practical tools for a constructive criticism of test theory.

Test scores, like all indicators of human performance, are multiply determined both by factors that educators and psychologists would consider directly relevant to the educative processes (such as the quality of teaching), but also by a variety of irrelevant factors (such as surface features of test design or the learner's emotional response to the testing situation). Cronbach's early work on response styles (Cronbach, 1946, 1950) demonstrated how aspects of tests that were completely irrelevant to the evaluation of the outcomes of learning could distort interpretation of test results if ignored. It became apparent that consistent individual differences in habitual styles of responding to test items were an important influence on the resulting test scores. Messick (1991) described the effect of this work: "Once Cronbach had opened the response-set floodgate, hundreds of empirical studies and dozens of research reviews inundated the measurement literature" (pp. 162–163). Despite later challenges and controversy about the validity and importance of the original claims, no educational psychologist can neglect to consider evidence on response processes. "For instance, if a test is intended to assess mathematical reasoning, it becomes important to determine whether examinees are, in fact, reasoning about the material given instead of following a standard algorithm" (APA, AERA, NCME, 1999, p. 12).

The consistency of test scores from repeated applications of the measurement procedure is the hallmark of the concept of test reliability. Cronbach's work on reliability, and later on generalizability had an enormous impact on the field of educational measurement. The most visible product of Cronbach's early work on issues of reliability was the "Coefficient Alpha" paper (Cronbach, 1951). The paper gave a new interpretation to an index of reliability that was based on the pattern of test inter-item correlations. From a practical standpoint, the proposed procedure enables analysts to calculate an estimate of reliability from a single administration of a test. The formula could be applied across a wide variety of tests and other measurement instruments, and has gained tremendous popularity among practitioners. It is a rarity to encounter an educational or psychological measure, from home-grown dissertation survey instruments to commercial achievement tests, that does not report Cronbach's Alpha. So much popularity caused Cronbach (1991) to lament about the "absurdly large fraction" of citations to the Alpha paper and about the fact that "[t]he conveniences of the label "Cronbach's Alpha" brought me a laughable status as eponym" (p. 387).

But the thinking that went into the question of test reliability, as manifested by the extent to which responses on different test items correlated, went beyond the technical. It brought real-world educational psychology considerations into psychometric work that often remained a detached abstract mathematical exercise. "Criticizing test theory thus becomes a matter of comparing what the mathematician assumes with what the psychologist can reasonably believe about people's responses" (Cronbach 1989, p. 82). From this perspective, the classical psychometric ideal of test purity was hopelessly restrictive. A deeper level of psychological processes underlying observed test behavior was obscured from sight.

> Many models for test development, past and future, reflect the idea that items contributing to a score should all "measure the same thing." Spearman could not observe pure *g* but did hope to isolate its effects by a statistical adjustment for impurities as well as for error of measurement. Thurstone and his followers sought "factorially pure" tests. My sympathies were with Binet's views: Problem-solving is an intricate and ever-shifting combination of processes. Influenced by Dewey and Judd, I looked for similar multiple processes in educational development. (Cronbach, 1991, p. 386)

The culmination of Cronbach's work on reliability during the 1950s and 1960s eventually found its fullest expression as a comprehensive generalizability theory (Cronbach, Gleser, Nanda, & Rajaratnam, 1972). Work on the theory started with relatively modest aspirations—Cronbach was to produce, together with Goldine Gleser, a handbook on measurement to help people attempting to apply "mathematical systems for transforming the flow of behavior and events into quantitative conclusions" (Cronbach, 1989, p. 84). The plan called for starting by explicating what was considered at the time a well understood topic—reliability. The classical formulation decomposed observed test scores into true score and error components, an idea that inspired numerous theoretical developments and practical applications for half a century (see Lord & Novick, 1968). In Cronbach's view, the model suffered from two serious weaknesses: True scores were ill-defined and errors were all-inclusive. The first weakness was addressed by Cronbach's proposals for test validation, to which I turn in a subsequent section. Generalizibility theory grew from Cronbach's concern that an undifferentiated error term concealed important information about systematic variations in test performance. Enlisting two other team members and armored with the newly developed "random model," a variant of analysis of variance introduced by statistician R. A. Fisher, Cronbach set out on an expedition to "the outer darkness known as 'error variance'" (Cronbach, 1975, p. 674).

Generalizability theory addresses the question of the relative influence on test performance of different aspects or *facets* of the testing procedure. Will students perform consistently on different occasions, with different test forms, with different item formats? A student excelling in a multiple-choice test in science, may perform poorer if a different test of the same content demanded her to provide more elaborate responses. Once the relative contribution of the various measurement facets has been estimated, the investigator can translate this information into specific design recommendations. For example, the test designer may conclude that more items are needed to reach a certain level of reliability, or that a revision to some items' format is required. Furthermore, the theory moves beyond examining the consistency in students' relative standing in a distribution—the hallmark of traditional reliability analysis. The theory recognizes that the particular items used in any given test are only a sample from a wider knowledge domain. Inferences from test scores are useful to the extent that they say something of value about the domain, beyond the particular set of items the student encountered on this test. A reading comprehension test, for example, may require the student to read and understand only a limited, small sample of text; yet, inference from the student's performance is used to draw conclusions about her reading comprehension in general.

In the end, the journey into the outer darkness of error variance produced far-reaching conclusions of the complexity of the endeavor to understand what a test was measuring. These conclusions would now serve the higher purpose of developing a framework for the theoretical and empirical validation of test scores. The extensions to reliability investigations afforded by generalizability theory allowed researchers to address more realistic educational problems and encouraged them to place substantive considerations at the forefront of their inquiries. This helped to demonstrate that validity was the most important consideration for evaluating the soundness of information extracted from test scores. Because error variance was not the random, uninteresting process once assumed, and substantive questions played a crucial part in unveiling systematic variation at the core of error variance, "[t]he investigator's theory, rather than an abstract concept of truth and error, determines which family contains tests that 'measure the same variable.' Analyzing generalizability becomes part of validating the construct represented in the chosen universe, hence studies of "error" have substantive importance" (Cronbach, 1991, p. 394).

Early conclusions were consolidated forcefully and brought into focus as a primary psychometric agenda item with the publication of Cronbach and Meehl (1955). The paper established the centrality of validity as the key theme around which inquiry concerning the meaning of test scores should be organized. The ideal expressed in the paper was that the process of validation should follow a path not unlike that of theory building. Whereas traditional approaches to test validity were limited to examining test content and simple correlations with other variables believed to represent adequate criteria, construct validation was to build a firm theoretical basis within which the measured construct can derive its meaning. Content analysis was unsatisfactory, as Cronbach demonstrated in his early studies of response sets; responses on tests and questionnaires may reflect the influence of many factors, some of which are irrelevant to the test's content—from the format in which information is presented to the respondents' motivation. Scores on an intelligence test, for example, may reflect examinees' perceptions of the threat posed by stereotypes about their capacity to succeed (Steele, 1998). Furthermore, the lack of adequate gold standards for most educational and psychological measures rendered correlations with various "criteria" as providing only partial evidence on validity.

In his later writings Cronbach acknowledged that the scientific principles of rigor expressed in the ideals of construct validity were too ambitious and did not serve well to advance the more modest aspirations of social scientists. Scientific rigor ought to be balanced by tolerance to a plurality of interpretations. Point of view, values, and beliefs are integral to how social scientists weave their theoretical stories from the raw material of empirical observations. Not because they are tender-minded but because such qualities are inherent in their subject matter. It is therefore unreasonable to expect a degree of consensus typical of natural science explanations. Cronbach (1986) went so far as to suggest that "[i]nterpretations arising out of scholarship ought to be afforded the tolerance afforded to art, and fortunately they sometimes are" (p. 97). The plurality of inquiry styles and theoretical constructions of contemporary educational psychology is indebted to Cronbach's efforts to align the scientific in social research with its age-old humanistic heritage.

THE INTERACTIONIST APPROACH

In two addresses to the members of the American Psychological Association Cronbach (1957; 1975) identified and described the fault line separating two intellectual continents that appeared to be drifting apart. A 1957 address tracked the historical, epistemological, and methodological roots of the widening divide between experimental psychology and correlational psychologies. Experimenters were mostly concerned with the statistical comparison of treatments and regarded individual differences in response to treatment as an inevitable annoyance. The correlational psychologists, on the other hand, focused their attention on individual differences and regarded individual and group variation as important effects of biological and social causes. The implications of this schism for educational psychology were far reaching. Cronbach's analysis made apparent the fatal flaws inherent in asking educational questions that artificially separated the role of the learner from that of the learning environment, such as considering either just a typical or average response to instruction or the correlations among aptitude or achievement variables.

Learners differ greatly in what they bring to the learning situation, and educational psychologists have to ask how individual learning histories and predispositions play a role in the learner's readiness to make progress and benefit in different learning environments. Solid knowledge and mastery of basic quantitative operations, for example, enhance a student's likelihood of making robust progress in algebra. Individual differences in response to educational treatments, argued Cronbach, were as important to understanding and improving educational programs as the typical response or average program effect. "Ultimately, we should *design* treatments, not to fit the average person, but to fit groups of students with particular aptitude patterns. Conversely, we should seek out the aptitudes which correspond to (i.e., interact with) modifiable aspects of the treatments" (Cronbach, 1957, p. 681, italics in original). Encouraged by efforts lead by Paul Meehl (and to which he was an influential contributor) to ground test validation in a network of interacting psychological constructs, Cronbach began to see the emerging interactionist paradigm as a key feature of a network of constructs that pertain to learning and instruction. Different forms of instruction should be matched to different types of learners. He was upbeat when he projected, "We may expect the test literature of the future to be far less saturated with correlations of tests with psychologically enigmatic criteria, and far richer in studies which define test variables by their responsiveness to practice at different ages, to drugs, to altered instructions, and to other experimentally manipulated variables" (Cronbach, 1957, p. 676).

Earlier work with Gleser (Cronbah & Gleser, 1957) on personnel-decision theory concluded that optimal placements must acknowledge the interaction of personal characteristics and job demands. For education it meant that the assignment of students, whenever based on their test scores or other standardized criteria, to different instructional programs must recognize that students with different scores may thrive in different learning environments. A decade after the first APA address, Cronbach, together with long-time collaborator, Richard Snow, embarked on an empirical research program in a quest to find tentative generalizations that would serve as a foundation for a theory of learner differences in response to alternative ways of teaching. A 3-year project turned into a 10-year search in the literature, laboratory, and field, for the elusive aptitude–treatment interaction (ATI) holy grail(s). The ATI formulation represented a formal analytic framework for determining the potential benefits of matching the right type of instruction to each student's ability or interest. The label referred to a method for statistically analyzing the results such as the model for comparing high- and low-aptitude students using structured versus unstructured instructional methods. Unfortunately, they discovered only rarely consistent ATI patterns in the literature, save for the conclusion that students with higher general cognitive ability typically profit from a learning environment that offers them autonomy, responsibility, and control. But the quest nevertheless led to profound insights about the scope of the challenge and the needed reform in thinking and methodology in order to support progress. It became clear that a rigid scientific ideal of a network of general propositions, grounded in a strong empirical set of quantifiable observations across many contexts, would fall short.

These lessons were reflected in the 1974 sequel address that offered a more sober evaluation of the nature of interactions and examined philosophically the ability of scientific psychology to portray a coherent, stable, and widely applicable picture of human affairs, in much the same way as the natural sciences were able to do for the principles that govern the physical world. The insights conveyed to the field were challenging: First-order interactions add precious little to our understanding of the learning situation; numerous factors engage in an intricate interplay to affect the learning outcome; even seemingly stable generalizations are bound by time, culture, and local settings. In sum: "Our troubles do not arise because human events are in principle unlawful; man and his creations *are* part of the natural world. The trouble, as I see it, is that we cannot store up generalizations and constructs for ultimate assembly into a network" (Cronbach, 1975, p, 123, italics in original). The inherent fragility of scientific generalizations, even when they claim to represent "laws of nature," have recently been dramatically underscored when a team of astrophysicists discovered that a basic numerical constant (involving strength of attraction between electically charged particles) may be changing slightly as the universe ages.

Cronbach's initial effort to discover general propositions about who would benefit from alternative methods of teaching and how learning environments could be designed to maximize benefits for all students, led him almost 2 decades later to suggest a radical shift in the goals of social science research toward a more contextualized approach (Cronbach, 1975):

> Instead of making generalization the ruling consideration in our research, I suggest that we reverse our priorities. An observer collecting data in one particular situation is in a position to appraise a practice or proposition in that setting, observing effects in context. In trying to describe and account for what happened, he will give attention to whatever variables were controlled, but he will give equally careful attention to uncontrolled conditions, to personal characteristics, and to events that occurred during treatment and measurement. As he goes from situation to situation, his first task is to describe and interpret the effect anew in each locale, perhaps taking into account factors unique to that locale of series of events. (pp. 124–125)
>
> Intensive local observation goes beyond discipline to an open-eyed, open-minded appreciation of the surprises nature deposits in the investigative net. This kind of interpretation is historical more than scientific. (p. 125)
>
> The special task of the social scientist in each generation is to pin down the contemporary facts. Beyond that. He shares with the humanistic scholar and the artist in the effort to gain insight into contemporary relationships, and to align the culture's view of man with present realities. To know man as he is is no mean aspiration. (p. 126)

Educational psychologists have benefited in numerous ways from Cronbach's quest for a better explanation of learning in response to instruction. First, he sharpened the sensitivity of educational research to the way different learners cope with the demands and affordances imbedded in different learning environments. Second, he advocated the use of intensive local studies and field methods that produced rich narratives of teaching and learning (for example, the use of video cases to facilitate rich descriptions of the learning process). Third, he helped refine research questions that seek to understand person–situation interactions in educational settings and the abandonment of strict scientism in favor of a more pluralistic philosophical and empirical agendas. Finally, he emphasized the role of context as essential to improved interpretation of educational processes (as expressed most strongly in a situative perspective).

PROGRAM EVALUATION

After spending most of his career on issues concerning the appraisal of individuals, Cronbach's last major undertaking was "clarifying the function of program evaluation and the choices to be made in evaluation planning" (Cronbach, 1991, p. 88). As foundation for this work, Cronbach adopted Ralph Tyler's ideas about how teachers should fashion their instruction to fit their students' needs rather than to implement a standard, rigid, externally-mandated curriculum. Assessment plays an important part, not as a yardstick against which students should measure and be ranked, but as a feedback tool to stimulate teachers' efforts to improve instruction in light of what assessment results told them about their students. Cronbach extended Tyler's ideas beyond the single classroom by applying similar principles to the evaluation of larger educational programs. Post-Sputnik efforts to improve American education produced many proposals for new programs of educational reform. The press for evaluation, coming especially from the National Science Foundation, motivated Cronbach to develop a framework for evaluation design, implementation, and analysis.

The dominant approach to program evaluation at the time was an "objective" methodology. Evaluators should be detached, analyze results apart from the field (preferably statistically), and then reach conclusions based on the results. Limited involvement with program participants was desired in order to ensure neutrality and minimize the evaluator's impact on the program. This approach, argued Cronbach, was wrong if the purpose of evaluation was to provide constructive feedback in real-time for program implementers and clients. Design, implementation, and analysis should reflect this feedback goal. The two contrasting views later came to be known as the "summative" and the "formative" approaches to program evaluation (see Cronbach, 1964, Scriven, 1967).

Cronbach saw the summative approach to evaluation as relying too heavily on experimental principles, thus creating an unacceptable imbalance by emphasizing those aspects of the program that lend themselves to experimental manipulation or random assignment and that could be measured by standardized instruments. Other, equally or even more important, pieces of the puzzle, remained concealed from view. Although other researchers have cautioned against overreliance on the scientific model in evaluation (e.g., Campbell, 1974; Rivlin, 1974), Cronbach's pronouncements went much further. He called for the evaluator to become an educator informed by empirical studies of the program rather than an impartial observer submitting a verdict and drafting a correctional order; he called for all program participants and others in the community who were likely to be affected by the program to give input and become active participants in the evaluation process; he recommended an open-ended style of inquiry, sensitive to unexpected issues or unforeseeable events that may present themselves during the evaluation; he urged evaluators not to hold their insights for the final report, but instead to share what they learn continuously with program constituents in order to foster improvement, even if such real-time adjustments spoiled the scientific elegance of the study.

Many of the ideas have been hashed out with colleagues and students who joined Cronbach in the Stanford Evaluation Consortium that operated between 1975–1979. A truly multidisciplinary group, the Consortium was engaged in practical evaluation work on diverse issues ranging from control of violence in schools to continuing education for lawyers. The group's ideas were first summarized in a volume published in 1980 (Cronbach et al., 1980). Two years later, Cronbach published an independent statement (Cronbach, 1982), as a "guide to practical social theory" (Cronbach, 1989, p. 90). He acknowledged Donald Campbell's ideas as central to helping him form his own: "My writing task became exciting with these strong colleagues to push against" (Cronbach, 1989, p. 90). In many respects Cronbach's formulations and proposals represent a shift toward an emphasis of the external validity of evaluations, which countered Cook and Campbell's (1979) emphasis on internal validity (and its insistence on tight experimental control). Internal validity is concerned with the soundness of the accounts of the particular operation under investigation, such as whether a rise in test scores is due to reduced class size for the schools who participated in an experiment. External validity addresses a broader question: Will this rise in test scores be replicable under different conditions, with different classrooms? Such concerns echo Cronbach's career-long attention to questions of generalizability and ecological validity.

In Cronbach's judgment, the ultimate test for successful evaluations should be "the extent to which they help the political community achieve its ends. The logic of science must come to terms with the logic of politics" (Cronbach, 1982, p. ix). This position has many implications for evaluation design, data collection and analysis, communication of results, and the process by which empirical findings are translated into program improvements. Cronbach's attention to the political realm stems from his conviction that the academic study of human affairs is not an exercise in abstraction. Research programs are valuable to the extent they serve the purpose of improving some aspect of the social reality. The distinction between "basic" and "applied" modes of research is rather blurry in the social sciences, and educational psychologists trying to evaluate the effects of educational programs must balance a set of conflicting demands. Cronbach provided a detailed roadmap for researchers and practitioners of the challenges and prospects of conducting program evaluations.

THE LEGACY OF LEE CRONBACH

Lee Cronbach's contributions to the discipline of educational psychology are many. A short list includes his work of response sets, the conceptualization and technical improvement of the concept of reliability, generalizability theory, the case for construct validation, the rational and evidence for person–situation interactions, the explication of test-based decisions and their evaluation, the formative approach to program evaluation, authoritative textbooks on educational psychology, and psychological testing. Each of these contributions should suffice to induct a scholar in educational psychology's Hall of Fame. Still, the sum is bigger than its parts. In the end, Cronbach's legacy includes empirical evidence, methodological and analytical tools, corpuses of arguments, and practical recommendations embodying a paradigm shift from a rationalist, atomistic, and simple cause-and-effect view of the world, to the realization of the importance of context, inter-connectedness, multiple interacting influences, and plurality of interpretations that characterizes contemporary thinking and practice.

Undoubtedly, the cumulative impact of Cronbach's thinking can be best appreciated from a broad perspective. The importance of his work and vision to educational psychology extends beyond his invaluable methodological innovations and improvements, beyond the many substantive insights he shared with the field regarding testing and evaluation, and beyond the specific conclusions he reached after each major research effort. It lies instead in his crucial contributions to the maturity of educational psychology as a discipline and of the social sciences in general.

Cronbach's influence on the field of educational psychology was clearly reflected in a statement by Gavriel Salomon (1995) as he concluded his term as editor of *Educational Psychologist*:

> Gone are the one-shot trial, short experiments carried out under highly contrived conditions; gone are the simple statistical analyses, and gone is the exclusivity afforded to the quantitative approach. Gone also are the simple-minded questions and with them the simple, two-group horse-race comparisons among ecologically strange treatments . . . " (p. 105)

In many respects the evolution of Cronbach's thinking during his lifetime mirrors broad trends in educational psychology itself, characterized by moving away from a monolithic, authoritarian, and at times simplistic worldview to a more pluralistic, open-ended model that shares as much in common with the humanities as it shares with the physical sciences. Commenting on the possibility of progress in the social sciences, Cronbach (1986) stated:

> It will be the kind of progress seen in architecture, music, and philosophy. Each of these fields has become richer in each century, the contributions of the past remaining a resource for the present. We are better off for having Descartes and Kant, Beethoven and Bartok, Piranesi and Le Corbusier. We do not store up truths or laws. What social scientists mostly harvest are additional concepts and inquiry skills, along with careful records of events observed. Rather than disparaging such inquiry as unproductive, we should cherish its power to nourish culture. (p. 104)

Clearly, educational psychology is better off because of the pioneering efforts of Lee. J. Cronbach.

REFERENCES

APA, AERA, NCME, (1999). *Standards for educational and psychological tests.* Washington, DC: American Psychological Association.

Campbell, D. T. (1974). *Qualitative knowing in action research.* (Occasional Paper). Stanford University, Stanford Evaluation Consortium.

Cook, T. D., & Campbell, D. T. (1979). *Quasi-experimentation: Design & analysis for field settings.* Chicago: Rand McNally.

Cronbach, L. J. (1946). Response sets and test validity. *Educational and Psychological Measurement, 6,* 475–494.

Cronbach, L. J. (1950). Further evidence on response sets and test design. *Educational and Psychological Measurement, 10,* 3–31.

Cronbach, L. J. (1949). *Essentials of psychological testing.* New York: Harper & Brothers.

Cronbach, L. J. (1951). Coefficient alpha and the internal structure of tests. *Psychometrika, 16,* 297–334.

Cronbach, L. J. (1954). *Educational psychology.* New York: Harcourt Brace.

Cronbach, L. J. (1957). The two disciplines of scientific psychology. *American Psychologist, 72,* 671–684.

Cronbach, L. J. (1964). Evaluation for course improvement. In R. W. Heath (Ed.), *New curricula* (pp. 231–248). New York: Harper & Row.

Cronbach, L. J. (1975). Beyond the two disciplines of scientific psychology. *American Psychologist, 30,* 116–127.

Cronbach, L. J. (1982). *Designing evaluations of educational and social programs.* San Francisco: Jossey-Bass.

Cronbach, L. J. (1986). Social inquiry by and for Earthlings. In D. W. Fiske & R. A. Shweder (Eds.), *Metatheory in social science: Pluralities and subjectivities* (pp. 83–107). Chicago: University of Chicago Press.

Cronbach, L. J. (1989). Lee J. Cronbach. In G. Lindzey (Ed.), *A history of psychology in autobiography* (Vol. VIII, pp. 64–93). Stanford, CA: Stanford University Press.

Cronbach, L. J. (1991). Methodological studies—A personal perspective. In R. E. Snow & D. F. Wiley (Eds.), *Improving inquiry in social science* (pp. 385–400). Hillsdale, NJ: Lawrence Erlbaum Associates.

Cronbach, L. J. et al. (1980). *Toward reform of program evaluation.* San Francisco: Jossey-Bass.

Cronbach, L. J., & Gleser, G. C. (1957). *Psychological tests and personnel decisions.* Urbana: University of Illinois Press.

Cronbach, L. J., Gleser, G. C., Nanda, H., & Rajaratnam, N. (1972). *The dependability of behavioral measurements.* New York: Wiley.

Cronbach, L. J., & Meehl, P. E. (1955). Construct validity in psychological tests. *Psychological Bulletin, 52,* 281–302.

Cronbach, L., Rajaratman, N., & Gleser, G. (1963). Theory of generalizability: A liberalization of reliability theory. *British Journal of Statistical Psychology, XVI*(2).

Cronbach, L. J., & Snow, R. E. (1977). *Aptitude and instructional methods.* New York: Irvington.

Lord, F. M., & Novick, M. R. (1968). *Statistical theories of mental test scores.* Reading, MA: Addison-Wesley.

Messick, S. (1991). Psychology and methodology of response styles. In R. E. Snow & D. F. Wiley (Eds.), *Improving inquiry in social science* (pp. 161–200). Hillsdale, NJ: Lawrence Erlbaum Associates.

Rivlin A. M. (1971). *Systematic thinking for social action.* Washington, DC: Brookings Institution.

Salomon, G. (1995). Reflections on the field of educational psychology by the outgoing journal editor. *Educational Psychologist, 30,* 105–108.

Scriven, M. (1967). The methodology of evaluation. In R. Stake et al. (Eds.), *Perspectives on curriculum evaluation* (pp. 39–83). Chicago: Rand-McNally.

Snow, R. E., & Wiley, D. F. (1991). Straight thinking. In R. E. Snow & D. F. Wiley (Eds.), *Improving inquiry in social science* (pp. 1–12). Hillsdale, NJ: Lawrence Erlbaum Associates.

Stanford Aptitude Seminar (2002). *Remaking the concept of aptitude: Extending the legacy of R. E. Snow.* Mahwah, NJ: Lawrence Erlbaum Associates.

Steele, C. M. (1998). Stereotyping and its threat are real. *American Psychologist, 53,* 680–681.

13

The Legacy of Robert Mills Gagné

Peggy A. Ertmer
Purdue University

Marcy P. Driscoll
Walter W. Wager
Florida State University

Asked once about how he developed his integrated theory of instruction, Gagné replied after a slight pause, "You just . . . think it up!" Gagné thought up many things over the span of his career. How he did so can be attributed to a multitude of variables, including his training and disposition to become a psychologist, the types of jobs he held, and the people with whom he worked and collaborated. We begin this chapter with an overview of Gagné's life and the many influences on it within historical and socio-cultural contexts. We hasten to point out that our use of the past tense stems from the fact that Gagné considers his career to be at its end. His final journal publication, a discussion of learning requirements and conditions within the specific context of job training, appeared in the *Training Research Journal* in 1995/1996. Even before then, however, Gagné gave away his professional library in preparation for taking up retirement life in the hills outside of Chattanooga, Tennessee, where he lives quietly with his wife, Pat. Despite their increasingly fragile health, the Gagnés are always pleased to see their friends and former colleagues and are visited with regularity.[1]

INFLUENCE OF HISTORICAL CONTEXT

Born in 1915 and raised in North Andover, Massachusetts, Robert Mills Gagné decided while in high school that he wanted to study psychology. His initial interest in the field was sparked by the popular books he was reading, but this interest was almost crushed by an introductory psychology course he took as an undergraduate at Yale University. Persevering despite the doubts this course raised, Gagné found greater satisfaction in advanced courses and went on to major in psychology, earning his Bachelor of Arts from Yale in 1937 and then his Master of Science and Doctor of Philosophy degrees from Brown University in 1939 and 1940, respectively.[2]

As an undergraduate, Gagné found intriguing the theory of Clark Hull, particularly because of the mathematical relations between adaptive behavior and hypothetical S–R connections that Hull proposed. Later, as a graduate student at Brown, Gagné indicated that his "knowledge of learning research and theory was broadened by courses with Walter Hunter, as well as by new acquaintance with other theorists such as Pavlov, Guthrie, Tolman, and Skinner" (Gagné, 1989, p. 1). Hunter was the department head at Brown and devoted much of his research to the study of cognitive processes. Clarence H. Graham, who was Gagné's graduate advisor, worked on visual mechanisms but shared with Hull an interest in whether mathematical formulations could be employed in the study of learning.

These influences came together in Gagné's doctoral thesis and early research on animal and human learning. He published two papers with Graham in 1940 and a study from his dissertation in 1941. Then came World War II and Gagné's enlistment in the United States Army, where he served in the Aviation Psychology Program until 1945.

Gagné's military service was only the beginning of his involvement with the military, which took various forms and influenced his work throughout his career. His experience in the Aviation Psychology Program, for example, led to a continuing interest in the learning of perceptual-motor tasks and transfer of training. Similarly, his nearly 10 years of work at two Air Force laboratories led to research on simulators and other training devices. Leslie Briggs, who worked closely with Gagné at several points in their respective careers, noted that Gagné's early work in the Air Force influenced the later development of his (a) taxonomy of learning outcomes, (b) concept of learning hierarchies, and (c) related concepts of instructional events and conditions of learning. Even after his official retirement from Florida State University in 1985, Gagné participated in training research projects at the Armstrong Human Resources Laboratory at Brooks Air Force Base in Texas, applying learning and instructional design principles to affect retention of motor skills involved in aircraft and weapon maintenance.

At Princeton University from 1958 to 1962, Gagné developed and studied the concept of the learning hierarchy and demonstrated the importance of prerequisite intellectual skills. During this period, he also became involved in developing a mathematics curriculum, collaborating with the University of Maryland Mathematics Project. This work must have contributed to Gagné's longheld and strong beliefs about teaching basic skills to students. Years later, when national educational reports were published criticizing the mathematical skills of American students and notions of constructivist teaching were creeping into math classrooms, Gagné could be heard to rail in exasperation, "These are basic, prerequisite skills! Students aren't being taught the prerequisites!"

Gagné became Director of Research for the American Institutes for Research in 1962, went on to the University of California at Berkeley in 1966, and moved to Florida State University in 1969. These years reflected a keen interest in school learning and marked the beginning of his contributions to the field of instructional design. During the 1960s, interest abounded in developing new curricula for mathematics and science. Gagné published papers on the implications of instructional objectives, varieties of learning, and the learning of specific capabilities, and he wrote the first edition of *The Conditions of Learning* (Gagné, 1965b).

From the 1970s on, Gagné focused on learning research, developing his ideas about learning capabilities and the internal and external conditions required for these capabilities to be learned. He was particularly interested in the learning outcomes of intellectual skills, and his research on learning hierarchies, problem solving, and conceptual learning reflected that interest. Gagné also emphasized the importance of articulating learning outcomes for instructional design as a basis for planning instruction, assessing performance, and conducting formative evaluation. With Briggs, he published *Principles of Instructional Design* (1974), which provided a systematic process for applying learning research to the design of instruction and training.

During the 1970s and 1980s, Gagné's work increasingly reflected cognitive information processing theory as it was developing in psychology. His third edition of *The Conditions of Learning* (1977) made specific reference to information processing theory and linked the nine events of instruction to the internal cognitive processes they were presumed to activate and support. Similarly, Gagné incorporated the notion of schema into his thinking and writing during the mid-1980s, discussing its importance in understanding how students learn from printed text and suggesting how instructional designers might use that knowledge to create better instructional texts (Gagné, 1986). With David Merrill in 1990, Gagné expanded the concept of schema to describe integrative goals for instruction.

Toward the end of his career, Gagné's work itself became integrative and reflective. His fourth edition of *The Conditions of Learning* (1985) included a chapter proposing an integrative theory of instruction, and his fourth edition of *Principles of Instructional Design* (1992) provided a comprehensive model for curriculum design. Finally, *The Conditions of Learning: Training Applications* (1996) illustrated the implications of Gagné's integrated instructional theory in the context of workplace training.

INFLUENCE OF SOCIOCULTURAL CONTEXT

In the early 1980s, Bob Gagné audiotaped 5-minute introductions to four learning theorists whose work students were assigned to read for one of his classes at Florida State University. He was one of those four theorists, and it is interesting to hear him describe himself in the third person and to note what he chose to say about himself. He mentions, of course, his work on learning hierarchies, his taxonomy of learning outcomes, and the nine events of instruction. But he also mentions, with a slight chuckle, the positions he held immediately before and after World War II at Connecticut College for Women. His initial appointment there was short, because he entered military service when the war began. "Although this period was intellectually stimulating," he wrote about his military service, "it provided little opportunity for independent research" (1989, p. v). His return to Connecticut College in 1945, then, enabled him to embark on a research program that launched his academic career. It is clear that he remembers this time with great fondness.

Besides Connecticut College, Gagné held academic posts at Princeton University, University of California at Berkeley, and Florida State University. He also had a short, temporary appointment at Pennsylvania State University, after leaving the service and before returning to Connecticut College, and he enjoyed a visiting professorship at Monash University in Australia after joining the faculty at Florida State. Gagné's career also reveals substantial time spent in nonacademic positions—8 years as a civilian employee of the Air Force and 4 years directing a nonprofit research organization. In the preface to *Studies of Learning: 50 Years of Research* (1989), Gagné wrote of his career:

> My publication history makes clear that since the time of graduate school, periods of vigorous pursuit of research, coupled with teaching, have alternated with periods dedicated to the administration of research and development.... Research itself often carries its own rewards—particularly seeing a novel idea come to fruition in a network of empirical validations. Teaching that grows out of such a solid foundation is a source of continuing satisfaction. Yet it is also true that administration of research, despite its theft of time for conducting investigations, has afforded me with some of my most memorable opportunities for appreciating the discipline of science and those who pursue it (p. vi).

Even when Gagné was not specifically employed as a research director, he was in fact directing research, whether with doctoral students working on dissertations or colleagues working on research grants. It is noteworthy that most of Gagné's research was collaborative, regardless of the setting in which he found himself. And it is in these collaborations that we can see best some of the specific sociocultural influences on Gagné's work and career.

Everyone who has ever worked with Gagné probably has a story to tell about his curiosity, forthrightness, and ribald sense of humor that all came out in, sometimes, unexpected ways. Bruce Tuckman, a graduate student of Gagné's at Princeton, described him this way: "He was a big man with a big round head, topped by sparse and rapidly disappearing tufts of hair. He wore a shaggy old sweater and strange looking shoes. He had a very loud and gruff voice . . . But he was direct, almost blunt you might say, and he was smart" (1996, p. 4). Tuckman goes on to note that Gagné treated him as an equal, exchanging ideas freely without fear of offense or intimidation.

Whether graduate student or colleague, those who worked with Gagné recall his openness to their ideas, his willingness to listen and to consider suggestions offered on collaborative efforts. It is hard to judge the effect others had on Gagné's thinking and writing, because most of his colleagues emphasize the impact he had on them. However, it bears noting that Gagné worked closely with his Florida State University colleagues throughout his tenure there. He wrote the third and fourth editions of *Principles of Instructional Design* with Walt Wager after Les Briggs' death in 1985, the second edition of *Essentials of Learning for Instruction* (1988) with Marcy Driscoll, and *Selecting Media for Instruction* (1983) with Robert Reiser. He also coauthored with Walter Dick an important chapter on instructional psychology in *Annual Review of Psychology* (Gagné & Dick, 1982). It seems likely, then, that Gagné's relationships with his Florida State colleagues were reciprocal and mutually satisfying.

In 1989, the Learning Systems Institute published a compilation of Gagné's work in *Studies of Learning: 50 Years of Research*, which was a capstone to his career as well as a tribute to his influence on the Instructional Systems program at Florida State and on the field. As Bob Morgan noted in the Foreword, "During the past fifty years, Bob has worked unswervingly on the problems of human learning. His studies have ranged from basic to applied and have examined virtually all the variables associated with the learning process. It is rare scholarship that retains its relevance and timeliness over so many years" (p. iii). It is this scholarship and Gagné's contributions to the field to which we devote our attention for the remainder of this chapter.

BUILDING A LEGACY

Gagné's interest in, and influence on, learning and instructional theory has extended over a period of more than 5 decades. When Gagné received the *Scientific Award for Applications of Psychology* from the American Psychological Association in 1958, it was noted that his "particular genius is the ease with which he moves between research and development, enriching both" (reprinted in Richey, 2000, p. 284). Although Gagné examined a wide range of variables associated with the learning process, his primary focus was on solving practical learning problems that occurred in school or the workplace. In particular, he sought ways to apply principles of learning to real-life instructional and training needs. As Gagné noted in 1962 (cited in Fields, 2000, p. 185) in his article, *Military Training and Principles of Learning*:

> I am not asking, how can a scientific approach be applied to the study of training? Nor
> am I asking how can experimental methodology be applied to the study of training?
> The question is, rather, how can what you know about learning as an event, or as a
> process, be put to use in designing training so that it will be maximally effective?

Beginning with Gagné's early work on transfer of training issues, continuing with his advancement of the cumulative theory of learning and instruction, and culminating in the foundation of the discipline of instructional design, Gagné's work has helped to shape educators' understanding of the entire learning enterprise: the nature of the learner, conditions of the learning process, and different types of learning outcomes. Evidence of his influence can be found in the application of his theories and research to a wide variety of content areas, age levels, and learning environments.

In organizing our discussion of Gagné's major contributions to the field of educational psychology, we have assumed a topical, rather than a chronological, approach. Although we might have examined how Gagné evolved from an experimental psychologist to an instructional theorist, we felt that it was more important to describe how his ideas, which were always focused on finding new ways to improve instruction, built and elaborated on one another. Table 13.1 illustrates how his interests evolved over the years; ideas that were tested in early experimental studies appeared later in his instructional theories and design prescriptions. In a building-block fashion, Gagné's ideas about transfer of training undergirded his idea of learning hierarchies, which, in time, incorporated the idea of classifying the different domains of learning and specifying the necessary prerequisites for learning, which then became the basis for specifying the internal and external conditions of learning. Finally, Gagné integrated all of these ideas within his recommendations for systematically applying the principles of instructional design.

Transfer of Training

In the early stages of his career, Gagné was an experimental psychologist, and his studies focused on the transfer of training. In this early research he studied which factors in the learning environment facilitated or hindered later performance on criterion tasks. He wanted to know how learning a complex skill would be affected if learners were first trained to perform *components* of the skill, and to what degree fidelity in the training situation contributed to later performance on a transfer task.

From 1949 to 1953, Gagné served as the Research Director of the Air Force laboratory that was producing research that guided the design of training devices. Most of the research being conducted at that time was for the military, and the types of tasks being trained were what Gagné called perceptual-motor tasks. These tasks involve the processing of external cues to guide motor behaviors, like typing,

TABLE 13.1

Fifty Years of Research: Gagné's Development as a Researcher

Time Period	Research Topics	Sample Titles
1930s–1950s	Animal and human learning	• External inhibition and disinhibition in a conditioned operant response • Transfer of a motor skill from practice on a pictured representation
1950s–1960s	Military training research	• Training devices and simulators: Some research issues • Military training and principles of learning
1950s–1960s	Aquisition of knowledge	• Some factors in the programming of conceptual learning • Factors in acquiring knowledge of a mathematical task
1950s–1980s	Problem-solving	• Human problem-solving: Internal and external events
1960s	Design of instruction and school curricula	• The analysis of instructional objectives for the design of instruction • Science—a process approach
1960s–1970s	Instructional design	• Some new views on learning and instruction • Formative evaluation applied to a learning hierarchy
1970s–1980s	Outcomes of learning	• Domains of learning • Expectations for school learning
1970s–1980s	Instruction and education	• Educational research and development: How to influence school practices • Planning and authoring computer-assisted instruction lessons

driving a car, or hovering a helicopter. Gagné was one of the first to observe that training devices served two major purposes: performance improvement and performance measurement. Furthermore, the requirements for each purpose were quite different. The criteria for a good measurement device are validity and reliability; that is, the extent to which the device accurately predicts performance on the criterion task. The criterion for a performance improvement device is transfer of training. The critical functions of an improvement device are practice and feedback on the components of the task being trained. In conducting his research on Air Force personnel, Gagné found that mediated representation of reality (e.g., pictures of control panels) served performance improvement functions as well as or better than more realistic physical mock-ups of real equipment. From these findings he concluded, "One may generalize from this example that the answer to the problem of what makes a training device effective is to be sought . . . in viewing [the] training device as a means of making conditions most effective for learning" (Gagné, 1989, p. 86).

TABLE 13.2
Early Taxonomy of Skills

Type of Skill	Examples
Discrimination	• Reading dials
	• Aligning dials and instruments
	• Distinguishing waveforms
Recall	• Identifying components
	• Remembering procedures
Use of symbols	• Reading or interpreting charts, diagrams, and tables
	• Performing numerical operations
Decision making	• Making complex judgments in which several possibilities must be successfully or simultaneously weighed
	• Systematic troubleshooting
Motor skills	• Tool using
	• Making fine adjustments of controls
	• Tracking

This early research set the stage for what later became one of Gagné's major contributions to the field, namely, the differentiation among types of learned behavior and the conditions that facilitate effective learning for each type. While at Princeton in the 1950s, Gagné conducted research on the acquisition of knowledge, including studies with seventh graders, that looked at vertical transfer of learning and prerequisite skills. It was this research that led to the notion of intellectual skills and learning hierarchies. Gagné (1955) developed one of the earliest taxonomies of learning behavior, which is outlined in Table 13.2 and illustrated with examples from early military training procedures. This list gradually evolved into the five major categories of learning and five subtypes of intellectual skills presented in the first edition of *The Conditions of Learning* (Gagné, 1965b).

Throughout his research Gagné focused on the psychological principles of learning. These principles first came from behavioral research and animal studies that primarily centered on the use of reinforcers, so it is not surprising that Gagné considered motivation and reinforcement a major principle of learning. However, he also emphasized a number of other important principles, such as the principles of repeated practice, component practice, establishment of learning sets, response precision, and performance feedback (Gagné, 1954).

In the mid to late 1960s, psychology began moving away from its emphasis on behaviorism to neo-behaviorism or models of cognition. Gagné realized the inadequacy of behavioral theory to explain some of the complex behaviors he was investigating, and so turned to the psychological theories of information processing, especially those of R. C. Atkinson and R. M. Shiffrin, as the foundation for his instructional theories (Gagné, 1965b). In doing so, he built on the assumptions that human beings process information in their environments in a series of stages, including stimulus reception, selective attention, rehearsal in short-term memory, encoding, and long-term memory. Each of these processes is influenced by conditions present in the environment as well as by previous learning. These ideas fit well with Gagné's notion that instruction comprises facilitating information processing for the purpose of developing human capabilities. The way to do this, he felt, was to attend to the external conditions that support internal processing of information—the environmental and mental conditions that facilitate learning.

Learning Hierarchies

In 1968, Gagné proposed the theory of cumulative learning. This theory was based on the premise that new learning depends primarily on combining previously acquired and recalled learned entities, as well as on their potentialities for transfer of learning (Gagné, 1968). According to Gagné, "There is a specifiable minimal prerequisite for each new learning task. Unless the learner can recall this prerequisite capability . . . he can not learn the new task" (1970, p. 29). This theory was in contrast to developmental theories of the time and, particularly, Piaget's theory of cognitive adaptation. The theory of cumulative learning was grounded in Gagné's research on vertical learning transfer and was consistent with the notion of an intellectual skills hierarchy (see Fig. 13.1). The hierarchy indicated which types of skills were prerequisites for which other types of skills.

The first skills in the intellectual skills hierarchy were perceptual discrimination skills that allowed learners to differentiate stimuli in the environment. Discriminations included visual, aural, tactile, and even taste and smell discriminations. Part of attaining discrimination skills depended on physical capabilities, such as the ability to see colors. A person with color-blindness couldn't possibly have the prerequisite capabilities for learning concepts based on the ability to differentiate colors. That would make it impossible to apply rules related to these concepts, and consequently to solve problems that required color discriminations. Yet, the physical capability is a necessary but not a sufficient condition for discrimination skills. An individual can learn to make finer and finer discriminations through a process of practice and feedback. It might take a wine taster many years to discriminate subtleties that others might never detect. Gagné classified these types of learned capabilities as the "ability to discriminate." While this might seem obvious today, it was cutting-edge thinking at the time.

The next level of skills in the hierarchy is concept learning. Gagné described two classes of concepts: concrete concepts and defined concepts. Concrete concepts defines the ability to put objects into classes through an analysis of their physical attributes. Thus, if a child sees a dog that she has never before seen, and on seeing it, calls it a dog; the child is exhibiting concrete concept behavior. The child has learned a rule, albeit not explicitly, for putting certain instances of animals into the category "dog" as a result of its physical attributes. One might ask, "What were the prerequisite discriminations that the child had to make?" The child had to be able to see that this animal was physically similar to other animals identified as dogs, and

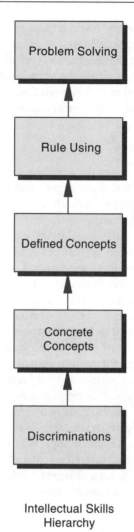

Intellectual Skills
Hierarchy

FIG. 13.1.   Steps in the intellectual skills learning hierarchy.

yet different from other animals identified as cats, horses, birds, and so on. If the child couldn't make these discriminations, she couldn't have learned the concept "dog." Gagné described this type of learned capability as the "ability to identify."

Next on the hierarchy are defined concepts. Defined concepts may or may not have physical referents. For example, consider the concept "seat." Much broader than a chair, couch, or stool, all are examples of seats. An object is classified as a seat if it fits the definition, "Something designed so that one sits on it." Now, one can see a seat, as it has physical attributes, but it isn't a specific set of physical attributes that are critical to proper classification. Rather, it is whether the object fits the classification criteria "was this object designed for someone to sit on?" Not all defined concepts have obvious physical referents. We might identify someone's political position as "conservative." This is a concept, and one could write a rule for classifying individuals as liberal or conservative, but they probably couldn't be classified by mere physical attributes. Instead, individuals would be classified by the verbal statements, opinions, or behaviors they expressed and that fit into the respective descriptions of the categories. The artifacts still have physical characteristics and require discrimination skills, but the link is not nearly as clear as in the case of concrete concepts. The learned capability verb for defined concepts is "classify."

The next highest skill is rule using. Rules are formal relationships among concepts, concepts and rules, or among rules. For example, consider the familiar spelling rule, "i before e except after c, and when sounded like a, as in neighbor and weigh." Here we have the concepts "before," "except," and "sounded" put into a statement that guides our spelling behavior. Gagné defined principles as a form of rules. So, a principle like, "thicker air moves toward thinner air," is a rule—a relationship among concepts. Whereas rules are often taught as verbal propositions, the evidence that individuals have learned a rule is that they can apply the rule in some way. Thus, the learned capability verb is "demonstrate." An example of an assessment of a rule-using objective is: "demonstrate, by use of an airfoil, that thicker air moves towards thinner air."

At the top of the intellectual skills hierarchy are higher-order and problem-solving skills. Gagné used these two terms interchangeably. A problem is a situation for which learners have no ready rule to apply to reach a solution. If they did, it would be rule-using. Gagné describes problem-solving as a generative learning process. What is being generated are new rules or procedures that lead to the solution of the problem. What is being learned is how to build new rules and combine old ones. The prerequisite skills are other rules and concepts. An example might be, "The student will generate a prediction of whether the stock market will rise or fall, based on five indicators of his choice." The learned capability verb is "generate."

Educational Implications. Gagné researched learning hierarchies extensively in the area of mathematics and his findings supported the principles of prerequisite learning. According to Gagné, readiness to learn depended on an individual's possession of the prerequisite skills for the skills she was about to learn. Thus, being able to complete a simple income tax return requires that the learner knows what income is, knows how to read a W2 form, and knows how to determine her filing status. For Gagné, this was a critical point, and prompted him to focus on the learner rather than the teacher. However, equally important for informing practice was Gagné's belief that the learner needed instructions to make the leap from one level of learning to the next. These instructions or instructional communications were thought to be most effective if they were designed to support the learners' internal events of information processing.

Design of Instruction

Gagné culled from the psychological literature what he called generalizable principles of learning. These principles, then, were used to guide the design of instruction. For example, Gagné (1972) described how principles from N. E. Miller—motivation, cue, response, and reward—were derived from behaviorist theories of behavior change, were frequently found in learning situations, and seemed to apply to many different types of learning. In the same chapter, he elaborated on B. F. Skinner's extension of these principles as well as other principles such as successive approximation, shaping, stimulus control, and schedules of reinforcement and chaining. These principles were used, initially, to train animals to make discriminations, and later as a foundation for programmed instructional materials to teach information. Yet, Gagné (1972) saw deficiencies in principles derived from behaviorist theories for developing instruction, especially instruction aimed at the development of concepts and principles. He wrote:

> In my view, these principles are only of general applicability to the learning of certain other kinds of tasks, particularly concepts and principles. For example, if one is concerned that a student acquire an understanding of the principle of separation of powers as defined by the Constitution, or an understanding of the principle of centrifugal force, the notion of successive approximation provides only a very general prescription for instruction. It says that one must bring such behavior under finer stimulus control, but it does not specify how to do this . . . It seems to me, therefore, that although some specificity about instruction in certain tasks is definitely gained from Skinnerian theory, for certain others of particular importance in college-level instruction, the suggestions remain highly general. (p. 28)

Later, Gagné made some very specific suggestions about the ways in which psychological learning principles might inform curriculum development efforts. In 1963, he published an article in the inaugural issue of the *Journal of Research in Science Teaching* (cited in Gagné, 1989, p. 243) entitled, "A Psychologist's Counsel on Curriculum Design." He stated:

> I was sometimes asked what psychological knowledge could contribute to such development efforts. I pointed out some broad principles derived from learning research, and emphasized in addition, the importance of behavioral objectives, the organization of learning content, and the need to assess learning outcomes.

Gagné's reference to these three additional components reflected his ongoing approach to the effective design of instruction. His emphases on behavioral objectives and the assessment of learning outcomes related to his ideas about the domains of learning and the need to match both instructional and assessment strategies to the type of learning involved. His emphasis on the organization of learning content referred to the use of learning hierarchies and the identification of the internal and external conditions that supported each type of skill in the hierarchy. Each of these is discussed in more detail in the following.

Instructional Objectives and the Domains of Learning. Gagné was not the first educational psychologist to stress the importance of instructional objectives. In a chapter written for *Teaching Machines and Programmed Learning* (1965a), Gagné emphasized the importance of previous work in this area by Tyler (1949, 1950), Skinner (1958, 1959), and Mager (1962), among others. Besides the programmed instruction movement, Gagné (1989) described additional roots for this movement lying within educators' interest in measuring educational achievement, which began at the University of Chicago, and in programs of research on military training, particularly the training of Air Force technicians.

While Mager (1962) may have popularized the use of objectives, Gagné helped identify the instructional implications of defining and classifying them. For Gagné, the primary purpose of objectives had less to do with determining what learners were expected to know or do after instruction than with *classifying* the type of behaviors to be learned. Gagné (1989) stressed that specifying objectives allowed designers to "draw distinctions among the different classes of behavior to be established as a basis for inferences concerning how modification of preexisting behavior can be undertaken" (p. 254). According to Gagné, "Unambiguous and complete statements of tasks to be performed when instruction is finished make possible the identification of certain categories of behavior to be learned" (p. 280).

By specifying and classifying objectives, designers could then determine the internal and external conditions of learning that would be most effective for facilitating learning. Over the years Gagné categorized types of learning in different ways, finally settling on the five major types: (1) Attitudes; (2) Motor Skills; (3) Verbal Information, (4) Cognitive Strategies, and (5) Intellectual Skills, which consists of the subtypes: (a) Discriminations, (b) Concrete Concepts, (c) Defined Concepts, (d) Rule Learning, and (e) Problem Solving (Gagné, 1965b). Definitions and examples are included in Table 13.3.

Gagné's classification was built around the prescriptive nature of the conditions of learning. Each of these forms of behavior carried a differential implication regarding the conditions of learning needed for its establishment. Gagné speculated that the type of mental processing required for achieving outcomes in each category was qualitatively different from the mental activities required in other categories. Depending on what the objective was at any point in the entire sequence, therefore, a learning program needed to make a particular set of provisions in order for learning to occur in an optimal fashion. Thus, defining objectives was important to Gagné because it allowed the designer to sequence them in such a way that higher-order skills were taught after lower-order skills. Furthermore, designers could, after classifying the objectives, make important decisions regarding how to teach each type.

Conditions of Learning (Organization of Content). Gagné believed that although general learning principles such as contiguity, repetition, and reinforcement, emphasized by learning theorists of the time, played a role in most types of

TABLE 13.3
The Domains of Learning

Type of Learning	Definition	Example
Attitudes	• Influence personal choices of action • Personal feelings or beliefs	• Chooses to recycle newspapers • Desires to do one's best
Motor skills	• Enable learners to perform movements • Physical capabilities	• Rides a bicycle • Pumps gasoline
Verbal information	• Enable learners to communicate names, facts, principles, generalizations • Declarative knowledge	• Names capital of Colorado • States definition of a theory
Intellectual skills	• Enable learners to make discriminations, identify and classify concepts, apply and generate rules • Procedural knowledge	• Distinguishes dogs from cats • Generates a rule for predicting rainfall • Follows steps in making lasagna
Cognitive strategies	• Enable learners to organize and monitor cognitive processes • Self-regulatory processes	• Initiates study strategies • Recognizes lack of comprehension

learning, there were specific conditions in addition to these that were appropriate for learning concepts, principles, and rules. He described those instructional conditions both as generalized events of instruction and as specific conditions of learning for each type of learning capability. According to Gagné (1989), "The *external* conditions for each particular type of learning form the basis for instruction. The *internal* conditions are retained capabilities of the student, which have been established by previous learning" (p. 29, emphasis added).

Gagné pointed out that once we know that a person is going to learn, for example, a concept, we know that certain conditions must exist both within the learner and external to the learner for that learning to take place. These required conditions of learning did not vary between people or even between subject areas. In other words, the psychological conditions required for learning a concept in mathematics were identical to the conditions required for learning a concept in grammar.

Internal Events.   After the objectives for a unit of instruction were defined and classified, the question to be addressed was, "what are the conditions which specify (so far as known) optimal conditions for learning the tasks that involve this type of behavior?" (Gagné, 1989, p. 266). In the case of each category, Gagné considered this answer in terms of a hierarchy of behaviors; thus, the most important condition for learning each type of objective was the preestablishment of a lower-order behavior in the learner. This implied that instruction should be sequenced such that associations preceded discriminations, which preceded concepts, which preceded principles, and so on. Thus, learners' previously acquired capabilities were of critical importance to the effectiveness of instruction. It was important to know, not only the various sub-skills involved in learning a certain task, but also the specific skills learners already knew when beginning the instruction.

External Events. Gagné (1962) noted that, 97% to 100% of the time, the acquisition of learning sets at successively higher stages of the hierarchy was dependent on mastery of subordinate learning sets. However, he noted that the establishment of prerequisite behaviors was a necessary but not sufficient condition for successive learning. To the necessity of prerequisites, he added the need for "instructions" (communications to the learner). This, in 1962, was the genesis for the "Events of Instruction."

Gagné believed that if there were to be a theory of productive learning, it must deal with the independent variables related to both subordinate capabilities and instructions, as well as their interactions, in bringing about changes in human performance. For example, one set of instructions might make it possible for the learner to *identify the required terminal behavior*, another to *identify the elements of the stimulus situation*, and yet another to establish *high recall*. Although these are expressed in the form of what the instructions might make it possible to do, they aren't far from some of the instructional components, now referred to as the Events of Instruction, that describe what instruction should do, such as *inform the learner of the objective*, *provide learning guidance*, and *provide practice and feedback*.

In the first edition of *The Conditions of Learning* (1965b), Gagné included a section entitled, "Component Functions of the Instructional Situation" which, in later editions, was referred to as the "Events of Instruction." These events, listed below, referred to instructional features that should be included in the teaching/learning situation, such as a description of the intended outcomes, the required prerequisite knowledge, and the provision for informative feedback. Gagné argued that these nine events should be considered as potential ways of providing external support for the internal act of learning. The events served as a major vehicle for incorporating the conditions of learning into an instructional situation and served as a framework for the design of lessons. These events were based on empirical observations of the procedures of instruction and the information-processing model of human learning and memory. They incorporated both behavioral and cognitive components and included:

1. Gaining attention
2. Informing the learner of the objective
3. Stimulating recall of prior learning
4. Presenting the stimulus
5. Providing learner guidance

6. Eliciting the performance
7. Giving informative feedback
8. Assessing performance
9. Enhancing retention and transfer

The nine events follow the typical sequence of a direct instruction lesson, and effective lessons are assumed to include all nine events in one form or another (McCown, Driscoll, & Roop, 1996). However, the nature of the instruction in any one event might be expected to differ depending on the category of learned capability expected as the outcome of instruction. For example, learning motor skills will require a different design of events than those required for learning verbal information or those required for learning intellectual skills. In addition, the order and who provides each event may change depending on the method of instruction.

Assessment of Learning Outcomes.   Gagné (1989) suggested that planning for assessment should occur *at the same time* that curriculum design is undertaken, rather than later and separately. Just as different types of learning outcomes re-quire different conditions for learning, so too do they require different forms of assessment. Thus, the development of appropriate tests is aided when curriculum designers think about objectives in terms of the learning category to which they belong, and then simultaneously consider how they will teach and assess each specific objective.

According to Gagné (1989), a test item "is expected to assess whether or not a student has achieved a kind of performance (like 'adding integers' or 'distin-guishing the functions of concave and convex lenses') that he could not do before instruction began" (p. 248). He continued, "Tests are needed to probe the students' capabilities, to determine whether these have in fact been changed by exposure to a curriculum and whether the objectives of the curriculum have been met."

Gagné (1989), like Glaser (1963) and others before him, advocated the use of criterion-referenced, rather than norm-referenced, tests that emphasized learn-ers' levels of competency following instruction, as opposed to determining their rank among fellow learners. In addition, he stressed the importance of systemati-cally avoiding "the pitfalls of restricted generalizability, over-verbalization, routine procedure-following, and unrepresentative performance outcomes" (Gagné, 1989, p. 247). Although there are a "number of places in a curriculum where learning verbalizations is the important thing to do, there are many other instances in which giving verbal answers to verbal questions is not the proper objective for learn-ing" (p. 246). Gagné believed that this was particularly true in science, in which concepts and principles must be applied to objects and events in the real world. He explained, "Objectives of instruction may include those of retention and, most significantly, of *transferability*. The latter kind of objective appears to be the aim of achievement measurement as typically employed. It is suggested that both forms of measurement are important for a full understanding of the changes in behavior effected by learning (1989, p. 281, emphasis in original).

Educational Applications and Implications. Gagné's ideas about learning hierarchies and the domains of learning, internal and external conditions of learning, and the design of instruction were applied to the curricular materials that Gagné helped design throughout his career. Besides math and science instruction, Gagné's theories have been applied in areas as diverse as program design, cooperative learning, military training, English as a second language, writing skills, social studies, and advanced economics (Fields, 2000). His theories also have been used extensively in training curriculum design in the private sector, as well as by governmental agencies.

One of most influential projects Gagné participated in during his career was the development of a program in elementary science called, "Science—A Process Approach," a project sponsored by the American Association for the Advancement of Science (American Psychological Association, cited in Wager & Driscoll, 2000). According to Fields (2000), this particular science curriculum was influential in schools and colleges during the 1960s and 1970s and provides one of the most pervasive examples of the application of Gagné's theories and research to school-based materials (American Association for the Advancement of Science Commission on Science Education, 1965). Furthermore, this particular orientation to teaching elementary science remained tremendously influential in science texts and other commercially published science materials, well into the 1980s. The process approach used in these materials was based on the idea that learners are taught to think and solve problems like a scientist. According to Gagné this was accomplished by helping learners master prerequisite skills prior to learning more complex skills. Following a systematic progression, learners were eventually advanced to a level where they were able to carry out scientific thinking that was disciplined and systematic and connected to the 'process of science' (cited in Fields, 2000).

Over the years, Gagné, together with Briggs, developed a wide range of instructional prescriptions that, taken together, constitute a theory of instruction because different methods of instruction are prescribed for different situations (Petry, Mouton, & Reigeluth, 1987). The Gagné–Briggs theory of instruction comprised three major sets of prescriptions: (1) different methods of instruction were required for each of the five categories of learning, (2) the nine events of instruction should be included to develop any desired capability, and (3) instruction for intellectual skills should be sequenced such that lower-order skills were learned prior to higher-order skills. Thus, a teacher, in applying these principles, would aim to determine the type of learning required and vary the instructional conditions for each type of learning; arrange for appropriate instructional conditions to support the internal processes involved in learning; and assure prerequisite skills, including identifying component skills, and carefully arranging and sequencing instruction to promote understanding, remembering, and transfer to new skills.

Summary. Gagné's instructional theory influenced the design of instruction at both the macro and micro levels. His ideas concerning learning hierarchies and the domains of learning represented his overall orientations to designing instruction, and thus can be thought of at the macro level. The events of instruction dealt with principles at the micro design level—that is, at the level of individual lessons. Gagné's thoroughness in specifying instructional conditions to support the transition process from initial to goal states for each type of learning had a tremendous impact on instructional theory of his time. Case and Bereiter (1984) suggested that the concept of sequencing intellectual skills and allowing instruction to move systematically toward higher-order skills while building on prerequisite skills catapulted Gagné beyond the behaviorists of that time.

Foundation of Instructional Design

In the early 1960s, the concepts that were being developed in the areas of task analysis, objective specification, and criterion-referenced testing were brought together and discussed in articles by Gagné, Glaser, and Silvern (cited in Reiser, 1987). According to Reiser, these individuals were among the first to use terms such as "system development," "systematic instruction," and "instructional system" to describe systems approach procedures similar to those employed today in the design of instruction. Gagné (with Briggs & Wager, 1988) defined an *instructional system* as an "arrangement of resources and procedures used to promote learning" (p. 19) and *instructional systems design* as the "systematic process of planning instructional systems" (p. 20). However, when designing small instructional systems such as courses, units within courses, or individual lessons, the term was typically shortened to *instructional design* to suggest that the focus was a piece of instruction itself, rather than the total instructional system.

Gagné, together with Briggs, was instrumental in developing a way to transfer laboratory-based learning principles, gleaned from military and industrial training, to create an efficient way of developing curriculum and instruction for schools. Gagné specialized in the use of instructional task analysis to identify required sub-skills and essential conditions of learning. Brigg's expertise was in systematic methods of designing training programs to save companies time and money in training their personnel. When they combined their talents, the result was a step-by-step process known as the systems approach to instructional design or systematic instructional design (Roblyer, Edwards, & Havriluk, 1997).

The main steps of the design process can be classified into three main functions: analysis of the learning situation (including specification of objectives), design and development of instruction (including the instructional strategy and materials), and

Analysis			Design/Development			Evaluate
Analyze Goals	Analyze Instruction	Analyze Learners	Develop Assessments	Develop Strategies and Materials	Choose Media	Evaluate Instruction

FIG. 13.2. Steps in the instructional design process.

formative evaluation and revision of the instruction. Each step is described in the following and illustrated in Fig. 13.2.

Analysis. In the analysis phase of the process, the designer learns as much as possible about the goal or task for which learners are being prepared (goal analysis) and about the learners themselves (learner analysis). During the goal analysis stage, the designer specifies the end-goal of instruction and then classifies it into one of the five categories of learning outcomes. This is considered critical to the other steps in the design process since different types of learning outcomes suggest different types of learning strategies and different types of assessment measures.

Following the goal analysis stage, the designer determines the specific skills or steps required for reaching the end-goal (instructional analysis). This instructional analysis takes the form of either a *task* or procedural analysis, which lists the skills involved in each step of the procedure, an *information-processing* analysis, which reveals the mental operations used by a person to complete a complex skill, or a *learning-task* analysis, which lists the subordinate skills needed to master a higher-order intellectual skill. A detailed task analysis also makes it possible to define specific and detailed performance objectives, which, in turn, can be readily translated into criterion-based test items, used to assess students' learning.

An important component of the instructional analysis is the categorization of each of the super- and subordinate skills into the five domains of learning. Completion of this step helps to ensure that designers will include, within their instructional designs, the conditions most effective for each of the different types of learning outcomes.

A learner analysis is conducted prior to, in conjunction with, or subsequent to the completion of the instructional analysis. The purpose is to determine which of the required prerequisite skills the learners have already mastered. In addition, designers identify abilities, traits, and attitudes of the target audience that might make instruction more or less difficult. As much as possible, instruction is designed to take advantage of what learners already know, while filling in critical gaps in knowledge, skill, or attitude.

Design and Development.   In this phase, the designer first determines, and then develops, the instructional strategy, that is, the plan for assisting learners with their study efforts for each performance objective. The instructional plan includes information about how the instruction will be presented, which learning activities the learners will complete, the sequence in which they will be completed, and the media that will be used to present the instruction. According to Gagné, "the purpose of all instruction is to provide the events of instruction" (Gagné & Driscoll, 1988, p. 28). It didn't matter who or what presented each event, as long as they were successfully performed. Depending on the learning domain of the intended goal of instruction, the events might be implemented in a slightly different order or receive greater or lesser attention. Once the plan is complete, the instructional materials (printed or other media) are selected or developed to specifically convey the specified events of instruction.

Evaluating and Revising Instruction.   The final design phase involves gathering formative evaluation data for revising and improving instruction so as to make it as effective as possible for the largest number of students. At this point, the focus is not on determining how to assess *learners'* performance (which is actually considered during the analysis phase), but on evaluating the *instructional materials*. This stage in materials development is probably one of the most frequently overlooked, yet without it, the instructional design process is considered incomplete. At this stage, the designer gathers information from target learners to determine where the instruction is inaccurate or hard to follow and then makes suggested revisions to improve the effectiveness of the materials.

Educational Implications.   Gagné's work has had significant impact on educational practitioners, in general, and on instructional designers, specifically. Gagné's approach to instructional design illustrates how he translated his instructional theory into practice. In general, Gagné equated the design process to lesson planning and noted: "the purpose is to ensure that the necessary instructional events are provided to the learner" (Gagné & Driscoll, 1988, p. 35). He continued, "Key steps in the planning process include: (1) classifying the lesson objectives by type, (2) listing the needed instructional events, (3) choosing a medium of instruction capable of providing those events, and (4) incorporating appropriate conditions of learning into the prescriptions indicating how each event will be accomplished by the lesson" (p. 35). These four steps highlight the practical applications of Gagné's work in terms of two main principles: the importance of classifying outcomes of learning and providing the appropriate internal and external conditions of learning needed to accomplish each type. Thus, if a physics teacher were developing a lesson to help her students understand the effect of friction on velocity, she would: first, determine that this involved an intellectual skill (although verbal information and psychomotor skills may also play a role); second, pay particular attention to the events of instruction related to gaining attention, presenting the stimulus material (the content), eliciting performance, and providing feedback; third, use a hands-on experiment that would allow the students to test their ideas about friction; and fourth, carefully consider which concepts and rules the students already understood and which would be presented by the lesson.

IMPACT OF A LEGACY

According to Richey (2000), "Gagné's career was eclectic—encompassing research, teaching, administration, and the practice of instructional design. His work pertained to the general study of human learning, military research and training, the education of children, workplace education and training, as well as higher education" (p. 144). When colleagues and friends are asked to reflect on the impact of Gagné's work, it is interesting to note the variety of roles they emphasize. While some point to Gagné's role as an instructional theorist, others emphasize his role in the foundation of instructional design, while still others note how he bridged the gap between behaviorists and cognitivists. Given the length of his career (over 50 years) as well as the diversity of his work, Gagné's impact is, indeed, pervasive. In the following sections, we highlight the impact of his work as it relates to our understanding of the nature of the learner, the learning process, optimal conditions of learning, and important outcomes of learning.

Impact on Nature of the Learner

Gagné helped educators understand that learners' ability to master higher-order skills depended on the acquisition of prerequisite lower-order skills rather than on a specific stage of intellectual development. Gagné (1968) emphasized the influence of learning, rather than growth, on human behavioral development. According to Gagné (1968), "the child progresses from one point to the next in his development, not because he acquires a dozen new associations, but because he learns an ordered set of capabilities which build upon each other in progressive fashion through the processes of differentiation, recall, and transfer of learning" (reprinted in Richey, 2000, p. 44).

Gagné stressed that students should be able to learn more advanced or complex skills as a result of their previous learning. Furthermore, he indicated that capabilities learned in school should provide students with the background and skills they need to accomplish practical things in their lives or future jobs (Fields, 2000). Although Gagné never referred to his instructional approach or theory as learner-centered, his belief that learners need to acquire practical and transferable skills suggests a genuine concern for meeting some of learners' most important needs.

Impact on Nature of the Learning Process

According to Gagné, people acquired all of their attitudes, values, skills, and knowledge through learning. Learning equipped humans with the capability to perform a variety of actions. Gagné classified these performances as five types of learning outcomes and suggested that different instructional conditions (both internal and external) were needed to promote each type of learning, and further-more, that different types of assessment were needed to adequately assess each type of learning.

Gagné's beliefs about the nature of the learning process led to the application of his instructional theories to the systematic design of instruction. Gagné's theory is considered foundational to existing "conditions-based" models of instructional design (ID) that are based on the assumptions that learning can be classified into cat-egories that require similar cognitive processes for learning—internal conditions of learning—and within these categories of learning, similar instructional supports are needed to facilitate learning—external conditions of learning (Smith & Ragan, 2000). Models that are based on this approach include those by Merrill (1983); Reigeluth (1979); Merrill, Li, and Jones (1990a, 1990b); and Smith and Ragan (1993; 1999).

Optimal Conditions of Instruction

As noted previously, Gagné's work, as an instructional theorist, focused on pre-scribing the components of instruction that supported learning. Drawing on knowl-edge generated by learning research and theory, he attempted to identify condi-tions of instruction that would optimize learning, retention, and transfer. Thus, Gagné explicitly described which, and how, features of the environment should be arranged to intentionally promote learning by relating specific instructional events to learning processes and learning outcomes. Gagné's ideas about learning hierarchies addressed the necessary *internal* conditions of learning, whereas his events of instruction addressed the necessary *external* conditions. His nine events of instruction included events directed toward motivating the learner; providing direction, guided practice, and feedback within the instruction; and identifying effective and meaningful ways to assess students and to promote the transfer of learning.

According to Smith and Ragan (2000), Gagné's instructional theory, and specif-ically his conditions-based propositions, have already spawned at least two gen-erations of instructional design theories. In addition, his influence has been noted as extending beyond ID theory into other areas of educational design, including curriculum design. In fact, many of Gagné's ideas have become so entrenched in practice that people fail to recognize them as originating with Gagné. Fields (2000) emphasized Gagné's prominent place within the field of instructional design when he stated:

His evolution from experimental psychologist to instructional and learning theorist, whose focus became one of application of cognitive theories to ID, is indicative of not only his flexibility, but also his interest in ID practice. His place in the history of ID practice is most certainly secure from both a foundational as well as an application perspective. (p. 202)

Important Learning-Instruction Outcomes

Gagné approached theoretical issues from an "applied science" perspective. He studied students' learning in demanding, realistic settings and maintained an ongoing emphasis on specifying performance objectives and establishing coherent links between goals and assessment measures. As Gagné noted, "The questions addressed in my research have usually been practical ones, or at least have been strongly influenced by practical considerations" (1989, p. 6). Always cognizant of the gap between theory and practice, Gagné advocated the importance of teaching and assessing real-world skills—not at a superficial level, but at the level of application and transfer. While his early research was directed toward helping military personnel acquire, retain, and apply perceptual-motor skills, later work focused on helping learners, of all ages, master intellectual skills, particularly problem-solving skills.

ASSESSING THE IMPACT OF A LEGACY

"It is difficult to overestimate the impact R. M. Gagné has had on instructional theory," Smith and Ragan (2000) concluded. "Although his has not been the only important voice in shaping the field, it has been an enormously influential one by virtue of the prodigious volume of original work which is at once bold in its conceptions and careful in scholarship" (pp. 173–174). In the final analysis, then, what can be said about the overall impact of Gagné's writing and thinking?

STRENGTHS OF GAGNÉ'S WORK

Perhaps the most notable strengths of Gagné's work are its comprehensiveness and its integration, and it is hard to speak of one without referring to the other. In her book on learning and instructional theories, Driscoll (2000) pointed out that most theories suffer from a limitation of scope. They focus on one or another aspect of learning, such as acquiring conceptual knowledge or developing self-regulatory skills, but ignore other aspects of learning. Gagné's theory of instruction, by contrast, is far more comprehensive, incorporating "a taxonomy of learning outcomes, specific learning conditions required for the attainment of each outcome, and the nine events of instruction" (Driscoll, p. 347). Gagné's instructional design model

(Gagné et al., 1992) further expands this scope with procedures for designing and developing course-level curricula.

Gagné (1989) noted that his taxonomy comprising five categories of learning outcomes describes "categories of human capabilities that result from learning, and that make possible certain distinctive types of human performance" (p. 483). He believed that these five categories account completely for the variety of capabilities humans can learn. Asked why he proposed five types of learning outcomes, Gagné once replied, "Because . . . [slight pause] . . . that's all there are!" In fact, although other taxonomic schemes have been proposed that bear similarity to Gagné's (e.g., Bloom, Merrill), none of the others included the cognitive, psychomotor, and affective domains.

Likewise, Gagné's work has set the standard for explicating internal and external learning conditions necessary for the acquisition of each learned capability. As noted earlier, Gagné's theory has served as the foundation for other models that have attempted to exemplify and elaborate on his ideas. Even these efforts, however, have typically focused on only a portion of Gagné's comprehensive approach. With Component Display Theory, for example, Merrill and his colleagues (e.g., Merrill, 1983) elaborated learning conditions only for facts, concepts, rules, and principles, which are all cognitive in nature and contained within three of Gagné's five categories of learning outcomes (verbal information, intellectual skills, and cognitive strategies).

Finally, Gagné's work is integrative in the sense that it is theoretically based (in applying psychological theories such as information processing), theory-building (in its articulation of learning conditions for specified outcomes) and empirical (in deriving the nine events of instruction from observations and testing the validity of learning hierarchies). As noted earlier, Gagné's work is also applied science; he expected the results of his work to have implications for educational practitioners, whether teachers or instructional designers.

LIMITATIONS OF GAGNÉ'S WORK

In some respects, the strengths of Gagné's work are also the source of its limitations. It is hard to be both broad and comprehensive and at the same time be specific and complete. Smith and Ragan (1999), for example, proposed supplementing Gagné's nine events of instruction with learner-initiated strategies because they believed Gagné's events are insufficient for self-learning. Likewise, Merrill's (1983) Component Display Theory and Reigeluth's (1979) Elaboration Theory extended and refined parts of Gagné's theory that were perceived to be incomplete.

The systematic analysis of Gagné's approach to instructional design has also come under criticism, especially in recent years. According to Orey and Nelson (1997) for instance:

A systematic approach such as that typified by the work of Gagné and Briggs (Gagné, Briggs, & Wager, 1992) is not particularly applicable to situations in which incidental learning, discovery-based learning or other forms of instruction are desired . . . [It] assume[s] that content can be sufficiently structured and that enough activities can be provided for the learners to acquire the desired knowledge and skills. . . . (pp. 283–284)

Lent and Van Patten (1997) argued as well that following systematic prescriptions for building skills is not always effective in teaching adult learners, citing Carroll's (1990) experience that "learners often tenaciously tried to accomplish real tasks, confounding the step-by-step guidance of their training materials" (p. 7). They further expressed concern that adult learners might refuse to cooperate during training and noted that the field of adult development and learning has been largely ignored by Gagné.

Errors of omission rather than errors of commission best characterize the limitations of Gagné's work. While he had begun to incorporate notions from schema theory into his framework, Gagné made little or no mention of the work of such people as Piaget, Bandura, or Donald Norman, whose ideas have clear relevance to his own. Perhaps it was a matter of time. Perhaps, as Smith and Ragan (2000) suggested, "Gagné has left some questions for future researchers and theorists to work out" (p. 173).

CONCLUSION

Robert Gagné has left a legacy that comprises over 50 years of research and publication contributions to the fields of educational psychology and instructional systems. His legacy is extended through the continued efforts of the students he mentored, many of whom have gone on to distinguish themselves in these same fields. Gagné crossed the line between basic research and applied psychology, and it is our good fortune that his interest was the total range of human learning, rather than just one type of learning. The Conditions of Learning provided a way to look at, not only how a particular type of behavior is learned, but also how the learning of one type affects the learning of other types. Gagné differentiated between behavior and the potential or capability for behavior, an important distinction, as was his differentiation between performance assessment and performance improvement.

The seemingly simple yet profoundly important connection he made between information processing theory and the external events of instruction served as a foundation for the development of a theory of instruction that will keep his name among the giants of psychology. The events of instruction appear in almost every instructional design text, in one format or another, confirming the belief that learning is a process that can be facilitated by instructional intervention. Gagné's research on hierarchies provided a foundation for practices related to learner readiness and basic skills education.

The work of R. M. Gagné may be slightly overlooked today as the pendulum swings toward theories of constructivism and practices based in social theory. However, we believe that Gagné's work is timeless. Gagné will be rediscovered, much in the manner of the current resurgence of interest in Dewey, as educators once again discover the practicality of his work for curriculum and instructional design. His research is meticulously documented and clearly written. His theories and principles are easily converted into rules for practice. The care he took in articulating not only those principles, but also his thoughts about how they relate to other theories of the time, provide a firm foundation for future research. Robert M. Gagné is truly one of the most influential educational psychologists of our generation, and he gave academic respectability to the practice of instructional systems design.

NOTES

1. On April 28, 2002, Robert Mills Gagné died peacefully in his sleep with his wife, Pat, at his side.
2. Some of the biographical information about Gagné was obtained from the *Distinguished Scientific Award for the Applications of Psychology: 1982* presentation that appeared in the January 1983 issue of *American Psychologist*.

REFERENCES

American Psychologist (1983). Distinguished scientific award for the applications of psychology citation. *American Psychologist, 38*, 24–29.

American Association for the Advancement of Science Commission on Science Education (1965). *The psychological bases of science—A process approach*. Washington, DC: AAAS.

Briggs, L. J. (1980). Thirty years of instructional design: One man's experience. *Educational Technology, 20*(2), 45–50.

Carroll, J. M. (1990). *The Nurnburg funnel: Designing minimalist instruction for practical computer skills*. Cambridge, MA: The MIT Press.

Case, R., & Bereiter, C. (1984). From behaviorism to cognitive behaviorism to cognitive development: Steps in the evolution of instructional design. *Instructional Science, 13*, 141–158.

Driscoll, M. P. (2000). *Psychology of learning for instruction* (2nd ed.). Needham Heights, MA: Allyn & Bacon.

Fields, D. C. (2000). The impact of Gagné's theories on practice. In R. C. Richey (Ed.), *The legacy of Robert M. Gagné* (pp. 183–209). Syracuse, NY: ERIC Clearinghouse on Information and Technology.

Gagné, R. M. (1954). Training devices and simulators: Some research issues. *American Psychologist, 9*, 95–107.

Gagné, R. M. (1955). Methods of forecasting maintenance job requirements. In Advisory Panel on Personnel and Training Research (Ed.), *Symposium on electronic maintenance* (pp. 47–52). Washington, DC: U.S. Department of Defense.

Gagné, R. M. (1962). The acquisition of knowledge. *Psychological Review, 69*, 355–365.

Gagné, R. M. (1963). A psychologist's counsel on curriculum design. *Journal of Research in Science Teaching, 1*, 27–32.

Gagné, R. M. (1965a). The analysis of instructional objectives for the design of instruction. In R. Glaser (Ed.), *Teaching machines and programmed learning: II. Data and directions* (pp. 21–65). Washington DC: National Education Association.

Gagné, R. M. (1965b). *The conditions of learning.* New York: Holt, Rinehart, & Winston.

Gagné, R. M. (1968). Contributions of learning to human development. *Psychological Review, 75*, 177–191.

Gagné, R. M. (1972). Learning theory, educational media, and individualized instruction. In F. J. Pula & R. J. Goff (Eds.), *Technology in education: Challenge and change* (pp. 20–43). Worthington OH: Charles A. Jones.

Gagné, R. M. (1973). Observations of school learning. *Educational Psychologist, 10*(3), 112–116.

Gagné, R. M. (1977). *The conditions of learning* (3rd ed.). New York: Holt, Rinehart & Winston.

Gagné, R. M. (1984). Learning outcomes and their effects. *American Psychologist, 39*, 377–385.

Gagné, R. M. (1985). *The conditions of learning and theory of instruction* (4th ed.). New York: Holt, Rinehart, & Winston.

Gagné, R. M. (1986). Instructional technology: The research field. *Journal of Instructional Development, 8*(3), 7–14.

Gagné, R. M. (1989). *Studies of learning: Fifty years of research.* Tallahassee, FL: Learning Systems Institute, Florida State University.

Gagné, R. M. (1995/96). Learning processes and instruction. *Training Research Journal, 1*, 17–28.

Gagné, R. M., & Briggs, L. J. (1974). *Principles of instructional design.* New York: Holt, Rinehart, & Winston.

Gagné, R. M., Briggs, L. J., & Wager, W. W. (1988). *Principles of instructional design* (3rd ed.). Fort Worth, TX: Holt, Rinehart, & Winston.

Gagné, R. M., Briggs, L. J., & Wager, W. W. (1992). *Principles of instructional design* (4th ed.). Fort Worth, TX: Harcourt Brace.

Gagné, R. M., & Brown, L. T. (1961). Some factors in the programming of conceptual learning. *Journal of Experimental Psychology, 62*, 313–321.

Gagné, R. M., & Dick, W. (1982). Instructional psychology. *Annual Review of Psychology, 34*, 261–295.

Gagné, R. M., & Driscoll, M. P. (1988). *Essentials of learning for instruction* (2nd ed.). Englewood Cliffs, NJ: Prentice-Hall.

Gagné, R. M., & Medsker, K. L. (1996). *The conditions of learning: Training applications.* Fort Worth, TX: Harcourt Brace.

Gagné, R. M., & Merrill, M. D. (1990). Integrative goals for instructional design. *Educational Technology Research and Development, 38*(1), 23–30.

Gagné, R. M., Mayor, J. R., Garstens, H. L., & Paradise, N. E. (1962). Factors in acquiring knowledge of a mathematical task. *Psychological Monographs, 76*, No. 7.

Gagné, R. M., & Smith, E. C., Jr. (1962). A study of the effects of verbalization on problem solving. *Journal of Experimental Psychology, 63*, 12–18.

Glaser, R. (1963). Instructional technology and the measurement of learning outcomes: Some questions. *American Psychologist, 18*, 519–521.

Lent, R., & Van Patten, J. (1997). Exploring the paradigm of instructional design: Implications in business settings. In C. R. Dills & A. J. Romiszowski (Eds.), *Instructional development paradigms* (pp. 141–154). Englewood Cliffs, NJ: Educational Technology Publications.

Mager, R. F. (1962). *Preparing objectives for programmed instruction.* San Francisco: Fearon.

McCown, R., Driscoll, M., & Roop, P. G. (1996). *Educational psychology: A learner-centered approach to classroom practice* (2nd ed.). Boston: Allyn & Bacon.

Merrill, M. D. (1983). Component display theory. In C. M. Reigeluth (Ed.), *Instructional design theories and models* (pp. 279–333). Hillsdale, NJ: Lawrence Erlbaum Associates.

Merrill, M. D., Li, Z., & Jones, M. K. (1990a). Limitations of first generation instructional design. *Educational Technology, 30*(1), 7–11.

Merrill, M. D., Li, Z., & Jones, M. K. (1990b). Second generation instructional design. *Educational Technology, 30*(2), 7–14.

Morgan, R. (1989). Foreward. In R. M. Gagné (Ed.), *Studies of learning: Fifty years of research* (pp. iii–iv). Tallahassee, FL: Learning Systems Institute, Florida State University.

Orey, M. A., & Nelson, W. A. (1997). The impact of situated cognition: Instructional design paradigms in transition. In C. R. Dills & A. J. Romiszowski (Eds.), *Instructional development paradigms* (pp. 283–296). Englewood Cliffs, NJ: Educational Technology Publications.

Petry, B., Mouton, H., & Reigeluth, C. M. (1987). A lesson based on the Gagné–Briggs theory of instruction. In C. M. Reigeluth (Ed.), *Instructional theories in action: Lessons illustrating selected theories and models* (pp. 11–44). Hillsdale, NJ: Lawrence Erlbaum Associates.

Reigeluth, C. M. (1979). In search of a better way to organize instruction: The elaboration theory. *Journal of Instructional Development, 2*(3), 8–15.

Reiser, R. A. (1987). Instructional Technology: A history. In R. M. Gagné (Ed.), *Instructional technology: Foundations* (pp. 11–48). Hillsdale, NJ: Lawrence Erlbaum Associates.

Reiser, R. R., & Gagné, R. M. (1983). *Selecting media for instruction*. Englewood Cliffs, NJ: Educational Technology Publications.

Richey, R. C. (Ed.). (2000). *The legacy of Robert M. Gagné*. Syracuse, NY: ERIC Clearinghouse on Information and Technology.

Roblyer, M. D., Edwards, J., & Havriluk, M. A. (1997). *Integrating educational technology into teaching*. Upper Saddle River, NJ: Merrill/Prentice-Hall.

Skinner, B. F. (1958). Teaching machines. *Science, 128*, 969–977.

Skinner, B. F. (1959). The programming of verbal knowledge. In E. Galanter (Ed.), *Automatic teaching: The state of the art* (pp. 63–68). New York: Wiley.

Smith, P. L., & Ragan, T. J. (1993). *Instructional design*. New York: Macmillan.

Smith, P. L., & Ragan, T. J. (1999). *Instructional design* (2nd ed.). New York: Wiley.

Smith, P. L., & Ragan, T. J. (2000). The impact of R. M. Gagné's work on instructional theory. In R. C. Richey (Ed.), *The legacy of Robert M. Gagné* (pp. 147–181). Syracuse, NY: ERIC Clearinghouse on Information and Technology.

Tuckman, B. W. (1996). My mentor: Robert M. Gagné. *Peabody Journal of Education, 71*(1), 3–11.

Tyler, R. W. (1949). Achievement testing and curriculum construction. In G. Williamson (Ed.), *Trends in student personnel work* (pp. 391–407). Minneapolis: University of Minnesota Press.

Tyler, R. W. (1950). The functions of measurement in improving instruction. In E. F. Lindquist (Ed.), *Educational measurement* (pp. 47–67). Washington, DC: American Council on Education.

Wager, W. W., & Driscoll, M. P. (2000). Preface. In R. C. Richey (Ed.), *The legacy of Robert M. Gagnè* (pp. xix–xxiii). Syracuse, NY: ERIC Clearinghouse on Information and Technology.

III

Educational Psychology in the Modern Era: 1960 to Present

14

Educational Psychology in the Modern Era: 1960 to the Present

Michael Pressley
Michigan State University

with
Alysia D. Roehrig
University of Notre Dame

When the editors approached us about contributing a chapter on the modern era (i.e., 1960 to the present) to this volume, the prospect seemed daunting. Educational psychology is an extremely complex subdiscipline of psychology, with the field encompassing a huge volume of theory and research. It is also a subfield that is very much contextualized by history—the history of psychology as well as American history, because so many of its leaders have been Americans.

One obvious possibility in organizing this chapter was to chronicle the era from the early years to the present. With that approach, the climax would be a summary of the nature of the field today. We chose an alternative organization, however. We begin with a summary of the field as it is now, and then reflect on it in light of work in the past 4 decades. We chose this approach because it highlights the uniqueness of the present relative to the past.

EDUCATIONAL PSYCHOLOGY AT THE CLOSE OF THE 20TH CENTURY

In this section we detail what the field of educational psychology is at the close of the 20th century. Specifically, we analyze two sources of evidence that are informative about the research being carried out by educational psychologists. First, we review the contents of three recent, substantial volumes overviewing educational psychology. Second, we take up the contents of the 1997 and 1998 issues of the *Journal of Educational Psychology*, the most recent volumes of the leading journal serving the subdiscipline at the time of this writing.

VOLUMES SUMMARIZING CONTEMPORARY EDUCATIONAL PSYCHOLOGY

There have been three major volumes published in the past few years that have detailed the field of educational psychology. In each, well-informed scholars detailed the diverse nature of educational psychology.

Handbook of Educational Psychology

The *Handbook of Educational Psychology* was sponsored by Division 15 of the American Psychological Association, the Division of Educational Psychology (Berliner & Calfee, 1996). We spent a great deal of time with this volume to discern the core topics represented in it. Eight major topics stood out.

Cognition. We found ideas from cognitive psychology prominent in many of the chapters of the *Handbook*, beginning with the two chapters, "Cognition and Learning" and "Problem-Solving Transfer". Cognition also was in some of the chapters dedicated to individual differences, including the ones concerned with development, individual differences in cognitive functions, affective and conative functions, and gender development. Discussions of cognition also occurred in chapters on school curriculum and psychology, including the chapters about teaching history, science, mathematics, literacy, and second-language. The cognitive theme was also very strong in chapters on teaching and instruction, especially those dedicated to learning to teach, teachers' beliefs and knowledge, teaching in a classroom context, situated social practice and instructional design, technology and education, and group processes in the classroom.

An unavoidable conclusion from reading the *Handbook* is that contemporary educational psychology is very much a cognitive psychology of education, with much work focusing on the cognition and cognitive development of various types of students and their teachers. For example, the nature of student thinking is preeminent in the thinking of a variety of curriculum and instruction reformers, who believe that instruction is best when meshed with the cognitive characteristics and proclivities of developing students.

Sociocultural Perspectives. To be certain, there were authors in the *Handbook* who argued that the field is now beyond cognition per se (Hiebert & Raphael, 1996). They reasoned that because thinking and cognitive development occur in social and cultural contexts, they are better conceived as sociocultural rather than simply cognitive, because the cognitive perspective emphasizes processes within the individual learner rather than processes that occur between people. The many references to Vygotsky in the *Handbook* drove home that the sociocultural perspective should probably be conceived as a separate subfield of educational psychology. It was striking, however, that although sociocultural theoretical perspectives were offered in the *Handbook*, there was little research cited from that perspective. This contrasted with the voluminous research summarized in the *Handbook* on most of the other topics that compose educational psychology.

Development. Developmental theory and research was prominent in much of the work represented in the *Handbook*. There were two separate chapters on development, but there was much developmental theory and research referenced in other chapters.

Motivation. In addition to two chapters on motivation (i.e., one on theories of motivation and the other relating motivation to instruction), motivation also figured prominently in both of the chapters concerned with development and in three of the chapters concerned with individual differences (i.e., the ones pertaining to affective and conative functions, culture, and gender). Motivation was particularly salient in chapters dedicated to teaching and instruction. In summary, the *Handbook* covered factors affecting student motivation, including classroom organizational factors (e.g., a classroom's goal structure—whether the emphasis is on competition with other students or learning of material).

Individual Differences. The section of the *Handbook* dedicated to individual differences was longer than any other part. Moreover, there was much concern with individual differences in other chapters. For example, the chapter on bilingualism and curriculum had a very strong individual differences concern. The chapter on teachers' beliefs focused on important differences between teachers in their cognitive processes. As the 20th century closes, educational psychologists are thinking about a variety of ways that people can differ that affect educational achievement.

Psychological Foundations of Curriculum. The chapters concerned with history, science, mathematics, literacy, and second-language curricula showed that psychological analyses are going far in redefining curriculum and research on curriculum.

Teaching and Instruction.   There were seven chapters specifically dedicated to teaching and instruction, with teaching also covered in chapters pertaining to curriculum (i.e., in chapters on teaching history, science, math, literacy, and second language). A chapter on the informal curriculum took up how instruction carries implicit messages that can affect students. The nature of teaching also was reviewed in chapters on individual differences, particularly in the chapters about exceptionality and gender.

Research Methods and Assessment.   One entire section of the *Handbook* was dedicated to research methods and assessment. There also was prominent discussion of assessment in the chapters on cognition and learning, exceptionality, mathematics teaching, literacy, and the informal curriculum.

Summary.   Based on reading the *Handbook* alone, we would conclude that educational psychology consists of theory and research on the following topics: cognition, sociocultural perspectives, development, motivation, individual differences, psychological foundations of curriculum, teaching and instruction, and research methods and assessments.

When we reflected on this list, it did not seem exhaustive, however. For example, there was no coverage of behaviorism in the *Handbook*, nor did we detect much coverage of research on educational media. Hence, it seemed unwise to rely on this one source, and thus, we reviewed two other volumes intended to cover the field comprehensively, hoping that by the conclusion of the 3-volume review, we would feel satisfied that all of the major topics in educational psychology had been identified.

International Encyclopedia of Developmental and Instructional Psychology (2nd Edition)

The *International Encyclopedia of Developmental and Instructional Psychology*, 2nd ed. (DeCorte & Weinert, 1996) consists of 171 articles arranged into 17 sections, with the first 7 sections concerned mostly with development and the latter 10 sections focusing on instructional (i.e., educational) psychology. (It is those latter 10 sections that are emphasized here.) Although all eight of the topics covered in the *Handbook* were also covered in the *Encyclopedia*, the instructional psychology section of the *Encyclopedia* included substantial work on some other topics as well.

Behavioral Learning.   There definitely was more emphasis in the *Encyclopedia* on behavioral learning than in the *Handbook*. This included coverage of operant conditioning, feedback, behavior modification, programmed instruction, behavioral objectives, and mastery learning.

Social Relations and Education. The *Encyclopedia* had chapters on home environment, peer relations, school social environments, communications, social interactions, and teacher expectations. Collectively, these entries covered the area of social relations and education.

Educational Media. An entire section of the *Encyclopedia* was dedicated to computers, media, and learning. In the late 1990s, studies of educational media effects became an important part of educational psychology.

Summary. By the conclusion of the review of the *Encyclopedia*, the list of subfields of educational psychology included the following: cognition, behavioral learning, sociocultural perspectives, social relations and education, development, motivation, individual differences, psychological foundations of curriculum, teaching and instruction, educational media, and research methods and assessments. Of course, these subfields are not mutually exclusive but rather overlap and interpenetrate one another.

Advanced Educational Psychology for Educators, Researchers, and Policymakers

Pressley with McCormick (1995) produced a graduate-level textbook that was intended to summarize exhaustively the field of educational psychology, especially documenting important research contributions in the field. The authors covered every important educational psychology research direction represented in the major journals serving the field.

The list of subfields of educational psychology identified from analyses of the *Handbook* and *Encyclopedia* contents were checked against the content of *Advanced Educational Psychology* (*AEP*). In fact, there was coverage in *AEP* of all 11 of the subfields identified in the analyses of the *Handbook* and *Encyclopedia*, with no new subfields identified by analyzing the contents of *AEP*.

Summary

Sources such as the *Handbook*, the *Encyclopedia*, and *AEP* provide good summaries of the field of educational psychology as conceived by some of its leadership. These volumes were intended to cover the waterfront, and the reader who spends time with them receives an impressive education about the diverse field that is educational psychology. Even so, these volumes are not about what is happening right now in educational psychology. For that, it makes sense to look at the journals that chronicle the field as it emerges. To the extent that there is connection between the recent past of the discipline and recent journal-published research, it would be expected that the 11 topics identified from review of the summary volumes would be represented in journal articles that recently appeared in the literature.

JOURNAL OF EDUCATIONAL PSYCHOLOGY: 1997–98

To appraise whether the 11 categories described in the last section were valid, we attempted to match them against the contents of the two most recent volumes of the *Journal* (1997 and 1998). Every article was reviewed and classified into 1 of the 11 categories identified.

Most articles fit several categories. For example, one paper on children's recall of television and print media pertained to cognition, educational media, and individual differences. Even so, the article seemed to both of us to be more about educational media than cognition or individual differences, and thus, was classified as a paper about educational media. Although there was some lively discussion, we were able to come to concensus in categorizing all 112 articles published in 1997 and 1998 as fitting into 1 of the 11 categories. The number of articles classified into each category is displayed in Table 14.1.

Almost two-thirds of what was in the *Journal* in 1997–98 was accounted for by three categories: cognition, motivation, and individual differences. Even more striking to us, however, was that a clear majority of the articles somehow related to cognition, even if that was not their main thrust, including most of the articles identified as being studies of motivation and individual differences. The *Journal of Educational Psychology* is a highly cognitively oriented journal at the end of the century.

TABLE 14.1
Number of *Journal of Educational Psychology* Articles Falling
into Each of the 11 Categories of Educational Psychological Research

| | Number of Articles ||
Category	1997–1998	1960–1961
Cognition	27 (24%)	1 (1%)
Behavioral learning	0 (0%)	22 (20%)
Sociocultural perspectives	2 (2%)	0 (0%)
Social relations and education	7 (6%)	6 (6%)
Development	7 (6%)	5 (5%)
Motivation	20 (18%)	4 (4%)
Individual differences	26 (23%)	21(19%)
Psychological foundations of curriculum	11 (10%)	0 (0%)
Teaching and instruction	11 (10%)	18 (17%)
Educational media	2 (2%)	3 (3%)
Research methods/assessment	9 (8%)	29 (27%)

We were also struck that much of the study of cognition in the *Journal* was in the area of literacy. For example, there were 17 articles relating to comprehension processing, and a dozen others about basic phonological and word-level processing. Also, the individual differences most reported in the *Journal* were in the area of literacy, with about a dozen articles focusing on students with reading and writing disabilities.

The only category not represented in the *Journal* that was identified in the analyses of the summary volumes was behavioral learning. Not only were there no articles in the 1997–98 *Journal* with behavioral learning as a focus, there was not a single article that seemed behaviorally oriented at all. Although behavioral research in education is still being conducted and regularly reported (e.g., *Journal of Applied Behavior Analysis*), such work is absent from the *Journal of Educational Psychology*, perhaps signalling that it is not mainstream in the field of educational psychology at the end of the 20th century. Alternatively, it may be that the methods preferred by behaviorists in education (e.g., single-subject designs) have not been favored by the *Journal of Educational Psychology*. As the most recent editor of the *Journal*, chapter author Michael Pressley can assert no bias on his part against such designs. He must also admit, however, that only a handful of single subject designs have been submitted to the *Journal* during his watch, probably reflecting that behaviorally oriented educational psychologists feel the *Journal* is inappropriate for their work.

There was little in the *Journal* in two other categories. First, there were only two articles that were primarily sociocultural. Although a few articles placed in other categories had sociocultural implications, little sociocultural work was reported in the *Journal* in 1997–98. Because sociocultural scholars believe there are qualitative differences between cultures that affect educational achievement, many of their analyses are more qualitative than quantitative. In contrast, educational psychology remains predominantly a quantitative discipline, with only a handful of qualitative articles published in the *Journal* in 1997–98. Thus, sociocultural scholars may be placing their work in outlets other than the *Journal of Educational Psychology* (e.g., *American Educational Research Journal, Cognition & Instruction*), even when their work has a psychological component, because they perceive a methodological mismatch.

Second, only a small number of articles were about educational media. In part, this probably reflects the presence of speciality journals (e.g., *Educational Technology, Journal of Educational Computing*), although we suspect that, for the most part, educational psychologists are not yet turning their attention to psychological analyses of student performance in media environments. For instance, when Pressley wrote *Advanced Educational Psychology*, he experienced difficulties identifying work on educational media carried out by educational psychologists.

In conclusion, the 11 categories of research identified in the content analyses of the summary volumes in the field of educational psychology captured the contents of the field in the late 1990s as defined by the leading journal in the field. Some of the categories were more prevalent than others, with cognitively-oriented studies and analyses of individual differences and student motivation predominating in the *Journal* in recent years. Other smaller categories are emerging or struggling to emerge, such as sociocultural analyses of educational achievement and studies of media effects in education.

In reviewing the categories of work represented in educational psychology, it is obvious that educational psychology is much determined by the larger field of psychology. Perhaps, most striking, the cognitive revolution in educational psychology is simply part of and influenced by the larger cognitive revolution in psychology. Similarly, fields like educational motivation and individual differences in educability are part of the general progress in psychology in understanding human motivation and differences. At the end of the 20th century, educational psychology is a decidedly multi-faceted subdiscipline of psychology.

EDUCATIONAL PSYCHOLOGY
IN THE EARLY 1960

As much as possible, we wanted to use the same procedures to construct an understanding of educational psychology in the 1960s as we used for the 1990s. Unfortunately, there were no earlier editions of the summary volumes used in the analyses of the 1990s. Thus, we had to identify books that would be revealing about the content of the field in the 1960s. After talking with several individuals who were in the field in the early 1960s, we decided to rely on educational psychology textbooks frequently used by graduate students in educational psychology. Of course, the *Journal of Educational Psychology* was published in the early 1960s, and thus, it could serve as the journal reference for that period.

Educational Psychology According to Cronbach (1962) and Klausmeier (1961)

Cronbach's (1962) *Educational Psychology* and Klausmeier's (1961) *Learning and Human Abilities: Educational Psychology* were two of the most respected educational psychology texts of their day. We reviewed these volumes to determine whether and how the 11 categories now defining educational psychology were represented in them, believing this would provide information about the cutting edge of the field in the early 1960s. Using the 11 categories identified here is what we found:

Cognition.   Both volumes had a little bit of coverage of cognition. For example, Piaget was covered in 3 pages in Klausmeier's book and 12 pages in Cronbach's volume.

Behavioral Learning. Both volumes were filled with behavioral conceptions of learning. Fully 40% of the chapters in each volume concerned topics in behavioral learning, with behavioral conceptions also interwoven into other chapters.

Sociocultural Perspectives. The closest that the Cronbach or Klausmeier texts came to coverage of sociocultural differences were a few references in both volumes to research on social class and cultural influences on learning and achievement.

Social Relations and Education. Both texts provided substantial attention to peer interactions in classrooms, mostly by discussing sociometry (i.e., measurement of who interacts with whom in a classroom). There was also some coverage of determinants of teacher and student interactions. In contrast, there was very little coverage of family influences or neighborhood effects on achievement.

Development. With the exception of brief coverage of Piaget, there was no coverage of other developmental theorists. Both Cronbach (1962) and Klausmeier (1961) reported on some specific age-related changes and acquisitions (e.g., physical maturation, vocabulary), with more emphasis on "readiness" (i.e., to read, go to school, learn, etc.) than any other idea related to development.

Motivation. Both volumes included considerable information on what was known about motivating students, with both volumes including a whole chapter on motivation and large sections of other chapters covering motivation. As with learning, the motivational theories of the day were behavioral, with an emphasis on needs, drives and drive reduction, goals, reinforcements, and punishers.

Individual Differences. There was substantial coverage of individual differences, although most of the discussion focused on individual differences in intelligence (i.e., IQ) as related to educational achievement.

Psychological Foundations of Curriculum. There was almost no coverage of how psychological ideas related to the curriculum, although Cronbach's text included brief discussions of research relating to reading and discovery learning in science, math, and other disciplines.

Teaching and Instruction. Both volumes included a good deal of theory and research related to teaching. For example, both volumes included chapters on the characteristics of more- and less-effective teachers.

Educational Media. Both volumes included brief coverage of learning from media (e.g., television, motion pictures). Both reviewed B. F. Skinner's ideas about programmed instruction and teaching machines (i.e., these were machines built to present programmed instruction, one little bit of information at a time, one test item at a time). Even so, very few pages were dedicated to theory or research on media.

Research Methods and Assessment.   Both volumes included a great deal of coverage of research methods (e.g., educational statistics) and several chapters relating to assessment.

Summary.   With the exception of psychological foundations of curriculum, all of the topics that compose contemporary educational psychology were represented in Lee J. Cronbach's and Herbert Klausmeier's books. Even so, just as cognition pervades contemporary summaries of the field, behavioral approaches pervaded the summaries of the early 1960s.

Another difference, however, was with respect to the salience of formal theory and research in any contemporary presentation of educational psychology compared to the presentations in the early 1960s. There were few great theorists cited in the Cronbach and Klausmeier volumes and very little research compared to even the least research-oriented educational psychology texts of the 1990s. Even so, as will become apparent in the next subsection, Cronbach's and Klausmeier's volumes were consistent with the educational psychology research of the day.

Journal of Educational Psychology (1960–61)

When the articles published in the *Journal of Educational Psychology* in 1960 and 1961 were analyzed with respect to the 11 categories identified for the 1990s, all seemed consistent with the categories, and each seemed to belong more in one of the categories than in any other (see Table 14.1). Some categories (sociocultural perspectives, social relations and education, development, individual differences, and educational media) had about the same percentage of the total articles in 1960–61 as in 1997–98. Some categories (cognition and motivation) had far less representation in the early 1960s than in the late 1990s. Others (behavioral learning, teaching and instruction, research methods/assessment) were more prominently represented in the *Journal* in 1960–61 than in 1997–98. In general, topics that were extensively covered in the Cronbach and Klausmeier textbooks were extensively covered in the *Journal* in 1960–61 (i.e., behavioral learning, individual differences, teaching and instruction, and research methods/assessment).

Before leaving this discussion of the *Journal* coverage in the early 1960s, there was a qualitative aspect of all the articles that was fascinating. The articles in the early 1960s were much shorter than the articles published now. For example, 2,500-word articles were not unusual in the 1960s; articles of less than 3,000 words are now the rare exception, with most articles in the contemporary *Journal of Educational Psychology* exceeding 6,000 words. Particularly striking were the brief introductions and discussions in the 1960s. There was much less theory and research then that could be used to frame a study; there was much less theory and research to which new findings could be related. The relatively long introductions and discussions in contemporary articles reflects the voluminous conceptual and empirical work in the field during this modern era.

Summary

If a student of educational psychology in the late 1990s were handed a copy of Cronbach's or Klausmeier's texts from the early 1960s or the 1960 and 1961 volumes of the *Journal of Educational Psychology*, she or he would be able to recognize the work as educational psychology. There has been consistency with respect to the categories of work that are considered educational psychology. Some of those categories have grown in importance, however, and some have diminished. For example, perspectives on motivation now represented prominently in educational psychology—many of them cognitive—were nowhere to be found in the early 1960s, with research on motivation in the 1960s inspired by behavioral theories.

In addition to noticing that *Journal* articles are longer now and more conceptually complex than in the 1960s, we noticed that there are many more educational psychology journals in the late 1990s compared to 1960–61. Moreover, it was clear that there was a book publication explosion in the field in the past 38 years, with many more books relating to educational psychology published in the 1970s, 1980s, and 1990s compared to the 1960s. What all that publication reflects was that many talented people made contributions to educational psychology during the modern era, with many more individuals working as educational psychologists in the late 1990s than in the early 1960s.

In reading Cronbach's (1962) and Klausmeier's (1961) texts, we were struck that the author indices were so short relative to the author indices in modern educational psychology texts. Moreover, the newer books have not just added the new names in the field while retaining the old ones. Rather, very few of the individuals cited in Cronbach (1962) and Klausmeier (1961) are cited in modern texts, with the much longer author indices in the newer volumes representing almost exclusively individuals who have worked in the modern era.

Consider Table 14.2. The left-hand column is a list of all of the authors cited at least four times in both Cronbach (1962) and Klausmeier (1961). The right-hand side is all of the authors cited at least four times in the 1996 *Handbook*, the 1996 *Encyclopedia*, and *Advanced Educational Psychology* (Pressley with McCormick, 1995). Despite the fact that the criterion for membership on the latter list was more stringent, there are twice as many names on it, reflecting a much larger group of educational psychologists who are active at the end of the 20th century compared to 1960. Notably, Benjamin Bloom and B. F. Skinner are the only individuals to make

TABLE 14.2
Cited Educational Psychologists

Cited 4 times in Cronbach (1962) and Klausmeier (1961)	Cited 4 times in Handbook (1996), Encyclopedia (1996), and AEP (1995)	
B. S. Bloom	J. R. Anderson	M. R. Lepper
W. A. Brownell	A. Bandura	R. E. Mayer
L. J. Cronbach	C. Bereiter	J. G. Nicholls
H. B. English	B. S. Bloom	A. S. Palincsar
H. J. Klausmeier	J. E. Brophy	D. N. Perkins
J. P. Guilford	A. L. Brown	P. L. Peterson
W. J. McKeatchie	J. C. Campione	J. Piaget
G. Murphy	C. S. Dweck	M. Pressley
S. L. Pressey	E. Fennema	M. Scardamalia
H. H. Remmers	H. Gardner	A. H. Schoenfeld
B. F. Skinner	R. Glaser	H. A. Simon
L. M. Terman	J. G. Greeno	B. F. Skinner
G. G. Thompson	W. Kintsch	R. E. Slavin
	L. A. Kohlberg	L. S. Vygotsky
		B. J. Zimmerman

both lists, reflecting distinguished early career contributions and contributions that continued well into the modern era. In general, however, the distinguished contributors of the 1960s were not cited extensively in the modern references if they were cited at all. Consider that only six of the 1960s list (i.e., Benjamin S. Bloom, W. A. Brownell, Lee J. Cronbach, J. P. Guilford, Wilbert McKeatchie, and B. F. Skinner) were cited four or more times in even one of the three modern summary volumes that were analyzed.

In studying the list of individuals who were cited in the summary volumes of the 1990s, there are a few salient features. At least one fourth of the sample are great theorists, whose contributions to educational psychology were principally theoretical, including John R. Anderson, Albert Bandura, Howard Gardner, Lawrence Kohlberg, Herbert A. Simon, B. F. Skinner, and Lev S. Vygotsky. Most of the rest also made some theoretical contribution but are better known for their distinguished programmatic research on an important problem or problems (e.g., Carl Bereiter for research and development efforts on early childhood education and writing; Richard Mayer for his work in cognitive analyses of educational problems; Alan Schoenfeld for his conceptualizations of mathematical cognition and math education; Barry Zimmerman for his research on observational learning and self-regulation). The clear majority of the scholars on the contemporary list made their distinguished contributions to some aspect of the cognitive psychology of education, reflecting the strong cognitive flavor of contemporary work. More than a quarter of the scientists on the contemporary list made contributions in educational motivation, reflecting the flurry of work in that area, especially in the last 2 decades.

A majority of the individuals on the modern list were students when the modern era began. Many of those modern era students, however, did not do their graduate study in educational psychology, but rather received their formal graduate degrees and education in an allied field (e.g., Ann L. Brown in developmental psychology, Annemarie Palincsar in special education, Robert Slavin in sociology). They found some exciting intellectual connection to education and psychology. Such cross-fertilization emphasizes, however, that educational psychology interacts with and is stimulated by larger fields, especially psychology.

THE COGNITIVE TRANSFORMATION OF EDUCATIONAL PSYCHOLOGY DURING THE MODERN ERA

In this section we discuss factors that shaped the field of educational psychology during the modern era. One of us lived and worked as an educational psychologist through much of the era, and hence, experienced first-hand some of the events covered in this section. In addition, we asked members of the current editorial board of the *Journal of Educational Psychology* for their perspectives on factors affecting the development of the field in the past 40 years, with a number of them responding in various ways to the request, from long prosaic letters detailing their personal histories to supplying lists of what they viewed as the most telling publications affecting the field between 1960 and the present. Finally, we talked to a number of senior educational psychologists directly about this topic, with those discussions also yielding many insights about ideas that affected the field. In the end, we had a long list of important influences and research directions in the field during the modern era. One of the most striking qualities of the list was that almost every item on it could be related to cognitive psychology. Moreover, it proved possible to relate every influence and direction on the list to the 11 categories of work identified earlier, and thus, this section is organized around those categories. Although we accept responsibility for the conclusions advanced here, these conclusions were based on the input of the many educational psychologists who communicated with us about the modern era.

Cognition: Major Cognitive Theories and Research Programs Were Developed

In general, psychology underwent a cognitive revolution in the past 40 years, and educational psychology was affected by that revolution. One book that excited many educational psychologists early in the modern era was Miller, Galanter, and Pribram's (1960) *Plans and the Structure of Behavior*. One source of its appeal was its accessibility, with it written in a style that made its ideas comprehensible to many social scientists. Moreover, Miller et al. (1960) took on some of behaviorism's most sacred assertions convincingly. Thus, S–R theorists long had contended that a psychology of thinking would have to appeal to an homunculus (i.e., a little man in the head) to explain decision making, with the homunculus concept, of course, being nothing but a circular explanation. Miller et al. (chapter 3) made the case that with the advent of computers, an internal information processing system could be specified in sufficient detail to account for the decisionmaking and behavior of a complex external machine. The authors forcefully made the case that concepts like intentions, plans, and images were scientific and promised much as potential explanations of human choices and behaviors.

Perhaps Miller et al.'s (1960) most memorable conceptual advance was the TOTE (i.e., test-operate-test-exit) unit. The authors contended that the performance of an action depended on a comparson between the state of affairs created by a present action and the state of affairs that was the goal of the actor. Thus, an individual wanting to pound a nail into a board would pound the nail and then compare the result of the pounding to the desired result. If the nail was not flush with the board, the actor would decide to pound again. In TOTE terms, the actor tested (i.e., looked to see if the nail was flush), operated (i.e., pounded if the nail was not flush), tested again (i.e., looked to see if the nail was flush), and exited (i.e., stopped pounding) when the goal (i.e., flush nail) was accomplished. Most readers came away from reading Miller et al. (1960) convinced that much of their actions on the world involved much testing, operating, testing, and exiting. Miller et al. (1960) was a much read, much remembered, and very influential book, inspiring many to think about thinking and how it could be conceptualized and studied.

Much of the new cognitive psychology would be about memory. There were a number of neo-behavioral conceptions of memory studied in the 1950s (i.e., S–R conceptions aimed at understanding memory in terms of what were conceived as internal stimulus-response chains), with prominent scientists such as Benton Underwood and Leo Postman leading the way. Their work on internal mediation in S–R terms was expanded by scholars who had more cognitive views of mediation. For example, a number of scientists contributed to a volume edited by Tulving and Donaldson (1972), *Organization of Memory*, making the case that memory was organized largely by categorical associations between bits of information. A primary piece of evidence favoring this perspective was that lists of words that could be organized into meaningful categories (e.g., some list items were vehicles, some foods, some toys) were more memorable than lists of unrelated words. A second example was Paivio's (1971) *Mental Imagery and Verbal Processes* in which he made the case that mental images could and did mediate much of memory. As supporting evidence, Paivio detailed how lists of words referring to concrete referents were more memorable than lists of words referring to abstract referents, how pictures were remembered better than words, and how instructions to construct mental images of words typically facilitated memory. This book definitely had an impact on educational psychologists, with a number of studies of imagery and its affects on learning and memory appearing in the *Journal of Educational Psychology* in the 1970s and 1980s.

In short, educational psychologists were influenced by basic cognitive theory since its first appearance. Indeed, a number of educational psychologists conducted research that resembled basic cognitive psychology, with the *Journal of Educational Psychology* carrying a number of articles on basic memory, conceptual development, and problem solving.

Behavioral Learning: Behaviorism Evolved Into Cognitive Behaviorism

Right up until his death, B. F. Skinner refused to acknowledge the importance of cognitive analyses of behavior (e.g., Skinner, 1990). Other behaviorists, however, were more open to cognitive theory, and in fact, transformed behavioral psychology into a cognitive-behavioral psychology.

Behavioral psychology was flourishing at the beginning of the modern era, largely because of successes in application of behavioral principles to applied problems, including problems of education. Behavior modification, in particular, was a well-known success near the beginning of the modern era, including its applications in classrooms. Although much of behavior modification was traditionally behavioral, involving only reinforcement and punishment of behaviors, a number of behavior modifiers experimented with cognitive techniques (e.g., imagery) that could be used in conjunction with the traditional behavioral techniques. Moreover, this work was covered respectfully in the most important early summary of research on behavior modification, Bandura's (1969) *Principles of Behavior Modification*, a resource that was mentioned prominently by several of the older educational psychologists who communicated to us about important publications during the modern era.

Albert Bandura's greatest fame, however, would come from his work on observational learning, work that was decidedly cognitive. Thus, in his 1977 book, *Social Learning Theory*, Bandura devoted about 20% of the book to the cognitive underpinnings of observational learning, particularly how observers represented what they saw and how such representations affected subsequent behaviors. There was prominent discussion of the attentional, memory, imagery, and language processes underlying behavior. This important theoretical work would be complemented the next year by Rosenthal and Zimmerman's (1978) *Social Learning and Cognition*. That book comprehensively reviewed all of the existing work relating social learning variables and cognition, including major sections on topics that were mainstream cognitive developmental psychology, including conservation and moral judgment.

That interventions amalgamating behavioral and cognitive mechanisms could be very powerful was an hypothesis advanced by several prominent theorists in the 1970s. One prominent volume was Donald Meichenbaum's (1977) *Cognitive*

Behavior Modification, which was filled with theory and data about treatments involving students talking to themselves to direct their own behaviors, imagining themselves performing behaviors, and reinforcing themselves for completing behaviors. Another volume detailing how people could self-direct their thinking in ways that affected behaviors was Michael Mahoney's (1974) *Cognition and Behavior Modification*.

These books were noticed by an entire generation of educational psychologists, with the result that many educational interventions were devised that combined behavioral and cognitive techniques (see Meichenbaum & Biemiller, 1998). For example, good teachers now are encouraged to reinforce adaptive behaviors in students, but they are also encouraged to promote student cognitions that motivate student self-regulation (e.g., encourage students to believe they can achieve through their own efforts). Good teachers encourage classroom-adaptive behaviors (e.g., paying attention, working quietly), but they also encourage student construction of understandings, for example, by providing hints about which aspects of a problem might be considered by students as they attempt a solution. Good teachers teach their students to self-reinforce themselves when they are active during learning, for example, when students self-instruct themselves to come up with a cognitive plan in advance of writing an essay, self-question themselves as they formulate and revise the plan, and carry out strategies to translate the plan into action (e.g., looking up information they do not know but need to know to write the essay). A who's who of educational psychology developed a variety of interventions combining behavioral and cognitive approaches, including, among others, Carl Bereiter, John Borkowski, Ann L. Brown, Don Deshler, Karen Harris, Steve Graham, Donald Meichenbaum, Annemarie Palincsar, Marlene Scardamalia, Alan Schoenfeld, and Noreen Webb.

In summary, although there were prominent behaviorists who never accepted cognitivism, others whose starting point was behaviorism discovered the greater power of combining behavioral and cognitive principles. A number of educational psychologists developed cognitive-behavioral approaches to teach reading, writing, and problem-solving, that is, to address the most important competencies that schooling is intended to develop.

Sociocultural Perspectives: Schooling Could Shape Cognition

From early in this modern era, it was recognized that cross-cultural studies could illuminate the effects of schooling on development, and, in particular, cognitive development. Cultures vary in the amount and types of schooling their children experience. If schooling matters in cognitive development, then thinking skills should vary as a function of the culture's schooling practices. In addition to cross-cultural comparisons that are informative about the effects of schooling, some cultures permit intracultural comparisons not possible in the Western world: That is, in some cultures, some children receive schooling and others do not; in some cultures, some children experience education aimed at increasing certain conceptual skills (e.g., memorizing religious verses and prayers) whereas other children experience education aimed at alternative cognitive skills (e.g., interpreting stories in sacred texts). If schooling matters in shaping minds, then children who go to school should think differently than children who do not go to school; children experiencing schooling aimed at developing particular cognitive skills should think differently than children experiencing schooling aimed at developing other cognitive skills.

Consistently, schooling has proven to matter. The cognitive skills that children display when memorizing, reading text, and problem-solving vary with the amounts and types of schooling the children experience, with the contributions of Michael Cole, Daniel Wagner, Jean Mandler, Barbara Rogoff, James Stigler, and Beth Kurtz-Costes particularly important. Cross-cultural data did much to convince that education had a fundamental impact on cognition and cognitive development, and hence, educational psychology should largely be about cognition and cognitive development through schooling and related variables (e.g., instruction).

That culture surrounding a developing child matters in the formation of mind was a central idea in Vygotsky's thinking, especially as depicted in the 1978 translation of *Mind in Society*. One of the most important ideas in that volume was that, as adults assist young children in their thinking, they begin to shape the child's thinking skills. Consistent types of interactions between an adult and a child over a problem are eventually internalized by the child and become the basis for the child's own thinking. Interpersonal thinking between an adult and a child, thinking driven more by the adult than the child, eventually becomes intrapersonal thinking, the type of thinking the child does for her- or himself.

That type of thinking provided much impetus for reconceptualizing instruction, with teachers encouraged to think with children and to support children's thinking more with hints and prompts that gets the child started on a solution path rather than teaching the solution path to the child. In a seminal paper, Jerome Bruner and his colleagues (Wood, Bruner, & Ross, 1976) referred to such support as scaffolding. As the child becomes more competent through interactions with the adult, the scaffolding can be withdrawn, with the child assuming more and more responsibility for the cognitive activity, much as the scaffolding is withdrawn from a building under construction as it becomes more and more self-supporting.

Perhaps the most influential instructional intervention conceived in Vygotskian terms was reciprocal teaching, an approach to development of comprehension skills in young readers who lacked them (Palincsar & Brown, 1984). With this approach, an adult teacher introduces a group of students to predicting, questioning, seeking clarification, and summarizing as comprehension skills that can be used during reading. Rather than the adult teacher directing students to use these skills, however, students take turns leading the group in the application of the skills to readings. The adult teacher provides some scaffolding, but only intervening when assistance is really needed, and then, only providing enough assistance to get the students back on track in their application of the comprehension strategies. Consistent with Vygotskian theory, skills that were first used in the group eventually seem to be internalized by the individual members of the group, with the result of improved understanding of text (Rosenshine & Meister, 1994).

Reciprocal teaching was only one of the instructional innovations inspired by Vygotskian theory, with many school reformers now attempting to reshape the schoolplace so that teachers interact with students more like masters interact with apprentices (Rogoff, 1990). The idea, of course, is that long-term apprentice-like interactions will result in internalization of the master's skills by the apprentice students.

In summary, the connections between culture and psychological development established by researchers such as Ann L. Brown, Michael Cole, Jean Lave, Sylvia Scribner, Annemarie Palincsar, and Barbara Rogoff, stimulated by theories such as Vygotsky's, inspired and continue to inspire educational innovation. That sociocultural environment proved to have such a profound influence on cognition contributed greatly to the increased interest in cognition by educational psychologists.

Social Relations and Education: Parents and Peers Affect Cognitive Development

During the modern era, it became clearer that relations with family and friends affect educational progress. For example, researchers in the area of emergent literacy determined that there was much that parents could do during the preschool years that would prepare their children for literacy instruction in school (Sulzby & Teale, 1991). Researchers such as Kathyrn Wentzel (1991a, 1991b, 1993) established clear relationships between social competence and academic competencies in middle school (i.e., academically competent middle schoolers are also socially competent middle schoolers). Lawrence Steinberg and his colleagues provided data establishing that a high school students' peer group makes a big difference with respect to academic achievement (i.e., the peer group can either be supportive or nonsupportive of academic efforts and accomplishments; Steinberg, Brown, & Dornbusch, 1996). There were important analyses of the relationships between home environments and achievement, for example, in the work of Robert Hess (e.g., Hess & Shipman, 1965) and Luis Laosa (e.g., 1978, 1980). A recurring theme in all of this work was that social relations and cognitive development were intimately intertwined, with this literature complementing well a large literature on cognitive development that related to education during the modern era.

Development: Cognitive Developmental Theorists and Researchers Studied Education

Cognitive developmental psychologists had a special impact on the field of educational psychology. When we talked with educational psychologists who were trained in the 1960s, they always mention the impact of Jerome Bruner's writings on their education, including *The Process of Education* (Bruner, 1960) and *Toward a Theory of Instruction* (1966). They also recollected J. M. Hunt's (1961) *Intelligence and Experience*, which, for many, was their introduction to Piaget. Without a doubt, however, John Flavell's (1963) *The Developmental Psychology of Jean Piaget* did more than any other volume to increase the awareness of North American psychologists, including educational psychologists, of Piaget's important stage theory of cognitive development. As a consequence, there were many studies of Piagetian phenomena (e.g., conservation) in the 1960s and 1970s, including a number of investigations by educational psychologists (Brainerd, 1978b).

A key question for many North American educational psychologists was whether conservation was a stage-dependent acquisition (i.e., it developed during the stage of concrete operations, corresponding to the elementary school years) or could be developed in younger children through instruction (Brainerd, 1978a; Rosenthal & Zimmerman, 1978, chapter 4). The North American educational psychologists concluded that conservation could be taught; even the most committed Piagetians eventually had to concede that some acceleration of conservation capacities was possible through experience, although they felt such acceleration was limited (Inhelder, Sinclair, & Bovet, 1974). For an excellent summary of how cognitive development related to educational psychology at the beginning of the modern era, Rohwer's (1970) chapter in *Carmichael's Manual of Child Psychology*, entitled, "Implications of cognitive development for education," is still a great read; so is Brainerd's (1978b) *Piaget's Theory of Intelligence*, especially for those interested in how Piagetian cognitive developmentalists investigated educational issues (see also Brainerd, 1978a).

Perhaps because of the prominence of research on adult memory as well as the obvious connection between memory and learning, children's memory and the general topic of memory development were research topics that especially appealed to educational psychologists. Whether children could be taught strategies that improved memory, and which strategies could be taught to improve memory, were questions that stimulated educational psychologists, with pioneering work by Flavell and his colleagues (e.g., Flavell, 1970) cited in many investigations of memory strategy instruction. The educational psychologists who studied children's memory in the first half of the modern era included, among others, John Borkowski, Ann L. Brown, Joseph Campione, John Hagen, Dan Kee, Joel Levin, Barbara Moely, Scott Paris, Michael Pressley, William Rohwer, Harriet Salatas Waters, Patricia Worden, and Steve Yussen.

Several very important findings emerged from the work on memory development (Schneider & Pressley, 1997): One was the children became more strategic with increasing development. A second was that when children did not use strategies on their own, often such strategies could be taught with large gains in children's memory as a consequence. A third conclusion was that strategies so taught often did not transfer. This third finding stimulated educational psychologists to think about metacognition as a mediating determinant of self-regulated use of memory strategies. Researchers including Borkowski, Brown, Paris, and Pressley did much work establishing that general use of strategies very much depends on children's understandings about when, where, and how the strategies they are learning can be applied and adapted (Borkowski, Carr, Rellinger, & Pressley, 1990).

Motivation: Academic Motivational Theory Turned Cognitive

At the beginning of the modern era, motivation in education was an entirely behavioral orientation, about rewards and punishers. Those interested in the intersection of personality and motivation made some impact in moving the field toward a consideration of inner states and academic engagement. For example, a number of distinguished educational psychologists considered how individual differences in anxiety affected student efforts and performances, including Sigmund Tobias (e.g., 1985) and Wilbert McKeatchie and his associates (Naveh-Benjamin, McKeatchie, & Lin, 1987).

Even so, modern conceptions of educational motivation have been much more cognitive theories than personality psychology, with cognitive theories of motivation emerging in the 1970s and being applied to education. Thus, Bernard Weiner (1979) made the case that the impact of student successes and failures on long-term motivation depended on how students explained their successes and failures to themselves. They could view successes and failures as reflecting ability, luck, or the difficulty level of the task, with such attributions possibly undermining motivation to work hard in the future. After all, if doing well or poorly is determined by ability, which is out of the student's control, why try in the future. Similarly, if success or failure is determined by luck, there is no reason to exert effort in the future. So, too, with believing that success or failure was determined by the difficulty of the test that was given. In contrast, if the student attributed successes and failures to effort expended, there was motivation to work hard in the future. Believing that you did well on today's test because you studied hard for it provides a reason to study hard in the future. Believing your failure today reflected too little study also motivates working hard the next time. Weiner's theory and supporting research brought to the fore student cognition as a powerful motivational force.

So did another conception of academic motivation that emerged in the early 1980s. According to goal theory (e.g., Ames & Archer, 1984), if students perceived that good grades depended on doing better than classmates, such a perception could undermine motivation. After all, only one student can be the best in the class, and only a very few can be at the top of the bell-shaped curve. Those perceiving that they could not make it to the head of the class have little motivation to try hard in a classroom with competitive grading. Moreover, those who easily make it to the head of the class also have little motivation to work hard, for simply by "cruising," they will do fine. In contrast, if the classroom is organized so that grades depend on individual improvement, students always have a reason for trying hard. That is, when students are rewarded for performing better next week than they did this week, there is plenty of reason to work hard.

In studies of goal theory, student perceptions of their classroom goal structures and their achievement orientations are critical. For example, within a classroom, there are differences between students, with some oriented toward doing better than others and some oriented to learning all they can. Students who have the former, competitive headset tend to be less motivated than those who are oriented to improving their performances (Ames & Archer, 1988).

Related perceptions were emphasized in other educational motivational theories, including Dweck's (e.g., 1986) entity theory of intelligence and Bandura's (1982) self-efficacy theory. According to Carol Dweck, students who believe their abilities are fixed (i.e., their intellectual abilities are innately determined and hence are not going to change) are not particularly motivated to try hard to improve themselves (Why bother? You either have it or you do not!). In contrast, students who believe their abilities are improved through learning new skills and information are more academically motivated. Albert Bandura's perspective was that academic motivation very much depends on the perception that one can do a task well, with such perceptions influenced by past successes and failures. Thus, students who experience a great deal of success in mathematics have high self-efficacy with respect to mathematical tasks, which in turn motivates effort in mathematics.

Although behavioral notions of motivation continue to be important in classroom management schemes at the end of the modern era (i.e., reinforcement and punishment are still mainstays of classroom management), the cutting edge in thinking about academic motivation is decidedly cognitive. One interesting twist has been an understanding that tangible rewards sometime undermine motivation, when they are provided for behaviors that are intrinsically motivating for the learner—with the work of Mark Lepper (e.g., Lepper, Greene, & Nisbett, 1973) and Edward Deci (e.g., 1971) stimulating much attention to this phenomenon. Lepper and Deci, however, were but two of a large number of exceptionally talented motivational researchers who developed cognitive theories of academic motivation that were both testable and tested in the past 2 decades. A great deal of support for various aspects of attributional, goal, entity, self-efficacy, self-concept, and other cognitive theories of academic motivation now exists, provided by, among others, Carole Ames, Albert Bandura, Susan Bobbitt Nolen, Martin Covington, Edward Deci, Carol Dweck, Jacqueline Eccles, Adele Gottfried, Sandra Graham, Susan Harter, Julius Kuhl, Mark Lepper, Martin Maehr, Herbert Marsh, John Nicholls,

Frank Pajares, Scott Paris, Julian Rotter, Dale Schunk, Deborah Stipek, Bernard Weiner, Kathyrn Wentzel, Alan Wigfield, and Barry Zimmerman.

Individual Differences: Much Ado About Cognitive Differences

Analyses of individual differences are prominent in the educational psychology literature, with huge subliteratures devoted to topics such as mental retardation and learning disabilities. Some of the more prominent analyses have been offered at the other end of the intellectual spectrum, however, with well-known studies of giftedness during this modern era, including the work of Nancy Jackson and Earl Butterfield (e.g., 1986), John Feldhusen (e.g., 1986), and Benjamin Bloom (e.g., 1985).

One salient individual differences variable among elementary school children is that some learn to read easily and others only do so with great difficulty. The prevalence of children who experience difficulties in beginning reading prompted much attention to reading during the modern era, extending well beyond the educational psychology community, from policymakers (including current President Bush) to millions of parents. As a consequence, psychological analyses of beginning reading have been among the most visible of the books published by educational psychologists, ones that sell in both the academic and popular markets.

A notable early-modern era book about beginning reading was Jeanne Chall's (1967) *The Great Debate*, which made the case that beginning reading instruction that included systematic phonics instruction was more effective than the whole word instruction that prevailed in schools in the 1950s and 1960s. The phonics versus whole word debate gave way as the modern era proceeded to a debate about phonics versus whole language, which emphasized that word recognition skills would be learned by beginning readers if only children had many experiences with reading and writing real stories, that explicit phonics instruction was both unnecessary and perhaps harmful.

There was a great deal of research relevant to these debates, with much of it supporting the conclusion that children, especially those who struggle with beginning read, do learn better if they are introduced systematically to letter–sound correspondences and are taught how to sound out words by blending the sounds represented by the letters of a word (Adams, 1990). An especially important finding was that many weak readers have a specific cognitive problem: They have failed to master the phonological skills emphasized in phonics instruction (e.g., Snow, Burns, & Griffin, 1998). That basic cognitive psychology went far in explaining the reading difficulties of beginning readers as well as in specifying a cure for word-level reading difficulties did much to increase interest in cognitive educational psychology, largely accounting for the high proportions of articles on basic reading published in the *Journal of Educational Psychology* in recent years. Researchers such as Marilyn Adams, Linnea Ehri, Maureen Lovett, Keith Stanovich,

Joseph Torgesen, Frank Vellutino, and Joanna Williams have made noteworthy contributions to the increased understanding of how development of phonological competence can improve reading at the word level for those beginning readers who are low in phonological competence relative to their peers.

If we were to attempt to identify a single article in the field of educational psychology that made the most news both within the field and beyond it, one obvious candidate would be Arthur Jensen's (1969) "How Much Can We Increase IQ and Scholastic Achievement?" published in the *Harvard Educational Review*. Jensen advanced a strong hereditarian perspective in that article, contending that individual differences in intelligence are much more determined by genes than environment, although that was not the Jensenian conclusion that produced all the attention for the paper. Jensen went on to argue that black–white differences in IQ were due to genetic differences between the races. It is possible that this paper attracted so much attention because it came in the turbulent 1960s, when there was great hope that racial differences could be explained by environmental deprivation and reduced through environmental interventions. That said, the strong hereditarian position continues to cause a stir, with its advocates still able to attract a great deal of popular attention (e.g., Herrnstein & Murray, 1994, *The Bell Curve*).

Despite the hereditarian arguments, there is now substantial evidence that IQ is very much affected by environment. The most complete summaries of the evidence on this point have been put together by Stephen Ceci. Particularly complementary to the cross-cultural work establishing the role of schooling in cognitive development, Ceci (1991; 1996, especially chapter 5) assembled the evidence that schooling matters in determining IQ: That is, IQ varies with the number of years spent in school; IQ falls during summer vacation away from school; when entry to school is delayed, there is a detectable effect on IQ; when children start school early, it is reflected in heightened intelligence. Yes, virtually all of the evidence of the quantity of schooling–IQ association is correlational, but the correlation is obtained so often that it is hard to believe that schooling is not responsible for increasing psychometric intelligence. That is, whenever there is more schooling, there is higher intelligence.

Jensen's hereditarian perspective could be discouraging to any would-be cognitive interventionist. In contrast, the Ceci analysis motivates optimism that intelligence and thinking skills are malleable. It also motivates the perspective that educational psychology should be focusing on how school affects the cognitive skills that are intelligence. Notably, new theories of intelligence were proposed during the modern era by Robert Sternberg (triarchic theory) and Howard Gardner (multiple intelligences theory), with both of these approaches inspiring school-based interventions hypothesized to promote intellectual functioning (e.g., Gardner, 1993; Sternberg, Torff, & Grigorenko, 1998).

In short, during this modern era, educational psychologists have focused on individual differences that are decidedly cognitive, such as reading and intelligence. Moreover, they produced explanatory theories of these individual differences that provided a role for the interventionist, with the clear message that schooling matters a great deal with respect to the development of skills such as reading and even global intelligence. We develop this theme further in the next subsection.

Psychological Foundations of Curriculum: Applying Cognitive Psychology in School

Robert Gagné's writing (e.g., 1977), and later the writing of his daughter Ellen Gagné (e.g., 1985), went far in introducing educational psychologists to cognitive theory as it related to education. Robert Gagné's *The Conditions of Learning* translated information processing theory into the basic research problems that were of greatest interest to the educational psychologists of the day (e.g., concept learning, cognitive strategies, transfer of learning). Ellen Gagné's *The Cognitive Psychology of School Learning* brilliantly summarized the research on reading, writing, and problem-solving that was inspired in the late 1970s and early 1980s by cognitive theory. The Gagnés' contributions were especially notable because their books were written for consumption by advanced undergraduates and graduate students, introducing many of the current generation of educational psychologists to the emerging cognitive educational psychology. We offer here a brief overview of some of the best-known efforts to illustrate that educational psychology during the modern era moved beyond basic cognitive theory, which dominated in Robert Gagné's book, to applied cognitive research and theory, which dominated in Ellen Gagné's text.

For example, Richard Anderson and his associates at the University of Illinois applied a cognitive conception known as schema theory (e.g., see Schank & Abelson's, 1977, *Scripts, Plans, Goals, and Understanding*) to the problem of text comprehension (i.e., reading above the word level). The basic idea was that a reader's prior knowledge can powerfully affect her or his understanding and interpretation of texts being read. In fact, that proved to be the case very reliably (Anderson & Pearson, 1984), with many studies detailing how a reader's schemata affect comprehension appearing in major educational research journals in the late 1970s and throughout the 1980s. This work has had a range of impacts, not the least of which is heightening awareness of the need to do everything possible to make certain that students are reading excellent literature, works filled with knowledge worth knowing. This, in part, accounts for the fact that every major reading series in the marketplace today is filled with excellent literature conveying important world knowledge rather than relatively contentless stories about Dick, Jane, and Sally.

The modern reading curriculum also contains many recommendations to teach students to use cognitive strategies to comprehend what they read. These recommendations follow directly from many investigations by cognitive psychologists confirming that reading comprehension and memory of text improves when students are taught to construct images as they read, summarize, and/or self-question about the content of text. This body of work was generated by, among others, Bonnie Armbruster, Carl Bereiter, Cathy Collins Block, John Bransford, Ann L. Brown, Jeanne Day, Gerald Duffy, Linda Gambrell, Joel Levin, Annemarie Palincsar, Scott Paris, Michael Pressley, Laura Roehler, William Rohwer, Elizabeth Short, Barbara Taylor, and Merle Wittrock.

Cognitive theory also influenced how writing is now taught in school (Flower & Hayes, 1980, 1981). Expanding on the Miller et al. (1960) notion of a cognitive plan, Flower and Hayes proposed that writing could be conceived as planning, drafting, and revising, with the writer recursively moving between planning, drafting, and revision activities. This conception inspired a great deal of research on student composition, including a number of demonstrations that the writing of very weak writers could be improved by teaching them how to plan, draft, and revise their writing (Harris & Graham, 1992). The impact of this theorizing and research has been striking. For example, as researchers who spend a great deal of time in classrooms, we cannot remember visiting an elementary classroom in recent years where there was not salient evidence of students being taught explicitly to plan, draft, and revise their compositions. Composition instruction, which used to begin in the middle school is now daily fare in kindergarten and Grade 1 classrooms.

Cognitive theory also has affected the problem-solving curriculum. Problem-solving fascinated psychologists throughout the 20th century and has been a central focus of basic cognitive psychologists during the modern era. In addition, some mathematicians, and particularly mathematicians interested in teaching, have gravitated toward cognitive conceptions of problem-solving (e.g., Polya, 1954a, 1954b, 1957, 1981; Schoenfeld, 1985, 1992). Without a doubt, the greatest theoretical influence on contemporary mathematics education reform efforts are the constructivist theories of cognitive development (e.g., Piaget). These conceptions emphasize that mathematical cognition develops best when students tackle problems just a bit beyond their current understandings. Consistent with Piaget, many contemporary math educators believe that understanding of problem-solving develops better when students are left to discover problem solutions on their own rather than be taught algorithms for solving them. Although this is a controversial position, it is an excellent example of how cognitive theory has had a profound impact on contemporary American curriculum, with constructivist math curricula now prominent in elementary and high school classrooms across the land (e.g., University of Chicago School Mathematics Project).

Cognitive psychology also has transformed the teaching of ethics. Lawrence Kohlberg's work (e.g., Kohlberg & Mayer, 1972), in particular, influenced a number of educators to encourage students to confront moral dilemmas as problems to be solved, ones that children could discuss with one another. When students debate alternative ways to solve moral dilemmas, their moral reasoning skills do improve, with them being more likely to see the perspectives and rights of others (Enright, Lapsley, & Levy, 1983). That is, consistent with Piaget's theory, such discussions result in cognitive conflict as a student's opinions are challenged by others, with a student's grappling with such conflict producing increased understanding of the particular moral problem and generalized improvement in moral reasoning abilities.

In summary, cognitive theory proved helpful in thinking about curricular problems that educators have always faced, such as how to teach students to read, compose, problem-solve, and confront ethical dilemmas. Educational psychologists devised and tested new theories of reading, composition, problem-solving, and moral education in recent years, with their efforts stimulating real educational reform, including transforming what and how children read, how they learn to write, how they are taught to solve problems, and how they learn to grapple with ethical dilemmas. These successes largely account for the domination of cognitive educational psychology at the end of the modern era.

If there is a single geographic locale responsible for much of the progress in cognitive educational psychology, it was probably the Learning Research and Development Center at the University of Pittsburgh. Its funding in 1967 by the federal government signaled widespread commitment to the inspiring visions of Robert Glaser, Lauren Resnick, and their Pittsburgh colleagues to cognitive learning conceptions of curriculum and instruction. It is impressive that as this chapter is being written, the Pittsburgh center continues to provide leadership in cognitive theoretically informed curriculum and instruction reform.

Teaching and Instruction: Teacher Cognitions and Student Cognitive Characteristics Affect Instruction

A number of shifts in teaching that were affected by cognitive theory and research were discussed already in previous subsections. There were a few others, however, that were mentioned prominently in the responses of members of the *Journal of Educational Psychology* editorial board to our inquiry about important influences in the modern era. One important discovery during the modern era was that teaching is affected by teachers' beliefs about learning, the curriculum, and students (e.g., Calderhead, 1996). For example, once teachers come to understand a students' cognitive abilities, they behave differently toward that student (e.g., Brophy, 1988). That is, teachers' expectations and beliefs about a student based on their experiences with the student come to determine the teacher's behaviors.

A complementary position that was developed during this modern era was that students do differ in their cognitive abilities in ways that should affect the instruction they receive. That is, whether instruction works well or not depends on the match between the instruction and a student's cognitive abilities, a position most completely developed by Lee J. Cronbach, Richard Snow, and their associates (Cronbach & Snow, 1977; Snow, Federico, & Montague, 1980a, 1980b).

As conceptually compelling as this perspective seemed, however, it proved extremely difficult to identify replicable interactions between cognitive abilities and instructional methods (i.e., it proved difficult to demonstrate that the effectiveness of particular forms of instruction varied with cognitive characteristics of learners).

At present, there continues to be much concern with the minds of teachers and students as determinants of instruction and instructional success. Not all such thinking has paid off as completely as had been hypothesized, but the search continues for cognitive differences of teachers and cognitive differences among students that are telling about instructional effects (Gustafsson & Undheim, 1996).

Educational Media: Cognitive Analyses of Educational Technology

At the dawn of the modern era, the technology most obviously informed by psychological analyses was programmed instruction. Although the conceptual and empirical analysis of this behavioral approach to teaching and learning would continue during the early part of the modern era (Skinner, 1981), prominent analyses of educational technology would be increasingly cognitive as the modern era proceeded. For example, under John Bransford's leadership, The Cognition and Technology Group at Vanderbilt (e.g., 1992; Van Haneghan, Barron, Young, Williams, Vye, & Bransford, 1992) developed an applied problem-solving curriculum using interactive videodisk technology. The curriculum stimulates students to plan as part of problem-solving, generate alternative solutions, and evaluate the alternatives before deciding on one approach over others, exploiting the flexible access of information that interactive videodisks permit. A second set of cognitively oriented analyses of technology emerged from Richard Mayer's group, which is evaluating the impact on learning and understanding of various types of visual and verbal presentations in computer microworld environments (e.g., Mayer & Moreno, 1998; Plass, Chun, Mayer, & Leutner, 1998). In doing so, Mayer and his colleagues are significantly extending the scope of basic cognitive theory (e.g., dual coding theory; Paivio, 1971), as they increase understanding of how technology can be used to teach a variety of content, from cause-and-effect sequences in earth science to foreign language vocabulary.

Research Methods: Analytical Advances That Served Cognitive Psychology Well

Early in the modern era, Campbell and Stanley's (1966) classic treatise on the design of experiments and quasi-experiments appeared. Their monograph put the true experiment, involving random assignment of large numbers of individuals to treatment conditions, on a firmer footing in the educational research community.

This proved to be an acceptable methodological framework for cognitively oriented psychologists, much more so than for behaviorists who continued to favor a set of designs emphasizing the analysis of behavior in individual subjects (Sidman, 1960). This methodological stance by the behaviorists distinguished them from much of the rest of psychology, for the Campbell and Stanley (1966) approach became the standard of research for many subdisciplines of the field. Hence, the cognitive educational psychologists who adopted this standard were much more mainstream in their methodological preferences than the educational behaviorists who resisted experimentation as defined by Campbell and Stanley (1966).

One product of the Campbell and Stanley revolution was the cognitive instructional experiment (e.g, Belmont & Butterfield, 1977). In one condition of such an experiment, a cognitive process is instructed (e.g., construct mental images of text content). A control condition is identical to the cognitive-process instructional condition except for the lack of cognitive-process instruction. If performance (e.g., text comprehension and memory) is better in the cognitive-process instructional condition than in the control condition, the inference is that the instruction induced the process and the processing that occurred in the instructed condition accounted for the performance difference. The pages of educational research journals have been filled with many such cognitive-instructional experiments during the modern era.

One of the big knocks on cognition that was made repeatedly by methodological behaviorists was that cognitive phenomena defied measurement, which contrasted with observable behaviors that were easily measured in comparison. That was true enough in 1960. During the modern era, however, cognitive psychologists developed a number of measurements of cognitive process during memorizing, problem-solving, or reading, from the quantitative exactness of reaction times to the qualitative fuzziness of think-alouds. Of course, what made the many measurements of process convincing was that they often correlated with other outcome measures (e.g., verbal think-alouds during reading correlate with memory and comprehension of text; Pressley & Afflerbach, 1995, chapter 2).

A potentially important development that is apparent in the educational psychology literature at the close of the 20th century is the use of qualitative methods by educational psychologists, most prominently, ethnographic approaches (e.g., Strauss & Corbin, 1998). The jury is still out on such work.

In summary, there was a methodological revolution in psychology during the modern era. There were advances in design of research and measurement of cognitive process that permitted cognitive educational psychology to flourish. In turn, educational psychologists generated much work that made the real-world relevance of educational psychology more apparent. Children are now taught to read, write, and problem-solve differently than before the cognitive revolution in psychology, educational psychology, and then, in education. Unlike political revolutions, however, methodological revolutions continue as the science advances in general, with qualitative methodologies now being explored by educational psychologists.

Summary

Educational psychology was transformed from a behavioral subdiscipline to a cognitive one during the modern era. This occurred because of multiple converging factors, including new and powerful theories of cognition and cognitive development, integrative theoretical work bridging cognitive and behavioral psychologies, cross-cultural research, new perspectives on motivation, interest in individual differences among students and among teachers that are decidedly cognitive, applicability of cognitive theory to curricular problems and educational technology, and methodological advances. These efforts were fueled further by the applied advances they produced, with the transformation of much of the American schooling curriculum in ways that are decidedly cognitive continuing to provide impetus for educational psychologists and others to reflect on the additional potential for cognitively based interventions in education.

FINAL COMMENTS

As part of coming to understand this modern era, we asked many prominent educational psychologists to indicate what they believed to be the books and individuals defining the era. A recurring theme in the responses was the shift from behaviorism to cognitivism during the modern era. Another recurrent theme, consistent with the conclusions offered in this chapter, was that there were many notable contributions and contributors to educational psychology offering diverse work, during this modern era. One senior educational psychologist, Vernon Hall, put it this way:

> I entered graduate school in 1960, so the period you are writing about is really my professional life. I have quickly jotted down a few references that have been important to me. I'm certain I have left out many others.
>
> When I look at the book I used to teach from in graduate school—by Pressey, Robinson, and Horrocks (1959)—I find over 1,000 references but only one for Piaget (1924; *Judgment and Reasoning in the Child*) and none for Skinner. Skinner did visit Ohio State while I was there and mentioned that Pressey was the first to use programmed instruction. At that time, some of Pressey's teaching machines were still in the department. We did read *The Analysis of Behavior*, which Skinner co-authored with Holland (1961) and later *The Technology of Teaching* (Skinner, 1981) and *Beyond Freedom and Dignity* (Skinner, 1986).
>
> We all had to learn about Piaget's theory somewhere. Hunt's (1961) *Intelligence and Experience*, and Flavell's (1963) *The Developmental Psychology of Jean Piaget* is where I acquired my initial information. We also had to learn cognitive psychology rapidly when verbal learning disappeared. I used Kintsch's (1982) *Memory and Cognition*. Paivio's (1971) *Imagery and Verbal Processes* was also important and has continued to influence contemporary educational psychology. I also think Tulving and Donaldson's (1972) *Organization of Memory* has been influential. Wittrock's

early work on generative learning has had much influence in educational psychology. Metacognition has been big. Credit Flavell again.

The arrival of the computer has also had an unbelievable influence on writing, theorizing, and education. I'm not certain who we credit here.

It is difficult to leave out Jensen's (1969) *Harvard Educational Review* article, "How Much Can We Boost IQ and Scholastic Achievement?," which led me to conduct a four-year longitudinal study of black and white boys....I can't leave out Rosenthal and Jacobson's (1968) *Pygmalion in the Classroom*, which led to a tremendous amount of research....The cooperative learning movement has had some influence and both the Johnsons and Slavin have had considerable impact.

We think Hall's story reflects the overall health of educational psychology during the modern era. Lots of individuals with expertise in some area of psychology found a connection to education that excited not only them but inspired others to do research. The books and articles Hall cited each stimulated voluminous research, with some of it landing in the *Journal of Educational Psychology* but with enough left over to provide substance for many books and new journals that define both a more cognitive and a more expansive field than existed at the beginning of the modern era.

In closing this chapter, we would be less than candid if we did not mention a curious slippage between the scholarly literature in educational psychology and the public perception of educational psychology. The most prominent educational psychology topic in the popular media is the analyses of standardized test results, with a typical theme being that American students' achievement lags behind students in other countries. For the most part, this work is not theoretically driven, and hence, such data are not collected in designs that permit testing of theoretical possibilities. Although there are broad claims made about the significance of such data by policymakers—and sometimes educational psychologists—rarely are the conclusions as definitively tied to the data and designs of the studies producing the data as is required for conclusions to be published in outlets like the *Journal of Educational Psychology*. This is not the best work of educational psychologists, although it seems to be the most prominent work of our fraternity in the contemporary marketplace of ideas. We probably should be thinking hard about how educational psychologists can provide data for the current great debates about student achievement that address the concerns of policymakers and the public as well as the professional educational psychology research community. Whether we like it or not, our worth as a profession in the eyes of the public and those who control the research purse strings probably depends to some extent on the perception that educational psychologists can provide important insights about trends in student achievement and how to improve achievement as indexed by the standardized tests that are the gold standard of the day.

That said, we also think that educational psychologists can point with pride to the many improvements in practice that have resulted from the work in the modern era. Moreover, based on the track record, they have a right to be optimistic that as educational psychologists continue to think about the ideas that have predominated in this modern era, more improvements in education will follow.

ACKNOWLEDGMENTS

When this chapter was written, Alysia Roehrig was supported by a fellowship from the Graduate School of the University of Notre Dame. Michael Pressley received endowment funds from the University of Notre Dame as the Notre Dame Professor in Catholic Education.

REFERENCES

Adams, M. J. (1990). *Beginning to read*. Cambridge, MA: Harvard University Press.

Ames, C., & Archer, J. (1988). Achievement goals in the classroom: Students' learning strategies and motivation processes. *Journal of Educational Psychology, 80*, 260–270.

Anderson, R. C., & Pearson, P. D. (1984). A schema-theoretic view of basic processes in reading. In P. D. Pearson, R. Barr, M. L. Kamil, & P. Mosenthal (Eds.), *Handbook of reading research* (pp. 255–293). New York: Longman.

Bandura, A. (1969). *Principles of behavior modification*. New York: Holt.

Bandura, A. (1977). *Social learning theory*. Englewood Cliffs, NJ: Prentice-Hall.

Bandura, A. (1982). Self-efficacy mechanism in human agency. *American Psychologist, 37*, 122–147.

Belmont, J. M., & Butterfield, E. C. (1977). The instructional approach to developmental cognitive research. In R. V. Kail, Jr., & J. W. Hagen (Eds.), *Perspectives on the development of memory and cognition* (pp. 437–481). Hillsdale, NJ: Lawrence Erlbaum Associates.

Berliner, D. C., & Calfee, R. C. (Eds.). (1996). *Handbook of educational psychology*. New York: Macmillan.

Bloom, B. S. (1985). *Developing talent in young people*. New York: Ballantine.

Borkowski, J. G., Carr, M., Rellinger, E. A., & Pressley, M. (1990). Self-regulated strategy use: Interdependence of meta-cognition, attributions, and self-esteem. In B. F. Jones (Ed.), *Dimensions of thinking: Review of research* (pp. 53–92). Hillsdale, NJ: Lawrence Erlbaum Associates.

Brainerd, C. J. (1978a). Learning research and Piagetian theory. In L. S. Siegel & C. J. Brainerd (Eds.), *Alternatives to Piaget: Critical essays on the theory* (pp. 69–109). New York: Academic Press.

Brainerd, C. J. (1978b). *Piaget's theory of intelligence*. Englewood Cliffs, NJ: Prentice-Hall.

Brophy, J. (1988). Research linking teacher behavior to student achievement: Potential implications for instruction of Chapter 1 students. *Educational Psychologist, 23*, 235–286.

Bruner, J. S. (1960). *The process of education*. Cambridge, MA: Harvard University Press.

Bruner, J. S. (1966). *Toward a theory of instruction*. London: Belnap.

Calderhead, J. (1996). Teachers: Beliefs and Knowledge. In D. C. Berliner & R. C. Calfee (Eds.), *Handbook of educational psychology* (pp. 709–725). New York: Macmillan.

Campbell, D. T., & Stanley, J. C. (1966). *Experimental and quasi-experimental designs for research*. Chicago: Rand McNally.

Ceci, S. J. (1991). How much does schooling influence general intelligence and its cognitive components? A reassessment of the evidence. *Developmental Psychology, 27*, 703–722.

Ceci, S. J. (1996). *On intelligence: A bioecological treatise on intellectual development*. Cambridge, MA: Harvard University Press.

Chall, J. S. (1967). *Learning to read: The great debate*. New York: McGraw-Hill.

Cognition and Technology Group at Vanderbilt (1992). The Jasper series as an example of anchored instruction: Theory, program description, and assessment data. *Educational Psychologist, 27*, 291–315.

Cronbach, L. J. (1962). *Educational psychology*. New York: Harcourt, Brace & World.

Cronbach, L. J., & Snow, R. E. (1977). *Aptitudes and instructional methods: A handbook for research on interactions*. New York: Irvington.

Deci, E. L. (1971). Effects of externally mediated rewards on intrinsic motivation. *Journal of Personality and Social Psychology, 18*, 105–115.

DeCorte, E., & Weinert, F. E. (Eds.). (1996). *International encyclopedia of developmental and instructional psychology*. Oxford, England: Pergamon.

Dweck, C. S. (1986). Motivational processes affecting learning. *American Psychologist, 41*, 1040–48.

Enright, R. D., Lapsley, D. K., & Levy, V. M. (1983). Moral education strategies. In M. Pressley & J. R. Levin (Eds.), *Cognitive strategy research: Educational applications* (pp. 43–83). New York: Springer-Verlag.

Feldhusen, J. F. (1986). A conception of giftedness. In R. J. Sternberg & J. E. Davidson (Eds.), *Conceptions of giftedness* (pp. 112–127). Cambridge, England: Cambridge University Press.

Flavell, J. H. (1963). *The developmental psychology of Jean Piaget*. Princeton, NJ: Van Nostrand.

Flavell, J. H. (1970). Developmental studies of mediated memory. In H. W. Reese & L. P. Lipsitt (Eds.), *Advances in child development and behavior* (Vol. 5, pp. 181–211). New York: Academic Press.

Flower, L., & Hayes, J. R. (1980). The dynamics of composing: Making plans and juggling constraints. In L. Gregg & E. Steinberg (Eds.), *Cognitive processes in writing* (pp. 31–50). Hillsdale, NJ: Lawrence Erlbaum Associates.

Flower, L. S., & Hayes, J. R. (1981). A cognitive process theory of writing. *College Composition and Communication, 32*, 365–387.

Gagné, E. D. (1985). *The cognitive psychology of school learning*. Boston: Little, Brown.

Gagné, R. M. (1977). *The conditions of learning (3rd ed.)*. New York: Holt, Rinehart & Winston.

Gardner, H. (1993). *Multiple intelligences: The theory in practice: A reader*. New York: Basic Books.

Gustafsson, J-E., & Undheim, J. O. (1996). Individual differences in cognitive functions. In D. C. Berliner & R. C. Calfee (Eds.), *Handbook of educational psychology* (pp. 186–242). New York: Macmillan.

Harris, K. R., & Graham, S. (1992). Self-regulated strategy development: A part of the writing process. In M. Pressley, K. R. Harris, & J. T. Guthrie (Eds.), *Promoting academic competence and literacy in school* (pp. 277–309). San Diego, CA: Academic Press.

Herrnstein, R. J., & Murray, C. (1994). *The bell curve: Intelligence and class structure in American life*. New York: The Free Press.

Hess, R. D., & Shipman, V. C. (1965). Early experience and the specialization of cognitive modes in children. *Child Development, 36*, 869–886.

Hiebert, E. H., & Raphael, T. E. (1996). Psychological perspectives on literacy and extensions to educational practice. In D. C. Berliner & R. C. Calfee (Eds), *Handbook of educational psychology* (pp. 550–602). New York: Macmillan.

Holland, J. G., & Skinner, B. F. (1961). *The analysis of behavior: A program for self-instruction*. New York: McGraw-Hill.

Hunt, J. M. (1961). *Intelligence and experience*. New York: Ronald Press.

Inhelder, B., Sinclair, H., & Bovet, M. (1974). *Learning and the development of cognition*. Cambridge, MA: Harvard University Press.

Jackson, N. E., & Butterfield, E. C. (1986). A conception of giftedness designed to promote research. In R. J. Sternberg & J. E. Davidson (Eds.), *Conceptions of giftedness* (pp. 151–181). Cambridge, England: Cambridge University Press.

Jensen, A. R. (1969). How much can we boost IQ and scholastic achievement? *Harvard Educational Review, 39*, 1–123.

Kintsch, W. (1982). *Memory and cognition*. Melbourne, FL: Krieger.

Klausmeier, H. J. (1961). *Learning and human abilities: Educational psychology*. New York: Harper & Row.

Kohlberg, L., & Mayer, R. (1972). Development as the aim of education: The Dewey view. *Harvard Educational Review, 42*, 449–496.

Laosa, L. M. (1978). Maternal teaching strategies in Chicano families of varied educational and socioeconomic levels. *Child Development, 49*, 1129–1135.

Laosa, L. M. (1980). Maternal teaching strategies in Chicano and Anglo-American families: The influence of culture and education on maternal behavior. *Child Development, 51*, 759–765.

Lepper, M. R., Greene, D., & Nisbett, R. E. (1973). Undermining children's intrinsic interest with extrinsic rewards: A test of the "overjustification" hypothesis. *Journal of Personality and Social Psychology, 28*, 129–137.

Mahoney, M. J. (1974). *Cognition and behavior modification*. Cambridge, MA: Ballinger.

Mayer, R. E., & Moreno, R. (1998). A split-attention effect in multimedia learning: Evidence for dual processing systems in working memory. *Journal of Educational Psychologist, 90*, 312–320.

Meichenbaum, D. (1977). *Cognitive behavior modification*. New York: Plenum.

Meichenbaum, D., & Biemiller, A. (1998). *Nurturing independent learners: Helping students take charge of their learning*. Cambridge, MA: Brookline Books.

Miller, G. A., Galanter, E., & Pribram, K. H. (1960). *Plans and the structure of behavior*. New York: Holt, Rinehart & Winston.

Naveh-Benjamin, M., McKeatchie, W. J., & Lin, Y. G. (1987). Two types of test anxious students: Support for an information-processing model. *Journal of Educational Psychology, 79*, 131–136.

Paivio, A. (1971). *Imagery and verbal processes*. New York: Holt, Rinehart & Winston.

Palincsar, A. S., & Brown, A. L. (1984). Reciprocal teaching of comprehension-fostering and monitoring activities. *Cognition and Instruction, 1*, 117–175.

Piaget, J. (1924). *Judgment and reasoning in the child*. London: Kegan Paul, Trench, Trubner & Co.

Plass, J. L., Chun, D. M., Mayer, R. E., & Leutner, D. (1998). Supporting visual and verbal learning preferences in a second-language multimedia learning environment. *Journal of Educational Psychology, 90*, 25–36.

Polya, G. (1954a). *Mathematics and plausible reasoning: (a) Induction and analogy in mathematics*. Princeton, NJ: Princeton University Press.

Polya, G. (1954b). *Mathematics and plausible reasoning: (b) Patterns of plausible inference*. Princeton, NJ: Princeton University Press.

Polya, G. (1957). *How to solve it*. New York: Doubleday.

Polya, G. (1981). *Mathematical discovery* (combined paperback ed.). New York: Wiley.

Pressey, S. L., Robinson, F. P., & Horrocks, J. E. (1959). *Psychology in education*. New York: Harper-Collins.

Pressley, M., & Afflerbach, P. (1995). *Verbal protocols of reading: The nature of constructively responsive reading*. Hillsdale, NJ: Lawrence Erlbaum Associates.

Pressley, M., with McCormick, C. B. (1995). *Advanced educational psychology for educators, researchers, and policymakers*. New York: HarperCollins.

Rogoff, B. (1990). *Apprenticeship in thinking: Cognitive development in social context*. New York: Oxford University Press.

Rohwer, W. D. Jr. (1970). Implications of cognitive development for education. In P. H. Mussen (Ed.), *Carmichael's manual of child psychology* (pp. 1379–1454). New York: Wiley.

Rosenshine, B., & Meister, C. (1994). Reciprocal teaching: A review of nineteen experimental studies. *Review of Educational Research, 64*, 479–530.

Rosenthal, R., & Jacobson, L. (1968). *Pygmalion in the classroom: Teacher expectation and pupils' intellectual development*. New York: Holt, Rinehart & Winston.

Rosenthal, T. L., & Zimmerman, B. J. (1978). *Social learning and cognition*. New York: Academic Press.

Schank, R. C., & Abelson, R. P. (1977). *Scripts, plans, goals, and understanding*. Hillsdale, NJ: Lawrence Erlbaum Associates.

Schneider, W., & Pressley, M. (1997). *Memory development between two and twenty*. Mahwah, NJ: Lawrence Erlbaum Associates.

Schoenfeld, A. (1985). *Mathematical problem solving*. New York: Academic Press.

Schoenfeld, A. (1992). Learning to think mathematically: Problem solving, metacognition, and sense making in mathematics. In D. A. Grouws (Ed.), *Handbook of research on mathematics teaching and learning* (pp. 334–370). New York: Macmillan.

Sidman, M. (1960). *Tactics of scientific research: Evaluating experimental data in psychology*. New York: Basic Books.

Skinner, B. F. (1986). *Beyond freedom and dignity*. New York: Knopf.

Skinner, B. F. (1981). *Technology of teaching*. Englewood Cliffs, NJ: Prentice-Hall.

Skinner, B. F. (1990). Can psychology be a science of mind? *American Psychologist, 45*, 1206–1210.

Snow, C. E., Burns, M. S., & Griffin, P. (Eds.). (1998). *Preventing reading difficulties in young children*. Washington, DC: National Academy Press.

Snow, R. E., Federico, P-A., & Montague, W. E. (1980a). *Aptitude, learning, and instruction: Cognitive process analysis of aptitude: vol. 1*. Hillsdale, NJ: Lawrence Erlbaum Associates.

Snow, R. E., Federico, P-A., & Montague, W. E. (1980b). *Aptitude, learning, and instruction: Cognitive process analysis of learning and problem solving: vol. 2*. Hillsdale, NJ: Lawrence Erlbaum Associates.

Steinberg, L., with Brown, B., & Dornbusch, S. M. (1996). *Beyond the classroom: Why school reform has failed and what parents need to do*. New York: Simon & Schuster.

Sternberg, R. J., Torff, B., & Grigorenko, E. L. (1998). Teaching triarchically improves school achievement. *Journal of Educational Psychology, 90*, 374–384.

Strauss, A., & Corbin, J. (1998). *Basics of qualitative research: Grounded theory procedures and techniques*. Newbury Park, CA: Sage.

Sulzby, E., & Teale, W. (1991). Emergent literacy. In R. Barr, M. Kamil, P. B. Mosenthal, & P. D. Pearson (Eds.), *Handbook of reading research* (Vol. II, pp. 727–758). New York: Longman.

Tobias, S. (1985). Test anxiety: Interference, defective skills, and cognitive capacity. *Educational Psychologist, 20*, 135–142.

Tulving, E., & Donaldson, W. (Eds.). (1972). *Organization of memory* New York: Academic Press.

Van Haneghan, J., Barron, L., Young, M., Williams, S., Vye, N., & Bransford, J. (1992). The Jasper series: An experiment with new ways to enhance mathematical thinking. In D. F. Halpern (Ed.), *Enhancing thinking skills in the sciences and mathematics* (pp. 15–38). Hillsdale, NJ: Lawrence Erlbaum Associates.

Vygotsky, L. S. (1978). *Mind in society: The development of higher psychological processes*. Cambridge, MA: Harvard University Press.

Weiner, B. (1979). A theory of motivation for some classroom experiences. *Journal of Educational Psychology, 71*, 3–25.

Wentzel, K. R. (1991a). Relations between social competence and academic achievement in early adolescence. *Child Development, 62*, 1076–1078.

Wentzel, K. R. (1991b). Social competence at school: Relation between social responsibility and academic achievement. *Review of Educational Research, 61*, 1–24.

Wentzel, K. R. (1993). Does being good make the grade? Social behavior and academic experience in middle school. *Journal of Educational Psychology, 85*, 357–364.

Wittrock, M. C. (Ed.) (1986). *Handbook of research on teaching*. New York: Macmillan.

Wood, S. S., Bruner, J. S., & Ross, G. (1976). The role of tutoring in problem solving. *Journal of Child Psychology and Psychiatry, 17*, 89–100.

15

Benjamin S. Bloom:
His Life, His Works,
and His Legacy

Lorin W. Anderson
University of South Carolina

In education, we continue to be seduced by the equivalent of snake-oil remedies, fake cancer cures, perpetual-motion contraptions, and old wives' tales. Myth and reality are not clearly differentiated, and we frequently prefer the former to the latter. . . . We have been *innocents* in education because we have not put our own house in order. We need to be much clearer about what we do and do not know so that we don't continually confuse the two. If I could have one wish for education, it would be the systematic ordering of our basic knowledge in such a way that what is known and true can be acted on, while what is superstition, fad, and myth can be recognized as such and used only when there is nothing else to support us in our frustration and despair. (Bloom, 1972, p. 332)

Rebels rarely look the part; that's their disguise. If they looked like Jack Palance, we would be on guard. They look like Tevye, the harmless milkman in *Fiddler on the Roof*. So when you meet Benjamin Bloom and you see this 73-year-old scholar in a business suit sitting across the table talking about education in soft, loving tones, it is easy to miss the fact that he is a kind of quiet rebel. . . . He believes that the educational system is structurally flawed and should be thoroughly rehabilitated, like an old house that is in danger of collapsing and killing its occupants. (Chase, 1987, p. 42)

HIS LIFE[1]

Benjamin Samuel Bloom was born in Lansford, Pennsylvania, on February 21, 1913, of Russian immigrant parents. His father was a picture framer and his mother, a housewife who loved flower gardening. He had three older brothers and a younger sister.

Bloom attended public grammar school and public high school in Lansford. He was an excellent student and a good athlete (particularly in swimming and handball). He was an avid reader, often frustrating the school librarian by attempting to return books on the same day he checked them out. (She refused to accept them.) In 1931 he graduated from high school as the class vale-dictorian.

After graduation he attended the Pennsylvania State University on a tuition scholarship. He completed his B. A. and M. A. degrees in psychology in 4 years, while working at several jobs to support himself. During his senior year, he was the intramural handball champion of the University.

His first job following graduation from college was as a research worker with the Pennsylvania State Relief Organization. After 1 year, he moved to Washington, D.C., where he took a similar position with the American Youth Commission. The move to Washington was to change his life forever.

During his second year with the Commission he attended a meeting at which Ralph Tyler spoke. At the time Tyler was involved in designing assessments for the Eight-Year Study (Aikin, 1942; Smith & Tyler, 1942). In addition, he was a reviewer of reports issued by the American Youth Council. Bloom was so impressed with Tyler that he decided to apply to the doctoral program at the Ohio State University, where Tyler was on the faculty. After he submitted his application, he found out that Tyler had taken a position at the University of Chicago, Tyler's *alma mater*. Despite his misgivings about attending a "city college," he withdrew his application to Ohio State and applied to the doctoral program at Chicago. He was admitted and began his studies in the summer of 1939.

Shortly thereafter he met his future wife, Sophie, in the education library. She was working on her M. A. degree at the University. He proposed marriage 1 week after meeting her; however, they did not become engaged until the following spring. They were married in the summer of 1940 in Detroit, Michigan.

While completing his doctoral program, Bloom served as a research assistant in the Office of the University's Board of Examinations under Tyler's supervision. In addition to his other duties, Tyler was serving as the University Examiner at the time. Bloom's affiliation with the Board of Examinations was to play a crucial role in his professional career.

The University of Chicago's Board of Examinations

The Board of Examinations was founded at the University of Chicago in 1931 and placed under the direction of L. L. Thurstone. Bloom explained the rationale for the establishment of the Board.

> In planning the new curriculum in general education, the faculty wished to separate the examining and judging functions from the pedagogical functions. They wished to have the instructor serve primarily to help students learn, and they believed that an ideal student–teacher relationship was impossible when the teacher also had the responsibility for judging and grading the student. (Bloom, 1981a, p. 245)

According to Bloom, the faculty also wanted to place greater responsibility on students for their own education. Class attendance requirements were eliminated and degree requirements were set exclusively in terms of students' performance on comprehensive examinations. The Board of Examinations was responsible for the quality of those examinations, as well as for their administration and scoring.

From 1931 through 1939 the Board's emphasis was on developing a technology of testing. Because each examination had to cover an entire year's worth of subject matter knowledge, the examinations were quite lengthy both in terms of the number of questions (from 400 to 600) and the amount of time required to complete them (6 hours or more) (Bloom, 1954a/1981). Furthermore, because of the length of the examinations, the focus was on students' recall of factual information using so-called "objective" item formats (e.g., true–false, matching, multiple-choice). Thus, during this time period, the Board addressed issues of test construction, test administration, scoring procedures, objectivity, validity, and reliability in both theoretical and practical terms (Richardson, Russell, Snalnaker, & Thurstone, 1933; Snalnaker, 1934; Thurstone, 1937; Richardson & Kuder, 1939).

Toward the close of this period, the faculty began to question whether subject matter knowledge should be the primary outcome of instruction. They began to believe that, as a result of instruction, students should learn how to reason and how to attack a variety of problems in specific academic disciplines. They regarded the fundamental task of general education as that of "enabling the individual to understand the world in which he [or she] lived and to attack the significant problems he [or she] encountered both as a [person] and as a citizen" (Bloom, 1981a, p. 251).

As the faculty increasingly accepted these newly defined learning outcomes, they began to teach in new and different ways. Quite naturally, they wanted different types of examinations that would help them determine how successful they were. In Bloom's (1981a) words: "Examining had to be seen as part of the total educational process and as having consequences beyond the accurate certification of achievement or beyond the production of good examinations" (p. 251). It was at this time, in 1940, that Tyler became University Examiner and Bloom went to work in the Office of the Board of Examinations.

Bloom remained with the Board of Examinations for 2 decades—from 1940 through 1959—eventually succeeding Tyler as University Examiner in 1953. The majority of Bloom's writings in the early years of his tenure with the Board focused on the relationships among educational outcomes, methods of instruction, and educational measurement (e.g., Bloom, 1944, 1947; Bloom & Allison, 1949, 1950). In the late 1940s and early 1950s, he began to explore alternative ways of measuring problem-solving (Bloom & Broder, 1950) and differences in problem-solving processes that resulted from different methods of instruction (Bloom, 1953c, 1954b). Also, during the late 1940s, the seeds for the *Taxonomy of Educational Objectives, Handbook I: The Cognitive Domain* were planted (Bloom, 1949; Bloom, Englehart, Furst, Hill, & Krathwohl, 1956; Krathwohl, 1994).

The Department of Education

Bloom spent virtually his entire academic life—over 50 years—at the University of Chicago.[2] He received his Ph.D. in the spring of 1942 and continued to work in the Office of the Board of Examiners. Two years later he was appointed as an instructor in the Department of Education. Over the next 2 decades, he rose through the ranks from assistant to full professor and was appointed the Charles H. Swift Distinguished Service Professor of Education in the late 1960s.

During his first 15 years in the Department, his writings reflected his ongoing work with the Board of Examiners (e.g., Bloom, 1957, 1958a, 1958b; Bloom & Heyns, 1956; Bloom & Statler, 1957; Bloom & Webster, 1960). Then, in 1959–60, he left his position as University Examiner and spent a year at the Center for Advanced Study in Behavioral Sciences in Stanford, California. This year marked a significant change in the direction of Bloom's research and writing.

During his stay at the Center, Bloom began work on what was to become *Stability and Change in Human Characteristics* (Bloom, 1964). In his words: "The freedom from the usual schedule and duties, the opportunity to explore a problem as deeply as possible, and the encouragement of the staff and other Fellows did much to help me get started on the problem of stability and change. The major outline of [the book] was completed at the Center" (p. ix). Thus began Bloom's shift from problems in testing, measurement, and evaluation, to problems in learning (e.g., Bloom, 1966a, 1974b), human development (1973, 1985), curriculum (e.g., Bloom, 1965, 1974a), instruction (Bloom, 1968a, 1984), and educational research (Bloom, 1966c, 1980).

The International Arena

Toward the end of his work with the Board of Examiners, Bloom began to take an active interest in international education. As Dick Wolf (2000) has suggested,

"Ben was one of the first people in the world to have a global view of education, long before the current notion of a 'global economy' became fashionable " (p. 1). Opportunities for international consultation arose in large part because of the publication of the *Taxonomy of Educational Objectives, Handbook I: The Cognitive Domain* (Bloom et al., 1956). In the late 1950s and early 1960s, he served as an advisor to the government of India on educational evaluation (Bloom, 1958a, 1961). In the mid-1960s, he served in a similar capacity for the government of Israel.

In the late 1950s, Bloom attended a meeting held at the UNESCO Institute of Education in Hamburg, Germany. One of the major results of the meeting was a recognition on the part of those in attendance of the need for cross-national studies that would enable educators to identify common factors related to enhanced educational achievement. Shortly thereafter, in 1959, the International Association for the Evaluation of Educational Achievement (IEA) was founded for the purpose of designing and conducting such studies. Bloom was one of the co-founders.

The first IEA study examined mathematics achievement in 12 countries (Bloom, 1966a; Husen, 1967). Bloom wrote the proposal to secure international funds for the conduct of the study and was deeply involved in the development of the instruments and the plans for data analysis (Wolf, 2000). Over the past 3 decades studies of civic education, computers in education, foreign language learning, literature, reading comprehension, science, written composition, as well as additional studies of mathematics, have been conducted under the auspices of the IEA (see, Degenhart, 1990, for a listing of IEA publications to 1990).

In 1971, Bloom brought together teams of educators from 29 countries to participate in a seminar on curriculum development, held in Gränna, Sweden. The seminar was led by an international faculty and featured Ralph Tyler. The basic text used by seminar participants was the *Handbook on Formative and Summative Evaluation of Student Learning* (Bloom, Hastings, & Madaus, 1971). The basic assumption underlying the seminar was that

> education must be increasingly concerned about the fullest development of all children and youth, and it will be the responsibility of the schools to seek learning conditions which will enable each individual to reach the highest level of learning possible. (Bloom et al., 1971, p. 6)

Following the seminar, each six-person team was to return to its own country and establish curriculum research centers. Such centers were in fact established in many of the participating countries (Bloom, 1994).

Finally, in 1986, Bloom, at age 73, was invited by the Honorary President of East China Normal University in Shanghai to be one of 25 exchange scholars between China and the U.S. This was a remarkable experience for Bloom. He described it in the following manner.

> One of my primary responsibilities was to conduct a series of seminars. During these seminars, the Taxonomy was described and discussed. Lin Fu Nian [the president

of the university] was so impressed with the *Handbook* that he had it translated into Chinese and distributed a million copies to educators throughout China. The magnitude of this effort is truly mind-boggling. (Bloom, 1994, p. 6)

HIS WORKS

A complete set of Bloom's published works is contained in the References in this chapter. In this section, six of his books and one brief article, spanning a total of 35 years, are reviewed. These pieces were selected because they reflect both the constancy and development of Bloom's ideas over time. Following a brief summary of the six books and the lone article, five "cross-cutting" themes are identified and discussed. The books are:

1. *Problem-Solving Processes of College Students* (Bloom & Broder, 1950).
2. *The Taxonomy of Educational Objectives, Handbook 1: The Cognitive Domain* (Bloom et al., 1956).
3. *Stability and Change in Human Characteristics* (Bloom, 1964).
4. *Compensatory Education for Cultural Deprivation* (Bloom, Davis, & Hess,1965).
5. *Human Characteristics and School Learning* (Bloom, 1976).
6. *Developing Talent in Young People* (Bloom, 1985).
   The article is "Learning for Mastery" (Bloom, 1968a).

Problem-Solving Processes of College Students

> Mental processes represent a very difficult and complex subject to study. To a large extent, we have been limited in this study by the wide-spread emphasis on overt behavior as the major acceptable type of evidence on the workings of the mind. This attempt to make an objective science of psychology not only limits the kinds of data acceptable to the psychologist but must necessarily make for many inaccuracies in his inferences about the nature of the mental processes. (Bloom & Broder, 1950, p. 1)

So begins the book. *Problem-Solving Processes of College Students*. This is a rather amazing set of statements in light of the fact that, at the time, behaviorism was the dominant theory in psychology; it would be 6 years until the "mythical birthday of the cognitive revolution" (Bruner, 1992, p. 780).

Problem-Solving Processes of College Students describes and presents the results of three studies conducted at the University of Chicago, beginning in the spring of 1945. The problems selected were limited to "questions and test situations taken from various academic tests and examinations" (Bloom & Broder, 1950, p. 8). Furthermore, "we attempted to select problems for which the subject would have clear-cut, although perhaps quite complex, goals to achieve and for which he could make a conscious plan of attack" (Bloom & Broder, 1950, p. 8). Individually, students were given a problem and asked to "think aloud" as they worked through the problem. As a student thought aloud, the interviewer took as complete notes as possible on everything the student said and did. In certain cases, the interviewer asked the students to recall what they had done while solving a problem after they had completed it.

The first study included 12 students, 6 who were academically successful (e.g., high test scores, good grades) and 6 who were not. The purpose was to examine the extent of the differences in problem-solving processes of the two groups. Differences were found in the students':

- Understanding of the nature of the problem.
- Understanding of the ideas contained in the problem.
- General approach to the solution of problems.
- Attitude toward the solution of problems.

The second study examined the differences in problem-solving processes elicited by different types of problems. The problems selected were classified according to their difficulty, their subject matter, and their format (e.g., true–false, multiple-choice). Common difficulties encountered by students attempting to solve the various types of problems were noted as were difficulties associated with specific types of problems. These difficulties provided the basis for a series of recommendations concerning the improvement of test problems (e.g., minimizing the use of relative terms in a problem, providing clear directions).

The third study focused on students whose "failure on the comprehensive examinations might be due in large part to poor problem-solving methods" (Bloom & Broder, 1950, p. 67). Specifically, these students (a) had scholastic aptitude test scores that were relatively higher than their performance on the comprehensive examinations, (b) devoted at least an average amount of time to study, and (c) claimed that the examinations did not adequately reflect their understanding and mastery of the subject. The attempt in this study was to improve the problem-solving skills of these students (that is, to remediate problem-solving deficiencies). A systematic approach to remediation was designed, implemented, and evaluated. Based on the results of the study, Bloom & Broder (1950) concluded that "the weight of the evidence is clearly that problem-solving remediation can help students" (p. 89). (See also Bloom, 1947.)

Taxonomy of Educational Objectives, Handbook 1: The Cognitive Domain

You are reading about an attempt to build a taxonomy of educational objectives. It is intended to provide for classification of the goals of our educational system. It is expected to be of general help to all teachers, administrators, professional specialists, and research workers who deal with curricular and evaluation problems. It is especially intended to help them discuss these problems with greater precision. (Bloom et al., 1956, p. 1)

Arguably, this is Bloom's most recognized work. Even today, more than 40 years later, there are few educators in the United States who are unable to recite the litany of knowledge, comprehension, application, analysis, synthesis, and evaluation. In addition, the *Handbook* has been translated into more than 20 languages (Anderson & Sosniak, 1994).

Bloom himself linked the development of the Taxonomy to his work in the Office of the Board of Examiners.

> Under President Robert Hutchins' General Education Plan, the undergraduate division of the University of Chicago was organized around interdisciplinary core courses and comprehensive examinations. The examinations . . . were to emphasize higher mental processes. . . . I was first College Examiner and then University Examiner with the Board of Examiners. It should be obvious why the development of the Taxonomy was of special importance to the faculty and to me. (Bloom, 1994, p. 2)

Bloom had high hopes for the Taxonomy from the very beginning. At the Allerton Conference, the first conference devoted solely to the work of the Taxonomy (Krathwohl, 1994), Bloom began by describing his vision of an empirically-built "examiners' taxonomy" designed to facilitate the exchange of test items (an early approach to item banking). He ended with a loftier challenge:

> There is a larger task which we may wish to consider. . . . A taxonomy of educational outcomes could do much to bring order out of chaos in the field of education. It could furnish the conceptual framework around which our descriptions of educational programs and experiences could be oriented. It could furnish a framework for the development of educational theories and research. It could furnish the scheme needed for training our teachers and for orienting them to the varied possibilities of education. (Bloom, 1949, cited in Krathwohl, 1994, p. 181)

The Taxonomy was developed in accordance with five guiding principles. First, the Taxonomy should focus on **intended** learning outcomes (rather than **actual** student learning processes). Second, the major distinctions among the taxonomic categories should reflect the distinctions that teachers make among them. Third, the Taxonomy should be "logically developed and internally consistent" (Bloom et al., 1956, p. 14). Fourth, the Taxonomy should be consistent with "our present understanding of psychological phenomena" (Bloom et al., 1956, p. 14). Fifth, the classification should be purely descriptive (in contrast with value-laden) so that every type of educational goal should "fit" somewhere. Based on these principles, the familiar set of six categories was identified. The categories were presumed to exist along a continuum of complexity, with each "higher level" category building on and incorporating the lower ones.

The Taxonomy influenced education and educators in several ways. One was to "provide a panorama of [educational] goals broader than might otherwise have been considered" (Krathwohl, 1994). A second was to offer "easily understandable guidelines for expanding both curriculum and evaluation beyond simple knowledge" (Postlethwaite, 1994, p. 179).

The Taxonomy may have had a greater impact internationally than it did in this country (Anderson, 1994; Sosniak, 1994). In large numbers of countries throughout the world, the Taxonomy was used as the basis for curriculum development, test construction, lesson planning, and teacher training (Chung, 1994; Lewy and Báthory, 1994).

Since its publication, the Taxonomy has not been without its critics. Criticisms have ranged from the likely neglect of important educational goals that do not lend themselves to precise specification, to the exclusive focus on process (at the expense of content), to the omission of understanding as a taxonomic category, to the questionable validity of the assumption of a cumulative hierarchy. (See Furst, 1994, for a useful summary.)

Stability and Change in Human Characteristics

> This book ... represents an attempt to identify "stable" [human] characteristics, to describe the extent to which such characteristics are stabilized at various ages, and to determine the conditions under which this stability may be modified. Hopefully, this work will enable us to understand how such characteristics may be identified, explained, and, eventually, modified. (Bloom, 1964, p. 2)

To accomplish these three purposes Bloom summarized the results of longitudinal studies pertaining to three sets of human attributes: physical (e.g., height, weight, and strength), cognitive (e.g., intelligence and school achievement) and affective (e.g., interests, attitudes, and personality). A single mathematical formula $[I_2 = I_1 + f(E_{2-1})]$ is used to frame his analysis of the data and to guide his interpretation of the results. In the formula I_1 and I_2 stand for measures of a characteristic at two points in time and E_{2-1} represents relevant environmental factors that were in place in the meantime. In other words the formula suggests that a person's height (or intelligence or aggressiveness) at one point in time is some combination of the person's height (or intelligence or aggressiveness) at some earlier time and the type of environment in which he or she lived during the intervening years.

In order to understand Bloom's findings, it is necessary to understand his definition of stability.

> Empirically, a stable characteristic is one that is consistent from one point in time to another. If pressed, one might further delimit this by specifying the time intervals

as one year or more and the minimum level of consistency as a correlation of +.50 or higher. Defined in this way, a stable characteristic may be one that is different quantitatively as well as qualitatively at the two time points if the change is predictable to some minimal degree. (Bloom, 1964, p. 3)

Thus, stability, according to Bloom, is **relative**, not **absolute**.[3] He illustrated his definition of stability using the characteristic, height.

A good illustration of a stable characteristic from this point of view is height, which changes from birth to maturity, and yet height at maturity is highly predictable from height at ages 3 or 4. That is, the *relative* height positions of a sample of boys or girls are highly consistent from one age to another. (p. 3)

According to the data summarized by Bloom, all of the characteristics he examined achieved a reasonable degree of stability by age 8, with most stabilizing between ages 3 and 4. Furthermore, for the characteristics studied there generally was an initial period of relatively rapid change followed by an extended period of relatively slow change. "With the exception of school achievement, the most rapid period for . . . development . . . is in the first five years of life" (p. 204).

Based on his data, Bloom suggested that the ability of environmental factors to influence change in human characteristics decreases as the characteristics become more stable. With respect to intelligence, for example, Bloom asserted that "marked changes in the environment in the early years can produce greater changes in intelligence than will equally marked changes in the environment at later periods of development" (p. 89). Similarly, Bloom interpreted the results pertaining to school achievement as suggesting the "great importance of the first few years of school as well as the preschool period in . . . developing . . . learning patterns and general achievement" (p. 127).

Prior to the publication of the book, but armed with his conclusions and supporting data, Bloom testified before Congress as legislators debated the structure and merits of the Economic Opportunity Act (EOA), one of the cornerstones of President Lyndon Johnson's "Great Society." In its final form, the EOA contained the early childhood education program, Head Start. When Bloom died in September, 1999, the writers of two of his obituaries emphasized his role in the creation of Head Start (Honan, 1999; Woo, 1999). Honan, in fact, referred to *Stability and Change* as the most influential of Bloom's books.

Compensatory Education for Cultural Deprivation

Very few problems in the field of education are as complex as the problems of cultural deprivation. An adequate attack on these educational problems requires that educational policy makers, curriculum specialists, teachers, guidance workers, and administrators have an appreciation of the many ways in which the social problems of our society bear directly on the development of the child and adolescent and influence the interaction between students and the schools. (Bloom, Davis, & Hess, 1965, Preface)

In the mid-1960s, two major pieces of federal legislation were passed. The first, mentioned in the previous section, was the Economic Opportunity Act (EOA) (1964). The second, was the Elementary and Secondary Education Act (ESEA) (1965). Whereas EOA established Head Start, ESEA established Title I and Follow Through programs. Follow Through was intended to build on the Heat Start programs by extending educational support from kindergarten through the third grade. Title I was a massive program that aimed to provide support to school districts that enrolled large numbers of disadvantaged, low-achieving students. In combination these three programs were grouped under the rubric of "compensatory education." It was within this national context that Bloom and two University of Chicago colleagues, Allison Davis and Robert Hess, convened the Research Conference on Education and Cultural Deprivation, June 8–12, 1964.

The funds for the conference were provided by the U.S. Office of Education. The purpose of the conference was to "review what is already known about the problems of education and cultural deprivation, to make recommendations about what might be done to solve some of these problems, and to suggest the critical problems for further research" (Bloom, Davis, & Hess, 1965, p. iii). The proceedings of the conference were published by Holt, Rinehart, & Winston under the title, *Compensatory Education for Cultural Deprivation*.

The conference report contains a series of recommendations, many of which found their way into public policy. The recommendations are organized into five sections:

1. Basic needs (e.g., each child should be assured of a adequate breakfast to help him begin the learning tasks of the day [p. 10]).

2. Early experiences (e.g., the parents must be sufficiently involved in the nursery school–kindergarten to understand its importance for their child and to give support and reinforcement to the tasks of these special schools [p. 19]).

3. Elementary school (e.g., the emphasis in the first three years of elementary school should be on the development of each child with careful evaluation records of his progress toward clear-cut tasks and goals. . . . The careful sequential development of each child must be one of continual success at small tasks [p. 25]).

4. Special case of the Negro student (e.g., especially in the early years of school all children must learn under the most positive set of human interactions. Where possible, teachers should be chosen because of their ability to help young children and because they can be warm and supportive of all children (p. 32).

5. Adolescent education (e.g., there should be work–study plans in which students can learn in relation to the work. This requires very effective co-operation between schools, industry, and public agencies [p. 38–39]).

Bloom, Davis, and Hess recognized that not all of the recommendations they offered would be accepted. At the same time, however, it was critically important to address the problems of properly educating culturally disadvantaged children and youth. "We would urge that groups which take exception to our recommendations provide alternatives which are as carefully conceived as we have tried to make ours. To do nothing is really not an alternative to the recommendations we have made in this report" (Preface).

Learning for Mastery

Each teacher begins a new term (or course) with the expectation that about a third of his students will adequately learn what he has to teach. He expects about a third of his students to fail or just "get by." Finally, he expects another third to learn a good deal of what he has to teach, but not enough to be regarded as "good students" . . .The cost of this system in reducing opportunities for further learning and in alienating youth from both school and society is so great that no society can tolerate it for long. Most students (perhaps over 90 percent) can master what we have to teach them, and it is the task of instruction to find the means which will enable our students to master the subject under consideration (Bloom, 1968a, p. 1).

Drawing heavily on John Carroll's (1963) model of school learning, Bloom laid out his strategy for mastery learning in this short newsletter. In the first half of this paper, Bloom summarized Carroll's model. Within Carroll's model is the conceptual shift that is needed to support learning for mastery; namely, the replacement of a fixed amount of time to learn with a fixed level of learning (i.e., mastery). If students who differ in terms of what they bring to a learning situation are given the same amount of time to learn (i.e., fixed time), they will leave the learning situation with different amounts of learning. If, on the other hand, students who differ in terms of what they bring to a learning situation are expected to learn to the same level (i.e., fixed learning or mastery), they must be provided with different amounts of time. The challenge for teachers, then, is to find the needed extra time, while at the same time, making better use of the time that is currently available.

In the second half of his paper, Bloom spelled out some of the necessary preconditions for mastery, the required operating procedures of mastery, and the likely outcomes of mastery learning. In combination, the preconditions and operating procedures became the essential features (Anderson, 1985) or critical elements of mastery learning (Anderson, 1985; Guskey, 1986).

As originally set forth by Bloom, these features or elements are:

- Specification of the objectives and content of instruction (precondition).
- Translation of the specifications into evaluation procedures (precondition).
- Setting of standards of mastery and excellence apart from interstudent competition (i.e., absolute mastery standards) (precondition).

- Breaking course or subject into smaller units of learning (operating procedure).
- Design and administration of brief diagnostic–progress tests (i.e., formative evaluation) (operating procedure).
- Use of alternative instructional materials or processes intended to help students correct their learning difficulties (as indicated by their performance on the diagnostic–progress tests) (operating procedure).

In combination, the last two bullets are generally referred to as "feedback/correctives." It is the feedback and correctives that require additional instructional time.

Over the years, numerous studies have been conducted investigating the effectiveness of mastery learning programs on student learning (both cognitive and affective). The results of these studies have been summarized in Block and Burns (1976), Guskey and Gates (1986), and Guskey and Pigott (1988). In general, the results indicate that students in mastery learning programs achieve at higher levels and have more positive attitudes and academic self-concepts than students in more traditional programs. These differences are particularly evident in tightly controlled studies and on achievement tests clearly aligned with the program objectives.

Human Characteristics and School Learning

The central thesis of this book is that variations in learning and the level of learning of students are determined by the students' learning history and the quality of instruction they receive. Appropriate modifications related to the history of the learners and the quality of instruction can sharply reduce the variation of students and greatly increase their level of learning and their effectiveness in learning in terms of time and effort expended. Where conditions for learning in the home and school approach some ideal, we believe that individual differences in learning should approach a vanishing point. (Bloom, 1976, p. 16)

In this book, Bloom laid out his theory of school learning. The history of the learner was defined in terms of cognitive entry behaviors (CEB) and affective entry characteristics (AEC). Quality of instruction (QI) was defined in terms of four elements: cues, participation, reinforcement, and feedback/correctives. The two aspects of the history of the learner (CEB and AEC) and the four elements of quality of instruction interacted within the context of a learning task (i.e., "a learning unit in a course, a chapter in a textbook, or a topic in a course or curriculum" [p. 22]). Within Bloom's framework, a semester or yearlong course consisted of a series or sequence of learning tasks. When the relationship among the learning tasks is sequential, the cognitive and affective outcomes of earlier tasks become the cognitive entry behaviors and affective entry characteristics for later tasks.

How are the components of the theory interrelated? Bloom suggested that differences in students' cognitive entry behaviors account for 50% of the variation in school achievement whereas differences in affective entry characteristics account for 25%. Because cognitive entry behaviors and affective entry characteristics are not completely independent of one another, they, in combination, could be expected to account for 65% of the variation in school achievement. Finally, when quality of instruction is added, the combination of cognitive entry behaviors, affective entry characteristics, **and** quality of instruction could be expected to account for more than 80% (p. 174) and as much as 90% (p. 169) of the variation in school achievement.

As in *Stability and Change*, Bloom used data from existing research studies to test his theory. He divided the studies into macro-level studies (i.e., relatively large-scale studies conducted over a fairly lengthy time period) and micro-level studies (e.g., smaller-scale, experimental studies conducted over a period of weeks or months). Whereas quite specific elements of quality of instruction (e.g., presentation of material, student involvement in learning, feedback and correctives) were included in the macro-level studies, mastery learning (as described in the previous section) was used as a composite indicator of quality of instruction in the micro-level studies.

The results of the studies supported the expected magnitude of the relationship between cognitive entry behaviors and school achievement. However, the relationship between affective entry characteristics and school achievement was somewhat smaller than expected, adding very little to the predictive power of cognitive entry behaviors alone. Furthermore, the multiple correlation of cognitive entry behavior, affective entry characteristics, and quality of instruction with school achievement was approximately 0.80. Thus, about two-thirds of the variation in school achievement was found to be attributable to the three major theoretical constructs (CEB, AEC, and QI) in contrast to the 80 to 90% that was hypothesized.

Developing Talent in Young People

Exceptional levels of talent development require certain types of environmental support, special experiences, excellent teaching, and appropriate motivational encouragement at each stage of development. No matter what the quality of initial gifts, each of the individuals we have studied went through many years of special development under the care of attentive parents and the tutelage and supervision of a remarkable series of teachers and coaches. (Bloom, 1985, p. 543)

The Development of Talent Research Project (DTRP) required slightly more than 4 years to complete, involved eight "major research workers" (p. 15), and included a sample of 120 extremely successful individuals divided into six talent fields. The fields were concert pianists, Olympic swimmers, world-class tennis players, award-winning sculptors, research mathematicians, and research neurologists.

All 120 individuals were interviewed, with each interview lasting from 2 to 3 hours. Shorter "follow-up" interviews were conducted as necessary. Virtually all of the parents were interviewed, as were many of the master teachers and major coaches. The parent, teacher, and coach interviews tended to be of shorter duration.

The results suggested that the process of talent development could be divided into three phases. The first phase, play and romance, was characterized by encouragement, interest and involvement, freedom to explore, and immediate rewards. The second phase, technical precision and discipline, was characterized by skill, technique, and the "habit of accuracy" (p. 434). Finally, the third phase, generalization and integration, was characterized by the development of individuality and the realization that a specific talent field can be a significant part of one's life.

Parents were found to play an important, perhaps critical role, in the development of talent in their children. They communicated to their children what was important (both the value of achievement and the value of the talent area). Early on, they introduced their children to the talent field. Later, they arranged for their children to receive formal instruction in the talent field. Early on, parents were intimately involved in their children's lessons and practice. Later, their role became more supervisory and supportive in nature. In most cases, the "family routine was ... arranged to accommodate the child's practice schedule" (p. 461).

Based on the results of the study, Bloom and his colleagues identified three general qualities that were shared by all of those studied. The individuals had a:

- "Strong interest and emotional commitment to a particular talent field."
- "Desire to reach a high level of attainment in the talent field."
- "Willingness to put in the great amounts of time and effort needed to reach very high levels of achievement in the talent field." (p. 544)

Common Themes

Five major themes can be found in Bloom's writings. First, Bloom was not influenced greatly by the prevailing educational *zeitgeist*. This can be seen most clearly in his early works. He was doing research on problem-solving processes at a time in which either thinking processes were not recognized at all or were being inferred from the solutions student offered or the answers they gave. In addition, he used a method, introspection, that, although popular early in the development of psychology, had fallen into disfavor and was little used. He demonstrated its usefulness.

Similarly, he helped to formulate a classification system for educational objectives that was remarkably eclectic in its psychological orientation. After examining the Taxonomy from five different theoretical perspectives, Rohwer and Sloane (1994) wrote the following.

We . . . find ourselves intrigued by the question of what psychological presuppositions the authors would make if they undertook to build the Taxonomy anew today. We doubt that their presuppositions would exhibit a docile adoption of the principles of cognitive science, despite the current dominance of that perspective. [In fact], we believe that the authors . . . would be no more inclined to temper their convictions to please the cognitive scientists today than they were to please the behaviorists when they were dominant. (p. 62)

A second theme pertains to the tremendous influence that different environments can have on people. In his introduction to *Developing Talent in Young People*, Bloom wrote:

After forty years of intensive research on school learning in the United States as well as abroad, my major conclusion is: What any person in the world can learn, *almost* all persons can learn *if* provided with appropriate prior and current conditions of learning. (p. 4)

With proper, powerful educational environments, students can be helped to improve their problem-solving skills (Bloom & Broder, 1950), overcome economic and cultural disadvantages (Bloom, Davis, & Hess, 1965), master the school curriculum (Bloom, 1968a; 1976), and develop their talents to an extremely high level (Bloom, 1985). "In spite of the many pessimistic notes about the lack of measurable effects of the teacher or school on learning, we are of the view that the *Quality of Instruction* students receive has a demonstrable effect on their achievement and learning processes" (Bloom, 1976, p. 171).

Educational environments are not limited to schools. Home environments, as educational environments, play an important role in student learning and development (Bloom, Davis, & Hess, 1965; Bloom, 1985). But, it is what happens in the home between parents and children, not the social or economic status, that makes the difference (Bloom, 1981b; Bloom, 1986b). In Bloom's (1981b) words: "It is what parents *do* rather than what they *are* that accounts for the learning development of children in the early years" (p. 75). In the talent development study (Bloom, 1985), parents changed jobs and moved to provide opportunities for their children to reach extraordinary levels in their talent field.

It is in *Stability and Change in Human Characteristics* that Bloom, the environmentalist, clearly emerges (Anderson, 1996a). "Although there must be some genetic potential for learning, the direction the learning takes is most powerfully determined by the environment" (Bloom, 1964, p. 209). Similarly, "whatever may have been the genetic potential for learning, there is little doubt that the environment will determine what is learned and even the extent to which learning does take place" (Bloom, 1964, p. 210).

A third theme concerns the vastness of human potential. In his final major work, Bloom (1985) stated: "Perhaps the major value of this study is that it documents many new insights into human potential and the means by which it is translated into actual accomplishment.... Underlying the entire study is the belief that the quality of life is dependent on individuals having a sense of fulfillment in one or more roles and fields of human endeavor" (p. 18). And what student of Bloom can forget the "mantra of the education field today: all children can learn" (Breslin, 1999, p. x).

People can change; they can learn; they can develop talents. They *can*, but *will they*? Consistent with the second theme, part of the answer to this question depends on the kinds of environments in which they find themselves. "The measurement of the culturally deprived child's intelligence at one point does not determine the upper limits of what he might be able to learn in the schools *if more favorable conditions are subsequently provided in the home and/or the school*" (Bloom, Davis, & Hess, 1965, p. 12; emphasis mine).

A second part of the answer to the above question is when people find themselves in particular environments. There is a "window of opportunity" in which powerful environmental interventions (Bloom, 1964) are most likely to be successful. For example, the "first three years of the elementary school are critical. If learning is not successful and satisfying in these years, the entire educational career of the child is seriously jeopardized" (Bloom, 1964, p. 22).

A fourth theme concerns the purpose of education. Over his entire career, Bloom remained true to the aims of general education he encountered while working in the Office of the Board of Examiners. "It is very clear that in the middle of the 20th century we find ourselves in a rapidly changing and unpredictable culture.... Under these conditions, much emphasis must be placed...on the development of generalized ways of attacking problems and on knowledge which can be applied to a wide range of situations" (Bloom, Englehart et al., 1956, p. 40). Furthermore, "there must be increasing emphasis on the higher mental processes of problem-solving rather than the existing stress on information learning.... In addition, there must be increasing emphasis on the basic ideas, structure, and methods of inquiry of each subject field rather than on the minutiae of the subject matter" (Bloom, Davis, & Hess, 1965, p. 3).

The fifth theme, one at least tangentially related to the previous one, concerns the purpose of schooling in our society. Throughout his writings, Bloom remained extremely critical of school systems that saw their primary responsibility as sorting and selecting students. "It is difficult at present to determine the exact ways in which educational institutions in the United States will be reshaped over the next decade. It is likely that one major change will be a shift in the conception of education from a status-giving and selective system to a system that develops each individual to his highest potential" (Bloom, 1965, p. 2). Two decades later, his conviction remained the same.

> A society which places such great value on education and schooling that it requires the individual to attend school for long periods of time must find the means to make education attractive and meaningful for the individual learner. Modern societies no longer can content themselves with the *selection of talent*; they must find the means for *developing talent*. (Bloom, 1985, p. 17)

HIS LEGACY[4]

What will Bloom's legacy be? I suggest that he will be remembered for three things. He introduced us to the world of possibilities. There are educational objectives that lie beyond rote memorization. All students, not just a select group, can learn and learn well. Talent is not something to be found in the few; it is to be developed in the many. If Bloom did nothing more than this, he would have made a tremendous contribution to education. But he did more.

He believed in the power of education, both for the welfare of individuals and for the betterment of society. Although education was likely to be more powerful when children were younger, it was never too late. "There is almost no point in the individual's history when his [or her] learning characteristics cannot be altered either positively or negatively" (Bloom, 1976, p. 137). As children became older, instruction had to be better. And, better instruction meant, among other things,

- Communicating clear learning goals.
- Promoting active student engagement in learning.
- Monitoring learning progress via tests and other forms of assessment.
- Providing feedback to students concerning their learning strengths and weaknesses.
- Helping students overcome learning difficulties before they accumulated to the extent they interfered with future learning. (Bloom, 1968a; 1976; 1977b)

To ensure that education was a powerful as possible, he challenged us to solve what he termed the "2 sigma problem" (Bloom, 1984). Based on available data, Bloom argued that the average student receiving tutoring scored two standard deviations higher than the average student receiving traditional group-based instruction on standardized achievement tests. Because the Greek symbol, sigma, is used to denote the standard deviation of a population, the problem of finding ways to design and deliver group-based instruction that was as effective as one-to-one tutoring became known as the "2 sigma problem." In reviewing the initial draft of this chapter, Tom Guskey suggested that the 2 sigma problem is the "classic illustration of the optimism of [Bloom's] work, the framework of his thinking, and his challenge to other educators."

Guskey's comment leads nicely to the third thing for which Bloom will likely be remembered. He gave us frameworks for thinking about and talking about educational problems: the Taxonomies, his theory of school learning, and his stages of talent development. In Krathwohl's (1994) terms Bloom provided us with a set of heuristics. According to Krathwohl, "heuristic frameworks are valued for the thought they stimulate, often leading to new insights and understanding" (p. 182). What greater legacy can anyone leave a field and those in it than to stimulate thought, promote new insights, and enhance our understanding?

ACKNOWLEDGMENTS

The author wishes to express his gratitude to Dr. Thomas Guskey, Dr. David Krathwohl, Dr. Richard Wolf, and Mrs. Sophie Bloom for their comments on an earlier draft of this chapter.

NOTES

1. The author is grateful to Mrs. Sophie Bloom for providing much of the information contained in this section.
2. Because the University had a mandatory retirement age of 70, Bloom technically retired from the University in 1983. For the next 8 years, he taught at Northwestern University. However, he maintained his office in the Department of Education at the University of Chicago until 1996.
3. In his comments on an earlier draft of this chapter, Dick Wolf remembered that Bloom used the term "constancy" to refer to absolute stability and the term "consistency" to refer to relative stability. Of Wolf, Bloom wrote in the Preface to *Stability and Change*, "Dr. Wolf, in particular, has contributed to this work to such a level that I have difficulty at present in differentiating his work and ideas from my own" (Bloom, 1964, p. ix).
4. Two of my colleagues who reviewed an earlier draft of this chapter, Dick Wolf and Tom Guskey, suggested that I comment on Bloom's legacy as a teacher and mentor. In Wolf's words, "The biggest oversight I noticed was that Ben's excellence as a teacher and mentor was not mentioned. Ben started the MESA (Measurement, Evaluation, and Statistical Analysis) program that was a real trailblazer. He trained a couple of generations of graduate students who are in leading positions, not only in the U.S. but throughout the world." While I agree with both of my distinguished colleagues, I believe that a comment would not be sufficient. Rather, I would encourage those interested in Bloom's legacy as a teacher and mentor to read my chapter in the book, *Teachers and Mentors: Profiles of Distinguished Twentieth-Century Professors of Education* (Anderson, 1996a).

REFERENCES

Aikin, W. (1942). *Adventure in American education, Vol. 1: Story of the Eight Year Study*. New York: Harper & Brothers.

Anderson, L. W. (1985). A retrospective and prospective view of Bloom's "learning for mastery." In M. C. Wang & H. J. Walberg (Eds.), *Adapting instruction to individual differences*. Berkeley, CA: McCutchan.

Anderson, L. W. (1994). Research on teaching and teacher education. In L. W. Anderson & L. A. Sosniak (Eds.). (1994). *Bloom's taxonomy: A forty-year retrospective*. Chicago: University of Chicago Press.

Anderson, L. W. (1996a). Benjamin Bloom, values and the professoriate. In C. Kridel, R. V. Bullough, Jr., & P. Shaker (Eds.), *Teachers and mentors: Profiles of distinguished twentieth-century professors of education* (pp. 45–54). New York: Garland.

Anderson, L. W. (1996b). If you don't know who wrote it, who won't understand it: Lessons learned from Benjamin S. Bloom. *Peabody Journal of Education, 71*, 77–87.

Anderson, L. W. & Sosniak, L. A. (Eds.). (1994). *Bloom's taxonomy: A forty-year retrospective*. Chicago: University of Chicago Press.

Axelrod, J., Bloom, B. S., Ginsburg, B. E., O'Meara, W., & Williams, J. C., Jr. (1948). *Teaching by discussion in the college program*. Chicago: University of Chicago.

Block, J. H., & Burns, R. B. (1976). Mastery learning. In L. S. Shuman (Ed.), *Review of research in education* (Vol. 4, pp. 3–49). Itasca, IL: Peacock.

Bloom, B. S. (1944). Some major problems in educational measurement. *Journal of Educational Research, 38*, 139–142.

Bloom, B. S. (1947). Implications of problem-solving difficulties for instruction and remediation. *School Review, 55*, 45–49.

Bloom, B. S. (1949). A taxonomy of educational objectives: Opening remarks of B. S. Bloom for the meeting of examiners at Monticello, Illinois, November 27, 1949. In D. R. Krathwohl (Ed.), *Summary report, college and university examiner's taxonomy conference.* Champaign, IL: Bureau of Research and Service, College of Education, University of Illinois.

Bloom, B. S. (1953a). Personality variables and classroom performance. *Journal of the National Association of Deans of Women, 16*(4), 13–20.

Bloom, B. S. (1953b). Test reliability for what? *Journal of Educational Psychology, 45*, 517–526.

Bloom, B. S. (1953c). Thought processes in lectures and discussions. *Journal of General Education, 7*(3), 160–169.

Bloom, B. S. (1954a). Changing conceptions of examining at the University of Chicago. In P. Dressel (Ed.), *Evaluation in general education.* Dubuque, IA: Brown. [Reprinted in Bloom, B. S. (1981). *All our children learning.* New York: McGraw-Hill.]

Bloom, B. S. (1954b). Thought processes of students in discussion classes. In S. French (Ed.). *Accent on teaching: Experiments in general education* (pp. 23–48). New York: Harper Brothers.

Bloom, B. S. (1957). The 1955 normative study of the Tests of General Educational Development. *School Review, 64*(3), 110–124.

Bloom, B. S. (1958a). *Evaluation in secondary schools.* New Delhi, India: All India Council for Secondary Education.

Bloom, B. S. (1958b). Ideas, problems, and methods of inquiry. In P. Dressel (Ed.), *Integration of educational experiences.* Chicago: University of Chicago Press.

Bloom, B. S. (1961). *Evaluation in higher education.* New Delhi, India: University Grants Commission.

Bloom, B. S. (1963a). *Report on creativity research.* In C. W. Taylor & F. X. Barron (Eds.), *Scientific creativity, its recognition and development* (pp. 251–264). New York: Wiley.

Bloom, B. S. (1963b). Testing cognitive ability and achievement. In N. L. Gage (Ed.), *Handbook of research on teaching.* New York: Rand McNally.

Bloom, B. S. (1964). *Stability and change in human characteristics.* New York: Wiley.

Bloom, B. S. (1965). The role of the educational sciences in curriculum development. *International Journal of the Educational Sciences, 1*, 5–15.

Bloom, B. S. (1966a). The international study of educational achievement: Development of hypotheses. In P. Dressel (Ed.), *Proceedings of the 1965 Invitational Conference on Testing Problems.* Princeton, NJ: Educational Testing Service.

Bloom, B. S. (1966b). Peak learning experiences. In M. Provus (Ed.), *Innovations for time to teach.* Washington, DC: National Educational Association.

Bloom, B. S. (1966c). Stability and change in human characteristics: Implications for school reorganization. *Educational Administration Quarterly, 2*, 35–49.

Bloom, B. S. (1966d). Twenty-five years of educational research. *American Educational Research Journal, 3*, 211–221.

Bloom, B. S. (1968a). Learning for mastery. *UCLA Evaluation Comment, 1*(2), (entire).

Bloom, B. S. (1968b). R & D centers: Promise and fulfillment. *Journal of Research and Development in Education, 1*(4), 101–113.

Bloom, B. S. (Ed.). (1969a). *Cross-national study of educational attainment: Stage 1 of the I.E.A. investigation in six subject areas.* Washington, DC: U.S. Department of Health, Education, and Welfare.

Bloom, B. S. (1969b). Some theoretical issues relating to educational evaluation. In R. Tyler (Ed.), *Educational evaluation* (pp. 26–50). Chicago: University of Chicago Press.

Bloom, B. S. (1970). Toward a theory of testing which includes measurement-evaluation-assessment. In M. C. Wittrock & D. E. Wiley (Eds.), *The evaluation of instruction*. New York: Holt, Rinehart & Winston.

Bloom, B. S. (1971). Affective consequences of mastery learning. In J. H. Block (Ed.), *Mastery learning: Theory and practice*. New York: Holt, Rinehart & Winston.

Bloom, B. S. (1972). Innocence in education. *School Review, 80*, 332–352.

Bloom, B. S. (1973). Individual differences in school achievement: A vanishing point? In L. J. Rubin (Ed.), *Facts and feelings in the classroom*. New York: Walker.

Bloom, B. S. (1974a). Implications of the IEA studies for curriculum and instruction. *School Review, 82*, 413–435.

Bloom, B. S. (1974b). Time and learning. *American Psychologist, 29*, 682–688.

Bloom, B. S. (1976). *Human characteristics and school learning*. New York: McGraw-Hill.

Bloom, B. S. (1977a). Affective outcomes of school learning. *Phi Delta Kappan, 59*(3), 193–198.

Bloom, B. S. (1977b). Favorable learning conditions for all. *Teacher, 95*(3), 22–28.

Bloom, B. S. (1977c). Only one-third of children learning. *Intellect, 106*(2390), 8–9.

Bloom, B. S. (1978a). Changes in evaluation methods. In R. Glaser (Ed.), *Research and development and school change* (pp. 67–82). Hillsdale, NJ: Lawrence Erlbaum Associates.

Bloom, B. S. (1978b). New views of the learner: Implications for instruction and curriculum. *Educational Leadership, 35*, 563–571.

Bloom, B. S. (1979). New views of the learner: Implications for instruction and curriculum. *Childhood Education, 56*, 4–11.

Bloom, B. S. (1980). The new direction in educational research: Alterable variables. *Phi Delta Kappan, 61*(6), 382–385.

Bloom, B. S. (1981a). *All our children learning*. New York: McGraw-Hill.

Bloom, B. S. (1981b). Early learning in the home. In B. S. Bloom (Ed.), *All our children learning* (pp. 67–87). New York: McGraw-Hill.

Bloom, B. S. (1981c). Talent development vs. schooling. *Educational Leadership, 39*(2), 86–94.

Bloom, B. S. (1982a). The master teachers. *Phi Delta Kappan, 63*(1), 664–668.

Bloom, B. S. (1982b). The role of gifts and markers in the development of talent. *Exceptional Children, 48*, 510–522.

Bloom, B. S. (1984). The 2 sigma problem: The search for methods of group instruction as effective as one-to-one tutoring. *Educational Researcher, 13*(6), 4–16.

Bloom, B. S. (Ed.). (1985). *Developing talent in young people*. New York: Ballantine.

Bloom, B. S. (1986a). Automaticity: The hands and feet of genius. *Educational Leadership, 43*(5), 70–77.

Bloom, B. S. (1986b). The home environment and school learning. In Study Group on the National Assessment of Student Achievement (Ed.), *The nation's report card* (pp. 47–66). Washington, DC: Author.

Bloom, B. S. (1986c). The international seminar for advanced training in curriculum development and innovation. In T. N. Postlethwaite (Ed.), *International educational research: Papers in honor of Torsten Husén* (pp. 145–162). Oxford, England: Pergamon.

Bloom, B. S. (1986d). What we're learning about teaching and learning: A summary of recent research. *Principal, 66*(2), 6–10.

Bloom, B. S. (1987). Response to Slavin's mastery learning reconsidered. *Review of Educational Research, 57*, 507–508.

Bloom, B. S. (1988a). Helping all children learn well in elementary school—and beyond. *Principal, 67*(4), 12–17.

Bloom, B. W. (1988b). Response to Slavin. *Educational Leadership, 46*(2), 28.

Bloom, B. S. (1994). Reflections on the development and use of the taxonomy. In L. W. Anderson & L. A. Sosniak (Eds.), *Bloom's taxonomy: A forty-year retrospective* (pp. 1–8). Chicago: University of Chicago Press.

Bloom, B. S., & Allison, J. M. (1949). Developing a college placement test program. *Journal of General Education, 3*(3), 210–215.

Bloom, B. S., & Allison, J. M. (1950). The operation and evaluation of a college placement program. *Journal of General Education, 4*(3) , 221–233.

Bloom, B. S., & Broder, L. J. (1950). *Problem-solving processes of college students: An exploratory investigation.* Chicago: University of Chicago Press.

Bloom, B. S., Davis, A., & Hess, R. (1965). *Compensatory education for cultural deprivation.* New York: Holt, Rinehart & Winston.

Bloom, B. S., Englehart, M. D., Furst, E. J., Hill, W. H., & Krathwohl, D. R. (1956). *Taxonomy of educational objectives, Handbook 1: The cognitive domain.* New York: Longman.

Bloom, B. S., Hastings, J. T., & Madaus, G. (1971). *Handbook on formative and summative evaluation of student learning.* New York: McGraw-Hill.

Bloom, B. S., & Heyns, I. V. (1956). Development and applications of tests of educational achievement. *Review of Educational Research, 26,* 72–88.

Bloom, B. S., Madaus, G. F., & Hastings, J. T. (1981). *Evaluation to improve learning.* New York: McGraw-Hill.

Bloom, B. S., & Peters, F. (1961). *Use of academic prediction scales for counseling and selecting college entrants.* Glencoe, IL: Free Press.

Bloom, B. S., & Statler, C. (1957). Changes in the states on the Tests of General Educational Development. *School Review, 65*(2), 202–221.

Bloom, B. S., & Rakow, E. (1969). Higher mental processes. In R. L. Ebel (Ed.), *The encyclopedia of educational research* (4th ed., pp. 594–60). New York: Macmillan.

Bloom, B. S., & Ward, F. C. (1952). The Chicago Bachelors of Arts Degree after ten years. *Journal of Higher Education, 23,* 459–467.

Bloom, B. S., & Webster, H. (1960). The outcomes of college. *Review of Educational Research, 30,* 321–333.

Brandt, R. (1979). A conversation with Benjamin Bloom. *Educational Leadership, 37*(2), 157–161.

Breslin, M. M. (1999, September 13). Benjamin Bloom, U. of C. prof who saw potential of all to learn. *Chicago Tribune.*

Bruner, J. S. (1992). Another look at new look 1. *American Psychologist, 47,* 780–783.

Chase, P. (1987). Master of mastery: This 73–year old scholar in a business suit would gladly ruin American education. *Psychology Today, 21,* 42–47.

Chung, B. M. (1994). The Taxonomy in the Republic of Korea. In L. W. Anderson & L. A. Sosniak (Eds.), *Bloom's taxonomy: A forty- year retrospective* (pp. 164–173). Chicago: University of Chicago Press.

Cox, C. H. (1979). Basic skills through mastery learning: An interview with Benjamin S. Bloom, Part I. *Curriculum Review, 18*(5), 362–365.

Cox, C. H. (1980). Basic skills through mastery learning: An interview with Benjamin S. Bloom, Part II. *Curriculum Review, 19*(1), 10–14.

Degenhart, R. E. (Ed.). (1990). *Third years of international research: An annotated bibliography of IEA publications (1960–1990).* The Hague, Holland: IEA Headquarters, SVO.

Furst, E. J. (1994). Bloom's taxonomy: Philosophical and educational issues. In L. W. Anderson & L. A. Sosniak (Eds.), *Bloom's taxonomy: A forty-year retrospective* (pp. 28–40). Chicago: University of Chicago Press.

Guskey, T. R. (1986, April). *Defining the critical elements of a mastery learning program.* Paper presented at the Annual Meeting of the American Educational Research Association, San Francisco, CA.

Guskey, T. R., & Gates, S. L. (1986). Synthesis of research on the effects of mastery learning in elementary and secondary classrooms. *Educational Leadership, 43*(8), 73–80.

Guskey, T. R., & Pigott, T. D. (1988). Research on group-based mastery learning programs: A meta-analysis. *Journal of Educational Research, 81,* 197–216.

Honan, W. H. (1999, September 13). Benjamin Bloom, 86, a leader in the creation of Head Start. *New York Times*.

Husen, T. (Ed.). (1967). *International study of achievement in mathematics: A comparison of twelve countries*. New York: Wiley.

Kellaghan, T., Sloane, K., Alverez, B., & Bloom, B. (1993). *The home environment and school learning*. San Francisco: Jossey-Bass.

Krathwohl, D. R. (1994). Reflections on the taxonomy: Its past, present, and future. In L. W. Anderson & L. A. Sosniak (Eds.), *Bloom's taxonomy: A forty-year retrospective* (pp. 181–202). Chicago: University of Chicago Press.

Krathwohl, D. R., Bloom, B. S., and Masia, B. (1964). *Taxonomy of educational objectives, Handbook 2: The affective domain*. New York: Longman.

Lewy, A., & Bathory, Z. (1994). The taxonomy of educational objectives in continental Europe, the Mediterranean, and the Middle East. In L. W. Anderson & L. A. Sosniak (Eds.), *Bloom's taxonomy: A forty-year retrospective* (pp. 146–163). Chicago: University of Chicago Press.

Postlethwaite, T. N. (1994). Validity vs. utility: Personal experiences with the Taxonomy. In L. W. Anderson & L. A. Sosniak (Eds.), *Bloom's taxonomy: A forty-year retrospective* (pp. 174–180). Chicago: University of Chicago Press.

Richardson, M. W., Russell, J. T., Snalnaker, J. M., & Thurstone, L. L. (1933). *Manual of examination methods*. Chicago: University of Chicago Board of Examinations.

Richardson, M. W., & Kuder, C. F. (1939). The calculation of test reliability coefficients based on the method of rational equivalence. *Journal of Educational Psychology, 31*, 681–687.

Rohwer, W. D., Jr., & Sloane, L. (1994). Psychological perspectives. In L. W. Anderson & L. A. Sosniak (Eds.), *Bloom's taxonomy: A forty-year retrospective* (pp. 41–63). Chicago: University of Chicago Press.

Smith, E. R., & Tyler, R. W. (1942). *Appraising and recording student progress*. New York: Harper & Brothers.

Snalnaker, J. M. (1934). The construction and results of a twelve-hour test in English composition. *School and Society, 39*, 193–198.

Sosniak, L. A. (1994). The Taxonomy, curriculum, and their relations. In L. W. Anderson & L. A. Sosniak (Eds.), *Bloom's taxonomy: A forty-year retrospective* (pp. 103–125). Chicago: University of Chicago Press.

Stern, G. G., Stein, M. I., & Bloom, B. S. (1956). *Methods in personality assessment*. Glencoe, IL: Free Press.

Thurstone, L. L. (1937). *Manual of examination methods* (2nd ed). Chicago: University of Chicago Bookstore.

Wolf, R. (2000). Benjamin S. Bloom. *IEA Newsletter, 26*, 1.

Woo, E. (1999, September 17). Benjamin S. Bloom; Education scholar's research influenced Head Start program. *Los Angeles Times*.

16

Toiling in Pasteur's Quadrant: The Contributions of N. L. Gage to Educational Psychology

David C. Berliner
Arizona State University

N. L. Gage has been one of the most consistent scholars in our discipline. He has made clear what he seeks. He seeks no less than a scientific basis for the art of teaching (e.g., Gage, 1978). Why not accept that teaching is a practical art? After all, teachers cannot strictly follow formulas, rules, or algorithms. Teaching regularly calls for individualization, improvisation, creativity, and emotional sensitivity. In short, teaching requires artistry, and to complicate the picture, that artistry must be displayed in real-time and in public settings. For many scholars, these are conditions of employment that preclude assistance from science. But N. L. Gage consistently has found such despair unwarranted.

> It matters greatly whether a mode of inquiry and a body of knowledge have scientific standing. Scientific method is recognized as the major avenue into valid knowledge about certain important aspects of the world. The victories of the natural sciences have led us to seek similar achievements in the world of human affairs by using the same general methods. (Gage, 1994, p. 565)
>
> But what do we mean by scientific knowledge? [It is] first, knowledge obtained empirically, through observation and experience, in ways that are public, that is communicable and, in principle, available to other persons with the necessary training and facilities. Second, scientific knowledge is relatively precise, clearly defined,

obtained with reliable instruments or procedures. Third, scientific knowledge is relatively objective in that it is determined by the data more than by the investigator's preferences, hopes, biases, or personal advantage. Fourth, scientific knowledge is replicable in that one investigator's findings can be obtained by other investigators who have the requisite competencies. Fifth, scientific knowledge becomes relatively systematic and cumulative in that it develops into an organized system of nonfalsified propositions, or a theoretical framework. Sixth, scientific knowledge makes possible the understanding or explanation of relationships between variables, the prediction with better-than-chance accuracy of the value of one variable on the basis of earlier knowledge of another variable, and control or improvement of one variable as a result of the deliberate change in another variable. Finally, scientific knowledge has survived attempts to falsify it. (Gage, 1992, p. 9).

Armed with examples, Gage points out that scientific investigations meeting these criteria have been employed numerous times in the field of education, and they yield findings that have the characteristics he finds so admirable in all scientific work (see, Gage, 1994; 1999). Moreover, Gage notes, these empirical findings can be intentionally employed to improve teaching. And that is precisely the goal that N. L. Gage set for himself and for our field of educational psychology. Professor Gage has toiled a lifetime in Pasteur's Quadrant (Stokes, 1997).

Motivation to engage in the work of science may be thought of as having its roots in one of four quadrants. Imagine a 2 × 2 table. One dimension of the table is labeled "The quest for fundamental understanding" and has the values "yes" and "no." The other dimension of the table is labeled "consideration of use," and it too has the values "yes" and "no."

The cell at the intersection of "no" and "no," where motivation to do science is not directed toward understanding or toward use, is empty. It is a cell where there is no motivation to engage in science. The other cells are far more interesting.

The cell where the quest for understanding is paramount, a "yes," and where there is no concern for the use of that knowledge, a "no," is characterized by the work of the "pure" scientist, say a Niels Bohr. The cell where there is no particular concern for understanding, a "no," but a tremendous interest in using our scientific findings, a "yes," is the realm of applied research. This is where we would place the work of Thomas Edison. The cell of most interest to us here is the cell where there is a great interest in scientific understanding, a "yes," *and* an equally great interest in doing the work of science so that it is useful, also a "yes." The "yes," "yes" cell is where Pasteur toiled. It is where there is a search for usefulness (say a vaccine to cure small pox, or the process we now call pasteurization) and a search for deep understanding of the processes involved (the germ theory, which revolutionized medicine). This is also the quadrant in which N. L. Gage has worked. His research is designed to improve teaching, *and* he also searches for understanding of the deeper processes involved in teaching, learning, and education. He studies teacher behavior, to improve it, and he works on a theory of teaching, to integrate that empirical work into a grander framework.

These postmodern times have revealed flaws in the conceptions of the science that were held earlier in the century, at the time when N. L. Gage received his training and decided to privilege science over all other ways of knowing. But to admit that science is flawed and that a reconceptualization of science was needed does not require that we abandon science, as some have concluded. Rather, postpositivist philosophy of science, as described by Phillips and Burbules (2000) and admired by N. L. Gage, can meet philosophic standards for establishing reliable knowledge and quieting the critics of science. Postpositivism provides the context for scientific, rational claims about causal relationships in the field of research on teaching.

Gage's empirical work and his theoretical defense of scientific research on teaching have been tenacious and are, in no small part, the basis of our contemporary faith that there is a role for traditional science in educational research, in particular, and the social sciences, in general (Gage, 1996). It is Professor Gage's achievements as an empirical scientist and as a defender of the role of science in education that brings him the respect of the community of educational psychologists. But I think that he is honored in our field, as well, for his decency, humor, affection, unfailing optimism, and for his mentoring of, and friendship with many other scholars in the field. The modeling of exemplary professional and personal behavior is what distinguishes Nathaniel Lees Gage.

BACKGROUND

As I write (Summer, 2001), Nathaniel Lees Gage (Nate, to his friends) has been associated with psychology for 65 years! For Nate, the journey to Pasteur's quadrant was not always clear.

N. L. Gage was born in New Jersey, just across the Hudson River from New York City, in 1917. His parents had independently emigrated from Poland as young adults, arriving around 1907. They met and married in the United States. Nate's father was a member of the working class by ideology as well as circumstance. He possessed, at best, a sixth-grade education. Nate's mother had even less formal schooling. They nevertheless provided an intellectually stimulating home, invigorated through political and social activism, and steeped in classical music. Nate's father, a self-taught violinist, played in the local symphony orchestra. Of his early years, Nate recalls unconditional love, library visits, and attempting to live up to the standards set by his brother—a super-academic-achiever, 4 years his senior.

Nate's brother was his primary model, finding resources to attend Columbia University, honored by making Phi Beta Kappa in his junior year, and continuing there to a Ph.D. in philosophy. Today he is professor emeritus at the University of Chicago. Similarly, N. L. Gage is now professor emeritus at Stanford University. These are remarkable contributions to the American intellectual community from the children of what have been called the "flotsam" of Europe.

Nate graduated from high school in 1934, in the midst of the great depression. Despite the fact that he was a good student, the lack of family funds forced him to put aside plans for college and join his father in the paperhanging trade. Luck intervened when Nate heard of a way in which he could get into the College of the City of New York—a free school—by taking an aunt's address within the city as his own. After 2 years at CCNY, Nate had decided that he was not cut out for employment in the physical sciences, although he had generally done well in the basic liberal arts and science program. At the suggestion of his brother he decided to leave New York and venture out into the world beyond the metropolis. He applied for admission to an inexpensive Midwestern university that he had vaguely heard about through friends, and thus entered the University of Minnesota in his junior year.

An Introduction to Psychology

During his first quarter at the University of Minnesota, N. L. Gage took the introductory psychology course, taught under the direction of Richard M. Elliott, who as chair had put together one of the country's distinguished psychology departments. Nate received a perfect score on the midterm exam, and on that basis was invited to join a special section of the course, taught by a new instructor from Harvard. This bright and productive scholar that everyone was talking about, but whom Nate had never heard of, was the youthful B. F. Skinner. Nate's experience in that course left him impressed, but not overly so.

Throughout this period Nate received financial support through the National Youth Administration (NYA)—a depression era work–study program—that paid him 50 cents per hour to score tests and do other clerical work in which he found himself inept. So he went to Skinner, who had an abundance of rats, cages, and kymographs, and offered his services. Since the NYA would pay for his work, he would not cost Skinner a penny. That was the kind of deal Skinner couldn't refuse, and for the next year and a half N. L. Gage made the little food pellets needed for reinforcing B. F. Skinner's rats. Nate's work also included counting words in various word lists, lettering captions for the figures in Skinner's *Behavior of Organisms*, and otherwise making himself useful. Nate received a footnote for his help in a study of verbal behavior by Skinner, his first citation in the psychological literature. Although Nate learned much from watching Skinner work, his heart was not in that kind of psychology. Gage was not comfortable in Skinner's domain of psychology primarily because it seemed too "pure" and irrelevant to human and societal problems.

At Minnesota Nate once studied statistics with another student who influenced our field—Louis Guttman. He also met Skinner's first doctoral student, John B. Carroll, who continues to make major contributions to our field. Ultimately, Nate accumulated five courses in statistics as an undergraduate, declared his major as psychology, made Phi Beta Kappa just before commencement, and graduated magna cum laude in 1938.

By that time Nate had applied for assistantships to attend graduate school in psychology at 10 universities, including Minnesota. Despite a record good enough to earn Phi Beta Kappa and undergraduate honors, Nate was *turned down by every one of the schools to which he had applied*!

Richard Elliott explained: From the universities' point of view it would be pointless to take him into a graduate program in psychology and waste resources training him, since he was Jewish. Even if he did, indeed, get a Ph.D., it would be difficult or impossible for him to find a job, given the depth of the depression and the prevalence of antisemitism. This experience brought Nate face-to-face with the ugliness of the self-fulfilling prophecy, though it had not yet been identified and named by social scientists. He was left with a concrete and personal understanding of this abstract concept. The year that this occurred was 1938, a time when the more violent forms of antisemitism in Germany were beginning to be reported, and a very discouraged N. L. Gage contemplated his immediate future.

Graduate School in Educational Psychology

Meanwhile, a socially liberal professor who had immigrated from Germany as a boy, and who had taken a doctorate in educational psychology at the University of Iowa, needed more graduate students in his new doctoral program at a different University. He approached his alma mater and was provided with the papers of all the applicants for assistantships at Iowa, one of the 10 institutions that had turned Nate down. The energetic, productive, personable, and unprejudiced H. H. Remmers offered Nate a readership in his doctoral program of educational psychology at Purdue University, without even having met him. Remmers and Joseph Tiffin, who became one of the nation's most eminent industrial psychologists, were creating an exceptional department of psychology at Purdue, and it was there that Gage went to pursue his doctoral studies.

In the fall of 1938, with a stipend of $25 per month, Gage began doctoral studies. He soon received an invitation to join John Stalnaker, research director of the College Board in Princeton, as a research assistant, and took leave to do that for 8 months. The experience gave him access to the evening seminars of Princeton's psychology department, involvement in the development and analysis of the SAT, and the possibility of gaining his degree from Princeton. But despite these advantages, Nate was not happy with his work. He returned to Remmers and Purdue in the fall of 1939, just as the Nazis were invading Poland, signaling the beginning of World War II.

Nate's first publications in our field, while still a student, were all concerned with aspects of testing and measurement, and almost all were done in collaboration with H. H. Remmers. Among those publications was a well-regarded book in educational measurement, published in 1943. Nate held a large number of assistantships in different areas during those years, though his work was focussed primarily on achievement and attitude measurement. The work provided him barely enough money to go to school and court Margaret Burrows—Maggie—whom he met in 1940 and married in 1942. But marriage and studies were interrupted in the winter of 1943, when Nate entered the Army.

Nate was first an interviewer in the Army, then joined the Army's aviation psychology program, developing and refining tests for the selection and training of airborne navigators and radar observers. The war years shaped a number of psychologists and moved them closer to educational psychology. Among the psychologists with whom Nate worked were Launor F. Carter, Stuart W. Cook, and Robert Glaser. In November 1945, with the promise of a job as a veteran's counselor at Purdue, but still without his doctorate, Nate returned to his studies. He also began editing and analyzing opinion polls for high school students. The data from one of those polls, concerning attitudes toward minorities, were used by Nate for his doctoral dissertation. His research entailed the use of Guttman scaling, factor analysis and a 2^6 factorially designed analysis of variance. In the era before statistical programs and computers, this was arduous and sophisticated statistical work. The doctoral degree was granted to N. L. Gage in 1947.

University Life

After 1 year on the Purdue faculty, Nate was hired, in 1948, by the University of Illinois, in what became its famous Bureau of Educational Research. Another bright new hire that year, with whom Nate at first shared an office, was Lee J. Cronbach, also honored in this volume. Cronbach's brilliance in psychometric work helped Nate to decide to move away from that area, and he moved closer to social-psychological research and studies of teaching. In his autobiography, Cronbach (1989) reports that he and Nate decided to split up the world: He would take psychometrics and Gage would take teaching. And that is exactly what they did, each influencing us all for over 50 years.

Over the next few years, as an assistant and associate professor at Illinois, Nate published in the *Journal of Educational Psychology*, *The Journal of Abnormal and Social Psychology*, *Psychological Monographs*, *The Psychological Bulletin*, *The Journal of Personality*, and other premier journals in our field. His coauthors during this time period included Bishwa Chatterjee, Lee J. Cronbach, George S. Leavitt, Phillip Runkel, George C. Stone, and George J. Suci. Among his major interests during this time (1948–1960) was the topic of person perception, an area that still remains of interest to scholars of social psychology. His explorations in this area resulted in a paper on social perception and teacher–pupil relationships that was unique enough to be reprinted twice (Gage & Suci, 1951). On the basis of this and related work (Gage, Leavitt, & Stone 1955), Nate and his students designed the oft-cited and replicated randomized experiment in which it was demonstrated that feedback to teachers, about what their students thought, influenced the teachers' subsequent behavior (Gage, Runkel & Chatterjee, 1960; 1963). This lengthy research program on person perception awakened Gage's interest in the study of teaching.

In 1951 Nate served as the junior member of a committee that was to profoundly affect his career and our field. This committee of the American Educational Research Association (AERA) was charged with examining the criteria of teacher effectiveness. After a 1-week meeting, the youngest of the attendees, Nate, was asked to edit the committee reports, published the following year in the *Review of Educational Research*. This work fostered in him a deeper interest in teacher effectiveness research, and provided him with visibility in this nascent area. Then, a few years after its first reports, the AERA committee on teacher effectiveness was resurrected with Nate as its chairman. Nate proposed to the committee that it should develop a handbook of research on teaching. This was the first of three salient events in which Nate took part, and which influenced our field in important ways.

By the end of the 1950s N. L. Gage had clearly established himself as a leading educational psychologist. He was elected president of APA's Division of Educational Psychology in 1960, and was elected president of the American Educational Research Association in 1962.

In 1962, after 14 years at the University of Illinois, Nate joined the faculty of Stanford University. He is still there, working vigorously as the Margaret Jacks Professor of Education Emeritus. An impressive list of his awards and honors, as well as his bibliography, were described in the published festschrift for N. L. Gage, celebrating his 70th birthday and official retirement from Stanford (Berliner & Rosenshine, 1987). But he has not lain fallow since his retirement, publishing regularly in major journals in the time since. Rather than provide that lengthy and impressive list, here I provide my analysis of N. L. Gage's three major contributions to our field, as well as some other noteworthy aspects of his career.

CONTRIBUTION ONE: THE HANDBOOK OF RESEARCH ON TEACHING

In fall of 1955 the AERA committee on Teacher Effectiveness prepared the first outline for a *Handbook of Research on Teaching*. A version of this work was submitted to AERA's council in 1956, and was greeted with lukewarm approval. There was fear that such a volume might compete with the third edition of AERAs *Encyclopedia of Educational Research*. Nate was asked to work on the proposal some more and to try to find funding. In 1957, with the help of the philosopher B. Othanel Smith, a small budget was obtained from Rand McNally Publishing Company, and Nate resubmitted the proposal. AERA then approved the *Handbook* project and appointed N. L. Gage as the editor. In early 1958, after a year of continual eye surgeries, Nate began work in earnest. Publication occurred 5 years later, in early 1963 (Gage, 1963a).

Nate, as anyone who has worked with him knows, is a compulsive editor. And each submission received his special treatment. Thus, the first *Handbook* is remarkably well crafted. But even more important is that the book was an intellectual milestone in the field of educational research, especially educational psychology. It structured the field of research on teaching, directed attention to important topics, influenced the research agenda for a decade, and affected government funding for 20 years. A remarkable 30,000 copies of the *Handbook* were sold. One of the more famous chapters was by Donald Campbell and Julian Stanley, on experimental design, which influenced both general psychology and other social sciences, not just the field of research on teaching. When published separately, over 100,000 copies of that chapter were sold. The chapter by Donald Medley and Harold Mitzel, also well known educational psychologists, presented a version of what would become generalizability theory, later developed more fully by methodologists such as Lee J. Cronbach. The chapter on historic exemplars of teaching methods by Harry Broudy is still used today in course work. And Gage's own chapter in the *Handbook*, on paradigms for research on teaching, was written without knowledge of Thomas Kuhn's book, *The structure of scientific revolutions*, written about the same time. Kuhn brought the concept of paradigm to the attention of the entire scientific community.

In education and educational psychology, the *Handbook* dramatically changed the kinds of research and the direction of thinking that were prevalent before 1963. Thanks to the *Handbook*, research on teaching came into the spotlight and became an extremely fruitful area of research for educational psychologists and other scholars. The fourth edition of the handbook has just been published attesting to the vigor of scholarship in this field that Nate so influenced, but it is unlikely that any subsequent volume can influence the field as much as did the first *Handbook*, the "Gage *Handbook*."

CONTRIBUTION TWO: THE STANFORD CENTER FOR RESEARCH AND DEVELOPMENT IN TEACHING

Lee Cronbach, who had moved to Stanford in 1964, opined to Nate in the summer of 1964 that the future of educational research would belong to the universities that won the relatively well-funded research and development centers being established by the U.S. Office of Education. Following Cronbach's suggestion, Nate and his colleagues, especially Robert N. Bush, developed a proposal for such a center. With the publication of the *Handbook* in 1963, and the infusion of large amounts of federal funds into educational research in 1964, a center for research on teaching was a natural choice for sponsorship by the government. In the fall of 1965 the Stanford Center for Research and Development in Teaching began operations. For almost a dozen years Nate served as codirector, acting director, or chair of the executive board of that center. Its substantive contributions to research on teaching were many, but in some ways its major products were well-trained, psychologically oriented personnel. The currently active educational psychologists who served at the Stanford Center as research assistants or associates include Christopher Clark, Richard Clark, Theodore Coladarci, Lyn Corno, John Crawford, Ronald Marx, Penelope Peterson, Gavriel Salomon, Richard Shavelson, Dale Schunk, Nicholas Stayrook, Philip Winne, and David Berliner. Educators associated with the center were eminent scholars such as Barak Rosenshine and the late Richard Snow. The people trained at the Center continue to focus attention on the scientific study of teaching, and they were all influenced enormously by N. L. Gage.

CONTRIBUTION THREE: THE DULLES CONFERENCE

In the spring of 1973, Nate supported an idea put forth by Ned Flanders; namely, the idea of coordinating planning among centers and laboratories interested in investigating classroom teaching and learning. Flanders and Gage discussed this idea with Garry L. McDaniels and Marshal S. Smith, who were then with the National Institute of Education. At their request, Nate moved to Washington for 8 months to plan a conference to formulate research agendas in teaching. Beginning in early January of 1974, Nate went to work deciding on priorities for topics and on the people who could address them. Eventually, a weeklong meeting of 10 panels, each with about 10 members, was held near Dulles Airport in the spring of 1974. The panel leaders—Lee Shulman, Richard Snow, Wesley Becker, Andrew Porter, Courtney Cazden, and other distinguished individuals—were joined by about 100 additional scholars from around the country. These individuals laid out the research agenda in such areas as clinical information processing, sociolinguistics, interactive teaching, research methodology, and theory building.

The conference resulted *directly* in four important outcomes. First, it served as the basis for funding of the productive Institute for Research on Teaching at Michigan State University, a center devoted to the study of teachers' cognitions, a previously low-priority area of funding. Second, the conference resulted in the funding of nearly 10 studies of sociolinguistics in classrooms, schools, and communities, another under-emphasized area at that time. Third, the conference provided one of the first opportunities for the voice of the qualitative research community to be heard by the government, because the conference promoted the use of ethnographic research in the study of teaching, learning, and language use. Fourth, the conference helped to reduce the funding in areas that seemed to have already been relatively well mined, such as behavior analysis, precision teaching, and other operant-like approaches to research on teaching.

The reports of the panels, all edited by Nate and Kent Viehover of the National Institute of Education, were seriously acted on by the National Institute of

Education. The character of research on teaching, indeed that of all educational psychology, was markedly changed by that conference. And that conference was influenced strongly by its organizer and recorder, N. L. Gage.

SOME ADDITIONAL CONTRIBUTIONS

These brief descriptions of Gage's influence on our field are not the sum of the man. Other contributions of N. L. Gage should also be noted.

Defending the Role of Science in Educational Research

Gage's two monographs, *The Scientific Basis of the Art of Teaching* (1978), and *Hard Gains in the Soft Sciences* (1985), both serve as carefully reasoned defenses of process–product research, teacher effectiveness studies, the usefulness of scientific approaches to what must always be a moral craft, and the potential of educational psychology for informing practice. In later writings it appears that these ideas have been refined, made more forceful and more generalizable, and also tied closer to mainstream philosophy of science (e.g., Phillips & Burbules, 2000). This can be seen in Gage's more recent rebuttals (1994, 1996) of those who despair of ever learning anything useful, practical, or widely applicable from the social sciences.

Theory and the Process–Product Paradigm of Research

Nate's continuing defense of the importance of theory in his monographs and journal articles gave rise to a descriptive theory by him for thinking about research on teaching, and the place within this domain of his preferred kind of research, process–product or teacher effectiveness research (Gage, 1999). This descriptive theory is presented here as Fig. 16.1, a framework in which to situate any particular research in the broad domain of research on teaching.

This framework defines six categories (A–F) of concepts or variables about which research on teaching is concerned. The six categories are arranged in a quasi-logical, chronological, and psychological sequence. The framework also shows the 15 possible two-way relationships or connections between pairs of the categories, and in this way defines the entire domain of research on teaching, the domain in which Nate works.

Box A is concerned with presage variables and might include variables such as teachers' experience, teachers' content knowledge, teachers' pedagogical content knowledge, and teachers' academic ability. These variables can be related to variables found under the headings of any of the other five categories of variables. The

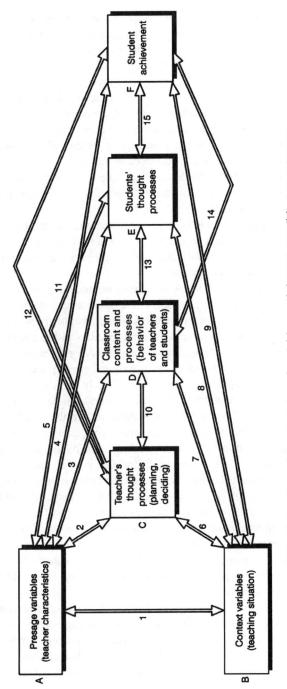

FIG. 16.1. Six major categories of variables and the 15 possible two-category relationships in research on teaching.

relationships between all categories are purposely designated as reciprocal—the arrows go both ways—acknowledging the complexity of research on teaching.

Category B includes context variables. These are such variables as the school's social class, the heterogeneity of the students, parents' educational levels, class size, and the motivations and values of the community.

Category C is concerned with the teachers' planning and thought processes during teaching. Research on teachers' thinking during instruction is concerned with the study of perception and adaptation to the moment-to-moment changes in classroom environments. The inherent unpredictability of classrooms creates interesting challenges for scientists who work in this area.

Category D includes the variables that describe the content and processes of instruction. These describe the observable interactions in the teaching/learning setting, the *process* in process–product research.

Category E is concerned about what students are thinking. Included here would be study of the engagement constructs—attention, time on task, depth of processing—and constructivist variables, such as the relationships of new knowledge to old and cognitive strategy use.

Category F is concerned with various kinds of student outcomes. These are the *products* in process–product research. These products include motivation to do more work, performance assessments, and of course, traditional tests and measures.

The domain of research on teaching includes studies within a single category, say the study of teachers' credentialing, in Category A; or the ways teachers plan, in Category C. It could also include relationships between variables in two of these domains. For example, a researcher could study the effects of high-stakes testing, Category B, a context variable, on teachers' thinking and planning of instruction, a Category C variable. This is illustrated in the link between these two categories, line 6. Process–Product research, so eloquently defended over the years by N. L. Gage, is of this type. It is found in the correlational or experimental studies joining variables from Category D and Category F. These would be the links between classroom behaviors of some sort and student achievement of some sort, as implied in line 14. Structural equations and path analysis can be used to study variables from three or more of the categories, such as the relationships of school context with teacher behavior and student achievement. This taxonomy of variables and concepts to describe research on teaching helps us also to see the links between basic and applied studies in educational research. Any basic work in one category may be capable of improving the study of relationships between variables in two or more categories.

Process–product studies are the equivalent of criterion-of-effectiveness studies, an applied psychology and functionalist research strategy with a long history, described by Gage (1963) in his *Handbook* chapter. Process–product research seeks to uncover "'processes' (teacher behaviors and characteristics, in the form of teaching styles, methods, models or strategies) that predict and preferably cause 'products' (that is, educational outcomes in the form of student achievement and attitude)" (Gage, 1978, p. 69).

For Gage the process–product paradigm for research on teaching is both appealing and robust. It is appealing to educators, in part, because it is practical, it deals with job-related effectiveness:

> What can be more natural than to seek to improve education through improving the work of the agents of society who come into contact with students? It is through those agents, namely, the teachers, that everything we do about curriculum, school finance, building construction, school administration, school–community relationships, and the rest, comes to the point—the point of making contact with the students through whom society will realize its schools' ideals. It is little wonder that the process–product paradigm has enlisted the allegiance of most of those who have done research on teaching during the past half-century. (Gage, 1978, p. 69)

And the process–product paradigm is robust in that it incorporates new ideas. As Gage noted (1978), new ideas, new concepts, new variables derived from other empirical and conceptual frameworks for research on teaching, or new conceptualizations about the nature of student learning must be converted into types of teacher behavior and types of student behavior to show effects or relationships. Thus, says Gage, most variables can be incorporated into the "process" or the "product" part of process–product research. Whether one's teaching is informed by phonics or constructivism, concerned about subject-specific pedagogy or generic teaching skills, the end point of the beliefs that teachers hold must be observable teacher behavior, one of the "process" variables that make up classroom life. Whether one's vision of learning is constructivist or behavioral, some student outcome will be seen as relevant to that theoretical perspective, and that is the "product" of process–product research. Is the process–product paradigm so inclusive that it provides us nothing special, as some critics suggest? Or, is the focus on classroom life that is inherent in process–product research forcing us to take our scientific sensibilities to where intended school learning is likely to take place, to observe where the rubber hits the road? The field has no consensus on these issues.

The criteria-of-effectiveness paradigm, from which the process–product paradigm is derived, is an eclectic one. The nature of the learner is unspecified, and so is the nature of the learning process. The process–product researcher, in deceptively simple language, seeks reliable relationships to guide practice. The researcher can be a constructivist or a behaviorist, a sociologist or a psychologist, seeking to create an open learning environment or following a scripted lesson in a program like *Success for All*. The same research strategy may be used by all, but of course would not be desired by an interpretive anthropologist, a critical theorist, or others who have different standards for defining reliable knowledge.

Because of the way they conceptualize their task, process–product researchers do not think about optimal conditions of instruction. They seek, instead, knowledge about reliable conditions for instruction to work, most of the time. That is no mean feat and not to be confused with being atheoretical. Theory first influences the choice of research paradigm. Process–product researchers must believe in a world that can be reduced, or simplified in some ways, in order to do their kind of research. Theory will also guide the variables that are chosen to be studied, and theory will guide the choice of the outcome measures to be studied, as well.

N. L. Gage has jokingly described himself as an eclectic purist (Gage, 1992). And so the process–product paradigm fits him like a glove—it is eclectic in all ways but one, the quality of the science that is used. That is where the purist comes in. The standards that constitute good science must be kept high. Nate does that well.

I know that Nate has and would always choose to study democratic and humane teaching methods, and he values student outcomes more complex than those we derive from multiple-choice tests. But choice of method and choice of outcomes is a decision of each individual researcher working within the process–product paradigm, with each scholar seeking better ways to teach, as they understand the meaning of that term.

Methodology. Beginning with H. H. Remmers, Nate has always had an interest in methodological issues. This showed in his early work on theory building, research reviewing, and meta-analysis, a technique that Nate quickly embraced and championed (Gage, 1978). He sees meta-analysis as a remarkable tool for making sense out of the (often) conflicting small-scale studies that characterize so much of educational research. More recently he has argued for the compatibility of qualitative and quantitative approaches to research—a position set forth in an article published in the *Educational Researcher* (Gage, 1989), and often cited in methodology classes.

His methodological efforts also helped the International Association for the Evaluation of Educational Achievement (IEA) to think through the ways to do international studies of classroom processes. From his initial work in the 1980s with Torsten Husén and T. Neville Postlethwaite, other scholars currently working on international studies have gone on to make his original point. That is, Nate was among the first to understand how critical it was to understand the within and between country differences in classroom processes if we wanted to interpret cross-national differences in student achievement. Recent video analyses of the Third International Mathematics and Science Study (TIMSS) demonstrate Gage's prescience. Without knowledge of the content and process of classroom instruction and the social contexts of schooling, we cannot sensibly interpret the between-country differences in student achievement.

Social Concerns. As a social psychologist with expertise in measurement, Gage could, and did, provide reasoned and elegant counterpoints to the strong genetic hypothesis that had been put forth to account for racial differences in IQ

(Gage, 1972a, 1972b). His scholarly and influential rebuttals to William Shockley's volatile pieces on race and learning helped to weaken those arguments.

Scholarly Communication.   There is a textbook coauthored by N. L. Gage that has been credited with changing textbook writing in the field of educational psychology through its inclusion of chapters on the psychology of teaching, as well as the traditional chapters on the psychology of learning. The success of this text—now in its 6th edition and 25th year—is credited by many in the field for having influenced other writers to make more explicit the research on teaching and the linkage between psychology and practice. It is considered both a scientifically grounded and a relevant text—where many earlier textbooks were much shorter on relevance (Gage & Berliner, 1998).

Another way that N. L. Gage fostered scholarly communication was by his founding the journal *Teaching and Teacher Education: An International Journal of Research and Studies.* It first appeared in 1985 with Nate as its editor. His stewardship helped the journal become a major high-quality outlet for the international scholarly community in research on teaching and teacher education.

A Model for Students.   An enduring, but less visible contribution to our field has to do with the ethical standards, scholarship, and habits of mind displayed by N. L. Gage. They have influenced many of the talented educational psychology students who have graduated from Stanford over a 35-year period. As one example of his modeling of scholarly behavior, I would like to note that *after* retirement, he took to going to classes in philosophy, and reading works on hermeneutics, in order to better understand the interpretive approaches to research—approaches with which he had been uncomfortable, given his training and experience. From that scholarly pursuit came his paper defending qualitative analysis and methodological pluralism (see Gage, 1989). That paper was a plea to end the paradigm wars, from someone who had been clearly aligned with the established methodological paradigm. N. L. Gage never gives up on science as a way of knowing, but he is catholic in his methodological tastes.

In 1957, in an elevator taking Nate and Harold Mitzel to a meeting room at the American Educational Research Association's annual conference, Nate made a joking remark. He said that if the elevator crashed all of the research on teaching at AERA would disappear, since they were the only two people giving papers on the subject that year! Now, just after the start of the new century, one of the fastest growing divisions of AERA is Division K, the Division of Teaching and Teacher Education. It now has about 4,000 members, many of whom are educational psychologists. Each year Division K, along with Division C (learning) and some other divisions, affords time for the presentation of hundreds of empirical and scholarly papers concerned with research on teaching. I believe the life's work of N. L. Gage has provided a cornerstone for much that occurs at the annual meetings of AERA, and he has influenced what occurs in Division 15 of the American Psychological Association, as well. N. L. Gage and Harold Mitzel are certainly no longer alone.

CONCLUSION

At the conclusion of this exegesis of N. L. Gage's contributions to educational psychology, we should also acknowledge the contribution of Margeret Burrows Gage to N. L. Gage's professional accomplishments. Maggie, trained in child development at the Merrill–Palmer School, insured, during the raising of four children and thereafter, that Nate had the time and the emotional support to devote his attention to our field. Thus, a host of graduate students and the field of educational psychology owe their debt of gratitude to her as well.

N. L. Gage is first and foremost a *scientific* psychologist. But his career has been marked also by pragmatism. It is the science of what works that has always interested him. Because the classroom environment is too complex to build an exact science, such as physics, he has sought instead to build a probabilistic science tempered by the political and social realities of schooling in America. These realities, Nate might argue, may even require a more complex science than that needed to study physical and biological systems. While science and pragmatism have influenced his career, Nate has also searched for relevance. He always wanted educational psychology to have an impact on the work and life of teachers, to help in transforming their profession by providing a more adequate scientific base for what they did, where there has been too little before. He sees the knowledge base on teaching as providing relevant information for a profession that does not receive the respect it deserves. He toils still in Pasteur's Quadrant.

Nate once said to me that he pursued research on teaching out of a belief that teachers should be liked and respected, and that they didn't seem to be. Of course it is hard to change such deep-rooted beliefs in our society, but in small ways the contributions of N. L. Gage do exactly that. This year, his 84th, he is still trying to meet yet another deadline, for yet another publication, to try once more to influence education and educational research. He works now on developing a general theory of teaching. As he engages in a quest for both understanding and for usefulness, he models what it means to be a deeply committed educational psychologist and a caring colleague.

ACKNOWLEDGMENTS

I take great pleasure in documenting the contributions to our field of educational psychology by my friend, colleague, and co-author, Nathaniel Lees Gage. I have known Professor Gage personally since 1964, and have worked closely with him since 1970. But only in the preparation of this chapter did I set out to systematically examine his achievements. The debt we owe this fine scholar is for directing contemporary educational psychology toward Pasteur's Quadrant (Stokes, 1997), areas of educational psychology in which good science about things that matter can be done.

REFERENCES

Berliner, D. C., & Rosenshine, B. V. (1987). *Talks to teachers*. New York: Random House.

Cronbach, L. J. (1989). Lee J. Cronbach. In G. Lindzey (Ed.), *History of psychology in autobiography* (Vol. 8, pp. 62–93). Stanford, CA: Stanford University Press.

Gage, N. L. (1963a). *The handbook of research on teaching*. Chicago: Rand McNally.

Gage, N. L. (Ed.). (1963b). Paradigms for research on teaching. In N. L. Gage (Ed.), *The handbook of research on teaching* (pp. 94–141). Chicago: Rand McNally.

Gage, N. L. (1972a). IQ heritability, race differences, and educational research. *Phi Delta Kappan, 53,* 308–312.

Gage, N. L. (1972b). Replies to Shockley, Page, and Jensen: The causes of race differences in IQ. *Phi Delta Kappan, 53,* 422–427.

Gage, N. L. (1978). *The scientific basis of the art of teaching*. New York: Teachers College Press.

Gage, N. L. (1985). *Hard gains in the soft sciences*. Bloomington, IN: Phi Delta Kappa.

Gage, N. L. (1989). The paradigm wars and their aftermath: A "historical" sketch of research on teaching since 1989. *Educational Researcher, 18*(7), 4–10.

Gage, N. L. (1992). Art, science, and teaching from the standpoint of an eclectic purist. *School of Education Review—San Francisco State University, 4,* 8–17.

Gage, N. L. (1994). The scientific status of the behavioral sciences: The case of research on teaching. *Teaching and Teacher Education, 10*(5), 565–577.

Gage, N. L. (1996). Confronting counsels of despair for the behavioral sciences. *Educational Researcher, 25*(3), 5–15, 22.

Gage, N. L. (1999). Theory, norms, and intentionality in process–product research on teaching. In R. J. Stevens (Ed.), *Teaching in American schools* (pp. 57–80). Upper Saddle River, NJ: Merrill.

Gage, N. L., & Berliner, D. C. (1998). *Educational psychology* (6th ed.). Boston, MA: Houghton Mifflin.

Gage, N. L., Leavitt, G. S., & Stone, G. C. (1955). Teachers' understanding of their pupils and pupils ratings of their teachers. *Psychological Monographs, 69* (Whole No. 406).

Gage, N. L., Runkel, P., & Chatterjee, B. (1960). *Equilibrium theory and behavior change: An experiment in feedback from pupils to teachers*. Urbana, IL: Bureau of Educational Research, University of Illinois.

Gage, N. L., Runkel, P. J., & Chatterjee, B. B. (1963). Changing teacher behavior through feedback from pupils: An application of equilibrium theory. In W. W. Charters, Jr. & N. L. Gage (Eds.), *Readings in the social psychology of education* (pp. 173–181). Boston: Allyn & Bacon.

Gage, N. L., & Suci, G. J. (1951). Social perception and teacher–pupil relationships. *Journal of Educational Psychology, 42,* 144–152.

Phillips, D. C., & Burbules, N. C. (2000). *Postpositivism and educational research*. Lanham, MD: Rowman & Littlefield.

Stokes, D. E. (1997). *Pasteur's' quadrant: Basic science and technological innovation*. Washington, DC: The Brookings Institute.

17

From *The Process*
of Education to *The Culture*
of Education: An
Intellectual Biography
of Jerome Bruner's
Contributions to Education

Nancy C. Lutkehaus
University of Southern California

Patricia M. Greenfield
UCLA

"I never felt I was going into education. If you didn't take into account this most powerful institution—schooling—how could you talk about cognitive development?" (Conversation with Jerome Bruner, October, 2000).

This quote expresses a link between the individual and the societal, between the cognitive and the cultural. Both these poles of educational thought have early roots in Bruner's undergraduate and graduate training. Bruner's early forays into the world of education were based primarily on cognitive psychology, particularly cognitive development. Over time, his educational thinking became increasingly grounded in cultural psychology and anthropology. While not forgetting Bruner's integration of these poles of the human condition, we see a shift of emphasis over time from the individual to the cultural, from psychology to anthropology.

This dynamism between psychology and anthropology provides the framework for the chapter. We organize our material chronologically, after first introducing our sources and perspectives on the material.

SOURCES AND PERSPECTIVES

Nancy Lutkehaus' sources are books Bruner has written, most importantly, his intellectual autobiography, *In Search of Mind* (1983a) and also an interview she conducted with him in New York City in October 1996.[1] Lutkehaus, a visual anthropologist who has written on the history of anthropology, was introduced to Bruner through the late Tim Asch, an ethnographic filmmaker who worked with Bruner on the visual component of the elementary social science curriculum, Man: A Course of Study (MACOS; Lutkehaus, 2002). She is also working on a book about the development of the MACOS curriculum and Bruner's impact on psychological anthropology (Lutkehaus, 2000).

Patricia Greenfield, a developmental cultural psychologist, traced Bruner's evolution as an educational theorist through analyzing his four major books on education, *The Process of Education* (1960), *Toward a Theory of Instruction* (1966), *The Relevance of Education* (1971), and *The Culture of Education* (1996). She also drew on her shared journey with Jerome Bruner (personal communication, October 2000), beginning as an undergraduate student at Radcliffe in the early 1960s, continuing into graduate school at Harvard in the early to mid-1960s, and as a postdoctoral researcher at the Harvard Center for Cognitive Studies in the late 1960s and early 1970s. A telephone conversation in September 2000 and an in-person conversation at Bruner's Manhattan loft in October 2000, part of their ongoing relationship, provided key orienting guidance.

PSYCHOLOGY AND ANTHROPOLOGY IN BRUNER'S BACKGROUND

Bruner was an undergraduate student in psychology at Duke University during the mid-1930s. While there he published a paper on "The effect of thymus extract on the sexual behavior of the female rat." At Harvard for graduate study in psychology, he had the psychologist Gordon Allport as an advisor. While he wrote in his autobiography that Allport "did not have a deep effect on my style of thinking" (Bruner, 1983a, p. 36), Bruner did end up sharing, in a later phase of his career, Allport's passionate interest in autobiographical narrative.

That is the more obvious psychology side of Jerome Bruner's intellectual roots. But there was an almost "underground" anthropology side as well. In his autobiography, Bruner mentions reading Malinowski and hearing Margaret Mead speak about cultural relativism (Bruner, 1983a, p. 26). He also had a roommate—Leonard Broom—who was an anthropologist.[2] Bruner visited him "in the field" during the summer of 1937 while Broom was studying change in dance forms among the

Cherokee produced by contact with their white neighbors. "It never occurred to me," Bruner wrote, "that there was any conflict between what anthropologists did and what I had been doing [studying the psychology of learning through exper-imentation with rats]. We psychologists (I was twenty-one) knew that whatever the anthropologists found would have to be explained by the very same elemen-tary processes we studied. The idea of the autonomy of cultural forms (one of Broom's great passions) never quite percolated into my psychologist's conscious-ness" (Bruner, 1983a, p. 29).

> The mainstream world of psychology that I entered as a student was dominated by sensationism, empiricism, objectivism and physicalism. But when I was an un-dergraduate, my heroes and mentors were almost to a man swimming against that mainstream. My heart was with them: Gestalt psychology, Sigmund Freud, the cul-tural anthropologists . . . [who] argued for the social origin of experience itself, that what we knew and experienced took its meaning from a world of culture, symbols and myth that had little to do with the world of physics and physical stimulation. (Bruner, 1983a, p. 59)

When Bruner arrived at Harvard as a graduate student, and again after the war, Culture and Personality theory was enjoying its hey-day there. The "torch-bearer," according to Bruner, was Clyde Kluckhohn, whom Bruner describes as "a romantic, a restless believer in the power of culture to shape mind, but too subtle an intelligence to embrace any simple generalizations about how the two were related" (1983a, p. 134). Both Margaret Mead and Ruth Benedict were frequent visitors to the campus and John Whiting was hard at work correlating culture traits with presumed basic personality characteristics.[3] The idea of culture, as anthro-pologists then saw it, was a new and compelling idea to Bruner (Bruner, 1983a, p. 178).

Bruner's contact with anthropologists grew even closer when in 1946 the old Department of Psychology at Harvard split in two. One wing, the more sociotropic, joined sociology and social anthropology to found a new Department of Social Relations.[4] Although he continued to have contact with the old Department of Psychology and to teach some courses there, the Department of Social Relations became Bruner's new home, until he and George Miller established the Center for Cognitive Studies in 1960.

Thus, from the very start of his career as a psychologist, Bruner said, he was juggling "two sets of maps," two models for thinking about and looking at the world and human psychology: one map from psychology, the other from anthropology. These two maps were soon to be joined in his work on education. But first he had to become involved in the world of educational praxis. Political events in the broader society drew him into this world.

EVENTS LEADING UP TO THE PROCESS
OF EDUCATION

Jerrold Zacharias and Postwar
Science Curriculum

In the aftermath of World War II and the climate of Cold War competition between the United States and the Soviet Union in the arena of science, the eminent MIT physicist, Jerrold Zacharias (who with Oppenheimer and others had worked on the development of the atomic bomb) turned his attention to the knowledge gap and the teaching of science to American school children. In 1956, with a seemingly modest proposal submitted to the president of MIT and the National Science Foundation to make short films titled "Movie Aids for Teaching Physics in High Schools,"[5] Zacharias launched what became known as the Physical Science Study Committee (PSSC), headed by himself and his colleague at MIT, physicist Francis Friedman (Goldstein, 1992, p. 152).[6]

A year later, in response to the Soviet launching of the Sputnik satellite on October 4, 1957, Eisenhower created the President's Science Advisory Committee (PSAC), of which Zacharias was a member. The next month Eisenhower established the position of special assistant to the president for science and technology and appointed James Killian, the president of MIT, to fill the position. In his State of the Union address for 1958 Eisenhower announced a fivefold increase in budget to the National Science Foundation (NSF) for science education. Shifting his focus from the study of atoms to the study of school children and how they learned science, also in 1958, Zacharias created Educational Services, Inc. (ESI), a private, nonprofit organization whose purpose was to carry out educational research and development. Funds were obtained not only from the NSF, but the Ford Foundation and the Alfred P. Sloan Foundation.

An important element of Zacharias' proposal for a new physics curriculum was that actual physicists would develop the films and the textbooks, problem books, question cards, and answer cards that were to accompany them, short-circuiting the usual role of education specialists. The success or failure of the films as teaching devices would depend to a large extent, Zacharias thought, on having the entire apparatus of the experiment really right: "Like a high fidelity phonograph," he said, "one must have besides the machine a good piece by a good composer played by an artist. The room must be good, not too noisy, and the people have to want to listen" (quoted in Goldstein, 1992, p. 152 and Bruner, 1983a, p. 179).[7] The scientists were to be the equivalent of the artists, the experiments the good pieces they were to play, and for the high fidelity phonograph, i.e., excellent quality films, Zacharias looked to film directors from the world of television and movies, rather than the traditional educational film industry.

Where Bruner fit into this project, he said, was to help his friends Zacharias and Friedman get people "to want to listen." The physicists, of course, hoped that

Bruner's research on cognitive development, especially his recent study of the work of Vygotsky and Piaget, would provide expertise on the psychology of learning. Little did Bruner realize in 1958 that this invitation and challenge, which started out over a lunch conversation, would eventually lead to what became a lifelong focus on "the culture of education." But, of course, that notion came much later.

At the time, Zacharias was aware that the goal of the Physical Sciences Study Committee was as much a cultural one as it was a purely technological one:

> In the minds of the committee, what they were trying to do was analogous to developing an appreciation of music, art or literature. It was commonly understood, they said, that one has to work at the liberal arts, to devote time and effort to them in order to get anything out of them. Educated people recognize the value and importance of the liberal arts, but only rarely do they appreciate science in the same way. People who would never countenance illiteracy in the liberal arts incline to a vast, unthinking tolerance of it when it comes to science. The committee had observed that parents, confronted with a child's inability to succeed at science in school, all too often react with an indulgent, "That's OK—I never understood science either." (Goldstein, 1992, p. 164)

What Zacharias and the other members of the committee meant when they spoke of wanting to develop an appreciation of science was "developing in the student the ability to distinguish knowing from opinion; to understand the meaning of probability; to recognize that uncertainty necessarily accompanies all observation and measurement, and to reject the false certainty of dogma" (Goldstein, 1992, p. 164). The goal of the PSSC curriculum was to make students familiar with the various modes of scientific reasoning. The facts of science were to serve principally as the means by which the goal was to be reached.

Thus Zacharias, Friedman, and Bruner shared a common goal—helping people learn to learn by learning how to think. As Zacharias said, "The reason I was willing to do it [PSSC] was not because I wanted more physics or more physicists or more science; it was because I believed then, and I believe now, that in order to get people to be decent in this world, they have to have some kind of intellectual training that involved knowing [about] Observation, Evidence, the Basis for Belief" (quoted in Goldstein, 1992, pp.164–165).

The Woods Hole Conference and Bruner's *The Process of Education*

In 1959 a 10-day conference was held at Woods Hole, Massachusetts, sponsored by the National Academy of Sciences. There, 34 scholars and teachers from a dozen disciplines gathered to review what had been learned in the newly launched science curriculum projects, of which PSSC had been the forerunner.[8] The Woods Hole conference was by Bruner's own account a response to the Russians' success in getting Sputnik up before the Americans. The Russians had won the first leg of the space race in the Cold War, and, so went the analysis, the Americans had lost because of their inferior education in science and math. At that point, improving math and science education became a national priority, something too important to be left to the educators. Out of this context was born the Woods Hole Conference.

The conference was primarily a gathering of psychologists and research scientists who came to discuss "the fundamental processes involved in imparting to young students a sense of the substance and method of science" (Bruner, 1960, p. vii) and to brainstorm about further applications of research science to the development of elementary and secondary school science curricula. Topics discussed at the conference included cognitive processes, the role of intuition and structure in learning, as well as aids to teaching, their relationship to intuitive and analytic thinking, and their stimulation of the motive to learn (Bruner, 1960).

Bruner was not only one of the participants at the conference, he was also asked to write a report that described the conference's findings. Out of the Woods Hole Conference came *The Process of Education*, Bruner's very personal account of the gathering (Bruner, 1960). Eventually translated into 20 languages, the book sold over 400,000 copies within 4 years and established Bruner as an international figure in educational reform. For example, in Italy, his publisher Armando Armando positioned Bruner as the successor to John Dewey. Encouraged, indeed, rather surprised it seems, by the response to the book, Bruner decided to continue his involvement with Zacharias and his group of science curriculum reformers as a researcher with ESI.

THE PROCESS OF EDUCATION: A STRUCTURALIST APPROACH

From an intellectual point of view, *The Process of Education* is a very structuralist account of education and cognitive development. It is structuralist because its central question is "What are the implications of emphasizing the structure of a subject, be it mathematics or history—emphasizing it in a way that seeks to give a student as quickly as possible a sense of the fundamental ideas of a discipline?" (Bruner, 1960, p. 3).

It is interesting to note that structuralism held sway in both anthropology and developmental psychology at that moment. In anthropology, the major structuralist was Claude Levi-Strauss, who, Bruner says, influenced him. The externality of the structure of a subject matter mirrors the externality of the cultural environment described by Levi-Strauss. But the idea was not just the external structure of the subject matter. The underlying notion of learning was a match between the external structure of the subject matter and the internal, cognitive structure of the learner. And the latter was seen to be a matter of cognitive development. Thus, Bruner wrote, "at each stage of development the child has a characteristic way of viewing the world and explaining it to himself. The task of teaching a subject to a child at any particular age is one of representing the structure of that subject in terms of the child's way of viewing things" (Bruner, 1960, p. 33).

The internal structure of cognitive development was based on Piaget's theory of cognitive development; indeed, Piaget was the major structuralist in the field of psychology (Piaget, 1970). Bruner devotes a few pages to Piaget's theory in *The Process of Education*. He saw the structured Piagetian stages of cognitive development as the bedrock of school readiness. So the two poles of Bruner's educational structuralism were subject matter structure on the outside and cognitive structure on the inside.

But there was also structure in the interaction between the two: the essence of education was, in his view, to grasp the structure of a subject: "Grasping the structure of a subject is understanding it in a way that permits many other things to be related to it meaningfully. To learn structure, in short, is to learn how things are related" (Bruner, 1960, p. 7).

The role of structure in learning and how it may be made central to teaching is the first and foremost theme in *The Process of Education*. In it Bruner argued for the importance of structure in relationship to knowledge. Knowledge is not merely performance, but understanding. Understanding consists of grasping the place of an idea or fact in some more general structure of knowledge. When we understand something, we understand it as an exemplar of a broader conceptual principle or theory.

THE ROLE OF COGNITIVE DEVELOPMENT

During this same period, Bruner was involved with what became known as "the birth of the cognitive sciences." In 1956 he published *A Study of Thinking* with Jacqueline Goodnow and George Austin. In 1960 he and his colleague George Miller got funding for a Center for Cognitive Studies at Harvard. Between 1960 and 1972, when Bruner left Harvard for Oxford, he split his time between "practical" work at ESI on the process of education and "theoretical" research at the Center for Cognitive Studies. The two foci of course were interrelated. His theory of cognitive development was, for example, the source of the famous dictum in *The Process of Education* that any subject could be taught to any child at any age in some form that was "honest."

Bruner's theory of cognitive development featured the ordered development of three modes of representation—the enactive, the iconic, and the symbolic (Bruner, 1965). Later modes depend on earlier ones, but they are not developmental stages, for earlier ways of making and decoding meaning are not lost, and adults possess the flexibility of all three systems. In this view, youngest children use action to represent the world; images are added later; and, last but not least, arbitrary symbol systems such as language and mathematical symbols are added to the representational repertoire. This is why and how any subject can be taught at any age: it is simply a matter of presenting a concept to children in a developmentally appropriate mode of representation.

For example, Bruner assisted the mathematician Z. P. Dienes in using balance beams and blocks to teach quadratic equations to a group of four 8-year-olds (Bruner, 1966).[9] Their instructional sequence incorporated an interesting mix of action (making the balance beam balance), image (use of the blocks to make equivalent squares) and symbol (developing notations to describe the images of loaded balance beam and blocks). In their instructional sequence, the separation of the different representational systems is not as clear as the integration of these systems. What is clear is the fact that 8-year-olds could not have learned quadratic equations in a meaningful way if it were not for the support of enactive and iconic representation.

CULTURE, COGNITIVE DEVELOPMENT, AND EDUCATION

During the period 1960–61, Jerrold Zacharias began three new projects, two of which involved Bruner.[10] Most relevant to culture, cognitive development, and education was a project on the teaching of science and math in Africa. The Steering Committee of Zacharias' African Education Program, which began to meet in 1961, included Bruner as the only psychologist. It yielded the highly influential *The New Mathematics in an Old Culture*, a path-breaking book on culture, cognitive development, and education in Kpelleland, Liberia, by Cole and Gay (1967).

Out of this involvement in Africa, Bruner secured funding from the Ford Foundation for the Institut d'Etudes Pedagogiques at the University of Dakar in Senegal. Working with Simone Valantin at the Institut, Bruner traveled to Senegal and did pilot studies on the development of the Piagetian concept of quantity conservation in Wolof school children. His notion was that Piaget's theory might be more culture-bound than Piaget had imagined. In1963, Bruner arranged for Patricia Greenfield, one of the authors of this biographical piece, to go to Senegal to follow up these pilot observations for her dissertation. For Greenfield, Bruner's thesis was an exciting one to explore and the trip to Senegal the opportunity of a lifetime. She was to do conservation experiments in the French language in the French-speaking schools (originally set up by the recently rejected French colonial government).

When she arrived in Dakar, she began to question some elements of this plan. Armed with some anthropology background from Bruner's Department of Social Relations at Harvard, she did not think it fair to test children in their second language, French, as the French educational psychologists were doing; so she set about to learn Wolof, the major language of Senegal and the *lingua franca* of Dakar. Then she made a discovery that enabled her to link culture, schooling, and cognitive development in her dissertation research: In the bush villages, there were many children who did not attend school.

Here was a natural experiment on the effect of schooling, and she seized the opportunity. The key to the design of her studies was to compare schooled and unschooled children from the same village on tests of cognitive development. These tests included both tests of quantity conservation inspired by Piaget and tests of categorization inspired by Whorf. All children, both schooled and unschooled, were tested in the Wolof language.

Greenfield's results astonished both herself and Bruner, who as a wonderful mentor, visited Senegal in the middle of the fieldwork. Greenfield found that school children in both the capital city of Dakar and in the bush village of Taiba N'Djaye were indistinguishable in their cognitive development from children in Cambridge, Massachusetts (Bruner, 1965) or Geneva, Switzerland (Piaget, Inhelder, 1962). In startling contrast were the unschooled brothers and sisters of the Taiba N'Djaye school children. Without schooling, cognitive development looked extremely different (Greenfield, 1966; Greenfield, Reich, & Olver, 1966). The insight relating to education was that cognitive development as Piaget had described it might be neither "natural" nor universal. Instead, it looked like a progression that unfolds in a particular cultural environment, the environment of the school.

These findings were a powerful experience that pushed Bruner toward seeing schooling as a cultural institution (Bruner, 1966). Chapter 2 of *The Relevance of Education* (Bruner, 1971) is a collaborative article originally published in 1967 (Greenfield & Bruner, 1967/1968/1971) called "Culture and Cognitive Development," where the findings from Senegal are discussed from a theoretical point of view.

Included in the article is one of Greenfield's most startling discoveries. This discovery, an incidental one, marks the beginning of Bruner's involvement in folk psychology or theories of mind, although these terms were unknown at that time. Greenfield found that unschooled children could not respond to questions (in Wolof) about their reasoning of the form, "Why do you *think* X is the case?" or even "Why do you *say* X is the case?" However, if she asked the exact same question, but in the form, "Why *is* X the case?," they answered in completely meaningful ways, along the lines she had expected.

Greenfield and Bruner understood the absence of response to questions about "thinking" as a lack of awareness of a distinction between thought and the object of thought; they saw it as a worldview or cultural logic that, instead, privileged self or person-in-world, a monistic worldview that lacked the dualism between the psychological and the physical self that is so fundamental to Western modes of thought (Greenfield & Bruner, 1967/1968/1971). They also concluded that literacy, as a mode of representation that physically separates thought (on paper) from the object of thought (in the world) was what caused the rapid change to the ability to talk about one's own thinking.

Greenfield and Bruner therefore wrote about the power of schooling (and literacy) to not only change the course of cognitive development, but also to put its stamp on naïve psychology or theory of mind (Greenfield & Bruner, 1967/1968/1971). Thus, both the power of schooling as a cultural institution and naïve psychology appear in one form in *The Relevance of Education* in 1971; they reappear in new transformations in Bruner's most recent book on education, *The Culture of Education* (Bruner, 1996).

In that book, folk pedagogy, the teacher's concern with how her students think, is a key element of teaching. And one aspect of describing how children think is metacognition—children's thoughts about their own thinking. Based on Ann Brown's pioneering study, Bruner attributes great educational value to children's ability to turn their inner eye to their own strategies for thinking and remembering. What Greenfield and Bruner wrote about in *The Relevance of Education* (but which may have been forgotten in the 25 years between the two books) is that metacognitive strategies are themselves a cultural construction brought about by schooling and external representations such as literacy.

This conclusion constitutes an integration between individual cognitive development and the cultural construction of mind that Bruner is searching for in *The Relevance of Education*. There he talks about the struggle between context-free conceptions of mind and context-sensitive ones:

> I suspect that both kinds of theory are necessary . . . The strength of a context-free view is that it searches for universal structures of mind; its weakness is its intrinsic anti-culturalism. . . . The weakness of most context-sensitive views of development is that they give too much importance to individual and cultural differences and overlook the universals of growth. Their strength, of course, is in a sensitivity to the nature of the human plight and how this plight is fashioned by culture (Bruner, 1971, pp. 153–154).

MAN, A COURSE OF STUDY (MACOS)

During the 1960s, Bruner also became involved with the development of an elementary-level social science curriculum called Man, A Course of Study, or MACOS as the curriculum came to be known. This project related anthropology and education in completely different ways. Under the directorial guidance of Jerome Bruner the curriculum used the subject matter of comparative anthropology as its core and engaged the participation of several major anthropologists of that era, including Robert Adams, Asen Balikci, Irven DeVore, Richard Lee, Lorna Marshall, Elsa Miranda, and Douglas Oliver, as well as filmmakers John Marshall and Timothy Asch.

History of MACOS and Bruner's Involvement with the Curriculum

Simultaneously with the work in Africa, Bruner had become involved in Zacharias' second project, an elementary school education program, which began as the Elementary Science Study (ESS) and later developed into MACOS by way of the Social Studies Curriculum Program. It became one of the largest and most influential—as well as most controversial—curriculum projects ever developed by Educational Services, Inc. (ESI).[11]

Zacharias' concern with elementary school science study resulted from the discovery of the teachers and developers of PSSC that if young people had not learned by high school age to explore and experiment, they were unlikely ever to do so. A focus on the practice and logic of science had to begin much earlier. Whatever program they might develop at the elementary school level, Zacharias insisted, "must manage to keep the essence of real science: the programs must be based on experiment and discovery, on learning by doing" (Goldstein, 1992, p. 200).

Bruner, who had been in charge of the Instructional Research Group at ESI, was trying to determine, by listening to children, which of the ESI materials were most effective. He had also spent many hours observing the teachers working with the early units. When the original director of MACOS, anthropologist Douglas Oliver, resigned in 1964, Bruner agreed to take over as project director (Dow, 1991, p. 71).[12]

Principles of the MACOS Curriculum and Pedagogy

The MACOS curriculum was built around the fundamental question, "What is human about human beings?" It was essentially a course in evolution and anthropology based on the comparative examination of the social behavior of salmon, herring gulls, free-ranging baboon troops, and a tribe of Netsilik Eskimos. According to Bruner, three basic questions recurred throughout the curriculum: In addition to "What is human about human beings?," there were also the questions, "How did they get that way?" and "How can they be made more so?" Thus, the course was also an exploration of human evolution and, specifically, the evolution of culture as human adaptation. The curriculum identified and focused on five great humanizing forces: tool-making, language, social organization, prolonged childhood, and the urge to explain one's world (Bruner, 1966, p. 87). The curriculum developers' interest in focusing on anthropology and other behavioral sciences, rather than the traditional subject matter of history in the elementary curriculum, was to be able to impart to students an understanding of general principles rather than overwhelming them with specific historical details. It was also, for Bruner, a challenge to present a body of knowledge in a form simple enough that any 10-year-old child could understand it.

Bruner identified the most persistent problem in social studies as the necessity to rescue the phenomena of social life from familiarity while at the same time not making it all seem either "primitive" or "bizarre" (1966, p. 92). To that end the curriculum developed four useful techniques, based on observations that Bruner had already ascertained and described in *The Process of Education*:

1. **The use of contrast:** The MACOS curriculum was based on four principal sources of contrast: humans versus higher primates, humans versus prehistoric humans, contemporary technological societies versus so-called primitive societies, and adults versus children. These contrasts were important in establishing conceptual categories. They can be seen as an application of his first book on cognition, *A Study of Thinking* (Bruner, Goodnow, & Austin, 1956), which equated thinking with the cognitive creation of categories based on binary contrasts. But the ultimate goal of contrast was to understand continuity and similarity—that what seemed like contrast at first is finally understood, at another level of abstraction, as continuity.

2. **Simulation and use of informed guessing, hypothesis-making, and conjectural procedures:** Here was where the introduction of scientific modes of thought would be developed, and film was an important tool in presenting information that could be used as the basis for guessing and hypothesis-making.

3. **Participation:** To be stimulated by the use of games, role playing, and the creation of models of reality. In a sense, Bruner said, a game is like a mathematical model, an artificial but often powerful representation of reality. And participation allows one the experience of learning by doing. It could be seen as an application of his theory of cognitive development, the use of enactive representation as a foundation for the iconic and symbolic modes of representing a particular domain.

4. **Stimulation of self-consciousness about thinking:** To be learned through mastering the art of getting and using information. This principle could be seen as an intensification of the self-consciousness about thinking engendered by schooling more generally, as discovered by comparing schooled and unschooled children in Senegal.

The Use of Film in the MACOS Curriculum

All four techniques, following Zacharias' lead with the PSSC curriculum, relied heavily on the use of film. First of all, film captured children's attention and facilitated the perception of contrast in teaching anthropology. In conjunction with anthropologists Irven DeVore and Asen Balikci, in the early 1960s film director Kevin Smith's ESI film studio began pioneering film studies of baboon troops in East Africa and Netsilik Eskimos in Pelly Bay, Canada, covering more than a year of their lives. Film could also be seen as a way of activating the iconic mode of representation, of grounding symbolic thought in an iconic reality. At the same time, Bruner also got a contract from John Wiley, the publisher, to make a series of films about cognitive development based on research going on at the Center for Cognitive Studies. Bruner hired Allegra May, the daughter of Rollo May, the famous clinical psychologist, to serve as filmmaker.

But Bruner was worried that too often films had a way of producing passivity. "How do you use film to get people to ask questions rather than to accept the surface of things?" Bruner pondered. Ruminating on the problem, he consulted his friend and colleague linguist Roman Jakobson, asking him how one could ask questions in film.

Jakobson replied "Look at the conventions of film-making, the sequences that are taken for granted. Perhaps that is what you can vary to make the viewer come awake in the mind. Go again to see Robbe-Grillet's *Last Year at Marienbad*. It is full of questions" (Bruner, 1983a, p.192).

And that is what Bruner did. After viewing the film, he decided to keep the films silent. There was sound, but it was the wind or the cracking of the spring ice or the laughter and animated talk of a Netsilik storyteller talking in Eskimo. He suggested the creation of short sequence films, 4-minute loops of film constructed from Eskimo, Bushman, and baboon footage with the intention of asking questions or posing riddles. For example, a loop might raise the question, "Why did the Eskimos gather moss, and what did they use it for?" This could then be followed by further material that illustrated how moss was used. Bruner called these films "*Marienbad* teasers" after the enigmatic French film. After some experimentation, a method of editing unnarrated films that depicted sequences of complete activities was developed that provided enough information to allow the viewer to follow a complex event involving several participants from beginning to end. The method also generated an interest in viewers in asking questions about what they had seen.[13]

There were sequences that violated American children's expectations as to how the world works. For example, a Netsilik child builds a bird snare, catches a seagull in it, and stones it to death. Later, Bruner recounts, "When Boston school children argued bitterly over whether little Zachary was a nasty brute, one of them said, 'Listen, he's got to grow up to be a hunter'" (1983a, p. 193). One assumes from this comment that this was neither the only nor the first film about the Netsilik that the children had seen. Rather, the comment was a logical conclusion drawn by the child based on previous observations and information about the life of the Netsilik in their particular environment. It was also exactly the kind of thinking that Bruner hoped the curriculum would develop in the children.

PROJECT HEADSTART AND THE SIXTIES

But let us now return to the political arena of education. The 1960s changed everything. We arrive at Project Headstart, the famous antipoverty educational program on which Bruner consulted. It was the Headstart experience, Bruner said recently (personal communication, October 2000) that made him see education as a cultural resource with relevance for social equity. He says that was when he began to realize that you cannot just look at education as curriculum but as an aspect of culture. Here culture takes on a more sociological meaning: For the first time in Bruner's work, it is related to power.

In the introduction to *The Relevance of Education* Bruner draws out the relevance of "our ruinous and cruel war in Vietnam" for education:

> How [could our society] wage a war in the name of a generous way of life while our own way of life included urban ghettos, a culture of poverty, racism, etc. We looked afresh at the appalling effects of poverty and racism on the lives of children and the extent to which schools had become instruments of the evil forces in our society. Eloquent books like Jonathan Kozol's *Death at an Early Age* began appearing. (1971, p. x)

Bruner concludes *The Relevance of Education* with a chapter entitled "Poverty and Childhood." He couches the problem in cultural terms, referring to induction into "the culture of failure." In this chapter he is very concerned with interventions that can counteract or prevent the destructive effects of poverty and racism. Chief among their characteristics, one stood out: "the importance of initiative in the community as a means of activating parents and caretakers to do something for their children" (1971, p. 157).

In line with this belief, Bruner supported an action project in community development at the Center for Cognitive Studies. In 1971 two center fellows, Edward Tronick and Patricia Greenfield, in consultation with a third Center Fellow, pediatrician T. Berry Brazelton, and under the guidance of Marilyn Clayton Felt at Educational Development Center, Inc. (EDC),[14] helped start a community-controlled infant childcare center in the Bromley-Heath Housing Project in Jamaica Plain. It was the first infant childcare center in the Boston area.

With Tronick and Greenfield as technical advisors, the community, comprised mainly of welfare mothers, started their center. In the course of training these mothers to be infant teachers, Tronick and Greenfield wrote a book called *Infant Curriculum: The Bromley-Heath Guide to the Care and Development of Infants* (1973). It applied the best developmental psychology of the day, including infancy research that was then the focus of the program led by Bruner at the Center for Cognitive Studies. Bruner's support for this project was expressed in a foreward to the book.

A description of the principles behind this curriculum closes Bruner's chapter on poverty and childhood in his book, *The Relevance of Education*. This theme of a curriculum representing a community who organizes their own cultural institution, the school, remains strong in his last book on education, *The Culture of Education*. For example, near the beginning of *The Culture of Education*, Bruner writes that "education is a major embodiment of a culture's way of life, not just a preparation for it" (Bruner, 1996, p. 13).

THE DEMISE OF MAN, A COURSE OF STUDY (MACOS)

From 1967 the MACOS curriculum began to be used in classrooms across the country from Boston to California and internationally in such far-flung places as Australia. By 1971, however, a backlash began among conservative parents in Florida, Maryland, and Arizona who challenged MACOS, saying it was not appropriate for the instruction of elementary school children.

By 1975 the issue of MACOS had reached the floor of the House of Representatives. Congressman John B. Conlan of Arizona, who represented a conservative district in Phoenix, charged on the House floor that the curriculum offered "stories about Netsilik cannibalism, adultery, bestiality, female infanticide, murder, incest, wife-swapping, killing old people, and other shocking condoned practices" (Dow, 1991, p. 200; Goldstein, 1992, p. 296). In Conlan's eyes the MACOS curriculum ultimately represented "a dangerous plan for the federally-backed takeover of American education" (Dow, 1991, p. 211). He introduced an amendment to the authorization bill for the National Science Foundation (NSF) budget that required Congress to review all NSF curriculum projects prior to implementation, shifting the argument from the content of the MACOS curriculum to the question of freedom of choice within the educational community.

The result of the controversy in Congress was the premature decline of the MACOS curriculum and of NSF's termination of several of its science and social science curriculum projects. Later Bruner concentrated his educational reform efforts in Europe, notably in England (while he was a professor at Oxford) and, most recently, in Italy (in Reggio Emilia).

NARRATIVE AND CULTURAL PSYCHOLOGY

We end this biographical essay with the most recent element in Bruner's cultural psychology and educational thinking: narrative. Still holding firmly to his earlier views about subject-matter teaching, he states:

> I want finally to leapfrog over the issue of school "subjects" and curricula in order to deal with a more general matter: the mode of thinking and feeling that helps children (indeed, people generally) create a version of the world in which, psychologically, they can envision a place for themselves—a personal world. I believe that story making, narrative, is what is needed for that . . .
>
> There appear to be two broad ways in which human beings organize and manage their knowledge of the world, indeed structure even their immediate experience: one seems more specialized for treating of physical "things," the other for treating people and their plights. These are conventionally known as *logical-scientific* thinking

and *narrative* thinking. Their universality suggests that they have their roots in the human genome or that they are . . . givens in the nature of language." (Bruner, 1996, p. 39)

This conceptualization nicely captures two cognitive cultures. Bruner makes it clear, furthermore, that schools privilege the logical-scientific mode. This conceptualization has broad applicability to cross-cultural issues in education. Recently, for example, in the course of a project called Bridging Cultures, Greenfield and colleagues discovered that Latino immigrant children use narrative in an omnipresent way to affirm and confirm their connections with their families. From the standard teaching perspective, it turns out that teachers do not know how to cope with these "stories," and they try to nip them at the bud, often in favor of the logical-scientific mode, which they recognize and reward. For example, in one observation in a public prekindergarten class, a teacher trying to teach a science lesson about eggs held up an egg about to hatch and asked the children to describe eggs by thinking about the times they had cooked and eaten eggs. One of the children tried three times to talk about how she cooked eggs with her grandmother, but the teacher disregarded these comments in favor of a child who explained how eggs are white and yellow when they are cracked (Greenfield, Raeff, & Quiroz, 1996).

The two features of this incident, the child's emphasis on a family-based story and the teacher's disregard and devaluation of the child's seemingly unscientific answer are a frequent occurrence in Latino immigrant classrooms. The child is responding in the narrative mode; the teacher expects the logical-scientific mode. As Bruner says, the value of logical-scientific thinking "is so implicit in our highly technological culture that its inclusion in school curricula is taken for granted" (Bruner, 1996, p. 41). It is so taken for granted that the other mode becomes invisible to the teacher.

Bruner hits on another point that is most relevant to this incident and its analysis: "Feeling at home in the world, knowing how to place oneself into self-descriptive stories, is surely not made easier by the enormous increase in migration in the modern world" (Bruner, 1996, p. 41). This is particularly so when one's stories are systematically devalued by the school, as Greenfield and colleagues have found them to be. Of the immigrant Latino children's stories, teachers typically say things like, "I can't stand it," etc. A major response to the Bridging Cultures teacher training project has been for teachers to revalue and use these stories in the educational process. They do so in writing, by giving writing prompts that use these children's strong motives to identify themselves by relating themselves to their families and their family activities. They do so in science by consciously constructing bridges between the narrative mode and the logical-scientific mode of thinking. For example, after a wetlands field trip, one Bridging Cultures teacher helped children make connections between narratives about family experiences with flora and fauna (e.g., watching a hummingbird stand still in the air) and relevant scientific facts (e.g., hummingbird wings beat very quickly) (Greenfield & Rothstein-Fisch, 1999).

In sum, Bruner's incorporation of the narrative mode of thought into a book about education provides an important theoretical rationale to make the many immigrant and other minority children who come from cultures that privilege the narrative mode over the scientific-logical feel at home in the world of the school.

Proving once again the breadth of his intellectual interests as well as the wide applicability of his theoretical insights into the role of narrative in human cognitive and social behavior, in his most recent book, *Minding the Law* (2000), written in collaboration with legal scholar, Anthony Amsterdam, Bruner demonstrates the importance of narrative to the way in which our legal system works. Through the analysis of key Supreme Court opinions, Bruner and Amsterdam explain how the tactics of narrative and rhetoric, along with the psychological appeal of deeply rooted mythic structures central to American culture, have shaped the Court's decisions about race, family law, and the death penalty. In doing so they also suggest that implicitly, as well as sometimes explicitly, the skillful use of the narrative mode of thought and discourse have been fundamental to the education of successful lawyers and Supreme Court justices.

LINKS BETWEEN EDUCATION AND CULTURAL PSYCHOLOGY

In the preface to *The Culture of Education*, Bruner suggests retrospectively how closely linked he came to see the problems of education and the questions that loomed large in creating a cultural psychology: "questions about the making and negotiating of meanings, about the construction of self and a sense of agency, about the acquisition of symbolic skills, and especially about the cultural 'situatedness' of all mental activity" (Bruner, 1996, p. x). Most importantly, education "presupposes that human mental activity is neither solo nor conducted unassisted, even when it goes on 'in the head'" (Bruner, 1996, p. x).

As Bruner has noted, during the late 1950s and 1960s, when the curriculum reforms we have described were being developed, little attention was paid by him or other reformers involved to the environment or cultural context in which kids in school were learning. It was assumed that students lived in some sort of "educational vacuum," untroubled by the ills and problems of the culture at large. Although Bruner writes that the "discovery of poverty" and the civil rights movement of the 1960s led him to become aware of the impact of poverty, racism, and alienation on the mental life and growth of children, the controversy surrounding Man, A Course of Study (MACOS) itself must also have provided a telling indication that what children were taught was also part of a larger social, political, and cultural context.

Even before the controversy erupted, MACOS prodded or forced Bruner out of his laboratory and into the observation of the real world, as far as learning and education were concerned. He began to observe teachers and students using the curricula developed by ESI in general and MACOS in particular. Thus, he was beginning to observe the cultural setting in which learning was taking place, as well as the interpsychic mode in which knowledge was being constructed and conveyed.

At the same time, his trip to Africa and the research it inspired moved him out of the mindset of Western thinking and developed an appreciation of cross-cultural variability in cognitive development. Most important of all, no longer could schooling be taken for granted as an unrecognized partner in cognitive development. In Africa, where schooling could not be assumed, its crucial role as a mind-developing cultural institution became clear.

Some of the tenets that Bruner describes as guiding a psychocultural approach to education have roots in the principles that underlay the MACOS curriculum or its praxis. These tenets were also highlighted by opportunities to observe children in African schools and, finally, to learn how children thought in a culture for which schooling was a foreign influence. Other tenets may stem from Bruner's studies at Oxford on the creation of joint meanings and culture in the mother–infant dyad. Still other tenets echo Vygotsky, whom Bruner introduced to American audiences in the early1960s (Vygotsky, 1962). Finally, others were very much influenced by his observations of the classrooms set up in Oakland by Ann Brown and Joseph Campione and by his experiences observing the progressive public schools in Reggio Emilia, Italy.

The guiding tenets for a psychocultural approach to education are:

1. **The perspectival tenet:** That the meaning of any fact or encounter is relative to the perspective or frame of reference in terms of which it is construed.

2. **The constraints tenet:** That the forms of meaning making accessible to human beings in any culture are constrained in two ways: by the nature of human mental functioning and the nature of the symbolic systems [i.e., language] accessible to human minds (Bruner, 1996, pp. 15–19).

3. **The interactional tenet:** Passing on knowledge and skill, like any human exchange, involves a sub-community in interaction.

4. **The externalization tenet:** The benefits of externalizing joint projects, or "oeuvres," as Bruner refers to them.

5. **The narrative tenet:** The mode of thinking and feeling that helps children create a version of the world in which, psychologically, they can envisage a place for themselves. This was indeed the primary thrust of the MACOS curriculum, to teach children what was human about being a human being. Bruner believes that story making and narrative is what is needed for that. An important aspect of the MACOS curriculum was to look at the myths and legends of other cultures and to understand the concepts of myth and narrative in our own culture.

BRUNER'S LEGACY TO EDUCATIONAL PSYCHOLOGY

Jerome Bruner's legacy to educational psychology is twofold. First, he was one of the first North American psychologists to utilize a cognitive approach to education and educational psychology. He drew attention to the importance of the structure of the subject matter, the representational skills of the learner, and the fit between them (Bruner, 1960, 1966). He also introduced Piaget to the educational community in the United States (Bruner, 1960), while later providing a critique of Piaget that opened up cognitive thinking in education to the role of the environment (Bruner, Olver, Greenfield, 1966). Through Bruner, the cognitive revolution hit educational thinking in the United States and around the world.

Second, Jerome Bruner called attention to education as a sociocultural enterprise. He began this enterprise in the 1960s when he wrote the preface to the first English translation of Lev Vygotsky's, *Thought and Language*, published in 1962. Vygotsky has since become a watchword in educational psychology, and his developmental theory is treated on a par with that of Piaget. The sociocultural thrust in education expanded with Bruner's use of cross-cultural data in the 1960s (Greenfield & Bruner, 1967), his role in the development of the MACOS curriculum, and his analyses of the role of poverty in educational development in the 1970s (Bruner, 1971). Finally, with the publication of *The Culture of Education* in 1996, Jerome Bruner firmly established educational psychology as part and parcel of cultural psychology. This gives it a pivotal position from which to address issues of educational psychology in a postmodern, multicultural world.

NOTES

1. Bruner wrote *In Search of Mind: Essays in Autobiography* (1983) as part of a series of books written by scientists that was sponsored by the Alfred P. Sloan Foundation to encourage a public understanding of science.
2. Broom, Bruner says, informed him of the parochial, culture-bound nature of Freud's view of the family, very "fin de siecle." (Bruner, 1983a, p. 134).
3. During the 1940s Bruner frequently interacted with anthropologists of the "Culture and Personality" group at conferences as well as at Harvard. For example, in a biography about Betty Friedan, Daniel Horowitz notes that Bruner as well as both Margaret Mead and Gregory Bateson were at a conference of the Topological Society in Northampton in December 1942 that Friedan, then a graduate student in psychology herself at Berkeley, attended with her mentor, Edward Tolman (Horowitz, 1998, p. 100). During the 1940s Bruner also worked with Mead on a Naval Research Panel, an interdisciplinary team assembled by Admiral Solberg, the Chief of Naval Research (Bruner, 1983a, p. 63).
4. Members of the new Department of Social Relations included Talcott Parsons, Gordon Allport, Clyde Kluckhohn, Pitirim Sorokin, and Henry Murray, among others.
5. Zacharias' memo, written to the president of MIT and then submitted to the National Science Foundation, stated that "In an effort to improve the teaching of high school physics I want to propose an experiment involving the preparation of a large number of moving picture shorts. In

order to present one subject, say physics, it is proposed that we make 90 films of 20-minute duration, complete with textbooks, problem books, question cards and answer cards" (Goldstein, 1992, p. 152).

6. The story of the development of the Physical Science Study Committee's (PSSC) physics curriculum is one that includes the role of the National Science Foundation (NSF), which funded the curriculum development. It also exemplified a quintessential "old boys" network at work as the individuals involved included scholars from MIT and Harvard and government officials in Washington, D.C. who knew one another from their earlier days of collaboration during WWII. In some cases, as with NSF, the officials there had been scholars at MIT themselves, or they conferred with the President's science advisors, who were MIT scholars. However, by its end, some 60 physicists, high school teachers, writers, editors, and filmmakers had taken part in the project (Goldstein, 1992, p. 168).

7. In the course of making the proposed films, Zacharias and his associates learned much about the difficulties of transferring on to film the excitement of doing science, as well as the difficulties of conveying the content. Cf. Goldstein for a discussion of the difficulty of getting physicists to appear interesting on film (1992, p. 152).

8. By the end of 1962 secondary school education in the U.S. included new curricula devised by the Physical Science Study Committee (PSSC), Biological Sciences Curriculum Study (BSCS), Chemical Bond Approach Project (CBA), Chemical Education Materials Study (CHEMS), Earth Sciences Curriculum Project (ESCP), School Mathematics Study Group (SMS), and University of Illinois Committee on School Mathematics (UICSM). All of these were well-established NSF-sponsored programs aimed at improving science and math education in the high schools. What these programs had in common, besides NSF funding, was the use of professional scientists and mathematicians, often drawn from the highest level, working alongside high school teachers and other educators to prepare new materials (Goldstein, 1992, p. 185).

9. S. Anderson, E. Duckworth, and J. R. Hornsby also participated in the study.

10. The third project was the development of a new college physics course.

11. Thus, the Social Studies Curriculum program was the intellectual heir of the Physical Science Study Committee. Support came from NSF, the Sloan Foundation, and the Victoria Foundation. Francis Friedman and Zacharias were among the signatories to the original proposal (Goldstein, 1992, p. 202).

12. When Oliver's wife died in 1964, he lost enthusiasm for the project (Dow, 1991, p. 71).

13. After initial problems with films of such short length, film editor Quentin Brown and anthropologist Asen Balikci abandoned the short loops and put together a longer film of 30 minutes, still without narration, titled *Fishing at Stone Weir* (1963). Pleased with the positive results the film received from both children and adults, Brown and Balikci continued to construct films from unnarrated sequences of complete activities. The key was to show complete activities that were designed to provide enough information to allow the viewer to follow a complex event involving several participants from beginning to end (Dow, 1991, p. 64).

14. In 1965 the Educational Services, Inc. merged with the Institute for Educational Innovation to form a new, enlarged corporation named Educational Development Center, Inc. (Goldstein, 1992, p. 262).

REFERENCES

Amsterdam, A., & Bruner J. S. (2000). *Minding the law*. Cambridge, MA: Harvard University Press.

Bruner, J. S. (1960). *The process of education*. Cambridge, MA: Harvard University Press.

Bruner, J. S. (1965). The growth of mind. *American Psychologist, 20*, 1007–1017.

Bruner, J. S. (1966). *Toward a theory of instruction*. Cambridge, MA: Harvard University Press.

Bruner, J. S. (1971). *The relevance of education*. Cambridge, MA: Harvard University Press.

Bruner, J. S. (1980). Foreward. In E. Tronick & P. M. Greenfield, *Infant curriculum: The Bromley-Heath guide to the care and development of infants in groups* (Rev. ed., p. viii). Santa Monica, CA: Goodyear. (Now distributed through Scott, Foresman.)

Bruner, J. S. (1983a) *In search of mind: Essays in autobiography*. New York: Harper & Row.

Bruner, J. S. (1983b). *Child's talk: Learning to use language*. New York: W. W. Norton.

Bruner, J. S. (1996). *The culture of education*. Cambridge, MA: Harvard University Press.

Bruner, J. S., Goodnow, J. J. & Austin, G. A. (1956). *A study of thinking*. New York: Wiley.

Bruner, J. S., Olver, R. R. & Greenfield, P. M. (1966). *Studies in cognitive growth*. New York: Wiley.

Cole, M., & Gay, J. (1967). *The new mathematics in an old culture: A study of learning among the Kpelle of Liberia*. New York: Holt, Rinehart & Winston.

Dow, P. (1991). *Schoolhouse politics: Lessons from the sputnik era*. Cambridge, MA: Harvard University Press.

Goldstein, J. S. (1992). *A different sort of time: The life of Jerrold R. Zacharias, scientist, engineer, educator*. Cambridge, MA: The MIT Press.

Greenfield, P. M. (1966). Culture and conservation. In J. S. Bruner, R. R. Olver, P. M. Greenfield, et al. *Studies in cognitive growth* (pp. 225–256). New York: Wiley.

Greenfield, P. M., Reich, L. C., & Olver, R. R. (1966). On culture and equivalence: II. In J. S. Bruner, R. R. Olver, P. M. Greenfield, et al. *Studies in cognitive growth* (pp. 270–318). New York: Wiley.

Greenfield, P. M., & Bruner, J. S. (1967). Culture and cognitive growth. *International Journal of Psychology*. Revised version in D. Goslin (Ed.) (1968). *Handbook of socialization theory* (pp. 633–660). Chicago: Rand McNally.

Greenfield, P. M., & Bruner, J. S. (1971). Culture and cognitive growth. In J. S. Bruner (Ed.), *The relevance of education* (pp. 20–51). New York: Norton.

Greenfield, P. M., Raeff, C., & Quiroz, B. (1996). Cultural values in learning and education. In B. Williams (Ed.), *Closing the achievement gap: A vision for changing beliefs and practices* (pp. 37–55). Alexandria, VA: Association for Supervision and Curriculum Development.

Greenfield, P. M., & Rothstein-Fisch, C. (1999, Month). *Bridging cultures in education: Implicit knowledge through explicit training*. Paper presented at the Biennial Meeting of the Society for Research in Child Development, Albuquerque, NM.

Horowitz, D. (1998). *Betty Friedan and the making of the Feminine Mystique: The American left, the cold war, and modern feminism*. Amherst, MA: University of Massachusetts Press.

Lutkehaus, N. (2000, November). *From image to narrative: Anthropology's role in the development of Jerome Bruner's cultural psychology*. Paper presented at the Annual Meetings of the American Anthropological Association, San Francisco, CA.

Lutkehaus, N. (2002). Man, a Course of Study: Situating Tim Asch's pedagogical assumptions about ethnographic film. In E. D. Lewis (Ed.), *Timothy Asch and Ethnographic film* (pp.___). New York and London: Routledge. In Press.

Piaget, J., & Inhelder, (1962). *Le developpement des quantitiés physiques chez l'enfant* [The child's development of physical quantity]. (2nd ed.). Neuchatel, Switzerland: Delachaux & Niestle.

Piaget, J., (1970). *Structuralism*. New York: Harper & Row.

Tronick, E., & Greenfield, P. M. (1973). *Infant curriculum: The Bromley-Heath guide to the care of infants in groups*. New York: Media Projects. Second edition in paperback. Santa Monica, CA: Goodyear. Now distributed by Scott, Foresman.

Vygotsky, L. (1962). *Thought and language*. Cambridge, MA: The MIT Press.

18

Albert Bandura: The Scholar and His Contributions to Educational Psychology

Barry J. Zimmerman

City University of New York Graduate Center

Dale H. Schunk

University of North Carolina at Greensboro

In June 1993, Albert Bandura's colleagues and former students surprised him by gathering in California's verdant Napa Valley for a 2-day Bandurafest. Months of secretive planning eluded his typically observant eye. He was lured to the event under a cover story. That so many people attended the gathering may seem remarkable because no papers were presented and no Festschrift publication was planned. Instead, the 2 days were spent in lively informal discussions, a sumptuous picnic in the vineyards, and a joyous celebratory dinner. People came from far and near to honor their esteemed mentor, colleague, and friend. He was affectionately described as the "jovial genius" by one of his former students for his wisdom, humility, and wonderful sense of humor. In this intimate gathering, joined by his wife Ginny and his daughters Mary and Carol, Al expressed his gratitude to those present and others who could not attend for enriching his life. In this chapter we attempt to recapture the spirit of the Bandurafest by reviewing Al's life and contributions to the enlightenment and betterment of human life. His theory and program of research have had diverse influence on many disciplines, but their impact on educational psychology will receive special attention in the present chapter.

THE SCHOLAR

Albert Bandura was born on December 4, 1925, in Mundare, a hamlet in northern Alberta, Canada, which is located about 50 miles east of Edmonton. He has described humorously the forbidding climate of his northern Alberta habitat as the place where arctic cold originates and descends unmercifully into the northern States (Stokes, 1986a). He was the youngest child and only son among six children in a family of Ukrainian descent. Interestingly, the name *bandura* refers to a Ukrainian 60-stringed musical instrument, which portended Al's lifelong love of classical music. His unique early educational experiences would prove formative to his subsequent view of learning as an essentially social and self-directed process. His entire precollegiate education was conducted in an eight-room school. Having but two high school teachers and few instructional resources, Bandura and his schoolmates had to develop their own academic skills at an early age. He described their adaptive academic self-directedness as follows, "The students had to take charge of their own education.... Very often we developed a better grasp of the subjects than the overworked teachers" (Stokes, 1986a, p. 2). This unusual reversal of academic roles produced several memorable incidents. For example, the entire curriculum of his high school mathematics class was comprised of a single textbook, which one beleaguered teacher tried to master ahead of her small but bright class of students. As a prank, the students got hold of the teacher's trigonometry answer book, reducing the teacher to desperate pleading and negotiation of homework concessions so that the class could resume. Although far off well trodden paths to academe, this meager academic environment produced some extraordinary dividends: Most of Bandura's circle of classmates went on to pursue degrees at various universities, which was unprecedented for that farming community. Bandura drew an important conclusion from his early educational experiences, "The content of most textbooks is perishable, but the tools of self-directedness serve one well over time" (Stokes, 1986a, p. 2).

Not all of Bandura's educational experiences were confined to formal schooling. During the summer of his senior year in high school, he sought to earn tuition money for college by repairing the Alaskan highway in the Yukon tundra from yearly ravages of freezing and thawing. As a member of a road crew, he encountered some truly colorful characters, "refugees from creditors, probation officers, draft boards, or alimony demands" (Stokes, 1986, p. 2)—the flotsam and jetsam of society who sought an honest day's wage with few questions asked. Needless to say, the ingenuity of this motley crew took some unusual forms. To supply themselves with alcoholic refreshment in their wild and isolated environs, they built a still for distilling vodka from potatoes and sugar. On one occasion, several resident grizzly bears arrived the day before the enterprising distillers and consumed their alcoholic mash. This brew was much more zestful than berries. This produced deep despondency in the distillers but great frolicking among the bears! The humor and yet pathos of these social learning experiences left an indelible mark on Bandura's understanding of the human condition—an enduring appreciation for the value of human agency, even among the dispossessed, in a world of real consequences.

To escape the severe weather of northern Alberta, Bandura enrolled in 1946 at the University of British Columbia in Vancouver, which enjoys a mild Pacific coastal climate and a fine intellectual reputation. Al's decision to study psychology was a product of fortuity rather than design. He commuted to the University in a carpool with several engineering and pre-med students who had enrolled in early morning classes. He decided to register for a psychology course to fill his early time slot. He was fascinated by the topic and decided to pursue it as a major. He was an exemplary student who graduated in just 3 years with the Bolocan Award in psychology. The impact of his fortuitous entry into the field of psychology would influence his theorizing later. In the seminal article "The Psychology of Chance Encounters and Life Paths," he discussed how personal initiative often places people in fortuitous circumstances that can shape the courses lives take (Bandura, 1982). Rather than treating fortuity as uncontrollability, Bandura focused on how to make "chance" opportunities happen through an inquisitive life and on how to exploit these opportunities through self-development.

For graduate study, Bandura sought the "stone tablets" of psychology, which he was advised resided at the University of Iowa. In the early 1950s, Iowa had a stellar faculty, such as Kenneth Spence and Kurt Lewin, who created a lively intellectual environment. It was also the scene of occasional clever pranks designed to elevate Spence's blood pressure, such as pinning on the departmental bulletin board a rat that had expired with an explanatory note, "This rat ran according to Tolman's theory" (Hilgard, 1989, p. 4). This drove Spence to explosive expletives.

Because of a close allegiance between Spence and Clark Hull at Yale University, students and faculty at Iowa followed closely the theorizing and research at Yale. In the 1930s, social learning theory was born at the Yale Institute of Human Relations under the direction of Mark May with the intellectual leadership of Hull. They sought to provide learning explanations for key aspects of personal and social development discussed by Freud, such as dependency, aggression, identification, conscience formation, and defense mechanisms. Among the key collaborators with Hull at the institute were John Dollard, Neal Miller, and Robert Sears. They sought to translate Freudian conceptions into Hullian principles. For example, to study identification, Miller and Dollard conducted a series of experimental studies of social modeling, which they conceptualized as a form of instrumental learning in their book entitled *Social Learning and Imitation* (1941). Bandura was not especially attracted to Hullian theory because of its almost exclusive focus on tedious trial-and-error learning. He felt that cultures transmitted social mores and complex competencies primarily through social modeling, although through different mechanisms than the ones proposed by Miller and Dollard.

While Bandura was pursuing graduate study at Iowa, another fortuitous event in his life resulted from a chance encounter. As he explained:

Seeking relief from an uninspiring reading assignment, a graduate student departs for the golf links with his friend. They happen to find themselves playing behind a twosome of attractive women golfers. Before long the two twosomes become one foursome and, in the course of events, one of the partners eventually becomes the wife of the graduate golfer. (Bandura, 1982, p. 748)

Had Al not sought to break the drudgery of that reading assignment by golfing or arrived at a slightly different time, he might never have met Ginny Varns, who was on the teaching staff in the College of Nursing. Following their marriage, they moved to Wichita where he completed a postdoctoral internship at the Wichita Guidance Center, and she worked as a supervisor in an obstetrics hospital. Bandura received his Ph.D. in 1952. This completed his academic odyssey from the meagre Mondare high school to a doctoral degree within 6 years.

In 1953, Bandura was recruited by Robert Sears to join the psychology department at Stanford University as an instructor. Bandura was very attracted by this offer, but he had already accepted a position at another institution. Sears pressed Bandura to ask for a release from the other institution, which he did reluctantly because he felt a strong sense of obligation to honor his commitment. This decision was path setting in Bandura's career. At Stanford, he had the opportunity to work with exceptional colleagues and students at that renowned institution in the resplendent San Francisco Bay area.

Influenced by Sears' work, Bandura undertook a systematic program of research on social and familial determinants of aggression with Richard Walters, his first doctoral student. They chose the unconventional challenge of explaining severe antisocial aggression in boys from intact homes in advantaged residential areas, rather than simply demonstrating that multiple adverse conditions tend to spawn behavioral problems.

This research underscored the key role of modeling influences in these advantaged families. They reported their findings in a book entitled, *Adolescent Aggression* (Bandura & Walters, 1959). Parents of "hyper-aggressive youngsters were modeling very hostile attitudes. They would not tolerate any aggression in the home, but they demanded that their sons be tough, that they settle disputes with peers physically if necessary, and they sided with their son against the school. They would go to school and become very aggressive toward the school system and toward peers that were giving their son a tough time. The youngsters modeled the aggressive hostile attitudes of their parents" (Hilgard, 1989, p. 11). The vicarious influence of seeing father modeling aggressive attitudes and punitive modes of social control promoted aggressive styles of conduct. These findings conflicted with the Freudian–Hullian assumption that parental punishment would inhibit children's expression of aggressive drives.

These results led Bandura to conduct a program of research with Dorrie and Sheila Ross on social modeling using the classic Bobo doll paradigm (Bandura, Ross, & Ross, 1961, 1963). At that time, it was widely believed, in accordance with the Freudian theory of catharsis, that modeled violence would drain observers' aggressive drives and reduce such behavior. Children who viewed aggressive models subsequently displayed the novel forms of aggression toward the Bobo doll whereas control children rarely, if ever, did so. This observational learning occurred in the absence of reinforcement to the observers. Bandura and his colleagues also demonstrated that children can readily learn any response or complex patterns of behavior vicariously without performing any response or receiving rewards. This line of theorizing was discordant with the views in vogue at the time that learning is a consequence of direct reinforcement. The results were also at odds with Miller and Dollard's (1941) conception in terms of instrumental discrimination learning. Bandura distinguished between the cognitive effects of modeling on *acquisition* and the motivational effects of rewards on imitative *performance*. The research on modeling was reviewed in a second book published in 1963 with Walters entitled *Social Learning and Personality Development*. They presented modeling as a pervasive and powerful process governing cognitive, affective, and behavioral forms of learning. They sought to free explanations of social learning from theoretical dependence on Freudian conceptions of identification and catharsis, and from Hullian and Skinnerian assumptions that learning requires direct reinforcement.

During the 1960s, Bandura launched a second major program of research on children's development of self-regulatory capabilities. This research foreshadowed his development of an agentic perspective in which people are viewed as self-regulatory and self-reflective organisms, not just reactive ones to environmental influences. Bandura and Carol Kupers (1964) demonstrated that children adapt modeled high performance standards for self-reward. Children are also better in sustaining their performance motivation by self-reward than through external reward (Bandura & Perloff, 1967). Bandura and a colleague at Stanford, Walter Mischel, found that children who observed a model forego small immediate rewards in favor of larger long-term rewards increased their preference for delayed rewards (Bandura & Mischel, 1965). These pioneering studies of the social origins of children's self-motivation and self-regulation provided a new and experimentally testable alternative to personality trait theories.

During the 1960s and 1970s, Bandura, along with a growing legion of students and colleagues, began to study the role of social modeling in children's cognitive and linguistic development. This theoretical and experimental work helped to shift descriptions of modeling from simple response mimicry (i.e., "imitation") to abstract modeling of rules and structures embodied in exemplars. He hypothesized that children's acquisition of abstract conceptual classes and linguistic rules could also be acquired vicariously from adult and peer models. In collaboration with another colleague at Stanford, Fred McDonald, Bandura conducted the first study of abstract modeling using Piaget's moral reasoning task (Bandura & McDonald, 1963). Piaget had discovered that the moral reasoning of immature children focused on the consequences of actions (such as the number of glasses broken), whereas the reasoning of more mature youngsters centered on intentions (whether a glass was broken purposely or accidentally). Piaget attributed preschoolers' deficiencies in moral reasoning to an their stage-related egocentrism (i.e., a first-person visual perspective) rather than their social learning experiences. Bandura and McDonald demonstrated that exposure to models who judged culpability by intentions of the characters in moral stories increased young children's use of intentions in their own judgments of culpability. Like children's acquisition of novel forms of aggression, their moral reasoning was strongly influenced by social learning experiences.

Bandura then turned his attention to children's language development through abstract modeling. With his student Mary Harris, they found that children could induce linguistic rules from diverse modeled exemplars embodying the rules (Bandura & Harris, 1966). Another of Bandura's students, Ted Rosenthal, with his colleagues Barry Zimmerman and Kathy Durning (1970), studied children's vicarious learning of a model's conceptual style of inquiry (e.g., asking cause and effect questions). Children exhibited high levels of conceptual learning with very little exact copying or mimicry of a model's specific behaviors. This series of studies included stringent transfer tests of observational learning. As Bandura noted in his book, *Principles of Behavior Modification* (1969), this transfer showed that observers modified their styles of behavior to new situations in accord with the model's dispositions even though they never witnessed the model's response to the same stimuli. By inducing rules underlying modeled exemplars, observers could create novel but rule-consistent behavior that extended beyond what was seen or heard. Modeling could also lead to abstraction of divergent ways of thinking, as when brainstorming by a model led observers to think unconventionally (Arem & Zimmerman, 1976; Harris & Evans, 1973; Harris & Fisher, 1973; Zimmerman & Dialessi, 1973).

Abstract modeling freed social learning accounts of modeling phenomena from the shackles of narrow conceptions of simple response mimicry. Evidence of abstract modeling of moral judgments, linguistic rules, and conceptual styles of inquiry attracted many adherents who were seeking alternatives to stage views of children's development. This research on abstract modeling was reviewed in the edited book *Psychological Modeling—Conflicting Theories* (Bandura, 1971). Bandura's analysis of the role of abstract modeling in conceptual development stimulated a wave of successful training studies in cognitive and linguistic functioning during the 1970s that challenged stage conceptions of development (Bandura, 1977; Rosenthal & Zimmerman, 1978; Zimmerman & Rosenthal, 1974).

To further understand the process of abstraction in vicarious learning, Bandura investigated the impact of observers' symbolic coding of modeling events (Bandura & Jeffrey, 1973). Symbolic coding greatly enhanced observational acquisition of complex patterns of motor behavior. Clearly the quality of observers' learning from a model was affected by their cognitive or linguistic facility. Bandura (1986) described the role of this symbolic capacity of learners in the following way, "Through their capacity to manipulate symbols and to engage in reflective thought, people can generate novel ideas and innovative actions that transcend their past experiences" (p. 1182). Through the recent revolutionary advances in the technology of telecommunications, symbolic modeling is playing a paramount role in the worldwide diffusion of ideas, values, and styles of behavior. Despite differences in place and time, learners can symbolically encode vicarious experience to better understand and transform their environments. Bandura put it this way, "Most of the images of reality on which we based our actions are really based on vicarious experience . . . We have a vast new world of images brought into our sitting-rooms electronically" (Stokes, 1986a, p. 3). Through symbolic modeling, people give structure, meaning, and continuity to their lives.

In 1974, Bandura unexpectedly received a letter from the American Psychological Association (APA) informing him that he had been nominated to the ballot for the office of the presidency. Because he had little contact with APA's administrative procedures and politics, he viewed the whole matter as an amusing fluke—his 15 minutes of Andy Warholian fame with little risk of election. However, one Saturday, while atop a mulberry tree trimming its engulfing branches, he received a phone call from APA headquarters. The executive secretary greeted him with the announcement, "You're it!" Later Bandura described his election to the presidency humorously as "the most rapid evolutionary descent on record from the trees into an organizational board room" (Hilgard, 1989, p. 15).

During Bandura's term of office, American psychologists were threatened by cuts in training grants by the Nixon administration, by efforts to exclude psychologists as providers of psychological treatment for dependents of veterans, and by sensational accounts of forced behavior modification. To combat these public policy issues, Bandura presided over the founding of the Association for the Advancement of Psychology (AAP). It served as a vehicle for psychologists to influence public policy initiatives and congressional legislation. This advocacy organization was viewed as very influential and became a model for other professional groups. The powerful senator from the state of Washington, Henry "Scoop" Jackson, was so impressed with the quality of the work that he invited the APA to assist his senate committee and staff on legislation having important social implications. In that same year, Bandura was awarded the David Starr Jordan endowed chair in Social Sciences in Psychology by Stanford University. He served as Chair of the Department of Psychology at Stanford during the 1976–1977 academic year.

At the time, Bandura had begun to extend his research on the acquisition of self-evaluative standards to other self-regulation processes, such as managing disabling fears. He and his students Bruni Ritter and Ed Blanchard developed a highly effective guided mastery treatment for people plagued with incapacitating animal phobias and recurrent nightmares (Bandura, Blanchard & Ritter, 1969). In this "participant modeling" approach, patients' were taught to overcome their phobic dread with the benefit of coping modeling and graduated performance induction aids. Participant modeling with guided performance mastery rapidly cured phobias and terrifying nightmares that haunted the people for a lifetime (Bandura, Jeffery, & Wright, 1974). In follow-up assessments, the participants expressed gratitude for

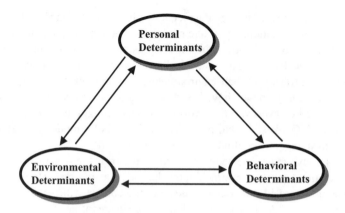

FIG. 18.1. Schematization of the relationship between the three classes of determinants in triadic reciprocal causation. From *Social Foundations of Thought and Action: A Social Cognitive Theory* 1986. Copyright 1986 by Prentice-Hall Inc. Adapted with permission of the publisher.

curing their phobias but explained that the rapid transforming experience had a more profound personal impact. It instilled a sense that they can exercise some measure of control over their lives. Unless people believe that they can attain desired outcomes by their actions, they have little incentive to act and persevere in the face of difficulties. The guided mastery approach was extended by Debowski, Wood, and Bandura (2001) to promoting competences for knowledge construction through the Internet.

Bandura's research on self-regulation and self-efficacy culminated in a 1977 book entitled *Social Learning Theory*, in which he analyzed human learning and self-regulation in terms of triadic reciprocal causations involving a complex interplay between personal (cognitive–affective), behavioral, and environmental determinants (see Fig. 18.1). Bandura summarized this triadic perspective as follows, "What people think, believe, and feel affects how they behave. The natural and extrinsic effects of their actions, in turn, partly determine their thought patterns and affective reactions" (1986, p. 25). In this model of reciprocal causation, people are producers as well as products of environmental conditions. This formulation avoided the pitfalls of classical cognitive approaches (Sampson, 1981), which minimized the interactive influences behavior and social environmental factors have on human thought.

During the 1980s, Bandura increasingly turned his attention to studying the impact of self-efficacy beliefs in new areas of functioning. With his student, Dale Schunk, he investigated the self-regulatory effects of personal goal setting in children's mastery of mathematical competencies that had eluded them (Bandura & Schunk, 1981). They discovered that students who set proximal personal goals developed higher self-efficacy, intrinsic interest, and competency than students who pursued only distal goals or no goals. Bandura shifted his program of research to shed light on the self-efficacy belief system: its origins, structures, and functions, diverse effects, and how this knowledge could be used for personal and social benefit. He viewed perceived efficacy as the foundation of human motivation and action.

This research on self-regulatory processes, such as goal setting and self-efficacy beliefs, led Bandura to integrate his earlier theorizing about modeling work with his later research on self-referent thought in a 1986 book, *Social Foundations of Thought and Action: A Social Cognitive Theory*. At the time, Bandura decided to re-label his theoretical approach as *social cognitive* because the breadth of his theorizing and research had expanded beyond just learning. The theory was increasing concerned with motivation and regulation of behavior. Moreover, the label had become increasingly misleading because it was applied to several theories founded on dissimilar tenets, such as Miller and Dollard's drive theory, Rotter's (1966) expectancy theory, and Gewirtz's (1971) operant theory. In this book, Bandura presented a social cognitive vision of the origins of human thought and action and the influential role of self-referential processes in motivation, affect, and action. He depicted people as self-organizing, proactive, self-reflective, and self-regulative rather than as merely reactive to social environmental or inner forces.

During the 1990s, Bandura undertook a series of studies of human development as highly socially interdependent and richly contextualized. "The capabilities of self-influence are developed, one is not born with them. They are developed by mastering experience, by modeling, and by what people persuade us we can or cannot do" (Stokes, 1986a, p. 3). Research with Barry Zimmerman and Manual Martinez-Pons revealed that students' beliefs about their efficacy to regulate their academic learning activities and writing were highly predictive of their academic goal setting and achievement (Zimmerman, Bandura, & Martinez-Pons, 1992; Zimmerman & Bandura, 1994). Shades of Mundare! The inclusion of perceived self-efficacy in path models increased prediction of students' academic achievement by more than 30% while controlling for their prior grades or performance on standardized achievement tests.

Bandura is not one to rest on his laurels. In 1994, he launched a large-scale longitudinal project in Italy in collaboration with Caprara, Barbarelli, and Pastorelli at the University of Rome. This multifaceted longitudinal project is examining the complex interplay of socioeconomic, familial, educational, peer, and self-influences in shaping the developmental trajectories of children. The findings of this program of research are documenting the pivotal role of efficacious agency in children's social, emotional, moral, educational, and occupational development.

Because of strong international interest in the construct of self-efficacy, Bandura was invited to organize a conference for researchers under the auspices of the Jacob Foundation on the role of youths' beliefs in their personal efficacy to manage the demands of rapidly changing societies. It was held in the beautiful Marbach Castle at the headwaters of the Rhine River in Germany in November of 1993. In this idyllic setting, the participants shared research findings, exchanged ideas, identified topics in need of further research during the day and wined and dined in the evening. In addition to sumptuous culinary offerings, Bandura's wisdom, wit, and humanity made the conference truly memorable. The papers presented at the conference were published by Cambridge Press in a 1995 book that Bandura edited entitled *Self-efficacy in Changing Societies*.

In 1997, Bandura published the volume entitled *Self-efficacy: The Exercise of Control*, which presented the theoretical foundations of the theory and the diverse applications of this knowledge to education, health, treatment of clinical problems (e.g., stress, depression, and substance abuse), athletic performance, organizational functioning, and collective efficacy of our social and political systems. In all of these diverse spheres of functioning, perceived self-efficacy predicts people's style of thinking, level of motivation, emotional well-being, and performance accomplishments.

BANDURA'S CONTRIBUTIONS TO HUMAN DEVELOPMENT AND EDUCATION

It should come as no surprise to readers to learn that the impact of Bandura's own program of research represents only a small part of his enormous influence in psychology and education. Apart from his own program of research, he had major impact through his modeling and writing on the work of his many colleagues, students, and followers. His immense social impact stems from the explanatory value of his theory and its ready social applicability. As a result, Bandura has achieved one of the highest citation indexes in the field of education as well as psychology (e.g., Gorden et al., 1984). The sections that follow illustrate sources of the ways in which his theorizing and research have added greatly to our understanding of educational processes and children's psychological development.

Understanding Children's Social Development

Before Bandura began his seminal research, educators' conceptions of students' aggression were dominated by the Freudian view that such behavior was the product of intrapsychic forces operating largely unconsciously. Students' aggression on the playground or in school was seen as a recurring expression of underlying impulses requiring release in minimally detrimental ways. Teachers and societal leaders who looked to psychologists for guidance in these matters received much misleading advice. In the early 1960s, the story lines in television programs and motion pictures became more violent. Network executives and movie producers defended this fare as socially beneficial by citing the Freudian theory of catharsis. Bandura's Bobo doll experiments disputed these claims, revealing instead the power of televised or filmed violence on children's aggressive proclivities. His pioneering studies led in considerable part to the U.S. Surgeon General's commissioning of a panel to evaluate the research in this area (Comstock & Rubinstein, 1972). The report acknowledged the adverse effects of televised violence and the conditions governing the magnitude of that impact.

The Bobo doll studies have achieved continuing fame because photographs of the modeling effects are included in introductory psychology books and virtually all undergraduates enroll in the introductory course. On one occasion, this high visibility begot Bandura an upgrade to a suite in a Washington, D.C. hotel when the clerk at the registration clerk discovered that the father of the Bobo doll studies was registering for the night. Clearly paternity has its benefits!

Bandura's modeling research also showed how social modeling could be used to diminish aggression, promote prosocial functioning, and foster adoption of moral standards of conduct. Bandura and his colleagues also showed how children could be taught through modeling prosocial forms of behavior, such as empathy, sharing, and altruism (Bandura & Rosenthal, 1966; Harris, 1968; Rosenhan & White, 1967; Zimmerman & Brody, 1975). In 1973, Bandura published *Aggression: A Social Learning Analysis* in which he compared social learning, instinct, and drive theories and discussed their implications for social policy and management of schools' social environments. Many current violence prevention programs in the schools are founded on social modeling and self-regulatory principles.

Much of theorizing on moral agency has focused on moral reasoning to the neglect of moral conduct. Bandura has suggested that students' moral conduct is rooted in their self-regulatory capability. That is, students monitor their conduct and the conditions under which it occurs, judge it in relation to their moral standards and perceived circumstances, and regulate their actions by the consequences they apply to themselves, and they do things that give them a sense of self-worth. They refrain from behaving in ways that violate their moral standards because such conduct brings self-condemnation. However, it is well known that otherwise considerate people can engage in cruel conduct in certain circumstances.

Bandura explains the breakdown in moral self-regulation in terms of people's selective disengagement of moral self-sanctions from harmful acts. He describes the fascinating account of Sgt. York, a deeply religious individual from Tennessee. He was a fervent conscientious objector to military service during World War I until a recruiter cited chapter and verse in the Bible to convince him it was his Christian duty to fight (Stokes, 1986b, p. 3). York went on to become the American sharpshooter who killed the greatest number of enemy soldiers in that war. Bandura has identified eight mechanisms of moral disengagement. They include moral justification, diffusion and displacement of responsibility, sanitizing language, advantageous comparison, minimizing, ignoring, or misconstruing consequences, and dehumanizing and attributing blame to the victim. Bandura warns, "You don't have to change a person's basic codes or transform their personality, all you have to do is to create conditions for disengagement of moral control" (Stokes, 1986b, p. 3).

Bandura proposed a dual regulatory model, which describes not only how people refrain from behaving inhumanely but also how they behave humanely at personal costs as they aid those who are in distress or make civic commitments to improve the lives of others. Individuals who invest their sense of self-worth in humane convictions and social obligations will contest social practices they regard as unjust or immoral even though their actions may incur heavy personal costs. Failure to do what is right according to their moral standards would incur self-devaluation. Many of these strong convictions emerge from direct or symbolic exposure to exemplary social models, such as Christ, Gandhi, and Martin Luther King. In addition to the powerful role of self-sanctions, people's self-efficacy beliefs about regulating their conduct play an important role in moral behavior. In studies conducted in Italy, Bandura, Barbaranelli, Caprara, and Pastorelli (1996b) found that low self-regulatory efficacy increased students' readiness to disengage their moral standards. In subsequent research (Bandura, Caprara, Barbaranelli, Pastorelli, and Regalia, 2001), students' perceived academic and self-regulatory efficacy concurrently and longitudinally deterred transgressions both directly and by fostering prosocial behavior and adherence to moral self-sanctions for harmful conduct. As expected, moral disengagement led to greater transgressions over time. Interestingly, prosocialness, such as cooperating, helping, sharing, and consoling, was highly predictive of not only social preferences by peers but also students' academic achievement (Caprara, Barbaranelli, Pastorelli, Bandura, & Zimbardo, 2000). Teachers and peers are attracted to prosocial children and provide them greater academic support and guidance. Prosocial students thus proactively create social environments that are conducive to their academic development.

Educators' views of children's prosocial and antisocial functioning have been heavily influenced by Bandura's research and writing. There is now widespread awareness that modeling experiences and self-efficacy and self-regulatory processes greatly influence children's coping with conflict, frustration, academic stressors, and failure.

Understanding Children's Cognitive Development

Educators' conceptions of children's cognitive and linguistic development during the 1960s and 1970s were greatly influenced by stage views. Piaget, Kohlberg, and Chomsky each made strong maturational assumptions about children's development and discouraged efforts to teach alleged stage-related competencies precociously, except perhaps during brief periods of stage transition. Some educators believed it unwise to teach abstract mathematical concepts to preschoolers because of their limited preoperational level of reasoning. Other educators believed that efforts to teach higher ethical reasoning to young children would be unsuccessful because of their stage-related egocentrism. Bandura and his colleagues challenged these stage views as insensitive to the role of social and cultural learning experiences in children's development and dwelling on constraints rather than potentials. "Most developmental models of human behavior presuppose a developmental predeterminism in which childhood experiences pretty much set the course of later development" (Stokes, 1986a, p. 2). "Stage theories have at best specified only vaguely the conditions that lead to changes in behavior from one level to another" (Bandura & Walters, 1963, p. 25). To address these issues, social learning researchers conducted numerous abstract modeling studies to demonstrate the acquisition of higher-order competencies (Zimmerman & Rosenthal, 1974). More specifically, they questioned claims that children (a) displayed homogeneous stage functioning across tasks and situational contexts and (b) could not be taught Piagetian concepts, grammatical rules, and Kohlbergian or Piagetian moral judgments precociously.

Mary Harris, Robert Liebert, Ted Rosenthal, James Sherman, Grover Whitehurst, and Barry Zimmerman among others, used abstract modeling to teach advanced stage functioning among children of a variety of ages (Rosenthal & Zimmerman, 1978). They showed that age-related shifts in children's functioning were influenced by changes in social learning experience, hierarchies of goals and knowledge, and motoric competence. They cautioned educators that shifts in children's functioning at the approximate ages of 2, 7, and 12 years, emphasized by stage theories, were better predicted by social learning experiences and accomplishments, such as the acquisition of speech and mobility, entrance into school, and experiences associated with the onset of puberty. Regarding later life-span development, Bandura (1982, 1998) emphasized the key role of life events in personal trajectories, like his own in education, marriage, and employment, rather than developmental stage indices. The paths that lives take are influenced by the interplay of diverse events in which individuals play an agentic role. In their highly regarded text, *Advanced Educational Psychology*, Pressley and McCormick (1995) document the role that Bandura and his colleagues played in the growing disenchantment with stage theories.

Understanding Observational Learning

Bandura and colleagues' research on observational learning provides considerable guidance for teaching by demonstration for both teacher training and student development. It should be noted that the root meaning of the word *teach* is "to show." Educators have acknowledged the importance of modeling to effective teaching from the time of the ancient Greeks (Rosenthal & Zimmerman, 1978). The Roman statesman and philosopher Cicero recommended placing students of oratory under the guidance of eloquent models. Despite its auspicious place in the pantheon of instructional methods throughout the ages, modeling received little scientific study before Bandura's theorizing and research on this pervasive mode of learning.

Among the different facets of observational learning, those dealing with abstract modeling are of special pedagogical relevance (Bandura, 1977). The research revealed first that, for abstraction to occur, students need multiple demonstrations of a conceptual rule across a variety of tasks and settings, such as different types of Piagetian conservation problems. The common instructional technique used by novice teachers is to model a single conceptual exemplar for students, but this procedure will not produce abstraction and transfer because irrelevant contextual features of the task are not varied systematically. Social learning researchers also showed that teachers' explanations linked to their demonstrations significantly enhance students' conceptual learning. Abstract modeling required functional adaptations for very young children. For example, preschool children experienced difficulty learning from extended modeling sequences because of limitations in attention and memory. But they were able to learn observationally from an alternating approach involving turn-taking on a series of tasks (Rosenthal & Zimmerman, 1972).

Bandura's research on participant modeling underscored the need for teachers to decompose complex or difficult tasks into component subfunctions. Task analysis and sequential demonstrations are especially important if the subfunctions are novel. In addition, coping models who gradually overcame difficulties through perseverant effort had greater impact than mastery models who performed flawlessly from the outset (Kitsantas, Zimmerman, & Cleary, 2000; Schunk & Hanson, 1985; Schunk, Hanson, & Cox, 1987). Coping modeling instills higher levels of self-efficacy and achievement through perceived similarity. Similarly, peer modeling by knowledgeable classmates builds higher efficacy and cognitive competencies than teachers' modeling the same activities (Schunk, 1987). How, when, and where to structure those peer interactions form an important part of social learning research on instructional modeling.

To translate knowledge of modeling into instructional practice, teachers need an informative theory. Bandura provided a theory specifying four subfunctions governing modeling: attention, symbol representation, production, and motivation. *Attentional processes* refer to students' attending to and extracting the key elements of modeled events. *Representational processes* are concerned with students' cognitive construction and rehearsal of modeled information of the symbolic codes. *Production processes* refer to students' representational guidance and corrective adjustment of enactments. *Motivational processes* refer to various types of incentives to act on what one has learned. In this conceptual formulation, defects in observational learning can be traced to breakdowns in one or more of these subfunctions. For example, a student may fail to learn a complex computer software program through modeling because of inattention to key features of the demonstration. Or the failure may be due to the observer's inability to analyze and encode the model's strategies. Or perhaps the failure resides in difficulty in converting the knowledge into proficient performance. Or finally, students may have insufficient motivation to put into practice what they have learned, such as fears of making a serious mistake. This type of particularized knowledge provides useful guides for instructional interventions (Bandura, 1986; Zimmerman, 1977).

Understanding Self-regulation

Historically, educators have attributed students' inability to self-regulate their learning to insufficient willpower in the face of more attractive activities. This led teachers to exhort their students to work harder and to resist the temptations of television, computer games, or phone conversations. These exhortations are not only ineffective, they can have a counterproductive self-fulfilling effect. Bandura (1986) has explained that students who rely on increased willpower to succeed often make self-debilitating attributions especially if they view "willpower" as a fixed trait they lack. Failure to learn leads students to make attributions to inherent personal deficiencies, which is demotivating and self-handicapping.

Willpower theories provide little guidance for teachers. Bandura notes, "Dualistic doctrines that regard mind and body as separate entities do not provide much enlightenment on the nature of the disembodied mental state or on how an immaterial mind and bodily events act on each other" (Bandura, 1986, p. 17). By contrast, Bandura's triadic model of causation posits a complex interplay between personal, behavioral, and environmental determinants (see Fig. 18.1). Through their thoughts and actions, people are able to exert self-regulatory control over their level of functioning and the events in their lives. "The degree of reciprocity in social transactions in part depends on the personal resources people have to draw upon and on the extent to which they exercise what is theirs to command. The more they bring their influence to bear on themselves and others, the greater the likelihood they will realize desired futures" (Stokes, 1986a, p. 2). Teachers can help students to monitor the impact of their activities and immediate environment on their cognitive and behavioral functioning and to enlist self-management strategies and self-incentives to increase their effectiveness.

Bandura (1986) has recommended teaching students how to self-regulate personal, behavioral, and environmental aspects of their lives through three essential self-management processes: self-observation, judgmental process, and self-reactive influence rooted in personal standards. *Self-observation* refers to monitoring various aspects of one's performance, such as self-recording of the quality of one's solutions to mathematical problems. *Judgmental process* refers to evaluating of one's performances against personal standards, referential performances, personal values, and performance determinants. *Self-reaction* refers to one's cognitive, affective, and tangible responses to those performance evaluations. The self-reactions may involve self-corrections and affective and motivational self-inducements. Deficits in self-regulation have been studied in terms of these three interdependent processes to determine whether their problems in managing students' learning activities stem from deficient monitoring, inadequate performance evaluations, or insufficient motivational self-incentives.

Bandura described the role of self-judgment standards in the following way. "It is through this internal source of guidance that people give direction to their lives and derive satisfaction from what they do" (Stokes, 1986a, p. 2). However, these personal standards have social origins according to Bandura, "The internal standards through which people influence their own motivation and actions are acquired through modeling and evaluative reactions by significant others" (Stokes, 1986a, p. 2).

Educational programs that address the three subfunctions of self-regulation have been highly effective in improving students' motivation, strategies, and academic achievement (Schunk & Zimmerman, 1994, 1998). Bandura comments on the diverse benefits of the capacity for self-directedness: "These [self-regulatory] types of personal resources expand freedom of action and enable people to serve as causal contributors to their own life course by selecting, influencing and constructing their own circumstances" (Stokes, 1986a, p. 2).

Understanding Self-efficacy Beliefs

From the outset of Bandura's career, he questioned reinforcement accounts of human motivation. He viewed reinforcement operations not as strengtheners of responses but as providing information for constructing behavior patterns and performance outcome expectations. "When [outcome] belief differs from actuality, which is not uncommon, behavior is weakly controlled by its actual consequences until repeated experience instills realistic expectations" (Bandura, 1977, p. 167). His research on the self-regulative role of beliefs of personal efficacy revealed that outcome expectancies alone are insufficient guides and motivators of behavior. People know that certain performances can produce desired outcomes, but they do not develop them because they doubt they have what it takes to succeed. Although self-efficacy and outcome expectations were both hypothesized to affect motivation, he assigned causal priority to efficacy beliefs: "The types of outcomes people anticipate depend largely on their judgments of how well they will be able to perform in given situations" (Bandura, 1986, p. 392). He argued that expectancy-value theories of motivation sacrifice explanatory and predictive power if they ignore efficacy beliefs.

The explanatory power of Bandura's self-efficacy construct is attributable in large part to its triadic behavioral and contextual qualities. Self-efficacy beliefs involve people's self-judgments of *performance capabilities* in particular domains of functioning rather than omnibus trait or a global self-concept. For example, students are asked to judge their capabilities for certain classes of mathematical operations not their concept of their academic self. Students' self-efficacy beliefs differ across domains of academic functioning, such as linguistic, mathematical, and scientific subjects. The contextual linkage of self-efficacy measures differs markedly from omnibus trait measures that dominated research on self-beliefs in the 1970s.

The predictive power of self-efficacy beliefs on students' academic functioning has been extensively verified (Pajares & Miller, 1994; Schunk, 1984; 1998; Zimmerman, 1995, 2000). A meta-analysis of the self-efficacy literature regarding academic achievement (Multon, Brown, & Lent, 1991) revealed an effect size of .58 for students' academic performance across a variety of student samples, experimental designs, and criterion measures. This effect size is considered as large according to indices of statistical power. In research by Kwon, Park, and Kim (2001), perceived self-efficacy contributes similarly to children's emotional well-being and academic achievement in the Korean collectivistic culture. Other meta-analyses corroborate the predictiveness of perceived self-efficacy in organizational functioning, health, and athletic performance (Holden, 1991, Holden, Moncher, Schinke, & Barker, 1990; Stajkovic & Luthans, 1998).

Bandura has analyzed how children's perceived efficacy, teachers' beliefs in their instructional efficacy, and schools' collective sense of efficacy contribute to academic achievement. Many educators have been particularly intrigued with research demonstrating the importance of teachers' self-efficacy beliefs. For example, Bandura has noted that teachers with high instructional efficacy devote more classroom time to academic activities, provide students experiencing difficulties with more guidance, and praise their students' accomplishments more frequently than teachers with low efficacy (Gibson & Dembo, 1984). Bandura (1997) put it as follows, "Teachers who believe strongly in their ability to promote learning create mastery experiences for their students, but those beset by self-doubts about their instructional efficacy construct classroom environments that are likely to undermine students' judgments of their abilities and their cognitive development" (p. 241). Teachers' perceived efficacy also affects their own vulnerability to stress, burnout, and commitment to the educational profession.

Bandura has extended the conception of human agency to proxy and collective agency. In many activities, people do not have direct control over social conditions and institutional practices that affect their lives. They seek to advance their well-being and security through proxy agency. In this socially mediated form of perceived efficacy, people try to get others with resources and expertise to wield influence on their behalf to obtain desired personal outcomes. Relatively little research has been devoted to proxy agency to date, but the study of collective agency has yielded important results. In collective efficacy, the focus is on the perceived capabilities of social subsystems such as families, communities, educational systems, business organizations, and social and political institutions. Being socially situated and interdependent, people form shared beliefs about their combined capabilities and aspirations. Bandura (1997) defined the concept of collective self-efficacy as "a group's shared belief in its conjoint capabilities to organize and execute the courses of action required to produce given levels of attainments" (p. 477). In the case of schools, Bandura (1997) has suggested, "The belief systems of the staff also create an organizational culture that can have vitalizing or demoralizing effects on the perceived efficacy of its members" (p. 248). School staffs with a high collective sense of efficacy have principals who "excel in their ability to get their staff to work together with a strong sense of purpose and belief in their abilities to surmount obstacles to educational attainments" (p. 248).

Bandura (1993) found that the collective efficacy of school staff play a key causal role in path analyses predicting school achievement in reading and mathematics. Characteristics of the student body, such as their socioeconomic and ethnic backgrounds, had a small direct role on school level achievement but a large indirect effect mediated through teachers' collective efficacy to motivate and educate their students.

Self-efficacy measures have been used successfully in educational settings to understand the motivational engagement and academic accomplishment of students and teachers (Bandura, 1997; Pajares, 1996; Schunk, 1984; Zimmerman, 2000). Advances in electronic technologies and growing globalization of human connectedness offer new opportunities for people to exercise some measure of control over their personal development and their national life. Web-based connectedness enables worldwide opportunities for distance learning, social "chat rooms," online library information, and business transactions. These rapidly evolving realities greatly expand human perceptions of collective efficacy.

Thus, the management of daily life requires a blend of individual, proxy, and collective agency. These diverse sources of personal agency to manage one's life circumstances also play a key role in effecting societal changes (Fernandez-Ballesteros, Diez-Nicolos, Caprara, Barbaranelli, & Bandura, 2002), such as improving the quality of schools.

EVALUATIONS OF BANDURA'S CONTRIBUTION TO THE FIELD OF EDUCATION

Bandura has created one of the few grand theories that continues to thrive at the beginning of the 21st century. He has defied the general trend in psychology and education toward mini-models by focusing on processes that are influential in diverse areas of human functioning, be they education, sports, health, organizational settings, medicine, mental health, and social political spheres. The broad scope of Bandura's theory stems from his diverse scientific interests and his theory's ready applicability. Social modeling, self-enabling beliefs, and self-regulation are pervasive across contexts and domains of human functioning.

The Nature of the Learner

Throughout his brilliant career, Bandura took issue with many prominent psychological perspectives, such as Freudian, Hullian, Operant, Trait-factor, developmental stage, and classic cognitive theories that focused on intrapsychic conflicts, uncontrollable drives, unfavorable environments, immutable personal dispositions, or reified cognitive stages or structures. In Bandura's (1997) view, these theories underestimate the power of people to contribute to paths their lives take: People are producers as well as products of environments. In his address as honorary president of the Canadian Psychological Association, he takes the psychological discipline to task for emphasizing theories of failure that grossly overpredict psychopathology. He documents how people can override adversity through the exercise of self-influences and social supports. Bandura's reciprocal view of functioning is not only more optimistic than other views about the possibility of personal and social change, it is broader in scope because it includes both proactive and reactive processes. Through proactive forethought, learners are able to increase their self-regulatory control over events that affect the course of their lives.

Bandura acknowledges the important role of biological forces in human development and functioning but rejects biological reductionism. In his view, biological endowment is a potential that allows diverse expression rather than a tight determinant of people's lives. His research elucidates the power of social experience and coping self-beliefs over basic biological systems. For example, he cites evidence that guided mastery through participant modeling raises perceived efficacy in phobics, which in turn predicts reductions in stress-related hormones (Bandura, Taylor, Williams, Mefford, & Barchas, 1985). Bandura (1997) reported that, "Perceived coping inefficacy is accompanied by elevated biological stress reactions, but the same threats are managed without stress when beliefs of coping efficacy are strengthened" (p. 266). Such findings give testimony to biological as well as psychological plasticity. Like personal environments, human biological forces are potentialities that must be activated by specific personal beliefs and actions (Bandura, 1999). By regulating their motivation and activities, students produce experiences that form the neurobiological substrate of functioning. These agentic actions shape brain development and foster brain cell growth underlying learning, memory, and other aspects of functioning throughout the course of life (Diamond, 1988; Kolb & Whishaw, 1998).

The Nature of the Learning Processes

From the outset of his career, Bandura has envisioned human learning as a socially embedded event in which children learn about the world around them through social transactions and media sources. Much of this social learning is not under the direct control of teachers or parents, but rather, arises from contact with siblings, peers, coworkers, and mass media sources. Bandura felt these vicarious sources of experience had many benefits compared to discovery learning, such as the avoidance of adverse consequences. Bandura has humorously warned learners who try to learn dangerous skills, such as driving or skiing, solely by trial and error to check their health insurance coverage first! His view of social learning was broader and more cognitive than the formulations of modeling and imitation that preceded him.

Bandura's conception of learning entails more than the acquisition of knowledge in a cognitively reactive way. It involves the development of self-beliefs and self-regulatory capabilities of students to educate themselves throughout their lifetime. Self-regulatory skills for acquiring knowledge is gaining primacy because of the rapid pace of technological change and accelerated growth of knowledge. However, these skills are of little avail if people cannot get themselves to apply them persistently in the face of difficulties, stressors, and competing attractions. Students' self-efficacy beliefs not only enhance academic achievement, they promote intrinsic interest and reduce academic anxiety. Contrary to common belief, academic anxiety is an effect of perceived efficacy, not a determinant of academic performance. Perceived efficacy shapes not only students' cognitive development but their subsequent career development (Hackett, 1995), which pretty much shapes life trajectories.

Thus, self-regulatory mechanisms are embedded in an agentic perspective regarding self-development, adaptation, and change. Bandura (1999) emphasizes the central role of consciousness in people's phenomenal and functional life. It provides the agentic base for making sound judgments about one's capabilities, anticipating the probable effects of different events and actions, ascertaining sociostructural opportunities and constraints, and regulating behavior. Agentic consciousness goes beyond mere knowledge of one's functioning to actually changing it. One's sense of identity is also rooted in one's phenomenal and functional consciousness. The identity people create for themselves derives, in large part, from how they live and reflect on their lives. For example, there is evidence (Steinberg, Brown, & Dornbusch, 1996) that students' identities as "nerds," "druggies," or "jocks" can profoundly influence their academic aspirations and accomplishments.

Optimal Conditions of Instruction

To facilitate students' learning, Bandura (1986) recommended a guided mastery approach. For each instructional step:

> A variety of opportunities are provided for guided practice in when and how to use cognitive strategies in the solution of diverse problems. The level of social guidance is progressively reduced as competencies are being acquired. Activities, incentives, and personal challenges are structured in ways that ensure self-involving motivation and continual improvement. Growing proficiencies are credited to expanding personal capabilities. Self-directed mastery experiences are then arranged to strengthen and generalize a sense of personal efficacy. Each of these modes of influence is structured in ways that build self-regulative capabilities for exploratory learning and strengthen students' beliefs that they can exercise some control over their intellectual self-development (pp. 226–227).

Drawing on knowledge from Patrick Suppes' research on computer-assisted instruction at Stanford University, Bandura and Schunk devised self-directed learning programs with proximal challenges for children who were markedly deficient in mathematical skills. These mastery experiences convert mathematical disinterest and deficiency into a high sense of mathematical efficacy and competence.

Instructional programs that have incorporated these principles have significantly enhanced students' self-efficacy beliefs and academic achievement on diverse educational tasks, such as mathematics, reading, and writing (Bandura, 1997). In an extensive series of studies using self-guided instruction, often with students having learning disabilities, Schunk (1989) found that students' self-efficacy beliefs, both during instructional sessions and after completion of instruction, are good predictors of subsequent academic attainments. Regression analyses reveal that efficacy beliefs make unique contributions to academic attainments over and above prior performance attainments.

The Nature of Important Learning–Instructional Outcomes

In order to capture the triadic interdependence of person-related processes during efforts to learn, Bandura (1986) has advocated microanalytic assessments of self-regulatory processes, such as self-efficacy beliefs, goal and aspirations, and self-incentives. He underscored the importance of his methodology, "Understanding how personal factors affect actions and situations is best advanced through the microanalysis of interactive processes. This requires measures of personal determinants that are specially tailored to the domain of functioning being analyzed" (p. 28). Bandura cautions that to be effective, microanalyses must capture transactions among all three triadic determinants (see Fig. 18.1)—especially, how sociostructural influences operate through psychological mechanisms to produce behavioral effects. Although many constructivist accounts envision intellectual development as situated in culturally proscribed contexts, they fail to specify the mechanisms through which sociocultural influences produce their effects, such as when a teacher's modeling influences students' self-efficacy beliefs. Because people are producers as well as products of social systems, researchers' need a methodology that can capture the dynamic interplay between individuals and the social systems they and others create.

Bandura's approach shifts the conception and assessment of personal determinants from traditional trait psychological measures to contextualized domain-related measures. "The study of trait measures derived from omnibus tests is a method of convenience which unfortunately sacrifices explanatory and predictive power" (Bandura, 1986, p. 28). Trait formulations, including "Big-Five" super traits (i.e., extroversion, agreeableness, conscientiousness, neuroticism, and openness to experience), are not equipped to predict variations in behavior in particular domains of functioning under variable situational circumstances. Attempts to enhance prediction by aggregating trait measures have met little success when focusing on actual behavior in different situations rather than self-reports of behavior. Traits are essentially clusters of habitual behaviors, not the structure of personality. Bandura's conception of the structure and mechanisms of personality resides in the self-system. This system includes (among other things) people's knowledge structures, their skills, self-efficacy beliefs, and self-regulatory capabilities, which operate through goals and outcome expectancies rooted in a value structure. An extensive body of research corroborates that measures of dynamic determinants, such as goal setting and self-efficacy beliefs, are not only good predictors of academic performance outcomes but provide informative guidelines for cultivating academic competencies (Bandura, 1997).

The availability of task-specific measures has enabled teachers to expand their instructional goals to include students' self-regulatory development. "Teachers face the challenge of adapting their instruction to students' differing levels of educational self-directedness in ways that build underdeveloped self-regulatory skills" (Bandura, 1997, p. 227). A focus on self-regulative instruction means that teachers need look beyond mere knowledge. "Students often know what to do but cannot translate that knowledge into proficient performance. Even if they can make skilled translations of knowledge, they often fare poorly when left on their own because they cannot get themselves to put in the necessary effort to fulfill difficult task demands" (Bandura, 1997, p. 227). Teachers who consider their students' self-efficacy beliefs, goal setting, strategy use, and other forms of self-regulation in their instructional plans not only enhance students' academic knowledge, but they also increase their students' capability for self-directed learning throughout their life span.

BANDURA'S LEGACY

Because of the scope and power of his research and theory, Bandura is one the most widely cited contemporary theorists in the fields of psychology and education. His list of prestigious awards has few peers. His vita includes nine authored or edited books and 230 articles and chapters, many of which have been reprinted in other anthologies in diverse specialties of psychology and other disciplines. He was elected president of the American Psychological Association (APA), president of the Western Psychological Association, and appointed honorary president of the Canadian Psychological Association. He has received numerous awards including the (APA) Distinguished Scientific Contributions Award, and the American Psychological Society's William James Award. He was given the Distinguished Contribution Award by the International Society for Research in Aggression, the Distinguished Scientist Award of the Society of Behavioral Medicine, and a Guggenheim Fellowship. He has been elected to the American Academy of the Arts and Sciences and to the Institute of Medicine of the National Academy of Sciences. He is the recipient of many honorary degrees from American and foreign universities.

Al Bandura has had a long and distinguished academic career (see a summary of milestones in Table 18.1). For his contributions to the field of educational

TABLE 18.1

Time Line of Bandura's Life

Year	Milestone
1925	Born in Mundare, Alberta, Canada
1946	Graduated from high school
1949	Completed B.A., University of British Columbia
1951	Completed M.A., University of Iowa
1952	Completed Ph.D., University of Iowa, Clinical Psychology
1953	Instructor, Stanford University
1959	Published *Adolescent Aggression*
1963	Published *Social Learning and Personality Development*
1964	Professor, Stanford University
1964	Fellow, American Psychological Association
1969	Published *Principles of Behavior Modification*
1969	Special Research Fellowship, National Institute of Mental Health
1969	Fellow, Center for Advanced Study in the Behavioral Sciences
1971	Published *Psychological Modeling: Conflicting Theories*
1972	Distinguished Scientist Award, Division 12, American Psychological Association
1972	Guggenheim Fellowship
1973	Published *Aggression: A Social Learning Analysis*
1973	American Men and Women of Science
1973	Distinguished Scientific Achievement Award, California Psychological Association
1974	President, American Psychological Association
1974	David Starr Jordan Professor of Social Science in Psychology, Stanford University
1976	Chair, Dept of Psychology, Stanford University
1977	Published *Social Learning Theory*
1978	Who's Who in America
1979	Honorary Doctor of Science, University of British Columbia
1980	President, Western Psychological Association
1980	Fellow, American Academy of Arts and Sciences
1980	Distinguished Contribution Award, International Society for Research on Aggression
1980	Distinguished Scientific Contributions Award, American Psychological Association
1982	Fellowship, Japan Society for the Promotion of Science
1983	Honorary Degree, University of Lethbridge
1985	Honorary Degree, University of New Brunswick
1986	Published *Social Foundations of Thought and Action: A Social Cognitive Theory*
1987	Honorary Degree, State University of New York, Stony Brook
1988	Sir Walter Scott Distinguished Visiting Professor, University of New South Wales, Australia
1989	William James Award, American Psychological Society
1989	Institute of Medicine of the National Academy of Sciences
1990	Honorary Degree, University of Waterloo
1990	Honorary Degree, Freie Universitat Berlin
1992	Honorary Degree, University of Salamanca
1993	Honorary Doctor of Humane Letters, Indiana University
1994	Honorary Degree, University of Rome
1995	Published *Self-Efficacy in Changing Societies*
1995	Honorary Degree, University of Leiden
1995	Honorary Degree, Alfred University
1997	Published *Self-Efficacy: The Exercise of Control*
1998	Distinguished Lifetime Contributions Award, California Psychological Association
1999	Honorary Degree, Pennsylvania State University
1999	E. L. Thorndike Award, American Psychological Association
2000	Honorary President, Canadian Psychological Association
2002	Honorary Degree, City University of New York

psychology, he was awarded the E. L. Thorndike Award in 1998. Despite his many accolades, he remains the consummate model of a teacher, researcher, and mentor. As he approaches his 50th year of tenure at Stanford, he remains genuinely dedicated to teaching and to providing the students under his guidance with the inquiring perspective and personal resources to make the most of their talents during their lifetime. He expects the same high quality scholarship from others that he demands of himself and provides them with the means to realize those standards. When not engaged in scholarly pursuits, he can be found dining at fine restaurants, hiking mountainous trails, enjoying symphonic and operatic musical events, sampling the noble grape, or traveling. He is cherished by his friends, colleagues, and students as one who lives his life according to the same agentic principles that he has studied throughout his extraordinary career.

REFERENCES

Arem, C. A., & Zimmerman, B. J. (1976). Vicarious effects on the creative behavior of retarded and non-retarded children. *American Journal of Mental Deficiency, 81*, 289–296.

Bandura, A. (1969). *Principles of behavior modification*. New York: Holt, Rinehart, & Winston.

Bandura, A. (Ed.). (1971). *Psychological modeling: Conflicting theories*. Chicago: Aldine/Atherton.

Bandura, A. (1973). *Aggression: A social learning analysis*. Englewood Cliffs, NJ: Prentice-Hall.

Bandura, A. (1977). *Social learning theory*. Englewood Cliffs, NJ: Prentice-Hall.

Bandura, A. (1982). The psychology of chance encounters and life paths. *American Psychologist, 37*, 747–755.

Bandura, A. (1986). *Social foundations of thought and action: A social cognitive theory*. Englewood Cliffs, NJ: Prentice-Hall.

Bandura, A. (1993). Perceived self-efficacy in cognitive development and functioning. *Educational Psychologist, 28*, 117–148.

Bandura, A. (1995). The exercise of personal and collective efficacy in changing societies. In A. Bandura (Ed.), *Self-efficacy in changing societies* (pp. 1–45). New York: Cambridge University Press.

Bandura, A. (1997). *Self-efficacy: The exercise of control*. New York: W. H. Freeman.

Bandura, A. (1998). Exploration of fortuitous determinents of life paths. *Psychological Inquiry, 9*, 95–115.

Bandura, A. (1999). Social cognitive theory of personality. In L. Pervin & O. John (Eds.), *Handbook of personality* (2nd ed., pp. 154–196). New York: Guilford.

Bandura, A., Barbaranelli, C., Caprara, G. V., & Pastorelli, C. (1996a). Multifaceted impact of self-efficacy beliefs on academic functioning. *Child Development, 67*, 1206–1222.

Bandura, A., Barbaranelli, C., Caprara, G. V., & Pastorelli, C. (1996b). Mechanisms of moral disengagement in the exercise of moral agency. *Journal of Personality and Social Psychology, 71*, 364–374.

Bandura, A., Blanchard, E. B., & Ritter, B. (1969). Relative efficacy of desensitization and modeling approaches for inducing behavioral, affective, and attitudinal changes. *Journal of Personality and Social Psychology, 13*, 173–199.

Bandura, A., Caprara, G. V., Barbaranelli, C., Pastorelli, C., & Regalia, C. (2001). Sociocognitive self-regulatory mechanisms governing transgressive behavior. *Journal of Personality and Social Psychology, 80*, 125–135.

Bandura, A., & Harris, M. B. (1966). Modification of syntactic style. *Journal of Experimental Child Psychology, 4*, 341–352.

Bandura, A., & Jeffery, R. W. (1973). Role of symbolic coding and rehearsal processes in observational learning. *Journal of Personality and Social Psychology, 26*, 122–130.

Bandura, A., Jeffery, R. W., & Wright, C. L. (1974). Efficacy of participant modeling as a function of response induction aids. *Journal of Abnormal Psychology, 83*, 56–64.

Bandura, A., & Kupers, C. J. (1964). Transmission of patterns of self-reinforcement through modeling. *Journal of Abnormal and Social Psychology, 69*, 1–9.

Bandura, A., & McDonald, F. J. (1963). The influence of social reinforcement and the behavior of models in shaping children's moral judgments. *Journal of Abnormal and Social Psychology, 67*, 274–281.

Bandura, A., & Mischel, W. (1965). The influence of models in modifying delay of gratification patterns. *Journal of Personality and Social Psychology, 2*, 698–705.

Bandura, A., & Perloff, B. (1967). Relative efficacy of self-monitored and externally imposed reinforcement systems. *Journal of Personality and Social Psychology, 7*, 111–116.

Bandura, A., & Rosenthal, T. L. (1966). Vicarious classical conditioning as a functioning of arousal level. *Journal of Personality and Social Psychology, 3*, 54–62.

Bandura, A., Ross, D., & Ross, S. A. (1961). Transmission of aggression through imitation of aggressive models. *Journal of Abnormal and Social Psychology, 63*, 575–582.

Bandura, A., Ross, D., & Ross, S. A. (1963). Imitation of film-mediated aggressive models. *Journal of Abnormal and Social Psychology, 66*, 3–11.

Bandura, A., & Schunk, D. (1981). Cultivating competence, self-efficacy, and intrinsic interest through proximal self-motivation. *Journal of Personality and Social Psychology, 41*, 587–598.

Bandura, A., Taylor, C. B., Williams, S. L., Mefford, I. N., & Barchas, J. D. (1985). Catecholamine secretion as a function of perceived coping self-efficacy. *Journal of Consulting and Clinical Psychology, 53*, 406–414.

Bandura, A., & Walters, R. H. (1959). *Adolescent aggression*. New York: Ronald Press.

Bandura, A., & Walters, R. H. (1963). *Social learning and personality development*. New York: Holt, Rinehart, & Winston.

Caprara, G. V., Barbaranelli, C., Pastorelli, C., Bandura, A., & Zimbardo, P. (2000). Prosocial foundations of children's academic achievement. *Psychological Science, 11*, 302–306.

Comstock, G. A., & Rubinstein, E. A. (Eds.). (1972). *Television and social behavior: Television and adolescent aggressiveness* (Vol. 3). Washington, DC: Government Printing Office.

Debowski, S., Wood, R., & Bandura, A. (2001). Impact of guided exploration and enactive exploration of self-regulatory mechanisms, and information acquisition through electronic inquiry. *Journal of Applied Psychology, 86*, 1129–1141.

Diamond, M. C. (1988). *Enriching heredity*. New York: The Free Press.

Fernandez-Ballesteros, R., Diez-Nicolos, J., Caprara, G. V., Barbaranelli, C., & Bandura, A. (2002). Determinants and structural relation of personal efficacy to collective efficacy. *Applied Psychology: An International Journal, 51*, 107–125.

Gewirtz, J. L. (1971). Conditional responding as a paradigm for observational, imitative learning, and vicarious-reinforcement. In H. W. Reese (Ed.), *Advances in child development and behavior* (Vol. 6, pp. 273–304). New York: Academic Press.

Gibson, S., & Dembo, M. H. (1984). Teacher efficacy: A construct validation. *Journal of Educational Psychology, 76*, 569–582.

Gorden, N. J., Nucci, L. P., West, C. K., Herr, W. A., Uguroglo, M. E., Vukosavich, P., & Tsar, S. (1984). Productivity and citations of educational research: Using educational psychology as the data base. *Educational Researcher, 13*, 14–20.

Hackett, G. (1995). Self-efficacy in career choice and development. In A. Bandura (Ed.), *Self-efficacy in changing societies* (pp. 232–258). New York: Cambridge University Press.

Harris, M. B. (1968). *Some determinants of sharing in children.* Unpublished doctoral dissertation, Stanford University, CA.

Harris, M. B., & Evans, R. C. (1973). Models and creativity. *Psychological Reports, 33,* 763–769.

Harris, M. B., & Fisher, J. L. (1973). Modeling and flexibility in problem solving. *Psychological Reports, 33,* 19–23.

Hilgard, E. (1989). *Presidents' oral history project interview of Albert Bandura, Ph.D. President 1974.* Unpublished manuscript, American Psychological Association.

Holden, G. (1991). The relationship of self-efficacy appraisals to subsequent health related outcomes: A meta-analysis. *Social Work in Health Care, 16,* 53–93.

Holden, G., Moncher, M. S., Schinke, S. P., & Barker, K. M. (1990). Self-efficacy of children and adolescents: A meta-analysis. *Psychological Reports, 66,* 1044–1046.

Kitsantas, A., Zimmerman, B. J., & Cleary, T. (2000). The role of observation and emulation in the development of athletic self-regulation. *Journal of Educational Psychology, 91,* 241–250.

Kolb, B., & Whishaw, I. Q. (1998). Brain plasticity and behavior. *Annual Review of Psychology, 49,* 43–64.

Kwon, U. E., Park, Y. S., & Kim, U. (2001). *Factors influencing academic achievement and life-satisfaction among Korean adolescents: With specific focus on self-efficacy and social support.* Manuscript submitted for publication.

Miller, N., & Dollard, J. (1941). *Social learning and imitation.* New Haven, CT: Yale University Press.

Mischel, W. (1968). *Personality and assessment.* New York: Wiley.

Multon, K. D., Brown, S. D., & Lent, R. W. (1991). Relation of self-efficacy beliefs to academic outcomes: A meta-analytic investigation. *Journal of Counseling Psychology, 18,* 30–38.

Pajares, F. (1996). Self-efficacy beliefs in academic settings. *Review of Educational Research, 66,* 543–578.

Pajares, F., & Miller, M. D. (1994). Role of self-efficacy and self-concept beliefs in mathematical problem solving: A path analysis. *Journal of Educational Psychology, 86,* 193–203.

Pressley, M., & McCormick, C. B. (1995). *Advanced educational psychology: For educators, researchers, and policymakers.* New York: HarperCollins.

Rosenhan, D., & White, G. M. (1967). *Journal of Personality and Social Psychology, 5,* 424–431.

Rosenthal, T. L., & Zimmerman, B. J. (1972). Modeling by exemplification and instruction in training conservation. *Developmental Psychology, 6,* 392–401.

Rosenthal, T. L., & Zimmerman, B. J. (1978). *Social learning and cognition.* New York: Academic Press.

Rosenthal, T. L., Zimmerman, B. J., & Durning, K. (1970). Observationally-induced changes in children's interrogative classes. *Journal of Personality and Social Psychology, 16,* 631–688.

Rotter, J. (1966). Generalized expectancies for internal versus external control of reinforcement. *Psychological Monographs, 80*(1, Whole No. 609).

Sampson, E. E. (1981). Cognitive psychology and ideology. *American Psychologist, 36,* 730–743.

Schunk, D. H. (1984). The self-efficacy perspective on achievement behavior. *Educational Psychologist, 19,* 199–218.

Schunk, D. H. (1987). Peer models and children's behavior change. *Review of Educational Research, 57,* 149–174.

Schunk, D. H. (1989). Social cognitive theory and self-regulated learning. In B. J. Zimmerman & D. H. Schunk (Eds.), *Self-regulated learning and academic achievement: Theory, research, and practice* (pp. 83–110). New York: Springer Verlag.

Schunk, D. H. (1998). Teaching elementary students to self-regulate practice of mathematical skills with modeling. In D. H. Schunk & B. J. Zimmerman (Eds.), *Self-regulated learning: From teaching to self-reflective practice* (pp. 137–159). New York: Guilford.

Schunk, D. H., & Hanson, A. R., (1985). Peer models: Influence on children's self-efficacy and achievement. *Journal of Educational Psychology, 77,* 313–322.

Schunk, D. H., Hanson, A. R., & Cox, P. D. (1987). Peer model attributes and children's achievement behaviors. *Journal of Educational Psychology, 79*, 54–61.

Schunk, D. H., & Zimmerman, B. J. (Eds.). (1994). *Self-regulation of learning and performance: Issues and educational applications*. Hillsdale, NJ: Lawrence Erlbaum Associates.

Schunk, D. H., & Zimmerman, B. J. (Eds.). (1998). *Self-regulated learning: From teaching to self-reflective practice*. New York: Guilford.

Stajkovic, A. D., & Luthans, F. (1998). Self-efficacy and work-related performance: A meta-analysis. *Psychological Bulletin, 124*, 240–261.

Steinberg, L., Brown, B. B., & Dornbusch, S. M. (1996). *Beyond the classroom*. New York: Simon & Schuster.

Stokes, D. (1986a, June 10). Chance can play key role in life psychologist says. *Campus Report*, 1–4.

Stokes, D. (1986b, June 11). It's no time to shun psychologists, Bandura says. *Campus Report*, 1–3.

Zimmerman, B. J. (1977). Modeling. In H. Hom & P. Robinson (Eds.), *Psychological processes in early education* (pp. 37–70). New York: Academic Press.

Zimmerman, B. J. (1995). Self-efficacy and educational development. In A. Bandura (Ed.), *Self-efficacy in changing societies* (pp. 202–231). New York: Cambridge University Press.

Zimmerman, B. J. (2000). Self-efficacy: An essential motive to learn. *Contemporary Educational Psychology, 25*, 82–91.

Zimmerman, B. J., & Bandura, A. (1994). Impact of self-regulatory influences on writing course attainment. *American Educational Research Journal, 31*, 845–862.

Zimmerman, B. J., Bandura, A., & Martinez-Pons, M. (1992). Self-motivation for academic attainment: The role of self-efficacy beliefs and personal goal setting. *American Educational Research Journal, 29*, 663–676.

Zimmerman, B. J., & Brody, G. H. (1975). Race and modeling influences on the interpersonal play patterns of boys. *Journal of Educational Psychology, 67*, 474–489.

Zimmerman, B. J., & Dialessi, F. (1973). Modeling influences on children's creative behavior. *Journal of Educational Psychology, 65*, 127–134.

Zimmerman, B. J., & Rosenthal, T. L. (1974). Observational learning of rule governed behavior by children. *Psychological Bulletin, 81*, 29–42.

19

Ann L. Brown: Advancing a Theoretical Model of Learning and Instruction

Annemarie Sullivan Palincsar
University of Michigan

Representing the work of a scholar as accomplished and prolific as Ann L. Brown would be a challenge under any condition. In this case, the task was all the more difficult because of Ann's untimely death on June 4, 1999, at the age of 56, while this chapter was being prepared. Being immersed in her work served as a constant reminder of this enormous loss to me personally and to the fields of psychology and education. Ann's contributions to educational and psychological research and scholarship were extraordinary, whether measured by their number, their generativity, or their impact. Perhaps more than most scholars, Ann's work can be characterized as a journey—a journey toward a theoretical model of learning and instruction—a journey in which she integrated and applied her vast knowledge of teaching, learning, curriculum, assessment, and the social contexts of classrooms and schools—a journey always focused on the goal of expanding learners' capabilities. In this chapter we will consider the various legs of Ann's journey, examining, in particular, the role that the analysis of learning played in her work.

Ann's life journey began January 26, 1943, in Portsmouth, England. She was the middle child and only daughter of Kathryn and John Lesley Taylor. Her own history as a learner is noteworthy as she failed the 11+ examination, experienced considerable difficulty learning to read, and did not attain fluency until the age of 13, an accomplishment that she attributed to a teacher who recognized Ann's potential and worked to unleash it. During her undergraduate education, she studied history, literature, and philosophy. Following the completion of her degree, Ann considered continuing her studies in history; however, intrigued by a television program on how animals learn in their natural habitats, Ann made an appointment with the chair of psychology at the University of London. The chair shared Ann's interest in 18th century literature, and they spent their 2 hours together discussing poetry; after which, Ann left with a scholarship to study psychology. She earned her degree in a psychology program steeped in behaviorist learning theory and completed her degree in 1967 with a dissertation study entitled, "Anxiety and Complex Learning Performance in Children."

Attracted by research in developmental psychology that was taking place in the United States, Ann took a leave from her first academic position at the University of Sussex and accepted a position as a visiting assistant professor in the Department of Psychology and an appointment as a research scientist at the Children's Research Center at the University of Illinois at Champaign-Urbana. In a rare turn in academia, but in a move that signaled Ann's talent, she was awarded tenure at the University of Sussex while in absentia!

Soon after arriving in the United States, while attending a meeting of the Society for Research on Child Development in 1969, Ann met Joseph C. Campione, who became her closest friend and collaborator, as well as her husband. After a brief time at the University of Illinois, Ann received a postdoctoral fellowship to work with Zeaman and House at the University of Connecticut. In 1971, she returned to the University of Illinois where she was active in the Department of Psychology, in the Children's Research Center, and eventually in the Center for the Study of Reading, which was awarded to the University of Illinois in 1975. In 1988 Ann and Joe left the University of Illinois for the University of California at Berkeley, where Ann held the Evelyn Lois Cory Chair in Cognition and Development. From 1996 to 1998, Ann and Joe assumed positions at the Harvard Graduate School of Education, returning to Berkeley in 1998. Ann had one son, Richard, who, with his wife Mary, provided Ann with one of the greatest joys of her life, her granddaughter, Sophie. We now turn to an examination of the program of research that Ann pursued in her prolific career, beginning with the ground work on which her scholarship in metacognition was built.

THE ROLE OF STRATEGIC ACTIVITY
IN POOR PERFORMANCE

Ann's initial research focused on human memory—in particular on the role that active memory strategies played in enhancing human memory and on developmental differences in memory tasks. Ann's studies revealed that developmental differences were not found in memory tasks that did not require deliberate use of mnemonics or anything more than the rudimentary use of strategies (cf. DeLoache,

Cassidy, & Brown, 1985). However, when the task was such that mnemonics could be used effectively, younger students performed poorly because they failed to adopt the appropriate strategy (Brown, 1974, 1975).

The distinction between mediational deficiencies and production deficiencies, a distinction championed by Flavell (1970) among others, was of theoretical relevance to Ann's early research. A deficiency was claimed to exist when the child performed poorly on a memory task because he or she failed to exploit the appropriate mnemonic mediators. If the child could be trained to produce the required strategy, this enabled a finer grained analysis of the deficiency; that is, if despite having produced the strategy, performance was not significantly altered, the deficiency was said to be mediational (i.e., the child does not use the strategy to mediate performance). If, however, performance was in fact mediated appropriately once the strategy was produced, then the initial deficiency was identified as a production deficiency. Ann and her colleagues used the training study as a theoretical tool to discern the relative contributions of capacity and strategic activity in explaining children's performance on memory tasks. Their research suggested that elementary-age students could be trained to make effective use of mnemonics, supporting the production deficiency explanation; however, the children seldom generalized these skills to new situations.

Curious about why children might display these production deficiencies in the first place and seeking an explanation for the failure to generalize the trained skills in novel contexts, Ann joined, and indeed led, a growing community of developmental psychologists who were raising questions identified as "metacognitive" in nature, inquiring about the role that knowledge about and control of learning played in children's learning.

These studies revealed that young children and children identified as slow learning did not engage in the metacognitive activities of checking, planning, self-testing, and monitoring attempts to solve problems. Ann argued that these were the very control processes prerequisite to the transfer of learning.

Again, Ann and colleagues employed training studies targeting the instruction of general metacognitive skills that she hypothesized to be easier to teach and likely to lead to transfer across task boundaries. The task they selected was a stop–test–study routine, specifically self-assessment of one's readiness to recall a list. A typical study (Brown & Barclay, 1976) would entail pretesting students' (identified as mentally impaired) ability to memorize a set of items, in a particular order. The set was determined individually and was designed to exceed by one and a half times the maximum number of items recalled consistently on practice trials. Participants were instructed to continue studying the items until confident that they could recall them all perfectly. The poor initial performance of the children was hypothesized to be related to their failure to use self-testing as a means of monitoring their test preparation.

The children were then grouped and trained in the use of three strategies: anticipation, rehearsal, and labeling. In both the anticipation and rehearsal groups, the participants were trained to pass once through the list, exposing and labeling each item in turn. On the remaining three compulsory exposures to the list, the participants in the anticipation group were prompted to attempt to label each item before exposing it. In the rehearsal group, they were instructed to "say the names of the items over and over again until you know them." In the labeling condition, the participants were trained to expose the items in a list in serial order, labeling each one in turn and repeating each list four times. Whereas the first two strategies engaged the child in self-testing, the third did not and essentially served as a control condition. Both strategy training conditions were determined to enhance performance when compared with the comparison condition. Furthermore, maintenance—even 1 year later—was revealed by older students (mental age = 8).

In the research conducted by Brown, Campione, and Barclay (1979), the students who revealed maintenance of the self-testing strategy (reported previously) were engaged in a task in which they were presented short stories and, without any reminding regarding the self-testing strategy to which they had been introduced, were asked to read and reread these stories until they were able to remember everything that happened in the story. They were then asked to retell as much of the story as they remembered. This task was designed to be more representative of the kinds of study tasks required in classroom activity—extracting and recalling main ideas from simple narrative text. The trained students, who had shown evidence of maintenance, were joined by a set of untrained students who were matched for chronological age (CA), intelligence quotient (IQ), and mental age (MA). The outcomes of this investigation revealed that the students who had participated in the earlier strategy training study performed significantly better than the comparison students. This finding was identified as evidence that these students had, in fact, transferred the trained strategies across tasks.

The significance of this research is best appreciated by placing it in the larger context of psychological research of this time. With the cognitive revolution, learners came to be viewed as active constructors, rather than passive recipients of knowledge. Learners were imbued with introspection, and were acknowledged to have both knowledge and feelings about learning and the capacity to control it—metacognition. The merger of behavioral and cognitive perspectives on learning was leading to questions about the efficacy of engaging learners in verbalized self-instruction for the purpose of self-regulation. For the most part, cognitive-behavior modification had been studied in the context of nonacademic tasks such as impulse control (cf. Meichenbaum, 1977). The application of verbalized self-instruction to academic tasks introduced new questions regarding the nature of the routines useful to promoting self-regulation. Brown and her colleagues hypothesized that more general problem-solving routines (such as self-testing) had an advantage over specific mnemonic instruction, precisely because they would generalize across distinct tasks. This research is also significant because it marked a shift from the study of recall of relatively meaningless material to the recall of connected discourse. Finally, this research was a transition to the next corpus of Ann's research: research on text comprehension.

FOUNDATIONAL STUDIES IN TEXT COMPREHENSION

The questions motivating Ann's initial research on text comprehension prepared the foundation for identifying effective strategies for comprehending text and effective conditions for engaging learners in the use of comprehension strategies. Initial studies (e.g., Brown & Smiley, 1978) were designed to assess the influence of the structural importance of idea units on readers' recall of stories. The method employed in this series of studies called for dividing narratives into idea units, which were then rated to determine their structural importance. College students and school-age students (in Grades 3, 5, and 7) were asked to read and recall these stories. While older students recalled more idea units than younger ones, the general pattern of recall was consistent across the two levels with the less important units being recalled less frequently than all the other units and the most important units being recalled the most often. When evaluating the rating data, there was a strong developmental trend, with students becoming more sensitive to idea importance as a function of age; however, it is important to note that Ann and her colleagues cautioned against drawing conclusions about the role that development alone plays in this type of metacognitive task. "We do not believe that there is a magical age at which children become able to indicate important elements of a text. This is obviously dependent on the intimate relation of the child's current knowledge and the complexity of the stimulus materials" (Brown & Smiley, 1978, p. 1087). These types of observations placed Ann among the forerunners calling attention to the interrelationships among learners, stimuli (texts), and criterial tasks in predicting and understanding performance. Furthermore, Ann and her colleagues were also among the first cognitive researchers to note the potential value of cognitive research for enhancing educational achievement; specifically, it was research of this nature that ushered in the next decade of strategy instruction.

For example, a series of experiments reported in Brown and Smiley (1978) were designed to examine the role that intentional learning played in the effectiveness of studying activity. In one study, college students were randomly assigned to treatment groups, which varied in terms of what the participants knew about the criterial task. While one group was asked to read for the purpose of identifying the moral of the story, another was asked to read for the purpose of recalling as much as possible about the story, and a third group read unaware that they would be asked to recall the story. Based on the proportion of idea units recalled across these groups, Brown and Smiley determined that the students who were aware of the criterial task, successfully engaged in intentional learning, and realized the benefit of doing so in their performance. Interestingly, when this study was replicated with young students (fifth graders) as participants, the students who were in the intentional condition did not look any different from the children in the incidental condition. Further analyses of the data from the fifth graders indicated that those who did profit from being in the intentional condition, used their awareness of textual importance to support their learning. Research, to date, that had been designed to enhance performance by engaging the learner in some strategic activity was, at best, equivocal in its outcomes. Ann speculated that these ambivalent findings suggested that researchers needed to attend not only to the activity that the learner was engaged in, but also to the learner's knowledge of the subject matter targeted for learning, knowledge of the strategies themselves, and knowledge of the interrelationships among these.

With the design and conduct of text summarization studies that Ann undertook with Jeanne D. Day, we see the merger of developmental, metacognitive, and text comprehension research. For example, in the study reported by Brown, Day, and Jones (1983), they examined how students across grade levels would perform on a summarization task when they were first provided the opportunity to learn the story very well. They found that strategic planning (which accounted for the differential success of participants) emerged gradually as a function of age; this difference was largely mediated by the nature of the activity in which learners at various ages engaged. However, there was also a close interdependence between the deployment of strategies and knowledge of the relative importance of ideas in the text: "the complex coordination of all these factors enables the student to plan, monitor, and evaluate her interactions with texts in an economical and efficient manner" (Brown, Day, & Jones, 1978, p. 978).

Another noteworthy feature of Ann's research at this time was the study of expert–novice differences on particular tasks as a window on human cognitive functioning. Brown and Day (1983) derived the macrorules for text summarizing (deleting, generalizing, and integrating across the text) from the theoretical model proposed by Kintsch and van Dijk (1978), in addition to their own informal study of summaries generated by learners representative of different ages and achievement levels. Ericsson and Simon (1980) had made the case that verbal reports were invaluable to informing our understanding of cognitive processing, particularly those verbalizations that were gathered concurrently with engagement in the actual task. The study reported in Brown and Day (1983) illustrates how verbal protocols collected in the course of summarizing were used to examine the robustness of these macrorules. The experts (graduate students in rhetoric), encouraged to talk about their decision making as they prepared summaries of text, provided evidence that the macrorules identified by Brown and Day were indeed apparent in the processing of these expert students. Brown and Day took this research one step further by examining the summaries generated by junior college students, hypothesized to have difficulty with tasks as complex as text summarization. Their data confirmed that the junior college participants looked not unlike the junior high students whose summaries Brown and Day had investigated. Consistent with Ann's tenet that the training study had a key role to play in confirming or disconfirming the theory, the summarization program of research included studies that were designed to determine the outcomes of teaching young students and students requiring remedial education to become more strategic in their summarization activity. The research reported in Brown, Campione, and Day (1981) illustrates this very process.

The summarization research that Ann conducted with her colleagues, most notably with Jeanne Day, has many of the attributes that characterize Ann's orientation to the design and conduct of research. It was both informed by theory and conducted to pursue theory development and refinement. In contemporary terms, it stands as an excellent model of social science research conducted in "Pasteur's Quadrant" (Stokes, 1997). Ann's research on learning from text took yet another turn with the launching of the program of research on Reciprocal Teaching, a program that unfolded over the next decade.

RECIPROCAL TEACHING RESEARCH

Reciprocal Teaching (Brown & Palincsar, 1989; Palincsar & Brown, 1984; 1986; 1989) refers to learning dialogues in which teachers and students took turns leading the discussion of segments of text. The discussions were organized around a set of strategies; namely, predicting, question generating, summarizing, and clarifying. The purpose of these dialogues was the collaborative construction of meaning; students were guided to consider the ways in which the text was advancing their understanding of the topic at hand and to use the strategies as a vehicle for both constructing the meaning as well as ascertaining when they were not able to make sense of the text. When teachers initially introduced their students to these dialogues, they were encouraged to draw on their skills as expert readers to model the use of these strategies. With each day of instruction, the students were encouraged to assume increasing responsibility for leading the discussion, while the teacher's role changed to one of coach, providing feedback to the students and stepping in to provide further support on the basis of need.

One noteworthy feature of this research was the shift reflected in the context in which the research was conducted. Training studies up to this time typically included very brief periods of intervention (few studies extended more than even a day or two). The form of teaching did not necessitate careful description because it was typically didactic in nature, and the interventions were typically one-on-one—hence there was no need to even consider the social context in which most learning in classrooms or other educational settings typically occurs.

While the piloting of reciprocal teaching took place with the researcher engaging individual children in these dialogues it quickly moved into classroom contexts in which teachers enacted the intervention in small ($n = 8$) to moderately ($n = 18$) sized groups, over a 20-day period. With this transition, a host of new issues arose: namely, an examination of the quality of instruction, and the relationships among the quality of instruction, the nature of the learner, the composition of the groups, the demands of the text, and the outcomes of instruction. This was the first time that Ann had worked with an educator, rather than a psychologist; this collaboration gave rise to new sets of issues. For example, we asked whether the intervention was making a difference not only in the context of the reading groups in which the students were experiencing the intervention, but also in the context of their subject matter courses, and we collected evidence that the learning was generalizing. Generalization was ascertained by administering comprehension assessments to the students in both the Reciprocal Teaching and Comparison conditions in the context of their social studies and science classes and comparing their percentile rankings with students who were not experiencing any form of comprehension intervention. Whereas reciprocal teaching consistently resulted in positive outcomes for students, the results were highly variable. This then led us to examine how heterogeneity of the groups facilitated learning when peers could join the teacher as additional models and how the skill of the teacher in scaffolding these dialogues influenced learning outcomes.

The research on Reciprocal Teaching took the most part of a decade and can be represented as generations. The first generation was designed to evaluate the efficacy of this instructional intervention when compared with more traditional forms of reading instruction and was conducted exclusively with informational text, working with upper elementary and middle school students. The second generation was a series of component analyses in which we asked questions about the relative value of reciprocal teaching when compared with modeling or explicit teaching of the strategies. A second componential analysis study compared the efficacy of introducing the four strategies simultaneously versus serially. Each of these studies was prompted by cost–benefit questions, as well as questions about tailoring the instruction for diverse learners. The findings pointed to the value added of dialogic instruction over direct instruction or modeling and suggested that students who were introduced to the four strategies concurrently attained criterion performance more quickly than did students who were introduced to the strategies serially.

The students for whom Reciprocal Teaching was designed were students with comprehension problems who, while adequate decoders at this point in their school careers, had a history of remedial reading instruction due to the delayed development of decoding skills. Their response to the Reciprocal Teaching intervention supported the claim that their activity as readers reflected poor metacognitive awareness to the extent that their efforts were focused chiefly on attaining fluency with little attention to reading for meaning. To examine this claim more fully, the third generation of Reciprocal Teaching research was conducted with primary grade students as a form of prevention (Palincsar & Brown, 1989; Palincsar, Brown, & Campione, 1993). Classroom teachers instructed small groups ($n = 6$) of students, the members of which were yoked based on language and comprehension assessments and randomly assigned to one of two conditions: reciprocal teaching or language development activities. Because the vast majority of students were not yet decoding conventionally, the instruction was conducted as a form of listening comprehension. In contrast to the earlier generations of reciprocal teaching research in which the children read disconnected texts, the texts used in the primary-grade research addressed simple biological themes of animal survival that engaged the students in knowledge building over time; for example, natural protection from predators through camouflage and mimicry. As the students listened and discussed the texts, they were also supported in identifying the theme across the experimental texts. The assessments included measures of recall and inference, as well as the ability to engage in analogical reasoning by applying the information in the taught-to-text to a novel problem that was presented in the assessment. The outcomes mirrored, in many ways, the outcomes attained from the study of older students: Reciprocal Teaching dialogues were productive in engaging young children in comprehension monitoring and the construction of meaning from text. Furthermore, students in the Reciprocal Teaching condition learned to recognize and apply the analogical information in the texts. These gains were not demonstrated by the students in the language development condition (Palincsar & Brown, 1989; Palincsar, Brown, & Campione, 1993).

FOSTERING COMMUNITIES
OF LEARNERS

Had Ann's career contributions ended with her research on text comprehension and teaching for self-regulation, she would have left an indelible mark on educational research and practice; but they didn't end here. In the last decade of her research with her husband Joe, while at the University of California, Berkeley, she launched a new program of inquiry, *Fostering Communities of Learners* (FCL), which had an amazing synthetic quality both in substance and form. The substance included the use of a diverse array of participant structures in which students—engaged as collaborative researchers—pursued deep understanding of content knowledge and domain-specific reasoning in the biological sciences. Working closely with educators in urban schools, Brown and Campione reconceptualized classrooms as contexts in which diversity was not only tolerated but was, in fact, integral to success. This research took the form of design experiments in which "first principles" guided the engineering and investigation of educational innovation. While these contributions were of significant value to advancing educational practice, they were all the more valuable for the ways in which they advanced learning theory. These were the kinds of studies that put flesh on abstract notions such as "constructivist pedagogy" and "socially mediated learning."

The theoretical concepts most central to the design of the FCL classrooms included the following. First, the classroom was conceived as being comprised of multiple zones of proximal development (Vygotsky, 1978) through which participants navigated at various rates and through various routes. Second, teachers and peers engaged in "seeding" the environment with ideas, knowledge, and other tools, which were appropriated by children in various ways as a function of the current zone of proximal development in which they were engaged. Finally, there was an ongoing process of mutual negotiation as members of the class engaged in shared activities and came to shared understandings of the activities in which they were engaged.

To understand FCL classrooms, in addition to these theoretical principles, one must also understand the primary features of these classrooms. The curriculum was a feature key to understanding how activity unfolded in FCL classrooms. The curricula were organized around thematic units; for example, biological themes included interdependence and adaptation; and environmental science themes included balance, competition, and cooperation. Children had access to a broad array of material to support their inquiry; examples included text, video, and a computer environment in which children corresponded with one another, as well as with expert consultants, and maintained a common database. Much of the activity in FCL classrooms occurred in the context of collaborative learning either using Reciprocal Teaching or the jigsaw method (Aronson, 1978) in which children were assigned part of the topic of study to learn and subsequently to teach to others; hence becoming expert relative to different aspects of the topic under study and then sharing their expertise with their peers.

Brown and Campione conceptualized the research regarding FCL as a design experiment, as captured in Collins (in press). In a paper Ann authored in 1992, she wrote: "As a design scientist in my field, I attempt to engineer innovative educational environments and simultaneously conduct experimental studies of those innovations" (Brown, 1992, p. 141). Both the nature of the curriculum and instruction, as well as the nature of this research, drove Ann and her research group to critically examine the nature of the assessments employed in this context and to press on the design of assessment practices that would serve the multiple purposes of accountability to the students, teachers, parents, and school administrators, as well as to the research community. In addition to using traditional measures of achievement, the Brown and Campione team employed a variety of dynamic assessments (Campione & Brown, 1990), conducted primarily through clinical interviews in which interviewers would probe student reasoning about problems that were central to the curriculum, as well as problems that provided the opportunity to assess transfer. Results of these assessments, as well as analyses of classroom discourse, were used to inform the redesign of the curriculum and instruction.

The elegance of the FCL research was enhanced by the interplay of classroom and laboratory research. For example, Ann drew on laboratory research she and colleagues (e.g., Brown & Kane, 1988; Goswami & Brown, 1990) conducted regarding children's analogical reasoning and explanation strategies to enrich her understanding of developmental patterns children demonstrated as they proceeded from merely noticing the occurrence of analogies to productively using these analogies to solve problems. This laboratory research served to focus the lenses the FCL team applied to the study of classroom activity and discourse. Reciprocally, classroom observations gave rise to the design of laboratory studies in which hypotheses could be systemically explored in relatively controlled environments. For example, Ann was interested in exploring what she regarded to be a developmental trend in the use of explanation; that is, that initially children engage in what she referred to as "impasse driven" explanations that arose out of breakdowns in comprehension. These kinds of explanations were followed by explanations borne of attempts to resolve annoying inconsistencies. Finally, explanations become a means for revising and deepening one's understanding of the phenomenon under investigation. These systematic studies arising from spontaneous classroom events constituted one aspect of Ann's research agenda at the time of her death.

Nature of the Learner and the Learning Process

The theories of learning that were prominent at the time of Ann's preparation as a psychologist were dominated principally by behaviorism and sought to yield laws of learning that were both general in nature and independent of species, age, content, and context. Learning was typically viewed as an individual enterprise that involved the formation of simple associations governed by external reinforcements. Through extension and combination, these simple associations were hypothesized to give rise to more complex behaviors. In the course of Ann's career, and informed in large measure by the contributions of her research, theories of learning and learners underwent significant change.

In the vanguard of psychologists who ushered in the cognitive revolution, Ann emphasized the active, reflective, and social nature of learning. From her earliest research on memory, Ann was concerned with the active role of the learner, the learner's capacity to be reflective, and to assume control of his or her activity. She advocated that students become critics of their own learning process but, admonished that this criticism must be constructive, mastery-oriented self-guidance, rather than destructive personal derogation (Brown, 1988).

Furthermore, she consistently asked questions about the nature of instructional opportunity before drawing conclusions about the capacity of learners. For example, in her research on young children's ability to reason by analogy, she demonstrated that children 3 to 5 years of age would demonstrate analogical reasoning and transfer if they were (a) given experience and practice with a series of pairs of analogous problems, (b) directed to attend to the goal structure of the original problem, (c) asked to reflect on similarities between pairs of problems, or (d) required to teach what they had learned to others (Campione, Shapiro, & Brown, 1995). This research contradicted views that were popular at the time suggesting that young children do not have the cognitive resources to engage in analogical reasoning and transfer.

Ann had enormous regard for the competence of young children and chose to view young learners as "intelligent novices" who, while not possessing the background knowledge in a field, could nevertheless learn how to get that knowledge, and how to think and reason in a variety of domains. However, she was also struck by the fact that the pace of development demonstrated by preschool children seemed to slow down during the school years (Gelman & Brown, 1986). Ann speculated that this might be explained in part by the fact that children's competence is increasingly tested on academic tasks that do not reveal what children are capable of. Furthermore, she wondered about the role that the shift away from natural learning to the intentional learning of decontextualized knowledge played in the profile of the school-age child. Observations of this kind explain Ann's keen interest in the optimal conditions of instruction, which are discussed next.

Optimal Conditions of Instruction

To address Ann's view of the optimal conditions of instruction, it is necessary to consider the goals for which the instruction is designed. Historically the goal of education was the production of graduates with basic literacy skills, but during Ann's career, the goal shifted to emphasize higher levels of literacy, to promote greater understanding of the subject matters and reasoning within the subject matters, to include powerful uses of technology, and to yield a citizenry capable of learning and adapting to workplace demands.

To attain the goals of critical thinking and reflection, Ann called our attention to the importance of deep disciplinary content as the grist for instruction. She was fond of quoting Jerome Bruner's call for the teaching of a few "lithe and beautiful and immensely generative" ideas (Bruner, 1969, p. 121). In hand with rich content, Ann was keenly aware of the role that expert others played in advancing students' ability to engage with these ideas. In the absence of knowledgeable others, students were unlikely to be pushed to higher levels of understanding or to confront and correct misunderstandings. Recognizing the burden this places on classroom teachers who are seldom subject-matter specialists (especially in the elementary grades), Ann was very interested in alternative ways of expanding the expertise of the classroom community with the addition of content area experts, accessible through electronic media or in person.

She maintained that schools are places where children learn to learn. Influenced by Piagetian and Vygotskian theories, she promoted—particularly in the second half of her career—instructional contexts that featured social interactions. She argued that in the context of conversation, whether in reciprocal teaching dialogues or FCL research groups, students were best positioned to assume responsibility for their learning, contribute and benefit from the collective knowledge capital that exists in classrooms, as well as talk about their learning.

The issue of transfer was central to Ann's program of research. As previously described, Ann did not subscribe to a stage-like theory of the spontaneous development of the ability to transfer, but rather advocated that instruction be designed to promote transfer. How does instruction promote transfer? Ann and Joe proposed that integral to promoting transfer in the classroom were opportunities for students to come to understand a variety of domain-specific concepts, as well as the more general processes useful to advancing new and continued learning. Such understanding would enable students to talk knowingly about these processes, as well as to use them flexibly. These tenets implied that instruction must first of all be about the task of mastering a rich domain of knowledge. A colloquial expression that Ann used to capture this was to suggest that there must be something worth "worrying about" in reference to text or curricula. In addition, instruction in this rich domain must include modeling that is designed to help students acquire the critical thinking and reflection activities that will guide their thinking as they entered new areas of learning. Finally, consistent with her belief in the social nature of cognition, Ann urged that students be provided with many occasions for explaining to others (and hence to themselves) the characteristics and limitations of what they are learning, and the reasons they are engaged in particular learning activities.

Ann was aware that *procedures* were integral to communicating educational innovations; but she worried that the dissemination of procedures might lead to the implementation of practices that addressed only the surface features of instructional interventions and might, in fact, fall far short of—or indeed misrepresent—the theoretical basis of the innovation. Hence, she called for instruction to be guided by a set of *first principles* (Brown & Campione, in press) that would enable educators to make informed decisions regarding the enactment of instruction that would be consistent with the theoretical premises of the instruction.

The Nature of Important Learning-instructional Outcomes

Consistent with the kinds of ambitious curriculum and pedagogy that were characteristic of their instructional research, Brown and Campione's research group consistently employed multiple, rigorous measures to understand learning-instructional outcomes. For example, in Reciprocal Teaching research, changes in comprehension were measured not by assessing students' understanding of the texts that were used in the context of the dialogues, but rather with texts that were read independently of the dialogues. Furthermore, the assessments included transfer measures, in which students could use the information from the curriculum to solve a novel problem.

Ann was very clever at identifying age-appropriate ways of determining what children were capable of. For example, one strand of the Brown and Campione research involved the use of dynamic assessment (Campione & Brown, 1987). In the course of dynamic assessment, students are provided increasing levels of support to successfully complete a task. Such a technique yields both an estimate of the child's current level of proficiency, as well as a prediction of the child's competence, provided instructional support.

Ann's early interest in analogical reasoning manifest itself in the design of assessments of learning outcomes throughout her career. A classic task, for example, in Brown and Campione's FCL research was to engage the learners in the design of an animal to fit a particular habitat, following the study of biological adaptation.

The Nature of Ann's Service to the Community

Ann's gifts were many and she gave of them generously. She served on the most prestigious boards and panels in our profession. The youngest scholar ever elected to the National Academy of Education, she was its president from 1997 until her death. She served as president of AERA and president of Division 7 of the American Psychological Association. She contributed tirelessly to the writing and dissemination of reports that would spur reform efforts and garner additional attention to and support for educational research; the most recent example being the report of the National Research Council, *How People Learn: Brain, Mind, Experience, and School* (co-edited with Bransford and Cocking in 1999).

In recognition of her seminal work in metacognition, her outstanding theoretical and practical contributions to the design of interactive learning environments, her contributions to our understanding of the development of reasoning in young children, and for the leadership she provided the research community, Ann was selected for AERA's Award for *Distinguished Contributions to Educational Research* in 1991. This award was followed by the *Distinguished Scientific Contribution Award for the Application of Psychology* by the American Psychological Association in 1996. Then, in recognition of her "... distinguished achievements in psychological science. For brilliantly combining the fields of developmental psychology, learning theory, and the design of learning environments in a career of theoretical and experimental work, and their applications to education," she was honored, in 1997, by the American Psychological Society with the *James McKeen Catell Award for Distinguished Achievements.*

Ann was a fellow of the American Psychological Society, Society for Experimental Psychologists, Spencer Foundation, Society for Research in Child Development, and American Psychological Association. In addition, she provided leadership on a number of editorial boards in education and psychology.

Chief among Ann's gifts was her ability to write. The clarity of Ann's writing reflected the fact that she wrote as much from her heart as from her intellect. For example, the children about whom Ann wrote, were not just the subjects of her research; thoughts of these children flooded her mind at night—fears of what they would confront as they matriculated to middle school, questions about the possible futures of these children who lived in poverty. When Ann wrote, "what most recent developmental theories ask of teachers is so hard," it was because she held a deep respect and appreciation for the work of teachers and the challenging socio-political contexts in which they do this work. Ann derived enormous satisfaction from her conversations with the children in her research and glowed as she recounted tales of their accomplishments, filing stories away to enliven future presentations and writing.

Fifth grader Florenzia captured Ann in the following way:

> Ann Brown—she's really very sophisticated. She knows a lot about a lot of things. It's no wonder people picked her to be president of AERA. She's good at organizing and she keeps track of all our work no matter how much we do. She spends a lot of time with kids. Yeah, that's what I like. When she comes to school she spends time with the kids instead of the adults. She listens to make sure that we have learned. To tell you the truth, she really is a big help. She makes you feel so proud of yourself. You know, your self-confidence gets better.

Ann Brown's work in cognition and instruction once inspired Lauren Resnick to suggest that "cognitive psychology has finally made a contribution to instruction." How is it that Ann's work was so helpful? Perhaps, from a researcher's perspective, it is because of the ways in which her work has advanced learning theory. Perhaps it is because of the nature of the questions she asked—questions that, to use a tired but very appropriate term, are the "authentic" questions that teachers wrestle with daily.

In closing, Jerome Bruner (1960) has suggested: "The shrewd guess, the fertile hypothesis, the courageous leap to a tentative conclusion—these are the most valuable coins of the thinker at work" (p. 64). Ann had an abundance of these coins, and we are all the richer for the manner in which she invested them. Ann's death at the age of 56 clearly brought her journey to a premature end; however, there is no question but that her legacy will endure in the work of so many of us who have inherited the powerful tools that are represented in her ideas and methods and in the challenges she posed to reveal and extend the capabilities of learners.

REFERENCES

Aronson, E. (1978). *The jigsaw classroom*. Beverly Hills, CA: Sage.

Brown, A. L. (1974). The role of strategic behavior in retardate memory. In N. R. Ellis (Ed.), *International review of research in mental retardation* (Vol. 7, pp. 55–111). New York: Academic Press.

Brown, A. L. (1975). The development of memory: Knowing, knowing about knowing, and knowing how to know. In H. W. Reese (Ed.), *Advances in child developmental and behavior* (Vol. 10, pp. 103–152). New York: Academic Press.

Brown, A. L. (1992). Design experiments: Theoretical and methodological challenges in creating complex interventions in classroom settings. *The Journal of the Learning Sciences, 2*(2), 141–178.

Brown, A. L., & Barclay, C. R. (1976). The effects of training specific mnemonics on the metamnemonic efficiency of retarded children. *Child Development, 47*, 71–80.

Brown, A. L., & Campione, J. C. (1996). Psychological theory and the design of innovative learning environments: On procedures, principles, and systems. In L. Schauble & R. Glaser (Eds.), *Innovations in Learning* (pp. 289–326). Hillsdale, NJ: Lawrence Erlbaum Associates.

Brown, A. L., Campione, J. C., & Barclay, C. R. (1979). Training self-checking routines for estimating test readiness: Generalization from list learning to prose recall. *Child Development, 50*, 501–512.

Brown, A. L., Campione, J. C., & Day, J. D. (1981). Learning to learn: On training students to learn from texts. *Educational Researcher, 10*(2), 14–21.

Brown, A. L. (1988). Motivation to learn and understand: On taking charge of one's own learning. *Cognition and Instruction, 5*(4), 311–322.

Brown, A. L., & Day, J. D. (1983). Macrorules for summarizing texts: The development of expertise. *Journal of Verbal Learning and Verbal Behavior, 22*(1), 1–14.

Brown, A. L., Day, J. D., & Jones, R. S. (1983). The development of plans for summarizing texts. *Child Development, 54*, 968–979.

Brown, A. L., & Kane, M. J. (1988). Preschool children can learn to transfer: Learning to learn and learning from example. *Cognitive Psychology, 20*, 493–523.

Brown, A. L., & Palincsar, A. S. (1989). Guided, cooperative learning and individual knowledge acquisition. In L. B. Resnick (Ed.), *Knowing, learning, and instruction: Essays in honor of Robert Glaser* (pp. 393–451). Hillsdale, NJ: Lawrence Erlbaum Associates.

Brown, A. L., & Smiley, S. S. (1978). The development of strategies for studying texts. *Child Development, 49*, 1076–1088.

Brown, A. L., Smiley, S. S., & Lawton, S. C. (1978). The effects of experience on the selection of suitable retrieval cues for studying texts. *Child Development, 49*, 829–835.

Bruner, J. (1960). The process of education. Cambridge, MA: Harvard University Press.

Bruner, J. (1969). *On knowing: Essays for the left hand.* Cambridge, MA: Harvard University Press.

Campione, J. C., & Brown, A. L. (1990). Guided learning and transfer: Implications for approaches to assessment. In N. Frederiksen, R. Glaser, A. Lesgold, & M. Shafto (Eds.), *Diagnostic monitoring of skill and knowledge acquisition* (pp. 141–172). Hillsdale, NJ: Lawrence Erlbaum Associates.

Campione, J. C., & Brown, A. L. (1987). Linking dynamic assessment with school achievement. In C. S. Lidz (Ed.), *Dynamic assessment* (pp. 82–115). New York: Guilford.

Campione, J. C., Shapiro, A. M., & Brown, A. L. (1995). Forms of transfer in a community of learners: Flexible learning and understanding. In A. McKeough, J. Lupart, & A. Marini (Eds.), *Teaching for Transfer: Fostering generalization in learning* (pp. 35–68). Mahwah, NJ: Lawrence Erlbaum Associates.

Collins, A. (in press). *Toward a design science of education.* In E. Scanlon & T. O'Shea (Eds.), New directions in educational technology. New York: Springer-Verlag.

DeLoache, J. S., Cassidy, L., & Brown, A. L. (1985). Precursors of mnemonic strategies in very young children's memory. *Child Development, 56*(1), 125–137.

Ericsson, K. A., & Simon, H. A. (1980). Verbal reports as data. *Psychological Review, 87*, 215–251.

Flavell, J. (1970). Developmental studies of mediated memory. In H. W. Reese & L. P. Lipsett (Eds.), *Advances in Child Development and Behavior*, (vol. 5, pp. 181–211). New York: Academic Press.

Gelman, R., & Brown, A. L. (1986). Changing views of cognitive competence in the young. In N. J. Smelser & D. R. Gerstein (Eds.), *Behavioral and social science: Fifty years of discovery* (pp. 175–207). Washington, DC: National Academy Press.

Goswami, U., & Brown, A. L. (1990). Higher-order structure and relational reasoning: Contrasting analogical and thematic relations. *Cognition, 36*, 207–226.

Kintsch, W., & van Dijk, T. A. (1978). Toward a model of text comprehension and production. *Psychological Review, 85*, 363–394.

Meichenbaum, D. (1977). Cognitive behavior modification: An integrated approach. New York: Plenum.

Palincsar, A. S., & Brown, A. L. (1984). Reciprocal teaching of comprehension-fostering and monitoring activities. *Cognition and Instruction, 1*(2), 117–175.

Palincsar, A. S., & Brown, A. L. (1986). Interactive teaching to promote independent learning from text. *Reading Teacher, 39*(8), 771–777.

Palincsar, A. S., & Brown, A. L. (1989). Instruction for self-regulated reading. In L. Resnick & L. E. Klopfer (Eds.), *Cognitive research in subject matter learning* (pp. 19–39). Washington, DC: The Association for Supervision and Curriculum Development.

Palincsar, A. S., Brown, A. L., & Campione, J. C. (1993). First grade dialogues for knowledge acquisition and use. In E. A. Forman, N. Minnick, & C. A. Stone (Eds.), *Contexts for learning: Sociocultural dynamics in children's development* (pp. 43–57). New York: Oxford University Press.

Stokes, D. (1997). *Pasteur's quandrant: Basic scientific and technological innovation.* Washington, DC: Brookings Institution Press.

Vygotsky, L. (1978). Mind in society: The development of higher psychological processes. In M. Cole, V. John-Steiner, S. Scribner, & E. Souberman (Eds.), Cambridge, MA: Harvard University Press.

Author Index

Subject Index